THE E-BUSINESS (R)EVOLUTION

Hewlett-Packard® Professional Books

THE E-BUSINESS (R)EVOLUTION

LIVING AND WORKING IN AN INTERCONNECTED WORLD

Daniel Amor
http://www.hp.com/go/retailbooks

Prentice Hall PTR
Upper Saddle River, NJ 07458
http://www.phptr.com

Library of Congress Cataloging-in-Publication Data

Amor, Daniel.
　　The e-business (R)evolution: living and working in an interconnected world / Daniel Amor.
　　　　p.　　cm.
　　Includes index.
　　ISBN 0-13-085123-X
　　1. Electronic commerce. 2. Electronic commerce--Management.
　　3. Internet (Computer network) 4. Business enterprises--Computer networks. I. Title
　　HF5548.32.A46　　　　　　　　　　　　　　　1999
　　658'.054678--dc21　　　　　　　　　　　　　　　　　　　　　　　　99-44842
　　　　　　　　　　　　　　　　　　　　　　　　　　　　　　　　　　　CIP

Editorial/production supervision: *Vincent Janoski*
Acquisitions editor: *Jill Pisoni*
Marketing manager: *Lisa Konzelmann*
Manufacturing manager: *Maura Goldstaub*
Editorial assistant: *Linda Ramagnano*
Cover design director: *Jerry Votta*
Manager, Hewlett-Packard Retail Book Publishing: *Patricia Pekary*
Editor, Hewlett-Packard Professional Books: *Susan Wright*

Published by Prentice Hall PTR
Prentice-Hall, Inc.
Upper Saddle River, NJ 07458

Prentice Hall books are widely used by corporations and government agencies
for training, marketing, and resale.

The publisher offers discounts on this book when ordered in bulk quantities.
For more information, contact: Corporate Sales Department, Phone: 800-382-3419;
Fax: 201-236-7141; E-mail: corpsales@prenhall.com; or write: Prentice Hall PTR,
Corp. Sales Dept., One Lake Street, Upper Saddle River, NJ 07458.

Printed in the United States of America
10 9 8 7 6 5 4

ISBN　0-13-085123-X　✓

Prentice-Hall International (UK) Limited, *London*
Prentice-Hall of Australia Pty. Limited, *Sydney*
Prentice-Hall Canada Inc., *Toronto*
Prentice-Hall Hispanoamericana, S.A., *Mexico*
Prentice-Hall of India Private Limited, *New Delhi*
Prentice-Hall of Japan, Inc., *Tokyo*
Prentice-Hall Singapore Pte. Ltd., *Singapore*
Editora Prentice-Hall do Brasil, Ltda., *Rio de Janeiro*

To Sabine,

for her love, patience
and understanding

Contents

III Internet Technologies   293

FOREWORD

Hewlett-Packard has been helping customers to implement information technology for 60 years. In the last years, most of these projects have involved Internet technologies although, in its own typical modest manner, the company has not talked too much about this to the outside world. But just consider the following examples:

- More than 70% of Internet nodes are managed by HP OpenView.

- Over 70% of all Internet bank transactions run on HP Servers.

- More than 120 Internet banks run on HP's secure Web-server HP Virtual Vault.

Half of the Secure Electronic Transaction (SET) infrastrucutures, being established by credit card processors, are being implemented by HP with its subsidiary Verifone. HP also provided and operated the complete IT set-up for the 1998 World Cup, handling everything from ticket management to electronic commerce. This was the largest and busiest single internet event in history (as documented in the Guinness Book of Records) and it went off "flawlessly", as the IT Manager of the French Organizing Committee commented after the event.

Now these projects are typically managed and implemented by local customer facing organizations, backed up with deeper technical expertise by a central organization for the European Region, as we call it, based in Böblingen, Germany. Daniel Amor has been part of this central team for several years, contributing to many different projects, in particular Internet business implementations at numerous customers, too numerous for me to mention. So he has gained a vast experience of electronic commerce implementations of all types.

Now in performing such a role as Daniel's, it is always very tempting to concentrate on the details only and to neglect the "big picture": why is the customer doing this, what difference will the project make to other aspects of its business. As this book shows, Daniel has always been aware of these aspects.

In fact, he combines the experience of someone who knows about Internet business "hands-on" (knows the pitfalls, what the products can really do and what they cannot do) with the general understanding that business are also fundamentally changing because of the endless possibilities of the Internet as a communications and transactional medium.

This combination is to be found in many Hewlett-Packard people and serves as the basis for our newly-announced E-Services strategy. Here, HP has articulated a compelling vision of where business are heading with new business models for all of us and new ways of delivering IT. HP has also substantiated this vision with an important new technological contribution: e-speak.

I would like to congratulate Daniel on this book and wish you, the reader, a pleasant and informative read as he takes you into this new world and helps you to understand how this will affect your businesses and your lives. I am confident that you will be much better prepared for this new world after reading the book.

Peter O'Neill

European Marketing Manager Electronic Commerce
Hewlett-Packard Enterprise Computing Organization
peter_oneill@hp.com

INTRODUCTION

The New Paradigm

Over the last few years the Internet has evolved from being a scientific network only, to a platform that is enabling a new generation of businesses. The first wave of electronic business was fundamentally the exchange of information. But, with time, more and more types of businesses have become available electronically. Nowadays we can buy goods online, book holidays or have texts translated over the Internet in an instant. Home banking, for example, is one application that is already provided by most banks around the world. Looking up your balance, transferring money and other transactions are done every day by millions of people. Public administration has discovered the Internet as a means to talk to the general public at election times. And it will not be long a time before we see general elections decided on the Internet.

The reason why I have called this book "The E-business (R)evolution" is that the approach is twofold. Technology has revolutionized the way we can do business. But business itself is only slowly adapting to the new possibilities. The New Economy needs a new paradigm, but the process of conversion will take some time to complete. The necessary technology is ready and waiting. The e-business in the title is not the same as IBM is seeing it, it is much more, as you will discover by reading this book, therefore the "B" in e-business is not written in capital letters as in IBM's case.

The Internet is changing the concept of programming applications. We are moving towards pervasive computing and towards electronic services. The Jini technology is one of the first implementations of what one could call "one world, one computer." Jini allows every device to talk to every other device in a common language. A device in this case can be anything with a silicon chip inside it and an Internet connection. Other companies have started to develop similar paradigms, technologies and visions, such as IBM's T Spaces technology and Hewlett-Packard's E-Services strategy.

Most probably you already know the example of the empty refrigerator that sends an e-mail to the grocery with a request for fresh milk that will be delivered to the doorstep before breakfast in the morning. Prototypes have already been built. A bar-code reader is able to detect which products are put into the fridge and taken out afterwards. For many people this won't be a necessity in the future. The grocery is more than just a place where people can buy food. It is a social place where people meet, which cannot be simply replaced by two chips. But for those who do not have the time to do the shopping or are not able to walk to the grocery, this may become an option.

New technologies are emerging slowly. In Helsinki, for example, it is already possible to pay for a soft drink with a cellular phone. Instead of inserting coins into the vendoring machine it is possible to call the machine with the cell phone with a special number which in turn releases a can of soft drink. In Europe more people have cellular phones than computers, therefore the crossover of communication technology and information technology is on the verge. Through cell-broadcast people with GSM cellular phones are able to receive news flashes, which can keep them up-to-date on the latest political and financial developments. The future of computing lies in devices and not stand-alone personal computers.

Other applications may be more useful to all of us, but the Internet is generally not designed to be a mass-media such as television or radio. The Internet is an infrastructure for many mass and niche markets. Two appliances, which may be suitable for many car owners, are the following:

1. **Cost Saving** – Imagine your car sending a request to all petrol stations within ten kilometers to find out which one is the cheapest. The navigational system of the car will then direct the driver to that petrol station.

2. **Life Saving** – After an accident the car is able to detect how severe the crash was and will call an ambulance and the police, if appropriate.

Pervasive Computing

Pervasive computing is therefore the next logical step in the evolution of computers. The Internet has enabled the connection of computers and allowed them to exchange information. Connecting all types of devices will create a network that is thousands of times larger than the current Internet, offering more than simple exchange of information. It will enable businesses to offer services, which can be basic such as "print something onto the nearest printer" or complex as "create a short document on the financial situation within the company".

In such an interconnected world everything becomes part of one huge system. This may sound like the evil Borgs in the Star Trek saga who tend to say: "You will be assimilated." The Borgs are a civilization that work and live in a collective; they have only one mind. Without the other members of the collective they are lost. Their mission is to assimilate all other cultures and to incorporate all other technologies into their own. They believe that resistance to change is futile.

Hopefully the introduction of new technologies will not be based on pressure but on agreements, understanding and co-operation. Otherwise it could be seen as very worrying if this goal is achieved on propriety standards, or it could be totally superfluous if this goal is achieved by wasting useful resources. It can also mean a leap into the future if this New World Order is built on open systems, open sources, open standards and open services. It remains to be seen if Jini will succeed, but the general direction is set and everybody will have to follow it over the next few years in order not to fall behind.

Pervasive computing is only just getting off the ground, but getting to know all about it will give you the edge over your competitors when it comes to implementing it. But before getting into pervasive computing, one should think about one's business idea. In order to be successful on the Internet it is necessary to get that right first, otherwise the best IT infrastructure will not be of any help.

Business on the Net Today

If you look at the current situation, you can divide the Internet presence of enterprises into six phases:

- **Phase 1: "Hello, I'm online, too"** – In this phase, the company has set up a web page. But in this phase, no real structure is provided. There is no search engine, there is only some of the product information and there is no link to the current stock price and no way to communicate with people within the company.

- **Phase 2: "Structured Web site"** – The web site now has a decent structure, you can use a search engine to search for keywords, you can see all the company information, you can exchange messages within the company.

- **Phase 3: "Trying E-Commerce"** – The company is trying to sell information, goods, etc. online. The system is not connected to the real databases on the Intranet. It is slow, costs a lot of money and is not really secure. There is no way to hook up your company's back-end system to the back-end of the other company.

- **Phase 4: "Doing E-Business"** – Your web site has a direct link into the legacy systems of your Intranet, it allows retrieval of information from internal databases and uses secure protocols to transmit data between your company and the customer or another business. You are able to save costs and start making a profit from your online business.

- **Phase 5: "Pervasive E-Business"** – Using any device that contains a chip (cellular phone, car, etc.) people are able to connect to your data and transmit or receive the desired information to do e-business.

- **Phase 6: "One World - One Computer"** – All chip-based devices will be interconnected and create one huge information resource. The devices are able to interchange any type of information on an object-oriented level. Applications will be transparent to these devices. Users won't know where the answer to their problems came from.

Most companies nowadays are somewhere near or between phase 2 and phase 3. Most of them are moving towards phase 4. One important part of this book is to show what will happen after phase 4. Pervasive computing is the most likely thing to happen. The book will show what such a world could look like and what the alternatives are. It tries to identify the standards and the owners, and tries to find out what the Internet will be like in five years time.

Who Should Read This Book

This book is intended for the electronic entrepreneur who is either thinking about setting up an e-business or has already set one up. It provides you with a checklist of all the important items in the e-business area. You can check immediately how much of your business is ready to go online. After having read this book you will be able to build up your own e-business or enhance it dramatically to make it not only yet another web page, but also a real financial stronghold for your company.

The book is the basis for your e-business decisions. The information given in this book is not technological hype that will evaporate next year; it will be the basis for your e-business over the next few years. The book covers all the topics required for a complete and secure e-business solution. On the other hand it does go into great depth in each topic, so that you will be competent enough to decide which of the solutions described fits your needs best, and you do not have to rely on someone else.

The major question for all technologies in this book is: "why should I use it?" There are enough books on how to use a technology and many people know how to do it, but many people forget to ask why. Sometimes it makes sense to avoid new technologies, as it does only add an extra overhead to the work that needs to be done. Whenever people come up to you and explain a new technology, do not ask how it can be done, but why it should be done.

The book contains many examples and links to web pages. As the Internet is changing every day, it cannot be guaranteed that every link will be available at the time of reading. As a convenience to the readers, a web site has been set up which contains a list of all examples used in the book. The list on the web site will be updated in regular intervals. In addition to this the web site will contain links to other e-business sites and more information on the topics in the book. The URL of the web site is `http://www.ebusinessrevolution.com/` and will be available from the time of publishing.

How This Book Is Organized

The book is divided into four parts. The first part is the foundation for all your online activities. It introduces the reader to the basic concepts of the Internet and how to do business via the Internet. It takes both, technology and business, into consideration and does not forget to talk about the legal aspects of doing business via the Internet. Finally it explains how marketing on the Web should be done in order to be successful. Without marketing your online business will lack the visibility it requires to succeed.

The second part talks about how e-business applications are used for Internet, Intranet or Extranet based applications. It looks at the questions from all perspectives, client software, middleware, and back-end systems. It's focus is on search engines, portals, shopping and ORM sites and last not least one chapter is dedicated to the communication possibilities via the Internet. Using this information you are prepared to go online and discover other businesses, what they offer and how they did it.

The third part explains the technologies that are below your applications. This is done from a technical point of view as well as a business point of view, in order to show you the business cases that are viable right now. Each chapter contains a set of business cases that are evaluated and it is explained how Internet technologies help to resolve issues with the business cases or how to extend one's business through new technology.

The fourth part is an outlook onto the future of electronic business and gets into more detail on how software and hardware will be developed in the future. The Open Source model is explained and how pervasive computing has been implemented. The last chapter of the book gives an outlook into the future on how it may happen.

Appendix A offers a glossary of e-business terms, which were used throughout the book. In case you do not understand a certain term, have a look here. Appendix B describes how a business can be moved to the Internet and what is required to do so. It does not only list the ideas, the required hardware and software, but goes also into detail regarding the costs and the benefits. Appendix C is a short list of my favorite web sites, ordered by subject areas.

Acknowledgements

There are many people I would like to thank as they helped me to make this book reality. This book is dedicated to Sabine, the woman I love. First of all I want to thank her for her love, support and understanding. I really tried to write as much of the book as possible, while she was asleep, but especially in the end I had not much time left for her. I worked on this book besides my real job as a consultant and project manager for Hewlett-Packard. Sabine, I want to tell you that I love you.

I also want to thank my family for their support and their suggestions and want to "apologise" to the English half of my family for using American English in the book. The original manuscript was written in pure British English. I want to thank my grandfather, father and mother for having already written books, which made it easy for me to follow their steps. At the same time I want to "apologise" to the Czech half of the family for not writing the manuscript in Czech.

I owe Hewlett-Packard, my managers, Isabelle Roux-Buisson and Albert Frank, and my colleagues a big thank you for their support and the many general discussions on business on the Internet that were conducted in the coffee breaks and during meetings that made me change some parts of the book while writing it. A special thank you goes out to Susan Wright and Pat Pekary at HP Press for managing the internal HP publication processes. I also want to thank Rosie Chiovari, Phil Mindigo and Peter O'Neill in the United States for supporting the crazy European writing a book on business on the Internet.

The people at Prentice Hall were also very responsive and helpful and I want to thank them for the continued support during the writing of the book without which this book would not have been possible. I want to thank Jill Pisoni, Linda Ramagnano, Gail Cocker, Camille Trentacoste and Vincent Jankoski.

At last, but not at least, I want to thank Uta Winter of MediaTechbooks[1], and Samantha Shurety of IBM[2] for reviewing my book at various stages of the development and for their invaluable support, ideas and suggestions.

---

[1]http://www.mediatechbooks.de/
[2]http://www.ibm.com/

Part I

The Foundation

Chapter 1

INTRODUCTION TO INTERNET BUSINESS

1.1 Being Online

file transfer protocol

1.1.1 The Basics

Flashback. When I first got in contact with the Internet in 1992 it was still a quiet place. Apart from sending and receiving e-mail, downloading software via FTP or chatting via "IRC," "talk" and "nn," there was not much one could do. Programs like "Archie" and "Gopher" were en vogue and using the Internet required a lot of Unix knowledge. All I had at that time was an ASCII-Text terminal that was connected via "telnet" to a HP Apollo Workstation. I did not have a web browser, because no browser software had been invented yet. Besides the Internet there were other computer networks, like the Fidonet that were far more attractive at that time because they had a colorful interface to the user.

Today, I start up my laptop and use a web browser to connect to the Internet, either via the Local Area Network (LAN) at work or via the modem at home and am able to do all I did in 1992 and even more. Fidonet[1] is still around, but its popularity has decreased a lot since the early days and most of it has been incorporated in the Internet over the last few years, just like most other computer networks, like BitNet and MausNet.

With this simple-to-use browser, I am able to do my e-mailing, up- and download of software, use online chats and search for keywords on the Internet. I am able to check my balance at the bank and buy flowers online. All services can be accessed with this single piece of software.

The software has become so easy to use that non-technical people have e-mail addresses. They buy and sell goods online. Exact figures are not available for the Internet. Neither do we know how many people are online nor do we know how many businesses there are. This is because of the structure of the

---

[1]http://www.fidonet.org/

3

Internet. It is different to anything we have seen before. Traditional methods of measuring audience just do not work anymore. With all other types of media the number of offerings is limited by region, for example 40 television stations or five larger newspapers for Tuscany, Italy. Counting viewers or sales is relatively easy, as the number of newspaper stands and televisions is limited in the region. This makes it easy to define prices for the advertising sections. On the Internet we have unlimited space and resources. People from Tuscany may choose from one of the 40 TV stations or choose any location in cyberspace. And everybody who wants to appear as someone who lives in Tuscany can do it by using masquerading techniques (choosing another virtual identity).

For the first time in the history of mankind a mass media has more offerings than potential users. And not only that: for the first time everybody is able to interact. People are able to change content, add information, link resources to logical structures and offer them to others. On TV we have a limited set of channels, on the Internet users have their own channels, moving through cyberspace at their own pace and in their own direction, guided only by their interest and curiosity. On TV, normally, one can watch one program at a time, on the Internet you can watch multiple web pages at a time. Sometimes I have more than forty browser windows open and flip through them while searching for something very specific or comparing something. There is no way to tell how much time I spent on a particular page or on the other.

It will be just a matter of years before everyone will be present on the Internet. The fear that it will replace real-life is unnecessary. Just as TV has not replaced the radio and books, the cyberworld won't replace the real world. But it will add a new dimension to human life, no doubt. The dream of the global village will eventually become reality. Everything and everyone will be only a click away. Prices for hardware and software are dropping making them available to the poorer people in the world, too.

1.1.2 Distant Learning

The University of Amsterdam has already created special online lectures for people who are not able to attend the regular lectures in Amsterdam. The Network University (TNU)[2] is a large scale project that aims to provide highly interactive, innovative Internet based distance learning to a global audience who opt for the advantages of a new form of academic education. The target group for this service are physically disadvantaged students and students from overseas, mostly from Africa and Asia, who are able to pay for the lectures. Some students may also not be able to pay to live in Europe, though, or may not be able to get a visa for the Netherlands. Through new Internet communication technologies and standard web pages the virtual lecturer talks to the students who in turn are able to communicate with the lecturer via the Internet and telephone.

---

[2]http://www.lwwl.com/tnu/

The master's degrees offered by TNU will be rooted in an interdisciplinary approach to the social sciences. It will be distinguished by their full use of the Internet as a medium providing access to vast amounts of information as well as a channel of communication that facilitates new ways of learning. The participants of TNU will not be at the receiving end of a one-way communication process but, through the mediation of technology, will actively contribute to the content and future development of the programme. The online learning process will be supported by access to an Internet-based "content call-center" that will offer 24-hour supervision and feedback. This feedback will eventually be offered in different languages.

Interactivity, global reach, the multi-lingual and multi-cultural approach and the nearly 100 percent availability are the key to success in this project. Especially with students from all over the world who live in many different time zones.

1.1.3 Space and Time on the Internet

The reasons for a success on the Internet is radically different to what we have seen in the past in business. It is not anymore the bigger fish swallowing the smaller fish, nor is it the faster runner beating the slower runner. In the information society the more knowledgable is making more deals than the less informed. Knowledge is quality and this is were the business is heading for.

Nicolas Hayek, the president of the Swatch Group [3], which produces the highly successful watch "Swatch"[4] has created a new time standard. Instead of dividing the day into 24 hours, in the Internet age a day is made out of 1,000 Swatch Beats. The Internet time uses its own meridian, the Biel Mean Time (BMT), named after a town in Switzerland. One Swatch Beat equals 86.4 seconds.

Although many people may think that the Internet time is a gag, it reflects the way work is done in the digital age. Instead of serving your customers from nine to five, the customers are served around the clock, whenever a customer feels like needing a product or service. Time zones and geographical boundaries have no importance anymore. Once someone has gone digital, everything is now and here. Although time zones are important for people to communicate with each other, it has become irrelevant for business. No matter if it is five o'clock in Boston or ten o'clock in Nairobi, the customers on the Internet want to receive the goods, information or service they have requested.

Through the Internet everything moves closer together, resulting in nearly zero response time and almost no distance. As the Internet is getting faster every day through new inventions and new programs, such as the Internet 2[5] initiative in the United States, every company will be as fast as its compe-

---

[3]http://www.theswatchgroup.ch/
[4]http://www.swatch.com/
[5]http://www.internet2.edu/

tition and just as near as the competition. Distance, size and speed become irrelevant. In order to be successful the service needs to be better than the competition. Quality of service becomes the ultimate success factor.

Through the Internet everyone is able to offer any service at maximum speed (converging to a delivery time of zero). As everyone is able to reach maximum speed, it does not make sense to try to be faster than the competition. A choice is not made anymore on the above mentioned factors, but mainly by choosing a brand, which has a positive image and a good quality. This simplifies the lives of the customers. Instead of choosing the objective best product, they choose the subjective best product.

The Internet reduces the three dimensions of the world and time to a single point, to the here and now of the customer. All customers have their own universe, which needs to be addressed when offering goods, information or services online. Through personalization the universe of the Internet appears differently to everyone. The Internet is constantly changing; making change the only constant one can count on. Products, ideas and prices, for example, are changing much faster than ever before, making them float.

1.1.4　The Web Is Not the Internet

Many people confuse two terms that are related but not identical in meaning. The Internet, which evolved from the military ARPANet has its roots in the 1960s. It's basic idea was to create a network that would continue to work as a whole, when parts of it collapse. The Internet means a network infrastructure that is built on certain standards, the Internet standards, which are used by all participants to connect to each other. The specification of the Internet protocol (IP) does not specify which type information, services or products should be exchanged. The IP defines how the flow of information is organized. Chapter 3 contains more information on IP and related standards.

These specifications reside on a layer above the Internet layer and one of these protocols for the exchange of information is the World Wide Web with its hyper-text transfer protocol (HTTP). Besides the World Wide Web there are other protocols that enable people to communicate via e-mail (POP3, SMTP, IMAP), chat online (IRC) or participate in newsgroups (NNTP). The web offers the exchange of documents via HTTP which are mainly in the HTML format, allowing browsers to display the content in the correct way.

The World Wide Web is just one the numerous services offered on the Internet and does not specify, if a certain web page is available on the Intranet, Extranet and Internet. It provides a simple-to-use interface that allows people with very little knowledge in computing to access web services all over the Internet. These web services including content, products and services, which can be viewed or ordered through the web browser. The web browser is a synonym to the first generation of the commercial Internet. It allows customers to self-service themselves over the web. The second generation of commercial

Internet usage will move away from "do-it-yourself" to "do-it-for-me." This new paradigm, also known as pervasive computing, will automate many processes customers were using web browsers for. Pervasive computing is still a vision and will take still quite a while to become reality. Therefore browsers will remain important over the next few years.

1.2 Defining E-business

1.2.1 Overview

One of the first to use the term E-business was IBM[6] in 1997. At that time they launched their first thematic campaign built around the term. Until then e-commerce was the buzzword used. The shift in terms also means a shift in paradigm. Until then selling was the only experience that people could reproduce on the web. Broadening the approach to allow more types of business on the web created the new term e-business. E-commerce is just one aspect of e-business like e-franchising, e-mailing, e-marketing. E-Business is about using the convenience, availability and world-wide reach to enhance existing businesses or creating new virtual business. IBM defines e-business as "a secure, flexible and integrated approach to delivering differentiated business value by combining the systems and processes that run core business operations with the simplicity and reach made possible by Internet technology."

IBM's E-business is what happens when you combine the resources of traditional information systems with the vast reach of the Web and connect critical business systems directly to critical business constituencies – customers, employees and suppliers via Intranets, Extranets and via the Web. By connecting your traditional IT systems to the Web you become an e-business. Most companies deploy applications on the Internet making it easier to do the things you already do.

Forward-thinking organizations are beginning to automate, organize, standardize and stabilize the services offered in order to create and maintain sustainable computer-mediated relationships throughout an e-business life cycle. At about the same time, other companies like Hewlett-Packard[7] also started to offer complete solutions for e-business, including software and hardware bundles and e-business consulting. Hewlett-Packard launched in April 1999 a new marketing campaign "Hewlett-Packard – The E-Service Company." More and more hardware companies move their business away from hardware and start to offer consulting and software as well.

The concept of electronic business had been invented before the Internet became popular. In the 1970s E-business was already popular for financial networks, for example, which used propriety hard- and software solutions. Electronic Data Interchange (EDI) was also available long before the Internet was

---

[6]http://www.ibm.com/
[7]http://www.hp.com/

used for it. But without the Internet E-business would not have been possible on such a large scale. The private networks, which were used in the seventies and eighties of the 20th century, cost too much for smaller enterprises and were not accessible for private use.

The Internet is not just another application; it is neither software nor hardware. It is the environment for the business and communication of the future. The Internet combines many existing technologies into one framework. Computer networks and communication networks, like fax, telephone and pager are already integrated into the Internet. Sending a fax via the Internet is just as easy as receiving a voice mail. Not only different types of communication are possible via the Internet, but also the conversion between them is possible. It is, for example, possible to convert a fax to an e-mail or an e-mail to a message for the cell phone. This enables businesses that use different methods of communication to come together more easily. In addition to this it is also possible to translate the communication text from one language to the other on the fly. Not only between human languages like English and Russian, but also between programming and database languages. Using these interfaces it is possible to connect a wide range of different types of hard- and software, which are the basis for very different businesses.

1.2.2 Communication Gateways

Hotels, for example, all over the world use the Internet without having a direct link to it. They use e-mail to fax gateways. People may go to the web site of the hotel and decide to send an e-mail to one of the hotels. The e-mails are collected at an Internet provider where the web site is located and sent on via fax to the hotel. This is done all automatically. The hotels then can then either respond via traditional fax or telephone or can respond via the fax the to e-mail gateway. Suddenly people from all over the world can reach that particular hotel, book rooms there or ask for information at the cost of a local phone call. This is a fraction of the costs it used to be. Instead of calling or sending a fax to the hotel, which may be located in another country, all you do is call your local Internet provider to connect to the Internet and send off a request.

Although this is clearly not the best way to communicate with your clients over the Internet, it is probably the cheapest, as you do not have to invest in new equipment. All you have to do is to Internet-enable your existing devices using gateways. For many companies it is the first contact when they are unsure about an online venture.

E-business, the Internet and the globalization all depend on each other. The more global players exist the more e-business they want to do. The more e-business is online, the more people will be attracted to get direct Internet access. And the more people are online the more global players will arise.

E-business can be divided into three areas. It can be within the organization using the so-called Intranet. The Intranet uses Internet standards for

electronic communication. People on the Intranet are able to see organization-specific web sites. These web sites are separated from the rest of the world by firewalls and other security measures. People from outside of the organization are not able to see these private pieces of information.

Apple[8], for example, built an Intranet web site to sell older Apple systems and accessories to its employees. Before that, Apple e-mailed special promotion details to employees who then ordered the products over the telephone. The Intranet web site now allows employees to obtain current information and place orders online, eliminating expensive and time-consuming phone calls.

IBM[9] is using its "Refurbished Computer Warehouse Web" site to sell PCs coming off leases. The site allows employees to view the machines' specifications and then purchase them online with credit cards or through traditional methods such as a telephone. These offerings are restricted to employees and therefore should not be accessible nor visible to the outside world.

As employees get special prices, putting these prices into the public would put pressure on the company to reduce the price for the rest of the world. Depending on the security policies of the organization or company, people may be allowed to connect over the Internet via virtual private networks (VPN) to the Intranet using encryption lines and strong authentication for identification purposes.

The second area is the business-to-business (B2B) deals that are done over the Extranet. The Extranet consists of two Intranets connected via the Internet, whereby two organizations are allowed to see confidential data of the other. Normally only small parts of information are made available to the partner, just enough to enable the business. Business-to-business networks have existed long before the Internet. Many organizations have had private networks to talk to their partners and customers. But maintaining them was very expensive. Through the usage of the Internet the costs have been cut dramatically. In order to keep the business transactions private virtual private networks (VPNs) are used in most cases.

Thirdly there is the business-to-consumer (B2C) area. This is the most prominent one, which most people already have seen on the Internet. The web sites of Quelle[10], a German Fashion retailer, Discolandia[11], an online compact disc shop, and Megazine[12] offer goods and services to anybody who comes to their web sites. Traditionally this is what most people know as e-commerce; selling products on the web, but as we will discover in this book, there is more than just this.

No matter in which of the three areas you want to do business, you should ask the right questions, before going online. Just having a web page or the

---

[8]http://www.apple.com/

[9]http://www.ibm.com/

[10]http://www.quelle.de/

[11]http://www.discolandia.com/

[12]http://www.megazine.ch/

infrastructure for the Intranet, Extranet or Internet is no help. You need to decide on your target group and think about the processes, which could be done electronically.

Technically there is no difference between the Intranet, the Extranet and the Internet. The Extranet and Intranet are subsets of the Internet, which can be viewed only by certain groups. Therefore the book does not make a distinction between these three forms of networks. The electronic business that can be conducted is basically the same. With a restricted group it is easier to force certain technical standards, but otherwise they are very similar. I will write about differences whenever appropriate.

1.2.3   E-business Statistics

While listening to presentations, talks or reading books about e-business you will hear or read about statistics on the Internet, its users and the prospective business. There are many problems with these statistics, so I tried to avoid them in this book and tried to concentrate on the things that really matter.

If you look at the numbers of online users, you will see that they are going up. Depending on which statistics you believe the numbers are increasing either faster or slower, but the tendency is clear, they are growing. The same applies to business. Every day more business is done via the Web. But how much exactly nobody knows. Even if somebody would know for a certain moment, it would already be false in the next. With millions and millions of servers and clients connected to the Internet it is almost impossible to get precise data. There is no precise definition what an Internet user is or what business on the Internet means. An Internet user can be anything ranging from a browser window, a cookie session over to a real person or a web proxy. It all depends on your view of the world. If I connect from work to a certain web page I have to use a web proxy server which relays my request and saves the pages in a cache, just in case somebody else in my company needs the same information. The web server sees the proxy address only, so those 6,000 people working at my company site can appear to be one.

Although many people use statistics to show how successful the Internet is, I don't want to use them in this book. Figures for such a fast changing medium look outdated immediately, even if they were correct. There is no doubt that the Internet is a success and can be used in a highly successful manner for your company, as well. Therefore the book contains a lot of real world (or even better cyberworld) examples from the Internet with companies that are successful or have failed.

Once you have built up a web site it will be useful to create statistics on the use of the web pages, but those statistics will help you only with your web site and will never give you an idea on the Internet as a whole.

The Internet is the first mass media that allows interaction. Radio, television, newspapers, catalogues deliver information to your home, but there is no way of direct communication back to the others involved in a certain process. You can send an order back to the catalogue company or send a letter to your newspaper, but this is not what you get when you go in a shop or walk into the newspaper office. There you get an immediate reaction on behalf of your request and this is what the Internet does. It moves everyone together, every piece of information, every service and every business to be instantly available anytime. The dream of the global village becomes true.

The winners of the Internet today are the UPS' and Federal Expresses of the world. Due to the fact that many products on the Internet are not digitized yet, someone needs to ship the products from the online merchant to the customers. This will change in the future, as books, music and videos, which are the bestsellers so far, are digitized easily. The problem with a digital video, for example, is the copyright issue. It is too easy to copy it without paying for it. Therefore new methods of shipping digital products will be needed. We will see later on in the book how this could be done.

1.2.4 Strategies for Digital Business

Just going online, because all competitors are, is the wrong strategy. There are many reasons to go online, so choose one or more to be your primary goals. Otherwise it will be difficult to measure the success of your online venture. See what you competitors are doing and look out for new competitors that are now closer to you through the Internet.

In order to set realistic goals for your e-business, it is necessary to find out what portion of the overall business will be conducted via the web in the next twelve months and two years. Although you are most likely not getting the figures right, as the Internet is moving far to fast to be able to deliver reliable forecasts, these figures can indicate a trend. Where do you want to be then? Do you want to go fully digital and use the Internet as the main channel for the business, or is it "just" the fourth channel for your business. This leads to the question of how fast you are planning to grow your company. Many Internet start-ups have managed to grow very fast in very short time. In order to do so, you need a working Intranet based on the same key technologies as the Internet (e.g. TCP/IP). Only if your business is fully digitized you are able to grow at such a rate, as eBay[13] or Yahoo[14] have grown in 1998 and that was more than a thousand percent. This is essential because the design of the electronic business and the support infrastructure must be able to handle growth effortlessly over time. Otherwise, the company may lose valuable time and money re-engineering a site after a few months.

The expectations within the company need to be set right, otherwise the online venture will not maximize your revenues. Other than expected in the early years of the Internet, it takes much longer to get an return on invest-

---

[13]http://www.ebay.com/
[14]http://www.yahoo.com/

Expectations

ment. Therefore your company needs some good financial backing, otherwise you may not succeed on the Internet, which will also have implications on the rest of your business. Amazon.com took five years until it could get back the investments it made up-front.

If the Internet is used for cost-reduction, it is necessary to measure the costs for every single item up-front, which may cost more than using the Internet. The re-engineering of the businesses processes will help more than using new technology in most cases. In many cases less staff is required to perform a task. With the free time of the staff it is possible to implement new business processes without additional cost.

Reasons for Going Online

Some of the most important reasons why a company needs to be on the Internet are the following:

- **Expand market reach** – Collect experience with a new customer segment.

- **Visibility** – Generate more visibility in your target market and gain mind share.

- **Responsiveness** – Increase responsiveness to customers and partners.

- **New services** – Provide new services for customers and partners.

- **Strengthening Business Relationships** – Real-time data increase the profit for every partner involved.

- **Cost-reduction** – Reduce cost of product, support, service and estate.

- **Channel Conflicts** – Prevent and resolve channel conflicts.

Table 1.1.

Table 1.1 contains a short list of good reasons why a company needs to go online. In the following subsection each of these reasons is explored more in-depth and online examples are used to verify the reasoning. There are more reasons to go online, of course, but most companies will have one or more of the above reasons, why they want to go online. But be careful, do not let your competitors drive you to this decision. Be there before the competition or take your time to develop a full business plan.

Once you have decided on the goals, you need to find criteria for measuring the success. Cost-reduction, for example, may not be really measurable. If a printer manufacturer is offering printer drivers on its web page, measuring the cost-reduction may be difficult, as the company may not have measured the costs before the introduction of the online service. Sending out floppy disks and CD-ROMs would have cost more, but were part of the price for the printer. Measuring now parts of the product separately may become difficult. Although measuring the cost-reduction may not be possible, the introduction of the online service will reduce costs for further products, as they require your company to put a price tag on parts of a product.

1.2.5 Strengths and Advantages of E-business

The strengths of e-business depend on the strengths of the Internet, which is the preferred infrastructure today and in the future. The Internet is available all over the world, twenty-four hours a day, seven days a week. It is simple to use and the transaction costs for the end user are low. The costs are also extremely low for the vendors on the Internet, compared to traditional distribution channels. The Internet allows two-way communications and is built around open standards. The two-way communication allows for direct feedback of the customers and the open standards mean interoperability between companies, web sites and services. It is fairly easy to integrate processes, services and products, once they have been digitized.

Using the latest software from BroadVision[15] and others, it is possible to customize your entire web site for every single user, without any additional costs. The mass-customization allows us to create web pages, products and services that suit the requirements of the user. A customized web page does not only include the preferred layout of the customer, but also a pre-selection of goods the customer may be interested in. Internet pricing becomes irrelevant, as all prices drop to the lowest possible level. The only chance to distinguish the products of your company from the ones of your competitor is to add services that increase the value of the product without increasing its price (or just slightly).

Although many people are afraid of security breaches on the Internet, it can be made very secure through encryption, digital signatures and firewall software and secure procedures. This will allow companies to offer private information to their customers and business partners without having to fear that an unauthorized person is able to see that particular information. Banks, for example, are able to allow customers to look at their account balance in real-time without having to worry that a hacker will be able to break into the bank's

---

[15] http://www.broadvision.com/

computer system. This is achieved through the use of the above-mentioned security components, which allow trade on the Internet to expand.

Companies need to protect their customer profiles, as this information is very private and should not be passed on from one organization to the other without written consensus from the customer. The customers should never get the feeling that they are followed around on the web site and that every click is saved into a database. Providing a link to the privacy policy from the home page is a must for all electronic entrepreneurs, but only few have done it so far.

Advantages of E-business

Getting into electronic business has several advantages:

- **Global Accessibility and Sales Reach** – Businesses can expand their customer base, and even expand their product line.

- **Closer Relationships** – Business-to-business sellers can grow closer relationships.

- **Free Samples** – Products can be sampled via the Web fast, easily and free of charge.

- **Reduced Costs** – Businesses can reduce their costly production by dynamically adjusting prices.

- **Media Breaks** – The Internet reduces the number of media breaks that are necessary to transport information.

- **Time to Market** – Shorter time to market and faster response time to changing market demands.

- **Customer Loyalty** – Improved customer loyalty and service through easier access to the latest information and a never closing site.

Table 1.2.

A web site is a good opportunity to reduce the cost of labor. By using a web site to answer questions of customers, one is able to reduce the number of calls to your service number and one is able to offer twenty-four hours of assistance. Your call center will be reduced and the people, who are now without any job, can be reused to build up an online database, which helps customers to find even more answers online. This can go so far that only one or two people are left to talk to customers on the phone and they get their answers from the company's web pages.

Companies who want to invest in electronic business are not restricted to the publishing, entertainment, information and software industries, as one could imagine. Every company will need to invest, as electronic business is more than just selling things online, it means moving processes and communication online, and this affects every company.

Today many work and communication processes have to deal with media breaks. This costs a lot of time. Consider someone calling a shop to order some products. The shop assistant will write the order down and pass it on to the person who is responsible for booking it. This person may type in the order and send out the goods. This simple process already has two media breaks: phone to paper and paper to computer. The information did not change, but the medium that carried the information did. Electronic business drives the information onto one digital platform, which can be shared by all the participants in the business process without having the risk of losing parts of the information in a conversion process. Digital information is not only more convenient, but allows also new applications, which were not possible beforehand.

Online tracking, for example, has become quite successful. This application could only be implemented because all relevant information were available electronically.

1.3 Reasons for Going Online

1.3.1 Expanding Market Reach

One of the major advantages of the Internet is its global availability. If you have a little company it is quite simple to expand the market reach beyond your geographic location and your current customer segments. Although this may relieve some of the pressure you experience in your current target market it will mean new pressure from competitors who are already on the Internet and are trying to get into your markets. The first phase would be to collect experience with a new customer segment and the new medium Internet.

Barnes & Noble[16], one of the largest chains of bookshops in the United States were forced to open a branch on the Internet, because they felt the pressure of Amazon.com[17], which is selling books over the Internet only and attracted more and more people who traditionally went into the shops of Barnes & Noble. The online venture started small for Barnes & Noble in order to gain experience, but grew fast after the initial pilot and has become since then number two in the online book selling market.

---

[16]http://www.barnesandnoble.com/
[17]http://www.amazon.com/

Tupperware on the other hand decided to ban all activities on the Internet. The Tupperware web site[18] only contains marketing information. According to the CEO of Tupperware, the Internet is a marketing medium and they do not want to use it for anything else. The personal contact in the form of Tupper parties is essential; it is part of their company culture. In my humble opinion Tupperware is losing a huge opportunity, especially with people who just want to order another Tupperware box or replace one and won't do so, as they have to go to the next Tupper party, which will take up a lot more of the customers' precious time than they may be willing to spend.

On the Internet every company that offers goods, services or information is reduced to the same size: to the size of the customer's browser window. Therefore it is easy for a small online translation service to compete with a large one. The customer will see differences in pricing, service and the way the company presents itself on the Web. This and what other people say about the online service are the basis for the decision. Marketing for the web site is important. Many people choose a web site because others are talking about it or because they have seen advertisements for it. If you had the choice to go either to Barnes & Noble's web site or to MediaTechBooks'[19] web site, you would go and visit the first one because the brand name is well known. But other than with traditional shops, the customer most probably will also visit the second to double-check prices and offerings. Moving from one bookshop to the other costs only a few seconds and the customer does not feel the pressure of a shop assistant who may help the customer in making his or her decision.

1.3.2   Generating Visibility

Another important goal, especially for small and medium-sized enterprises (the so-called SMEs) is to gain more visibility. The Internet allows a company to present itself at very low cost. Although buying a computer and setting up an Internet connection may not be cheap, once you have it, setting up new web pages and adding prices, products and information costs very little and the costs for reproduction are practically nothing. You do not need to replicate a catalogue, a brochure or a flyer. Put it onto the Internet and it replicates itself. Each user generates its own copy when accessing your web server. This is especially true when you use one-to-one marketing tools that allow the customer to see a personalized view of your products, services and information. Through co-branding, you are also able to present your products and services on other web sites.

Generating visibility is substantial for every company. The better known your company is, the more people will be interested in doing business with you. In the early years of the Internet being online was a synonym of being cool and forward-thinking, but it was in no way a must to be online. This may

---

[18]http://www.tupperware.com/
[19]http://www.mediatechbooks.de/

be true for certain industries, although it is difficult to find an industry where this is still true. Missing the opportunity to present your own company on the Internet, even with only a simple web site, is something nobody can do today. Several years ago the Security First Network Bank[20] wanted to become the first Internet bank in the US. Now it is one of the largest electronic banks in the Internet business.

Early adopters have the advantage of getting to know technology in advance of the competitors. Therefore new technology enables small start-ups to become large organizations. Dell[21], who was selling in the early nineties computers over the phone, wanted to become the biggest computer reseller on the Internet. There is no doubt that they have achieved this goal. For Dell it was easy to move from telephone business to Internet business. As they do not have a channel, which involved shops and resellers, they did not have to resolve a potential channel conflict. All they did was move from one communication medium to another one, which offered them more possibilities.

With the traditional telephone business Dell had to send out catalogues to its customers. Using the Internet they have a web site which can be reached twenty-four hours a day with a lot of technology and little human resources behind. Once the web site has been set up, it is able to accept orders and offer instant help without any user interaction. As they still have their traditional telephone business, they have a call center, which can also be used to help web customers.

1.3.3   Strengthening Business Relationships

Implementing business-to-business communication on the Internet has a huge potential. In the past many industries have been using electronic data interchange (EDI) to simplify business processes and reduce the cost of communication between the business partners. Through EDI suppliers, manufacturers, distributors and retailers are able to share information on the inventory and enhance the flow of information and goods through the supply chain. Passing on the information electronically reduced the cost of communication and the number of errors.

The disadvantage of EDI is that it is very expensive and time consuming to implement, therefore many SMEs have not implemented it. Once a company has implemented it, every partner that uses it needs to implement it as well. Even if two companies have an existing EDI infrastructure, the special connection between these companies needs to be implemented. Consider a manufacturer with 50 suppliers; the costs are enormous for the manufacturer as it has to implement 50 EDI infrastructures.

The paradigm of EDI is good, but the technology was too expensive. With the Internet it has become accessible for all companies. Costs that have been

---

[20]http://www.sfnb.com/
[21]http://www.dell.com/

reduced by fifty times are not seldom and EDI on the web allows for more content. Exchange of multi-media information has been made possible and fosters much tighter relationships among participants. The real-time capabilities of the Internet provide a sense of teamwork and shared goals. EDI via the Internet enables all components and systems of a virtual value chain to communicate with each other automatically.

Early EDI implementations on the Web were proprietary standards, but more and more implementations do EDI via the Web by using XML documents. For further information on XML see Chapter 9.

1.3.4 Responsiveness

The Internet can support increased responsiveness to your customers easily. Increasing responsiveness to customers and partners is very important to tie customers to a company. Being responsive gives customers the feeling that they are treated well by the company. Trans-O-Flex[22], for example, a logistics and shipping company in Germany gives customers the possibility to check the location of their shipments at any time. Although this feature nowadays is a must for all companies, it was something revolutionary a few years ago. Instead of calling your logistics partner and asking what happened to your goods, you can just go to their web site and check yourself, which means a cost reduction for yourself and even a greater one for the shipping company.

Responsiveness means also that when you give out e-mail addresses to your customers, somebody needs to answer these e-mails fast and competently. If they do not know the answer to the questions, they should know whom to ask within the company. As a rule of thumb, e-mail should be responded within one working day, even if you do not have the answers ready. Send a short notice that you have received the e-mail and that you will try to help to resolve the queries. Offering up-to-date information on your company to partners is also very important. GemPlus[23], one of Europe's leading smart card manufacturers, for example, provides partners with sensitive up-to-date information via a secured web connection (using basic authentication and SSL encryption). Partners are able to see this information using their logins and passwords. This part of the web site is GemPlus' Extranet area. As you can see, technically there is no difference between Extranet and Internet, except for the limitation on the viewers.

1.3.5 Offering New Services

Offering new services is also a reason to go online. Introducing new services in traditional markets is difficult and expensive. The Internet on the other hand offers the possibility to introduce new services with very little start-up

---

[22]http://www.trans-o-flex.de/

[23]http://www.gemplus.fr/

costs. New services should not only be provided for customers and partners, but also for employees. A service for the employees could be for example a search engine for the Intranet. The larger the company grows the harder it is to find relevant information on the internal network. A search engine is only helpful if all employees put their documents online. Even if they are not able to create HTML documents, it is fairly easy to upload existing word documents to the Intranet, which can be indexed by the search engine as well. The search hit-rate for non-web documents is lower than with HTML documents, but still much higher than not putting them online at all.

Hewlett-Packard provides specific configuration bundles to resellers over its order@hp.com web site[24]. This is also a new service to Hewlett-Packard's offerings. Up to then Hewlett-Packard did not offer pre-configured bundles online. The next step was to offer an online configurator where partners, resellers and end customers are now able to configure their PCs and Unix Servers using a simple web page. Complex configurations need special configurator tools. More information on configurator tools can be found in Chapter 7.

AutoByTel[25], the "Dell of the car industry," offers a complete set of car services online. It is possible to buy, to rent, to insure and lease a car from a single web site. AutoByTel as the name suggests used to sell cars via telephone, so moving to the web was a natural thing to do.

1.3.6   Cost Reduction

The cost for estate, service support and production can be reduced greatly through the use of the Internet. So it is another very good reason to move business to the Internet. Printer manufacturers such as Canon[26] or Epson[27] use the Internet to distribute printer drivers and updates. The cost for replicating floppy disks or CD-ROMs is not very high, but because of the high volume of printers they sell, it is a very large sum in the end. The replication cost on the Internet are nearly zero. Although downloading the driver does not cost anything, the infrastructure to do this needs to be paid for. By generating new business on the Internet, these infrastructure costs become irrelevant to these companies, as they are generating additional business and offer an instant solution to missing printer drivers as one new service. This results in more content customers and less overhead.

The ExhiBit Gallery[28] in Pisa, Italy, a small gallery focusing on contemporary paintings closed down its showrooms shortly after it moved to the Internet. The costs for the showrooms were too high to maintain and someone had to be there every day, just in case some visitors came by. As only very few visitors

---

[24]http://euros.external.hp.com/

[25]http://www.autobytel.com/

[26]http://www.canon.com/

[27]http://www.epson.com/

[28]http://www.gallery-net.com/individuals/

came during normal business hours, there was no reason, why someone should be there all the time. Their first reaction was to reduce the opening times, but this didn't help much. Moving to the Internet did help a lot. The showrooms are now open 24 hours a day and about four hundred visitors a day from all over the world are visiting the online gallery.

Costs can also be reduced in the customer care center by offering frequently asked questions (FAQ) pages, where customers can find answer to frequently asked questions about a product or service. Newsgroups where customers can ask questions can also be very helpful. Other customers may be able to share their experiences and reduce the work load for the customer care center. In addition, companies can support employees and business partners over their corporate Intranets, keeping them informed and soliciting their feedback.

A company web site can also help to reduce inventory costs by shortening the sales and supply cycles. By distributing information in electronic form, you can reduce material costs by saving on paper, the printing and the manual distribution. The customer is taking over parts of the distribution costs.

Cost saving should not be seen as the primary goal in the long term. In the long term everybody will have saved cost and increased the profit. In order to survive it is necessary to have a deep relationship with your customers. This will allow you to charge more money for a service than others do, because service quality is what matters, not the base product.

1.3.7   Just in Time Inventory

As price pressure is very high on the Internet, it is necessary to reduce operating costs by reacting much faster to demand, as demand is created in real-time. Therefore it is necessary to cut down inventory to reduce the cost and adapt more dynamically to the wishes of the customers. The longer it takes to reach suppliers, the more inventory a company needs to hold to account for errors and delays.

Having large quantities of one product is not helpful, if your customer's have highly dynamic demand for certain products. Therefore it is necessary to build stronger relationships with your suppliers and integrate them into your digital ordering process. Estimates on the product sales for the next day, week or month (depending on your inventory cycle) also helps to keep the overhead low. Therefore digital communication between factories, marketing and purchasing departments becomes essential.

In the United States an initiative called "Collaborative Planning Forecasting Replenishment"[29] (CPFR) has been set up by retailers, wholesalers and manufacturers. It is in the process of setting up standards and guidelines for better forecasting. Using this system retailers and suppliers are able to exchange their forecast electronically and in real-time in order to change orders or production.

---

[29]http://www.cpfr.org/

Online bookshops, such as Amazon.com have only very limited stocks. They rely totally on their suppliers to deliver the books in real-time, which they then pass on to their customers.

Time management

1.3.8 Preventing Financial Loss

This lead us to the last reason we want to discuss here to go online. Preventing financial losses is one of the most important reasons. Although the Internet may pose a financial threat to your company it means also a great opportunity. The first few years, many companies need to invest heavily into a new infrastructure. But once you have made the break-even, it is much easier to resist the changes of the future. Amazon.com was in red figures until 1999 and only then a break-even was reached. Although being highly successful, marketing and infrastructure have cost more than the company received in revenues. In order to grow, Amazon.com needed to invest a lot in new customer segments.

invest & gain

One of Germany's largest shopping malls, My-World[30] had to re-launch its web site in early 1998, because of lacking success. Since then it became an important online shopping portal for Germany. IBM's WorldAvenue[31] had to be closed down, as it generated no revenues. These two examples show also quite clearly that it is not sufficient to convert existing environments to the Internet. They need to be adapted to have an impact and to be a success. In Chapter 7 we will see how shopping malls can be transformed to portal sites and become highly successful.

impact in the market

Although the Internet may pose a financial risk to your company, it should be no obstacle for you. Not investing into e-business will kill your company for sure. In order to make your e-business venture a success, the guidelines in this book may be helpful. As with most guides, this is not the only way to conduct business, but it is a way, which balances risks and investments in such a way that you will be highly likely to succeed.

Survival hint!

1.3.9 Relevance to IT

Although your IT department should not need to be the driver for your business decisions, without them you are nobody on the e-business side of life. Your IT needs to adapt to understand the new needs for the New Economy. They need to employ Internet experts without reducing people with knowledge for the systems currently used. The IT department can gain experience in the Internet world by implementing an Intranet first. If you do not have an IT department or you do not want to invest directly into Internet technologies, then you should consider outsourcing the whole operation. If you have your own IT department and want to implement your own e-business strategy, keep in touch with them to learn what can be done and how much it would cost.

IT Dept.

---

[30]http://www.my-world.de/
[31]used to be http://www.worldavenue.com/

For some new services it may be better to outsource the development and just maintain it on the own network. Your existing IT infrastructure should be able to cope with the changes that come along with the Internet. The Internet is changing all the time, so you need the right people with the right skills to move on into the right direction.

As more traditional electronic services, such as e-mail, remote access and web server hosting have become commodities, or off the shelf products, these services can be outsourced to third party services who specialize in these areas. This frees up resources in your IT department to deal with new services and technologies that are not commodities yet. Part of the IT department would start to act as a broker for services between the internal customers and the external service providers. This would allow IT to maintain control over the services, without having to keep up operations on a daily basis.

1.3.10 Concerns for Going Online

Traditional companies may have concerns for going online, as they have established processes and channels, which would require investments for the digital age. Many conservative companies are reluctant to invest into new technologies, processes and ideas, as they are successful in their businesses and fear that the investment will do more harm than good.

Employees in companies fear also that with the introduction of the Internet they may lose their jobs, as they are not qualified to work on the Internet. The Internet changes the work of many employees drastically. It requires the employee to adapt to the ever changing Internet. Long-life learning becomes more important in order to keep up with the latest developments on the Internet. Other than with traditional business were maybe nothing changes for ten years, technology and paradigms on the Internet change must faster.

In 1997 push technology was expected to take off and become the next big thing. Many companies were heavily investing in this technology and disappeared soon after. In 1998 nobody knew anymore why there was such a fuss about it. Push technology is still being used, but it has been integrated into many products, such as newsfeeds or automatic software updates which are triggered by the server and not by the user (which is called pull). The certainty on which many businesses relied in the past is gone. Only the companies that are prepared to invest will survive the challenges of the 21st century.

Resellers and merchants fear that disintermediation will ruin their business. Through the Internet it has become easy for a manufacturer to get in direct contact with the end customer. But most manufacturers cannot do this without conflict between the company and the traditional channels. Therefore manufacturers may be reluctant to go online, in order to prevent a channel conflict. More forward-thinking manufacturers may use the Internet, but not to reach out for the end customers, but increase their relationships with their resellers, for example.

Concerns on the Internet

When going online people have many concerns. If you want to provide a solution, you need to take them into account.

- **Channel Conflict** – Disintermediation may happen.

- **Competition** – The competition is growing from a local competition to a world-wide competition.

- **Copyright** – Once information has been published on the Internet, it becomes easy to copy it and use it for own business.

- **Customer Acceptance** – Many companies are afraid that their customers won't accept the new channel.

- **Legal Issues** – There is no legal framework for the Internet that is binding on a world-wide basis.

- **Loyalty** – The Internet is less personal, so people are not bound to a certain vendor.

- **Pricing** – The New Economy makes it easier to compare prices. Prices will drop, so quality and add-on services become more important.

- **Security** – Most companies are very concerned about security on the Internet.

- **Service** – A customer can compare the offerings of a certain company much easier with another one.

- **Viability** – Many companies are unsure about the viability of their digital business case.

Table 1.3.

Companies offering information and soft products on the Internet are concerned about copyright issues. Compact disc sales are dropping although more people are listening to music, the reason for this are the CD recorders, which make it easy to duplicate audio CDs and the file format MP3, which allows transfer of songs over the Internet in a highly compressed way. Typical files in the MP3 format are compressed at a ratio of 1:10, resulting in a 3 minute song to be 3 MB instead of 30 MB. New appliances such as the Rio MP3[32] player replace disc man. Although unauthorized copying music over the Internet is illegal many sites offer the files. Search for your favorite music and you can be almost sure that you will find something.

A successful online business needs to be accepted by the customers. If none of your customers has access to the Internet then providing an online service is no good, if your company does not try to target new customers. Providing your current customers with Internet access and Internet-enabled equipment may cost too much. In order to move your customers to the Internet you need to offer additional services that were not available without. Online ordering should offer the possibility of tracking the order, for example, which would not have been possible without the Internet.

Without a global consent on the legal framework that needs to be implemented on the Internet many companies are reluctant to invest, as they are not sure what the consequences may be for them.

1.4   Differentiating between E-business Categories

1.4.1   Overview

Electronic business is a super-set of business cases, which have been digitized and work now on the Internet. An e-business category is defined by the business case and not by the technology used to implement it. Over time more and more types of business will be converted to a digital form, even though it may seem impossible today. Technology is moving fast to make things possible tomorrow, which seemed impossible today.

1.4.2   Categories

The following categories have been selected, because of their proven success on the Internet. Many other categories exist and in order to make one of these categories successful it needs to interact with the other categories. Commerce, for example, without marketing and communication does not make a lot of sense. These categories need to work together, both offline and online. The Internet offers huge possibilities to integrate the categories and automate the interaction between the processes.

E-Auctioning

Auctioning on the Internet has become a new dimension. In traditional auctions a number of people turned up at the auction house and some people were

---

[32]http://www.diamondmm.com/

allowed to bid over the phone. Getting to the auction house or bidding over the phone did involve costs, which may be higher than the value of the goods. Either auctions were restricted to a location or to a very exclusive circle of people.

The Internet makes auctions more democratic allowing everyone with an Internet connection to bid for any good offered. Everyone is able to go to the auction web site with a click, no matter where the server is located physically. The Internet also speeds up the bidding process. In the real world it can take quite a while until a final bid has been made. On the Internet most live bids are over in a few seconds. During the live bid an auctioneer registers the bids and hands over the goods to the highest bidder.

Besides the live bid, the larger sites offer bidding for everyone. The auction sites offer the possibility to present goods on a web page, which belong to individuals and that they want to sell. These private auctions are not live, the bidders place their price onto the web page and the auctioneer waits until a certain value has been reached or a time limit has been passed and then hands out the goods to the lucky one. Suddenly everyone does not only become a bidder, but also has the possibility to organize an auction.

eBay[33], QXL[34] and Ricardo[35] offer the possibility for everyone to become either a bidder or auctioneer, or both at the same time for two different products. The web site becomes an infrastructure for exchanging goods based on the auction model, which works basically by setting the prices by demand.

The whole Internet is transforming the fixed price structures to a more dynamic pricing. Auction web sites are only the beginning. In a few years time, individual prices based on customer demand will be on every web site offering goods, information or services.

E-Banking

Electronic banking is one of the most successful online businesses. E-banking allows customers to access their accounts and execute orders through a simple-to-use web site. There is no special software to install other than a web browser and many banks do not charge for this service. Some banks even lower costs for online transactions versus real life banking transactions. Electronic banking saves individuals and companies time and money.

Online banking puts the power of banking into the hands of the customer and allows the customers to self-service themselves with all their banking needs, just as customers have become used to getting money from an automated teller machine (ATM) instead of walking up to the cash desk in the bank. With this online service, customers can view their account details, review their accounts histories, transfer funds, order checks, pay bills, re-order checks and get in touch with the customer care department of the bank. The

---

[33]http://www.ebay.com/
[34]http://www.qxl.co.uk/
[35]http://www.ricardo.de/

only transaction that currently can't be done is the withdrawals of cash, but banks are working on resolving this problem.

To get started the virtual banking customer needs a computer or embedded device connected to the Internet and a browser. Depending on the security strategy by the online bank, you may need to install a plug-in or enable Java to increase the level of security in your browser. The plug-in or Java applet are used to increase the level of encryption to make sure nobody can intercept your banking transactions. Even more sophisticated systems use smart card technology to allow secure access for their customers. Another option to make banking more secure is used in addition to the ID and login; a list of transaction numbers (TAN), which are one-time passwords that can be used for a single transaction.

Many people use PC banking software such as Quicken, which are personal financial management software packages, which are not the same as electronic banking. The major difference is that with PC banking, software is loaded onto your computer and all your transactions are handled through a third party vendor, adding security issues to the e-banking service.

Electronic banking is an online service that allows customers to perform the same banking functions as in Quicken except that they can access their accounts directly over the Internet.

E-Commerce

If we look back, commerce in the pre-Internet age was very restricted compared to the possibilities the information technologies and the infostructure (information infrastructure) offers. The major limiting factors were time and space. Even if shops were open twenty-four hours a day, only a limited amount of customers can come to the location of the shop. The shop can also offer only a limited selection of goods, as space is limited on the premises of the shop.

A shop on the Internet is unlimited in space and time. There are no limits in the amount of products a shop can offer. Amazon.com offers more than 4.7 million books. Imagine a bookshop, which has 4.7 million books in stock. The comparison may not seem fair, as Amazon does not stock the books, but orders them on demand. But Amazon.com does offer information on every single book.

Online retailers (sometimes also called e-tailers) offer either more products than traditional retailers do or more service for the same products. On the Internet books, compact disks and tickets are outselling their traditional counterparts, as these products are bought because of their content and not because of their design. The look and feel of a flight ticket is not important, the price and the service are what really matters. New technologies make the Internet also attractive for goods that are bought on an emotional basis, because of their design and not their content.

The Internet is changing the traditional sales model, which is tactical in nature. The companies used to produce a deliverable, either a product, service or piece of information and then employ the 4P's of marketing (price, product, promotion and placement) as the foundation of their efforts to sell it. Internet commerce, on the other hand, is far more strategic. While most companies view their products purely in terms of the demand conversion stage, Internet commerce will force them to increasingly view the entire sales cycle (market development, demand creation, fulfillment, customer support and customer retention) as their product. In the tactical model, these above mentioned phases in the sales cycle are just extras that aid in pre- and post-sales. In a strategic model, however, they are building blocks of the entire sales message.

Many people think that e-commerce is the same as e-business, but as defined here it is only a subset. This may be true for many end customers who only deal with companies when buying goods. E-commerce was one of the first business types to become digitally available, but the Internet offers more than just buying and selling products and services.

E-Directories

Directories have always played an important role in finding a particular service or product. Telephone directories, the so-called white pages for private telephone numbers and the yellow pages for businesses have been essential in locating a person or business. In addition to the directories in book form, the telephone companies allowed people to call in to ask for information.

These two functionalities have been merged on the Internet. The database is located in a single place, providing a centralized functionality, but offering it to anyone at any time, making it a decentralized solution.

The Internet offers the possibility to replicate the phone directories without many hassles, but it can do more than just search for a name and receive a phone number. On the Internet, for example, it is possible to enter a phone number and get the name. Moreover new directories are necessary to locate the web pages of people and businesses and their e-mail addresses.

The Internet makes the retrieval easier and more difficult at the same time. Easier, because the means of searching are more powerful. But finding a particular piece of information has become more difficult as the amount of information has increased dramatically with the introduction of the Internet.

E-Engineering

Engineering has also changed dramatically over the last few years. Just a few years ago, engineers working on a draft needed to be all in the same office to work effectively. If a design needed to be sent out to another location, large prints needed to be made, which were sent via postal service to the other location. There the design was refined, checked or processed. All these processes involved a lot of manual work, making them slow and error-prone.

The Internet changed the speed of design. It enabled electronic collaboration to a much higher degree than was possible ever before. The location of the engineers does not play a role anymore. Everyone with an Internet connection is able to take part in the development. New tools for concurrent development have been developed to support the possibilities of the Internet.

Through the Internet is has also become possible to develop continuous engineering by letting engineers participate from all over the world. Open source development is done that way very efficiently. Anybody is able to take part and can donate a piece of code whenever there has been some time to program it. This will vary for every person involved.

E-Franchising

In the past big traditional franchising companies like McDonald's[36] and Benetton[37] have made their money by vending their products and brands to resellers who sell exclusively the products of the franchising company. These resellers are called franchising partners. By offering a set of products and brands the franchising company guarantees a certain success for the retailer, as people tend to like buying these products, as the brands are well-known. The advantage of the franchising companies is that they do not need to invest in shop personnel, for example. The franchising partner is responsible for the employees and the financial success of the single outlet.

Electronic franchising works very similarly. It has become actually much easier on the Internet. Moving digital products, processes and brands is extremely easy. The affiliation programs of the large booksellers on the Internet are one example. They are not truly franchisers, as the large booksellers have their own store. But they allow franchising partners to exclusively distribute their products on the partners' web sites. The advantage of this system is that there is no distribution costs involved. It is possible to link to the original products without letting the customers know. Quelle[38], for example, is selling books on its web site. Books are not part of their core product set, but through a co-operation with Libri[39], they are able to offer more than 1.5 million books on their web site.

E-Gambling

Although there are moral issues about gambling, it is one of the most profitable businesses on the Internet. In the real-world gambling is restricted by many laws, making it difficult to access the casinos. The owners of the games often need to pay high taxes to the state, which make it also difficult to create competition. Per state only a certain amount of casinos are allowed.

On the Internet this has changed dramatically. Gambling is still not legal in some states and the taxes are still high in these states, but the business

---

[36]http://www.mcdonalds.com/
[37]http://www.benetton.com/
[38]http://www.quelle.de/
[39]http://www.libri.de/

has moved to places where gambling is legal and only low taxes need to be paid. Most gambling web sites have moved to the Caribbean or South America, where no laws on gambling have been implemented.

The companies who operate the gambling web sites are able to operate the full program of games, without any restrictions. As the owners have their companies in countries where gambling is legal, they are able to operate without fearing the intervention of the state. But other than real-world casinos, which are restricted to the geographical location, online casinos are able to attract gamblers from all over the world with a mouse click. Companies such as 123Gambling[40] and CasinoPlace[41] attract hundreds of thousands of gamblers every day.

E-Learning

The constant change on the Internet requires also a change of learning. In the industrial age, the subjects and the content taught did not change a lot. Changes to the curriculum did occur over the years, but compared to the Information age change was extremely slow. Having a job for forty years, working in a steel plant, for example, is not possible anymore. Fluctuation between jobs is much higher, which requires a readjustment of the job focus. New technologies appear in Internet time, which require learning new technologies, paradigms and processes all the time. Long-life learning has become a necessity, as teachers need the same time to learn a new subject just as long as the pupils need to. As knowledge becomes a major income factor, it is often not possible to wait and learn a thing in a school.

Computer-based training (CBT) has been introduced a few years ago, making it possible to learn via computer. Software is used to explain the subject and then tests the pupil. Although this is an effective way of learning some subjects, there is nobody you could ask, in case of a misunderstanding.

Electronic learning sometimes also called Internet-based training (IBT) offers a new dimension in digital learning. Instead of receiving an executable file, which is used to explain and test a subject, the material is presented online. Tests are executed in real-time together with other participants and the pupils are able to exchange ideas and questions. In addition an online teacher can be offered, which is a real teacher, who may explain topics to anyone attending a course, no matter where the people are located. This can all happen in real-time. Instead of waiting for the next hour, the students can connect to the learning network, whenever they want, making the learning experience more individual, allowing people to learn at their own pace.

An Internet-based training can also be offered to students, before the complete course is available. For hot topics the course can be developed at the same time as the students start to learn.

---

[40]http://www.123gambling.com/
[41]http://www.casinoplace.com/

E-Mailing

Many people do not think about e-mail when talking about digital business. But communication is the basis of all business. The Internet breaks into the traditional communication markets. Postal services and telecommunications companies are losing market share to the electronic communication, especially e-mail. E-mail combines the strengths of phone calls and letters. The advantage of a phone call is its immediacy and the letter has the advantage that everything is in written form. The Internet enables instant communication in written form, either by e-mail or online chat.

More and more businesses are talking digitally to each other. Other than a phone call, e-mails can contain more than just the text. It is possible to attach files, which may, for example, contain formatted documents, presentations, images or sounds. Information can be shared much more easily.

E-mail does also change the way people communicate. Instead of writing down every aspect in a single letter, thoughts may be spread over multiple e-mails. The advantage is that a thought may evolve through instant response, but it also means that you expect instant response to every e-mail that has been sent out, just as everyone expects a response from you.

E-Marketing

Traditional marketing was focusing on target groups and creating a positive image for that particular group. Communication in advertising was one way only. The marketing team could not get immediate results on the customer reaction. In the pre-information society this was fine, as there was time to do surveys and publish the results, which influenced the company strategy and the products.

In the information society everything has started to flow. Products, strategies, prices, everything depends on the customers' needs. Everything becomes much more customer centric. The demands of the customer directly affects product design, marketing strategies, and the product pricing. As marketing traditionally has direct ties to the customer, the information flowing back from the customer in real-time needs to be passed on to the appropriate department within the company to react in real-time to the ever faster changing demands of the customers.

The Internet allows companies to react to individual customer demands. All customers can be treated in their preferred way. One-to-one marketing has become the standard way of dealing with customers over the Internet. One-to-many marketing does not work anymore in Internet time.

E-Operational Resources Management

Besides the goods that are needed for production, companies need to buy operational resources. These are the non-production goods and services that are required and managed on a daily basis to run the day-to-day business. The areas for operational resources include capital equipment (such as computer equipment), maintenance, repair and operating (MRO) supplies (such as office supplies) and travel and entertainment (T&E) (such as travel services).

The process of acquiring the operational resources involves many organizations and departments within the company, which deal with many different suppliers. The suppliers are providing services, goods and information. Although the operating resources do account for a large amount of company spending, the buying process is often not well organized and managed. In many cases a paper-based process is used for ordering new pencils and phone lines. Due to its decentralized approach in many companies, every department is able to handle the operational resources on an individual basis, which results in higher prices than through a central buying organization. Once a central buying organization has been put in place, the paper-based process needs to be digitized in order to automate, control and leverage it. As long as the process is not digitized, the company is not able to control the spending and the suppliers involved in the process.

Operational Resources Management (ORM) allows companies to manage operational resources more strategically, by using the Internet and its connectivity to provide a communication infrastructure, where buyers and suppliers can work together on a direct basis without losing control over the spending. Actually the company gets more control over the spending through the electronic management system. Introducing ORM does not require additional hardware or software to be installed, as many systems run on standard web browsers, which can be run on any computer platform. Through the use of electronic communication the cost per transaction can be lowered significantly and the process can be strongly automated.

E-Supply

Numerous independent companies and customers form a supply chain. Manufacturers, logistics companies, senders, receivers and retailers all work together to co-ordinate the order generation and order taking. The offer fulfillment and the distribution of the products, service, or information are organized through the supply chain management. By digitizing the products, the processes and the communication, the Internet has a great potential in linking and managing these organizations. Although EDI was able to link up the companies, it never really took off, as small and medium sized companies could not afford an EDI link to each partner they worked with.

The Internet reduced significantly the cost for starting up the digital business-to-business communication. Through the use of open standards, such as XML and Java, supply chain partners are able to share and exchange information more easily and with lower costs involved. The supply management process may even be contracted to a third party instead of developing one's own applications and investing in separate systems. In this intermediated market, sophisticated logistics management and automated supply-chain management are available almost universally.

E-Trading

Before the Internet, buying and selling stocks was restricted to people with access to financial networks, in order to buy and sell the stocks at the right moment. Others could only get the stock quotes in the newspaper, which was fine, if you did not want to make money fast with the stock market.

The Internet has changed the way stocks are traded. E-trading, often also called E-brokering offers the real-time stock prices to every desk throughout the world. People are able to react in real-time to changes in the stock market. Everyone with an Internet bank account is able to buy and sell stock. This enables anyone to participate in the stock market and earn money by investing. Although the stock market is more risky than ever through the computer based trading, it also offers access for people who did not even know what a stock option was a few years ago.

1.5 Using the New Paradigm of E-business

1.5.1 The Interoperable Network

In the early nineties a strong concentration on the computer market appeared, the so-called Wintel (composed of the software Windows[42] and the hardware Intel[43]) monopoly was at its height. In order to exchange information with business partners everyone was forced to use the same operating system, the same word processor and the same hardware.

With the introduction of the Internet, incompatible devices have learned to talk to each other. This allows interchanging products and integrating processes. This is achieved through the use of digital technologies based on open standards. Moving everything to the same basis started to converge networks, markets, products, technologies and business processes.

The convergence of the networks was the first segment. Telephones, broadcast networks, satellite and wireless networks are now all able to send and receive digital signals. Sending information from a mobile phone to a standard telephone network is possible. It has become totally transparent to the user, which networks are used to route a phone call. A phone call from the United States to Asia may be routed through satellite networks, the Internet and normal telephone networks.

Through the Internet several regulated monopolies face competition from those who used to be in different markets. Suddenly telephone companies, ca-

---

[42]http://www.microsoft.com/
[43]http://www.intel.com/

ble television operators and power supply companies have become competitors to offer access to the Internet and web site owners and television broadcasters start to offer competitive products. Market boundaries are breaking down, just as geographical boundaries have started to collapse.

More and more products are now available in digital form: audio signals, such as voice and music, video signals such as television and video broadcasts, textual information, such as books, magazines and news. All these pieces of information from other media have been moved to a new medium, the computer platform, where databases, computer software, such as office applications and games were in use. Through the use of networks, which all evolved into the Internet, all these types of information could be easily transmitted to any place in the world.

Different types of technologies, such as printers, computers, cameras and mobile phones, are moving closer together to offer the users a wider area of appliances. Using a mobile phone to communicate with a digital camera and a printer without a computer as an intermediary is already possible. The Internet makes it possible.

By digitizing processes, different types of processes in a value chain are integrated into a seamless process. A digital process can be much easier mass-customized by using digital feedback from the customer. Through the feedback mechanism it is also possible to streamline processes much more easily than it would have been possible in the real world.

The convergence brings many new opportunities for start-up companies and many uncertainties for established companies. Start-ups will use the new technologies to implement new processes and products, while many traditional companies will try to convert their current success to the digital world without enhancement. A dictionary in book form and on the Internet will use the same base of data, but presentation and functionality will be very different than if a company just replicates the book by providing a web page with all the content. The Internet-based dictionary will have search and link capabilities that exceed the cross-indexing features a book can provide. Some companies do not add these new functionalities the Internet offers, in good faith their current set of features are satisfying the needs of their customers. Start-ups will see their opportunity to get into the dictionary market and will win market share by offering new digital products. These new products mean new uses, new customers and new ways of doing business. Traditional companies focus on the opportunity to expand their business, but start-ups focus on the novelty of the Internet and its possibilities.

1.5.2   The New Economy

Digital business is causing an upheaval that is shaking the foundations of traditional business. More and more companies recognize the opportunity the Internet offers and start to establish an online presence with a sound business model behind it. Increased revenues and additional customers who return voluntarily to the company are drivers that bring more and more companies to digitize their offerings. Through the Internet it is possible to invent new and innovative ways to add value to existing products and services without necessarily spending a lot of money.

Over the last few years the Internet has established itself as a mainstream medium. With the publication of the Starr report on Monica Lewinsky[44], which was released first on the Internet, everyone was made aware of this in the traditional media. Television news broadcasts were showing online excerpts, as no other information was available. Many sites replicated the report and newspapers printed parts of it.

Internet technologies are advancing to support commercial transactions and in addition to this, new commercial transactions have been invented by these new Internet technologies. Companies need to move fast in this New Economy. But speed is not the only factor that is important to succeed in electronic business. Careful planning and execution are just as important as moving on quickly. This requires the combination of a variety of skills and disciplines, many of which are new and unfamiliar. Computer companies, advertising agencies, Internet providers and service providers come together and act on an equal level of expertise. In the industrial age, every company had expertise in one field. In the information age, every company has a lot of expertise in its own field and at least some expertise in the fields of the others.

---

[44]http://www.house.gov/icreport/

Chapter 2

PREPARING THE ONLINE BUSINESS

2.1 Competitor Analysis on the Internet

2.1.1 Locate your Competition

The company's existing competitors may already have a web site up and running and may already be doing business via the web. In order to be successful on the Internet, it is essential to check out regularly your competitors on the Web and to identify what these competitors are doing. Some may be aggressively pursuing electronic business, while others have just a marketing web site up and running.

Learn what they are trying to achieve, how they stay in contact with their customers and use their ideas in your online initiatives. Find out if they are only extending their existing offerings to the Internet or if they are creating new business. Don't copy your competitors, but use their ideas as a basis for new online ventures for your company. Don't forget to look at companies which you would not classify as your competitors, as they may be in a totally different business. They may also offer some new ideas how to make your online business even more successful.

Although current competitors are a threat, this threat is more or less calculable as you have had time to get to know your competition. Digital start-up companies are the big unknown in business, because they are the companies that find new ways to deconstruct and reconstruct traditional value chains. One bright idea may propel them in front of the established competition by using the Internet for their business, especially with competitors that simply move their existing business processes to the Internet.

The Internet offers new possibilities in competitor analysis. Every company that goes digital becomes transparent at the same time, as every company needs to show what it is doing, otherwise the customers would not have the possibility to compare. This basic feature of the Internet can also be used to monitor the competition.

In most cases your competitors offer similar products, services or information. Therefore they also have similar customers and objectives. This competition is normally very tough, as every company tries to gain more customers and market share. Therefore it is necessary to understand the competitors. It is important to find out what they think. The difference between profit and loss is small in today's economy, so finding out the leading edge is the important question. A little advantage over the competition may lead to a larger market share. Finding out the little secrets of your competitors is crucial for business survival. Only by comparing one's strategies with those of the competition can one win. By knowing the competitors one may be able to predict their next moves, exploit their weaknesses and undermine their strengths.

2.1.2   Collecting Competitive Information

With the Internet collecting information about the competition has become much easier. On one hand you can gather information directly on the web pages of the competitors and on the other hand it is much easier to gain information from customers. Do regular customer surveys on your web page and ask them what they think about your products compared to the ones of the competition. Use all of your traditional methods to gather information, as well. Sales people, for example, can use customer visits to hear about the competition. All these pieces of information need to be categorized, interpreted and analyzed. Using computers this can also be much quicker. The collected intelligence can then be used to stay ahead of the competition.

Some companies collect business information and offer these pieces of information as a service on their web sites. Yahoo offers on its financial pages[1] information about many companies around the world. Another company specialized is Dun & Bradstreet[2] with information on more than 35 million companies. Another important area to monitor is research and development, so checking out the number of patents a company delivers each year will help you find out what is going on in that particular company.

Monitoring the competition and adapting your own enterprise to be ahead of the market are crucial things to do, especially in an interconnected world as we already have today. The fights with competitors should always be operated within the law. Engaging hackers to break into the systems of your competitors may give you the edge over the competition, but is highly illegal, as you can imagine. And any illegal activity will result immediately in bad publicity and loss of revenue. The Internet enables your competition to show your errors to your customers in an instant and there is no way to hide anything anymore. And don't expect any favors from your rivals.

Besides news services, online surveys and competitive web pages there are other means of gathering intelligence about your competition. Subscribe to

---

[1]http://finance.yahoo.com/
[2]http://www.dunandbrad.co.uk/

mailing lists of your competitors and listen to what the customers are talking about. There may be new ideas, which are very interesting for your company and you can learn from errors your competitors have made and do not need to repeat them.

2.2   The Fourth Channel

2.2.1   Understanding the Fourth Channel

Traditionally buyers and sellers conducted trade through three channels: face-to-face, mail and phone. Channels are a set of independent organizations that are involved in the process of making a product or service available for use or consumption by the consumer or a business.

Wholesalers and retailers provide essential services in the physical market. Imagine needing to visit the factory of every manufacturer to buy a certain product. By going to a local store, you save traveling costs but pay the margins for distributors. In many businesses, that margin for wholesalers and retailers is extraordinarily high. If there is a more efficient way of distributing goods, it would lower prices and increase consumer benefits.

On the Internet, customers can visit manufacturer's Web sites and order goods directly. There are no physical or geographical obstacles for the direct factory-to-consumer interactions. Therefore, at least that portion of the markup (distribution costs) will disappear. Intermediaries won't be able to get margins from passing on a certain good.

The Internet has become the fourth channel for trade. Internet trade is booming and this can create conflicts with the other channels. The Internet allows businesses to sell more and at a lower cost. The sales forces and distribution partners may not be able to keep up the pace of the Internet. As we've already seen before, some companies have been forced to withdraw their Internet venture in order to prevent the total collapse of the other channels.

The Internet offers a great opportunity over traditional channels as it has some advantages. Information can be exchanged on a world-wide basis without the need to respect time zones or holidays. The distribution of content can be done at a much lower cost and products, information and services can be customized to meet the requirements of the customer.

Companies with well established channels need to be careful before launching their electronic business as this can create problems with their existing channels. Before launching the new channel it is important to find a way to resolve the channel conflict. If online sales reduce the sales volumes in the existing channels, then it needs to be determined which impact it will have and what can be done against it. One way would be to redefine the role of all channels by splitting up the market into four different segments or by creating new businesses for certain channels. Partners should always be incorporated into the online venture and new business should be distributed over the Internet.

The Internet can support the ordering process between producers, distributors and end customers.

Unlike traditional methods of doing business, the value chain is also used to give customers access to products regardless of the location of the manufacturer. Without this system a car could only be bought directly at the factory, which would require everyone to go to a single location, which would be too much for the car manufacturer and too much for the customers. With the Internet things are changing rapidly. Customers are able to choose their preferred company, no matter how near or far it is located. This give you the opportunity to change the way you supply your customers and deal with your suppliers.

The Internet allows a more direct communication at all levels along the value chain, allowing more detailed information to be passed on without additional cost. Through the use of technology it is possible to reduce costs for the communication and the delivery and every company becomes instantly a global player, if the software used for the web site is internationalized and the processes in place are able to handle international orders.

2.2.2   Preventing Channel Conflicts

A myth about the Internet is that it will eliminate intermediaries. The disappearance of physical distribution chains as people move from buying through distributors and resellers to buying directly from manufacturers. Disintermediation was proposed by many in the early years of the Internet, but web experience has shown that this is not the case. The reality is that the Internet is transforming the distribution chain, but is not eliminating it.

The traditional value chain is linear. The manufacturers build the products, distributors buy products from multiple manufacturers and bring them through several levels of distribution in small lots to resellers who deal directly with consumers. The value-add of the distribution chain lies in shipping, warehousing and delivering products.

Some channel partners are not prepared for the Internet and can create channel conflicts. Channel conflicts arise, for example, if manufacturers sell goods on their web sites, although they have a network of resellers and alienate their sales forces and the stores that sell their products. A similar channel conflict may arise if the larger resellers go online to sell directly to the end customers. With the Internet every partner in the value chain is able to contact the end customers. If the channel conflicts are not resolved, partners in the value chain may decide to leave the chain. Let's have a look at two examples where things went wrong in the past.

A few years ago Levi Strauss & Co.[3] started to sell women's jeans on its web site to North American customers. They were actually so successful that jeans shops started to boycott the producer, as sales dropped. Levi-Strauss had to remove the offering from their web site and had to think about a new strategy.

---

[3]http://www.levistrauss.com/

A story appeared in the International Herald Tribune[4] in February 1999 on
their new strategy. They decided to re-open their online shop with a much
wider selection of jeans than are available at department stores and banned
all retailers from selling its brands on the Internet. Every web site that was
offering Levi's jeans had to remove their offering.

KLM[5], the Dutch airline, had a similar problem when it started to sell space
on cargo planes directly to end customers. Large customers that also act as
resellers of cargo space decided that they did not want this and chose other
airlines for their business. KLM had to close down this particular business
again, as well, and had to rethink their strategy.

The most important thing is to contact all partners in the value chain and
decide on whom sells what to whom. If everybody targets the end customers,
nobody can win, as all partners try to have the lowest prices for one and the
same product. Manufacturers may resell to end customers via the web, for
example, but only if they sell to customer segments that are not in the reach
of the resellers. Ideally manufacturers will use the web to receive orders of
the resellers, just as resellers receive orders of the shops. This keeps the value
chain intact, but reduces the ordering costs.

2.2.3 High Emotions

Emotions run high when a channel conflict arises and the relations between
the channel partners are damaged. A channel conflict damages the business of
all channel partners and even the end customers are confused, pushing them to
competitors. The channel conflict is not only a problem on the Internet. It was
already around before and is a normal issue while doing business. A channel
conflict can be tolerated until the competition becomes unfair, meaning that
a company is cannibalizing the business of other members in the same value
chain. If the partners stick to the rules, the best will win and the customer will
see this in lower retail prices.

Some retailers worry that low-cost Internet operations of manufacturers
will undercut traditional store sales and hurt their online business. At least
for now, most manufacturers that are online are selling at or near retail price.
This keeps most resellers happy.

The difficulty lies in understanding the difference between fair and unfair
competition. Preventing a channel conflict will result in a stable or growing
market share position. In order to resolve the channel conflict you need a clear
market segmentation for all channel partners. To reduce the damage the unfair competition creates, there are some steps that can be taken. All channel
partners need to be able to deal with a channel conflict in order to survive. Just
complaining about the threat won't resolve the problem.

---

[4]http://www.iht.com/, 9th February 1999, "Virtual Stores, Real Clout, Cyberspace Sales Pressure Traditional Retailers"

[5]http://www.klm.com/

Resolving the Channel Conflict

Channel conflicts are a natural thing in business. The following checklist should help all intermediaries to handle and resolve a channel conflict.

- **Market Check** – Resellers and vendors should regularly check the target markets of each other and talk to each other in order to determine if the channel conflicts can be resolved.

- **Channel Strategy** – Prepare a strategy for channel conflicts and look out for partners in case you lose in the channel conflict.

- **Conflict Documentation** – Document the circumstances of a conflict. This helps you to remain calm and not get emotional about the unfair competition.

- **Time Limit** – Define a limit. If the partner in the channel conflict does not respond to your complaints, abandon the product set.

Table 2.1.

Manufacturers who have until now dealt with resellers and dealers should not use the Internet to remove the intermediaries to the end customer. The reason why manufacturers used to deal with intermediaries are explained easily and are still important for businesses, even in the information age. Intermediaries are often more efficient in making goods available to particular target markets. Through their contacts, experience, specialization and scale of operation, intermediaries usually offer more than a manufacturer could achieve on its own. Resellers and dealers play an important role in matching supply and demand. Most manufacturers have narrow assortments of goods, but the end consumers want a broad range of choices. But the Internet is starting to blur the differences between manufacturers and resellers.

By going online a manufacturers is not automatically able to take over the functions mentioned above. The manufacturer is able to earn more on a single sale as it is not necessary to feed a long value chain, but this brings also a change for manufacturers, as the customers are now requiring direct support

from the manufacturer, which was performed by the intermediaries before and in which they were specialized.

Still many manufacturers decide to sell their products online. If done correctly it will increase the overall volume of sales and does not hurt the channel partners. Manufacturers should never use their advantage to offer lower prices than their channel partners. They could use the new medium to reach new target groups and pass them on to the channel.

Never!! unless you want to do the work all by yourself.

2.2.4 Reconstructing the Value Chain

In order to prevent the above mentioned channel conflict it is necessary to change the model of distribution and adapt it to the possibilities of the Internet. With the Internet, distribution models are being deconstructed and reconstructed in a different manner, into so-called value webs.

During the construction of the value web a new class of intermediaries comes up. Other than in traditional chains where additional value is created through sophisticated logistics in the New Economics value is created by adding information. Consumers come to these sites looking for information and opportunities to purchase.

focus

New intermediaries such as flug.de[6], TISS[7] or Travel Overland[8] are selling flight tickets over the Internet and are becoming part of a new value chain. They are changing the traditional model of selling goods and services. On the Internet everybody is able to become an intermediary easily. The chances for traditional companies and Internet start-ups are about the same. As a manufacturer the Internet offers the possibility of breaking up old structures and creating relationships with new intermediaries. In order to be a successful intermediary on the Internet, it is necessary to add real value to the core product, as the Internet offers much more possibilities to compare product and service offerings of different online businesses.

Resolving the channel conflict is possible; just one short example. Libri[9], one of Germany's largest online bookshops is at the same time one of the largest resellers of books. Instead of selling the books directly to the customers, the orders from the end customers are redirected to the nearest bookshop in Germany. The customer is then able to pick up the books at the bookshop or it will be sent to the customer via mail. As you can see quite clearly from this example, the channel has not been cannibalized. Libri could have sold the books directly to the customers via the web with the result that the bookshops would choose another distributor. The bookshops are taking part in the Internet experience of the distributor and everybody is gaining new customers through the web site.

Example

the publisher has to leave some margin to the intermediaries in order to keep the value chain functional and in balance.

---

[6]http://www.flug.de/
[7]http://www.tiss.com/
[8]http://www.travel-overland.de/
[9]http://www.libri.de/

Who is Customer

Instead of by-passing the traditional resellers to talk to the end customers directly, manufacturers should treat their immediate partners as customers. Offer them a dedicated web site, where they can order their products and allow them to customize the appearance of the web site, just as you would expect an end customer web site to look like.

Many surveys show quite clearly that the fourth channel Internet does not only attract customers from traditional markets, but also generates new business, which then can be brought back to the traditional markets. The Web offers a great opportunity to expand the business.

Michael Dell, the owner of Dell Computers[10], said once when asked about how to resolve the channel conflict, that the Internet posed no threat to the traditional channels. All that was needed to keep everyone happy was to increase the number of orders.

By implementing new processes and opening up communication, the supply chain is converted to a true demand-pull supply of goods and services which removes the traditional channels. The Internet may remove the need for intermediates in the current form, but new intermediaries will be necessary as we have already have seen earlier in this section.

By failing to recognize the significance and the possibilities of the Internet, many businesses will be forced out of traditional value chains while their customers and suppliers start to communicate in a more direct way and experience increased margins by dealing directly. By embracing the Internet, its technologies and the new ways and means of dealing with others, every company is able to offer a better service to existing customers and build profitable new businesses.

2.2.5 New Intermediaries

Retailers offering undifferentiated products, which have a high price, are going to disappear rapidly. New players will emerge rapidly as the Internet has very low barriers to entry. Information-based services are the key to success for becoming an intermediary for the New Economy. Information and appropriate processes can help to increase response time. The Internet is becoming fast an important factor in business decision making. New players appear, such as IndustryNet[11], which is one of the representatives of the new emerging industrial marketplace. Suppliers are using the Internet for presenting their products and pricing. New intermediaries will aggregate information from various locations into a central location. This allows the new intermediaries to offer a greater customer convenience while pushing product prices down.

Another new intermediary is Food.com[12], which is a match-making service for online pizza buyers and sellers. Rather than searching for an appropri-

---

[10]http://www.dell.com/
[11]http://www.industry.net/
[12]http://www.food.com/

ate online pizza shop, customers can order pizza directly through the Cyberslice.com web site. The system locates the shop, which is located nearest to the customer and sends an automated voice message to the pizza service. The restaurant uses touch-tone prompts to take the order, paying Cyberslice.com a small fee in commission for every pizza transaction.

On the Internet two types of intermediation will survive. The Internet as a new sales channel allows customers to be charged for services to meet the expectations of the customers; those who extend services from the physical world and those who evolve from the new capabilities of the New Economy. The first group will implement services such as digital telephone directory services and certification authorities, which are identity-issuing agencies on the Internet.

The second group are the real new intermediaries and will be based on knowledge and connectivity. Products will be bought on demand for customers who are interested in a service. The product itself becomes less valuable, if no service is associated with it driving costs for products down to nearly zero. In Germany, for example, costs for mobile phones are nearly zero, for 1 DM (about 50 cents) it is already possible to buy a mobile phone. But in order to use the phone, the customer needs to buy services for it, such as a pre-paid phone card or a GSM card which is debited on a monthly basis.

2.3   Paradigms in the New Economy

2.3.1   The One-To-One Enterprise

This section shows two paradigms, which change the way business is done. The impact of the one-to-one marketing paradigm and the dynamic trade idea does not halt at the frontiers to the real world, but will eventually be part of the overall economy.

As we will see in Chapter 5, a one-to-one marketing strategy needs to be implemented in order to make your company successful on the Internet. Mass-customization is a must on the Internet as more and more companies make this as a standard.

In order to support one-to-one marketing it is necessary to transform your whole company to support the new paradigm. Therefore it is necessary to look at the products, services and information your company is offering right now and decide which of them gain value through the one-to-one approach. Digital goods, such as news are easy to customize to the individual reader, whereby other products such as perfumes cannot be customized as this would cost far too much. But this may change in the near future; therefore it is necessary to repeat this step of evaluating the assets of your company. The vision of the dynamic enterprise needs to be updated on a regular basis to encompass more and more customized products. Even products like petrol at a petrol station may be customized in the future, although this may not seem likely right now, but it eventually will happen.

The dynamic enterprise is a long term goal for most established companies, as it requires many organizational changes within the enterprise. The major difference of the one-to-one approach is that there are no target groups or product segments anymore, but individuals you have to deal with, which want products designed to their needs and not to the needs of the average customer.

In the real world this is not possible, as it would take up far too many resources, but in the digital world with the support of computers and the Internet, it is possible for a company to build up truly individual relationships which each of their customers. Most companies just use the Internet as a one-to-one marketing vehicle but forget to use the data that they have gathered when talking in real life to the customer.

As the dynamic enterprise does not have target groups it is not possible to measure success for a certain product with traditional means. Instead of measuring success by product segments or target groups, the success is measured for every customer individually. How successful has the company been on a particular customer is what really matters, not how many units of a certain product have been sold.

This change of focus may result in lower product sales, but this should not worry you too much. The focus on the customer has a lot of advantages, as you get more detailed information on the customers and are able to adapt to their needs. Customers are more willing to spend more on a certain product and its associated services as it is customized to their specific needs. Mass-customization keeps the costs down while customer satisfaction will rise and this will eventually increase the profits.

Traditionally many companies use marketing for 95 percent of their customers and one-to-one marketing for the other 5 percent. The traditional one-to-one marketing meant that a dedicated person would build up a relationship with the customer and would adapt the products to the needs of the customer. This is extremely cost intensive both for the companies and the customers. So only very large customers could afford this type of marketing and companies have had no interest in extending the personal marketing initiative.

With the Internet and the new possibilities in one-to-one marketing companies are able to extend the customized approach to all customers and reduce the cost for information technology at the same time. Typically businesses won't allow everybody to be part of the one-to-one marketing offensive at one time, but offer these capabilities over time to more customers. Therefore the shift is performed by steadily moving one target group after the other to the new paradigm.

The biggest obstacles to overcome are to convince everyone in the company to adhere to the new paradigm and to convince the customers that this new paradigm is the best for them as well. One-to-one marketing and production perfects the trend to mass-customization.

2.3.2 Dynamic Trade

The digital economy is driven by several factors, which change the Internet environment constantly. Customer demand is changing, as soon as one site offers an added value to its services and products, customers expect that added value from all others as well, otherwise they will abandon a particular web site. The pressure from customers has increased as they are more willing to change. The growing globalization is also a driving factor on the Internet and works both ways. The more the economy is globalized, the more the Internet is used for business transactions. The same is true the other way round as well. The more the Internet is used for business transactions, the more global the economy becomes. The Internet ubiquity, new technologies and intermediaries are also driving forces on the Internet that change the conditions constantly in which companies operate.

Waverly Deutsch of Forrester Research[13] stated in a speech[14] that the constant change on the Internet is creating a New Economy which Forrester calls "Dynamic Trade." This dynamic trade is "leveraging technology to satisfy current demand with customized response". Other than in traditional shops where prices are decided in advance, the Internet offers the possibility of creating highly dynamic prices for a certain point in time, customized to the request of a certain customer. As comparing prices has become easy on the Internet, especially if customers use shopping agents, fixed pricing does not fit anymore into the New Economy.

Dynamic trade will change relationships between organizations (especially between buyers and sellers) and alter the processes used to do business transactions. Established organizations will change. Instead of static organizations, more and more virtual organization will appear that get together for a certain task and reorganize themselves for the next task.

The constant change alters the way business is done over the Internet. Instead of using a price list, the market decides on the price of a product. Product attributes become buyer-selected, instead of being seller-selected in the traditional market. The production of goods in the era of dynamic trade is initiated after the sale has been complete, as the product is highly customized and cannot be produced before the customer has ordered the goods. Customer relationships are strongly customized and the company asset is the customer database with detailed information on the customers preferences. The customers get much more power through the dynamic economy.

It requires also more flexibility from your partners. Instead of having one partner that delivers a certain service or product, you will more likely have a few of them delivering the same product or service and will choose the one, which will have the best price for a certain point in time. Contracts become more flexible and do not contain fixed pricing.

---

[13] http://www.forrester.com/

[14] Forrester Forum, "Preparing For Dynamic Trade In The Internet Economy," Amsterdam 1999.

In the dynamic economy added value is provided in form of services. The core product becomes less important while the services around the product become more important, both for the company selling it and for the customers buying it. By linking real-time demand into production, the supply chain has become highly dynamic as well. The production therefore moves closer to the customer and is able to respond to demand much faster and more exactly.

The real change comes from the new pricing model, which now matches market conditions. This pricing model is based on the auction and bid model, which is already used by some companies on the Internet.

Airlines already offer seats at dynamic prices. If there is a lot of interest in getting tickets for a certain flight, the prices will go up for the seats and for other flights where many seats are still empty, the prices will drop, as it is better to have a fully-booked flight. It happens quite often that people sit side-by-side in an airplane with totally different prices, depending on the time they bought the tickets. Last-minute sales already work this way and have for some years. Tickets for planes that are not booked out are sold at a lower price. Today all tickets are sold on a dynamic basis.

Another industry that is already highly dynamic is the telecom industry, where capacity on international carriers is sold on a dynamic price. Depending on the time of the day and the number of interested companies, the price for a minute of a phone call may go up or down.

In order to prepare your company for the dynamic trade, a flexible execution environment is required. Therefore your strictly hierarchical company needs to reorganize to a hyperarchical company, which consists of many virtual teams that are able to reorganize at any time. A fluid restructuring of internal and external processes will become the goal. A corporate process audit team will be necessary to monitor all ongoing activities and to establish process metrics with partners.

2.4 Driving Business Process Re-engineering

2.4.1 Changing Business Processes

With the introduction of high-speed networks, businesses are able to execute much faster without having to change business processes. One example is the processing of EDI messages. The introduction of the Internet has made it possible to deliver EDI much faster. EDI is communicated in a store-and-forward principle that can take up to a day to arrive at the computer of the recipient. An e-mail over the Internet arrives in most cases within seconds at the destination. EDI is used, for example, to notify manufacturers that their shipment has arrived, but if the information arrives the next day its usefulness is limited. Replacing private EDI networks with EDI over the Internet speeds up processes significantly without requiring a change of the process and without increasing turnaround times.

Through the increased speed of traditional business processes the economy has been put into a position to offer real-time delivery of processing information. Customers expect to see results twenty-four hours a day, seven days a week, no matter where the company is located. The expectation of a rapid response means that there is less time for organizational navigation through a company. Direct questions require direct responses. And customers want direct access to their response. They want to be able to access an enterprise system directly or speak to the responsible person directly. Real-time processing is becoming a major factor in the market, while the number of batch process systems decreases.

2.4.2   Introduction to Business Process Re-engineering

The general idea of business process re-engineering (BPR) is to provide means for optimizing and enhancing business processes, both in the production area and in the administration. Using information technology in general and in the Internet in particular many processes can be streamlined reducing time and costs for every single step. By digitizing the information flow, for example, costly media breaks can be prevented. A media break occurs every time information is moved from one medium to another and that requires cost for the conversion. A hand written document that needs to be typed into a computer is one example.

In the early nineties many consulting companies have started to use the term business process re-engineering, especially after James Champy and Michael Hammer[15] have written a bestseller on the topic. In order to explain what is needed to re-engineer a business, they use a set of terms to describe the needs for BPR. The terms they are using are: "radical", "fundamental", "business process" and "increase by factors."

Radical means that it is not enough to scratch at the surface and modify existing processes, but that it is necessary to create completely new processes to deal with the change. BPR questions existing processes, rules and structures and replaces them with completely new processes, rules and structures to increase the revenues or effectiveness by factors.

Fundamental in BPR means that the reasons for the business are questioned, such as: "Why are things done in a certain way?", "What are the reasons for using a certain process?" or "Do we need this product or service?"

The term "increase by factor" means that the goal of BPR is not to enhance existing processes and increase revenues by five percent, but it means that effectiveness and revenues are supposed to jump by factor two (one hundred percent) or higher as a result of the business process re-engineering.

The focus on BPR is to reorganize companies to fit the new processes. Instead of creating organizations based on products or location, the organizations are defined by the business process. The business processes are defined in a

---

[15]M. Hammer and J. Champy, Re-engineering the Corporation, New York 1993

customer-centric way. Every person in the process that receives input from you needs to be considered a customer and every person giving you input is viewed as a supplier.

In many companies the employees are working very efficiently within their organization, but viewed from a customer's standpoint, the results are very inefficient. The problem is the co-ordination of resources for a process and the management of information. Even simple processes involve several departments of a company in order to be executed. Instead of fixing itself on these departments, the BPR tries to reorganize the departments to fit the process. In many cases virtual organizations fit best, as the processes change without necessarily changing the work for the single employee.

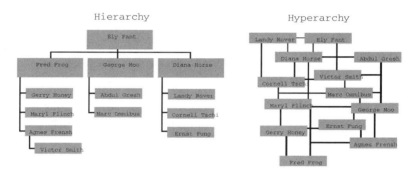

Figure 2.1. A typical hierarchy compared to a hyperarchy

In order to make organizations more flexible, it is necessary to get rid of the strict hierarchical organization and move on to a hyperarchical system, which allows every department to communicate directly with every other and decisions are made by the person who is collecting and evaluating all the relevant information. Figure 2.1 shows the differences between a hierarchy and a hyperarchy. The World Wide Web is the best example of a hyperarchical system. There is no root page from where everything starts. Each single web site may decide to have a hierarchical system for its documents, but between web sites there is no hierarchy. Every web site has the same priority on the web.

2.4.3 Methods of Reorganization

There are two possible ways to reorganize a business. A change can be initiated by the employees or by the structure of the company. In order to get the maximum out of the reengineering process, both approaches should always be combined and executed at the same time, as both approaches have the same goal, but come from different angles.

Changing processes through the employee means that it is necessary to influence key persons throughout the company. A more positive work environment is created through training of these people, which results in a more friendly atmosphere that enables the employees to work more efficiently. The goal is to build a team out of several individuals working for the same department. Only then the work can be done in time, if these people are able to communicate the necessary information within the department. As a result the structure of the company is changing.

The structural approach is working the other way round. By applying structural changes within the company, employees are moving from their actual position to another position that fits better into the new structure of the company.

2.4.4   Planning Systems

Manufacturing resources planning systems and material requirement planning are able to compute the actual requirements for material and resources in a highly dynamic way. In order to be able to do these calculations, they need detailed and accurate input data. So far this has been difficult and many systems have failed, as it was not possible to keep all the systems up-to-date because data was delayed for one or the other reason. This resulted in inconsistent systems and forced people to manually change requirements to meet the demand. Human interaction is often inaccurate and leads to more delays as humans are much slower in moving data. The data on demand was coming from many different sources, in many different formats, on many different types of media, forcing people to convert information manually.

Electronic business has the advantage that all information on customer demand is already in digital form and can be easily sent to the inventory management system. The necessary data can be gathered, formatted and presented in such a way without much work that the inventory system can handle the data and deliver the right output. If the two computers are directly linked, the inventory system can be fed with real-time information. But even if the systems are not directly connected, because of security concerns, for example, the data fed into the inventory system has a much higher quality than from other sources. The reason is on one side the technical possibilities and the consistent media, but also the direct contact to the customer, which enables you to receive detailed information.

In order to use the full impact of the Internet for the digital planning systems new processes need to be put in place, which replace or enhance the old processes, structures and resources.

2.4.5   Just In Time

The ultimate goal of every digital company is to move to just in time inventory management. Software companies, which distribute their goods over the Internet have already achieved this goal. The product is created in the instant a demand for the product is generated. In the case of the software company, it would be the moment a customer has paid for the software. Other companies, such as a digital bookshop will try to avoid any inventories and pass on the order from their customers on a just in time basis to the publisher. The publisher then sends out the books to the virtual bookshop, which in return passes the goods on to the customers. In this process the publisher still has to produce books in advance of demand.

In order to make every part of the value chain just in time, it is necessary to change the way external relationships are managed and requires the change of many internal processes. In order to implement a just in time environment an effective exchange of information between supplier and purchaser is required. Organizations need to become much more tightly integrated in order to achieve this level of co-operation and meet the requirements for the input and output. Electronic shopping systems are the first step in that direction, as they are able to facilitate the level of interaction and exchange information at a fraction of the cost of the proprietary systems developed and used by the major retailers before the world-wide introduction of the Internet. With the world-wide deployment of electronic business, businesses are able to take all the advantages of the digital era to implement complex just in time systems.

Suppliers, on one hand, will benefit from the frequent and direct communications with customer organizations and are able to feed the incoming information directly into the production systems; in the first step to make production predictions better and then later on create a real just in time environment. Through strong relationships with your customers you are able to adopt even more demanding supplier performance criteria, which result in higher levels of service to your (potential) customers and propel your company in front of the competition. Companies that supply others with products that are easily digitized such as software and music will be able to deliver the products directly and immediately to their customers. Inventory, production and shipping costs go down to zero.

Purchasers, on the other hand, are able to manage the supply chain more easily as a result of the introduction of the electronic business. More information about the customers is becoming available and a more accurate demand-forecasting is possible. The demand from customers can be fed easily into the inventory control system and the demand passed directly on to the suppliers. The whole process of ordering can be automated and accelerates not only the inventory management process, but the overall process throughout the new virtual value chain.

By connecting purchasers and suppliers directly to each other, purchasers will be able to automate the order process and the delivery schedules by routing the orders automatically through based on the customer's demand. The purchaser is also able to check inventory levels in-house and at the supplier sites, offering customers a far better service. Companies, which are not willing to adapt to this new paradigm will have a tough life in the future.

2.5   Designing, Developing, and Deploying the System

2.5.1   Identifying the Online Business

After the World Wide Web had been invented, information sellers saw the opportunity to distribute their goods on a world-wide basis without spending much money in infrastructure. Therefore these businesses were the first to open a web site and start doing business over the Internet. Slowly, but steadily more and more businesses that do not sell or provide information were doing business over the Net. Information providers offered their information for free in the beginning, as the Internet had been designed for the exchange of scientific information.

First of all it is necessary to identify the type of business you are in. Companies can be divided into three categories: providers of soft goods, hard goods and service providers. These providers produce, distribute and sell their goods via the web. Soft goods are products that can be easily digitized, such as software and information. These products can be delivered over the Internet. Hard goods on the other hand, such as food and toys are not easily digitizable and need traditional methods of delivery. The service providers offer products, such as translations or advertising, which can be done both, online and offline. Depending on the type of product your company represents a different strategy is necessary to be successful on the Internet.

If the company is in the soft goods and service business the Internet can become a sales and distribution channel. It needs to be evaluated if the Internet business can become the fourth channel. If so, then it should help to reduce costs. Companies that deal with hard goods won't see the Internet as their primary goal for expansion as it is not possible to digitize these products. The Internet still can help reduce costs for these companies. Manufacturers, resellers and online shops can reduce costs by digitizing the value chain and the orders between the partners.

Set realistic goals for your online business, the next section discusses some of the most important reasons for going online. The online business can help to reduce pre-sale costs such as marketing and post-sale costs such as customer care. Online marketing can be much more direct than traditional marketing and the success of marketing can be measured much easier. But the main cost reduction will come from the sales costs. Online distribution of goods can reduce these costs too almost zero. The order costs will also go down to nearly zero. The order information is provided by the customer in digital form and can be easily processed by your company.

Direct revenues from your online business may come from point of sale revenues, subscriptions to online services and revenues from other advertisers. Traditional business will not want to base their revenues on advertising online, but many start-up online businesses live off banner advertising only until they are profitable enough to base their income on the actual product sales.

Depending on the size of your company you should decide if you want to have your web site in house or if you should outsource the web server or even the whole business. The advantage of outsourcing are the lower costs, but you may lose control over your business. As companies today need an Intranet, putting web servers in front of the firewall would not increase costs largely. Outsourcing online business may be useful if your company does not have the resources to implement and maintain the solution. A section is dedicated in Chapter 5 to finding the right ISP.

Electronic Business Analysis

Before launching your electronic business on the Internet it is necessary to analyse the situation your company is in.

- **Identification** – Identify the type of business you are in.

- **Evaluation** – Evaluate the Internet as your sales and distribution channel.

- **Goals** – Set realistic goals for your online venture.

- **Reduction** – Use the Internet to cut costs.

- **Sales** – Use the Internet to make sales.

- **Location** – Place your site either at your Internet connection or at the ISP.

- **Shopping** – Design the appropriate shopping experience for your customers.

 - **Profiling** – Get to know better the needs of your customers.

- **Public Relations** – Advertise and promote your site.

- **Payment** – Accept online payment.

- **Laws** – Keep up with international laws.

Table 2.2.

Depending on your customers you need to design the appropriate online experience. Online shoppers want an efficient and easy-to-use web site that offers the lowest prices possible, without decreasing the service. Online business will want direct access to databases of the partners and integration and co-operation between the legacy systems.

In order to understand the needs of your customers better, you should track the visits of the customers on your web site and save the information in a database. This profiling helps to improve the business, the navigation on the web site and can help to find new areas of business, which can change or extend the focus of your company.

Other than with traditional business that was restricted to national laws, online businesses need to keep up with international laws. Online businesses that restrict business to only one or very few countries will not work very well. Your company will receive many requests from customers in other countries asking why the web site is restricted, resulting in an overload for the customer care center and harming the online image of the company.

2.5.2 Developing a Business Plan

In order to develop a successful electronic business plan, it is necessary to embed the e-business strategy into the overall enterprise strategy. More forward thinking organizations will work to make the electronic business strategy the overall enterprise strategy in the end. Several issues need to be taken into concern, which we will look at in this section.

Electronic business over the Internet is not just a platform that enables existing customers use, but will also result in new customers. Although these new customers are very interesting to your business, it needs also to be taking care of the existing customers. They already have business relations with your company and can also benefit from moving to the Internet. Therefore they need to move from physical channels into the electronic channel. This move does cost money; depending on the type of company it may range from installation of new software to buying hardware and hooking up an Internet connection. Therefore it is necessary to add value to the electronic channel. If your customers do not gain anything from it, it is not very likely that they will use it.

If you are an Internet start-up or want to reach new customers via the web this won't be that important, but this, of course, is risky, as you do not know your customers yet. Relying on strong relationships and moving the communication between the partners involved will result in much higher revenues, but only if all parties involved are of the same opinion.

It is necessary to do some research and ask your customers what they really need and how the existing service can be improved. The use of the Internet will most probably require you to create new processes and depending on these new processes people will accept the online offering or reject it. Technology should be used to improve existing processes or create new ones, but business should not be driven by technology, as it makes the business case too much dependent on one piece of software or hardware.

A sound business plan can be implemented in several ways, which are interchangeable and do not restrict the business to accept the policies of a software vendor, for example. The other issue with relying on technology is that in the Internet world technology and user preferences change very quickly. A technology that is cool today can be out tomorrow. It is not possible to plan for twelve or eighteen months in advance. The business case must be flexible to adapt to the expectations of the customers and the evolving technologies on the Internet.

On the Internet new companies appear rapidly creating a vast supply of new choices. Any business plan for the Internet needs to take into account that not only technology and customer's expectations are changing very fast, but also the competition. There is no time to do extensive competition analysis by comparing oneself to other companies. It is necessary to compare ideas instead of companies. We will see how competition analysis is done on the Internet later in this chapter.

In order to implement such a business case, the management, the employees and the business partners need to be aware of this shift and get their input if the processes involved are supportable by them. It is also important to understand how it will affect such areas as performance reviews and sales targets.

One of the primary tasks is to define the customer segment the electronic business wants to target. Depending on the type of network you are using to create the electronic business the target group will be different. If you are using your company Intranet as the foundation for the proposed electronic business, you will have an internal audience, such as marketing, sales, finance or any other internal department. If the business plan is to communicate with partners, suppliers or resellers in order to exchange information, products or services over a network, creating an Extranet will resolve the technical issues. When using the Internet, you will most likely reach external customers. Depending on the target audience you can start to implement the electronic business system, as this element in the business plan has an effect on many other aspects, ranging from interface design to marketing.

In order to make the electronic business system attractive to the target group, it is necessary to develop an effective online marketing campaign. All departments involved in running the system need to understand the target audience. They need to know who they are and how they spend their time on the web site. In order to develop a sound business plan it is necessary to know what factors are important for the target audience. It should also identify the needs and expectations of the customers as well as how the company and its services and products can address these needs and services more effectively than the competition.

There are, of course, risks involved, as with any business initiative and therefore it is important to identify any risks in advance and create backup plans to relieve negative effects that may impact your company because of these risks. The electronic world usually has some very special risks, such as a defective web server or a dead connection to the Internet, which in itself may not be difficult to resolve, but which can bring down your whole business, if the problem cannot be resolved in a short time. The main risk comes from security breaches, from people who try to steal, delete or change information that are the basis for your business. Although most people think that an Internet connection makes your company vulnerable, the biggest security risk comes from within the company. Security technology is able to secure the access from the Internet, but employees are able to send out information with the click of an e-mail to outsiders.

hacker from within

The business plan should also evaluate possible channel conflicts by investigating attitudes and perceptions in existing channels and then provide solutions how to resolve the conflicts.

Another important property of the business plan is to provide a road map with all major milestones in it for all phases of the project, from the design phase through to the operating phase, from the strategic level through to the tactical level. It should cover the next twelve to eighteen months in detail, as this is the maximum time for deploying a new electronic business. A project that takes longer to deploy will most probably have difficulties succeeding, as the technology is moving far too fast to make a project competitive with technology older than two years. To define milestones for the next few years will make sense on a business level, but should not incorporate any dependencies on a specific hardware or software technology as this will be superseded by something else in no later than two years time.

12-18 months

The business plan needs to address the issue of integrating the new electronic business processes with the old real-world processes, and with the processes of your partners and customers. Only if this is addressed in a reasonable manner it is possible to create a complex network of business processes. The goal of your e-business initiative in the end will be to integrate all communications and move it to the Internet to make them more automatic and direct.

Inventory, accounting, sales forecasting, order processing, customer information and operational resources management will be integrated into your digital business therefore the business plan needs to state when and how these services can be integrated into the overall plan. Only if it is possible to integrate the existing services and partners into the electronic business it will be truly successful, as the viability and profitability depends upon the efficiency of the value-chain-wide system implementations.

2.5.3   Preparing for the Electronic Revolution

When implementing electronic business in your company you should get all departments in your company going. Electronic business will transform the way you conduct business, therefore it is necessary to get everyone involved. They need to support the Internet initiative and to support the necessary redesign of the business processes.

For the three major phases, the design, the development and the deployment, every department needs to be involved to understand what impact the Internet will have on their daily business. Marketing, sales, customer service, engineering, operations and information technology will benefit from the decision, if implemented correctly. The departments are able to assist in re-engineering the business processes with their specific knowledge and by asking them to send a representative to the project team, they will be more willing to participate in the changes in the company. The project team provides ideas and input for the functionality and the design requirements of the future digital business. In order to make the project team work effectively, everybody should have some knowledge on the Internet. Therefore provide introductory courses for employees who haven't had contact with the Internet, in order to make their contributions more valuable and reduce their fear for the new medium. The course should give them a feeling for the possibilities and some basic applications, such as e-mail and creating HTML pages.

In order to survive in the Internet age, technology should be able to support heterogeneous systems architectures. Therefore it is necessary to use component technology that can be used to build new applications by re-using existing building blocks. Every application needs to be Internet enabled and connections to the applications of your partners need to be established, just if they were your own systems.

The computers of the employees should be connected to each other so that people are able to exchange files, information and e-mails. One or more Intranet servers should be set up, that run not only a mail service, but also a web server with company information and departmental information. Through the introduction of the Intranet, all employees have the possibility to play around with technology while being at work. This reduces the amount of time introducing new technologies. Technology is changing much faster; every day updates of existing programs or completely new programs appear. Therefore the business plan needs to discuss the paradigm and how the company is able to cope with the rapid change.

In order to foster the vision of the Internet business, it is necessary that every employee does understand the impact. Every single employee needs not only know how to browse some web pages and send some e-mails, but should have its own web page up and running, both on the Intranet and on the Internet. To put it more drastically, get rid of all people who are not present on the Web. Designing a web page is simple and can be done by everyone. Do not expect that everyone will have an extensive web site up and running, but a single page can be done by everyone and should be enforced. This should not exclude the managers.

2.5.4 Design and Development

Technical aspects and business processes need to be combined during the design phase. In order to deal with other businesses and customers, it is necessary to exchange data. Therefore security has the highest priority. In most cases it is necessary to reveal some data to customers and business partners, but a company needs to be sure that the right data arrives at the right person. ✓ Protecting the sensitive information from others becomes a critical issue in the design and development phase.

In order to provide a valuable service to your customers the data presented to them should be up-to-date. Mission-critical information is the most valuable to the customer but requires you to add some extra protection to your company Intranet, as the information can easily be used against you.

The project teams needs to determine which technologies can be used to implement the business processes and which business processes need to be re-engineered to become more valuable. If Internet technologies are already used on the Intranet, it needs to be determined how your company can connect the Intranet with the Internet.

The visual presentation on the company's web site is also very important. Marketing should develop a visual strategy for the web site, which takes into account the needs of the customers and the business processes of the company.

To succeed in the electronic world, the employees in your company are required to adopt new skills, knowledge and expertise in three disciplines: creativity, strategy and technology. Other than with normal business, the digital business employees need to constantly update their knowledge, as technology is changing all the time. Long-life learning becomes a must for everyone involved in the Internet. Only if everyone is up-to-date about the latest technology, can new creative business models be created and an ever-changing strategy be developed. It is not possible anymore to create a long-term strategy, as new competitors and technologies emerge all the time and constantly change the business model.

Strategic planning needs to be approached very differently because of the dynamic nature of the Internet. Using the Internet to start investigations on the competition has been made easier, not only for your company, but also for any other company. The existing business processes need to monitored and analyzed around the clock and need to be adjusted to the changing environment by the introduction of new business models and new technologies. Many existing processes can be streamlined and enhanced by Internet technologies.

The Internet technologies are rapidly evolving every day. In order to keep pace with the new breakthroughs it is necessary to have a core team of experts that is able to understand the hardware and software solutions and needs to evaluate new technologies. Technologies for site development, systems integration and security issues also need to be addressed by this group, which must consist of technical and business people.

The creative people need to understand more than just design, in order to develop an appealing user experience. This requires the creative department to understand the business models and the technical implications of emerging standards. They also need to understand what customers see on a web page and how to use it. User tracking has become easy and helps companies to evaluate business processes and to streamline the process and the web design. The web design will also have impact on the audience development activities, as it will drive traffic to the web site from web surfers. Although they are not the preferred customers for a company they are prospective customers who may be willing to try out a new business; therefore they need to be taken care of, as with your regular customers, which you may have already acquired.

Marketing and promotional techniques that are effective in traditional media don't always translate well into the online marketplace. The creative area involves understanding the most effective online marketing techniques and applying the ones that make the most sense for the specific product and the audience. The best technologies need to be evaluated in your business plan.

As most businesses do not have in-house expertise in all disciplines, it may be helpful to have a partner for the start-up phase. This will reduce the delay for developing and deploying the electronic business and the advantage competitors may gain through a delay is reduced. The partners are able to provide skills, knowledge and expertise in the area of electronic business and the Internet. Many companies offer consulting in this area, and depending on the size of the consulting firm the direction will be different. The big five consulting companies are more focused on strategic planning and less on technical details. Many companies get the big five involved for developing a strategy, but get smaller companies involved as soon as they start the design, development and deployment of the solution, as the big five lack the in-depth Internet expertise and the creativity that is necessary to build up an electronic business.

For many companies the big five are too expensive and so they will choose smaller consulting companies. In order to find the right one, you should look for a company that is able to show reference projects and experience in strategy, creativity and technology. Depending on the knowledge within your company, the consulting firm should be able to support the electronic business through its entire life cycle, from planning to deployment and operation. Depending on your plans the company should also offer the possibility to hand over the project at the time you are ready to do so. Having a partner that is able to support the entire life cycle will offer you a fall back strategy in the event of problems, even though you decided to outsource only a part of the business.

2.5.5 Building a Pilot *phase*

Once the design has been completed and the first implementation has taken place, it is a good move to start with a pilot, which proves the integrity and the effectiveness of the design concept. During the pilot phase the departments

Implementation Strategies

In order to succeed with the Internet business it may be helpful to get through the following steps:

- **Find a champion** – Get the management involved and explain the benefits.

- **Plan for change** – Technology will change the corporate culture.

- **Define a pilot project** – Don't try to change everything at once.

- **Estimate the costs** – Training, maintenance and support will be the majority of costs.

- **Measure productivity** – Measure it before and after the pilot has been implemented.

- **Re-engineer business processes** – Make technology part of the business re-engineering process, but don't let it dominate.

- **Learn as you go** – Make adjustments while you implement.

- **Prepare for resistance** – People won't change overnight and organizations are even slower.

Table 2.3.

and some selected customers should have the possibility to test the system and give feedback about the quality and usefulness of the system. A feedback form on the system should allow users of the system to report eventual bugs and logical errors in the system. Performance issues should be resolved during the pilot phase and the seamless integration into legacy systems needs to be checked. Another important point is to see if the system is scalable or if it crashes with fifty users online at the same time and the effectiveness of the processes defined on the system need to be verified.

During the pilot phase it is possible to bring more customers into the system, if you see that it works, but be careful about letting everyone from the public in without extensive testing. Although a few months of piloting may seem a long time and a waste of money, it is still cheaper than going into full production with a faulty system. If you let all customers in, mark the site clearly as beta so that nobody associates your beta site with your brand and their awareness of quality.

There are no rules how long a pilot phase should take. It depends on the size of the project and the importance of it. If you just plan to set up a few web pages to inform your customers about your company then this can be done with a short pilot phase, as the information can be exchanged rather easily or the server can be switched off without doing real harm. If you plan to digitize complex business processes and want to rely on that service, then it is necessary to do extensive testing, which will take some months time. More and more companies decide not to do a pilot phase, but go directly online with a beta version of their site and then let the general public test the site. Although this provides your company with zillions of bug reports, it may not be the best way of doing it, as a system that needs to long to be fixed will ruin the image of your company. *too*

2.5.6 Going into Production

Once the feedback from the pilot phase has been evaluated and modifications have been introduced to the pilot system, your company is ready to deploy the complete system to the public. Although still all departments will be involved, the IT department will be responsible for the roll-out of the service. It will also be responsible for the availability of the service and need therefore be trained in the technology used for building the business, but also needs training on the business itself, in order to understand the requirements of the customers and users better. This is necessary to maintain the system and the components involved and is necessary to extend the system based on the upcoming requirements of the users. Therefore costs and goals for the IT personnel need to be included into the business plan. For some services it may make sense to outsource the service operations. Calculations for both scenarios should be made. There is no simple rule to decide for or against outsourcing, the calculation will be able to provide the answer.

In order to generate service awareness the marketing staff needs to develop an audience. The audience then needs to be attracted to the site and the customer relationship needs to be fostered. The key success factor is to create customers that return to the site and do business, and increase the number of visitors and customers through the awareness campaign. Other than with traditional businesses, the increase of customers does not automatically mean that you need to increase resources, such as employees or machines. The virtual business can expand by adding new hardware in the simplest case and the customers won't notice even a delay or disruption of service because the company is growing.

To accomplish a growth in customers and business, the marketing and communications department needs to use a combination of proven audience development techniques, such as special promotions, PR campaigns and advertising (both online and offline) that leverage the unique characteristics of the Internet. This could include special prices by ordering online and up-to-date information. The marketing paradigm on the Internet is different than in print and broadcast media. The Internet has its own specialized promotional tools, which we will get to know in detail in Chapter 5 and in order to be successful, a company needs to create online communities and stay always on the cutting edge. In order to be successful, the subtle complexities of the online culture needs to be appreciated and leveraged. Activities like spamming are not welcome on the Internet and are a factor for losing market share. The business plan needs to create a vision for the development of new marketing strategies for the Internet and the risks associated with going online.

2.5.7 Connecting the Intranet

In order to be successful on the Internet, you should have a working Intranet first. The Intranet allows companies to digitize internal business processes and also allows the communication between all employees of a company. This is extremely helpful especially if your company has several sites that are geographically separated. The experience the company and each single employee get from the Intranet are very valuable for getting to know new technologies and new processes. It enables the employees to digitize existing processes and to invent new processes to simplify the work. It also enables new ways of communication via e-mail and chat between them and prepares them for the Internet.

As soon as your company goes online, the employees will start to talk to their clients via e-mail and chat as well. Just putting up some web pages will most probably not return any investment. Only when you and your company start to digitize your processes will you be seeing the revenues from the Internet flowing back into the company. Much of this depends on the company culture and the personal culture of each employee to accept and understand the importance of electronic communication in order to adapt the working habits to accommodate radically revised ways of working. An Intranet, which is readily adopted, often becomes a seat of innovation and the development of new and better business practice, much of which will be related to internal company communication rather than the business of trading.

Federal Express[16] built a tracking and tracing functionality into their external web page for their customers, which became very successful. Instead of calling FedEx you could enter your tracking number and you would see where your package was. After a short while the employees noticed how useful this service was also to them. They started using it as well and soon it replaced

---

[16]http://www.fedex.com/

the old process, which existed within the company. Now everybody is using the same system, customers, partners and employees. They may see different views of the same data, e.g. the employee may see all shipping records, while the customers can only see their own, but using only a single data source reduces costs massively. In addition to this, it also offered a new service to customers and partners. It also gave FedEx an edge over the competition. Customers suddenly preferred FedEx to other services. UPS and the other companies had to implement a tracking service as well to stay in business. See Figure 2.2 for the order tracking system of FedEx rival DHL[17].

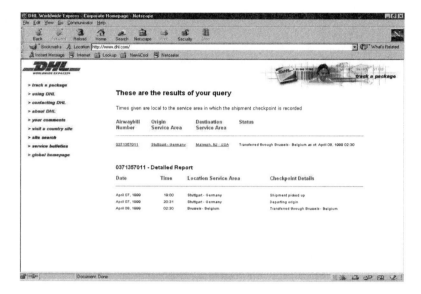

Figure 2.2. Order Tracking at the DHL Website

2.5.8   Verifying the Results

As the Internet is changing constantly it is not possible to find a point in time to verify the results of your electronic business. The results are changing just as fast as the building blocks of the business. Therefore a new paradigm for verification is necessary. A constant verification is necessary. As soon as your electronic business starts to become visible to customers you are able to detect success and failure of the service.

Other than with traditional business, where you check results once a year, once a month, or once a week, it is possible to detect change in your online business in the instant of change and can adjust the business process to minimize

---

[17]http://www.dhl.com/

the loss or increase the profit. Constant monitoring of the highly dynamic business has become a must. Therefore a mission-critical operations center that follows the sun is something larger companies cannot afford to miss. Smaller companies won't be able to afford a twenty-four operations, they will rely on algorithms that adjust their business processes to the needs of the changing environment.

Monitoring

cannot afford to lose the market.

Chapter 3

SELECTING
THE TECHNOLOGY

3.1 Internet Networking

3.1.1 The Internet Infrastructure

Over the last few centuries governments played a key role in building and regulating the transportation, communication and energy infrastructure. Technology was driven by politics. Although it helped to move society from agriculture to industry, it hinders now the transition from the industrial society to the information society. Technology is driven nowadays by the private sector and governments have more and more trouble keeping in touch with the latest developments in order to create appropriate regulations.

In many industries, such as transportation, e.g. airlines and railways, communication, e.g. mail services and telephone companies, and energy, e.g. power plants and petrol stations, have been privatized over the last decades, splitting politics from economy and vice versa.

For the Internet four technological key areas play a large role in future expansion of the Internet: the traditional telecommunications companies, satellite technology vendors, wireless networks providers and cable companies.

The traditional telecommunication companies are moving fast from providing simple services, such as phone calls to more technological companies that provide solutions for all types of customers. They are developing new technologies for higher-bandwidth communication across existing networks, such as xDSL technologies and faster switches. In addition to this software companies have developed new types of compression technologies to reduce the amount of data that is sent over the network. In addition to enhancing existing networks, new types of networks are being set up. Fiber optic networks, which use optical amplification and photonic switches, are more powerful and more efficient. Not only telecommunication companies are laying these new fiber cables, but also electric utility companies spend a lot of money in providing a fiber optic Internet backbone.

New broadband networks with a global reach are being set up by satellite
companies, who work closely together with electronic and aerospace corporations to get the satellite up and running. These new broadband networks will
connect all the people who live in areas where telephone service over normal
copper wire is not available. These new broadband networks will be much
faster than current technology at a much lower price, making network access
accessible for people with very little income.

Most of the industrial countries have spent a lot of money and effort in
building up cable networks for television over the last decades. The cable wires
can be used for more than just television, so that many cable providers started
to prepare the networks for two-way Internet traffic, by introducing so-called
set-top boxes, which act as converters and separators for the inbound and out-
bound traffic, as data is sent besides voice and video.

Wireless networks are the latest type of network that is being converted for
Internet use. Local wireless networks will be soon found in every household,
where all devices will be able to communicate via wireless Internet protocols.
New standards for mobile phones will increase the throughput, and aiready
today it is possible mobile phones receive and transmit voice, data and Internet
traffic. The older mobile phone one can only pass the Internet traffic on to a
computer, but newer ones are able to process the data themselves, allowing
users to receive and send e-mail and browse the web.

3.1.2   The Internet Architecture

The Internet is actually a network of computer networks. It does not only
consist of one network, but of many networks, which are physically separate
and linked together only at very specific points. Every network that wants to
participate in the Internet needs to adhere to a set of communication protocols,
known as the Internet protocols (IP).

A network consists of nodes and channels, which provide the basic communication infrastructure. Two different type of nodes are available: end-nodes
and intermediary nodes. The so-called end-nodes are servers and clients in
most cases, providing either a set of services or requesting a set of services.
Clients are most probably computers, from which users communicate to other
nodes and servers are centralized service providers that offer services for the
clients, such as web server and mail server functionalities.

Intermediary nodes are normally scaled-down computers which forward
traffic between network segments. These devices are called routers and bridges.
Sometimes they offer the possibility of filtering certain requests out and restrict access to certain devices within a network, but neither clients nor servers
can access any service an intermediary nodes offers.

End-nodes and intermediary nodes do not necessarily need to be different
devices. Servers can also be clients at the same time, just as they can be a
router simultaneously (and vice versa). Every node has a unique identifier

called IP-address. Larger systems may have even more than one IP-address and normally a domain name is assigned to the IP-address, as the domain name is easier to remember.

The channels required for the communication between nodes can be implemented by many different means. In most cases a piece of cable is used, which connects end-nodes via intermediaries. The cable can be either co-axial, fibre-optic or good old copper wire. Depending on the type of cable you will get different connection speeds, but as the protocols for transmission are the same, the applications do not need to be rewritten for the different transmission channels. In additional to physical connections, wireless transmissions can be conducted. These electro-magnetic transmissions are done at different frequencies, such as infrared transmissions, microwave links, cellular phone communication and communication over a satellite link.

In general it can be said that any node is able to communicate with every other node on the Internet. As this behaviour is not always desired, intermediary nodes can refuse connections to particular nodes. These so-called firewalls protect company-only networks (Intranets) from the general public. As Intranets use the same set of protocols anybody would be able to get access to internal data, which is company confidential. Firewalls are also used to protect governmental data and any other set of information you want to make available to a certain group over a network.

ARPANet, from which the Internet evolved, was created by the US government. It's basic idea was to create a network that would continue to work as a whole, when parts of it collapsed due to a nuclear attack, for example. In order to make this work, the network cannot be based on a hierarchical structure. Redundancy is the key to this type of network. Neither ARPANet, nor the Internet do provide rules on how nodes need to be connected. In most cases clients will have only a single link to other nodes, but servers and routers will have more than just one link. Through this "chaotic" structure, the Internet offers for every connection between two nodes, in most cases, more than only one way of connection. In case one intermediary node fails, the connection can be re-routed over other network segments, without any user interaction. The network is able to reorganize itself.

The Internet Protocol Suite, which needs to be implemented on every node, enables every pair of nodes to communicate directly without needing to know much about each other, except for the IP address or the domain name. The protocols are pieces of software that run on every node. Today every operating system provides the basic Internet functionality.

As the Internet apparently does not belong to anyone in particular, it seems astonishing that it still works so perfectly. One reason is that today networks are not connected directly to each other anymore, but use backbones. These backbones are high-speed connections that connect network segments that are physically separated and offer connection to networks that belong to others through interchange points or gateways. The Internet backbones are the part that can be really called the Information Highway. The local networks are more like cities, where the roads are more crowded and narrower.

The basic protocols on the Internet are planned and controlled in a hierarchical manner. Although anybody can contribute to the development of new technologies and protocols, only very few organizations have an influence on what will be in the set of Internet protocols.

The Internet Engineering Task Force (IETF)[1] is the driving force for new standards. It is an open international community of companies, who design and operate networks, do research in new technologies and sell products based on these technologies. Although it is open to anyone, the task force is driven by companies, which try to agree on new standards, which enable new services on the Internet, while running smoother. Internet Standards proposed by the IETF are the so-called Request for Comments (RFC)[2]. Although the RFCs are drafts, they keep their name when they become a standard.

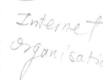

The Internet Engineering Steering Group (IESG)[3] is responsible for technical management of IETF activities and the Internet standards process.

The third group having an influence on new standards, is the Internet Society (ISOC)[4], which is an organization of Internet experts that comments on policies and practices. It oversees a number of other boards and task forces dealing with network policy issues.

The well-known World Wide Web Consortium (W3C)[5] has no direct influence on Internet standards. This organization is responsible for Web standards, which are built on top of the Internet standards. This is just a side note for people who think the Web is the same as the Internet.

3.1.3   The Internet Protocol Suite

In order to keep up communications, a set of rules has been established that take care of the communications between the nodes connected to the Internet. The rules contain a wide number of functions that are grouped into protocols. This family of protocols is called the Internet Protocol Suite (IPS) or sometimes just TCP/IP.

The protocols are based on the layers of the OSI/ISO model of layers. The lower layers of the OSI/ISO model perform deep-nested, technical functions, while the layers in the middle are used by applications and rely on the fact that the functions in the lower layers work flawlessly, without having to know how they work. The upper layer protocols are based on the functionality an application requires and reduces therefore the complexity of the applications drastically. A connection over the Internet can be established easily by any

---

[1]http://www.ietf.org/

[2]http://www.ietf.org/rfc/

[3]http://www.ietf.org/iesg.html

[4]http://www.isoc.org/

[5]http://www.w3.org/

application without having to know anything about the hardware, which is used to access the Internet, such as a modem or a router.

Other than the complete OSI/ISO model, which consists of seven layers, the IPS model uses only four of those layers: The link, network, transport and application layer. The link layer is the lowest layer and is responsible for the network access. It connects the node and the channel and specifies how the node connects to the communication channel. It results in a signal being transmitted on a channel. The signal has been converted from packets, that are made of a series of bits, which contain the information. The signal is transmitted through a physical port (such as a parallel or RJ-11 port) onto a channel, which can be an optical fibre cable or a copper wire, for example. Typical protocols for the link layer are FDDI (Fibre Distributed Data Interface), which is used to create Ethernet networks and PPP (Point to Point Protocol) for token ring networks. The software for the link layer is also known as the device driver and is normally embedded on the network card.

The network layer is the next layer above the link layer. It is responsible for data addressing and the transmission of information. The protocols define how packets are moved around on the network, i.e. how information is routed from one start node to the end node. Information is represented in segments and packets. A packet is composed of a set of bits or bytes. The protocol used for the network layer is the Internet Protocol (IP). Another protocol used at this level is responsible for multi-casting, which sends out a single message to multiple recipients, reducing the required bandwidth for sending out the information. This protocol is used for audio and video broadcasts over the Internet and is called Internet Group Management Protocol (IGMP).

The next higher level, the transport layer is responsible for the delivery of the data to a certain node. It ensures whether and how the receipt of complete and accurate messages can be guaranteed. Information is represented in messages and segments. Messages are composed of a group of packets. The transport layer breaks down larger messages into segments, which then can be transported. On this layer two protocols are of importance. The Transmission Control Protocol (TCP) is the key protocol and provides a reliable message-transmission service and the User Datagram Protocol (UDP) offers a stateless, unreliable service, which works with the paradigm of best effort.

The application layer ensures the delivery of data to a certain application from another application, which is located on the same or on another node in the network. This layer uses messages to encapsulate information. The protocols on this level include the Hypertext Transfer Protocol (HTTP), which ensures the transmission of HTML documents, for example, the Simple Mail Transfer Protocol (SMTP), which is able to transfer mails from one node to any other and the File Transfer Protocol (FTP), which transfers files between nodes.

Although this structure may seem complicated, it actually simplifies the implementation of the whole IPS. By segmenting information in messages, packets, bytes, bits and signals, depending on the layer, it becomes easier to develop software that incorporates the required protocol more easily. Every layer can be implemented separately without knowledge about the other layers, making the software more simple and robust. It makes it also easy to integrate software from different vendors into a single solution, even if they operate on different levels. Through the use of the common protocol they can be used transparently.

3.1.4   The Domain Name System

As we have seen above the network layer is responsible for addressing the nodes and how they are connected. Every node on the Internet has a unique IP-address. As IP-addresses are difficult to remember, domain names have been put on top of the IP-addresses, which are far more easy to remember. For most people it is far easier to remember "www.hp.com" than its corresponding IP address (192.151.11.13). "hp.com" actually has more than one IP address assigned, through a so-called round-robbing mechanism customers are delegated to one of the four machines to keep the load levels on all computers more or less equal.

Every domain name maps to one or more IP address and every IP address can map one or more domain names. If there are more than one IP addresses per domain name this means that there are several servers at the same location, which share the incoming load of requests and if several domain names point to a single IP address, then most probably several customers are sharing one large web server at the site of an ISP.

In order to map the domain names to the IP address a specialized service is required, which is called the Domain Name System (DNS). The hierarchical name-space of the DNS is used to map domain names to IP addresses and vice versa. It consists of a sequence of names, from the most specific to the most general (left to right), separated by dots, for example "www.ferrari.it."

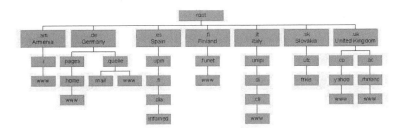

Figure 3.1. The DNS Hierarchy

As you can see in Figure 3.1, the root of the system has no name. Below the root, there is a set of top-level domain names (TLD), which consist either of the

two-letter country codes, as described in ISO-3166 or are of a more generic nature, such as ".edu", ".com", ".net" and ".org". Most countries such as Germany
(".de") do allow the registration of individual organizations directly below the
TLD, which makes the hierarchy flat. For other countries, such as the United
Kingdom (".uk"), there is an additional layer of generic categories below the
TLD, reflecting the generic TLD. In the United Kingdom, for example, these
second level domains are ".ac" for academic institutions, such as universities,
".co" for commercial companies, ".org" for all sorts of organizations and ".gov"
for governmental sites. The TLD ".us", for the United States, is based on geographical second level domains. The ".us" domains tend to become very long
and unusable.

Nodes that are connected permanently to the Internet do not change their
IP address or domain name over time. But many people connect over modems
to the Internet and do not require permanent connections. As the number
of addresses using the Internet Protocol is limited, dynamic connections do
not get assigned a permanent IP address, but use dynamic addresses as well.
Every time you connect via modem to the Internet, you will get assigned an
IP address from a pool of addresses. This allows ISPs to connect thousands of
people with only a few hundred IP addresses, as not everybody is online at the
same time.

During the early years of the Internet, the DNS system was stored in a
single master-file, which all nodes had to download from time to time to keep
up-to-date. As more and more nodes connected to the Internet, it became quite
clear, that this solution scales not at all. Therefore a new decentralized approach needed to be implemented[6]. Instead of getting the information from
one resource only, the decentralized approach allowed it to retrieve the information from thousands of servers, which are connected to the Internet.

The new system allows the direct query between the source DNS and the
target DNS. When looking up a web page located at the domain "www.rus.uni-
stuttgart.de" from a computer with a domain name "tmbbvaf1.bbn.hp.com" the
node with the host name "tmbbvaf1" sends a request to the local DNS server.
The DNS server is able to see that the domain name is not a local address and
passes the request on to the authoritative server for the ".de" domain. By the
way, domain names in the "bbn.hp.com" domain can be resolved locally and do
not need a connection to the outside world. The authoritative servers for all top
level domains are the only files that are distributed from a central point and
are highly unlikely to change over the time. The ".de" server passes the request
on to the DNS server of the University of Stuttgart ("uni-stuttgart.de"), which
then in turn passes the information on to ".rus.uni-stuttgart.de", which is able
to return the IP address to "tmbbvaf1.bbn.hp.com".

Although this seems highly complicated, the IP address is within fractions
of a second at the client. The process is sped up by keeping a local cache of IP

---

[6]http://www.ietf.org/rfc/rfc1034.txt

address information. If you try to connect to a certain site and someone else
from your local network wants to do the same a little bit later, the local DNS
will hold a copy of the request in memory. This reduces the network load and
speeds up the process even further.

3.1.5   IPv6

The Internet is currently based on the Internet Protocol version 4 (IPv4), which
is able to address about 4 Billion IP addresses. In 1990 about 20 percent of the
available IP addresses where already assigned and the number of assignments
were doubling at that time already every fourteen months. Without changes
in paradigms the complete range of IP addresses would have already been exhausted in 1994. At that time work started on IPv6.

IPv4
↓
IPv6

In 1999 most of the Internet is still using IPv4 and there are still IP addresses available. The reasons therefore is the introduction of dynamic IP addresses for Internet users, who are not connected all day to the Internet. My
first Internet Service Provider gave me a static IP address, which was great at
that time, but today would be impossible. The advantage of static IP addresses
is that if the connection breaks down and you reconnect you can continue with
all your activities as if nothing has happened; downloads etc. were put on hold,
but not stopped. Today ISPs use a range of IP addresses, which are assigned to
certain users, at the time of the login. Another reason that the IP address range
is still not exhausted is that most companies do use network address translation (NAT). NAT means that the company's Intranet uses a certain range of IP
addresses, which may be used by someone else on the Internet. These internal IP addresses are not visible to the outside world. At the company firewall
the internal IP addresses are translated to Internet IP addresses, which the
company has bought officially. This does not only reduce the risk of a break-in
attackers never see the original IP address and the complete internal network
architecture is hidden by this mechanism.

NAT

Hewlett-Packard is one of the few companies who have bought a complete
Class A network, which includes the complete IP-Range starting with 15.*.
A company today buys parts of a Class C network and hides the rest of the
required IP addresses behind a NAT service. A short explanation what Class
A, Class B and Class C networks are, can be found in Table 3.1.

Although it is not expected that there will be a shortage of IP addresses in
the near future, there are still many valid reasons for implementing the next
generation of the Internet Protocol. The IPv6 standard is defined in RFC1726[7].
As we have seen the original reason of creating IPv6 was the limited IP address space. With IPv6 the address space has increased from 2^{32} (4294967296,
a number with 11 digits) to 2^{128} (a huge number with 39 digits) allowing to
support 10^{12} nodes and 10^9 networks. In order to enhance the flexibility of the
network topology the routing algorithm should have no knowledge of how the

---

[7]http://www.ietf.org/rfc/rfc1726.txt

Networks in IPv4

The IP address range were originally subdivided into three different classes, depending on the size of the company. Today most companies get only small fractions of a Class C Network.

- **Class A Networks** – A Class A Network gives access to 16,777,216 (2^{24}) IP addresses.

- **Class B Networks** – A Class B Network gives access to 65,536 (2^{16}) IP addresses.

- **Class C Networks** – A Class C Network gives access to 256 (2^8) IP addresses.

Table 3.1.

network has been made. In IPv4 each node needs to be connected to the other with less than 256 devices in between (the so-called hops). Another important requirement is that the performance should not decrease with the introduction of a new protocol and the robustness of the service should not degenerate.

In order to make transition to IPv6 possible, it is necessary that IPv6 supports and accepts IPv4 packets. The new protocol needs to be backward compatible to allow older systems and devices to work on the new protocol stack. In order to make IPv6 a viable solution for the future, it needs to be independent of the network media. No matter if the transmission is done over a high-speed network with 500GBit/s or low-speed networks with 300 Bit/s, it should be possible, just as with IPv4.

As IPv4 does not only allow TCP, but also UDP, it is necessary that IPv6 needs to support this unreliable datagram service as well, in order to allow applications using this protocol to work on IPv6 as well. The configuration, administration and operation of IPv6 should become easier than with IPv4 and security needs to be introduced, as this is a requirement for electronic business.

As IPv6 has such a large IP address space one of the goals is to use every IP address only once. The basic multicast features, introduced in IPv4, need to be enhanced to support better broadcasting over the Internet, such as radio and television streams. Packet headers should be extensible to hold additional information required for the particular transmission and the data structure should be independent of the actual protocol. As a result it would become possible to create new types of packets and network services, which are able to implement quality of service (QoS). QoS means that packets belonging to different applications will get a different priority on the transit via the Internet. Voice may have a higher priority than e-mail, for example.

The current implementation of the Internet protocol is based on the premise that devices and networks are immobile. But more and more mobile devices are connecting to the Internet and even complete networks are becoming mobile. A mobile phone is such a device and a car stuffed with computers, printers and scanners forms a network, which is highly mobile for example, the MegaCar[8]. MegaCar is using 16 multiplexed GSM-Mobile Phone channels to connect to the Internet. Although international roaming will keep the car connected, no matter to which country you are going, the prices will go up. First of all, because you suddenly pay international phone call rates back to the ISP in the originating country. An automatic switch over to a local provider would reduce costs a lot, but requires a reconnect.

Through the mobility, the devices and networks need to connect to different hosts in different locations, in order to keep costs low and to have the maximum speed available. Therefore the connection to the Internet needs to be highly dynamic. With IPv4 it is necessary to disconnect and reconnect. In order to have a better control over the network, the new IPv6 protocol should support debugging and control protocols.

Based on this proposal most companies who are involved in network technologies have created software or devices that support IPv6. The Internet 2 project[9] in the United States is based on the new protocol stack to allow the introduction, development and testing of new services and applications.

3.1.6   ATM Networks

Another interesting technology which has emerged over the last few years is the Asynchonous Transfer Mode (ATM), which is a new networking technology designed especially for next-generation, multi-media communications, just like telephony, video or computer generated data.

Other than TCP/IP ATM offers new protocols, which are especially designed to handle time critical data, such as video or audio. These new protocols are able to provide a homogeneous network for all types of traffic. The protocols are independent of the content that is transported.

The information is transported in constant-sized cells that permit rapid switching so that time critical data can be sent over the same network as computer network traffic. Instead of providing a fixed data rate, each application can decide how much bandwidth is required and request for it on the network. Bandwidth on demand has become now really possible.

The ATM protocols are very scalable. Although ATM is used mostly for backbones right now it is being based on fiber cabling. It is possible to imple-

---

[8]http://www.megacar.com/
[9]http://www.internet2.edu/

ment ATM over OC-48, which offers a bandwidth of 2.488 gigabits-per-second. But ATM is not restricted to fibre optic cabling. If implemented properly ATM can run over any media.

The ATM protocols are developed and maintained by the ATM Forum[10], which is an international non-profit organization formed with the objective of accelerating the use of ATM products and services through a rapid convergence of interoperability specifications. Once a standard has been developed and approved, it is presented to the International Telecommunications Union (ITU)[11].

There are many reasons why ATM will be the networking technology for the near future and beyond. One reason is that it has been engineered in a manner to pro-actively address the problems that will be encountered with next-generation networks.

As multimedia applications proliferate, technologies such as ATM have a good chance to succeed, as it is able handle all aspects of multimedia, video, audio, and data. Another reason is that this networking technology will provide for sufficient improvements in capability to justify the expense of the investment in new technology. The scalability in bandwidth allows for true gigabit-per-second networks, and is much more scalable in number of network nodes because of the switched network architecture.

The most important reason for the success of ATM in the future is that this technology is standards-based. Standards and interoperability are the most important factors behind internetworked communications. Networking standards that are technically sound and rigidly followed are more important than many technical limitations within a system.

3.2   Exploring the IT Infrastructure

3.2.1   The Platform

Choosing the right platform can become a religious war within the IT department. No matter which platform you choose, you will find strong supporters and many people who will fight against the decision. Although it is not quite logical, choosing a computer platform is often not based on facts, but on feelings. Remember the clashes between user groups of the Commodore 64 and the Atari 800, between Commodore Amiga and Atari ST, between Windows 3.1 and Macintosh and more recently between Windows NT and Linux?

In many companies the hardware dictates the solutions, because people in the IT department are not willing to support another platform. Although it is easier to maintain a homogeneous network, the problem with this approach is, that it may not be possible to get the best solution for a given problem. But on the other hand it does not help to have the perfect platform for the solution, if the people who are responsible for running it are unwilling to do

---

[10]http://www.atmforum.com/
[11]http://www.itu.int/

so. Although such a behaviour is not professional at all, it happens all over the world. Another issue with homogeneous networks is that if an error occurs on one system it is highly likely that all other system will also fail. Hackers and viruses also have much greater impact in homogeneous environments.

The Internet has changed the face of applications dramatically. It does not matter anymore, which hardware and software are used to implement a solution. In order to make it Internet-ready the output needs to be platform independent. Many companies have acquired different software and hardware platforms in the past, because of a missing or changing platform strategy. Internet technologies enabled these platforms to talk to each other and exchange information and services.

For electronic business two types of platforms are interesting. High-end commercial Unix systems and low-cost Intel/Motorola-based operating systems (including Linux, Windows NT, FreeBSD, MacOS X and NetBSD). Windows 95/98 and MacOS, which are highly popular among end customers, are not suited for hosting electronic services.

Internet start-ups are most likely to by a low-cost solution, which is easily extensible. Building a complex solution can be done either by creating a server-farm of low-cost platforms or by using one or few high-end systems. The advantage of many little boxes is the higher availability and reliability of the whole system. If one little box has a downtime because of a software or hardware problem, the service can continue to run (if configured well). If only one large box is available, a downtime of this server will cause the provided service to stop. The disadvantage of many boxes is the highly complex system management, which is required to run the service.

Every platform has its advantages and disadvantages and I don't want to start yet another discussion on which platform is the best. If you need arguments for or against a certain platform, then choose among the thousands of papers on the Internet, why a certain platform is the best. Just to name some examples, the unix-vs-nt[12] homepage is something for Unix fans, DHBrown Associates[13] has published a paper, why Linux is not as good as Windows NT. I won't try to convert you to a particular operating system. In my opinion the right operating system is supporting the needs of the user, so this depends on the expectations and requirements of every single user. The operating system is just as good as the person using it. This book, for example, has been written in LaTeX making it totally OS independent. I kept the files on a server and used it to add text on any platform that supports Internet connectivity, files and text editors, no matter where I was.

I will try to present some of the major advantages and disadvantages of each group of platforms, but keep in mind, that the platform should not be your major issue. Get the business idea right, implement the business processes and

---

[12]http://www.unix-vs-nt.org/
[13]http://www.dhba.com/

then get the platform that suits your needs best. By using Java and XML it is possible to create applications and services which do not depend on a certain platform, but can run from any platform depending on the requirements of the electronic service.

The high-end Unix systems are the most expensive investment up-front but offer some features that other platforms will not be able to deliver. For these reasons the large majority of web servers connected to the Internet are running on Unix servers. People who need scalability will be delighted by the prospect to start with a single processor machine and end with up to 64 processors in a single box. As commercial versions of Unix scale very well over several processors, it is possible to reach the maximum boost for your online venture. New technologies such as NUMA allow you to share resources over a set of computers creating a very tightly integrated cluster.

Today the Unix world already offers 64-bit operating systems, such as HP-UX 11, which increases the amount of addressable memory and enlarges the file system size, besides other newly implemented functionalities. These systems also provide support for large disk arrays and clustering. This offers a high available solution, which is critical for most electronic businesses. The concept of clustering means that you are not only running one box but several servers as if they were one, sharing processing load and providing automatic redirection of traffic if one of the servers goes down. While the low-end systems require additional software and hardware for clustering, the high-end Unix systems provide built-in support for clustering.

If Unix knowledge is already available within the company and among the administrators these systems make a lot of sense, as the cost for running the systems are very low. They run fast and stable and cause only very few problems. But if no knowledge is available on Unix, you should consider a system you already know or send your administrators to an extensive training. A misconfigured Unix system will give you just as much pain as any other system, with the difference that it may have cost a lot more to set it up, in the first place. During the start-up phase, the hardware vendor should provide a consultant who will check if the system has been installed right and if the system is running as it should. Otherwise it can happen that the system is not performing well, causing a lot of financial troubles.

It is also important to mention that an administrator who is able to administer one flavor of Unix also needs a training for the other flavor. This training will be much shorter than for the newcomer, but is necessary as there are subtle differences between the Unixes. To mention one example, threading is implemented in totally different ways on Solaris and HP-UX. In order to get the maximum out of each system, the administrator need to fine-tune the settings, which are different for each of the systems.

Low-cost servers, based mainly on PowerPC and Intel-Architectures, on the other hand, have the advantage that more people are able to get one of these computers and create software that will run on one of these platforms. Anyone buying a low-cost computer today has the possibility to choose from a series of operating systems and is able to contribute to the large pool of software, either commercially or by putting software into the public domain.

There is a lot of discussion, which operating system is most suitable for the PowerPC/Intel-architecture, and there is no right answer to this discussion. In my opinion Linux[14], MacOS X[15], Windows NT[16], FreeBSD[17], BeOS[18] are similar in function and reliability. If a system works for your online venture depends on how much knowledge you have about the platform and about the products used. The standard products are available for all of these platforms, such as a web server, a database, word processor, HTML editors, mail server, firewall software, anti-virus software and so forth. The operating systems are all providing a multi-threaded kernel and offer modern graphical user interfaces, which make it easy to administer. Even less experienced users are able to administer a digital business running on such a system.

These operating systems also offer limited support for symmetric multiprocessing (SMP), allowing them to put more than one processor into a box. But these operating systems do not scale well over more than one processor. Clustering possibilities are reduced and these operating systems provide less stable service than the before-mentioned high-end systems. This leads to a less scalable solution, so that more boxes need to be managed.

Most commercial applications are available for Microsoft's Windows NT and Apple's MacOS X operating system, but the other operating systems are catching up. Oracle[19] and SAP[20], for example, have started to support Linux.

The size of your online business will dictate the size of the server you need to get. The service will decide which solution and platform is needed to implement it and if you ask five different companies, you will get (at least) five different answers. There is no simple answer to your Internet business platform requirements and in order to find the optimal solution, pilots should be in place to test the availability and reliability of the proposed service, instead of putting it untested into production and risking an image loss.

3.2.2 Basic Internet Software

The Internet protocols described in the last section are required for the basic Internet software that is running on most computers today. This subsection gives a short overview on the available software and its use on the Internet. E-mail and web clients are the most prominent pieces of basic software customers are using each day to conduct business over the Internet. They connect

---

[14]http://www.linux.org/

[15]http://www.apple.com/macosx/server/

[16]http://www.microsoft.com/ntserver/

[17]http://www.freebsd.org/

[18]http://www.be.com/

[19]http://www.oracle.com/

[20]http://www.sap.com/

to e-mail and web servers for the exchange of information. These software packages can be run on all Internet nodes, not only on client computers, but also on servers and intermediating hosts, as these types of nodes can always be also clients. Actually any network-enabled device can be client and server. Pervasive computing makes this possible (see Chapter 15 for more information).

Internet protocols are implemented by software that runs in all Internet nodes, including workstations, hosts and intermediating nodes. In some cases, the software that implements a particular protocol may be a stand-alone tool, in others it may be a function within application software, and in others it may be embedded within systems software. Moreover, a particular piece of software may implement protocols in only one layer, or in several.

On the lowest layer, the link layer, the PPP protocol is most widely used to connect to the Internet via modem. This piece of software is embedded into all modern operating systems and setting up a connection has been made easy. A phone number, a login name and a password are everything that is required by modern PPP implementations.

The protocols on the network and transport layer (TCP/IP) are also embedded into the operating system and work transparently in the background. People who want to communicate via the Internet do not need to know how the TCP/IP protocols work. On some systems it is necessary to add information for these protocols manually (the IP address, the DNS server, the default gateway and the netmask). A new type of server, the so-called DHCP server is able to resolve all these information from a server, making human interaction for setting up the Internet connection superfluous.

On servers and routers additional commands are implemented that allow you to configure routings and other rules related to the network. These tools are very powerful, but not required any more for non-technical people to set up an Internet connection.

On the application level the end-user programs are written and use the above described protocols. Services that you offer to your customer are running on this communication layer. Computers that run web servers (such as Apache[21] or Roxen[22]) use the HTTP protocol to distribute their documents. A file server (built into all Unixes by default) uses the FTP protocol to allow access to files and mail servers use the protocols SMTP, POP3 and IMAP4 to service mail to customers.

On the client side, the customers need applications that connect to the services offered by the server. E-Mail clients (such as Eudora[23]) pick up the customers' mails using the same protocols the mail servers use (SMTP, POP3 and IMAP4). A web browser (such as Netscape Communicator[24] or the Internet

---

[21]http://www.apache.org/

[22]http://www.roxen.com/

[23]http://www.eudora.com/

[24]http://www.netscape.com/

Explorer[25]) uses the HTTP protocol to download HTML documents and FTP clients use the FTP protocol to up- and download files to and from a server. More in-depth information on browsers can be found in Chapter 9.

In order to provide a valuable and well-accepted service to your customers, you should try to find out, which protocols are supported by the installed software base of your clients. If you are writing an application that requires a new protocol, then try to integrate the new protocol into a Java applet that can be executed from within a web browser before offering a stand-alone solution, which needs to be downloaded and installed separately by the user. The customers will be more than reluctant to install another piece of software, as not everyone knows how to do this and installation of new software always puts the whole installation at risk.

3.3 Deciding on the Enterprise Middleware

3.3.1 Mail and Collaboration

On the Internet we can see two areas of users for mail and collaboration. On one hand there are the private mail systems, which are used in companies and run by themselves and the public mail systems, which are used by individuals and are mainly hosted by service providers. While the functionality of the mail and collaboration software is similar, we see totally different products in both areas. While the private mail systems are dominated by Lotus Notes, Microsoft Exchange, Novell, Hewlett-Packard's OpenMail and Netscape the public mail systems are run by Software.com's InterMail[26], Netscape, Sun SIMS, Sendmail and MCIS.

More than one third of the Internet's public mailing is handled through InterMail even though almost nobody knows about it. The mailing system offers a web-based front-end, which has become very popular over the last few years. Instead of using applications such as Eudora, Pine, Elm, or even the Netscape Messenger, which is part of the Netscape browser, more and more people have started to use web-based e-mail programs. The major advantage is that the e-mail client is very easy to use. Anybody who is able to use a browser is able to send and receive e-mail, without any configuration, which would be required by all other types of e-mail clients.

The second advantage is that the e-mail can be read from any terminal that has a web browser installed and is connected to the Internet. This feature has become also very interesting for business people who are traveling a lot and need to access their e-mail. Therefore we will see a convergence between the corporate and private mailing, which will result in unified mailing solutions, which allow both, web based reading and e-mail client reading, depending on where the user is.

---

[25]http://www.microsoft.com/windows/ie/
[26]http://www.software.com/

Web-based mailing has already become the preferred method of reading and sending e-mail for individuals and traveling business people accessing the Internet. So more and more companies are looking out for solutions to allow their employees secure access to their internal mailing. Today many employees forward their mails to Excite[27], MyOwnEmail[28] or any other of the thousands of free web mailing services on the Internet. This poses security risks, as one can imagine. The e-mails are transported to another server and are not necessarily heavily protected on that server, as you would like your corporate e-mail service to be.

While InterMail in its standard configuration is more for the traditional web mail to meet the needs of the service providers and their customers, OpenMail Anywhere[29] sets a new standard in secure web access to corporate mailboxes.

InterMail is the standard of carrier-class messaging with its massive scalability, high performance, and a host of features designed to insure reliable operation, uninterrupted access, smooth administration, and customized integration with other systems and services. Three different versions are available to meed the needs of the service provider, ranging from 25,000 customers to unlimited customers.

The InterMail software is designed to enable consumer, business, and Webmail messaging services within a single integrated architecture. Service providers are able to create and customize classes of service at varying price points for consumers and business customers. Service providers can further differentiate their products by offering service level agreements (SLAs). These capabilities help service providers to expand market share, retain subscribers, lower total cost of ownership, and derive increased profits.

While InterMail is trimmed on efficiency it lacks the secure integration into the corporate mailing infrastructure. OpenMail Anywhere on the other hand offers a tight integration into HP's trusted web platform Virtual Vault, which makes it easy to allow employees access their e-mail either from within the company and their standard mailing application or over the Internet through a web browser.

The integration of OpenMail and Virtual Vault eliminates the need for remote users to rely on dial-up networking or carry a laptop to access e-mail from remote locations. OpenMail users simply access an SSL-secured URL from any device with an Internet browser, including PDAs, Web phones, walk-up terminals and PCs. The browser accesses OpenMail Web client software located on a Virtual Vault server. The server then connects users to their OpenMail accounts on OpenMail servers inside the corporate firewall.

With this solution, companies can reduce their investment in remote-access systems, private networking, and associated support and help-desk staff. Virtual Vault uses trusted mandatory security mechanisms to block sophisticated

---

[27] http://www.excite.com/

[28] http://www.myownemail.com/

[29] http://www.openmail.hp.com/

attacks on the OpenMail client, the boundary Web server and internal corporate OpenMail servers. Attackers cannot modify Web pages nor modify legitimate application code.

3.3.2 Network and Systems Management

Today companies face enormous challenges in managing their infrastructures. There are three reasons why this is happening. First of all the existing infrastructure is growing rapidly, the Internet and its services require new devices and new software, which become part of the business within a very short time. The second reason is that technological approaches to networking, database, application, hardware and software platforms continue to diverge. And finally business success in today's economy is predicated on keeping costs in line while delivering more timely and better targeted, goods and services than the competition. These reasons require you to have a solid network and systems management solution in place.

This effective network and systems management architecture allows you to manage all networks and systems centrally. This means that you are able to control every single system and every component of the network and will also receive immediate response from the system in case of an error, so that it can be either corrected over the network or if this is not possible locally.

Such a solution should support open systems multi-vendor environments and multi-platform infrastructures, meaning that all types of hardware and software should be able to be managed through this central interface, including all operating systems and all network protocols. It is quite uncommon to find a company who is running exclusively one type of hardware and one type of operating system. Over time legacy systems have been introduced into the company, which cannot be replaced easily with newer systems as they have become mission-critical. Changing strategies of the company will lead to different hardware and software equipment over time. Therefore the network and management solution needs to take this into account.

The management system should integrate all necessary functions, such as inventory, storage, scheduling, and security. It needs to be open to extension by third parties and allow customization by the enterprise staff as well as service providers. Comprehensive control of the enterprise requires end-to-end management of the entire IT infrastructure. Issues in enterprise management are not bounded by specific technologies. Therefore an end-to-end management system must address all types of resources: systems, networks, desktops, databases, and applications.

A consistent user interface will help the administrators to detect anomalies on the network and on the systems easily and take action, if necessary. A global view of the network should be provided, which can also be drilled-down to single components. An early warning system should be integrated to support the problem management module.

Over the years Hewlett-Packard's OpenView software has established itself as the industry standard. More than half of the servers on the Internet are managed through OpenView systems, as it is a proven product and very tailorable to the needs of each single organization. OpenView meets the needs of troubleshooters, help desks and administrators and supports distributed heterogeneous environments. It expands the effectiveness and productivity of IT organizations by increasing the up-time of networked systems and by decreasing problem resolution time. The OpenView system collects, consolidates and selectively presents only the most critical information to the central management system.

Besides OpenView there are two other highly successful products on the market. Unicenter TNG[30] by Computer Associates and Tivoli Enterprise[31] by IBM provide a similar functionality.

Tivoli Enterprise is a suite of management applications that gives you the power to manage your entire enterprise application architecture, including your data center, your distributed system, and even your laptops. Tivoli Enterprise unites these disparate environments and enables you to manage them together as a single business system, treating each as a strategic component of your complete enterprise.

Tivoli Enterprise is an open, object-oriented framework that includes a set of managers, brokers, and agents that conform to the CORBA specification. CORBA technology allows major differences between computer operating systems to be hidden from the Tivoli Enterprise user, and it allows key services to be encapsulated in objects that can be used by multiple management applications. The Tivoli Management Framework provides platform independence, a unifying architecture for all applications, and the ability for third-party vendors to easily adapt to, or plug into, the framework. It also provides a rich set of application program interfaces (API) and services. This enables customers to write new applications that also plug into, or leverage, the Tivoli Management Framework and can be easily monitored over the network.

Unicenter TNG (The Next Generation) is a comprehensive, open, and scalable solution that provides the management of all IT resources in an enterprise. It delivers a rich set of management functions, which are built on top of an object-oriented, open architecture and a highly scaleable, manager/agent infrastructure. Unicenter TNG allows IT organizations to manage all of their enterprise resources through a single management interface, which encompasses heterogeneous networks, systems, applications, databases and even non-IT devices, such as door openers. The network management function in Unicenter TNG uses the common object repository to store information. This shared repository is instrumental in ensuring uniform enforcement of management policies, user interface, and interaction.

---

[30]http://www.cai.com/unicenter/
[31]http://www.tivoli.com/

Besides the big three in network and systems management there are many smaller solutions that work exclusively on the Simple Networking Management Protocol (SNMP) level. Many applications use this protocol to output management data, which can be then collected by these SNMP savvy application and be processed to inform the administrator about the status of these applications and devices. The big three do understand SNMP as well. Depending on the size of your company you should decide, if you need a simple solution, based on SNMP only, which is not secure or if you go for the full-blown management system, such as OpenView.

3.3.3   Security Software

The communication over the Internet is by default open and uncontrolled and conflicts with the business needs of digital businesses. Privacy, confidentiality and integrity of the business transactions is a problem of the Internet, if no additional security layers are implemented. The growing demand for electronic business also raises the awareness for security issues and concerns about achieving this goal. The news are full of reports on Internet security that are hyper-critical and increase the fear. Network-based fraud is growing dramatically, and has made Internet security a business issue and not just a technical issue to be resolved in the IT departments of companies considering an Internet business strategy.

Today technology is able to make a system secure, but more than pure technology is required. Many problems have been reported in the past and it is sure that we will see even more incidents in the future. But if you look more in-depth into the problems behind the attacks, you will often find human error, missing procedures and wrongly configured software as the main problems. These errors can't be eliminated by technology, instead they require intensive training for every single employee.

Security is often not a technical issue, but a political and process-related issue. The software solutions for ensuring privacy, confidentiality and integrity are available and have proven themselves over the last few years, but often companies forget the human component in their security strategy. The weakest link in the chain will break, no matter how strong the other links are.

To protect your company information from hackers it is necessary to have a firewall solution. The solutions in the market range from free software products (FreeBSD[32] has some basic firewall functionality built in) and FreeStone[33], which offers a fully-functional freeware implementation of a firewall to highly complex multi-layered solutions (using software such as Firewall 1 by CheckPoint[34] depending on the needs and financial possibilities of your company. But still hackers can easily steal information from within your company,

---

[32]http://www.freebsd.org/
[33]http://www.soscorp.com/products/Freestone.html
[34]http://www.checkpoint.com/

by sending an e-mail to one of the employees and requesting a certain document. If the employees have not been educated about social engineering and other forms of attack, the best software solution will not be able to protect your intellectual property.

The HP Praesidium firewall[35] provides a boundary protection environment. This provides control for allowing or denying all network connection into or out of a particular network. It provides for active online authentication of who is getting through using either the strong techniques of multi-factor authentication using token cards or weak passwords to establish sessions. The firewall also provides an audit of all activity that insures non-repudiation and detection of misuse events. The firewall is running on a conventional operation system that has been strengthened by the removal and disabling of many applications and services that are not required on a firewall. For example the sendmail, or the finger daemons are not run on the firewall machine; actually everything has been disabled to the outside except for the firewall service. This makes it more difficult for attackers.

The Praesidium firewall provides for network connections with a single solution that gives access to the LAN, to the perimeter (the DMZ) and remote access using the VPN. The Praesidium Firewall provides access to basic back-end services and it can reside in parallel with a Praesidium Virtual vault providing access to more sensitive mission critical environments on the inside.

IBM's eNetwork Firewall[36] contains all three critical firewall architectures in one product. Filtering, proxy, and circuit level gateways provide customers both a high level of security and flexibility. The virtual private network support is based on the IPSec standard and offers therefore a high level of security. There are many other firewall products and the software you choose should fit best to your security concept and not the other way round.

If you have the right procedures and technologies in place to protect the intellectual property, you are in shape to try to set up a true electronic business on the web with a connection to your internal data. If we remember the phases from the preface we would be moving towards phase four with such a strategy.

Information security is necessary to prevent unauthorized access to electronic data. The result of unauthorized access can be disclosure, the alteration, substitution or destruction of information.

Once the company Intranet is secure it is possible to start communication over the Internet. Organizations and people describe their needs for information security and trust in terms of five major requirements: Confidentiality, integrity, availability, legitimate use and non-repudiation. Confidentiality is necessary to control who gets to read the information and to conceal the information to all others. Integrity needs to assure that information and programs are changed only in a specified and authorized manner and that the

---

[35]http://www.hp.com/go/security/
[36]http://www.software.ibm.com/security/firewall/

data presented is genuine and was not altered or deleted during transit. The availability needs to ensure that authorized users have continued access to information and resources. Legitimate use means that resources cannot be used by non-authorized persons or in a non-authorized way.

These five components may be weighted differently depending on the particular application. A risk assessment must be performed to determine the appropriate mix. A number of different technologies can be used to ensure information security.

Confidentiality and integrity can be implemented through cryptography, which offers a high degree of security. By encrypting the data no one is able to tell what the information is about. Through strong authentication it is possible to ensure that nobody sees, copies or deletes a certain piece of information. Using strong authentication and strong encryption the only way to break in is to have the necessary certificate for authentication and the key for the encryption. An authorization system is able to prevent access in a non-authorized way by authenticated people. Non-repudiation requires a trusted third-party which time stamps the outgoing and incoming communication and which is able to verify the validity of a digital signature. By time stamping the communication it is easy to find out if a certain e-mail had been sent out in time.

To ensure end-to-end security this does not suffice. It is also necessary to protect the computer of the customer. First of all they need to be educated as well about the security issues on the Internet. While they normally do not need additional technology to secure the communication (the browser and the mail program are capable of doing this), a digital certificate will make life easier for customers and businesses to make deals over the Internet.

The digital certificate allows customers to identify the real identity of the business and vice versa, making it possible to build up a trustworthy relationship between the two. The digital certificates are issued by trustworthy third party organizations that are able to verify the identity of the holder of the certificate. The so-called certificate authorities issue the certificates and allow users to verify the certificates at any given time. The only problem for digital certificates are the missing legal frameworks in the countries. Actually the Internet requires a global legal framework. More information on the legal issues on Internet business can be found in Chapter 4, while an in-depth review of the security issues can be found in Chapter 10.

3.3.4 Payment Solutions

As more and more companies do business over the Internet, electronic payment becomes more important. For many businesses online payment is the bottleneck for the fast completion of transactions. Everything is digitized except for the payment. Offline payment is in most cases very slow and expensive, compared to what is possible on the Internet. Therefore many companies have started to offer digital payment solutions.

In order to make electronic payment solutions accepted by a world-wide audience it needs to fulfill certain requirements. The most important issue with digital payment systems is the acceptability. If a customer pays using an electronic payment solution, the company on the other end needs to be able to accept the payment via that particular solution. If this is not the case customers may go off to another online business, which supports their preferred online payment solution.

The electronic payment solution should be open to different requirements of the customers and very flexible. If desired by the customers, their identity should be protected, just as with cash. Nobody knows where the money came from and where it goes. Although this may sound a lot like criminal behaviour it reflects also part of the privacy issue on the Internet. If money can be followed around, it enables advertising agencies to get a detailed picture of a certain customer, such as the buying pattern.

A successful online payment solution needs to be convertible, meaning that I can interchange one form of currency into another form of the same currency or another currency. In the real world it is possible to exchange a 10 Euro banknote for some coins or for some Dollar notes. This mechanism needs to be provided on the Internet as well. The transition between virtual funds and real money especially needs to be ensured.

In order to make the transaction interesting for customers the cost per transaction should be zero or near zero. Paying by credit card or cash does not pose additional costs on the buyer. Another important point for efficiency is the tight integration with existing applications. Only if payment can be tightly integrated into the business application can it reduce costs for the business and speed up the whole transaction.

In order to make customers feel good about using a certain payment solution it needs to be ensured that it is highly available and avoids all single points of failure. As an analogy one could see a customer going into a shop, wanting to buy a book. At the cash desk the customer hands over the money to the cashier. The customer puts the money onto the desk and disappears before the cashier can pick it up. Although this is highly unlikely in the real world, it can happen very easily on the Internet. Therefore it needs to be ensured that there is not point in time where the money is neither at the client nor at the merchant.

Scalability of the payment solution allows to add new users to the online business without bringing down the service. The security architecture allows financial transactions over open networks, such as the Internet. Digital payment systems are a prime target for criminals all over the world. In the real world, copying coins or bank notes is hard, but not impossible, if you have the right equipment. But replication takes up time and money, and false bank notes are in most cases easy to detect, as they all have the same serial number. On the Internet, replication costs are near zero and changing the serial number is made easy. Therefore one must ensure that the payment system is secure, otherwise it will not be accepted by the customers. The Internet is an open network, which allows anybody to eavesdrop on the traffic, so modification of messages needs to be prevented by the use of digital signatures.

On the Internet three types of payment have been established: Micro-payments, consumer payments and business payments. Micro-payments are cash transactions with a value of less than approximately 5 Euro or Dollar. Suitable payment solutions are based on the electronic cash principle, as the transaction costs for these systems are nearly zero. Consumer payment solutions are based on the premise that transactions have a value between about 5 and 500 Euro or Dollar. Typical consumer payments are executed by credit card transactions. The business payment solutions are designed for transaction with a value of more than 500 Euro or Dollar. Direct debit or invoices seem to be the most appropriate solutions. Each of these payment systems has different security and cost requirements, depending on the payment paradigm that is used. Please read Chapter 13 for in-depth information on electronic payment solutions, products and paradigms.

3.3.5   Database Management Systems

Although the majority of web pages are still static on the web, more and more companies start to use dynamic web pages, which get their content from internal databases. Databases are also used on the Intranet for storing larger portions of data in a structured way. Most applications today use or require a database to run fast and efficiently.

The database server is in most cases a separate box, which contains the databases of a company. If the company is large, then you can expect a whole data center equipped with database servers. By moving the data onto these dedicated servers, clients are able to send requests to that server and the server responds with the requested data. This allows clients to work in a client/server or distributed environment, making the data independent of the creator or a special computer. Any device with a database connector is able to add, modify or delete information in the database, if the user of the device has the authorization to do so.

Another advantage of a distributed database environment is that the clients do not need to perform the database queries and that only the required traffic is going over the Internet. The clients processing power can be used for other tasks faster this way. Today's Database Management Systems (DBMS) are highly sophisticated and are even able to take on part of the applications processing burden.

Databases are able use to stored procedures, triggers and rules for better integration with applications. A stored procedure is predefined sequences of SQL statements, which can be compiled and stored on the system as a database object. The enterprise applications access these stored procedures for functions they perform more often, reducing the load on the application server. The triggers are stored procedures used to perform automatic actions. They are activated automatically by events, such as insert, delete and update, that the database server runs across in the normal course of database processing. Rules are a special type of triggers, which are able to verify data before it is inserted into the database.

By running parts of the application on the database management system, it is possible to balance the processing load in a typical three-tier Internet application. The three tiers are the database server, the web/application server and the client browser.

A simple trigger would be: Add a new set of data into the database and a trigger adds automatically the data and the user who entered the data to the database. A more complex trigger could do calculations on input and so forth. DBM systems are also supporting rules for data, making it easier to find false input in the database. Multi-user access is a must for all systems, as several clients will try to access the same data at the same moment. A locking mechanism prevents that data is overwritten by someone, if someone else is already working on it. Although stored procedures, triggers and rules are very powerful, the disadvantage is that they are not portable from one system to the other, as the capabilities vary largely.

Another important feature is the so-called two-phase commit, which ensures that a server crash will not result in a loss of data. The data is therefore stored in a redundant and recoverable process.

Just as with the right platform, there is actually no way to tell which DBMS is the best one. Most DBMS run on all major platforms making it independent of the platform layer below. The most commonly used systems are the following: DB/2 by IBM[37], Informix Online Dynamic Server by Informix Software[38], Interbase by Inprise[39], OpenIngres by Computer Associates Inc.[40], Oracle Server by Oracle Corporation[41], SQL Server by Microsoft[42] and Sybase SQL Server by Sybase[43]. All of these systems are available on most Unix platforms and Windows NT, with the exception of Microsoft's SQL Server that is available for Windows NT only.

Depending on your needs and your applications you should choose the database management system in conjunction with the underlying platform in order to get the fastest combination possible. Depending on basic features of the operating system, such as caching and network services, the speed of the system will be high or low. But not only the underlying platform is important, the application layer, which is above more or less dictates the DBMS. It does not help to have the ultimate platform/DBMS configuration if your applications do not

---

[37] http://www.ibm.com/

[38] http://www.informix.com/

[39] http://www.inprise.com/

[40] http://www.cai.com/

[41] http://www.oracle.com/

[42] http://www.microsoft.com/

[43] http://www.sybase.com/

support it. Buying an additional server for the DBMS costs less than buying a new platform for the applications in most cases.

High-end Unix systems are predestined for database management systems, as they provide multitasking and multithreading capabilities. These can be exploited to offer a huge number of simultaneous connects from the clients. DBMS servers handle the connections from clients either by using a process per client, a thread per client or a combination of both. The advantage of processes is that if one client connection dies because of an error, all other connections won't be affected, as each process runs independently on the system. In multi-processor environments the processes can be distributed evenly over the set of processors available without much overhead. The disadvantage of this system is that many concurrent processes will eat up your resources fast.

A thread on the other hand is a lightweight process running within a process. A process will spawn several threads that share the same address space on the system. Threads use up to twenty times less resources on the system and are faster because of the memory sharing. Another advantage is that programming threads is more portable across platforms than inter-process communication. The major disadvantage is that if all threads run in a single process, a crash within the process will kill all threads as well. Threads also do not scale so well over several processors as processes do.

Most modern database management systems use a combination of both paradigms to get the most out of the system. By running a small set of parallel processes, which spawn threads the above mentioned issues can be resolved greatly. If a process crashes it will take down a set of transactions, but not all of them. With some intelligence it is also possible to reroute the threads to another process.

As more and more customers tend to get a low-end solution, such as Windows NT, which does not handle threading that perfectly, the client connections are handled through a single thread, making it possible to get the most out of these systems. The reliability of such a system is of course much lower due to the nature of the low-end operating systems.

The performance of most database management systems in the market is improved by bypassing the functionality of the operating systems. Instead of using the operating system to write to the hard disk, the DBMS is often able to write directly to the hard disk. This has the advantage that disk access is much faster resulting in a faster query. The major disadvantage of this idea is that if something goes wrong, you cannot use standard disk tools to repair the disk and therefore need to rely on the DBMS vendor to provide the necessary tools. The same applies to backups. Standard backup tools won't be able to backup the database data.

Another way of increasing the speed of the DBMS is to pack it into the system at Kernel level, meaning that it runs as part of the operating system. The advantage of this is that is has a higher priority on the system and will result in a better performance. The disadvantage of this method is that if the database software crashes it will pull down also the operating system. On Unix normal programs terminate without touching the operating system, making it possible to restart the application immediately after the crash. In the case of an crashed operating system a reboot is often required in most cases, which may take a while.

Today most DBMS are still based on the relational model. This model is rather simple to understand as it uses only two-dimensional tables linked by a set of common fields. This make the model perfect for most problems in the current client/server world of the Internet. As we are moving to the more distributed Internet world, multi-dimensional and object-oriented database management systems are becoming more important. This has also to do with the change in programming paradigm. Old style programming in C or Pascal are superseded by object-oriented programming languages, such as C++ and Java. Using an object-oriented database makes programming easier for the newer languages as everything is implemented using a consistent paradigm. This new breed of DBMS is able to store more complex data structures and therefore contain more intelligence, which is critical for the New Economy. They can also be used for online analytical processing (OLAP). Objectivity[44] and GemStone[45] are two of the software manufacturers. Although these new systems are slowly gaining market share, the traditional relational model won't become obsolete in the near future.

The most important standard in connection with database management systems is SQL. At the moment there are three flavors of it: SQL-89, SQL-92 and SQL3. These standards are defined by ANSI[46]. SQL-89 is supported by all database management systems, but as you can see it has been developed in 1989 and is not up-to-date anymore. It can be used to interchange data between different databases, as it can be seen as the lowest common denominator. Most of the functionality of modern system is lost in the transit, though.

SQL-92 is the current standard for databases and supports features such as embedded SQL support for modern languages, dynamic SQL and standardized error codes. SQL-92 supports intelligent agents, which can interact automatically with the database and generate output. More information on intelligent agents can be found in Chapter 6.

A third standard is currently being developed and is code-named SQL3. The most outstanding features is the support for Object SQL capabilities, enhancing relational database systems in such a way that they can include features such as encapsulation, methods, user-defined data types and inheritance. The gap between relational and object-oriented databases is getting smaller.

In order to decide which DBMS suits your needs best, you should also look at the additional software bundled with it. The administration and monitoring tools, for example, may be important for some companies, while others have

---

[44]http://www.objectivity.com/

[45]http://www.gemstone.com/

[46]http://www.ansi.org/

only simple databases, which are not mission-critical. Tools for backup and restore should be available, both for the system that uses the operating system for accessing the hard disk, as well as for the system that bypasses the operating system. For the latter case special programs for administering the raw hard disk should also be included. As the requirements for every customer are different, tools for performance tuning should also be available in order to calibrate the database parameters for the optimal performance.

Security is a major issue and should not be neglected. Users should be authenticated before letting them access the database and authorization should provide the necessary means to allow or disallow access and modification to certain tables, columns or rows within the database. The standard implementations of database management systems are not designed to be highly secure and therefore rely on other middleware components to secure the database. Packet filters, routers, firewall and application gateways help to ensure security for the databases. Please refer to Chapter 10 for more information on information and Internet security.

If you want strong security built into the DBMS, you need to look out for special versions of the standard DBMSs. These systems have additional audit features and intruder alarms. The disadvantage is that they are slower because of the additional security. In any case it needs to be evaluated if it is necessary to have the security on the database level or on another level of the system, such as the operating system.

To find the right DBMS for your company, you should first find out what your business processes are like and how the DBMS is going to be integrated into it. Although the above mentioned database management systems have all the same core features, the additional features vary a lot and will help you decide which DBMS is the right one for you. Don't start buying the database server first and then think how you can solve your business problem. I've seen companies buy a DBMS because they had people who knew something about that particular DBMS. In the end they had to buy a new DBMS and send the employees to expensive product training in order to implement the business process. This approach requires changes in your IT organization. A business savvy person needs to work closely with IT or even work for IT. IT should not dictate the business solution, they should implement it by using the most appropriate platform and middleware.

3.4 Choosing the Right Enterprise Applications

3.4.1 Imaging Technologies

The Internet is a huge library of information, mostly textual information. But reading on the screen is hard, therefore most texts are rather short and images are used to present content in a very condensed way. On the Internet two types of images are used: static and dynamic image formats. All web browsers

*Graphic
Interchange
Format
1994*

support natively the static image formats. Static means in this case that the image itself cannot change its colors, perspective or resolution. All browsers understand the static file formats GIF, JPEG and PNG.

The GIF and the JPEG formats have been in use since the introduction of the World Wide Web. The reason for the invention of PNG is simple. The other two formats have problems. The GIF was developed by CompuServe and has a bad reputation for being the format of choice for pornographic images that were exchanged on the CompuServe network. GIF uses the patented LZW compression algorithm from Unisys, so that actually every GIF-supporting program would require paying licensing fees. As far as I know this was never enforced, but this could change anytime, so it is better not to rely on this format. GIF images support only up to 256 colors. This was fine until true color graphic cards became the standard in all computers.

JPEG on the other hand is a so-called "lossy" image format. Depending on the strength of compression, the image loses information. The compression algorithm tries to remove data that cannot be distinguished by the human eye, so that makes it a good format for viewing. But as soon as you try to change a JPEG image, you will notice that this hidden information is missing. When applied to photos you won't notice the loss, but with clip arts, text, etc. you can see the difference immediately. The advantage of JPEG is that the files are compressed at a ratio of 1:10 or more, so that your 500 kilobyte images become less than 50 kilobytes to download.

When CompuServe announced at the end of 1994 that the GIF format uses a patented algorithm, the Internet society started developing a new format (after the obligatory inflammatory weeks on Usenet) that would be free of charge and better than GIF and JPEG together. The PNG project is a perfect example of Internet co-operation and efficiency (similar projects are Linux, Mozilla and Apache, see also Chapter 14 for more information on open source projects). Using mainly E-mail and Newsgroups, developers from all over the world have designed and implemented this new standard.

Static images are the best choice for images that do not contain content, but are for web page design purposes only, for low-quality images or non-interactive pictures. Static image formats are not designed to deliver high-quality and interactive imaging. A simple example would be to offer a small thumb nail of an image on a web page and then by clicking on the image, you could get a higher resolution image of the same picture. Many people think that this may be a good solution, but it becomes highly complicated as soon as one has thousands of images on the web site. The use of interactive image formats can simplify the administrator. From a business point of view, static image formats will be important to your web designers but won't help increase sales over the Internet. The future of static image formats is PNG. It provides the best solution quality with the smallest image size. Other formats may be in development, but nothing that would revolutionize the area of static images.

If we now look at dynamic image formats, we can see that there is a whole range of different products on the market right now. Dynamic image formats are able to change their resolution, change the perspective, the lights, colors, etc. In the context of Internet imaging dynamic does not mean Java applications, Director movies or Active X controls that can also deliver dynamic and interactive image formats. They need additional programming. Dynamic image formats do not require programming. They do require design, though.

Dynamic images contain meta-information about the picture itself, allowing one to modify its appearance without having to create a new picture. Think, for example, of an apple that can be viewed from all sides without having to reload the web page. Looking at an apple in GIF format one cannot change the perspective of the apple; one cannot view the apple from the other side, because the GIF format hasn't stored any information on what the other side may look like. Adding meta-information to the data is crucial for processing it and for creating added value to the customer. See Chapter 6 for an in-depth discussion on this topic.

FlashPix, QuickTime VR and VRML are three breakthrough technologies, which provide a profound basis for dynamic Internet imaging. There are many other formats out there, but none of them fit as well into the business requirements of today's online businesses. Chapter 12 discusses the static and dynamic formats in depth.

3.4.2   Content Preparation

Content preparation has become more complex over the last few years as customers expect more from your online business and technologies change the face of the web site just so often. Although many sites are still pure HTML to contend all customers in the same way, some web sites do not care about the average customer. Look at kimble.org[47]. This site requires a T1 connection to the Internet and a high-end PC with the latest release of a browser and the flash plug-in installed. Kimble, the "0wn3r" of the web site prefers a few cool visitors with the right equipment on his web site.

But even businesses that create HTML web sites only won't do this with Notepad or a similar tool anymore. The good old days of simple, static HTML pages are over. The problem is less the missing HTML knowledge with the web designers but more the dynamic management of HTML pages, which makes it impractical to work with simple tools for large sites. Today's web sites do not only contain HTML text, but also graphics, animation, interaction and sound. To manage these "multimedia" sites it is necessary to have four basic types of software: Web Page Editors, Graphics software package, multimedia tools and sound software. The word "multimedia" is put in brackets as I do not like the word very much, as it is much over-hyped.

---

[47]http://www.kimble.org/

Web Page Editors

As we already have learnt, the increasingly sophistication Internet technology demands of web pages require more sophisticated. One of the goals is to make coding pages unnecessary for novices and easier for more experienced programmers. But more important is the consistent look of all web pages and the control over change and links.

Two types of web page editors are available. On the one side the pure text editors that give HTML a rich set of code-entry, manipulation and management tools (such as Sausage Software's[48] HotDog). On the other hand there are pure wysiwyg (what-you-see-is-what-you-get) editors that look and behave much like modern word processors (such as Netscape Composer), with the difference that the output is saved as HTML format. Some editors are a cross-over of text and wysiwyg editors, such as NetObjects Fusion[49]. These products make it possible to design an entire web site without even a superficial acquaintance with HTML.

At the time of writing there were more web page editors than HTML commands available, making the decision very difficult. To find the right solution look out for the following features. The availability on your preferred platform should be given. Your graphic design department will most likely use Macintosh computers for the artwork, so expect them to do the web design part as well. As the graphic design department is not an IT department the software should be easy to set up and user-friendly.

More important are the site management features, that are included. The content and the design should be kept in separate places in a database, in order to make it easy to add new pages and change the design of the complete site in one go. Therefore the content should be saved in database and the design should be stored in templates. Most sites will manage with less than ten templates for the whole web site. In order to make the publishing as easy as possible it should be possible to upload the content to a staging site first, where the changes can be tested before they are put online for the visibility of the public.

As many pages appear and disappear over time, it is necessary to ensure that all links that point to pages that have been deleted need to be removed with a single mouse click. If new pages appear it is also necessary to ensure that they are linked into the rest of the web site. You cannot expect that customers will be able to guess the name of the web page.

A good web page editor offers a set of standard client-side scripting programs that can be included into the web page to make it more interactive. In addition to the pre-designed pages the web page editor should support the inclusion of self-written scripts, and therefore should offer some syntax checking on the script, just as it should provide syntax checking for the HTML code. The

---

[48]http://www.sausage.com/
[49]http://www.netobjects.com/

HTML code should be checked against HTML 3.2 and HTML 4.0 and in addition to this, the syntax check should provide a check for each browser to ensure that the output will look good in every browser, as they are not one hundred percent HTML standard compliant.

Another important issue is code efficiency. If you work in wysiwyg mode, you lose control over the underlying HTML code, resulting in many software packages in very overblown code. Instead of real HTML output of one kilobyte, some programs deliver the same web page with 10 kilobytes or more. Although this may not seem a lot, it will amount to a large sum, if your web site is well visited, resulting in less content customers and higher transaction costs for your company and your customers, if you have an ISP contract where you pay for each megabyte transferred between your server and the rest of the Internet. A spell checker is also often very useful to do a first spelling check of the web site. With this feature it is possible to find many typos, which occurred during the text input.

One of the best web page editors is DreamWeaver[50], which has some very nice features such as dynamic HTML, which allows you to create animations and transitions on a web site without much trouble. Word.com[51], for example, is one site that features some nice JavaScript animations, called JavaScript Sprites, developed in DreamWeaver.

Content Management

The significance of content on the web is increasing rapidly. With the increasing number of available documents on the web, traditional methods of maintenance become more and more inadequate. The only alternative that guarantees structuring and administration of information is content management. A content management solution therefore needs to offer co-ordination of users as well as automation of document publishing thus ensuring sound and up-to-date online publications.

Traditional web page editors are not able to handle the automatic generation, control and organization of content. Content management systems need to handle large quantities of documents. Over time every company is collecting more and more information and often the information cannot be removed as customers and partners rely on it. Another important factor is workflow management for the coordination of the course of business. This allows the content management to become part of the day-to-day business for every employee. The import of external documents should be supported, allowing documents from word processors, for example, to be converted and included into the web publication. The process of versioning of documents makes it possible to track changes over time.

---

[50]http://www.dreamweaver.com/

[51]http://www.word.com/

While general document repositories such as Documentum[52] offer the above mentioned features, they are not designed for the web. But there are dedicated content management packages such as NPS from Infopark[53], which offer a tight integration of content into web servers, electronic business applications and other online services.

Graphics Software

There are many graphic software packages on the market available, but two programs have become the most popular graphic solutions, not only for the Internet. Adobe's Photoshop[54] and Paint Shop Pro[55]. The major difference between these software tools is the fact that Photoshop is a commercial tool, while Paint Shop Pro is distributed as Shareware, meaning that you can get a free evaluation copy of it for a certain period of time and then register. This reflects also in the price for the tools.

Photoshop is the standard tools for graphic designers and offers a rich set of features, such as layers, which make it easy to compose images and move single elements around on a page, making it also a viable tool for designing web pages. Through guidelines it is easy to position elements very exactly on a page, even though this requires cascading style sheets on the browser.

Photoshop will not output HTML directly, but if you are only interested in making HTML mock-up pages, then it is a good tool for evaluating different designs. The typographic control of Photoshop is not as good as in Adobe Illustrator, for example, but good enough for most web pages, as the typographic control on web pages is also restricted through the underlying HTML code.

Photoshop can also be used to create single elements on a web page. Selected items can be rotated, flipped and scaled. This allows designers to create bevelled buttons, for example, very easy, which are used on many web sites. This can be done by making a circle on one layer, then copy that layer and scale the circle down and the bevelled box is ready. In addition to creating elements, Photoshop can also be used to define patterns, which can be used as background graphics.

For newcomers Photoshop has a relative steep learning curve, but as your graphic design department will have worked with it, there should be no issue with it. Compared to most Microsoft products the program itself is also relatively small with its eighteen megabytes, so that enough memory on the computers should be available.

Paint Shop Pro on the other hand has evolved from being a graphic converter to a full blown design and paint program. Therefore it offers some conversion features that are not available in Photoshop, making it an ideal tool for

---

[52] http://www.documentum.com/

[53] http://www.infopark.de/

[54] http://www.adobe.com/

[55] http://www.jasc.com/

converting images from TIFF to JPEG, for example. As a result of this heritage it also offers a nice picture browser allowing you to preview large sets of images through a rather simple interface.

Although Paint Shop Pro has some filters built-in, it does not offer the wealth of filters Photoshop offers, which can be used to create special effects for the web. If you look closely at the features you can see that these two programs actually do not contend with each other, but enhance each other, as each of them has invaluable features the other application is missing.

But deciding on the graphical toolbox should not be part of your business problem. The imagination of your artists is far more important than the tool they use. A simple-to-use tool will increase the efficiency, but it won't make a bad designer create new web design elements. While it may make sense to define a standard for word processors and spreadsheets throughout an enterprise to reduce work and hassle with these documents, it does not make sense to impose restrictions on the graphics design department. They should be free to use any tools they need. The files they create need to be converted to a web compatible format before they leave the department anyway.

Besides these two applications, which are the most commonly used application for graphics and design, there are many others, such as MetaCreations Painter[56] or Corel PhotoPaint[57], which offer similar functionality.

Multimedia Tools

To define multimedia tools for the web is very difficult. Actually every web browser provides the functionality required to create multimedia applications through the use of HTML, JavaScript and Cascading Style Sheets. This is often referred to as DHTML or Dynamic HTML.

Although this is very powerful, it requires web designers to learn how to program in a traditional way. Many web designers have little or no knowledge in this area. Therefore many designers will want to use traditional multimedia tools, such as MacroMedia's Director[58] or Flash, which they used for CD-Rom productions, for example.

While director is the ultimate tool to develop complex applications for the web, Flash[59] is used to create beautiful, resizable, and extremely small and compact navigation interfaces, technical illustrations, long-form animations, and other dazzling effects for Web sites and other Web-enabled devices (such as the WebTV[60]). Flash is far more easy to learn for Web developers of all skill levels. Flash graphics and animations are created using the drawing tools in Flash or by importing artwork from your favorite vector illustration tool.

---

[56] http://www.metacreations.com/

[57] http://www.corel.com/

[58] http://www.macromedia.com/software/director/

[59] http://www.macromedia.com/software/flash/

[60] http://www.webtv.com/

Director has been extended to become the premium software package for the World Wide Web. The software has been enhanced to understand all the Internet formats, such as MP3 and JPEG. The software's intuitive visual development metaphor makes it easy to create, import, animate, and control media. When you need sophisticated interactivity, leverage Director's easy-to-use drag-and-drop behaviours or powerful object-oriented scripting language. The final multimedia application is then saved in the Shockwave for Director file format, which requires the appropriate free plug-in from MacroMedia to be installed to view the content.

Sound Software

If you look at the file formats that are common on the web you will find only very few that are used very commonly. While ".wav", ".aiff", ".au" are standard audio sample formats which have been used in the past on Microsoft, Apple and Sun platforms respectively, they have become over time the standard formats for exchanging high quality snippets of audio over the Internet. If you have a short piece of audio that you want to make available, then you would choose one of those three, as they are all understood by the browsers. One could imagine that a click on a button will cause a sound to be played. This can be done easily through a JavaScript program, which controls the sound associated with a certain web page.

Besides the sample formats, the MIDI is very common on the Internet. Many web sites start MIDI files in the background. This can be very irritating, when you sit in your office and look at a web page that makes a lot of noise without having asked for it. The MIDI format was actually used by musicians to exchange tunes and control music hardware that understands the MIDI format. It allows you to save a complete song in very little memory. MIDI files are between 10 and 100 kilobytes for songs up to 10 minutes, making it a very convenient way of transportation. The downside of MIDI is that you will hear only the electronic representation of the original song and there is no voice that really sings the song. In order to get the real audio, you would need to have the real audio hardware, but for many areas MIDI output is sufficient.

Gallery-Net[61], for example, offers to its customers classical music, while they are browsing through the web site. Unlike other sites, the customers are not forced to hear the music (they have to select it actively) and they have the possibility to choose the music they like.

The Beatnik Player[62], another very common player offers a mixture between the sampled format of AIFF and WAV and the MIDI format, where the song is already structured. David Bowie[63], for example, has used the Beatnik technology to allow his fans to remix his song fame on the Internet.

---

[61] http://www.gallery-net.com/

[62] http://www.beatnik.com/

[63] http://www.davidbowie.com/fame/

The RealPlayer[64] offers the possibility to hear streaming audio via the web. Streaming audio means that audio content that is created at the time of hearing is transmitted in real-time to the customer. It can also be used to transport content that is not live, but it's real strength lies in this feature. Radio has become part of the web with the RealPlayer and many people will not want to live without it anymore.

For recorded content, which does not need to be played in real-time, the MP3 format has become the format to use. It compresses audio files with a compression ratio, which is on average about 1:10, and allows everyone with an MP3 player to replay the recorded content. It can be compared to the standard sample formats, such as AIFF, but does not require as much space on your hard disk as it uses a compression format.

Depending on the needs of your application and your customers you need to decide on which type of delivery you require and then decide on the format. Today's sound applications are all able to convert the sounds into each of these formats, so this should not be a problem. The business issue is here the only critical issue.

3.4.3   Data Warehousing

Data warehouse is becoming a popular business application, which is used in many companies already. A data warehouse is a copy of the business transaction data specifically structured for query and analysis. The operational system cannot hold their data for infinite times, therefore data is moved to the data warehouse. With the Internet the amount of transaction data is increasing rapidly. Data warehouses are used in two areas. First they can support decision makers in the process of deciding and they can be used to verify the results of a decision. Using live data for these applications would bring down the application server. The computations required for the decision making process are very heavy and require a dedicated system, where data can be shifted around, depending on what results are required. In most cases it is not acceptable to have business analysis interfere with the operational systems and decrease their performance.

Vivek Gupta has written a good introduction on data warehouse solutions[65]. His definition of a data warehouse is "a structured extensible environment designed for the analysis of non-volatile data, logically and physically transformed from multiple source applications to align with the business structure, which is updated and maintained for a long time period, expressed in simple business terms, and summarized for quick analysis."

The introduction by Mr Gupta starts with a historical view on how data warehouse systems evolved. In the past the functionality of the data ware-

---

[64]http://www.real.com/

[65]An Introduction to Data Warehousing, Vivek R. Gupta, Chicago, 1997, http://www.system-services.com/

Decision Support Systems

Decision support or executive information systems, which are widely seen as the precursors of data warehouse systems have the following characteristics:

- **Consolidated Views** – Consolidated views are available for product, customers and markets, for example, which also allow for more details.

- **Descriptive Terms** – The systems convert the names of the data fields from cryptic computer terms to descriptive standard business terms to make it easier to understand by the managers.

- **Pre-processed Data** – The available data is pre-processed in order to match the standard rules better.

Table 3.2.

house was buried in legacy systems that offered some tools for the graphical representation and analysis of the data. With the emergence of the personal computers data moved from legacy systems to personal computers making it easy to analyze the local data, but with the disadvantage that it became more difficult to get the whole picture. As networks were not very common, data could not be shared with other systems. The third group of systems that was used before the introduction of data warehouse systems were decision support systems and executive information systems, which provided partly the functionality of data warehouse systems.

While decision support systems used to tend to focus on details, useful for lower to mid-level managers for their particular decision problems, the executive information systems provide a high-level view of the data. The basic data for this group of systems is normally the same, but is processed in different ways. This group of systems can be viewed as a precursor to the data warehouse systems. The reason why these systems never became really popular was the fact that they were very expensive. Table 3.2 gives a short summary on the functions of these systems.

The data warehouse systems, which evolved from these applications provide analytical tools, which are able to satisfy more general requirements. Not only analysts, managers or executives are targeted by the system, but everyone

is able to use the system to analyze portions of data based on specific requirements. It is far easier to buy a standard product and integrate it with the
overall business structure.

In order to make the data warehouse system a useful and successful tool
for the business analysis, data from more than one operational system needs
to be combined. In order to integrate the data from different sources the data
needs to be transformed into a single data format which makes it possible to
analyze the combined data in a consistent way. This of course cannot be done
to the real production data. A copy is used, transformed and analyzed. Data
warehouse systems can combine data, for example, from sales, marketing, finance and production applications. Once the data is combined it is possible to
cross-reference data and get the bigger picture.

Data in the data warehouse is organized around time, as this dimension is
often used a the primary search filter criteria. Most people will want reports
based on a given week, month or quarter and compare the results with other
weeks, months or quarters. The time attribute is also used to cross-reference
data between different operational data sources. This allows users to establish
and understand the correlation between activities of different groups within a
company. This unique feature make data warehouse systems so powerful and
precious to its users.

Data warehouse systems do not only integrate data from multiple sources,
but can also analyze multiple versions of the same source. This allows users
to verify, for example, if an upgrade of an existing application has improved
the performance or if new employees are able to generate more revenues than
other employees. By changing application software the data warehouse can be
used to combine software from the old and the new application to maintain a
single business view of the whole company.

Once the data has been imported into the data warehouse it becomes non-
volatile, meaning that no modifications are made afterwards to the information. Data that comes from operational systems that is triggered to go to the
data warehouse is in its final state. Orders or production data are completed
before going into the data warehouse. By moving this data to the data warehouse you free up resources on the operational system and create an archive,
which can be used for multiple purposes. Keeping the data in the data warehouse for long times does not cost a lot of money. Once the data is in the data
warehouse, it keeps the operational system from filling up thus saving costs on
down-times. In addition to data in their final state, data warehouses can be
used to compare snapshots of data, which change all over the same time. Data
warehouse systems are not designed to host dynamic data.

As you can imagine every application provides different types and different
formats of data. In order to make the data warehouse a success the source data
needs to be logically transformed to match the data formats coming in from
other sources. Therefore the architecture of the data warehouse is crucial. It
needs to consider all lines of business in a company. The data warehouse ar-

chitecture outlines the logical and physical structure of the data. The architect needs to structure the data independent of any relational model of any of the operational systems that are used as sources.

Normalization of Data

Before data modelers de-normalize the relations for performance or other reasons, they try achieve the "Third Normal Form." The following three levels of normalization exist:

- **First Normal Form** – If a relation describes a single entity and it contains no arrays or repeating attributes.

- **Second Normal Form** – If a relation has in addition to the first normal form properties, all attributes are fully dependent on the primary key for the relation.

- **Third Normal Form** – If a relation, in addition to the adhering second normal form, has all non-key attributes are completely independent of each other.

Table 3.3.

In many companies information is available from different resources. Information on prices and product numbers, for example, are stored in different types of operational systems that use different databases and formats. In order to make the data warehouse system work effectively these items need to be consolidated. There are two ways to consolidate the data, either at the source or at the destination. If you consolidate the data at the data warehouse, you save a lot of cost and time in the beginning, but will need to repeat the exercise for every change on the source system. If you consolidate at the source system this will take longer, but will bring all your systems in line over time and reduce costs in the long run. The model of the data warehouse needs to be extensible so that data from different applications can be added as a business case. It is highly unlikely that you will be able to incorporate all data right from the beginning.

The logical model of the database is aligned with the lines of business in the company. The entities in the warehouse model are based on actual business entities, such as customers and orders. This allows the person who is analyzing the data to get exactly the business view that is required. Thus make the data warehouse independent of the source application data models.

In order to improve performance of the system the database model needs to be de-normalized. The maximum performance gain can be achieved when the data has been normalized first in order to achieve the maximum flexibility (see Table 3.3). De-normalization reduces the need for database table joins in the queries. Another reason is that the relationship between many attributes does not change in this historical data.

When entering new data into the data warehouse it is necessary to "scrub" and to "stage" the data. "Date scrubbing" is a very tedious process and means that the date needs to be homogenized and purified before entered into the data warehouse. "Data staging" means that the data is put into a staging area before it really ends up in the data warehouse. This reduces the risk of wrong data in the data warehouse.

The summary of the business views are in most cases simple aggregations based on predefined parameters, such as the sales figures of a certain product, which can be viewed for a week, month or quarter. In order to reduce the processing power of the data warehouse server, the results of the most common summary views are stored on the server and updated on a regular basis.

The simplicity of the data warehouse system makes it a valuable tool for everyone and reduces the cost significantly for the analysis of business decisions. A lot of care has to be taken on the data that is entered into the data warehouse, as invalid data will falsify the results. A well-implemented data warehouse system is the key for understanding the business decisions of yesterday and making the right decisions for tomorrow. Especially in the rising light of the Internet business these features are highly important as fast decisions are required.

3.4.4 Enterprise Resource Planning

With the introduction of the Internet the world has become very small indeed. The global village is electronic reality already. As many organizations now confront new markets, new competition and increasing customer expectations the manufacturers needed to find new ways of reacting to these business threats.

Business Process Re-engineering and the Information technology helped these companies to resolve the problems. In the 1960's digital manufacturing systems were already available, but were only able to handle the inventory control, meaning that a manufacturer had only a very limited view on the production process. Ten years later the focus shifted from inventory control to material requirement planning (MRP). These systems allowed manufacturers to control the flow of components and raw materials and offered ways of planning in advance.

Around 1990 the MRP was evolving into a system which allowed it to cover all business activities within a company, such as human resources, projects management and finance. These highly complex systems were called Enterprise Resource Planning (ERP).

ERP is used nowadays to manage the important parts of the business, including product planning, parts purchasing, maintaining inventories, interacting with suppliers, providing customer service, and tracking orders, which provide all information that can be very interesting for the online business and automatic exchange.

By digitizing all these business processes, the manufacturers were able to lower the total cost in the supply chain and shorten the throughput times. The stock could be reduced to a minimum by implementing a just in time process and the product assortment could be enlarged. Through the digitization manufacturers were able to improve product quality without raising the prices and provide more reliable delivery dates. ERP allows them to co-ordinate global demand, supply and production very efficiently.

The efficiency of an enterprise depends on the quick flow of information across the complete supply chain, i.e. from the customer to manufacturers to supplier. ERP systems therefore need to have a rich functionality in all areas of business. Large companies used Electronic Data Interchange (EDI) in the past to speed up communication with trading partners. Parts could be ordered automatically or customers could order goods from the manufacturer. Although EDI was a good system it meant a large investment for every participating company, making it unavailable to smaller businesses. The costs for EDI were high because there were repeated costs for every installation. A company trading with fifty partners had to install fifty EDI interfaces and each of the companies involved, too, making it one hundred installations. EDI is a two-way protocol, which was fine in the client-server area, but in the emerging pervasive computing area EDI in its traditional form will not survive. XML is replacing the functionality of EDI in more and more businesses (see Chapter 9 on more information on XML).

As many manufacturers are working on a global scale they will have a lot of different suppliers around the world and the ERP system needs to take this into account, just as they need to have multi-site management capabilities for companies that are organized in a decentralized manner. An ERP system should be able to address all the requirements of the financial accounting and management accounting of the organization. The ERP system should contain an Enterprise Information System in order to analyze the performance in key areas fast and correctly.

The deployment of an ERP system typically requires first a business process analysis, employee retraining, and then the development of new work procedures. Some people say that the company needs to adapt to the ERP system, as the software is so complex that it cannot be adapted directly to the needs of the company.

Selecting the right ERP software is difficult and requires a lot of planning. Some of the most important criteria for the selection can be found in Table 3.4. Rapid implementation will lead to a shortened ROI period. Many companies start with a business process re-engineering cycle before starting to implement the ERP system. As a result the BPR cycle does not always match the changing processes within the company and a de-coupled BPR and ERP implementation will take far longer to implement. The consequence of this is that additional customizations are required and higher costs occur.

Evaluation of ERP Software

When selecting ERP Software for your company you should consider the following topics:

- **Business Processes** – The Software should support all the business processes of your company.

- **Component Integration** – The software should have a high degree of integration between the various components.

- **Flexibility** – The ERP system should be adjustable to the changing needs of your company.

- **Internet Connectivity** – A component should be available to integrate the ERP system with your online business, making it secure and feasible.

- **Multi-Site Support** – Global and local planning and control facilities need to be supported.

- **Quick Implementation** – A short implementation period will also reduce the wait for the ROI.

- **User Friendliness** – The ERP system should be usable and manageable by non-technical people.

Table 3.4.

In order to reduce the time for implementation two strategies can be used. The first strategy is to make the technical implementation based on the current business processes and enhance the processes after the first phase. This requires a very flexible ERP system, but makes it easy to start with. In order to keep the implementation simple, only a single site should be considered at a time. This can be done if improvements of the business processes are not required immediately.

The second strategy would be to implement the ERP system with business improvement in mind. In this scenario only certain parts of the business are considered, but improved and implemented over all manufacturing sites and then the whole process is repeated for other parts of the business.

The Internet has changed the way ERP systems operate and interoperate with other ERP systems. It allows rapid supply chain management between multiple operations and trading partners. An ERP system, which does not support Internet connectivity is not acceptable by most companies anymore. By linking multiple ERP systems together it is possible to create virtual supply chains and therefore provide the possibility for the end customer to monitor the production of a particular product.

The Internet has introduced a secure and direct self-service model for accessing the ERP system, which allows customers and suppliers to interact with your company without getting in touch with a sales representative. This requires a highly secure connection to the system, as the ERP is the heart of the company, once it is in place hackers are able to intrude and change order values or bring the ERP system to a halt. More on security can be found in Chapter 10. Only if the security can be guaranteed the business partners will have trust and confidence in the system.

From a fully installed ERP system three groups of users will gain benefits: The customers, the suppliers and the employees. Customers are able to place orders and trace the orders. In addition to ordering products, they can also get additional information on the products. The Internet offers a unique platform for all these services. It allows users to incorporate workflow components easily to create real business transactions on the web. Shipping information, inventory balances and engineering specifications become available in an instant making the production faster and easier.

The ERP system also offers some advantages for the supplier. Sharing manufacturing data with the suppliers allows them to anticipate services and products required by the manufacturer without adding costs to the components. Changes in manufacturing will be broadcast to all suppliers automatically in order to change order volumes and products. Contracts can be put online and included into the workflow and revised whenever appropriate.

ERP is also useful for internal use as it enables companies to expand their internal automation. Standard paperwork from human resources, expense reporting, approval processes and purchase requisitions can be automated and stored in a single system. The reduces the resources your company expends to support employees while offering them automated methods for performing tasks that might otherwise take hours or days to complete. Employees can update their personal human-resources information automatically by using a simple web browser. Self-service has become a standard for many enterprise business applications.

Through the Internet the access to the business systems of your own company or of those of your trading partners has been unified and allows the self-service of information. This has helped to improve the service, reduce the operating costs, compress the cycle times, open new sales channels and make it dramatically easier for people to do business with you and your company.

The best-known software providers of ERP solutions are Baan[66], Oracle[67], PeopleSoft[68] and SAP[69]. Which solution fits best to your company needs to be decided by your business needs. Again the hardware and software platform should not dictate the solution. The ERP system, which you implement should offer interfaces to the ERP systems of your partners, no matter what solution they are using. Otherwise you will have a big problem. Having the same system will help a lot, but you can't choose your partners because of their ERP system or your ERP system because of your partners. Find common data formats, for example, in XML for the exchange of information and you will be on the safe side.

3.4.5 Call Center Solutions

More and more companies are under constant pressure to innovate in the development and provision of new services for their customers. The Internet adds even more pressure. Every service that is put online requires a call center so that people are able to call in, in the case of problems. The calling does not mean automatically a phone call anymore. The Internet makes it possible to offer many different possibilities, but the telephone cannot be neglected. It offers a very direct way of communication and many people have got used to it over the past decades.

As companies move towards digital customer contact, customers often feel like they get a less personalized service, put on hold too long, transferred from agent to agent, department to department and at each step along the way they need to repeat information. A dissatisfied and frustrated customer results. Your customers have several options today at the click of a mouse button. If it's not a positive experience and their problems are not solved, you're at a competitive disadvantage. The service provider needs to improve the image when at the same time they are being asked to reduce costs and run a more efficient operation.

Regardless of what "customer care" is called in your company, it is the process when your customer contact you when they only have their particular problem in mind. Typically it's a question about their bill, a repair problem or a need for information about a new service. What your customers want is a single point of contact providing convenience and satisfaction. They want the person that they contact to be able to handle their needs without a lot of hand-offs and call-backs. This requires a call center solution.

---

[66]http://www.baan.com/

[67]http://www.oracle.com/

[68]http://www.peoplesoft.com/

[69]http://www.sap.com/

The financial industry, for example, sees a major change occurring. Customers do not want to go to a branch to be served, but expect that their wishes are executed from anywhere and they want more direct access to their assets. They want, for example, to pay their regular household bills, order travelers checks, buy and sell stocks and shares, arrange insurance, and order and pay for goods, all through direct electronic services accessed from the home or office.

This change does not only bring benefits to the financial industry, as the cost per transaction is lower as part of the labor is executed by the customer instead of the employee. Therefore financial services are moving away from branches to very specialized call centers, which are cheaper to operate, more efficient, and can offer the full range of services.

Customers want to be able to manage all aspects of their account through a single, consistent and efficient service process. This process could be handled over a phone, a pager or an Internet terminal, for example. This means having a single point of contact, whether they are moving money from one account to another one, reporting a problem with the current account balance, or are interested in new services.

If we stay with the example of the financial industry, you will see that although a bank, for example, is able to handle all the above mentioned processes, they are all handled through different business units. A bank clerk who is responsible for your bank account will not be able to handle your stocks. These two processes are handled internally by two different lines of business. As a customer you are not interested in how the processes are handled internally. A bank that offers several types of services should also be able to serve you from a single point of access.

The Internet can hide these departmental issues quite well. When accessing a bank's web site, you will not see which line of business is responsible for which part of the web site. But once a problem occurs and you need to get in touch with the company the so-called call center needs to aggregate all the information to help the customer.

This will not only assist customers and gives them a higher level of service, but will also help to identify cross selling opportunities. This information can also be brought back to the web site to let the customers help themselves with these opportunities. The same systems can be used to offer customer service representatives a simple and intuitive interface, to access information across the organization on.

In order to make a call center effective it needs to access multiple data sources within the company and carry out concurrent processing in different applications, without delaying the customer who may be waiting on-line for a response. These customer service functions also require powerful client processing characteristics at the desktop, if implemented in a traditional telephone call center.

In order to make a call center successful it needs to be highly integrated and needs to create a single customer view through the integration of all relevant databases. The call center becomes the unique point for marketing, sales, customer management, distribution and solutions.

Hewlett-Packard offers an integrated customer call center, named Smart Contact, which is divided into five focus areas: Contact Management Services, Enterprise Data Integration, Business Applications, the Integrated Desktop and Integration Services. Smart Contact is able to integrate not only multiple database, but also several channels, such as telephone, the web, fax and e-mail. The solution is not only suitable for in-bound calls, but also for out-bound calls, such as tele-marketing efforts, which can be integrated into all the key business applications that manage a sales campaign.

Besides Smart Contact there are many other solutions on the market. One other solution called Remedy[70] allows companies to build up a centrally managed telephony based call center, with the integration of other communication channels, in a similar way to Smart Contact.

While it may be appropriate for large companies to build up their own call-centers using the mentioned solutions, many smaller companies will outsource this activity to a call center provider who will be able to manage the whole infrastructure in a very cost-efficient way. The Internet is able to reduce these costs even further, as it had a large impact on telephone costs and the introduction of new technologies has reduced the need for a standard telephone-based solution. The Internet reduces the need for telephones in general and traditional call centers in particular.

LiveAssistance[71] offers a web-based call center solution, which allows customers to click on a button on a web site, which will connect the customer with a person in the customer care center via the Internet. A new window pops up, where the customer is able to enter a text-based online chat, which allows the customer and the employee to communicate very efficiently. The call center is able to push URLs to the customer, which may be of help, for example. This chat based solution offers a very convenient, but inexpensive way to build up a customer care center. Other companies add Internet telephony to their offering to extend the possible communication ways with the customer. The Internet telephony solution does require the customer to have speakers and a microphone to communicate with the call center, but does not require expensive add-ons for the call center architecture.

3.5   Building the E-business Applications

3.5.1   Putting the Building Blocks Together

Now that you have an overview on the building blocks for an Internet business, you need to find the right blocks that fit together. A problem are legacy systems, where standards are not available to the public. There are still enough

---

[70]http://www.remedy.com/

[71]http://www.liveassistance.com/

companies who are not willing to share their standards with other companies, requiring you to select a certain piece of software in conjunction with another piece of software to make it work on a certain platform.

It is expected that this will change over the next few years. As more and more technology is built upon Internet technologies, it will become easier to integrate these building blocks into a seamless working solution. Before choosing your building blocks look at the rest of the book for more in-depth information on available formats and protocols that have become standards on the Internet and then choose the applications with your business model in mind that support the appropriate standards.

As the computing paradigm shifts towards pervasive computing, the single application becomes less important and the service behind the application becomes more important. Today people think application-centric, in the future people will think service-centric. They won't care anymore about the application that provided a service but specify the service they require. Instead of ordering Star Office, the will order a text input, layout and print out service. These three services may come from different sources, the customer will decide on the features and the pricing for the usage of that particular service. Applications will most likely also not be sold anymore, but rented or leased for a certain period of time.

3.5.2 Integrating the Enterprise

In order to improve customer satisfaction and increase the speed of the product delivery, many companies have started to link disparate applications within their enterprise. By integrating the strategic business applications, such as e-business applications, virtual supply chains and customer care center, they are also able to cut costs drastically and simplify the business integration with customers and partners.

By tying together all enterprise applications, one is able to create an environment that is able to withstand the changing electronic world. It makes it easier to exchange or add applications, as the basic messaging system, which links these business critical applications together does not change. This makes the architecture very flexible and allows it to adapt rapidly to the changing needs of the customers. The developers are able to focus on the business logic, rather than on the architecture.

The integrated enterprise is able to support the flow of information across multiple business units, IT systems and companies. An online order starts at a certain company and goes into the web server, from there on to web application servers and into a database. This system then often interacts with an accounting system, an inventory management system and a shipping application. All these systems live on different platforms and often do not speak the same language. The applications often have different APIs and file formats and can't exchange information directly with applications from other manufacturers.

While many companies have tried to integrate these applications already in the past, it was mostly a very expensive project, which required them to write some integration code between each application. It required a lot of programming and system knowledge. Although these complex architectures have become business critical systems, they are difficult to maintain.

Three types of application integration software are being used to make the manual integration of these business applications simpler. The first type is the messaging middleware, which allows applications to exchange data in real-time. This type of integration software is used in traditional mainframe and transactional environments. One such product is MQ Series developed by IBM.

On the level above messaging is a new type of business process integration tool, which links the business critical application on a business process level. BusinessWare developed by Vitria[72] allows developers to design graphically business processes, which may require several applications to complete. The software generates the underlying application logic and middleware needed to link the applications and allow the exchange of data in real-time.

On the top level a set of tools allows the integration of a company into a virtual supply chain. They allow the automated connection of a company to its partners' systems over the Internet. One such product is developed by Extricity[73].

The integration of business critical applications is not only interesting in order to link up existing systems within the company or with partners, but especially when mergers or acquisitions occur. Two companies that merge often have totally different IT infrastructures, but the same or similar business processes. In order to complete the merger the integration of these two infrastructures is a key point, as it reduces the duplicate processes and costs. Through the above mentioned layers of integration this can be achieved very fast and efficiently.

As a result of the business application, integration manual and batch processes can be replaced by automated processes. This dynamic business requires a tight but flexible integration among in-house enterprise applications, and between partner and customer applications. A more in-depth view on the integration of enterprise applications can be found in Chapter 9, where web application servers are discussed, which do not only offer the integration, but also a unified web front end, allowing clients to access the enterprise applications through a web browser.

---

[72]http://www.vitria.com/
[73]http://www.extricity.com/

Chapter 4

AVOIDING LEGAL
ISSUES

4.1 Global Contracts

4.1.1 Legal Preface

Due to the uncertain state of a global legal framework for the Internet, the information in this chapter should be not construed as legal advice or opinion on any specific facts or circumstances. There is a lot of movement on regulations regarding the Internet, both on a national and international basis; therefore I would advise you to contact a qualified lawyer for specific advice. The contents are intended for general information purposes only and will most likely change at short notice.

4.1.2 Doing Business over the Internet

Paper contracts are not the ideal document form in the global village. I found out myself the hard way. I got the contract for this book from Prentice Hall and had to sign it and send it on to HP Press. Unfortunately HP Press moved on the day I sent out the contract so it never got to the destination. I waited for two weeks and sent out a new set of contracts to HP Press. The day the new contracts arrived at HP Press the old ones arrived there as well. You can imagine that this is not how it should have happened.

Although all information regarding the book were transmitted electronically from Southern Germany to Northern California the contract could not be signed electronically. It was technically possible to sign the document electronically, but legally there was no way that such a signature could be validated and authenticated, in the event of a problem.

As the Internet is available world-wide, business does not stop at national borders. An online offering, for example, in a web store can be seen from any country and anybody is able to buy the goods. If everything goes well, nobody has to bother about laws and regulations, but what needs to be done, if something goes wrong? If we look at our simple example of the web store we can identify several possible issues between a merchant and a customer in this e-commerce online shopping scenario, which you can find in Table 4.1.

Legal Disputes on the Internet

Disputes on the Internet in an online shopping scenario occur often because of one of the following reasons:

- The customer pays, but the merchant does not deliver.

- The customer pays, but the merchant delivers the wrong goods or in less quantity or broken.

- The customers pays, but the money does not arrive at the seller.

- The merchant delivers, but the customer refuses to pay.

- The merchant delivers, but the customer has not ordered anything.

Table 4.1.

These are the most common issues between buyer and seller. In order to resolve them, laws are in place to support one or the other. The problem that arises with the Internet is that other than in a local shop the buyer and the seller may be in two different countries, whereby the web server could be in a third country.

The important thing for the courts to decide is where the business transaction has taken place. Depending on the country where the transaction has taken place the laws are enforced. In most cases the country in which the web server is placed is not taken into consideration. It is also not always clear where a server is located. The top-level domains (TLD), such as ".de", ".uk" or ".com" can be bought by anyone who is willing to spend money. There are no legal restrictions on where such a TLD can be used and where not. What counts is the country where the seller is located.

In many countries, casinos need special regulations to open. The same applies to online casinos, so that many entrepreneurs have decided to move their business venture to a country where gambling is allowed. Many Caribbean countries have an excellent connection to the Internet, and many online casinos are hosted there. Just putting the web server there is not enough however, in order to make this a legal offering for American entrepreneurs, for example. An American company needs to establish a subsidiary in the Caribbean in order to pursue this venture. The same applies to many other countries. Some countries in Europe, for example, have high taxes on gambling; the casinos have to pay more than 90 percent of the income to the state. Moving the digital business to another country may help.

4.1.3   Jurisdiction on the Internet

As the Internet creates a global village without global laws, jurisdiction on the Internet is a very important topic. If business is done over the Internet it is important to know, if it is caught by the jurisdictions of other countries. The concept of extra territoriality is critical for any type of business on the web.

If the electronic business is located in the France and the customer is in Italy and Spain, it is necessary to know which jurisdictions will catch. In the real world, there are many regulations which support the customers by making the laws of their countries rule.

Most businesses in the real world have terms and conditions, which fit the country the customers and the business are in. On the Internet suddenly customers from all over the world are able to deal with a particular company. There the electronic business needs to create online terms and conditions that will comply with the laws of every country.

Putting up a web page and starting an online business without any limitations regarding terms and conditions will most probably infringe the laws in most countries around the world. As there is no way to restrict a web page to a certain country a global solution is required. Global terms and conditions not available, therefore it is necessary to look into all countries where you expect to make business.

For all other countries it is important to draw the attention of a customer to the terms and conditions of your country of origin with information on how to enter a contract or reject it and which law will be applied in the event of a dispute. Therefore this text should be presented on the home page and a link should be provided from any web page.

In August 1999 Amazon.com was accused by the Simon Wiesenthal Center[1] of selling banned books in Germany. In Germany Adolf Hitler's "Mein Kampf" and other hateful literature is banned. While Amazon.com offers these books on its web site, its German subsidiary Amazon.de doesn't. Other online bookshops, such as Barnes & Noble[2] also offer these books on their web site.

Amazon.com is of the opinion that international customers who order books at their site are treated like tourists who are responsible for the import of books into their country. Amazon.com has no program or person looking into each sales and checks if the book is banned in one or the other country. But

---

[1] http://www.wiesentahl.com/
[2] http://www.barnesandnoble.com/

Amazon.com is risking of losing a process in Germany. Amazon.com is exposed to German laws because it has a German subsidiary. It is not clear who should is violating the law. Amazon.com for offering the book to German customers, DHL for delivering it to Germany or the Germany customer for ordering it.

4.2   The Web Site

4.2.1   The Domain Name Battle

Once a company decides to move on to do electronic business, it needs to register a domain name, which translates the numeric IP address into a more friendly form of text. Instead of typing xxx.xxx.xxx.xxx most people prefer to type www.wired.com, which is much easier to remember and less error-prone. Registering a domain name is not difficult, but getting the one that fits to your business name, logotype or trademark can be difficult.

On the Internet every domain name needs to be unique to avoid communication errors. But they are assigned on a first-come, first serve basis, meaning that anybody can register the domain name, which you would like to use for your company or product.

Internet domain names are composed of two distinct elements, the top-level domain (TLD) and the second-level domain (SLD). The TLD contains information on the origin of the web site, such as ".it" for Italy, ".jp" for Japan and ".za" for South Africa. The SLD completes the domain name by adding a company name, trademark, acronym, abbreviation, noun or any other word to the TLD.

The problem with domain names is that they are not trademarks. Anyone can register a domain name for an established trademark. And many people have registered domain names with trademarks without relationship to the trademark owners. In some cases people have been using the trademark without knowing about the trademark and in most of these cases a court battle was not necessary. One example is "altavista.com". A small company called Altavista Technologies used to own the trademark to represent the company. Digital[3] started to offer a highly successful search engine with the name Altavista, as the domain name was already registered, Digital was using altavista.digital.com for the search engine. In 1998, shortly after Compaq acquired Digital, it paid more than three million dollars to the owners of the altavista.com domain in order to expand their search engine business.

Other companies buy domain names with trademarks in order to sell them to their rightful owners. Prices for these registered domains ranged from a few hundred dollars to a few million dollars, compared to the approximately one hundred dollar fee for two years. In the early years there was no court interested in a legal battle over domain names, so that it was quite easy for these companies to get the money they were requesting.

---

[3]http://www.digital.com/

Preventing Domain Name Issues

In order to prevent domain name issues you should consider the following steps:

1. **Check for Existing Trademarks** – Conduct a trademark search prior to applying for a domain name to determine whether the proposed domain name would infringe on an existing trademark used in connection with goods or services similar to those that you propose to offer.

2. **Check for Famous Marks** – A name or trademark, which is very famous, can't be used in any other product or service. Offering "Coca-Cola translations" would be a violation of this law.

3. **Register Trademark** – In order to make sure that your domain name is secured, register the domain name as a trademark and start using the domain name at the same time.

4. **Check Foreign Countries** – Register the trademark and the domain name in all countries that are relevant to your business now and in the future.

Table 4.2.

　　The domain name for MTV[4], for example, was acquired by a former employee of the company at a time when MTV had no plans to go online and even supported the use of MTV.com by the employee. Very soon later the company wanted to go online themselves and were not able to use the domain name anymore. Hasbro[5] attempted to register the domain name "candyland.com" for use in connection with its popular children's game, but the name had already been registered by a company to identify a sexually explicit adult Web site. In the early years there was no way to get these domain names back.

　　In the mean time things have changed. An individual who had registered panavision.com had to hand over the domain name to Panavision[6], because the

---

[4]http://www.mtv.com/
[5]http://www.hasbro.com/
[6]http://www.panavision.com/

defendant was violating the Federal Trademark Dilution Act in the US. Many similar cases have happened in the US and all over the world. Although a domain name is still not a trademark, it has become much easier for trademark owners to re-register the domain names that contain their trademark names. See Table 4.2 for a short introduction to acquiring domain names.

New regulations for the registration of domain names have also helped resolve court battles. Depending on what has been registered first, the priority will be given to the owner. If a trademark, such as panavision.com has been registered before the domain name, the trademark owner will also be granted the domain name. On the other hand, if the trademark has been established after the domain name has been registered, such as altavista.com, the owner of the trademark has no rights to obtain the domain name.

In order to prevent legal issues for your company check both the availability of domain names and registered trademarks, before applying for your domain name. If you want to be on the safe side, register the trademark if you have a domain name, and vice versa.

Besides the legal issues on a particular domain name it often happens that unhappy customers of a particular web site get a domain name that puts a negative light on the company. Chase Manhattan Bank, for example, owns the domains Chasesucks.com, IhateChase.com, and ChaseStinks.com, while Walker Digital, a company founded by Priceline.com chief executive Jay Walker, registered Priceline-sucks.com and Pricelinesucks.com to prevent customers from using these domains to express their views on these companies.

It is not possible to ban people from using these domains, especially in the United States, where they are protected under the law of free speech. It is also not possible to register all domains which contain a certain keyword, therefore randomly buying domain names is not very effective and does only cost money. The better way is to understand the needs of your customers and try to resolve their issues. There will always be some customers who are never satisfied.

4.2.2 Linking and Framing Issues

The hypertext format allows the interlinking of documents on the web. The links are not restricted to a particular part of the web. Any web page can be linked to any other web page without restrictions. Links are provided, for example, as a service to other information resources with similar content, or as a means to link advertising into a web page.

As there are no legal grounds for the web, everybody is interlinking with anybody without restrictions. It is common practice to provide links to other sites. The problem arises as soon as links are used to pretend to provide pieces of information that have been created by others. It is very simple to create a news-service by providing headlines to the latest news on other servers. People will come to your site, because you have the latest news headlines, but all you did was provide links to the work of others.

Although there are no rules regarding linking, over the past few years it has become clear that so-called deep linking (i.e. direct linking of a particular web page) is considered as pirating a web site, if done in large scale. But providing a single link to a particular document is no problem.

In 1997 Microsoft was sued by Ticketmaster[7] as it was providing direct links to the ticket sales portion on the web site. Through the direct link it was bypassing the Ticketmaster homepage, its associated advertising and the disclaimer. Many customers were not aware that they were moving on to another site and to another company. Hewlett-Packard is also linking to other companies from its homepage[8], but displays a disclaimer before leaving the Hewlett-Packard homepage. This ensures that the customers understand that they are leaving a certain site and that the owner of that particular site is not responsible for the content, services or products of the sites that are outside of its realms.

Framing is considered to be even worse. Frames have been invented to partition a web page into several parts, which can be loaded individually. With frames it is possible to separate the navigation bar from the content. It also made it easy to place a different banner ad every thirty seconds on the screen without the need of reloading the complete window. Although the idea was not bad, frames create more problems than they are able to resolve. With frames it is also very easy to create a navigational bar with your company logo and then link to other sites. As people see your logo, they will think that the document in the other frame is also part of the site. Web sites owners will object in most cases if they find their content being framed at another site, particularly if their content is surrounded by paid banner advertising.

Some students in Germany tried to circumvent paid advertising on the *Spiegel* homepage[9]. The site consists of three frames, the upper frame contains advertising, the left frame is used for navigational purposes, while the lower right frame contains the content. The students created a no-advertising *Spiegel* web page, which allowed anyone to navigate through the *Spiegel* site without looking at the advertising. This reduced download times and increased the number of visits to the web site. The *Spiegel* advocates brought this case into court and tried to remove the other site from cyberspace, which eventually was ordered by the court, as *Spiegel* was losing money on banner advertising. In order to prevent "attacks" from other sites; a small JavaScript checks now, if the site is being framed or if frames are missing and resets the browser windows to the original URL of the *Spiegel* company.

Search engines such as HotBot[10] are not only able to search for content, but also for sites that link to your site. Check these sites on a regular basis to see if they are linking to or framing your site in a manner that is not appropriate.

---

[7]http://www.ticketmaster.com/

[8]http://www.hp.com/

[9]http://www.spiegel.de/

[10]http://www.hotbot.com/

4.2.3 Online Disclaimers

A problem with having a web site is that everyone could become an adversary in the event that a difficulty arises from relying on information, services or products that you have provided. In order to prevent financial loss and damage every web site needs a properly worded disclaimer. It needs to be written in a clear and unequivocal manner, in order to be understood by anyone in the world. But because of differing national laws a disclaimer or parts of it may not be valid in all countries.

If your web site contains only some contact information then a simple disclaimer will be enough, but as soon as you provide information, products or services that businesses rely on or act upon, the disclaimer on your web page needs to be as watertight as possible. If your company deals a lot with French and German speaking countries, it is advisable to translate the disclaimer, as it may not be understood correctly by non-native English speakers. A simple translation will not do it. It is necessary to check the local law and see if the disclaimer applies or if it needs to be adapted.

Once the wording of the disclaimer has been completed, it is necessary to find a good place on the web page, in order to make it easily accessible. On some sites the disclaimer is almost hidden, which renders it very ineffective. In some countries, such as Germany it may even be illegal, if the disclaimer is not presented in a highly visible manner. Putting the disclaimer on the home page on the other hand will be overkill. Typically a link from all pages should be provided to the disclaimer and in the case of accepting a business transaction of any kind, the customer should be notified about the disclaimer and the text could be presented in a text box on the web page, as done, for example, by Lufthansa Cargo when customers order the SameDay online service[11].

4.2.4 Content Liability

The liability for content will vary in different countries. If your web site contains only information about your company it is necessary to create a process for the automatic verification of the content. Other than a magazine, for example, which is published periodically the Internet content is updated constantly. Therefore the publishing processes need to be adapted to support the Internet presence. If you have to wait a week until you can publish anything on the Internet, you will lose eventually. Your company is liable for the content, which makes it rather easy to sue.

If you are an Internet provider things become more complicated, as you are hosting services, information and products of other companies. In order to prevent your company from damage it is necessary to create a disclaimer and rules, which explicitly forbid certain material on your servers. Although most countries consider Internet providers to be in a similar position as telephone

---

[11]http://www.sameday.de/

companies, in some cases they are considered to be responsible for the content of the servers.

In 1998, Felix Somm, who headed the CompuServe[12] operations in Germany until he was indicted in 1997, was convicted in Germany of violating local pornography laws. Mr. Somm has been accused of trafficking pornography and neo-Nazi propaganda, which is forbidden in Germany by law and was blamed for not blocking access to pornographic pictures that were available on the Internet. By convicting Mr. Somm, the court appears to be saying that Internet service providers in Germany are responsible for Internet content and must take affirmative steps to block access to objectionable material. This verdict fortunately is based on the German legal system nd does not affect the laws as it would in the United States, for example.

Although a judge who apparently did not understand how the Internet works made the decision. It is an indication that illegal content can be a problem for every party involved in providing the information.

4.2.5 Intellectual Property on the Web

Copyright protection on the Internet has several fundamental limits, defined by international agreements. Only an expression can be protected, but not ideas or facts. A work that is very similar to another work does not infringe copyright either. Before the Internet arrived these rules where easy to handle, as copying in many cases was at least as much work as rewriting it with one's own words. On the Internet information is copied very easily. Just copy the information from a site and paste it into your web page. This can be done in seconds and even automatically by specialized programs.

Brad Templeton has written a highly interesting article about intellectual property on the web[13]. His article, entitled the biggest myths about copyright, gives a good overview on the issues with copyright. Today almost every piece of information is copyrighted, no matter if a copyright statement is visible or not. Using that material is a violation of the copyright, no matter if you charge money for it or not. This applies especially to the Internet. Although information is accessible freely it does not mean that the information can be reused for commercial purposes.

Many companies have started suing people who are running fan sites on the web, if they use copyrighted material. In the beginning, everyone was setting up fan pages, without thinking about copyright issues, as these fan pages where mostly created for fun and not for making money. But as trading banner advertising became more popular, many fan pages started to make money, which was not in the interest of the copyright owners. One example is Star Trek[14]. The owner of the Star Trek logos and images asked all fan page own-

---

[12]http://www.compuserve.com/
[13]http://www.templetons.com/brad/copymyths.html
[14]http://www.startrek.com/

ers to remove the copyrighted information from their pages, leaving most pages blank. The number of Star Trek fan pages has decreased since then. This has angered many of the fan groups, which started to protest against this decision on the web.

Other copyright owners try to bundle the fan pages into a single site. Look at ACMEcity[15], which allows fans of various comic figures to create their own web pages on that particular server. The fans are able to use a set of a few thousand images, sound and other media as long as the pages remain on that particular server.

The awareness of copyright issues has increased over the last few years, but information on the web wants to be free. Web technology enables the free transfer of information and restricting it is difficult. The major advantage of the web is that copyright owners can use search engines to discover copyright breaches easily.

The biggest problem on the Web does not come from text based content, but from copied images, sounds and programs. Images are easily scanned in and put onto a web site. Many images come from a books or magazines. The JPEG image format allows images to be presented on every screen of any type. The images are compressed, therefore it does not take a long time to download. The music business is fearing the MP3 format, which compresses similar to the JPEG format with a ratio of 1:10 or even higher. It allows complete compact discs to be copied over the Internet in reasonable time. The files can be downloaded onto a computer and from there copied onto a cassette or another compact disc.

Distributing pirated versions of software has been made much easier with the Internet and many sites offer pirated software for download. This is also one of the reasons why more and more companies offer free software, as protecting the software would cost more than distributing it for free. Until a few years ago copying software was not protected by a law and only very recently a law has been introduced to protect databases (in Germany, for example, in 1998). Many countries still do not have copyright laws.

Most web sites today consist of a database that contains, for example, travel information, e-mail directories or product information. Copying databases over the Internet is just as easy as copying information or software. Copying the database of Yahoo is easy (as it is publicly available on the Internet) and without the copyright protection of the database we would see many replicate sites popping up on the Internet.

The law does not apply for all types of databases. In some countries databases that contain all information about a certain topic without sorting them systematically and methodically are not included, as they do not contain any added value. But this again is not true for all countries, therefore do not assume that you have the right to copy the database from a web server. If you

---

[15]http://www.acmecity.com/

only use small parts of a database than this is considered fair use. Copying the complete database onto a private system is not allowed without the permission of the database owner.

4.3   Encryption Algorithms

4.3.1   Key Escrow

Discussions in many countries are going on about encryption algorithms and privacy issues. Encryption algorithms allow transmitting information using code that cannot be read by people who do not have the right key or password. Law enforcement agencies and governments all over the world discuss the possibility of disallowing encryption in order to keep up public safety. Many politicians think that criminals are the only ones using encryption technologies. But this is not true.

Encryption algorithms are essential for e-business. See Table 4.3 for a simple encryption algorithm. Without the possibility of privacy, every business transaction over the Internet could be heard over and used against the participants in the transaction. Would you want to show your competitors how much business you are doing with your customers or even let them know who your customers are? Would you like to share the e-mails you have sent to your spouse with the public? I don't think so, but still many politicians think that it is better to ban encryption.

Some countries, like France, already only allow the use of encryption if a copy of the keys, which are used for the encryption, have been sent to a governmental agency. This concept, called key escrow, allows the government and the police to decipher encrypted messages. The idea behind it may be good, but it won't work. People and businesses won't trust encryption algorithms, if they know that the government is able to read your information. And it won't keep criminals and terrorists from using it.

In most countries the possession of weapons is illegal, but criminals are still using them. Making encryption illegal will be even worse. All business transactions over the Internet become public and using this information will be used by other companies to ruin businesses. Even if encryption would become illegal all over the world, gangsters would still use it, as they are already outlaws and don't care about what politicians or the law says.

4.3.2   Legal Issues on Export

Strong encryption is what the governments all over the world fear. It uses complex mathematical algorithms to encode text, which was originally developed for the military. In 1991 Phil Zimmermann wrote a 128-bit encryption program called PGP[16] (Pretty Good Privacy). The program was distributed over the In-

---

[16]http://www.pgp.com/

A Simple Encryption Algorithm – ROT13

One of the simplest encryption algorithms is ROT13. With this algorithm every letter gets a number assigned. A becomes 1, B becomes 2, etc. If you now write "HELLO", you assign each letter a number and add 13 to it, then replace the number with a letter again. If the number is larger than 26, subtract 26 in order to stay within the range of the alphabet. "HELLO" becomes 8, 5, 12, 12, and 15. Now add 13 to each of the numbers and you get 21, 18, 25, 25, and 28. 28 is larger than 26, so we subtract 26 from 28 and get the following 21, 18, 25, 25, 2 which becomes eventually "URYYB", which has no resemblance with "HELLO". This is an example of a very simple encryption algorithm. It is sufficient, if you are afraid that someone is scanning your mails in transit for keywords. Using this simple encryption, they won't find the keywords anymore. But even this won't be really secure; adding a little decryption algorithm to the scanner can be done without too much trouble.

Table 4.3.

ternet and suddenly people from all over the world where able to encrypt and protect their data.

In the United States, ammunition is treated like ammunition and requires a special export license. As Zimmermann did not request such a license before releasing PGP over the Internet, he was arrested, as publishing on the Internet is the same as exporting it to other countries. Anybody throughout the world is able to download the application. After three difficult years in court, the government relaxed the restrictions on encryption algorithms.

In 1996 encryption algorithms were dropped off the list of controlled ammunitions. But it is still illegal to export any technology that uses encryption algorithms that are stronger than 40 bits, without the written consensus of the US government. In order to export strong encryption algorithms you need to leave the keys with the government. The only exception is the banking sector. There exists a special regulation, which allows exporting 128 bit keys for banking applications. But the laws on exporting encryption algorithms in the US are not very logical at the moment.

In 1994 Phil Karn requested permission to export his book, Applied Cryptography. The book discussed encryption algorithms and had a floppy disk that contained all of the source code. The book was approved for export, but the floppy disks were not. The export of encryption algorithms in digital form is forbidden, but exporting it in book form, is not. Karn sued in order to find out what the difference was. Although the case is still pending, others are using this hole in export restrictions to get algorithms outside of the US.

PGP, for example, is developed in the US. In order to ship it to international customers, the source code has been printed out. The resulting book of more than 5,000 pages has been exported to Finland where some people scan in the source code and put the program back together. PGP supports key lengths up to 4,096-bits in the version 5.5. It is actually no problem to extend the number of bits to a higher number, but with each additional bit encryption and decryption take longer to complete. Although 1,048,576-bits may be really safe, it is impractical as it takes too long to encrypt. Not even your grand children would see the result of the encryption and decryption.

Breaking Encryption Algorithms

Using the brute force method, it is nowadays possible to hack a code encrypted with 40 bit within very little time. There are even screen savers that use the free time, when a user is not working at a certain computer, to hack 40-bit encryption algorithms. Just recently even a text with 56-bit encryption was cracked within three days.

By adding a bit to the key it doubles the strength of the key. If it takes three days to crack a 56-bit key, then it will take approximately six days for a 57-bit key. A key with 64-bits can be cracked in 768 days. Faster computers will eventually decrease the time to crack these keys; therefore it is important to use keys with more bits. At the time of writing 128-bit keys are safe, but soon we will have to switch to 256-bit keys in order to be sure that nobody can break into your information.

Table 4.4.

There are two types of encryption: Symmetric and asymmetric. With symmetric encryption 40-bit keys are allowed to export, and with asymmetric, it is possible to export 512-bit keys. Browsers use symmetric encryption and PGP, for example, asymmetric encryption algorithms. A more detailed discussion on encryption algorithms can be found in Chapter 10, Security on the Internet.

As exporting encryption technologies in book form is very time consuming and error prone, encryption algorithms developed in other countries become more important for e-business transactions. Some of the most important companies are Baltimore Technologies[17] in Ireland, which develops public key infrastructure software, Brokat[18] in Germany, which creates online banking software, Softwinter[19] in Israel, which programs encryption software for Windows NT and C2Net[20] in Australia, which develops the "Stronghold" web server, which allows SSL-enabled transactions at 128 bit. These companies offer encryption algorithms that use any bit-rate your application requires, without any restrictions on export. They can also be imported into the US, as there is only a restriction on export.

The US congress receives pressure from the software industry to change this policy, as it destroys the encryption technology market for US American companies. It hinders free trade and the development of new technology in the US. While American companies try to find a compromise together with the government, companies in other countries move on to develop and introduce new technologies, which gives them the leading edge over their competitors in the US.

4.3.3 National Encryption Laws

This subsection can only give an indication on the national laws in different countries around the world. Governments have only realized recently that laws and regulations are needed. As the knowledge and awareness is still in the progress of being built up, laws are changing constantly and quickly at the moment. Just remember the former Chancellor of Germany, Helmut Kohl, who was asked a few years ago, what he thought about the information highway and thought the questioner was talking about the German "Autobahn". Since then, awareness has increased significantly within the governments and parliaments. But due to the global nature of the Internet, it is difficult for single governments to be able to solve the legal issues on their own. The Internet poses a threat to the powers of national governments.

Please do not refer to the information given here as being valid for the time of reading. France, for example, has just recently abandoned its policy of disallowing the use of encryption. Great Britain, on the other hand, has been talking for a while about introducing regulations on encryption technologies. On the book's web page[21] you will find up-to-date information on national encryption laws. National laws on encryption regulate the use of encryption and if the export or import is prohibited or not.

---

[17] http://www.baltimore.ie/

[18] http://www.brokat.de/

[19] http://www.softwinter.com/

[20] http://www.c2.net/

[21] http://www.ebusinessrevolution.com/

Table 4.5 has a list of some the larger countries around the world with national regulations on the use of encryption and how import and export are handled by these countries.

National Encryption Regulations

Country	Use of Strong Encryption	Export of Strong Encryption
Australia	No restrictions on use.	Some restrictions on export.
China	Not allowed.	No information.
European Union	No restrictions on use.	No restrictions on import and export.
India	No restrictions on use.	No restrictions on export. License for import is required.
Israel	License is required, but almost always granted.	Regulations for import/ export exist and are handled case-by-case.
Japan	No restrictions on use.	License for export is required. No export of encryption software is allowed.
Russia	A license to use encryption is required.	No restrictions on export. License for import is required.
Singapore	No restrictions on use.	No restrictions on import and export.
South Africa	No restrictions on use.	No restrictions on import and export.
South Korea	Not allowed.	Import/Export of encryption is prohibited.
United States	No restrictions on use.	License for export is required for encryption software with more than 56-bit.

Table 4.5.

4.3.4 Digital Signatures

Encryption technologies cannot only be used to ensure that nobody else other than the authorized persons are able to read a certain message, it is also possible to ensure the authenticity of any given message through a digital signature. Internet services offering public key infrastructures (PKI) offer both functionalities as part of their service.

Contrary to public belief, it is possible to sign digital documents in a similar way that you can sign traditional documents. A digital signature is not a scanned image of a hand-written signature or a typed signature. The digital signature is an electronic substitute for a manual signature. Technically spoken, it is an identifier composed of a certain sequence of bits, which is created through a hash function and the result is encrypted with the senders private key (which can be decrypted by anyone who is in possession of the public key). By adding the digital signature to the digital document, it can be easily verified who signed it, when it has been sent off and whether the document has been altered during transit.

Once the encrypted message has been sent out, the recipients are able to decrypt the message using their private key. If a signature is found, the same hash function is invoked, as the sender was using and the message digest of the recipient is compared automatically with the result of the sender. If the two results match, the message was really sent by the sender. And it can be verified that nothing has been changed in transit, by checking the integrity of the message.

As digital certificates are difficult to forge, non-repudiation has become possible on the Internet. If a person has sent out a certain message, it can be traced back much more easily through a PKI and the signatures. The PKI is used to store the time when a certain message has been sent out, which can be very important in some business cases.

Digital signatures form the basis for formally legally binding contracts in the course of electronic business, since they provide electronically the same forensic effect that a traditional paper document and a hand written signature thereon provides. In order to use digital signatures legally a framework needs to be created in all countries that defines exactly what a signature is and how it can be created. In the European Union several initiatives have started, both on a Union wide level and on a nation wide level, such as the "Signaturgesetz" in Germany. But it is unlikely that national legislative initiatives can be used on the global Internet.

A prospective directive for establishing a legal framework for the use of electronic signatures[22] has been presented in 1998 by the European Commission. By defining the minimum rules for security and liability, the proposal ensures that digital signatures are legally accepted throughout the European Union. It creates a framework for secure online transactions.

---

[22]http://europa.eu.int/comm/dg15/en/media/infso/com297en.pdf

4.4   Developing a Dark Site

4.4.1   Reasons for Crisis Management

When selling products or services online, they may possibly be defective or have some sort of a problem. If it is more than a single incident, the manufacturer or retailer will get in trouble. If such a disaster happens to your company, you have two possibilities. Either cover it up and hope that nobody will notice, or go public with all the information you have, warning people and giving them advice on how to resolve the problem.

The first choice is no longer an option, especially nowadays with the wide use of the Internet. You just cannot keep something secret, normally too many people are involved and someone will leak it to the Internet. So the only thing you can do is to go public and let everybody know that you are aware of the problem and take the responsibility for that particular issue.

In order to be prepared for such a situation you need to create a dark site that can go online in case of a problem or an emergency. A dark site is not a sort of voodoo site, but a site that is kept secret until it is necessary to use it. The dark site contains information on your product you would not have released, but may be helpful in case of defects.

But not only defects in your products may cause problems. Unhappy or angry online users are able to put up a web site with negative information. Due to its infrastructure, every web page has the same priority on the Internet. If someone puts something up against you, you had better take it seriously. It takes only a few people with a web site to set back the whole production of a company. But even worse than web sites are e-mails, which are sent out to other Internet users at speed of light. In the real world one bad experience is relayed to less than fifty people in most cases. Bad experiences on the Internet are sent out to thousands of people with a single mouse click.

4.4.2   Disaster Recovery

Ulrike Brandt has written has a very informative article on Internet crisis management in the German financial magazine *Wirtschaftswoche*[23], where she discusses this topic and where you can get additional information. The topic is very important, but unfortunately not many managers are aware of it.

Just look at the case of Intel[24]. In 1994, Thomas Koenig, a mathematician found out that the newly released Pentium chip did not calculate correctly. Under certain conditions divisions, remainders, tangent and arctangent floating-point instructions can produce results with reduced precision. He reported this error to the chip manufacturing company, but they put him off. First they denied the existence of the bug, then they stated that the problem affected only

---

[23]http://www.wirtschaftswoche.de/, "In Sekunden zerstört", *Wirtschaftswoche* 45/29.10.1998, pp. 157-160.

[24]http://www.intel.com/

very few users. And then they wanted the users to prove that they needed that special calculation to certify for a replacement.

All this created a huge outcry on the Internet, web sites had been put up and heated discussion threads started in the Internet newsgroups. The result was a huge avalanche that fell back on Intel. The media talked about the problem; users sent angry e-mails to Intel wanting them to replace their chips, and the chip sales dropped. As a result Intel gave up in December 1994 and offered to replace all faulty Pentium chips[25] and had to stop the complete production of that particular chip, even though they were right about their claim that only very few were affected. But giving up production of that particular chip was not so difficult, as faster chips were already in the pipeline. The next generation of Pentium chips, without the error, was already designed and the roll-out phase began soon after.

The Pentium FDIV Bug

The first release of the Pentium did contain a bug in their floating point processor which returned a faulty result when performing a floating point division (FDIV). To see if your Pentium has the FDIV bug enter the following formula in the Windows calculator:

$$x = \frac{4195835}{3145727} \times 3145727 - 4195835$$

The result should be $x = 0$. On faulty Pentiums you will get $x = 256$ instead. In this case you are entitled to receive a free replacement for your faulty Pentium chip.

Table 4.6.

Since then Intel has changed its strategy. Even though they still cannot guarantee that their chips are error-free, they are now more open to customer issues and maintain an online database with known errors of their chips. With the introduction of the Pentium II, they also have invented a possibility to update some parts of the micro-code on their chips so bugs can be removed without replacing them.

Their latest chip, the Pentium III, on the other hand, seems to end in a marketing disaster. The Pentium III chip contains a digital ID that is unique for every processor. The reason for it was to provide a means to check the identity

---

[25]http://www.intel.com/procs/support/pentium/fdiv/

of a particular user for online transactions. Intel's serial number is appealing to corporate customers, because they can more easily track technology assets because of the identifying serial code.

Although many online companies like the idea of identifying the customers, privacy groups have called for consumer boycotts and legal action and created a web site called "Big Brother Inside"[26], which resembles the motto of Intel with "Intel Inside". Many people (hackers and software companies) have started to crack the safeguards imposed by Intel to make the serial number secure. Although at the time of writing nobody was able to crack the highly secure ID number, the message that gets out to the customers is the wrong one.

Other companies do not seem to be affected by angry users. Microsoft[27], for example, does not seem to have this problem. Although there are many anti-Microsoft sites on the Internet, Microsoft is not losing market share because of these sites. Ford[28] had similar problems 1995 as Intel had one year earlier. Due to a technical problem, some Ford drivers claimed, the car could go up in flames. The online activists, calling themselves the "Association of Flaming Ford Owners", decided to put up a web page[29] (with the image of a burnt-out Ford on the main page and flames in the background).

In April 1996, Ford had to recall more than 8.7 million cars and trucks in the United States and Canada to have the ignition switches replaced (with potentially up to 26 million cars and trucks that may need a replacement). The action cost Ford more than 1.5 billion dollars. In this case I do not know if their claims were right or not, but that is not the point here. The incident happened in 1995, but the Flaming Fords web site is still up and running in 1999. Today more than 20,000 links exist to that particular web site. People may stumble over it and decide not to buy a Ford.

In December 1998 Ford had a short press release that it had to recall more than three million cars because of a possible corrosion problem. I found this snippet on Yahoo's "dailynews" site[30] (search for "Ford Recall Issued", December 23rd 1998) and went then directly to Ford's homepage to check if they have a press release with more information on the incident, but was not able to find anything. Neither their search engine gave me more information nor was there a link from their homepage as one might have expected. Maybe there was information online, but I couldn't find anything within ten minutes of searching. It may also be that because of the holiday season no webmaster was around to update the information. But not being there during holidays may ruin your business even faster, as more people have time to surf on the Internet.

The Internet enables consumers to talk more freely about their experience with a certain product or service. So it becomes vital for all companies to keep

---

[26] http://www.privacy.org/bigbrotherinside/
[27] http://www.microsoft.com/
[28] http://www.ford.com/
[29] http://www.flamingfords.com/
[30] http://dailynews.yahoo.com/

an eye on the web to track down people who are not amused about their products. If you think you can just shut down the web site of that particular consumer, you have not understood how the Internet works. Once information has been put online, it is virtually impossible to get rid of this piece of information. If you cut off somebody's web site, they will find fifty others who will replicate their content immediately. The more pressure you put on people the less effective it becomes, as more and more people join in to support them.

There is no way you can stop people publishing their opinions on the web. No matter how right or wrong they are. The only thing you can do is set up a web site that tells the consumers you are aware of the allegations. If the allegations are true, you had better put some additional information online about how to solve the problem. If the claims are false put some evidence online to prove you are right. In any case, respond fast or you will lose out, no matter if you are right or not.

4.4.3 Negative Campaigning

Not only angry consumers can mean a bankruptcy for your company. Negative campaigning by your competitors can also ruin your image with the public. Instead of showing the advantages of their own products, they will start to find all the disadvantages of your products.

In December 1998 Sun[31] launched a web page with information on Hewlett-Packard's newly introduced Unix Server HP V2500[32]. Depending on your point of view, the information presented on that particular web page is either positive for Sun or negative for Hewlett-Packard. In the European Union, law prohibits for example, negative campaigning and comparative advertisement. But on the Internet national laws are not always applicable. Putting up the information on a web server in another country is fairly simple. Countries like Bulgaria just recently introduced laws against software pirates, so there are still enough countries where the Internet is something beyond the scope of the law. But in our example, merely putting the desired page onto an American web server would resolve all legal issues regarding the content.

Another problem may be the media. Due to the amount of information a magazine or newspaper receives each day, it is virtually impossible to check if all of the data is correct or wrong. Especially in the US we can see a tendency to print information without double-checking it. Together with negative campaigning it will have a negative impact on your products and/or your company. Therefore always keep an eye on the Internet. Look out for tendencies within your user groups, keep in touch with them, seek dialogue and, in the case of an emergency, react fast and offensively. In our interconnected world there is no way to avoid a disaster if you are not open to your customers. Everything becomes transparent. This is also a reason why dictators fear the power of the

---

[31]http://www.sun.com/
[32]http://www.sun.com/realitycheck/headsup981215.html

Internet. They just can't control information anymore, which is their only real power over the people.

Risk management

In the event of an emergency your company needs to act fast. Therefore you have to take some steps before, during and after the crisis:

- **Risk Audit** – Do a risk audit of your company on a regular basis.

- **Documentation** – Develop plans for documenting tasks and responsibilities for the emergency.

- **Keyword Monitoring** – Monitor constantly the Internet (especially web sites, mailing lists, newsgroups and chat areas) for special keywords.

- **Crisis Manual** – Develop a crisis manual and put it on your Intranet.

- **Dark Site** – Design a dark site with all the necessary information.

- **Simulations** – Do simulations of emergency situations on a regular basis.

- **Up-to-date** – In case of emergency always keep the dark site up-to-date.

- **Information** – Inform your target group and the media via e-mail about the emergency.

Table 4.7.

4.4.4 Online Experience

In October 1996 a 16-month-old baby died from an infection of E-coli bacteria. The baby had drunk apple juice made by Odwalla[33], a California-based juice

---
[33]http://www.odwalla.com/

company. The apple juice was suspected of being the source. Within twelve hours the management of Odwalla called back the apple juice from more than 4,500 shops and set up a web site with information on the incident. It contained a statement by the management, a frequently asked questions (FAQ) page on E-coli bacteria, written by doctors, to help the victims. A team of experts was online to calm down the frightened consumers. The site also provided links to the web site of the Food & Drug Administration (FDA)[34] which contains additional information on emergency situations. Although another sixty-six cases of E-coli infections were registered, a survey showed afterwards that almost ninety percent of Odwalla customers are willing to drink their apple juice in the future. The investment in releasing all information and creating the dark site had been spent wisely.

After the horrible crash of the MD-11 off the Canadian coast in September 1998, Swiss Air[35] set up a first press release on their web site within hours. Important phone numbers, a condolence web page and some other statements were available on the Internet the same day. On the following days more information was released, including the radio chats between the tower and the pilots and the names of the deceased. The very efficient webmaster rescued Swiss Air from losing its highly successful business as a result of this single, though extremely tragic, incident. It also helped the relatives of the victims to find out more on the incident without having to search for information all over the place, as it often happens.

The Deutsche Bundesbahn[36], the German rail service company, lost a lot of credibility after the derailing of one of its high-speed trains ICE in May 1998. Information was not available on the incident immediately after the accident (neither online nor offline), nor was the Bundesbahn responding to the families of the customers in a sensible way. A general letter was sent out to each of the families with advertising on rail journeys. The company was not prepared for handling such an incident. It seemed that they thought that it could never happen. *Der Spiegel*[37], the most-read German news magazine, compared this accident to the tragic incident of the Titanic in 1912.

In the case of an emergency it is too late to start thinking about a strategy. You need to start thinking about a strategy long before the emergency. You should do a risk audit for your company, analyzing what could go wrong with your products. You should develop plans where the tasks and responsibilities are documented for the emergency situation. In order to learn about emergencies in advance you need to monitor the Internet seven days a week, twenty-four hours a day. First you need to create a list of keywords and then check web sites, newsgroups, search engines and databases on a regular basis. Mailing lists and chat areas should also be visited, if your target group is using

---

[34] http://www.fda.gov/
[35] http://www.swissair.ch/
[36] http://www.bahn.de/
[37] http://www.spiegel.de/

these types of media. This is the only way to find out about dissatisfied customers and aggressive competitors. Your emergency plan should be available on your Intranet, so that people know what to do whenever they need to and a printed copy should also be available in case of a technological breakdown.

4.4.5 Digital Complaint Services

Another factor that needs to be taken into account are online complaint services, which are hoping to make money by resolving consumer disputes with Net retailers. These services are able to bundle complaints against companies and create class-suit actions in a very simple and effective way. Consumers will get access to a brand name and experience in linking up with major companies to make sure the complaint goes to the right person quickly.

Complain.com[38], Fight back[39] and Complain To Us[40] are three service companies in this area. These companies charge a flat fee if they get involved in writing a letter and following up complaints. Fight Back, for example charges $25, while Complain.com charges $19.95 for any case that is pursued personally, while all other complaint resolutions are free of charge.

Consumers can fill out a form with information about the product or service they purchased, what went wrong, the actions they have taken to resolve the dispute, and the resolution they are seeking. In order to qualify for the online complaint service, customer must have tried to contact the customer care department themselves before.

Complaint.com does send a letter of complaint to the company and will receive a confirmation within four weeks, if the issue has been resolved. If the problem persists, the letter will be sent once more to the company, but this time to the chief executive. If that does not help, consumers will be referred to partners, such as law firms to pursue further action.

While single complaints won't be very effective, the aggregation of complaints and the publicity on the web site will drive companies to respond to the issues of their customers. The above mentioned companies have also plans to publish the contents of their complaint database onto the web, making it easy for customers to look up complaints from the past and find out how to resolve a particular issue.

4.4.6 Strategic Planning

A dark site needs to be developed that contains basic information about your company and your products. It should inform your customers on security measures and should contain a list of experts that they can contact in the case of an emergency. The dark site should replace your normal web site within an

---

[38] http://www.complain.com/
[39] http://www.fightback.com/
[40] http://www.complaintous.com/

hour, or even better within thirty minutes. The management needs to be informed about the Internet presentation, and they need to release statements as soon as possible. The web site needs to be updated as soon as new information emerges about the emergency.

The dark site should also be put on removable media, such as a CD-ROM or ZIP disk. Just in case your company gets cut off the Internet, you can send the information to an Internet Service Provider (ISP) who is able to set up an emergency site very fast. In this case inform the public immediately via TV, radio or newspapers about the incident and tell them about the emergency URL. Many of these steps need to be taken, even if your company is not presently on the web. But with the Internet you have to be even faster in your communication of the crisis. If you don't talk about it, then someone else will for sure. The competition is tough on the Internet.

Doing all this is not cheap, but not doing anything is far more expensive as we have learnt from the first two examples. Larger corporations have special task forces for emergency situations. That is overkill for small and medium sized enterprises, but they also need to keep an eye on the Internet.

Specialized search engines will monitor the web for them. They only need to key in their desired keywords and these search engines will monitor the web day and night. As soon as something happens, an e-mail will be sent off that triggers a beeper or something else to get the attention of the responsible person so that the company can react to the threat from the Internet. Two web sites that offer this service are "The Informant"[41] and "Mind-It"[42].

Many small to medium-sized companies will most likely outsource the task of monitoring the web. Specialized companies will take over the task. They will become the watchdogs over content and they will also react in the case of a crisis. Investment in such a company is a good bet for net investors. These services are needed and their revenues will increase fast in the future.

Although dark sites and other means of prevention won't reduce the liability for an error in a product, it will help to limit the financial damage, which can ruin a company.

---

[41]http://informant.dartmouth.edu/
[42]http://minder.netmind.com/

Chapter 5

MARKETING STRATEGIES ON THE WEB

5.1 Internet Marketing Technologies

The Internet offers a whole range of new technologies to increase your marketing activities on a global around-the-clock basis. The basis for your business should be the corporate Internet web page, which may link to Internet and Extranet applications. Your marketing initiative should focus on presenting your web page, as this is what everyone can remember and access with a simple browser. From there on you need to guide your customers to the particular places they are allowed to go and to carry out the transactions they require.

The Web, Mail, Newsgroups and Chat applications have established themselves to allow communication between companies and customers, These applications are highly available, robust and simple-to-use. Therefore it is very important to understand the way they work and to know what to look for, in order to make these tools successful.

Digital measurement of the customers' experiences is also very important, but also very difficult and different online. Customers are not bound to a limited set of offerings, as they are used to with newspapers, magazines or television channels. The Internet offers an unlimited number of channels, so measurement of the Internet as a whole does not make any sense.

The Internet also offers a much higher degree of interaction. Customers and partners also have different expectations; they expect that your offerings will be available 24 hours a day, without interruption and that they can ask questions whenever they feel like it. The Internet allows customers to talk directly to the manufacturers of the products and can easily bypass the shop where they bought the goods. This means that a manufacturer needs to set up an online call center as soon as their web site goes live. People expect to be able to ask questions directly. If you are not able to fulfill the expectations of your customers and the customers of your customers, then you should not go onto the web. But this would mean the immediate death of your business.

Marketing Strategy on the Web

A strategy for marketing on the Internet should follow the subsequent rules:

- **Brands** – Your web site becomes your most important brand.

- **Change** – The rules on the Internet are changing.

- **Conciseness** – Keep your pages short and spread information on several pages.

- **Content** – Content is king, don't bore your customers.

- **Dynamic Sites** – Create dynamic sites that use new technologies to adapt information based on user profiles.

- **Finances** – Try new markets with low advertising pricing schemes.

- **Free Give-aways** – Create freebee offerings for your loyal customers.

- **Global Village** – Think global, but localize.

- **Live Events** – Online events create awareness fast.

- **Niche Markets** – The Internet is a series of niche markets and mass markets.

- **Promotion** – Promote your site everywhere.

- **Syndication** – Co-brand your services and products.

- **Technology** – Use Internet technology to maximize your marketing objectives.

Table 5.1.

Online advertising moves commercials into new dimensions as you are able to place your advertisement in real-time on the desktops of a particular target group. Everything becomes more dynamic. Those who don't get going and remain static will lose out. The companies who are prepared to change their web sites, adapt their businesses and marketing strategies will have the best chances for being very successful in the Internet age.

In order to be successful on the Internet your company needs to to focus on the five Ps: Products, Promotion, Presentation, Processes and Personalization. Review your products and choose the products that are the most suitable for your online business and put them first on your web page. Promote your site through advertising and offer cross-selling on your web site. The presentation of your online business needs to have an easy to use site navigation, the look and feel should be based on corporate logos and standards. Customer supports need to be integrated into your online web sits. Prepare your order management, logistics and technical infrastructure to cope with the orders from the Internet and customize the web site for every single customer.

A typical sales and marketing cycle for an online shop requires the business to look out for the target customers and their needs. The next step is to create awareness and start an advertising campaign to attract customers to your on-line business. Before doing so, be aware that you need to have the web site up and running. "Under Construction" sites will lead your potential customer base to other online sites that offer what they promise. Merchandising is also an important task to complete. It is necessary to decide which products or services can be sold over the Internet and how they should be positioned. Promotions are very common, so they need to be taken into consideration, as part of your marketing campaign. They help to promote merchandise and services to give customers incentives to make purchases.

To make your customers return to your web site, a sales service is necessary that is able to answer the questions of your customers fast and reliably and help them solve their problems in an instant. In order to learn from your existing customers and orders it is necessary to save marketing data and analyze it, to support decisions. To further enhance your service you need to establish post-sales service, which allow your customers to find out about the order status after the sale has been made, for example. These are some of the topics discussed in this chapter.

Other important issues in the sales cycle are transaction processing, which defines the way orders, tax, shipping and payment processing are handled; and fulfillment, which defines how orders are passed to the fulfillment center. These topics will be discussed in Chapter 7 in depth.

5.2　Web-Design

5.2.1　The Power of the Internet

Your web site is the basic marketing message on the Internet. From there you and your company can start the marketing offensive. Be sure that your marketing people understand the full potential of the web. It offers more possibilities, but also more dangers than other media do. The rewards for doing marketing the right way on the Internet are immediate, just as failures may result in an instant loss of customers. The web site is from a marketing point of view like the business card of your company.

Therefore it is important to comprehend the power of the Internet, for everyone in your company. Everyone becomes involved in electronic marketing instantly, as soon as one receives access to the Internet. Your customers may view every online activity as a company activity, even though it may be the result of the initiative of a single employee. If one of your employees writes an e-mail to one your customers, this e-mail may be re-sent to anyone, anywhere in the world, without much work. Even e-mails that are sent within the company reach non-corporate mailboxes very quickly. So you should set up some guidelines for your company e-mails. Chit-chat mails from employees to their friends are no problem and it keeps the employees happy. If you do not allow your employees to write private e-mails, they will start using web-based e-mailing services, which waste far more resources and time than a little e-mail to a friend will ever do.

5.2.2 Content Is King

The most important thing on your web page is content; never let users leave your web page without giving them information. This increases the probability that they will return to look for new information. Clicking on fancy graphics which take ages to download may win a design prize, but functional web pages with content in the foreground are more important. Respect the wishes of the customer and remove irrelevant images or text. Offer the possibility to customize the appearance of the web pages.

Pictures and illustrations can be worth thousands of words, if used correctly. Many images on the web were designed for print media and offer too much detailed information which cannot be seen on the web. Use graphics that add real value to your site, where appropriate. In order to present high-quality images on the web, use technologies such as FlashPix or VRML, described in detail in Chapter 12.

In order to build up a web site fast you should re-purpose your existing materials. Many companies think they can just copy their existing paper documents to the web server. This will fail. It is necessary to adapt the material and make them suitable for online use. Other than traditional documents, which are linear, documents on the web are non-linear. On the web there is no pre-defined sequence of reading. Adding links within and across documents further simplifies navigation and is common practice on the Internet.

The design of your web sites is very important, as it is the first thing your customers are going to see. In order to make it attractive to your customers you should stick to the following rules: Although a nice graphics and large buttons are good, well-produced content is what will bring people back. The

Internet lives off the information it provides to the users. On any given web page the customers should be able to find a summary of the content in the title of the page and in the URL. This methodology is also used by search engines to classify a web page according to these entries.

Don't put more than ten links onto one page, except for link lists. Usually it is enough to provide only two or three links to other pages. The user wants to be guided and not confused by your offering. Information should always be instant, understandable and accessible. Try to create web pages with less text but without reducing the amount of content.

Instant means that the web pages should be downloaded very fast even with older computers and slower modems. Understandable means that the information should be presented in a way that everyone is able to get the message within very short time and very little effort. Accessibility is the largest problem currently on the web. People with disabilities have a hard time on the web, as the information is presented in a very visual way and not necessarily in a logical structure. Using tables on a web page will create nicely layouted web sites, but make it difficult for blind people, for example to read the text in the right sequence. Before going online with a web site, the site should be checked by Bobby[1], an online and offline application that analyzes web pages for their accessibility to people with disabilities. Bobby is the full implementation of the 1998 working draft of the W3C Web Accessibility Initiative[2].

Have you ever created slides for a presentation? This method of presenting information in a very dense way should also be applied to web pages, with the difference that you do not follow a linear sequence as with presentations. Users should always have the possibility to create their own sequences. To reduce information overload or data burn-out web sites should give users the information they have requested and nothing else. If users require more in-depth information, then give them the possibility to download the information in a useful format, such as a spreadsheet format for a database. Offer your customers several alternatives for document download. Text, for example, should always be available in HTML and ASCII format. In addition to these two formats you can offer Postscript, Acrobat and Word, for better viewing and printing.

If you offer other information be sure to serve the customer first. Users should not be forced to scroll down an endless page of irrelevant information before reaching the information they are looking for. Give users more control over the way they view your site and make it more of an interactive experience. Create a user-friendlier place to visit.

Another common design problem is to avoid having too much company information and not enough product information on the web site. Although company information is also very important, very few customers need detailed informa-

---

[1]http://www.cast.org/bobby/

[2]http://www.w3.org/WAI/

tion. Most of the customers want to buy products and services and not the company. Information that is on your web site needs to answer the potential questions of the customers and not the needs of the company. See Table 5.2 for an overview on design rules.

Web Design Rules

In order to have a successful business online, the visual presentation of your web site needs to adhere to the following rules:

- **Content** – Focus your attention first on content and then on design.

- **Consistency** – Design your site consistently without varying the content.

- **Density** – Break up content into little pieces without tearing it apart.

- **Design** – Use few colors without designing a monotone web site.

- **Size** – Use small graphics with large impact.

Table 5.2.

5.2.3 Feedback and Online Surveys

Every web site should offer the possibility for customer feedback. A feedback form should be provided on a separate feedback page that enables the customer to choose the reason for the feedback and some fields for the name and e-mail address and the feedback itself. By offering feedback reasons, the feedback can be directed automatically to the appropriate department and reduces the size of the customer care center, as the customers provide the information required to classify the feedback. Figure 5.1 shows EuroSeek's[3] feedback form, which allows customers to enter a statement on the usefulness of the web site.

In addition to the simple feedback form, extended feedback in the form of a survey could help your customers express their needs better and your customer care center will be able to help much faster and respond to the needs of the

---

[3]http://webdir.euroseek.net/page.cfm?page=feedback

Figure 5.1. EuroSeek Feedback Form

customers in general (in the form of a FAQ, see below). Typically a single web page is used to give feedback and fill in a general survey. Customers should not be forced to fill in the survey, if they only want to give some feedback.

In addition to the general survey about the web site, from time to time you should offer specialized surveys on topics around your company to learn more about your customers. These surveys should be combined with a prize in order to make it attractive to people. Offering a book or a compact disc as a prize will make people more willing to give more information such as their address.

5.2.4   Frequently Asked Questions

In order to build up an online service it is necessary to have a customer care center in operation. Large sites, such as eBay[4] receive more than 60,000 mails a week. Many of the senders ask the same questions. In order to reduce the workload of the response team and enhance the time of the reply it is helpful to build up a database with frequently asked questions (FAQs).

A frequently asked questions web page consists of questions and their responses, which may be interesting for most customers. On large sites it makes sense to create separate FAQs for every service and product online. On the feedback page you should also provide the link to the FAQ page or database and it needs to be presented very prominently.

---

[4]http://www.ebay.com/

You should ask your customers to consult the FAQs before sending an e-mail to your customer care department. The FAQ needs to be updated regularly to include all questions that arise around a certain product or service. In addition to the FAQ you could use a set of newsgroups where all questions are shown to other customers together with the answers. I used the Hewlett-Packard's "User Group Forum" for the HP Deskjet 340 to find out how to connect the printer to the Apple PowerBook. The question and the answer are still both on the web and may help other customers who want to do the same.

5.2.5   Corporate Design Rules

Every company needs corporate rules for e-mails, newsgroup postings and web design. The layout should be defined there, so people are able to recognize postings, e-mails and web pages from a certain company at a glance. All e-mails need to be responded to very fast; no matter to whom it is sent in the company. If the person is out of office, an auto-reply needs to be sent out to let people know that the mail has arrived at the destination. Employees should be informed about chain letters and virus hoax warnings on the Internet, as they can ruin the image of a company with a few mouse clicks. See Chapter 10 for more information on this topic. If your company has products for which special newsgroups exist, then some employees need to be present there, read through the questions and answer as many as possible to help the customers with their problems. Spamming, the action of sending out information to people who did not ask for it, in newsgroups and on mailing lists is not an option for your company. These methods of direct marketing will ruin the image of your company.

5.2.6   Navigational Aids

The web site should have a clear and simple-to-use interface, that helps users contact the right people, find information and to offer the services customers require whenever they are needed. The more interactivity you offer to your customers, the better received the web site will be. A search engine for the company web site is a must. Enhance your existing web site to become a portal (see Chapter 6).

The navigation and the graphics need to look the same throughout the whole web site. Make it simple and clear. Have a navigation bar that every user can understand and replicate all graphical navigation bars in textual links, in order to support non-graphical browsers.

Design a simple navigation, which is consistent throughout your web page, in order to guide your customers and give them control over your web site. Use labels for sets of web pages, so users know which area they are in. Define special logos for each of your areas (or channels) making it easy to identify them. Don't overuse graphical logos or icons, a simple label in the form of a word may be sufficient as well. As your site can be viewed globally, there are only very few icons that can be understood on a world-wide basis.

Provide guides throughout the site in order to help users find their way around. The user should always have the possibility to jump directly back to the beginning of a channel or to the main home page. Don't make customers look for the navigation bar all over the page. Integrate it into your design, but make clear that the navigation is separate from the content. Otherwise your customers will waste time finding what they are looking for and may decide to go for a competitor.

About 80 percent of people read only 20 percent of a web page. Most people never scroll down web pages, but they like clicking on buttons. New web pages also offer the chance to present new banner ads. But be sure that if you offer one chunk of information over several web pages that the user always knows what is still to come; choose your section titles wisely.

5.2.7   Color Schema

Choose two or three colors for your web site and stick to them throughout the site. To check that your web site has a good color design, print a page out on a black & white printer. If the page is still readable, you are doing it right. Depending on the focus of your site, you should know about the effect colors have on the users. Some colors are more aggressive, other calm them down. The colors you choose should try to support the message of the web page.

Red, for example, is a very aggressive color, full of energy, determination and passion. It can be used to promote a new product aggressively. If you use orange you invite your customers to remain longer on a given web site and relax. Orange is the color of happiness, courage and success. Blue is a tranquil, intuitive and trustworthy and therefore a preferred color for company logos. Colors can be used to influence the way users see a web page.

On the Internet there are some web pages that talk about colors. Two well-done examples can be found on myth.com[5] and on artomatic.com[6]. Both sites explain colors and their meanings extremely well.

5.2.8   File Size

Don't use large graphics for the design of the web page. Many users still connect to the web using a modem. The more seconds users have to wait, the more users will just go on to another site. Use larger graphics or videos where you cannot offer the content in any other way. Always try to provide a low-bandwidth solution. All images on the web should have an alternative text for people who switch off the automatic image loading. This option is also very important for search engines, as they are able to index images as well.

---

[5] http://www.myth.com/color/
[6] http://www.artomatic.com/color/

The same applies to other types of documentation. If you offer a 10 MB presentation on your web site, you should also allow the user to browse through it online. The conversion of large files to low bandwidth versions is very important. Although the quality of the low bandwidth document may not be good, it allows the customer to get an impression of the content. In many cases there are more than two file sizes possible.

Real Media's RealPlayer[7], for example, adapts its speed exactly to the speed of the modem. The quality of the sound depends on the modem speed, but does not influence the content, which is always the same. As the RealPlayer has its own preferences it is possible to set the speed of the connection. The hypertext protocol does not have the ability to adapt quality to the speed of the modem, no matter how fast the connection is, the same data is transported. Therefore other means of selecting the speed must be invented. Many sites ask the user to fill in a profile and try to match the entered data. If the user enters a certain connection speed (such as 56k), the web server will try to send data that best matches the requirements.

The major disadvantage is that every piece of information needs to be saved in a different quality, resolution or density. RealPlayer for sound and OpenPix[8] for images are two solutions that try to solve the problem by offering a quality independent format that stores the content and is able to deliver the appropriate quality at any given time. OpenPix is described in more detail in the section "Dynamic Image Formats" in Chapter 12 and RealPlayer in the section "Streaming Media" in Chapter 9.

If you provide file formats that need additional components installed such as plug-ins or help applications then always provide a direct link to download the software component. Don't link to the site of the software provider, link directly to the download page, otherwise people will get distracted and forget why they wanted to download a certain piece of software. Ask permission, if you can host the software directly on your server which would least distract the customers.

All this is important for the image of your company. Brand names and the corporate identity become more important on the Internet, as prices and services become nearly identical.

When introducing electronic marketing into your company, be sure to use the technology and the possibilities the Internet offers, otherwise the Internet initiative of your company may fail.

5.2.9   Delivering Content to Network Appliances

In addition to the desktop computers and servers that are connected to the Internet right now, over the next few years new network appliances will appear. Pervasive computing will become reality. The difference with these appliances

---

[7]http://www.real.com/
[8]http://image.hp.com/

is that they have less memory, a limited display, less storage and lower transmission rates. In order to send information to these devices and exchange data these restrictions need to be taken into account.

Jupiter Communications[9] has identified three different types of network appliances evolving from stand-alone products:

- **Personal-based** – Portable devices that customers carry around and use to connect to the Internet. Examples are mobile phones adhering to the GSM standard such as the Nokia Communicator[10], personal digital assistance such as the Psion V[11] and other wireless information devices. Europe is leading in the introduction of personal devices.

- **Passenger-based** – These devices are built into transportation vehicles and provide services such as route planners, traffic or weather reports in cars, shopping networks for duty free shopping on planes and excursion programs on a cruise ship.

- **Place-based** – A variety of non-PC terminals and Internet appliances that can be found in the public. A set-top box in a hotel room or web-based kiosks at a train station are typical examples.

Depending on the type of Internet appliance restrictions need to be considered. Mobile phones have only a very small display and no colors or sound, and the communication speed is very low compared to traditional modems. Battery life is also an issue; the application should not use a lot of the battery which is required for the actual task of phoning. On mobile phones there is no space to put in a hard disk, so very little information can be stored on the phone itself. It needs to be provided in textual form and should use only very few graphics in black and white.

A route planner in a car has other requirements. The information should be provided in audio and use only very few graphical interactions as it may distract the drivers from their task of driving the car. The connection speed is as low as with mobile phones, but the graphical display and processor speed will be much higher, as there is enough space in a car. Installing a hard disk into a car won't be an issue so that storing information in the car is possible.

A kiosk at the airport will most likely be a standard PC with a standard monitor and a modem or network connection, so that restrictions there are not to be expected, except for the fact that these devices will most likely have touch screens. Set-top boxes for TV sets have the restriction low resolution. Small text will become illegible on the TV screen.

In a hotel, you will get Internet often delivered over the TV set. As television has a much lower resolution than typical computer monitors, one thing

---

[9]http://www.jup.com/

[10]http://www.nokia.com/

[11]http://www.psion.co.uk/

that is a problem, are white background, which can be found on many web sites, combined with dark text. Although it appears perfectly on a computer monitor, this type of backgrounds can cause severe screen distortion on a television screen. Dark backgrounds with light colored text are better for viewing on television as the picture is calmer.

These are just some of the restrictions for the Internet appliances. These will become more and more important in the future, as this market will be growing very fast. HTML in its current form is not able to cope with all these different devices, so XML will replace HTML in the near future as information is strictly separated from the layout.

5.3   Attracting Visitors to your Site

5.3.1   Gaining Market Share through Content

Keep your content up-to-date, so people come back regularly to check for news and updates. The Internet is changing; therefore your company and your web sites need to change as well and adapt themselves to the new influences. Some time ago I talked to someone and suggested to him that his web pages needed an update, as they were out of date. His response was that there was no need for that, as the web pages were created only two years ago and he did not want to change anything or add information, as this would only cost money. I don't think I need to mention that he is out of business now. If you do not invest in information, content and intelligence, you will fail.

The Internet is used by many companies to offer real-time, up-to-date information. If you fail to offer the same, you will lose out eventually. What is the advantage of looking at your bank account if the data is three days old? What is the advantage of looking at a news site when the news is one day old? It is like reading yesterday's newspaper.

In order to keep customers coming back, and spread the word about your site, you need to offer something new each time they come back. All pages should contain the date when they were last changed. This puts some pressure on you to update them on a regular basis and your customers have a simple way of checking how new certain information is. Using personalization and one-to-one marketing technologies it is possible to show users what has changed since their last visit.

5.3.2   Offering Free Information

In order to get a loyal customers base, you need to offer free information, products and services to everyone who comes to your web site. To those who come back the next time you should offer some form of incentives and discounts, in order to tie them to your company. Customers will not to go to another company if they are treated well by your company.

Most people who come to a certain web page do this, because they have certain expectations of the service, content or products. The number of surfers who look at web pages just for fun is decreasing. The users with expectation want a piece of information, a service or a product. Offer free give-aways, like screen savers or mouse pads for customers who are willing to register for your site. Once users have registered you need to offer some sort of personalization, like greeting them when they return.

5.3.3 Personalization

Once you know who your customers are, you can start to collect information on them. The more you learn about your visitors, the better you will be at marketing to them. Add information to your site that may interest your user group without having a direct relationship to your company (thus creating a portal). This will keep them coming back again and again. If you don't give away "freebies", in whatever form, you will loose customers to other companies.

Using data mining technologies you are able to offer an effective marketing program to particular target markets. Once you have understood the needs of your customers, you can create better products, content and services. On-line marketing can be used in a powerful, cost-efficient way to build up a very complex and efficient customer database.

At the same time it is necessary to ensure that the privacy of the personal customer information is ensured. In the European Union and Canada special laws have been established to ensure the privacy of the information. Don't forget to put up a privacy notice on your web site and keep the information confidential.

By recognizing the value of returning customers your online offerings become more valuable for them, as the customers do not need to re-enter information, for which were asked already in a previous session. Internet Explorer 5 and the Mozilla pre-release offer a function which remembers input made into a form on the client side, making automatic form completion possible. Once you have entered your credit card information somewhere, the browser is able to add this information to other forms as well. Although this may reduce the typing for the user, it also increases privacy issues on the client. A well-protected server-based personalization system is therefore preferred.

5.3.4 Support Online and Offline Reading

As reading on the screen is more difficult than reading a newspaper or a brochure, you should condense the information to a much greater extent than you would do for printed media. The first paragraph of each web page should contain a summary of the overall web page. Use concise, straightforward language. Offer the possibility to download and print information. News.com[12]

---

[12]http://www.news.com/

and Wired[13] offer news services, which contain longer articles on a given topic, but they offer the possibility to print out the text without a special web layout. They offer information in two versions. One specifically designed for the web and one for printout.

5.3.5   Cross-Marketing and Cross-Selling

When offering goods, information and services over the Internet it is quite easy to follow users around on a web site. The marketing departments is able to create cross-references between products and services. This feature is used widely in online bookshops, for example. If buying a certain book, the customer is presented with five other books about the same topic or by the same author or books that other people have bought after buying that particular book.

This technology can be extended to virtually any business. It requires the marketing department to think about possible cross-references for the online products; not only a few times a year, as they were used to with catalogues. Cross-marketing on the Internet becomes highly dynamic. If one of your competitors decides to start a promotion for a certain product and displays the price reduction on the web, you can counter the attack with a few mouse clicks by adjusting your price or adding value to the article.

Although adding, changing or removing cross-marketing initiatives has become very easy to the algorithms can be highly complex and if your software does not allow the automatic checking of your cross-selling, it may result in losses for your company.

5.3.6   Be Faster than Your Customers

When you design your web site, customers want to find what they are looking for fast. Don't hide information; offer a simple-to-use search engine. Help your customers to where they want to go as fast as possible. Using one-to-one marketing technologies, it is possible to anticipate the needs of the users. With every visit it is easier to find the relevant information before the user has entered any request. Provide simple but powerful navigational aids on all web pages to make it easy for customers to find their way around.

Your web site needs to be designed in such a fashion that every single piece of information on your web site can be reached with three clicks. People don't have time to click through all the pages on a given web site. Once customers have reached the information (products or services) they were looking for you can add additional information on that page with links to related subjects, but give the information first.

The most important rule on the Internet is that everything is subject to change. Be prepared that the rules for marketing will change with every new technology that is introduced. This does not only mean a passive preparation

---

[13]http://www.wired.com/news/

for change, but active contributions to change, in order to stay ahead of the competition.

5.3.7 Event Marketing

Special events attract many new users and bind existing users to a certain web site. Governmental web sites in the UK[14] and in Germany[15], for example, offer online chats and interviews with important politicians at regular intervals. These special events attract a lot of customers who would not have come otherwise to a particular site. Infotainment and edutainment are means to attract customers and present information in an informative and entertaining way. As people remain interested in what the government is doing, they are able to subscribe to mailing lists announcing new events, where the citizens are able to participate.

In February 1999 Victoria's Secret[16] broadcast their fashion show live on the Internet[17]. The event was a big success for the company although many users were disappointed by the quality and availability of the streaming video. Victoria's Secret underestimated the interest by online surfers to see models in underwear so that the server broke down. To transport the streaming media the RealPlayer[18] was used. An estimated 250,000 copies of the software were downloaded per hour on the day of the event.

The idea was good, but the technology was not ready. The Internet was not designed to be a real-time media. And new standards emerge only slowly. The server crash could have been avoided by many different servers transmitting the event, in many different locations.

The State of the Union address by US president Bill Clinton in January 1999 could be seen without interruption as this event was transmitted by many different servers all around the world. Television stations around the world broadcast the event live on the Internet, such as CNN[19] in the United States, the BBC[20] in the United Kingdom and RTL[21] in Germany. The television pictures were transmitted via satellite to the television stations, so that intercontinental Internet traffic was not affected by the broadcast.

But still the first event attracted more people. Not because Clinton was less interesting, but because they could see something that was not transmitted via television. Internet technology makes it easy to create video and audio items, but they won't have any impact if the customers do not see something special or useful.

---

[14]http://www.number-10.gov.uk/
[15]http://www.bundesregierung.de/
[16]http://www.victoriassecret.com/
[17]http://webevents.broadcast.com/victoriassecret/fashionshow99/
[18]http://www.real.com/
[19]http://www.cnn.com/
[20]http://www.bbc.co.uk/
[21]http://www.rtlnews.de/

5.4   Virtual Societies

5.4.1   Affiliate Networks

In order to market your online products, you need to syndicate your content or technologies to other sites or even to other media. Portals are a good place to offer your content, products or services. The Internet is an infrastructure for many niche and mainstream markets. Split up your marketing offensive into narrow target markets which correspond to zones or channels (see also Chapter 6, Portals).

Affiliate networks are a special form of customizing your online products; this time not to end customers, but to resellers, who want to extend their offerings by adding your services, products or information. Your services, information and goods need to be totally separate from the design of your web pages. The resellers should be able to configure your offerings the way they need them, online and on-the-fly.

Create a special reseller section, where you not only offer the customization of the digital products, but also marketing material that the resellers can use to promote your electronic goods.

Another good reason to create an affiliate network is to create brand awareness. The more web sites you are able to recruit for your network, the more people will become aware of your offerings. Amazon.com's affiliate network is probably the most known. Thousands of web sites have become resellers of Amazon.com's books and the owners of these web sites get up to fifteen percent of each sale. Other than in real life where manufacturers seek to build up a limited number of resellers that are geographically separated, entrepreneurs on the web try to get as many affiliates as possible as this increases profit.

The affiliate network of Amazon.com has created many niche bookshops on the Internet that focus on one or more topics. These niche bookshop have additional information on the books and concentrate more on the surrounding topics of the books than Amazon.com could, but still Amazon.com is the big winner, as the books are purchased in the end from them.

Special online directories, e.g. Top Reseller[22] or Refer-It[23], list affiliate networks, but be careful. Many companies try to appear as affiliate networks but are in reality companies based on the pyramid scheme. The pyramid scheme is forbidden in many countries, as it does not make money from selling goods, but by recruiting others.

5.4.2   Internet Communities

Try to map your target groups into Internet communities. Building up these communities on your web site will not only enhance your one-to-one marketing

---

[22]http://www.topreseller.com/
[23]http://www.refer-it.com/

ut will also allow one-to-many and many-to-many communication
user groups. It is also easier to customize products for certain com-
nd present them in a special way to them.

g-lover community on your web site, should be able to get all the
nformation about frogs without having to click through a series of
that contains no value to them. Saving your customers' profiles will
make everybody happy, as they are treated in a very special way, and your company gets detailed information on the target group. But be careful about the
information you gather, the customers should know what you are doing with
the material. Your privacy regulations should be visible very clearly. Otherwise you may have trouble with online privacy activists, who will try throw a
bad light on your company. Provide a link on every page to your privacy information where you state what your intention is with the private information
your customers provide.

One of the most famous communities on the Internet is the WebGrrls community[24]. The Webgrrls International community provides a forum for women
interested in new media and technology. It is basically a network for exchanging job and business leads and helps to form strategic alliances. The mission is
to mentor and teach, intern and learn the skills to succeed in an increasingly
technical workplace and world.

5.4.3   Interactive User Groups

Other than with traditional media, communication via the Internet is much
faster and is not restricted to one-way only. Customers are able to talk directly
to your employees and the other way round is just as true and possible. No matter who initiated the conversation, responding to it by the other party involved
is easy, using e-mail, chat or newsgroups.

In order to attract customers it is necessary to build up a dialogue between
your company and the customers. The customer needs to experience interactivity in order to stay with a particular company. Focus on the target group
and try to convince them to stay with your company. Internet surfers who just
browse by accident through your pages should not be ignored, but they should
get only general information about your company. If they are really interested
they should register with your site to access more information.

In order to offer your customers an interactive experience put up links to
contact e-mail addresses. For every type of request there should be a different
e-mail address. If your visitors want to know about advertising prices then
they should send their mail to another e-mail address than they would if they
wanted to comment on the web site in general. Although the mail may be read
by the same person, it makes it easier to classify the type of communication the
user requests. A real dialogue between your company and your customers will
enhance the loyalty of your customers and the awareness for your company.

---

[24]http://www.webgrrls.com/

Your company on the other hand gets valuable information on the customer base and is able to enhance products, services and content to please the customers even more.

Other simple measures to increase the interactivity of your web site include offering contests or sweepstakes on your web pages. Giving away one of your products does not cost much, compared to other methods of promotion. Not only does the number of users increase significantly, you also gather information on interested users. And users love to take part in a contest. They will check back regularly to see if they have won.

Offer additional free information, products or services by inviting customers to register on your web site. Customer service is also very important. Give them, for example, real-time information on product order status. If you sell digital products and services, offer demo or limited versions on your web site that everybody can use. This helps the customers in their decision to buy a certain product. Offer feedback forms and provide search engines for your site.

5.5 Localization

5.5.1 Act Global, Think Local

Being online means that you compete with competitors on a world-wide basis, but need to target individuals from all over the world. The Internet has enforced the era of globalization, which is the expression of deterritorialization and a borderless world. While globalization has become a fact it is not true that a global culture has been established. The more the people get in touch with people from other countries, they see their own culture as becoming more important. It is part of their identity, which they are about to lose in a global culture. The effect can be seen quite clearly in Europe, where fifteen countries are moving together to form the European Union. While national boundaries have been lifted, the identity with the region where the people live has risen to new levels. For many people it has become less important to be German, French or Italian. They see themselves as from Bavaria, from Bourgogne or from Tuscany. In the early years of computing it had been expected that all programs need only be written in English, but the mistake was that in the early years only well-educated people, who were native English speakers or learnt English at school, had access to these resources. With the Internet everybody is able to use it.

In order to cater for this change in society, be sure to have country- or region-specific web sites in the local languages. Customers from China or Russia may not be able to speak English or another Western language, such as French or German, so if you target such markets, make sure you have translations online and you know the customs of doing business in these countries.

As pages can be seen on a world-wide basis, you need to think about your target groups and your future target groups. You should try not to offend other cultures or religions by the content or the graphics on your web pages. Although this does not mean that you cannot display anything that may be viewed differently in other countries, you should be aware about possible issues when dealing with these countries.

The decision to translate or not to translate depends on two basic considerations; business and legal. In order to make a product more attractive, it is necessary to localize a product or service in order to compete with a local manufacturer. In some countries there are laws that require all imported goods to have the warnings, the safety instructions and user installation information translated into the local language. Even if translations are not required, because the country you are exporting the goods to shares the same language, it may be necessary to localize the product or service.

The format of dates, for example, is different in the UK and the US. Certain words that are shared among these two countries may have different meanings. While the title "esquire" is still commonly used in the UK as a synonym for "mister", it is not used in this sense in the US anymore. And while English speaking countries do not expect to have a field in the address form for the academic title, it is highly desired in Germany and Italy. A "Herr Professor" wants to receive mail addressed to "Herr Professor" and a "dottore" in Italy will expect a personalized web page to greet her or him with the academic title.

The currency is different in Germany and Austria, although they share the same language. Although the Euro has been introduced in both countries in 1999, the people of Germany and Austria still have their own currencies until 2002. Austria and Germany are in the European Union and share mostly the same legal framework. The North of Switzerland, which also speaks German is not part of the European Union and has other tax and law regulations.

Another issue may be the form where customers need to fill in their postal address. Postal codes have different formats in different countries and the field "state", that is used in the US, is not needed in most European countries. This not only misleads the customers, but also results in bad records in your database. An address form, which is not conforming to the local use may keep customers from using the offered service, meaning that this results in missed deliveries. I have come across many web site that offer their goods to European countries from the US, which require to fill in the "state" field. If you leave it empty, the order cannot be processed, as the validation tool used checks if all fields are filled in. What makes this even worse is that many sites just output a general error message leaving the customer in doubt whether the web server failed or if the entry was wrong.

5.5.2 Cultural Differences

Although it may be hard to understand, other cultures will have difficulties with behaviours that are common in one's own area/country. They will have totally different expectations that may lead to misunderstandings. A simple example would be the way people order drinks in a bar. In Germany you are served and pay when you leave, in Italy you have to pay first and then order and in Ireland you order first and pay immediately. A German in Ireland or Italy would sit down at a table and wait until a waiter comes. But neither in Ireland nor in Italy would anything happen. The expectations are totally different. The German may think that the Irish and Italians don't like Germans and therefore gets nothing to drink. The Irish and Italian on the other hand may think that the German is not interested in anything to drink and will just ignore the person.

Although these countries are all in Europe, they have a lot of cultural differences and varying customs. It is therefore easy to imagine the differences in countries that are far more distant than Germany and Italy, for example. The Asian countries, for example, have difficulties in using standard applications like a word processor from the United States, not because it has not been translated properly, but because the logic and the habits are those of Americans and not of Asians. Therefore programs such as RichWin[25] are very popular in China, for example, as it modifies standard applications on Windows to fit in with the way the Asians think.

Disney[26], for example, had large problems with cultural differences, when they opened their theme park near Paris, France. Charles Hill uses this example to describe the dilemma many companies get into when extending their business to other countries[27]. The American managers thought that they could use their existing business model and values and introduce them into the French market. It soon became quite clear that the company needed to adapt to the local market. Other than expected; the customers to the EuroDisney were mostly Americans living in Europe and Japanese tourists. The Europeans coming to the theme park were also not staying as long as their American and Japanese counterparts. Instead of staying four days in the theme park, most Europeans came for one day, making it difficult for Disney to fill all the hotels that they built around the theme park. These errors are often repeated by online businesses. Just because you know your local market does not mean that you are able to repeat the success in other markets or even create a global market for your products and services.

Not only will providing a business model that will work in every country fail in most cases, but also a single advertisement for several countries can easily fail, if local laws are not taken into consideration. In an article in *The Economist*[28] Kellogg was cited as an example. Kellogg's[29] made a television commercial in the UK, which was highly successful there, but could not be

---

[25] http://www.richwinusa.com/

[26] http://www.disney.com/

[27] International Business, Charles W. Hill, Washington, 1998, pp. 64

[28] http://www.economist.co.uk/, "Advertising in a Single Market", *The Economist*, March 24, 1990, p. 64

[29] http://www.kelloggs.com/

used in any other European country. The commercial featured a child wearing a Kellogg's t-shirt promoting the iron and the vitamins in the product. The key line was "Kellogg's makes their cornflakes the best they have ever been." In France the commercial could not be shown, as it is against the law to show children in product endorsements. The Netherlands forbid the commercial because the reference to the vitamins and the iron were claims to health and medical benefits, which is forbidden. In Germany the spot could not be shown, because of prohibition against competitive claims.

When localizing Internet applications do not only translate the texts and adjust currencies, but think also about local habits. If you have, for example, a French hotel on the Côte D'Azure, you could offer an online reservation service. French customers who want to book a hotel may want to take their pets with them, as this is very common in France. So there should be a check box where they can click, if they want to bring their dogs or cats along. If you now translate the pages into Japanese then it would not make much sense to have the pet option, as it would be very unlikely that Japanese tourist would bring their pets to France. This option may confuse them, especially if the translations are not perfect, which happens quite often on the Internet. Badly translated texts destroy more business on the Internet than they generate.

Many Americans especially are not aware of the cultural differences and expect that their way of conducting business will be accepted throughout the world. Most non-Americans, though, will prefer to do business with people who are accustomed with the local habits and rules. This is also reflected on the web. Amazon.de[30] is a success in Germany, because it uses a German top-level domain, the web site is all in German and because it sells German books and is run by Germans who know how to conduct business in Germany and not because many people know Amazon.com.

In order to be successful in local markets it is necessary to know how people react to your offerings. In Southern Europe, for example, people are far more responsive to spoken words, while Northern Europeans prefer a written order. A phone conversation with people from Southern Europe is often more effective than sending an e-mail.

When expanding your companies to cover other countries, get to know the local customs. The Internet offers the advantage that you can go to local web sites and see how they do business. In order to build up a subsidiary get in people from that particular country who know better what to do. If you are planning a major investment then consider learning some phrases and visit the country. Otherwise the investment may result in a failure, which can result in financial trouble for the whole company.

The National Forum on Cultural Differences[31] is also a good place to start investigations. The forum offers the opportunity to ask questions about cul-

---

[30]http://www.amazon.de/

[31]http://www.yforum.com/

tural differences and people who seem to know more about the other culture are able to respond. Although I have also seen some wrong answers there, the place is in general a good starting point for your world-wide expansion.

5.5.3   Translation Requirements

Depending on your budget you should think about translating your web pages into other languages. Many smaller companies use automated translation services to produce foreign language web sites. Babelfish[32], for example, allows automated translation on the web into many different languages, such as Spanish, French and German. Many people use this service to get a fast, but rough translation of a certain web page (which the system was designed for). Some companies use the output as the basis for their localization efforts and are laughed at by the foreign speaking online community. To offer automatically translated web pages to serious customers is a good way of destroying business.

Figure 5.2 shows the web page of MediaTechBooks[33], which has been translated with Babelfish from German to English. "Newsletter", for example, which is actually borrowed from the English word, becomes "New Type Character" in the English translation, which doesn't make any sense anymore.

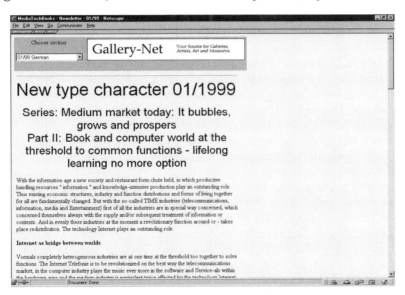

Figure 5.2. Automated Translation of MediaTechBooks' Web Page

If you are serious about extending your business, then get professional translators and localizing experts. A professional translator tries to capture

---

[32]http://babelfish.altavista.com/
[33]http://www.mediatechbooks.de/

the exact meaning of the source text without compromising the integrity of the author's style of expressing ideas. This cannot be done by simple algorithms on a computer. The bad translation will fall back on the image of your electronic business. The software that you are using should support localization, otherwise it will become quite difficult to add new languages, currencies and customs.

5.6 Promoting Your E-business

5.6.1 Choosing the Right Domain Name

Before you can start to promote your web site, you should choose a domain name that fits your business and needs. If you have a company that is well-known you should have your company name in the domain name. If you are offering services for a particular target group try to find a domain name that matches a keyword people would search for. Of course, two or more domain names would be the best solution.

Let's say your company is called Spaghetti Inc. and produces Italian style pasta. The most obvious domain names for the company would be "spaghetti-inc.com", "spagehtti.com" or "pasta.com". If your company has subsidiaries all over the world, the top level domain should be also bought for all target countries, i.e. for your subsidiary in Germany you would choose "spaghettiinc.de", "spaghetti.de" and "pasta.de" and for the subsidiary in Taiwan you would select "spaghettiinc.tw", "spaghetti.tw" and "pasta.tw". The use of ".com" suggests that your site contains information in English. If you use other country codes, such as ".se" you need to translate all information into Swedish, otherwise you do not live up to the expectations of your customers. A complete list of the available top level domain names can be found at many places on the Web[34] and can help to identify the number of TLDs you need to target.

If you are choosing more generic terms such as "spaghetti" or "pasta", there is no need to create a new web site for every domain name. You can easily link several domain names to one web site. By using different TLDs, such as ".de" and ".fr" you could directly link to the German and French pages with the option of switching back to the English pages at any given time. Lufthansa, for example, is using multiple TLDs in this way. The .de-domain[35] points to the German site and the .com-domain[36] points to the English site. Ca5ino.com[37], on the other hand points to the same company and web site as CasinoPlace[38]. Through the use of two different domain names, more customers are likely to be attracted by the content.

---

[34]e.g. http://www.iana.org/top-level-domains.html

[35]http://www.lufthansa.de/

[36]http://www.lufthansa.com/

[37]http://www.ca5ino.com/

[38]http://www.casinoplace.com/

Of course, domain names are not always available having already been taken by some other company. In this case you should check if these companies are infringing your trade marks. If you have a company with a certain name and someone else is using the domain name without apparent connection, then you can get the domain name back without too much hassle.

A few years ago people bought domain names in order to sell them on, which worked in the beginning, but nowadays almost all court rulings are in favor of the company which holds the trademark name.

To check the availability of domain names, you can go to InterNic[39] for American domains, Ripe[40] for European domains and APNic[41] provides domain names for the Asia and the Pacific region. Your ISP is also a good place to check for domain name availability but compare prices with the domain name registries, as ordering a domain name is simple and can be done in five minutes. You have to be especially careful, if you order domain names through your ISP. Some IPS register the domain in their name, instead of your company's name, making it difficult to switch provider, as they have become de-facto the owners of the domain name and not your company.

In addition to the domain name it is necessary to apply for an IP address, as all domain names need to be mapped to an IP address. In most cases a range of IP addresses is ordered, which enables a company to grow in the future more easily. Due to an error in the IP address database I was the owner of approximately one third of the Internet for a few days (the range from 195.125.0.156 to 255.255.255.255). This happened on June 20th, 1998 and was corrected soon after, as it became impossible to chase hackers and spammers and I did not want to take responsibility for them. But it felt good to "own" a large part of the Internet ;-). Unfortunately I was not allowed to put the excerpt from the IP database into the book for copyright reasons.

Some people try to participate in the success of certain web sites, so they register domain names that are very similar to the successful ones. "whitehouse.com" has nothing to do with the US American White House web site "whitehouse.gov". The purpose of "metacralwer.com" is totally different than the meta search engine "metacrawler.com". And finally the owners of "office21.com" have nothing to do with the German project "office21.de", which tries to create the office for the 21st century .

Many companies are not bound to a country or region and use top level domains (TLDs) as part of their name. Even small countries in the Pacific ocean are participating in the domain name game. Tuvalu, owner of the ".tv" domain, Niue, owner of ".nu", Tonga, owner of ".to" have TLDs that are used very frequently. ".tv" is used by many sites centered around television. ".nu" is pronounced in the same way as "new" to suggest to people that you have a new site. The people of Tonga have become rich with the ".to" domain. Many

---

[39] http://www.internic.net/

[40] http://www.ripe.net/

[41] http://www.apnic.net/

sites have registered this domain, such as cryp.to[42], go.to[43], come.to[44]. Even Armenia (".am") is attracting foreign businesses, such as the i.am[45] web site, which allows customers to build URLs, such as http://www.i.am/danny/ (which is, by the way, not my site).

What is a URL?

The URL (Uniform Resource Locator) is a means to locate a resource on the Internet. Most common are URLs in the form of http://www.hp.com/. The "http:" is the type of protocol used for the connection. Commonly used protocol types are the following. You can try them out by typing them into a web browser.

- **http** – Standard hyper text transfer protocol (HTTP), which provides a connection to any given web server (example: http://www.realhamsters.com/).

- **https** – Encrypted HTTP connection to a web server (example: https://lg.homebanking.de/).

- **ftp** – Standard FTP (File transfer protocol) connection (example: ftp://ftp.apple.com/).

- **telnet** – Telnet protocol to connect to a server (example: telnet://delos.lf.net/)

- **mailto** – Mail protocol to send out an e-mail (example: mailto:president@whitehouse.gov)

Table 5.3.

Such use of the TLD shows that the current system is not good anymore and needs to be replaced by a more sophisticated solution in the future. Adding new TLDs won't help much. The whole system of domain names needs to be reviewed. Several new systems have already been proposed; Netscape's system being maybe the best-known. Netscape has a feature known as smart browsing, based on "keywords" that link to locations within Netcenter and on partners' sites. Netscape's idea is to replace the domain names with keywords

---

[42]http://www.cryp.to/
[43]http://www.go.to/
[44]http://www.come.to/
[45]http://www.i.am/

or trademarked names. This would unify the concept of a search engine with the domain names, but Netscape's model is no use at the moment, as their proposal works only with the Netscape browser and they want to host the name database. This would put at a disadvantage all other browser producers and would put the control into Netscape's hands.

Another system that has been proposed is called RealNames[46]. The aim of the service is to simplify using the internet by replacing complex URLs with memorable words and phrases in any language. Instead of typing "http://www.buecher.de/", one can simply type "Bücher" to be redirected to that web site. The RealNames system is based on the Unicode code set, that does not only contain the Latin character set, but all character sets in the world such as the Russian, Chinese, Hebrew and Arabic character sets. The advantage is that Arabic native speakers, for example, are able to enter an Arabic name in Arabic and will be redirected to the appropriate web site. But RealNames has the same disadvantage as Netscape's smart browsing; the database is managed by only one group or company. They define the policies of use and the policy of "appropriate use" on the RealNames web site is not clearly defined. It cannot be ensured that your names will be accepted, as only RealNames decides on your submission. Another issue with RealNames is that it works on top of domain names. It means an additional layer of complexity.

A new system is still required, but it needs to be open, secure and should not depend on a certain vendor. An independent body such as the World Wide Web Consortium[47] will eventually come up with a solution that can be supported by the majority of Internet users. In any case it should be browser independent and replace the current solution of the domain name system. Such a solution needs to allow a smooth transition, otherwise the chances are high that many customers will not be willing to switch.

5.6.2   Announcing the Web Site

The best site is useless if nobody knows how to get there. The domain name should be everywhere your company logo is. Be present in all search engines and online directories. Add meta-tags to your web pages, which give general information on the content of a certain web page and contain a set of keywords that increase the success of finding a particular web page in a search engine. Additional information on search engines and meta-tags can be found in Chapter 9. Get the attention of the press and use traditional media to promote your web site.

There are many strategies to increase the visibility of your offerings. Find other sites that share a similar target audience and exchange banner advertising and links. Register your web site with all search engines and directories. Some companies offer this service for money, but doing it yourself is easy and

---

[46]http://www.realnames.com/
[47]http://www.w3.org/

you retain control over your marketing initiative. Use the "Add URL" button which is provided on all search engines and directory web sites or use one of the free services that add your URL to many search engines in one go, like SignPost[48] in the United Kingdom or MultiSubmit[49] in Austria.

Submit only the main page to web directories. If you start submitting every single page to a directory, chances are high that all of your submissions will be ignored. Give precise information on the content of your web site, its services, the information contained and products offered. Submit to web crawlers the most important pages, as the crawler is able to find the rest of the pages. If you, for example, have added a new subdirectory to your web site, then submit the first page of that subdirectory to Internet crawlers and they will fetch all the other pages automatically. For them meta-tags are important to collect the relevant data.

It is possible to post information about your new site to mailing lists, but be careful about this. There are some dedicated mailing lists for announcing new sites, but most general mailing lists will not accept this form of advertising.

Your site should be promoted not only online on other pages, but also off-line using traditional media and should appear in advertising, press releases, corporate literature, trade shows, letter heads and business cards. As a rule of thumb: Either give out the domain name, such as "www.mycompany.com" or the complete URL, such as "http://www.mycompany.com/". Do not omit the slash at the end. Although web browsers add the slash if you forget it, everybody should enter it. It requires two connections to the web server, because the first request will return a request to the web browser to add the slash. Although this may not seem important it also distinguishes companies that know what they are doing from the rest.

Tell everyone that you have a web site up and running; tell it to your customers, clients, suppliers, partners and tell it to your competitors. And don't forget to mention what it offers and can do for them. But do not give out the information before your site is ready. Once you let users onto your site, you must be sure that nothing is missing and all links are clickable and lead to another web page. A page which says "Under Construction", can mean the death of your online business. If you don't offer a service right away, don't tell people. If your customers are able to click on a link then you set expectations. They expect to receive the service behind the link. If you fail to offer the service, they will go to another web site.

5.6.3   Managing Your Image

As the competition on the Internet gets more and more cluttered, consistency is one of the most important things on the Internet. A consistent image in form of standard web pages, e-mails and newsgroup postings is essential. It

---

[48]http://signpost.merseyworld.com/

[49]http://www.multisubmit.at/

needs also to be consistent with all your traditional communication methods, like television, radio, magazines, newspapers and direct mailings. The world-wide branding program of a company must be able to cross the boundaries of the traditional and new media and join them into one.

Not doing so, may result in self-competition. Instead of selling more goods using all channels, the Internet may take away existing customers from newspapers, for example, thus not increasing the profit. Customers may not recognize which web sites, brands and companies belong together. The web sites may have little or no relationship to the rest of their marketing communications efforts. All types of media must be part of an integrated marketing strategy. New media should always try to attract new target groups or convince existing target groups to stay with a certain brand, but never should a target group be forced to change the media to stay in touch with a certain company.

Just as your letter heads adhere to the corporate or brand image in design elements and colors, your web site should use the same elements. Anyone looking at your web site should be able to associate it with your company or product in an instant. But remain innovative; don't just replicate your printed documents to the web. Use Internet technologies to display your information in a new way, become more interactive and add new services. This would not have been possible without the Internet.

Some companies try to control the images of their brands online by banning their products from all other web sites. Levi Strauss[50], for example, has found out in the real world, that they can better control their brands by operating their own stores. Instead of selling jeans to retailers, they sell them in their own shops, where they have greater control over their goods and the interior design. This, on the other hand, encouraged retailers to create their own brands. So the line between manufacturers and retailers has been blurred.

This behaviour is typical of manufacturers who are not sure about their online strategy. While more and more digital companies spread their services over portal sites to create awareness of their brands and make money with them, traditional manufacturers try to protect their brands by banning the sale of their products on other web sites. This does not help their brands and will only work if the brand is strong enough.

5.7 Banner Ad Campaigning

5.7.1 Basic Strategies

As many providers of information have failed to make money with selling the information directly to the customers, they use banner advertising as a revenue stream. The problem with information is that it is very easy to copy. A company that charges for information on a web site will attract other sites to offer the

---

[50]http://www.levis.com/

same or similar information for free. The technologies required to sell content over the Internet, such as standard content encryption and authentication, are not ready yet.

While companies with specialized content, such as the *Encyclopaedia Britannica*[51], make this model work, more frequently companies are finding that the netizens (the citizens on the net) typically refuse to pay for general information, which they can find at other sites for free. So, many site owners switched to selling advertising to cover costs.

Banner advertising is one of the easiest ways of advertisement on the web. Following some simple rules makes banner ads also very efficient and a constant stream of revenues. Just putting some form of graphics onto some web site won't be enough. You need to develop a strategy for your advertising projects. You will find lots of web sites that contain banner ads nobody will ever bother to click.

Users will be very upset if they have to wait for a banner ad. The ad never should slow down the speed of the content related page. The users will go on to other sites where they can get all the relevant information in less time. This is bad for your banner advertising, but also for the content provider. In order to be safe with banner ads, use last years technology to design them. The less bandwidth, colors and processor speed is required to display the banner ad the better it is.

An ugly banner will reduce the chances of someone clicking on it. Not only does the web page design to be done right, but also the banner ads need a clear design that fits into the design of the web sites. You may have to engage a designer for the banner, but it will pay back immediately.

Complex animations may be cute, but most users won't appreciate them. They take too much time to download and are not helping to attract people to click on the banner ad. If you use animations in your banner, use them wisely. Be sure that the message has the top priority.

Many banner ads contain text and fonts that are illegible. This again will not get your message to the user, even though your designer thought that this particular design was cool. The more you keep it simple, the more consumers are able to understand what you want to achieve.

Even the best banner will fail, if the link to which it points is not available. If you change the destination on your web server, remember to tell all other sites of a link to that particular page. To reduce the probability of a dead link, link the banner directly to the home page. Dead links are very bad for the image of your company. Do an automatic check every few days of all banner links pointing to your pages in order to be sure nobody has messed something up and all customers get to see the information you have prepared for them.

If you want to animate people to click on your banner ad, you need to create a catchy message. Remember that your ad is a representative of you and your

---

[51]http://www.eb.com/

Banner Advertising Rules

In order to implement a successful online banner campaign the following rules may help:

- **Keep banners small** – The message must be visible within a few seconds on slow connection.

- **Invest in Design** – Use a concise design to display your message.

- **Avoid complex animations** – Animations are cute, but take up a lot of time for downloading.

- **Make it readable** – Don't use funny fonts. Display your message in such a way that everyone is able to read it.

- **Make sure the link works** – The best banner ad is useless if the link leads into Nirvana.

- **Design a compelling message** – Make a short, compelling statement on your product or service.

Table 5.4.

company, containing a smattering of your personality and ability. Keep the message clear rather than clever. Never try to code a message. It does not help to have a good banner if nobody understands the message.

In order to put your banners onto other pages, special agencies have been set up to provide the infrastructure to put banners onto a certain web page at a specific time. Traditional advertising agencies missed the Internet opportunity, so new companies emerged. Two types of banner management agencies have been established on the Internet.

5.7.2 Banner Exchange

Banner exchange agencies are a new service that have been enabled through the Internet. Every webmaster is able to sign up with a banner exchange service. The webmasters need to provide a banner promoting their own web site in a specific format and need to allow other banners to appear on the web site. In exchange for a certain amount of views (just looking at the banner ad) or click-throughs (clicking on the banner ad) on the webmasters' own web page, their own banner is displayed on other web pages or the webmaster is rewarded with some money. Banner exchange sites can be divided into two different types.

One focuses on a very narrow target market, like for example, Anthrotech[52], who exchange banners on anthropologically related sites only, the Christian Banner Exchange[53], as the name already suggests, exchanges banners only between sites that are related to the Christian religion. On the other hand there are some general-purpose banner exchange agencies, like 1-For-1[54] or Banner-Mania[55], which offer to put your banner on a wide array of sites, but also have the possibility to target your banner to a certain type of web site. The banner services also keep logs of the people who looked at the banner and clicked on it. An example can be seen in Figure 5.3 on the site of IndiaConnect[56].

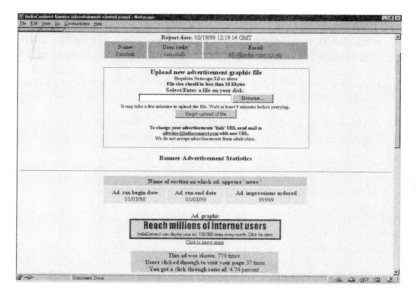

Figure 5.3. Banner Administration on IndiaConnect

Banner selling agencies on the other hand offer the more traditional approach of selling advertising to known publications. Instead of selling ads to a newspaper you sell ads to a certain web site, that very many people go to each day, for example; the CNN[57] homepage. ClickThrough[58] allows advertisers to

[52]http://www.anthrotech.com/banner/

[53]http://www.cbx2.com/

[54]http://www.1for1.com/

[55]http://www.banner-mania.com/

[56]http://www.indianconnect.com

[57]http://www.cnn.com/

[58]http://www.clickthrough.com/

place their banner ads on certain web pages for a certain period of time. You have to decide in advance where you want to put which banner on which web site. The solution is not very flexible.

Flycast[59], on the other hand, allows you to buy and sell web-advertising space in real time. Other than with "normal" agencies, where you can order 100,000 page views within a month, Flycast offers the possibility of putting banners onto a certain web page at any given time. It allows you to watch the click-throughs happen in real time. This allows you to make changes to your marketing campaign on the fly. Whenever the click-through rate is dropping, you can move your banner ads on to another web site.

Using this innovative technology it is also possible to try out banner ads on new sites with a very low risk. Just place it onto a certain site and watch the click-through rate. In many cases it may work out, so your company does not need to pay the high prices for the "must have" sites, but still reaches its potential customer base. You can use this technology to put banner ads on ten niche sites at a lower price than it would have cost to put it onto a major site.

If you have a consumer base, which is online at a certain hour (e.g. office hours), you are able to increase the number of banner ads at a certain time. Using this method is it also possible to reduce the costs during the time when your target market is offline (e.g. because they are asleep in a certain region).

5.8 Online Measurement

5.8.1 User Tracking

The Internet combines the tracking capabilities of direct mail and the instancy of TV and radio broadcasts with the addition of interactivity. But as I already mentioned in Chapter 1, measurement methods on the web are still quite immature. It is not possible to make exact measurements on the Web, but some methods have been established which will be presented here, as accountability becomes more important. Measurement services and web sites use these methods to sell advertising space to their advertising customers.

Mainly the methods, used on the web today are counting, auditing and rating. Therefore it is essential to understand the differences between these measurement methods.

Counting is the process, which is normally done by the web site owners. It consists of monitoring and reporting user activity. The measurement is done on the basis of the web server log files. The log files are then processed. The processed figures are then sent out to the advertisers. Because the figures are based on the log file of the web site, advertisers can't be sure that the data is comparable across web sites.

---

[59]http://www.flycast.com/

5.8.2 Avoiding Problems

The problem is to count users. There is no clear definition of how to count one user. The problem is spiders, little robots sent out by search engines, and proxy servers; special servers that allow access to web sites and save them in a cache in order to improve performance for other users that use the same proxy server. To speed up the browsing experience, Internet Service Providers (ISPs) and online services save copies of web pages and images (including banner ads) on specialized servers and provide the data from their servers rather than yours. That means the banner ads are not counted in every case. The same goes for ads and pages stored locally in your browser cache file. The result is that you get inflated and under-counted impressions. Depending on your user base, it could well be that twice as many people have seen your web pages, but only half of them were connected to your site. Although this reduces the cost for the advertising (as you pay only for the impressions that reach the server), it does not give a complete picture of the online activity.

Spiders appear like users on the web site and may take up to 25 percent of the online activity. Proxy servers relay requests from users, so that the web servers see only the address of the proxy, thus letting 1,000 people appear to be one. In order to overcome both problems, it is possible to use cookies. But nobody can force the users to accept cookies from the web server.

The measurement units used for online advertising are called page views and visits. Page views are all pages that were viewed by the online consumers and a visit consists of all page views by a single customer.

The best way to overcome these problems is to ask for auditing. This is the process of verifying the counting; i.e. checking the log files. Auditing is done by an impartial third party organization, which is trusted both by the advertiser as well as the web site owner. On the basis of audited numbers, advertisers are in a good position to buy space on certain web sites.

5.8.3 Log File Analyzer

Every web server is able to keep track of the users accessing its web pages by saving the action into a log file. To analyze log files on highly-frequented sites is manually not possible, as it is difficult and time-consuming to mine, and the sheer volume can be overwhelming. Therefore automatic log analyzer tools have been implemented, which allow a graphical output of the data to make its analysis simple.

In order to analyze log files, it is necessary to import the data into the proprietary database of the analyzer. Filters can be used in most products that allow you to analyze traffic for a certain period of time or certain user groups or areas on the web server. Once the data has been imported, the filters have been chosen, the data is processed and the analyzer creates graphical reports such as tables and charts. These reports make it easier to spot trends and patterns of the users on your web site.

It is possible to see if people have trouble finding certain information and it is possible to see where they were coming from (see Figure 5.4). The so-called referrer log tells you which site people have seen before coming to your site. Many analyzers have a database of search engines, making it easy to spot people who found your site on a certain search engine.

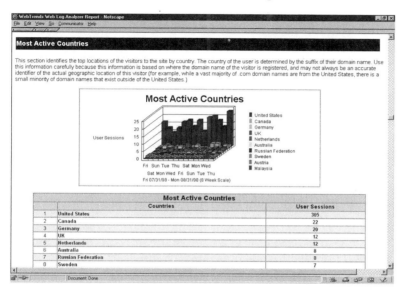

Figure 5.4. Sample Report in WebTrends

5.8.4 Online Rating Agencies

In order to gather even more information, advertisers are able to subscribe to online rating agencies. These agencies use special software that monitors the activity of the customers. The software needs to be installed at the users' computers. The activity includes web site visits, online chats and other services on the Internet. The advantage of this approach is that everything is recorded at the user level and not at the service level, allowing a better overview of the users' activities. The technology used is similar to the rating services on television. It is clearly not the best way of achieving demographic information, as the selected users cannot be representative, nor is there a limited number of available channels. It may well be that 1,000 users go to 1,000 different sites. You could, of course, choose a group of people who visit certain sites regularly and monitor the way they use the site. This may help you to organize the site in a way that makes it more usable for your customers.

As already mentioned above, the Internet is not a mass-media. So it is not possible to have a representative user group for the whole Internet. It

Measurement Units

The most commonly used measurement units are the following. The results can be very different, so be careful. One visitor, for example, can be equivalent to ten visits, fifty page views and two hundred hits. One ad click can be equivalent to one thousand ad impressions. So get the web server log files and verify the results yourself.

- **Page View** – An HTML page that has been successfully downloaded, including all embedded elements (such as graphics).

- **Hits** – Every access to the web server, including HTML pages, graphics, sounds, frames.

- **Visits** – A sequence of page views performed by a single visitor. If the user does not view a page for fifteen minutes then the visit is over.

- **Visitor** – A visitor is a user that can be identified by certain properties, such as e-mail address or cookies.

- **Ad Impression** – Number of banner views on a certain web page.

- **Ad Click** – Number of clicks on a banner for a certain web page.

Table 5.5.

is possible to select a niche group and monitor their activity, but the results cannot be valid for the Internet as a whole.

Another drawback from these services is the fact that most users that are monitored through these services are home-based, as corporate firewalls, other security measures and corporate privacy policies do not allow the installation of the rating software on company computers. This blurs the results, as most companies today offer their employees the possibility to connect to the Internet and to surf the Web.

Special software that monitors web server log files and cannot be tampered with has already been developed and helps to ensure that webmasters do not try to forge the results of their own log files. These log files are authenticated by a third party and can enhance the predictability of the accounting. Advertisers who use all of the above mentioned methods can paint the most revealing picture of a certain web site activity.

5.8.5 Third Party Auditing

As more advertisers and agencies go online, large sums are spent for marketing. On request of the advertisers more and more web sites, for example, Deja News[60] and Snap[61], are now being audited through third parties. Measurement needs to be as exact as possible and needs to inform the advertisers in order to make the right decisions.

As mentioned above the problem is to count the users who sit behind firewalls and access web sites through proxy servers. Some new software programs promise to solve this problem. I/Pro[62] and MatchLogic[63] are two companies who offer such programs. Both of their solutions are written in Java. Therefore you gain greater control over your customers, but even those systems are not perfect, as they require a Java-enabled browser. Some customers still use older versions of a browser, others just switch off the Java functionality and some firewalls just don't let Java applets through. So these systems are better than nothing, but not good enough to really trust what they have counted.

5.9 One-to-One Marketing

5.9.1 Information Technology

Although I have mentioned one-to-one marketing strategies throughout the chapter, this section goes into more detail about it. A web site that does not use one-to-one marketing won't be successful in the future, as it ignores the needs of the customers. Information technology provides electronic businesses with the following possibilities: Identification, Interaction, Differentiation, Tracking and Customization. In order to develop a successful one-to-one marketing strategy these possibilities need to be combined.

The Internet offers many possibilities to identify a customer, such as using login and password to enter a certain web server. Digital certificates can also be used to authenticate a customer which contain information about the user, either stored in the browser or on a smart card. Browser cookies (personal information stored in the browser) and the IP address are other means to identify customers. Once a customer has been authenticated, the server should look up the personal record in the database to add new information about the cus-

---

[60]http://www.dejanews.com/

[61]http://www.snap.com/

[62]http://www.ipro.com/

[63]http://www.matchlogic.com/

tomer and understand the buying patterns of the customer, in order to present interesting products to the customer.

The Internet offers a wide range of communication possibilities, such as interactive chats, e-mail and newsgroups. These services allow customers to talk to digital businesses fairly easily and the companies need to respond very quickly, as customers have higher expectations of exchanging ideas with the companies. Back in the industrial age, customers were not used to talking to businesses directly. Businesses used to talk to the customers through advertising, but communication between the business and customers was not as direct as it is now with the Internet.

Differentiation is very important, especially if you are a reseller and offer a set of products that you have bought from various manufacturers. In order to differentiate your offerings from the other offerings on the web, you need to add value to the goods, such as additional free services. Treat all customers on a personal basis. Address the values and needs of each single customer.

Digital business makes it easy to keep track of the customers. This tracking information can be stored in a database and can be used to create special offers on the web site for a certain user, based on the previous visits to the site. The information that is collected on the web site can also be used to understand the needs of customers when talking in person to them or when customers call in via telephone. Therefore the information should not only be available to the application that sits on the web server, but to everyone within the company who is in contact with the customer.

Information technology makes mass-customization easy. Instead of offering a product that appeals to the "average" customer, the offerings on the web can be highly customized to the needs of the customer. This is especially easy if your company is offering digital goods, such as online services, information or products. Without computers, customization is impractical and far too expensive and without the Internet the amount of customers cannot be reached automatically.

In the near future it will be possible to offer customized software packages to customers. Instead of buying a word processor that includes functions for every type of business, you will order a word processor that suits your needs. You will choose the 20 percent of functionality that is relevant to your business. This will not only reduce the cost for the customer, it will also increase the execution speed of the program and reduce the required memory. Modular design is the key to such products. It is not restricted to software but can be extended to any type of business. Componental design becomes more and more important.

5.9.2 Developing Customer Relationships

As already briefly described in Chapter 2 the focus shifts from developing segments of information, products or services for a target group to servicing indi-

One-to-One Marketing Strategies

In order to develop a successful one-to-one marketing strategy you need to follow the principles of one-to-one marketing.

- **Identification** – Identify your customers in order to understand the buying patterns for every single customer.

- **Interaction** – Offer your customers automated assistance by pre-selecting goods, information and services that may be valuable to a particular customer.

- **Differentiation** – Treat all customers on a personal basis. Address the values and needs of every single customer.

- **Tracking** – In order to understand your customers better it is necessary to track down every transaction for every individual customer.

- **Customization** – Build product module, information part and service components that can be adapted to the needs of every single customer.

Table 5.6.

viduals, whereby individuals may be end customers or businesses. The digital enterprise needs to focus on differentiating customers instead of creating differentiated products.

In the dynamic economy it is not possible to sell standard products anymore. The products need to be built highly dynamically based on the needs of the individual customer. Traditional companies focus on creating a highly sophisticated product that suits the needs of as many people as possible. The more additional functionality is built in, the larger the market potential may be for a certain product. But this also increases the complexity of the product, which in turn increases the price and the time to understand it.

The one-to-one approach simplifies the use of the products as only the functionality is built in; reduces the amount of information to read, as only the information that is required is presented and it reduces the amount of time a service requires, as it only executes the services required by the customer. But this can only be achieved by fully understanding the needs of the customers.

Communication with the customer becomes more important and needs to be refined. Customers nowadays have many means of communicating with a certain company. Telefax, Phone and E-Mail are just a few ways of communication. No matter how a customer contacts the company, the information needs to be brought together into a single database where special programs are able to extract exact customer profiles.

For every product segment in traditional companies there have existed different electronic databases (and other forms of data storage) where the information about customers is stored, therefore it was not possible to track the buyer profile throughout the company and offer the customers special offers due to the profile. There was no way to know if the customers tried to contact the company or to whom they talked. The companies where focused on the products and not on the customer relationship.

As Don Peppers puts it in his book "Enterprise One To One"[64]: The customer base is the primary asset for the companies in the New Economy. The intelligence gathered about the customers enables your company to create the right offer for the right customer at the right time.

5.9.3 Customer-Centric Marketing

In order to provide customer-centric marketing we need to shift the focus from the business to the customer. A business needs to view every product in the digital age from the customers point of view to be successful. The judgement on the quality of service is shifted from the business to the individual customer. If a company produces digital cameras it used to define quality by the production environment and the general satisfaction of the target group. In the one-to-one society the satisfaction of every single client needs to be measured.

Customer satisfaction is linked to the expectations of a particular customer, which are highly dynamic. If your competitors offer a product at 200 Dollar or Euro then the customer will expect a comparable product from your business in the same price range. If one of the other companies decides to half the price then you will need to adapt fast, otherwise you will lose your customers, if you cannot convince them that your product quality is much higher.

In order to measure customer satisfaction it is necessary to put service quality in the context of the competition. If you have the time and the financial resources, then you could even go forward and measure the customers' satisfaction of your competitors. Through the Internet is has become much easier to measure customer satisfaction. Every point along the way that an electronic business touches a customer can be tracked and collected in a database. Every interaction is an opportunity to delight or disappoint a customer. Asking customers after each step about the satisfaction would be overkill and would annoy customers, but by tracking quietly it is possible to gather information on the success or failure of an online venture.

---

[64]Don Peppers and Martha Rogers, Enterprise One To One, Currency Book Publishers, 1997

If you have a series of web pages a customer needs to go through in order to do business with you, you can detect how much time a single customer has spent on every page. This information can be used to find out what is wrong with a certain web page. The purpose may be unclear or the design difficult to understand. The gathered data will tell you which aspects of a given process work well and which ones need to be improved.

Measuring Customer Satisfaction

Traditionally the following types of customer satisfaction measurement have been used:

- **Attribute Importance** – Every service attribute contributes diversely to the overall satisfaction of the customer. Therefore it is necessary to establish which attributes have which priority for a given customer and try to strengthen the most important attributes first. Every customer will have other priorities, so the system can become quite complicated.

- **Customer Satisfaction** – Every dimension of satisfaction gets its own score, which then can be compared to evaluate the strengths and weaknesses of your electronic business. The results can be used to plan quality improvements and launch immediate updates of the service in case of problems. The data can be gathered by evaluating log files and by asking customers to fill in a survey either on the web or via e-mail.

- **Customer Value Added** – This index is generated by dividing your business' overall customer satisfaction by the scores of all businesses competing in a certain market segment. This will give you an idea where your company is positioned in the market.

Table 5.7.

Damage control on the Internet is also very important, as we have seen in Chapter 4. A customer that is not satisfied is able to tell thousands of people with a few mouse clicks. So keeping customers happy is very important and will ensure a steady revenue stream.

Traditionally three types of customer satisfaction measurement have been used. The relative importance of attributes, dimensions of customer satisfaction and added customer value. Table 5.7 explains the types in more depth. These reports have been issued periodically to keep the business managers up to date. With the introduction of the Internet, these reports are not produced periodically anymore, but are updated in real-time, therefore offering the possibility of dynamically changing the marketing initiative.

The value of every business in the future will be two-fold. Intellectual property within the company and the customers of the company. The intellectual property will contain a lot of information on the customers, therefore it is necessary to keep this information up-to-date in order to strengthen the relationships with the customers. The information on the products and services the company offers are also extremely important as they are needed to refine the manufacturing process for the products and the extend the range of services. Products will become less important in the future, services to the customer will become more important and require more people who are able to resolve the problems of the individual customer.

5.9.4 Advanced Personalization Technologies

In addition to the standard personalization technologies, there is rules-based filtering, whereby the customer needs to answer a set of questions and gets the appropriate information presented. The rules can range from the country the users come from and set up the correct language to specific needs of each customer. Many sites ask for a zip code, for example, to find out which local news you may be interested in (such as weather and sports).

A new approach is becoming more popular. Known as learning agent technologies and collaborative filtering, it is able to help you refine the process of customizing a particular web site to the customers. This technology tries to serve relevant material that may be of interest to you by combining the preferences of the customer with the preferences of a group with similar interests. This way customers automatically recommend products, services and information to others with similar interest. Firefly[65], for example, is using this technology to create automatic recommendations between users with similar interests. On their web site customers are able to rate music on a scale. If customer one like music from A and B, and customer two likes music from B and C, the system will recommend music from C to customer one and music from A to customer two.

This system is also used by Amazon.com, for example. If you choose a book, it recommends a set of other books that have been bought by people who also bought that particular book. In order to maximize the one-to-one approach not a single technology should be used, but a mix of several technologies. Offering learning agent technology in conjunction with rules-based filtering offers the

---

[65] http://www.firefly.net/

One-to-One Technologies

More and more companies offer solutions that implement or include one-to-one technologies. A selection of software technologies can be found here.

Product	Description
BroadVision	The high-end tool recognizes customers and displays products and services relevant to that particular customer. **http://www.broadvision.com/**
Cold Fusion	Tool for rapid application development and site design. **http://www.allaire.com/**
Edify	Product specialized for electronic banking solutions. **http://www.edify.com/**
GroupLens	A collaborative filtering solution with rating services for content or products. **http://www.netperceptions.com/**
WebObjects	A framework for developing e-business applications that need to access legacy databases. Provides a strong one-to-one technology to serve data to visitors. **http://www.apple.com/webobjects/**

Table 5.8.

possibility of guiding the customers while offering them the possibility to adjust the guidance to fit their needs even better.

More and more product are becoming available. Some of the better known products can be found in Table 5.8. The software solutions are able to simply play back some data that the user entered, such as the first name of the customer (e.g. "welcome back, Ralph"). The information collected on the user can also be used to calculate discounts or trigger special offers. The more advanced functionalities of one-to-one marketing include functions such as making suggestions. The idea behind making suggestions can be either up-selling (e.g. "Perhaps you would rather be interested in this?") or cross-selling (e.g. "This t-shirt matches perfectly to the trousers").

One-to-one marketing can even go further by asking the customer a direct question. After having bought a car on the web, for example, the customers could be asked, if they need insurance and a new license plate. Some companies keep track of all the items purchased and are able to check if new items fit together with the existing equipment. Imagine a computer retailer where you have bought your Macintosh computer and now want to buy a Hewlett-Packard printer working together with the Mac. The online retailer knows what type of computer you have and will be able to show you a list of all Hewlett-Packard printers that are compatible with your computer.

In order to make one-to-one marketing work, business rules need to describe how the automated personalization works. A rules engine is used to solve problems using facts (e.g. "employees of Hewlett-Packard are first-class customers") and rules (e.g. "first-class customers get a discount of 15 percent"). Facts and rules are contained in a knowledge base. Rules engines and knowledge bases were first created for artificial intelligence systems. They are typically designed to seek out and acquire knowledge. Rules engines can work with information that is incomplete or appears incomplete. This is not usually the case with conventional transaction processing or database systems, so the addition of a rules engine makes the system appear to be more intelligent to the customers.

5.9.5 Beyond the Internet

The Internet was the first media to become fully customizable. Other media, such as TV, radio or newspapers are not yet that far. A radio or TV program nowadays is developed by a TV station and may fit your needs or may not. If you want to see or hear a certain program you are forced to tune in at the time of broadcast.

With the imminent introduction of digital TV and radio, consumers are able to customize the program. Instead of offering a 24 hour program, TV and radio stations will offer building blocks that can be accessed whenever the customer wants to. Instead of having the news update on the hour, the customer may choose to receive it at twenty past. Instead of presenting a program that tries to suit the majority, TV and radio stations will present a personalized program that suits the needs of the individual.

Newspapers will most likely become individualized in the near future. The first step will be to offer an updated version of the newspaper at any time of day. On trains and planes in Germany, for example, the newspaper is printed out on board to be always up-to-date. Newsagents have no printers so far, but the prices for hardware is dropping fast, making this possible. Instead of issuing a newspaper daily, hourly updates will become possible. Individualizing the newspaper will then be the next logical step. When subscribing to a newspaper you will eventually choose which type of information is interesting to you. Not many people have time to read through a complete newspaper.

It will be very difficult to customize books, but eventually it will become possible. One possibility may the type of book a person will buy. A book on E-business may become customizable in such a way that it will have 100 pages with high-level information for managers or be 600 pages with in-depth information for technical people. Some additional information would be needed, such as which section is relevant for technical people and which for managers, but it would make one book interesting for very specific needs.

5.10   Direct Marketing

5.10.1   Spam

Direct marketing on the Internet is very powerful, but one has to be very careful not to misuse the power. Sending out an e-mail to millions of people has become very simple, but although this brute force method may be effective it is no good at the same time.

If you send out 5 million e-mails, you may have ten thousand people who may be interested, which is more than you could reach with traditional methods, but you will have 4.99 million angry users. Unsolicited mails can be compared to unsolicited faxes, but never with radio or television spots or newspaper or web site advertising. Maybe just 5 percent of the 4.99 million users start to complain back to your company that they did not want to receive information from you. But this would result in 249,500 mails, which is far too much to be able to detect the ten thousand who were really interested in your products or services.

The behaviour of sending out millions of e-mails is called "spamming". The senders of the e-mails are usually asking the recipient to buy a product or service of some kind or participate in a get-rich-quick scheme. The senders do not ask their recipients beforehand if they want to receive such mail. Spam mail is often referred to as bulk e-mail, unsolicited e-mail, or junk e-mail.

Spammers collect e-mail address from various sources like newsgroup postings, web pages or from mailing lists. I often receive spam mails offering lists with up to 10 million e-mail addresses for just 500 Dollars. As these addresses are collected automatically by special programs, I suspect that at least half of them are invalid.

Most people consider spamming to be very rude. The Netiquette, a set of rules for the Internet, condemns the activities of spammers (derived from net and etiquette). Legislation in the US and in Europe has not decided yet how to handle spam mails. There has been a lot of activity in the court rooms, but there is no clear guideline in sight. Most countries in Asia, Africa and South America have no regulations on spam mails, so far.

The true problem is the large majority of people who do not know why they received a certain e-mail. Many mails are also cleverly written, as if they were sent to the wrong recipient. These e-mails normally contain tips for online or

Direct Marketing Rules

The following rules help you with your direct marketing offensive:

- **Audience** – On the Internet the audience targets you and not the other way around.

- **Clarification** – Question and confirm any message that appears to contain a critical mistake in typing.

- **Cross-Borders** – The Internet is open to any culture and nation. Be sure not to offend your target audience.

- **Customers** – Use one-to-one marketing technologies to gain information on your customers.

- **Lists** – Don't rent or sell customer lists without written permission.

- **Log Files** – Don't rely on web server log files. Try to find more meaningful data.

- **Privacy** – Privacy is important. Treat any personal information as confidential.

- **Spam** – Never misuse e-mail to spam, it provokes more anger than response.

Table 5.9.

phone services which cost a lot of money. As a rule of thumb: Don't reply to such mails, it just confirms the spammer that the e-mail address is valid and someone is dumb enough to respond. Never buy anything from spammers, no matter how good the offer seems to be. Spammers use false e-mail addresses in most cases. They cannot be trusted; otherwise they would have a web page or a shop somewhere, where people could get more information on the products and services. And even if the spam contains a valid web site, you should send an e-mail to the ISP of the spammer, typically abuse@isp.com.

Most spammers use either completely false addresses, mostly when offering telephone services, or e-mail addresses from free web-based e-mail services, which cannot be traced back to the sender. The worst thing that can happen is that the account of the user will be closed down, but it takes only minutes to set up a new one with the same or a similar service.

One of the most prominent spammers is Sanford "Spamford" Wallace, who also fought in court for his right to use spam for marketing activities. He was famous for sending out mails to millions of people so that complete networks broke down. Spamming activities have decreased over the last few years, as more anti-spamming-tools and new legislation has become available.

Just before Christmas 1998 my father's account was put on hold because someone was using it to "promote" casinos on the Internet. During the holidays no one was available to explain to us why the account was put on hold. It took five days, several e-mails and a phone call to re-activate the Internet connection. Spamming activities are monitored on the Internet, so the Internet accounts of people who do spam will be closed down immediately. In our case someone broke into the account and used it to appear as someone else on the Internet (sometimes called spoofing).

In order to get rid of spam you need to inform your postmaster about the spam mails you have received. In any case you should also send a copy of the mail to the postmaster of the sender's domain.

Typical Spam

```
Hello Folks,
Making Money Could Never Get Easier!
GET EXCITED!!  XXX launched 27 Feb.  Check out the
FASTEST growing Internet Marketing on the Internet.  If
YOU ever wished you were at the beginning of the other
successful online marketing ventures!
NOW is your chance to get in early.
XXX started promoting in the Major Magazine's and USA
Today!!
All spillovers, will go to your downlines.
DON"T GET LEFT BEHIND!!!!!
For more information, click on lower email address and
send it Today!!!
Committed to your Success!
```

Table 5.10.

A little example will demonstrate what needs to be done. Let's say your e-mail is danny@danny.cn (sending e-mails to this address won't do much, as

I haven't got an Internet account in China, and the domain name is not registered at the time of writing); and you have received the spam from spam@spam.org. You should forward the mail that you have received to postmaster@danny.cn and postmaster@spam.org, in addition send mails to the user abuse at these domains. These two people may able to trace back where the e-mail originated and are then able ban the user from the Internet. If the spam contains illegal activities such as a pyramid scheme or phoney investment offers you should contact the appropriate law enforcement authorities.

Have a look at Table 5.10 for an example of spam. This example shows what type of unwanted messages arrive in mail boxes every day. I removed the name of the company and replaced it with XXX, otherwise people will start suing me for spamming in this book ;-). Typical for Spam is writing sentences completely in upper case to get the attention of the reader. Sentences in upper case are like shouting at people, which is considered rude in Netiquette. References to well-known institutions such as USA Today[66] are often cited to add credibility to the offering.

E-mail advertising is still possible using the opt-in mailing service. The opt-in e-mail advertising distribution is a viable option to attain your target market. Other than spam (unsolicited e-mail), an opt-in list only sends e-mail to persons who asked to receive e-mail about that particular subject.

5.10.2 Mailing Lists and Newsletters

Fortunately there are other ways of using direct marketing on the Internet. It is highly important that you provide free information about your products and services to your customers. This can be done via mailing lists, newsletters, newsgroups and chat areas. In any case, the customers must agree to have their e-mails used for newsletters and nobody should be forced to subscribe to a newsgroup or a mailing list.

Although e-mail and chat have been around for quite some time, they are still the most used applications on the Internet. Therefore they are trusted applications which are simple-to-use and can be used by virtually anyone who is online. Although many companies offer products that allow one-to-one marketing on the Web, e-mail was always destined for that kind of business.

E-mail discussion lists and newsletters are explained easily. These e-mails normally are focused around one topic, so people can read news, comments and information provided by other participants of the discussion list. The main difference between the discussion lists and newsletters is that a discussion list has participation from its subscribers, while a newsletter is more of a one-way editorial product. There are discussion lists and newsletters for almost every imaginable business and consumer interest. One such mailing list is the Bugtraq[67] mailing list, which talks about bugs on Unix systems.

---

[66]http://www.usatoday.com/
[67]http://www.bugtraq.com/

Once you have signed up, you start to receive e-mails that are sent to a special address. Anybody who is signed up is able to send in a submission. Some lists also have a moderator who sifts through the incoming messages and sends them on to the subscribers, if appropriate. The e-mail traffic created by mailing lists can vary from a few each day to hundreds each day. When Netscape put up its Mozilla[68] site, I subscribed to their Mozilla mailing list and received up to 500 mails a day. This was overkill. There were too many people who sent out e-mails without any value to me. So I signed off that particular list. The Mozilla people recognized the problem and split up the mailing list into several subtopics, which were more specific and produced less garbage. In addition to this a gateway between mailing lists and newsgroups has been established in order to support push and pull from the users.

The push technology used in this case is the mailing list that sends all messages on to all subscribed users. The pull technology is the newsgroup where users can go to and choose interesting topics and read them. Asking a question works similarly, it can be either sent to the mailing list or posted in the newsgroup. As a result, the subscriber to the mailing list will receive all answers automatically while the newsgroup reader must actively go back to the newsgroup and check for answers.

Newsletters on the other hand are written by the maintainer of the mailing list or by several authors and then collected by the maintainer. The newsletter is sent out periodically, for example each day, each week or each month. The topic of the newsletter is also very specific. I am, for example, signed up to the news.com and the MediaTechBooks[69] newsletters. Back issues of newsletters can normally be retrieved at their respective web sites.

By setting up mailing lists and newsletters about a certain topic you do appear as a qualified person in that particular topic. You may help your user group to understand better one your products or services. If you offer a forum for your customers make sure that a qualified and trained person is on the list as a moderator to represent your company.

Being on mailing lists created by others is also very useful. By contributing helpful information, you can establish yourself and your company as qualified experts. This does not automatically increase your business, but maybe someone will remember your expertize and come back to you in the future.

Implementation of such a discussion list or creating a newsletter is quite simple and does not cost anything, as you already have the infrastructure in place to serve it. All you need to invest is time and some ideas. Before starting up your own newsletter or mailing list, subscribe yourself onto some other mailing lists in order to learn how such a service works.

Mailing lists and newsletters do not have to be for free, but keep in mind, that if you send out information customers have to pay for, it is highly possible

---

[68]http://www.mozilla.org/
[69]http://www.mediatechbooks.de/newsletters/

that they send it on to colleagues and friends without paying for another copy. The enforcement of copyright laws is too expensive if your document is sold at a very low price.

5.10.3 The Power of E-Mail

E-mail can be used to promote your services and products. Just be sure not to spam. Using some more subtle methods will have a much greater effect. One of these methods is to use a signature file for every e-mail that is sent out. Signatures are tolerated on all mailing lists, newsgroups and ordinary e-mail, if you stick to the conventions. The signature should be separated from the mail by adding a line with two dashes, i.e. "--". The signature should not be longer than two lines. Put your name and your business into the signature, include your web site address and you are able to promote your business without harassing anybody. Table 5.11 contains a sample signature. By contributing useful answers in newsgroups, you can very effectively and gently plug your business. It may make sense to create different signature files for different media or target groups, such as different newsgroups or mailing lists. Avoid larger signatures as they annoy many other readers. Although adding graphics may be fun for you, it does not necessarily add value to the readers.

```
          Example: Newsgroup Posting with
                     Signature

Dear Fred,

By holding the mouse button pressed over the back
button of your browser you will see a list of the
previously visited sites, which makes it easier to
jump back more than one site.

I hope this helps,

Danny
--
Danny Amor, Kangaroo Management Centre Ltd.,
Visit http://www.kamacltd.cz/ or send mail to
info@kamacltd.cz.
```

Table 5.11.

Auto-responders are also a very helpful application for your business. If people need, for example, a price list for a certain service or information on a certain product, then they may choose to go to a web site or send an e-mail to a certain address and receive the information via e-mail. Although this may not seem to be helpful, it actually is. Sometimes information on web sites is divided up into several sections, which make it difficult to grab the information and put it into a document. By offering auto-responders it is possible for customers to request information in text format without formatting for the web and graphics. If customers send queries in the form of e-mails to your customer care department, an automated mail should respond and tell them that the e-mail has arrived. And don't forget to put in the URL of your FAQ page, as it may help the customers in finding a response to their question until a human being from the customer care department is able to respond to an e-mail.

You also have better control over your content by offering back issues of a newsletter only via auto-responder. It is then possible to track down all users who are interested in it. You can use this information to offer them a subscription to the newsletter and other products or services you might offer. All these pieces of information must be in the same mail as the newsletter. Do not start sending dozens of e-mails to your customer base. If users request one piece of electronic mail, don't upset them with mail flooding.

Any e-mail arriving in your inbox should be confirmed. If the mail appears to include a critical mistake in typing it should be questioned by sending back a confirmation mail. E-mail messages do not convey voice tones, body postures or other non-textual cues, therefore it is difficult to find out if the content should be taken literally. Some mails contain emoticons such as ":-)", but they may be misunderstood if the other party involved does not know about the meaning of these symbols.

An emoticon (or smiley) is a sequence of ordinary characters, which you can find on your keyboard. Emoticons are often used in digital communication to express an emotion. The Table 5.12 contains some of the more popular emoticons. For a very complete list look at the web site of Smilies Unlimited[70] or check with your favorite search engine for more information.

5.10.4   Opt-in Mailing Lists

A special form of the newsletter is the opt-in mailing list, which was already mentioned briefly. It provides consumers with specific product or service information on request. Unlike spam, the customers have expressed interest in receiving the information. Companies often ask for your e-mail address before you are allowed to download a piece of information or a file. A small tick box is provided, which allows the request of additional information. In many cases it is already ticked, meaning that without additional interaction you will be put onto these opt-in mailing lists.

---

[70]http://www.czweb.com/smilies.htm

Emoticons

As it is difficult to express emotions on the Internet, emoticons have been invented. The following list shows some of the most common emoticons.

:-) Laughing. Joking. Being satisfied.

:) Laughing. Joking. Being satisfied. For lazy people without noses.

:-(Crying out loud. Sad. You aren't joking. You are not satisfied.

;-) Winking Smiley. You don't mean it, even if you are joking.

:-> Follows a really sarcastic remark.

(-: Left handed Smiley.

:-* Kissing Smiley.

Table 5.12.

The major difference between opt-in and spam is that addresses that have been passed on to opt-in mailing list owners are only used for one purpose. Spam mailers reuse the same set of e-mail addresses for any type of product or service abusing the idea of e-mail. Opt-in mailing lists have become the de-facto standard for customer-oriented mass-mailings on the Internet. It is the only form of mass-mailing that is tolerated by customers and governments around the world.

5.10.5   Building an E-Mail Address Database

In order to reach out for new customers you need to know who is online and how they can be reached. A list of people who want to hear from you and your company needs to be built up. The problem is to convince the people to give you their e-mail address and convince them that you are not sending rubbish only, but also some useful information.

Getting people to your site is relatively easy, but convincing them to come back is the more difficult task. Sending a short e-mail to the visitors as a little reminder may help. Customers who have used your services or bought your product are much more willing to buy another service or product from your company, because they already know you and trust your company and the products you manufacture, sell or rent.

The trouble is getting hold of the e-mail address and the permission of the recipient. One of the simplest ways of collecting e-mails is to have a link to an info mailer in your company, e.g. info@yourcompany.com. Invite people to send messages to this address, but without any reason most people won't send you anything.

Adding some type of interaction to your web site makes it easier to convince people to leave their e-mail with you. The quicker the action and the simpler it is to use, the more people will use it. Offer the possibility to receive updates on the web site or offer a free catalogue or a free sample of your product or service in exchange for the e-mail address. Newsletters and mailing lists automatically show the e-mail addresses of the participants. Be careful, though. Many people won't give out their addresses if you do not state clearly what you intend to do with the it. Your privacy policy should be available from every page.

Another way to receive e-mails from customers is to ask their opinion. Either have a set of yes/no questions or request for specific input from them. The customers can express their opinion on a given topic, such as a product or the web site.

Surveys are another possible way to receive information on the users and their addresses. As surveys tend to be more complex, offer something in return, like the results of the survey or a free sample of a product.

Once you have collected a certain amount of e-mail addresses you need to decide what to with them. You need to find a piece of software that allows you to manage the mailing list. Every time you send out a message to your subscribers, try to tell them something that is useful to them, in addition to what is useful to you.

5.11 Choosing the Right ISP

5.11.1 Direct Access to Your Company

Another important issue for your online marketing activities is where the web pages are hosted. Some companies have a direct connection to the Internet via a leased line, other use dial-up lines, which create temporary connections for the time someone is accessing the Internet, so they prefer to have an Internet Service Provider (ISP) to host their web pages.

No matter where your web pages are hosted, you need to be sure that you have direct access to them 24 hours a day, seven days a week. As we have learnt in Chapter 4 in the section on "Dark Sites", changing the information whenever necessary is vital for your company. This applies not only to emergency situations, but also to when there are new products, news or changes within your company. The worst thing that can happen is that news about your company can be found on the web sites of the competitor before it is available on your own web pages.

There are some minimum requirements that you should ask for from your ISP, no matter if the ISP connects your existing or planned networking infrastructure to the Internet or hosts the web pages and your e-mail accounts only. You need to ask your ISP to provide you with information on the reliability of the service. Your connection must be available twenty-four hours a day, seven days a week. In your contract you need to define how much downtime is acceptable for your company per year and what the ISP is willing to pay, if the service is down for a longer period. If this is not defined, you and your company may run into financial trouble, once your online business has become the portal to your company.

Choosing an ISP

When choosing an ISP, check out the following:

- **Reliability** – An ISP should be up and running more than 99.9 percent of the time each year.

- **Performance** – Don't believe the marketing hype of the ISPs. Get performance data from third parties.

- **Tech Support** – Establish the ISP as your partner. Create strong links between your company and the ISP.

- **Price** – Price is not everything. Look out for an ISP that offers complete service.

Table 5.13.

5.11.2   Dial-up Connections

A dial-up connection is suitable for companies that have outsourced their web activities and require Internet connection for downloading mails and accessing some web pages daily. With this style of connection, you use a modem and existing phone lines to reach an ISP. There are thousands of ISPs who provide dial-up access to the Internet. The cost for a dial-up connection range from fifteen to thirty Euro or Dollars and do not depend on the type of connection you want. Analogue modems and ISDN connections do not differ in access cost.

The List[71] contains a very large list of providers on a global basis. ISPs can be searched for by country, state, or area code.

Before picking an ISP you should check if the ISP has a point of presence (POP) in your town or near enough to allow you to make a local phone call. In the United States then only the cost for the ISP would need to be paid, in Europe and other parts of the world, the phone cost needs to be added.

Another important issue with dial-up is the availability of the service. It does not help if the service is very cheap, if the line is busy all the time and you cannot get through to check your e-mail and look for a web page. A good ISP will not have a busy line. Once you have decided on an ISP, pick up the phone and dial the phone number of the Internet access several times a day during the times when you hope to get online. This will help to ensure that you made the right decision.

Most ISPs offer additional services, such as additional e-mails and web hosting. Although this is very useful it is not really necessary, as you can get these services for free on the Internet. If you do not need your own domain name then it will be sufficient to have access to the Internet, but once your company web site is up and running all your employees will get an e-mail belonging to your domain. The web site may not necessarily be hosted by your local ISP, which grants you access to the Internet. Often local access and web hosting are provided by two different companies. The Internet makes it easy to go for a company on the other side of the globe to provide web hosting. This may be much cheaper than a local provider.

5.11.3 Leased Lines

Organizations with a significant number of employees requiring access to the Internet for their e-mail and for web access will be more interested in a dedicated line. This will give them constant access to the Internet, which may be cheaper in the end, if much traffic is generated throughout the day.

Many companies start with a dedicated line consisting of two ISDN b channels, giving your company the maximum of 128 kilobytes/s. Although this speed is good enough to handle e-mail and some web access, it will break down as soon as you get more than twenty people who are heavily browsing the web. A local web cache and proxy will help you to reduce the amount of traffic that is generated, but you won't get around the fact that you will need at least a "T1" connection, which provides up to 1.5 Mb/sec of throughput. The ISP charges a flat monthly rate for the connection, which includes their fee and the cost of a dedicated line from your location to their nearest POP. The dedicated line will be provided usually by the local phone carrier. Most ISPs will be able to arrange this for you.

To be sure that your provider does not become the bottleneck in your Internet connection, you should only consider those ISP's who have significant

---

[71]http://thelist.internet.com/

backbone capacities and who are directly connected to the Internet's Network Access Points, or NAPs. Although there are many ISPs available only very few operate their own high-speed backbone networks. The other ISPs are connected to these backbones via larger ISPs. The choice of the right ISP will guarantee you the best speed possible.

This can be done by examining their backbone network. It just does not make any sense to buy a dedicated line from an ISP who is not capable of passing through the traffic fast enough. Therefore ask your ISP to provide you with a backbone diagram showing you how their POPs are connected to the backbone. This allows you to understand how your connection enters into the backbone and how your traffic will be routed to other parts of the Internet.

The ISP should provide you with the required hardware to set up the leased line, such as an preconfigured router that just needs to be switched on to enable Internet connectivity. The ISP should also offer you a selection of security products, such as firewalls to protect your company Intranet, which you make vulnerable by a direct Internet connection. Although it costs less to operate a firewall yourself, you may not be in the position to do this, because of missing knowledge or resources, just as with web hosting. Because of the dedicated line, you would be able to handle the web site yourself, except where resources are missing.

5.11.4 Performance Issues

The performance of your provider needs to be excellent, for your services and for the connection of your customers. Don't get mislead by ISPs offering 155 MBit/s connections. 155 MBit/s is very fast, but do you really know how many customers share the bandwidth of 155 MBit/s at the same time? If there are ten thousand customers hooked up to the line, the average speed will drop to 0.0155 MBit/s (or 16 KBit/s). If you have ten concurrent visitors each of them will get an average of 1.6 KBit/s (Normal modems did 56 KBit/s at the time of this writing). In most cases some people will get higher connection rates, and others won't get through to the server at all. This can disrupt your service and will anger your customers.

The ISP should also be connected directly to an Internet backbone, which allows much higher transfer rates; the more computers are in-between the ISP and the backbone, the slower the connection will be.

The ISP should also offer good tech support, both reachable via telephone and Internet. In your company you need someone who understands the issues of connecting to the Internet. But this person needs a counterpart on the ISP side. Select one from your staff and one from the ISP staff to act as a team. Most problems with your Internet connectivity can only be resolved if both parties involved solve the problem together.

5.11.5   Keeping Internet Costs Low

There are very many cheap offerings, but in most cases, some extra money for higher quality services is well invested. ISPs should also be able to help you implement your business strategy. Check out if your ISP offers more than just pure hosting and connectivity. Some ISPs offer to increase traffic to your site by submitting it to search engines or directories. If you have to pay for it, stay away from these offers. Good ISPs submit your URL to at least some of the most popular search engines for free.

If you are not able to calculate the monthly costs for your Internet connection, because an ISP has a very complicated pricing structure, then there may be many hidden costs involved. Always ask for flat-rate fees. These prices may seem to be higher, but in many cases they turn out to be cheaper in the end. Many companies forget to add the costs for the telephone company. Although this may not be an issue in the US, it is certainly one for other countries.

Dial-up connections are not useful in most cases. A leased line will have higher initial costs, but the monthly costs are much lower and are fixed. The costs for dial-up connections cannot be calculated in advance, so expect the highest price possible. If your dial-up connections costs 5 cents a minute, the maximal costs are $5 \times 60 \times 24 \times 30 = 216000$ cents (or 2160 Euro or Dollar). Of course you would not expect to use the line 24 hours a day, but don't be surprised if your costs are around this limit every month.

Part II

E-business Applications

Chapter 6

SEARCH ENGINES
AND PORTALS

6.1 Searching the Internet

6.1.1 Finding Something on the Net

Searching for information on the Internet is difficult for many people, so this section will try to explain how search engines work and how to find the item that one is looking for. For your online business it is very important to understand how search engines search and how people try to look for certain things on the Internet.

Some people who use a web browser just enter a keyword where the URL is normally entered. Sometimes this leads to good results. The reasons are explained easily. If you enter a word into a web browser, the browser first adds "http://" to it and tries to find a web page. If that does not work, it adds ".com" at the end and then "www." after the "http://" part. So entering "motorcycles" will lead you eventually to "http://www.motorcycles.com/", which leads to the Honda web site in the US. If you search for Harley Davidson motorcycles then you could enter "Harley-Davidson" and the browser would expand the name to "http://www.harley-davidson.com/", which leads you to the web site of the Harley Davidson manufacturer. Some older browsers do not support the expansion of keywords, so people need to add these attributes manually, but adding "http://www." and ".com" to the keyword is not that difficult. That was the reason why in the early years so many people registered domain names without using them, they had recognized the value it will have in the future.

The fact that web browsers try to guess what you are doing is used by a new service called HTTP2[1]. They seem to have invented a new protocol for transferring information between a web server and a web browser, but in reality they do something completely different. You can go to their web site and register a domain name that uses http2// instead of http://. The trick is that

---

[1]http://www.http2.com/

194

they omit the colon. So if you have a site registered at http2, the "URL" may look like this: http2//ebusiness. The idea of http2 is exploiting a feature of most browsers, that if they do not find an address http://http2//ebusiness, it expands it to http://www.http2.com//ebusiness, which is then redirected to the site you have registered at HTTP2.

If you are looking for a specific item, just type in the name and see if there is a web site with the corresponding information. If there is not such a web site, then try out brand names associated with your search. If you are living in Germany and require Information on ties ("Krawatte" is a tie in German), you could try http://www.krawatte.de/ and you will go to an online shop that sells ties and gives information on how to use ties properly. If you are interested in getting more information on Philips products in the Netherlands you could try http://www.philips.nl/ and will land on the web site of Philips consumer products, Ferrari fans in Italy go to http://www.ferrari.it/ in order to buy merchandise or become a member in the Ferrari fan or owners club. Depending on the country you live in you will have other ideas how to find your information. Some companies, especially smaller-to-medium enterprises, prefer to use the top level domain (TLD) of the country of origin. As a rule of thumb: American companies use mainly .com, all others may use it, but not necessarily. If you search for a company in France, then use ".fr" as the suffix.

Most search engines on the web have a basic search form and a more complex search functionality that allows more in-depth search. Most search engines allow Boolean operations, by combining terms using "AND", "OR", or "NOT". If you want all words to be present in a document you are looking for, you can link the keywords with the "AND" command. If you use the "OR", any of the keywords need to be present in the document you are looking for. By using "NOT", you are able to exclude words, which you do not want to appear in the search results. If you do not give any Boolean expression, most search engines will default to "OR".

Some search engines allow the use of "+" and "-", which basically allows you to perform the same actions as the Boolean expressions. A "+" preceding a term means that it must be present in the search result. A "-" means that you do not want it to be present.

In addition to these standard search features, it is possible to truncate words and use an asterisk ("*") to complete the word and find multiple forms of a given word. Using quotes around several words it is possible to specify that words must appear next to each other in retrieved items. These advanced search tips vary from search engine to search engine. Before using any search engine, it is helpful to read the FAQ of the search engine you are going to use. The search results get much more exact and the amount of time required for searching is reduced significantly.

6.1.2   Different Types of Search Engines

If you do not find the required information using the tips from the previous section, then you need to consult an online service to find the piece of information you were looking for. Three different types of services have been established over the years: Crawler, directories and meta search engines.

The first crawler was created back in 1993. It was called the World Wide Worm. It crawled from one site to the next and indexed all pages by saving the content of the web pages into a huge database. Crawlers or spiders visit a web page, read it, and then follow links to other pages within the site and even follow links to other sites. Web crawlers return to each site on a regular basis, such as every month or two, to look for changes. Everything a crawler finds goes into a database, which people are able to query.

The advantage of the web crawlers is that they have an extensive database with almost the complete internet indexed in it. The disadvantage is that you get thousands of web pages as a response for almost any request.

Web directories work a little different. First of all they contain a structured tree of information. All information entered into this tree is either entered by the webmaster who wants to announce his new web page or by the directory maintainer who looks at the web pages submitted. The directories where webmasters can submit both the URL (Uniform Resource Locator) and the description normally contain more misleading information.

Getting into most web directories is a combination of luck and quality. Although anyone is able to submit a web page, there is no guarantee that a certain page will be included. Some directories charge for submission, which is basically a rip-off.

Some crawlers maintain an associated directory. If your site is in the directory, the ranking of your web site normally will be higher, as it is already pre-classified. Many directories work with crawlers together, in order to deliver results, when nothing can be found in the directory.

Meta search engines do not have a database with URLs and descriptions. Instead they have a database of search engines. If you enter your keywords into a meta search engine it will send out requests to all the directories and crawlers it has stored in its database. The meta search engines with a more sophisticated application in the background are able to detect double URLs which come back from the various search engines and present only a single URL to the customer.

6.1.3   Net Robots

In the early stages of the Internet web surfing had been a nice hobby by individuals who could choose from a handful of useful web addresses. But with the growth of the Internet it has become more difficult to find the right information through simple browsing. Programs that behave like web browsers are far more efficient by browsing through the information and storing the content at the same time in a form that makes it easy to retrieve afterwards. These programs are called crawlers, robots or spiders.

A crawler retrieves a document and then retrieves recursively all documents linked to that particular document. While traversing the document, the crawler indexes the information according to predefined criteria. The information goes into searchable databases. Internet users are then able to query these databases to retrieve certain information. The robots crawl the Internet 24 hours a day and try to index as much information as possible.

In order to keep the databases up-to-date, the crawlers revisit links in order to verify if they are still up and running or have been removed. Dead links happen, when users move information or give up their online presence. In this case the information in the database needs to be removed.

Some specialized crawlers wander around and collect information for statistical analysis, such as the NetCraft[2] (see Figure 6.1) robot that collects information on the web servers used on the Internet.

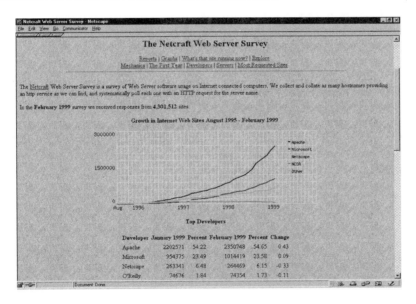

Figure 6.1. Result of the NetCraft Robot

Other robots perform site mirroring activities. Software archives, for example, are mirrored on a daily basis, to reduce the load on a single server and spread it out to many servers, which are on the Internet. Another reason is that it is easier to copy the new information once and then make it available to customers in a special country, instead of letting them download the infor-

---

[2]http://www.netcraft.co.uk/

mation from a far more distant server. Tucows[3] uses this technology to mirror shareware and freeware programs throughout the world, in order to guarantee fast download times for every user.

The Robots Exclusion Standard

The Robots Exclusion Standard defines how robots should behave on the web and how you can prevent robots from visiting your site. Although these rules cannot be enforced, most Internet robots do adhere to this standard. If you want robots to ignore some of the documents on your web server (or even all documents on the web server), you need to create a file called `robots.txt`, which needs to be placed in the root directory of the web server. You can go to any web server and try to see if there is a robots.txt available (just try http://www.gallery-net.com/robots.txt, for example).
A sample robots.txt could look like this:
```
User-agent:  *
Disallow:  /cgi-bin/
```
This simple file disallows access to the `/cgi-bin/` directory on the web server for all (marked by the asterisk) robots scanning the site. By protecting the /cgi-bin/ directory you make sure that no documents from that directory are read by robots and prevents these documents from appearing in search engine results.

Table 6.1.

Crawlers perform a very useful task, but they consume a large part of the bandwidth on the network, which can create frustration to the end user. Crawlers with programming errors can also create unwanted denial of service attacks on certain web servers, as they are trying to retrieve information at a speed rate that is far too high for that server. But the major problem is the lack of intelligence. A crawler can't really decide which information is relevant and which isn't. Therefore combining web crawler results with results from online directories will give the end customers the best search results.

There are also some problems with robot technology on the Internet. Certain implementations of robots have willingly or unwillingly overloaded networks and servers in the past. Some robots had bugs and started to flood

---

[3]http://www.tucows.com/

servers with requests, other robots have been tuned intentionally to behave like this. Human interaction can also be a problem, as a human may misconfigure a robot or not understand what impact the configuration will have for contacted servers.

Although there are several problems, you can protect your site by implementing the Robot Exclusion standard on your web page (see Table 6.1). Most robots are managed well and cause no problems. They offer a valuable service to the Internet community.

6.1.4 Using a Search Engine

The usage of all three search engines is the same and actually very simple. You are normally provided with a text field, where you enter your keywords. The important things are the keywords. Get them right and you will get the answer right. It is best to start with general keywords and then add details.

If you are, for example, looking for camp sites in Italy, try the following: Use the following keywords "Camping Italy", then if this does not produce a useful response add some more details like the region "Camping Italy Tuscany Pisa Beach". The more keywords you add the fewer results you will get (in some cases you won't get any results, so just retry with some other keywords or less keywords). Also try keywords in different languages (e.g. "Toskana", "Toscana" instead of "Tuscany" or "Italien", "Italia" instead of "Italy"). This is often very useful, but has the disadvantage that you need to speak that particular language to understand the web page.

Which search engines suits your needs best, depends on your requirements. It also depends on the quality of the material you want to gather. If you need a large number of web pages with many different aspects of the desired topic, then go for the crawlers. You can collect the information and use data mining procedures to evaluate the content. If you prefer only some good pages then go for the directories and if you need a mixture of both then go for the meta searches. Prefer local search machines to global ones if you are searching for country or language specific information.

Finding the web pages of relatives and friends is easy. Just use any of the above described search engines and enter the first and last name as keywords. Provide additional information like the names of the kids, the street address or anything else you connect to the person. If a person has got a homepage you normally will find the e-mail address on that page. If the person does not have a homepage you can look up e-mail addresses on e-mail search engines.

In order to find the telephone number, you may find it on the homepage. If the person has an e-mail address, just send an e-mail and ask. Otherwise have a look into the telephone directories on the Internet.

Finding files is easy. If you know the producer or distributor then go to the appropriate homepage. Patches for PhotoShop can be found at Adobe's web page. New levels of the game Worms can be downloaded from the web site of the producer Team 17[4]. If you are looking for shareware, freeware and public domain programs than go to one of the program search engines.

6.1.5   Adding Information to Search Engines

Web sites need to be announced in order to appear in the search engine results. Therefore the webmaster has to go to the search engine and submit the URL. Depending on the type of search engine, either a human being or a computer will look at your web pages and will decide if it will add it to the database. It takes a few seconds for a crawler to look at all your pages and store the relevant information into the database. A directory will need up to a month to check out your web pages. Submitting the URL to every single search engine will take up too much time, so some people started developing submission tools. Most of them want a lot of money for submission, but some are free, such as the Broadcaster[5] service in the UK.

Chapter 5 contains more information on submitting URLs to search engines. In this subsection we want to concentrate on the way search engines classify a web page. Most search engines first look at the number of appearances of a certain keyword on a given web page. The next thing they look for is if the keyword appears in the domain name (such as www.keyword.com) or in the URL (such as http://www.blabla.com/keyword/bla.html). Then the search engine checks the title of web page and looks to see if it can spot the keyword there. The important thing is the meta-data that you can add to every web page (see next subsection). If the search engine is able to find a particular keyword in every field mentioned here, the page will be classified as very useful to the customer.

Professor Attardi[6] at the University of Pisa[7] developed a methodology for search engines in order to weigh the relevance of web pages. The first search engine to implement this methodology was Arianna[8] in Italy. In addition to the above-mentioned requirements, it counts the number of links pointing to a given web page. The more people link to a certain web page, the more important and relevant it is. This helps presenting the most relevant pages first.

Having an affiliate network that points back to your company therefore will result in a much higher relevance for your company compared to all your affiliates, as they do not link between each other.

6.1.6   Adding Value through Meta-Data

By adding meta-data to every single HTML document on your web site, you enhance the probability that a search engine shows your page for a certain re-

---

[4]http://www.team17.com/
[5]http://www.broadcaster.co.uk/
[6]http://www.di.unipi.it/ attardi/
[7]http://www.unipi.it/
[8]http://www.arianna.it/

quest. The meta-data is stored in the so-called "meta-tags". Meta-tags contain information which is not rendered visible by the browser, but contains additional information on the document, such as information on the content, the author, the software that was used to create the document or the keywords that are relevant on that particular page. The <meta> tag is used within the <head> tag to embed document meta-information not defined by other HTML elements. The META element is used to identify properties of a document (e.g., author, expiration date, a list of key words, etc.) and assign values to those properties. At least two meta-tags should be present on all pages: description and keywords.

Using Meta-Tags

The following example shows how meta-tags could be used on a web page about FlashPix. Four meta-tags are used:

- **author** – The author of the content.

- **generator** – The program used to create the web page.

- **description** – A short description of the content.

- **keywords** – Keywords related to the content.

```
<HEAD>
<META HTTP-EQUIV="Content-Type" CONTENT="text/html; charset=iso-8859-1">
<META NAME="Author" CONTENT="Daniel Amor: daniel_amor@hp.com">
<META NAME="Generator" CONTENT="BBEdit 4.5">
<META NAME="Description" CONTENT="This page explains the usage of Flashpix. There is a demo and links to other
Flashpix pages.">
<META NAME="Keywords" CONTENT="FlashPix, Java, JavaScript, Demo, Usage">
<TITLE>Flashpix</TITLE>
</HEAD>
```

Table 6.2.

The description tag contains one or more sentences describing shortly the content of the web page. The summary is shown as the search result, instead of the first few sentences which are on the page, resulting in a much faster understanding of what the page is about. The keywords tag helps search engines to decide on the relevance of a certain web page for a given keyword. If you add the right keywords to the search, the search engines will show your page much earlier in the listing. Add keywords in all languages that are relevant to you. Other meta-information that is useful to know is the author of the web page. Add the author tag and enter the name and e-mail of the responsible person for a certain web page and people will know who to ask if they have questions about the web page.

Infoseek[9], for example, is able to search for meta-tags. It is possible to look for all web pages which have been written by a certain person. By entering "author:amor" you will get a list of web pages that have been created by people with the name of "amor", such as myself. Programmers of web utilities are able to see how many web pages have been created with their tool. Bare Bones Software[10], the maker of BBEdit, may count the web pages by using "generator:bbedit", for example.

Meta-Tags should also be multi-lingual. Add keywords in all languages you or your friends, family or employees know. Look up keywords in dictionaries in order to extend the reach of your information. Especially if your information is of value to many customers around the world as multi-lingual and cross-lingual search engines are not the standard yet.

6.1.7 Specialized Searches

In addition to general web searches, many specialized search engines have established themselves. These search engines focus on a special file type and produce far better results than general search engines ever could. Before the invention of the world wide web, FTP sites had been very popular. These sites contained lots of files that could be downloaded. At that time a program called Archie was very popular which allowed the search for file names. Today nobody knows Archie anymore, but file search engines are still very popular. Sites such as shareware.com[11], filez.com[12] and Aminet[13] allow the search for computer programs and data (images, sounds, fonts, etc.). Every file that is uploaded to one of these sites is accompanied by a short summary of the function and some keywords, which make the search simple.

One of the most popular file formats is MP3, which contains music. The music is stored in a highly compressed format and has almost CD quality. Although distributing copyrighted music over the Internet is illegal, many sites offer complete sets of CDs that can be downloaded. No matter what you are looking for, on the Internet it is possible to find any CD. It is possible to download the music and put them onto your hard disk or burn them onto a CD. The music industry opposes the creation of these search engines, but can't do much about them. One of the most popular MP3 search engines can be found at Ly-

---

[9]http://www.infoseek.com/

[10]http://www.barebones.com/

[11]http://www.shareware.com/

[12]http://www.filez.com/

[13]http://www.aminet.org/

cos[14]. A meta-search engine for MP3 is also available at 123mp3.com[15], which allows not only to search over several dedicated MP3 search engines, but also to search for videos, lyrics and web sites.

Newsgroups are very popular, but without a search engine it is not possible to find a certain thread on a given subject. Every day tens of thousands of messages are posted on the newsgroups, therefore high quality full text search engines are needed to retrieve the relevant data. DejaNews[16] is one example, that not only allows you to search for online postings, but also enables the users to post new messages.

6.1.8   People Search Engines

Private investigators are able to use the Internet to research personal information on people. Finding postal addresses, telephone numbers and e-mail addresses has become very easy through the use of specialized search engines. Generic search engines will find this information only, if it is stored on web pages, but most databases use dynamic web page creation to present the data, which cannot be crawled by web spiders. Four11[17] allows the entry of a first and last name to retrieve the e-mail address of a person, TeleAuskunft[18] allows customers to search for telephone numbers and postal addresses in Germany. So far no telephone book has been established on the Internet that has phone numbers from all countries around the world. A meta-search engine on phone books will be able to resolve this problem rather quickly, but nobody has thought about that yet.

Although none of the databases at present compromise the privacy of a person, the sum of the results can present a very detailed picture of a person. In Europe only telephone numbers are available on the Internet due to very restrictive privacy legislation. The United States has a very lax privacy legislation which allows very private investigations.

Infospace[19], for example, allows the retrieval of phone numbers, postal addresses, financial data, such as credit card limits, if a person has been in court, driving license information and even the names of neighbors. Although the service is not free of charge, it enables anyone with a credit card to become a private investigator without even leaving the house. By using chat groups it is possible to talk to friends, neighbors or even the target person directly using masquerading techniques. Tracking people around the net has also become possible through new technologies.

This information can be used to track a person. Using the social security

---

[14]http://mp3.lycos.com/

[15]http://www.123get.com/

[16]http://www.dejanews.com/

[17]http://www.four11.com/

[18]http://www.teleauskunft.de/

[19]http://www.infospace.com/

number it is even possible to go to other databases that are restricted to the person with the number. Just enter the number and you will be presented with some personal data.

The web site of DigDirt[20] goes even further. It researches even more private details, such as visits to the doctors' and credit card invoices, which make the person even more transparent. How often a person has been to the doctors' tells something about the state of health and the credit card invoice shows quite clearly, where the person has been over the last few months, for example, and how much money has been spent.

Additional information can be found in the local newspaper. Most newspapers offer online search functionality where you can access the complete database of the newspaper, where you may find more information on a certain person.

This information could be used by an employer to evaluate if a candidate is suitable for a certain job. An online retailer could do some background checking on a customer before sending out the ordered goods. Many privacy organizations are worried by this development. More information on privacy issues on the Internet and how to resolve them can be found in Chapter 10.

6.1.9 Tracking Search Result Positions

As every search engine returns a whole set of web pages for every query it is important to appear within the first ten results. Therefore it is important to verify from time to time the position of your web site in every important search engine. In order to move up in the ranking of the search engine, check out the web pages which are ranked higher than your site. Download the web site and look through the HTML code, the content and write down the URL. All these pieces of information influence the position of a web site, as we have already learned before.

If you are interested in increasing the position on various search engines, then you need to keep track of what you have submitted. Every time you change your web site you should re-submit the URL to every search engine. Web crawlers will automatically come back to your site at regular intervals, but by re-submitting the URL, it will be updated in that particular instant.

This, of course, can also be done automatically. Several Internet applications allow the automatic tracking of positions in search engines. One is called WebPosition[21]. This program allows you to find the exact position of each of your pages in every major search engine. In addition to this it gives automatic advice on how to improve the current position by comparing your page with the rules of the search engine for an exact match.

Reports are generated automatically and search engine positions can be compared between the reports. WebPosition has a special function built in,

---

[20]http://www.digdirt.com/

[21]http://www.webposition.de/

which is called "Mission Creation". With this feature it is possible to create web pages that are ranked very high on a given search engine for certain keywords. If you want to move a certain web page into the top ten of Altavista when people enter a certain keyword, then the program will help you through a simple process of changing the current web page to become the top addresses for that keyword.

In combination with a submission tool, you are able to increase traffic on your web page and direct more relevant people to your web site. One such tool is Submit-It[22], which enables online and offline submission. All the relevant information is entered into a form, which is then sent out to a large bunch of search engines. The program does nothing else than you could do by manual submission, but the automatic submission is much faster.

6.2 The Future of Searching

6.2.1 Issues with Search Engines

Searching by keyword is the most common method of using a search engine, but the problem with keywords are the relatively imprecise results and the return of a lot of irrelevant information. Keywords may have more than one meaning and search results may be found only by using a synonym of the keyword. The method of browsing on the other hand takes too much to find the relevant information. Directories like Yahoo try to circumvent the problem, but the manual process of classifying material on the web takes up too much time, resulting in very few search results, as not everything on the web can be classified. Therefore new paradigms of searching are needed as well as new software that is able to categorize web sites automatically.

The majority of search engines come from the United States and have specialized in English resources and information reflecting the American culture. People who do not speak English or who are non-native speakers have therefore many disadvantages on the web.

The centralized approach to information retrieval has extreme difficulty in coping with the multi-lingual and multi-cultural nature of the Information Society. The Internet has become a success throughout the world, but the American search engines operate with a US-centric company structure and tend to concentrate upon the English language. Although many search engines have subsidiaries in many other countries, like Japan or Italy, the way the information is presented is the American way and may not reflect the logic of the people who are using it.

National search engines in Russia or France, for example, have to deal with far smaller sets of information and specialize in the cultural and linguistic environments which they know best. Their disadvantage is that the queries

---

[22]http://www.submit-it.com/

are in Russian or French and the search results contain only a small subset of possible results on the web, as they are restricted to the language. This strongly reduces the possibility of using the Web as a source for the world wide diffusion of information.

Larger search engines, such as Altavista are able to perform multi-lingual searches, which presents search results in multiple languages. This is good, if the searcher knows all the languages, but if, for example, an Indian finds a Japanese web site on the search topic, this may not be helpful.

Text documents that are in special formats (such as Postscript or Star Office Documents) are unreachable for many search engines, as the textual information is embedded into the binary structure of the particular file format. The same applies to scanned documents, Java applets and video/audio clips. The content of these file formats is hidden from search engines today. Only if the description of the file format is known and included into the search engine is it possible to add the content for certain document types. This is relatively easy; just a matter of work. Infoseek[23], for example, is able to index the content of Word documents. More difficult is the inclusion of content that is hidden in applications, as there is no way to tell where the information may be hidden.

The research and development in information and data retrieval is aimed at improving the effectiveness and efficiency of retrieval. Individual and parallel development for database management systems has left this sector without a centralized vision and co-ordination between the different types of search engines. Search engines on the Internet are very specific and not able to cope with multiple database formats and file types. In order to make searches complete a search engine needs to search over text, documents, images, sounds and all other media formats. So the database integration will be the single most important objective for the future of intelligent search engines.

In order to receive better search results, it is not only necessary to improve the search engine technology, but also the user interfaces, depending on the type of user (such as casual, researcher, users with special requirements).

Neural networks will be used more commonly in the future to organize large, unstructured collections of information. Autonomy[24] is a search engine that uses the model of the adaptive probabilistic concept to understand large documents. The system is able to learn from each piece of information it has discovered. By putting together a set of not so relevant resources, the set should get the large picture by reading through all the documents. Therefore it is necessary to rank information by importance.

This allows zones in a portal to be created automatically (for an explanation of zone see later in this chapter) or with a minimum of manual intervention, instead of manually creating the zones in a way Yahoo, for example, does it. In order to achieve this goal, such systems need to employ technologies for concept

---

[23]http://www.infoseek.com/
[24]http://www.autonomy.com/

clustering and concept profiling.

6.2.2 EuroSearch

One project to overcome the above mentioned limitations of search engines in the EuroSearch[25] project. EuroSearch is a federation of national search engines which gives much better results and is more suited to the challenges of the multi-lingual and multi-cultural global Internet. The founding members are national search engines from Italy, Spain and Switzerland. The multi-lingual approach allows a query to be entered in the preferred language of the researcher and the search engine takes care of the search on the search engines in the other languages.

Every national site that is part of the federation remains in the country of origin and is maintained by a native-speaker who will ensure that the search works in their own language. At the same time, the EuroSearch framework tries to remain open to other countries and services who would like to become part of the initiative.

The framework allows provision, access and retrieval of documents that are not only in English, but also in a variety of other European languages. This makes it easier to find information provided in other languages than English that may contain the information the searcher was looking for. It enables people who do not speak English to retrieve information and information providers to present their information in their mother tongue, as they can express themselves more clearly in that language.

Other than with search engines that retrieve information only in one language, the cross-language search results need to be presented in a form that the searcher understands. The description of the documents should be presented in the language of the query. Cross-language retrieval is not the same as multi-lingual. The multi-lingual systems support many different languages, but cross-language retrieval systems provide the increased functionality of retrieving relevant information written in a different language than the user's query. The query is translated to the target language and then the search engine is queried. In order to broaden the search a thesaurus for every language needs to be incorporated into every search engine and automatic classification procedures need to be implemented.

The EuroSearch project wants to develop techniques and resources to implement a cross language search engine and to improve retrieval and classification technologies. The ultimate goal is to create a federation of national search engines that work together in order to deliver better search results. A prototype is currently being built that provides an interface to formulate queries and present understandable results in the users' preferred languages. This requires the system to translate not only the queries into a meta-language, but also translate the results and the resulting web pages into the query language

[25]http://eurosearch.iol.it/

to make it accessible to the user. This approach makes the whole web more accessible to non-English speakers.

EuroSearch will simplify the access to information on the Internet in and across different languages. A simplified and multi-lingual access to the wide variety of information on the Web will improve cultural exchanges and knowledge integration between European countries. This means a significant improvement in the quality of the available information for every user. This will not only have an impact in Europe, but in all non-English countries on the acceptance of the Internet.

6.2.3   Natural Language Searches

The idea of natural language access to a database is not new, but still hasn't been achieved. Most search engines are not able to handle questions such as "Where can I get light bulbs?" or "How many legs does a horse have?" The answer to the questions can be found for certain on the web, but the search engines are not able to understand the questions. If you have a page that has a question and an answer on it, then you may succeed, but this is a rare case. Instead of receiving the answer "At shop XY in Z" or "four", you would receive a long list of search results, as the search engines split up the question into keywords. Every word in the question is then searched for.

The difference between conventional and natural language search engines is the way pages get indexed. Unlike a conventional database, the symbolic approach to natural language processing involves treating words as nodes in a semantic network. The emphasis is then placed on the meaning of the words instead of the single words.

A natural language processor (NLP) that is required for an Internet search engine needs a large and concise dictionary. Words are represented then by the way they are used (this approach is called case-based reasoning). Each occurrence of a word is treated in an individual way, resulting in extremely large databases, as every word can have up to a few thousand individual meanings. The strength of case-based reasoning is in it's flexibility. Since databases are based on semantics, imprecise querying may still retrieve information which is close to the answer but does not exactly match the question.

The second approach to natural language search engines is to add a thesaurus to the database. A query on "plant" will also look up "factory" and "flower" as both of them are related to "plant", even though they have totally different meanings. This entails a significant improvement in precision and recall rates over current search methods. Improving the syntax analysis is also very useful. By analyzing the syntax of a given query, it is possible to compare it with stored patterns in the database. Altavista supports natural language queries, and the results get better every day. Figure 6.2 shows the results for the question "Where can I find information on natural language?" Only simple questions are supported, but it is already the next step to complex natural

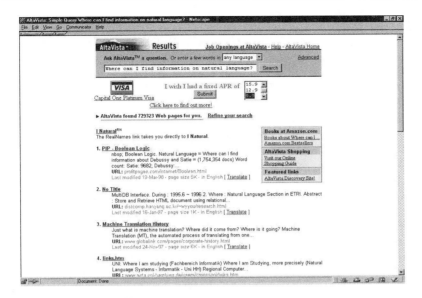

Figure 6.2. Natural Language Search on Altavista

language search engines.

6.2.4 Image Search Engines

On the Internet are many images, but unfortunately it is not possible to search for them in a similar way, as it is possible to search for web pages or music files. Other than with web pages, where I can use text to describe what I am searching for, and music, where I can name the artist or the title (I would have trouble if searching for a sequence of notes), images on the web are in most cases not of artistic value, otherwise it would be possible to search for the artist or the title.

In many cases people search for a boat, a house, a dog to illustrate a text, for example. Image search engines on the Internet today are using the information that accompanies a picture, such as the file name (e.g. "href='cat.jpg'"), the alternative text (e.g. "alt='this is a picture of a cat'") or the text that is next to the image ("the following image displays a cat"). As long as your search is very generic, the existing image search engines work very well. More and more people add the HTML alt-tag to provide additional information on the image, which helps finding the right information. But unfortunately the provision of alternative text (i.e., using the ALT tag) for textual WWW images is in most cases wrong or incomplete.

The problem arises, as soon as you search for more specific images. "A red cat with a little ball" could be a very common request. Although it is highly unlikely that the filename will contain all this information, the alt-text may contain it and the accompanying text as well, but don't be too sure. Another issue may be that the cat with the red ball is on a picture among many other things. It could well be that the web page is talking about balls and will not the mention the cat, or talk about a table, where the cat and the ball are placed on top. In these cases image search engines that rely on textual information will fail miserably. Many images contain text that could help to index the image correctly, the problem is extracting the textual information from an image. The logo of Tucows[26], for example, contains the alt-tag "Moooo...". This information is not helping anyone. Extracting the text from the logo would help indexing the image correctly.

Apostolos Antonacopoulos[27] of the University of Liverpool in the UK started a project in 1998 to extract textual information from images on the web. Although humans are able to extract the information from images very easily, there is no way to automate the analysis on such text at present.

In order to index and validate the information in an image, the characters embedded in the image need to be extracted and then they need to be recognized. The task of identifying the text appears to be similar to the traditional techniques in optical character recognition (OCR). But there are several differences. The text in images has the advantage over scanned text, in such a way that it contains no distortions from digitization. But other than scanned documents, the backgrounds on images tend to be complex (compared with a white paper) and the characters are very small, in order to keep the resolution low. A web image is presented in 72 dpi, while scanned documents are at a resolution of 300 dpi. If using a lossy compression algorithm, such as in the JPEG format, compression and quantization artifacts appear, making it more difficult to extract a character and then recognize it.

Previous efforts to analyze text in images restricted themselves to single color text and ignored very small characters. As they were globally analyzing the image file, the performance was bad and it took a long time to complete. As only very few characters use a single color and very many texts are small this approach was not resolving the problem. Mr Antonacopoulos' approach is different. The algorithms used allow the identification of text with gradient color or textures on complex background textures. This allows the retrieval of textual information from images.

The results are achieved through several steps. First of all, the number of colors needs to be reduced. Although GIF images use only 256 colors, JPEGs use up to sixteen million colors. By reducing the number of colors, it is easier to detect text within the image. By dropping bits, the number of colors is reduced to 512 colors. After having reduced the number of colors, a color histogram is created, that shows which color is used how often in the image. By identifying

---

[26]http://www.tucows.com/
[27]http://www.csc.liv.ac.uk/ aa/

the differently colored parts of the image, the colors present in the image have to be grouped in clusters according to their similarity.

After the algorithm has determined the main colors, the regions which share the same color are extracted and a special technique is used to identify the connected components. This allows the contours of particular image regions to be identified that form closed shapes. By examining the relationships between regions potential character components are extracted. The proposed system is working very well. So good actually that is has found its way into a commercial software package.

The next step will be to implement a search engine that recognizes objects in an image, but this is highly difficult and requires a lot of computing power, as a cat may be painted, photographed or drawn. The cat can run, sit, jump and the perspective can be varied. Although a human is able to detect a cat very easily, expressing the looks of a cat mathematically is very difficult, so don't expect anything on the Internet soon. But then again the first rule on the Internet is still valid, expect the unexpected.

6.3   Intelligent Network Agents

6.3.1   Little Helpers on the Web

Intelligent agents are widely used in computer science and are part of the research in the area of artificial intelligence. Areas of agent research include user-interface agents, such as personal assistants and information filters, which perform networking tasks for a user. Another area of agent research are multi-agent systems, such as agent communication languages, systems for co-ordination/co-operation strategies. Autonomous agents are programs that travel between sites and decide themselves when to move and what to do. At the moment this type of agent is not very common as they require a special type of server, where the agent can navigate. This section focuses on network agents, which are also known as "knowbots", little robots that gather information on a network.

As we've seen in the last section search engines can help us find information, but the problem is to remember where this information was, when we looked at it last and to know if something has changed since we last visited the site. It sounds easy to save every interesting page in the bookmarks of the browser, but soon you will have hundreds of bookmarks on your computer whereby many links will be dead.

The major disadvantage of search engines is that they require human interaction, which leads to incomplete sets of information. Even with good search strategies it may take some time to locate the information desired, and time is money. In many cases people are not able to locate content although it is available on the Internet.

In order to reduce the amount of time needed, intelligent agents have been developed that are able to search on the Internet without user interaction (except for the entry of the keywords). Let's look at an example. You look for information on Shakespeare's literature. No matter how hard you search on the Internet, you always miss some information, as there are far too many sites, newsgroups, portals and chats to check out.

The idea of intelligent agents is to search for a set of given keywords (in our example: Shakespeare and literature) not only once, but repeatedly every hour, day or month in order to be always informed of the latest developments about your topic. Simply putting together a query for a given set of databases would not resolve the problem, as the set of databases changes on the Internet all the time. New sites appear and existing sites disappear. The agent will keep you always up-to-date.

Intelligent agents should not only collect data, they should also be able to classify the data. This can be achieved by counting the times a certain word or synonyms appear or by the structure of the document. The difficulty is to characterize the importance and relevance of keywords that were found in a certain document.

6.3.2 E-Mail Agents

One of the first applications for intelligent agents was to sort out unwanted e-mail from the inbox. Although it is possible to delete automatically mail from certain e-mail addresses, this does not help anymore, as spammers use fake addresses that change every time they send out something. Therefore it is necessary to develop agents that are able to detect spam automatically because they contain certain keywords or a certain structure.

Another application in the area of e-mail for agent software is to prioritize e-mail by importance. This type of agent moves the most important mail to the top of your mail folder, so that you can read it first. The priority can be defined by sender, content or structure.

In the first case it is rather simple to build out-of-the box products to prevent spam, as spam is seen by most people in a similar way. In the second case it is necessary to customize the agent in order to support personal needs. This is much harder as it requires the person who uses the agent to think about their priorities. Although this exercise is really helpful and will help to save a lot of time, especially if you receive a lot of e-mail every day, many people do not take the time to think about their priorities.

6.3.3 News Agents

Over the past few years more and more news agents have established themselves. These news-agents are able to create a sort of customized online newspaper, which displays only news that is interesting to the customer. The agents therefore need to visit all news sites and decide which of the offered news may be interesting to the particular customer. It then collects the information and passes it on via e-mail or web front end.

In Germany two companies are competing in the business of news agents. Paperball[28] and Paperboy[29]. The competition between these services is getting them to add more online newspaper resources to their database to create an even more detailed personalized newspaper, which can be viewed either on a web page or where the headlines with some additional relevant information are sent out to the customer automatically via e-mail.

In the past there have been some disputes between the newspapers and the digital news agents, how the information should be presented on the news agents' web sites. In the past the digital news agents collected the raw information and included it into their own layout, adding their own advertising. This is no longer possible; the news agents can only produce the headlines and some lines of text and then they need to link to the original newspaper site, in order to stay away from legal trouble.

There are still many privately owned sites that offer collections of news links which strip away the advertising. Depending on the popularity of these sites, online news services sue the owners and try to stop these sites. But for every site that is shut down ten new ones appear, making it difficult for Internet news providers to stop it. It is part of the Internet culture to make information available for free, even without advertising, but there is no technical way to stop it and only limited legal power. See Chapter 4 on the legal aspects.

6.3.4   Personal Shopping Agents

The most interesting agent is the personal shopping agent that scans the Internet for the lowest price for a given product. The shopping agent consists of a database with merchants on the web and how to access their databases. Once customers decide on a product they are able to key in the product name, part number, ISBN number or a keyword that relates to the product and the shopping agent starts checking all the merchants for the product. If the search word is too generic, the customers will be presented with a selection of possible products. If the customers then decide for a certain product the shopping agent will query all databases for the prices and availability. The prices displayed normally do not only contain the price for the product, but also for shipping, so the total price is displayed as well as the time for delivery.

Acses[30], developed by some German students, has become highly successful. It has specialized in searching for books on the web. By entering the title, the author or the ISBN number, the shopping agent looks out for the book and presents the results in a list. The books are sorted by price, including postage and packaging. Besides the price, the time of delivery is presented. I use

---

[28] http://www.paperball.de/
[29] http://www.paperboy.de/
[30] http://www.acses.com/

the system very often and have already found some books to be cheaper in Australia than in Germany, where I live. Sending the books from Australia may take some weeks, but if the price difference is large enough then it is a viable option.

Jango[31], a shopping agent developed by the American company Netbot allows the price comparison of computer products. As with Acses the price list is not stored at the site of the agent but is retrieved in the moment of the customer's interest, therefore providing the actual price. The difference between Jango and Acses is the way payment is handled. Acses sends the customers to the bookshop where they can pay using the bookshop's payment system. Jango on the other hand offers the possibility of paying at their site without direct access to the Internet shop that provides the product.

As more and more shopping agents become available, a special portal for shopping agents has been set up. SmartBots.com[32] is a directory offering information on shopping agents from all over the world. See Table 6.3 for an overview on some of the most used shopping agents, which can also be found on SmartBots.com.

Shopping agents work for mass products, such as software, compact discs and books, as they require no customization to the individual customer. Other products, such as cars or complete computer systems won't be targeted initially by these agents, as the offerings differ too much on every web site, just as do the requirements by the customers. Cross-promotion and service are other points that cannot be dealt with by the shopping agents as they cannot be expressed simply by value.

In order to allow these advanced features, the shopping agents themselves need to become highly complex configuration systems. Then such a shopping agent could be implemented that is able to find a complete computer system at the lowest price possible by comparing all the components individually and looking for cross-promotions (e.g. a hard disk becomes cheaper if bought with a certain type of memory). This will require a large investment on the shopping agent site, as it needs to know which components work together and which of them exclude each other. This information is different for every product. The shopping agents eventually become true brokers.

6.4 Portal Sites, the New All-in-One Mega Web Sites

6.4.1 Growing Together

A portal is a "World Wide Web site that is or proposes to be a major starting site for users when they connect to the Web or that users tend to visit as an anchor site" (as defined by the whatis online dictionary[33]). Portals contain lots

---

[31]http://www.jango.com/

[32]http://www.smartbots.com/

[33]http://www.whatis.com/

Overview on Shopping Agents

The following list contains a selection of shopping agents that were available at the time of writing. For an complete and updated list, please go to http://www.smartbots.com/.

Name	Description, URL
Acses	The ultimate shopping agent for online bookstores. **http://www.acses.com/**
Auction Watchers	This specialized agent allows you to scan prices on Internet auctions for computer equipment. **http://www.auctionwatchers.com/**
Bargain Finder	Specialized in finding compact discs. Uses nine online shops for comparing products. **http://www.bargainfinder.com/**
E-Smarts	Complex Internet Guide with shopping agents for bargain shopping on the Web. **http://www.esmarts.com/**
Jango	Offers price comparison of computer products. **http://www.jango.com/**
MySimon	MySimon can be taught to shop in new online shops with guidance of the customer. **http://www.mysimon.com/**
Shopper.-com	Compares 1,000,000 prices on 100,000 products, which are available online. **http://www.shopper.com/**

Table 6.3.

of content in the form of news, information, links and many services, such as ordering flowers, books and CDs or free e-mail and web space. As locating desired material on the Internet becomes more difficult, the value of fast, reliable and simple-to-use portals increases.

Portals are actually nothing new to the web. AOL[34] and CompuServe[35] in

---

[34]http://www.aol.com/
[35]http://www.compuserve.com/

the United States, T-Online[36] in Germany and Ireland Online[37], for example, have offered something similar for years. All online services have had a private web site with special services for their customers, like online banking, free e-mail, search engines, chat forums and online shopping malls. The difference between these first generation portals and the current wave of portals is the target audience. With the first generation, only subscribers to AOL could see the AOL portal pages. The second generation which is already online is not restricted to availability for subscribers of a certain online services only, but can be accessed by anyone with a web browser.

The reason online services have opened up their private portal sites is that search engines, like Excite[38], and directories, like Yahoo[39], have started to offer services in addition to being a directory or a search engine. These services are accessible via a web browser from anywhere without the need of being a subscriber to a certain online service. Digital's search engine AltaVista[40], for example, added instant online translation to its search engine as an additional service, whereby any web page can be translated on the fly while downloading them from their respective server. Yahoo offers free e-mail and a news service. You can even download a little program from Yahoo's web site that displays a ticker in your task bar on Windows computers, where you can see the latest developments in politics, finance and sports.

The search engines and directories had to add new services to distinguish themselves from the vast number of similar services. There are more than 100 international search engines and more than 15 – 20 search engines per country, ranging from hundreds for Germany (like web.de[41]) and the UK (such as GOD[42] to Fiji-Online[43]. The result was that they entered the domain of the portal web sites. The search engines were already the most attractive sites on the web, but with the addition of new services they were able to enhance their customer loyalty.

By offering additional services through registration, portals know quite well who their customers are and are able to respond to their wishes fast, which is very important if you live off banner advertisements. One-to-one marketing is the key to customer loyalty.

The third large group that became portals is the group of software distribution sites, like Netscape's NetCenter[44] and Tucows[45]. The former is the largest portal in the world, worth more than $ 4.3 billion (this was the price AOL paid

---

[36]http://www.t-online.de/

[37]http://www.iol.ie/

[38]http://www.excite.com/

[39]http://www.yahoo.com/

[40]http://www.altavista.com/

[41]http://www.web.de/

[42]http://www.god.co.uk/

[43]http://www.fiji-online.com.fj/

[44]http://www.netscape.com/

[45]http://www.tucows.com/

Netscape for NetCenter in November 1998) and the second is one of the largest archives for shareware and public domain software on the web. They were facing the same problems. They needed to distinguish themselves from their competitors. On the Internet there are only few ways to distinguish oneself from the competition; i.e. by price, speed or service. If you do it right, you are cheaper, faster and offer a better service.

The fourth large group of web sites that became portals were the sites offering free services, like e-mail and web space; Global Message Exchange[46] and Xoom[47], to name one service from each of the two categories. As users tend to come to these sites on a regular basis to check their e-mail or to change their web sites, they have a high potential for becoming a portal.

Jim Sease offers a "meta-portal" on his web site[48]. He links to all sorts of portals where users can get additional information. This may be useful for selecting a portal but once you have found "your" portal, you will most probably stay with it and ignore the others.

Converting traditional shopping malls to digital shopping malls failed in most cases, because they only replicated the environment and not the information. Having twenty shops within one domain is no help to the customer; a link to a page within the domain is just as far away as a link to another country. Portals combine shopping and information and pass the relevant information on. Users enter their requirements once and are guided through the possibilities of the portal. Most portals save user profiles to make them look even smarter. They remember what particular users did last time and are good at guessing what they may want to do this time by presenting to them information and products that they are most likely interested in.

6.4.2   Digital Neighbourhoods

Free web space providers such as GeoCities offer a wide range of neighbourhoods, where customers can find other people with similar interests. Adding services, information and product offerings to these neighbourhoods will create a zone with added value for every participant. The zones create a virtual market space which is highly specialized. The zone on a certain portal can act as an umbrella for many companies of all sizes. These virtual marketplaces also make it easier to sell advertising space to potential advertisers, as the viewers are most likely to be of a certain target group.

If you look at various portals you will find services there which you have already seen in other places. Portals tend to buy existing services and incorporate them into their web sites. This is so-called co-branding. Netscape, for example, uses the Florists Transworld Delivery service[49] on its homepage, so it is now

---

[46]http://www.gmx.net/

[47]http://www.xoom.com/

[48]http://www.sease.com/

[49]http://www.ftd.com/

possible to buy flowers from Netscape. At first glance you will not even notice that you are using a third-party service, as FTD uses a special co-branded site with the design of Netscape's web page. Snap uses the mapping service of Vicinity[50] and Excite uses the e-mail address book from WhoWhere.com[51]. Building up such services would break the financial neck for most portals, so they co-operate with existing online service providers. For users there is no big difference if they click on Altavista's news section (which is provided by ABC-News) or on ABCNews web site[52]. The real advantage is the tight integration of different services. Read a news story on Altavista and search for sites related to that topic with one click or search for a certain keyword on Yahoo and get a list of reference books from them (with kind support from Amazon.com).

Another start-up service provider is ConSors[53], an online brokering service company. To their direct customers, who come to their web site, they do not offer any support. They want only the "intelligent customers" who are able to help themselves. But at the same time they are offering the brokering service to online banks, who can include the raw service into their product portfolio and offer consulting and other things around this raw service. This new paradigm of providing core services to portals has been taken on-board by Hewlett-Packard's E-Services[54] campaign. An in-depth review of the paradigm can be found in Chapter 15.

6.4.3 Becoming a Portal Player

Becoming a portal player is not difficult. All you need is interesting content, which is unique on the Internet, and a good search engine to start with. With some HTML knowledge you can build a simple portal by adding your favorite links, a search mechanism, links to free e-mail and chat and news feeds, thus creating a homepage of your favourite bookmarks. Your browser bookmark file is a form of private portal. As every page on the web has the same priority, there is no reason why five million people should not access your homepage instead of AOL's. All you need is good marketing and a solution for these five million people.

In order to become a successful portal you need to add services that tightly integrate into your online offering. Integration is the main reason why so many people choose portals over individual sites. Once you have registered with a portal, the information can be reused for all services within the portal. Although some may not like the idea of cross-selling personal information, most people do like the idea of their own personalized portal site. Once you have entered your credit card information for buying a book via a portal, this in-

---

[50]http://www.vicinity.com/
[51]http://www.whowhere.com/
[52]http://www.abcnews.com/
[53]http://www.consors.de/
[54]http://www.hp.com/e-services/

formation can be reused to pay for something else within the portal or offer the same customers other products to complete the last buy. The user does not need to re-enter information. Being a major browser producer will help a lot establishing your portal. Netscape and Microsoft have highly successful portals because their homepages are the default homepage of their browsers.

The Go Network[55], for example, invites their customers to use a web directory search for web pages. The news headlines and financial data are on the page and it is possible to get a free e-mail account. It is possible to sign in and customize the page to the needs of the individual subscriber. In Figure 6.3 you can see my customized page on the GO portal site.

Figure 6.3. The Portal Site of GO Networks

While building up your portal it is helpful to offer free services like web space, free e-mails, chat rooms, newsgroups, and free software for download. This will get the users attention in the first place. They will come to your portal and try it out. In order to keep the customers attracted to your web site, you need up-to-date news feeds, games, online help and some online shopping possibilities. It does not matter if you build up your own service or if you buy it from someone else. Customers won't notice in most cases, but they will notice how easy (or difficult) it is to navigate within your portal and find information on a certain topic. Although portal owners have services directly included in their system, they should never exclude other services from their search engine. The customers should never have the feeling that the search engine only

---

[55]http://www.go.com/

shows the preferred suppliers. If the customers want to get in touch with another company the search engine must be able to provide the users with the required information, otherwise they will go on to the next portal where they feel that their requirements are met in a better way. The services which are offered on the portal site should always be available as a suggestion and not as a must.

Search capabilities must have the top priority for your portal. This is the most frequently used service on the Internet. Information on the site needs to be organized in zones (sometimes called channels or guides) on general topics like Computer, Travel, Arts and Cars.

Each zone combines all offered service for that particular topic. If, for example, you select the Entertainment section on Yahoo, you will not only get the directory entries for that particular topic. You will also get links to related news and current events. You are able to join a virtual community using online chats, clubs or message boards and you get a list of online services that are related to entertainment, like online auctions, a classified section, yellow pages and online shopping (with a direct link to CDNow[56]). It is even possible to see a listing of cinemas with timetables. All these services are offered by clicking on a simple link that says "Entertainment". Two or three years ago you would have found only a long list of web sites where you could find more information on the topic, but no service at all.

6.4.4   Portal Owners and Service Providers

Portals have two major players: The portal owners and the service providers who add functionality and services to a portal. Depending on the structure of your company and your plans for the future, you should become either one or the other, ideally both.

There are two different types of portals on the Internet. The horizontal ones which cover a lot of topics and the smaller ones, the vertical portals with a tightly focused content area geared towards a particular audience. Gallery-Net[57], for example, offers a directory for artists, art-related sites, online galleries and virtual museums. In addition to this it offers free e-mail and a chat, web space and a shopping area. It appeals mainly to art-lovers and artists, but still offers a wide range of activities from this one site thus being the portal for many people around the world

Another example is the web site of Gravis[58] in Germany. I visited their site in December 1998. Although they are the biggest resellers of Apple Macintosh products in Germany their web site consists mainly of scanned images of the printed brochure. There is no way to get any additional information on the products or on prices. It is not even possible to buy anything online. There are

---

[56]http://www.cdnow.com/

[57]http://www.gallery-net.com/

[58]http://www.gravis.de/

no online chats, no newsgroups, no FAQs, just a few 100-200 KB images and that's it. They have an extremely high potential of becoming a major Mac portal for Germany, but unfortunately they did not see the potential of the Internet when I contacted them back in December 1998. I asked them about their new G3 accelerator boards. It took me three mails to explain what I was looking for on their web site. Finally they thought that they had understood and sent me the URL of the producer Phase 5[59]. I don't think that I have to comment on this reaction. The people in their customer care center have to learn how the Internet works.

If you and your company have an interest in only one specific topic it is quite easy to build up a portal using your knowledge and your products. If, for example, a company is selling dog food, creating a vertical portal web site would consist of adding a search functionality not only for that particular site, but Internet-wide. It would need to offer online chats, e-mail, web space, newsgroups and all the other things which we have discussed above, tailored to meet the needs of dog owners. Create a portal that would be the kind of service all dog owners would come back for. The vertical portal could be a zone in a horizontal portal, but with more detailed information and services than a general portal like Yahoo or NetCenter could offer. As a dog food company one could ask Excite, for example, to include the services provided by the dog food company for dog owners in their portal or even offer to outsource the dog zone on Excite's portal web site.

As you can see, becoming a small portal is easy and can be a threat to the large ones, if done well. Be careful about offering services that are not related to your company. If these services fail, your company will be held responsible for it. So choose your partners carefully.

6.4.5 Personalizing the Online Experience

To return to personalization or one-to-one marketing (personalization is typically driven by the customer and one-to-one marketing is driven by the business), portals use these techniques to deliver precisely the information the customer needs in the way the customer wants it to be presented. The user profile that consists of information the customers have entered and information they gave while browsing the site is used to organize the portal in the most convenient way for them. The simplest form of personalization is described above. All services that are available are focused on the customer's search topic. The next level would be to provide local weather reports and other local news of interest (e.g. movie listings). This would require that the users enter their home town or the zip code and the country they live in. Giving only so little information about them allows the portal to become even more personal. The more information the customer is willing to give the better the portal adapts to the needs of the customer.

---

[59]http://www.phase5.de/

Most portals have personalized home pages for their customers where they are greeted with their names and get the latest information on their stocks, the latest news headlines on certain topics, see if they have received new e-mail and get a weather forecast for the next few days. Birthdays within the next five days of all your relatives pop up and you are able to see if you're chat partners are online as well.

All this pops up automatically each time the customers enter their portal. From there on they are able to search for topics and use online services. Most probably they will use the search engine offered by the portal and use the on-line services proposed by the portal. Tracking the movement of the users gives feedback on the usability of the web site. Some pieces of information, for example, need to be put onto the home page, because 80 percent of the users want to know about it, but only 20 percent are able to find it. It also gives feedback on the preferences of the users (for example, all users go to the "Cars" zone). This in return helps the portal owner to enhance the services and the information flow. The major obstacle is to persuade the users to provide the required information to deliver the services onto their personalized homepage. See the section on "Privacy on the Internet" in Chapter 10 for more information on this topic.

6.4.6 Must-have Features for a Portal

Besides the search engine, e-mail and online chats are the most interesting things for Internet users. Offering free e-mails may seem to be superfluous, as everybody gets a free e-mail account with his or her online access, but there are several reasons why they would need additional e-mail accounts.

Firstly, it could well be that several family members share one account and want to send and receive private e-mails without paying for an extra account from their online service provider.

The second important reason to have e-mail accounts available through a web browser which do not require a special e-mail program, is that they are a very attractive offering for people who travel a lot. Just walk into the nearest Internet café or ask someone in an office with an Internet connection and within seconds you can read your mail and respond. Although web based e-mailing is far from being comfortable and fast, it offers a way to stay in touch while traveling and it is very simple to use. More advanced users may prefer to telnet to their accounts and use old fashioned Unix programs such as pine or elm to check their e-mail (or even telnet to the mail-server on port 110, which opens the standard pop3 connection).

Thirdly, people who are moving from one location to the other more often may not be able to move their e-mail account with them, because their online service provider is not available in the new location. Now having such a virtual e-mail address, they have one address that is valid for any location.

A fourth reason is to have fun accounts. MOE[60], for example, offers a wide range of different domain names, ranging from for-president.com to tweety-bird.com (my e-mail address could look like this danny@for-president.com or danny@tweety-bird.com). They are now in the process of becoming a portal as well, by adding new services such as web space (if we use my example I could receive the following URL, if desired: http://danny.for-president.com/) and weather reports.

Giving away free web space was what GeoCities[61] offered in the first place. Now it is one of the largest portals on the Internet, offering everything from virtual communities, online shopping and a search engine to stock quotes and many other things.

Online chats are something really wonderful for telephone companies and online services that charge per minute or per hour. Once you have started a chat, it takes quite a while until you really get engaged in a conversation (unless you know the people already) and once you have started it is difficult to stop. Every portal offers online chats, ranging from Java-based chats to CGI chats. In-depth information on online chats can be found in Chapter 8.

---

[60]http://www.myownemail.com/
[61]http://www.geocities.com/

Chapter 7

SHOPPING AND ORM
SOLUTIONS

7.1 Online Shopping

7.1.1 Reasons for Online Shops

In order to sell products through the electronic channel, the Internet, it is necessary to think about the means to bring the products, services or information to the customers. The Internet does not offer the possibility to present these goods in a show room and in most cases no shop assistants are available that customers could ask for more information.

Online Shopping solutions are more adequate for selling products than services. Products require a catalogue where the customers can browse and order some of the products. The products can then be shipped to the customer (such as furniture) or directly downloaded from the Internet (such as software). The major difference between products and services is that products are mass-produced and may be mass-customized. Services in most cases require individual work by the service provider, which looks totally different for every customer. A translation service does translate texts for customers, but every text is totally different. These services cannot be easily replicated or even stolen. A strongly personalized service helps the customer and the merchant, as the service is not useful for other customers in other situations. It is not even useful for the same customer in a different situation.

Before deciding which shopping solution is the right one, it is necessary to find out which products you want to sell on the Internet. Are you planning to offer standard products or highly customized services. The number of products you are planning to place on your web site is also important.

If your company offers only very a products and has very low order volume, there is no need for a complex shopping system. A few web pages with a description of the products will satisfy the needs of the shop owner and the customers. Each of the pages will contain a link to an HTML form, which can be used to process the order. This approach does not cost very much and enables everyone to go online. Small art galleries are offering their pictures to the customers over the Internet. If the order volume or the number of products increases, it is fairly easy to extend the system to process the orders automatically if the web site is implemented in a modular fashion.

As soon as you start to offer a wide range of articles this system becomes difficult to handle for the shop owner and for the customers as well. The shop owner will have difficulties keeping the web pages up-to-date and consistent and the customers will have trouble finding a certain product fast. Therefore a shopping solution is required to handle the increased flow of information that is the basis for the online transaction. It should automate the process of selling goods over the Internet.

A software shopping solution should be easy to use for the customer in such a way that is saves the preferences and personal data of the customer, if so wished, for example. This simplifies the order process for repeat customers and creates customers satisfaction. Customers should have different possibilities for finding a certain product, either by browsing or by searching.

An important question to answer is when the return on investment (ROI) can be achieved. Ask yourself what your goals are. Are you planning to be profitable in the short term or are you planning more strategically and accept that the ROI will take years to pay back? Amazon.com needed five years to become profitable, but now it is the largest bookstore on the Internet.

7.1.2 Setting up the Shop

Choosing the right shopping solution is not easy, as there are hundreds of different software solutions available on the market, and every day more and more appear. In order to select the right solution, three areas need to be examined.

It is necessary to know how difficult the set-up of the shop is, in order to determine if your current staff is able to handle the set up, or if external partners or new employees are needed. Then you have to find out how easy it is to process orders through the shopping solution and then it is important to find out how difficult or easy the administration of the system is.

Depending on the skills of the shop designer it is possible to find shopping solutions that are able to create complete online shops via wizards and templates. This is something for people who do not have much knowledge about creating HTML pages or writing CGI applications, in which case this type of online shop will be sufficient. The disadvantage is that the shops are not as flexible as the more complex solutions, which use HTML templates that can be easily extended by the shop designer.

But more important than the skills of the web master are the basic technical features which then result in the business cases a solution can help to resolve. A good online shopping solution will have the ability to connect to existing product databases or at least allow the import of the data into a new database. Electronic commerce cannot be conducted if data needs to be replicated manually all the time. In the electronic world it is important to be fast and fast means that most steps, except for the decision making ones, need to be automatic.

In order to create a successful online shopping experience, it is important to track users. Tracking users is necessary in order to know which goods a certain customer has chosen and in the field of one-to-one business, it helps to determine what preferences a certain user has stored.

There are several ways of doing this. Most web sites use cookies to store information about the user. A cookie is a string of text which contains a user ID and maybe some user preferences, such as preferred language and the preferred layout of the web site, but this information can also be stored on the server. A cookie needs to contain only the user ID to help identify and track the user. A cookie is created by a web server and is then saved in a file on the customer's computer. The cookie can only be read by the web server that put it onto the customer's computer, so there is no way that other sites can gain information on your shopping and browsing. But therefore the customers need to have installed the latest browser versions, as earlier versions had bugs which allowed cookies to be read from other web servers. Some companies do not allow their employees to use cookies, for privacy reasons and therefore there should be another way to authenticate a user.

Using basic authentication, users can log in to a site using a login name and password, which allows the web server to identify that user. If cookies cannot be used to track the user, the login name can be added to the URL to identify a customer. Another way to track customers is to log their domain name or IP address and save this information into a log file.

Amazon.com, for example, is using cookies, basic authentication and user-based URLs, in order to make sure that everyone is able to use their web pages. The cookie contains a user identification number which is read when the customer logs onto a web page. The customer then is passed onto a URL which contains this identification number. In case a customer has switched off the cookies or is logging onto the web site from another computer, customers can alternatively use basic authentication to identify themselves. If the login and password match the data in the database the customer is passed on to the personalized URL, making the shop usable for anyone. During set-up it should be possible to determine the way tracking should occur.

One of the most important issues for e-commerce software is internationalization. Internationalization should not be mistaken for localization. Internationalized software allows the shop owner and the customers to be anywhere in the world. It should allow the conversion of currencies to display the payable amount in the local currency and sales taxes and shipping charges need to be adapted to every country and state. The simpler solutions use tables in database with pre-defined values for shipping, taxes and currency conversion, but the more advanced systems allow the integration of shipping companies

Tracking Customers

On the web several technologies can be used to track customers. In order to track customers they need to be identified first. Identification can be achieved through:

- **Basic Authentication** – Customers identify themselves through a login and password procedure.

- **Cookies** – A web server stores personal information on the customers' computer and retrieves this information whenever the customer returns to the server.

- **Domain Name** – Customers are identified through their domain name.

- **IP Address** – Customers are identified through their IP address.

- **Personalized URLs** – Customers access a web server by using personalized URLs, i.e. every customer gets another URL.

- **Strong Authentication** – Digital certificates are used to identify a customer, which reside either on the hard disk or on a smart card.

Once a customer has been identified, tracking occurs through the same means.

Table 7.1.

like UPS. The logistics partner will determine how much it will cost to ship a certain good to a given place on earth and how long it will take, and an interface to a bank exists to have up-to-date currency information. Some service providers may also keep a tax database up-to-date, which can be accessed automatically through the shopping system. The set-up process should help in choosing the right logistics partner and the right bank.

There are many additional features an online offering needs to include, such as auto-responders, chat rooms, and newsgroups and automatic search engine submission should be an option in the set-up process.

7.1.3   Processing the Order

Once the online shop has been set up, several features for processing the order are required, the most basic being a shopping basket functionality, which collects all the items a customer has chosen. The shopping basket should allow the customer to add items, remove items and change the amount of items included. When the custome shopping process has completed, the customer is presented with a list of all products and can do last changes and proceed to check-out where they need to pay. A shopping solution should support several payment methods, such as credit card payment through secure socket layer (SSL) and secure electronic transaction (SET), paper and electronic cheques, invoice and cash on demand (COD) (see Chapter 13 for further information on payment models).

Accepting only one payment method will not be sufficient, especially if your price range is very broad. In order to maximize sales in your web shop, you should not only accept several payment methods, but also several order methods, such as ordering via web page, e-mail, fax, telephone and normal mail. Companies who already sell through traditional channels will require these payment and order models and for digital start-up companies these features will enable them to penetrate the traditional channels. This also leaves flexibility to cope with future growth. Depending on the company culture it may be necessary to check if the customers' addresses are valid and if the credit card limit is not reached.

Automation of the order and payment process is also a very important feature of online shopping solutions. Automatic acknowledgements via e-mail or fax should be delivered after the customer has ordered an item from your shop. The acknowledgement should contain all information that is relevant to the order, such as shipping address, all ordered items, date and time of the order and contact addresses for your company, in case of questions.

The online shopping software should take care that the privacy of the customer is guaranteed by storing all customer related information in a secure place, which cannot be accessed by hackers. When sending out acknowledgement mails, the credit card information should not be included or only the last few or first few digits should be included for the verification of the customer, as hijacking e-mails is very simple on the Internet.

Cross-selling and cross-promotion should also be standard features of your shopping solution. These features present merchandize, which is related to the items a customer already has chosen. A customer, for example, may decide to buy a dining table. The online shop should propose, for example, chairs, plates, forks and knives that go well with the dining table and offer a discount, if the customer decides to buy all the goods together.

Repeat or high-volume customers should receive automatic or negotiated discounts for certain products and online order tracking is also a feature your online solution needs to include right from the beginning. Customers should be able to check the status of their orders at any time. The tracking feature and a customer feedback feature reduce the load on the customer care center and reduce costs as it is growing slower than the company, as more customers are able to use the self-service.

In order to further automate the process of restocking, an inventory management module should automatically re-order goods that drop below a pre-determined level.

7.1.4 Administration of the Shop

In order to make the online shop successful it is necessary to adapt to change very fast, therefore the administration of the online shop needs to support all required features for fast change and should be easy to use at the same time.

Some products allow changes to be made offline, test and then upload them to the server. This method restricts changing information to a certain computer, which has the required software and the data installed. Avoid solutions that require all changes to be made offline and then for the whole database to be re-loaded on to the server. Another way would be to use an online administration interface and update the information in real-time. This is also not the optimal solution, as changes cannot be tested before showing them online. A wrong price can affect your sales, as in the case of buy.com[1].

This online retailer claims to have the lowest prices on the web and offered in February 1999 a Hitachi 19-inch monitor for 164 dollar, which is more than 400 dollar below the right price of 588 dollar. Customers called in to verify that the price was correct, as the wrong price was in the database the customer care center confirmed the price and within very little time hundreds of orders were made, as the word was spreading very fast on the Internet. Buy.com first refused to honor the orders, but then decided to sell the remaining monitors in stock (about 150) at the low price and cancelled all other orders and offered the customers a monitor in the price range of 164 US dollar. Immediately after the event, buy.com changed its sales policy and added a section about typographical errors, which basically stated that wrong prices on the web site do not have to be honored by the company. As a result a group of customers filed a class-action lawsuit against the company.

In a different incident, ShopNow.com[2] lost an estimated \$50,000 when it accidentally sold a number of Palm V organizers for \$79, which was \$300 below the regular asking price. The company received about 250 orders for the Palm V at \$79. In the interest of customer relations, ShopNow sold one Palm V at the discounted price to each of the customers who placed orders.

Although pricing errors on retail Web sites are not a trend in online commerce, they can damage the business of single online merchants. They are an indication that online companies are under more scrutiny than their tradi-

---

[1] http://www.buy.com/
[2] http://www.shopnow.com/

tional counterparts, where such mistakes could go unnoticed except by a handful of customers. A wrong price is communicated within an instant into chat groups, newsgroups and mailing lists, flooding the online shops with orders.

Therefore database quality assurance and a staging area for a web site are critical for the success of an online shop (these two points are important prerequisites for any type electronic business, by the way). Database quality assurance includes automatic procedures to verify the content of a database by defining a set of rules, such as the minimum prices for a set of products and the maximum range of allowed changes. In addition to this, a person needs to verify the changes made before going into production. A staging area should be available, which is an exact copy of the online shop and that can be used to test changes. Moving the new online shop from the staging to the production area should be done automatically.

A shopping solution should not force the company to invest in new database technology and use the existing database infrastructure for the online shop, instead. If only one database for the products is used errors in replication are minimized. The shopping solution should contain interfaces to other applications that are necessary for the buying process, such as the back-end ordering system and the payment process. Direct links to other in-house systems enable additional services to the customers, such as order tracking and availability of products. In order to minimize investment into new technology, the shopping solution should be available for your preferred operating system and hardware platform.

The existing inventory system should be tightly integrated, in order to allow your customers to check on stock availability before ordering. Even if you do not want to offer this functionality to your customers, then you need this functionality internally to organize re-orders of goods. Certainly, it is essential to check out the costs of integrating your Internet ordering system with your inventory control system before committing to it.

The HTML presentation of the online shop should be done through templates, which contain variables which will be replaced by product names and prices, which are stored in the database. This allows the layout to be changed for the whole shop by changing only very few templates, instead of thousands of web pages.

Marketing should be able to add, delete and change product information. Changing data in order to create a special price promotion, for example, needs to be so easy, the marketing department is able to do it without technical training. Other marketing instruments, such as customer buying history, web server log files, user preferences, direct mail and affiliate program management need to be standard in the product you are choosing.

Some companies prefer to divide their merchandise into several online departments to make it easier for customers to find products. Quelle[3], for ex-

---

[3]http://www.quelle.de/

ample, does not have one shop on its web site, but a row of smaller shops are available. One shops is for fashion, one is for technology, and one is for books. Although a central catalogue and one shopping solution is used, the approach of Quelle shows competency in every field by having an extra shop.

Reporting is also a very important feature. Customer behaviour and buying patterns need to be presented in a visual way so that managers are able to base decisions on these reports. The reports can show how many customers visit the shop every day, how effective the shop works, how easily customers find the products and how satisfied they are. The reports should be customizable and need to show results from different perspectives, such as based on time, product and person.

7.1.5 Quality of Service

To support the growing businesses of the Internet the selected solution needs to be scalable, offering your company growth over time without having to replace the underlying solution. The solution you choose should be able to handle fifty products and five orders per day, just as well as five million products and fifty thousand orders a day. Additional hardware and a better Internet connection will be necessary, just as other pieces of the architecture will need to be updated, but the basic business process should not be changed and the shopping experience of the customer should not be affected. This leads us to another important issue, which is performance. Although you are online twenty-four hours a day, seven days a week, you won't experience the same amount of customers every day and every hour. You will certainly have peak times, where more customers flow into your online shop and quiet times, when almost none visit your shop.

Quality of service on the Internet becomes even more important. In the real world customers have only a limited selection of shops they can visit; in many cases there is only one shop nearby selling a certain product. So service is sometimes a problem, but the shop owner just doesn't care, as people are still buying the products. On the Internet dissatisfied customers will have a choice. Therefore do something about your quality of service. A customer who is looking for a certain item and is slowed down by your web site will eventually go off to another site which is faster. A customer, who is in the process of paying, will not come back if the web server crashes in that particular moment.

Today many web sites overprovision the hardware in order to ensure the availability at peak times. As this does cost a lot of money, alternative techniques are discussed here to solve the problem with the peak. First of all you need to analyze why your server is experiencing problems at peak time. Are there paying customers who are locked out at this time? What pages are most frequently visited during this time? Do you offer large files for download?

Once you have answered these questions it becomes quite apparent what needs to be done. If there are customers who lose connection while paying, it is necessary to implement a sort of service prioritization, meaning that the payment service on your web server will have more dedicated resources than other services running on the same server, such as browsing the catalogue or searching for items. During the peak time, this won't resolve the overload of the server, but it will prevent that customers who are in the process of doing business with you from being disconnected. If you have web pages that are visited in a very frequent manner or offer large files for download, then think about mirroring these parts to other servers around the world. Either use one of the thousands of free web space services, or ask one of your business partners not only to exchange banners, but also web space, making the download more local for the customers. This way a customer from the United States does not have to go to a European web site for the download of a particular program, but can download it from a mirror in the United States.

The second step to ensure the quality of service is to prioritize certain user groups. It often makes sense to give known customers a higher priority on the web server than passers-by. When you have a successful web site up and running with lots of returning customers you especially want to make the shopping experience as comfortable as possible. By providing a better quality of service for registered customers you are able to attract new customers to your site.

Through the better management of resources on the web server it would now be possible to prioritize services and user groups. This would ensure that registered and known customers would experience a better service on your web site, but it still does not solve the problem at peak times, as an overload may lead to a server crash. In order to prevent a server crash, the connection to the web server needs to be restricted. The restriction can be implemented through different mechanisms. The most simple is to display a web page, saying the server is overloaded and to ask the client to come back later. This is, in fact, not much better than letting the server crash. In addition to telling the customer to come back later, it is possible to reserve a time slot in the near future, where some resources will be dedicated to that customer. The web site would still say that the server is too busy right now, but it would ask the client to wait for thirty seconds. A little JavaScript would then automatically re-connect to the site after thirty seconds and the customer would be able to buy something. Another way of restricting access would be to redirect all new customers to another server, which contains the same content. This requires you to mirror the complete server to another location or create a local cluster where several servers contain the same solution. This will be only justified if the online shop is large enough. Another means of restricting the access to the site is to disallow access for all unknown customers during peak times and invite them to register in order to continue shopping on that site.

Although it seems quite complicated to implement the above-mentioned measures to enhance the quality of service, it actually requires only a small program called WebQoS[4] to be installed on the web server and to feed it with the rules. The program has been developed by Hewlett-Packard and can be downloaded for free from the web site for the HP-UX, Linux and Windows NT platforms. It does help to increase the level of service, while reducing the required hardware in many cases.

This little piece of free software was first used during the Soccer World Championships in France in 1998 and helped the web page[5] to enter the Guinness Book of Records for the most visited web site in history.

7.2 Shopping Solutions

7.2.1 Business Requirements

Not every shopping solution includes every feature mentioned above. Depending on your requirements one or the other solution will fit well, but in most cases some additional programming is required to implement special processes that are not supported by the software.

The minimum requirements are the components which can be found in Table 7.2. A customer entering an online shop should immediately grasp what type of shop it is, just like in a real shop. In order to make shopping easy, a shopping basket is required, otherwise the customer needs to go to check-out with every single item. The order and payment process should be implemented analogous to the real world process in order to make it simple to use and understandable for everyone.

In many countries selling goods is illegal if the customer does not know what the terms and conditions are. Therefore it is necessary to display the terms and conditions on the screen, before accepting the order. Although this may not be valid for all countries, offering the terms and conditions will ensure that you do not get into trouble if people from other countries buy in your online shop. An example can be see in Figure 7.1, which displays the terms and conditions page of Lufthansa Cargo's SameDay[6] service.

The shopping solution needs to provide interfaces to enterprise and legacy applications in order to reduce costs significantly. Most important are the interfaces to existing databases, as your company does not want to handle product sales for every channel in a total different way.

7.2.2 Taxation of Internet Products

Adding taxes to the online order can become quite complicated if you try to sell services and products on a world-wide basis. Just knowing how to apply taxes in the United States alone is a very complicated task. In California alone there

---

[4]http://www.hp.com/go/webqos/

[5]http://www.france98.com/

[6]http://www.sameday.de/

Features of an Online Shopping Solution

Online shopping solutions should at least include the following features. Many products offer additional features, but the following are essential.

- **Database** – Product information needs to be stored in a database, separate from the layout.

- **Interface to Applications** – The shopping solutions need to provide interfaces to other applications, such as a payment processor and the ordering system.

- **Payment** – The shop should support several payment models, for supporting different business models and user preferences.

- **Reporting** – Through reports it should be possible to determine what customers really want.

- **Search Engine** – Customers should find a particular item with one mouse click.

- **Shopping Basket** – The tool of the customers for collecting the products they want to order.

- **Terms and Conditions** – In order to make contracts legal, it is necessary to display the terms and conditions.

- **Web Design Templates** – Use of templates to simplify the design process.

Table 7.2.

are hundreds of different sales tax rates. Different counties also have different rates and on top of this, some cities add a percent or so as well. The sales tax in San Francisco is 8.5 percent. In Marin, which is just next to San Francisco it is 7.25 percent. Berkeley, which is also near San Francisco has a sales tax of 8.25 percent.

In one part of Canada, tax is taxed, making tax calculations even more complicated. In Europe on the other hand, you have differing sales taxes, de-

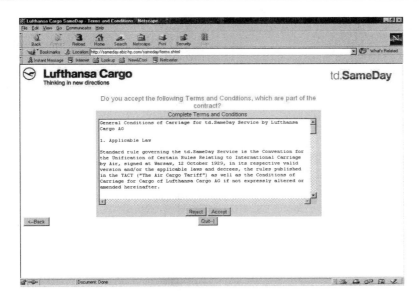

Figure 7.1. Terms and Conditions at Lufthansa Cargo

pending on the type of goods or service you are selling. Trying to keep up with the latest tax regulations manually is not possible.

Besides dealing with varying tax rates all over the world, you also have to deal with the so-called "Nexus". The Nexus is a legal term meaning, "where you have a presence doing business". In the United States, for example, you are obligated to collect, report, and pay sales tax in states where you have a Nexus. The important thing is that nexus is a legal term, so you should seek the advice of your tax attorney on this issue. You need to find out if having a web server in the United States requires you to pay sales tax or not. Many companies have web servers in the US without being physically present there, as the servers are cheaper and connection is better in general.

Many online businesses don't calculate the sales tax online, but put a sign onto their web page that the sales tax will be added to the order. The fulfillment center then has the task of figuring out the correct sales tax. Although this may be ok for a while, many customers will turn away and go to other sites where they get the full price and don't have to expect hidden costs. This is especially necessary if you want your customers to pay online. You cannot expect them to pay twice, once for the product and once for the tax.

Therefore it is necessary to introduce software that automatically calculates the correct tax. ClearCommerce[7] offers a tax calculator as part of its hosting

---

[7]http://www.clearcommerce.com/

solution. The Intershop[8] shopping software allows taxes to be added manually for every country and every product. Another good software solution is Taxware[9], which offers tax calculations for US and international jurisdictions either over the Internet or as an independent software module. CyberSource[10], on the other hand, integrates tax and other transaction features through their online service, meaning that you tap into its software via the Internet rather than installing the software on your own system.

7.2.3 Shopping Products

There are literally thousands and thousands of different online shopping solutions available. This subsection does contain some pointers to systems, which can be used as a foundation. Describing every available solution in detail is not possible, so I have chosen some products, which have proven themselves in the market.

Basically you have three options for choosing the right shopping solution: Buy a ready-made solution, rent space in an e-hosting solution or build the system from scratch with components and parts exactly to your specifications.

It is a difficult decision to make and to find the right option for your solution. I will try to make it easier for you. A ready-made solution is best for companies who have the money and the know-how to install a complete solution on their own and to maintain it. It does not only require HTML knowledge, but also some programming knowledge to set up the shop and maintain it. These solutions have all the required e-commerce features with a few additional business rules built in as a bonus. If your business needs closely match what the package offers, buy it, as this will save you money and a good deal of time. The appropriate IT infrastructure needs to be set up, but as a reward you have total control over the availability and the content, making it a good solution for live transactions, which require up-to-date information and an order tracking system. The costs for setting up and maintaining the system are not to be neglected, but a company with an online shopping strategy will have to invest. If the system is lacking some of your businesses critical features, you may need to rethink. The solution may be a good fit right now, but will likely become obsolete as more and more features become necessary later on in development. Adding non-standard features to a software solution can become difficult, if not supported by the software vendor. Make sure that you choose an extensible solution. While the initial costs are pretty high, the customization is easy enough so that hidden charges won't be a problem for your site afterwards.

Smaller companies will often not have the financial backing to implement and maintain a complex shopping solution, so they should look out for electronic hosting solutions, meaning that they rent an online shop from an ISP,

---

[8]http://www.intershop.com/
[9]http://www.taxware.com/
[10]http://www.cybersource.com/

which has paid for the software and hardware, and has the infrastructure to operate the online shop. The company would only provide the layout and the products for the online shop. Setting up the shop is easy, because the whole store is administered through a web front-end. Besides your web browser no additional software needs to be installed. It is possible to configure some settings and you're ready to go. This makes it more difficult to integrate with an existing fulfillment system, but small companies won't have an automated fulfillment system in most cases and the number of orders will be low, so that they can be processed manually or semi-manually. A hosting solution can also be appropriate for larger companies who do not see the Internet as their key strategy for the moment, but need to start using the Internet in order to learn more about the medium and its possibilities.

When evaluating the available solutions, you should not only consider the cost of the package but how much it will cost to customize it to suit your individual needs. Often what looks like an inexpensive setup at the outset can end up eating away at your budget as you try to add new features or redo the design. E-hosting services in general are fairly cheap to get going, but there's a pretty steep cost for configuring them to work and look the way you want.

The third option can be divided into two sub-options. Hewlett-Packard calls them "Chapter one" and "Chapter two". Chapter One shops would be built from scratch using tools, such as Allaire's Cold Fusion[11] or Pandesic[12], which offer building blocks for setting up online businesses. These tools make it easy to create complex sites, if the appropriate programming knowledge is available. Through these products the complete solution does not need to be coded in Perl, Java or C++, but only the missing parts, but still it requires a lot of hard work. The next generation, called "Chapter two" businesses, do not require these services to be build from scratch. Instead of using components from a single vendor, these e-services can come from any source on the Internet and be built into a complex online shopping solution with very little programming. The advantage of this approach is that if one of the components from another vendor provides more functionality or has become cheaper it is possible to exchange the building block on the fly without disrupting the service.

Once this new class of online businesses start to appear, the above mentioned options will fade away. Companies will start to offer very special services, such as tax calculation, shipping or product presentation on the Internet and anybody who uses the same standards will be able to use these services.

Beans Industry Cappuccino

The German company Beans Industry[13] offers an innovative solution based on Java. Other than most other shopping software Cappuccino cannot be bought,

---

[11]http://www.allaire.com/products/ColdFusion/

[12]http://www.pandesic.com/

[13]http://www.beansindustry.de/

it can only be rented. Depending on the size of the online shop (in this case the number of products) a rental price is paid each month. The pricing is very moderate allowing small companies to go online very fast.

The concept of Cappuccino is to download the complete shopping solution in one go using a Java applet (see Chapter 11 for more information on Java). Instead of having to reconnect to the server for every single page, all product information is downloaded in one go. This is useful, if the product catalogue is small, otherwise the initial download time would be too great.

The advantage is the speed of the navigation, once the applet has been loaded. The disadvantage is that the applet is not as customizable as a web page could be. It is possible to add elements, such as the company logo, but it still always looks like a very technical shop, which may not be appealing to everyone.

BroadVision One-to-One Commerce

BroadVision One-To-One Commerce[14] is an extensible and flexible electronic commerce application that helps you sell more efficiently to your online customers, whether they are consumers, businesses or channel partners. With its instant personalization feature, it enables fast-moving, high transaction companies to instantly change the products, prices, promotions and other content to better meet user needs, as demand changes. The software is very scalable offering a high throughput in transactions, without having to give up the strong personalization.

The comprehensive shopping engine allows you to create the best shopping experience for your customers. The system enables the full integration of enterprise, payment, and shipping systems to leverage your existing investments and service relationships. The site management tool is easy to use and allows business managers to change incentives, adverts, products and other content without having to know much about the underlying technology. The content and catalogue management tools enable business managers to add, change, stage and publish content from wherever they are through a simple-to-use visual interface.

HP Emporium

HP Emporium[15] offers a cheap online shopping solution. It is totally managed and hosted by Hewlett-Packard, meaning that the customers do not have to worry about the operation and maintenance for the first phase. The fixed price is a low risk for the customer, while offering the company growth over time.

HP Emporium allows companies to explore, experience and evaluate the power of the web for six months, where the shop is hosted by Hewlett-Packard

---

[14]http://www.broadvision.com/

[15]http://www.hpemporium.com/

and where several workshops are held to allow the company to expand their business after the six weeks. With Emporium companies are able to go online almost immediately with the chance to pick up the required knowledge in the meantime. This allows a timely entry to e-commerce.

The online store consists of the shopping solution in the front-end and payment processing, shipment and marketing management modules in the back-end. The six months online are accompanied by five workshops. The first workshop is the kick-off workshop, which is set up to develop the project plan and the teams required within the company and Hewlett-Packard to support the shopping initiative.

Once the resources and the project plan are decided on, a marketing workshop will be used to develop the marketing plan. Right after this a workshop is on the agenda that will explain the e-commerce solution to the company. After the completion of these three workshops, the digital shop is ready to go online.

After three months an intermediate workshop is planned, where the interim results are discussed and analyzed. And after six months the analysis of the final experience is performed and the next steps are discussed. Thereafter the company is prepared to deal with online shopping and is able to let Hewlett-Packard host their solution, move on to an ISP or host the solution in their own environment.

IBM Net.Commerce

Net.Commerce[16], developed by IBM, is a complex shopping system with shopping basket and full search functionality. It is fully localized, making it a good solution for shops with lots of products.

It provides a set of integrated software components to sell goods and services through an electronic catalog on the Internet. This out-of-the-box solution gives companies the ability to start simple and grow fast. It comes complete with catalog templates, setup wizards and advanced catalog tools to easily build effective and attractive electronic commerce sites. Net.Commerce can be used both in business-to-business and business-to-consumer applications.

The product comes in three flavors. START, which is suitable for small-to-medium enterprises, the PRO edition, for large online retailers and a version for hosting servers for ISPs. The software supports both, single or multiple storefronts and is scalable over single or multiple machines. Net.Commerce is available for many different platforms and offers a good system integration with databases and legacy systems. Both, static and dynamic web pages are supported, to enable multi-languages, for example.

In addition to the storefront it also contains a payment module suitable for accepting credit card payments using the SET and SSL standards. A wizard makes it easy to set up shops. A module for order tracking and personalization support is integrated as well.

---

[16]http://www.software.ibm.com/commerce/net.commerce/

i-Cat Electronic Commerce Suite

The electronic commerce suite by i-Cat[17] is a complete solution, which consists of ready-to-use templates, which can be used to create the layouts for the shop. The standard search functionality and an index is available. In addition to this, customers are able to register and the information is saved for returning customers. The standard shopping basket is also available and resellers are able to register and will get special prices.

Promotions can be created through the simple-to-use administration interface. It is also very simple to change the pricing of the products. In addition to the typical shopping functionalities, i-Cat has built in security features that allow secure payment over the Internet. CyberCash, CheckFree, First Virtual, Open Market, OM-Secure Link, SET and SSL payments are allowed (see Chapter 13 for more information on payment solutions). In addition to these pre-installed payment solutions, it is possible to create new ones using a standardized API. i-Cat runs on all major operating systems and works together with the most common web servers. User identification is done by password and not by cookie.

Intershop Online

The Intershop[18] solution offers another complete, open shopping software package. Like i-Cat it uses templates to create the web shop front-end. Search and index functionalities are also available. Customers are able to register their address and preferred payment method. Promotions and pricing can be configured easily through the web administration interface.

Payment methods, which are already pre-integrated include SET and SSL credit card payment, invoice and cash on delivery. The payment methods can be easily extended, as our team at Hewlett-Packard has proven. We integrated a smart card identification and payment solution into the existing software without too much trouble, making it an easy to use software package, that can be easily extended with some programming.

Internet Factory Merchant Builder

Merchant Builder by the Internet Factory[19] is a flexible solution, which uses templates and is easy to administer. It is cheaper than Intershop and offers a good starting point for start-ups, which do not want to sell thousands of products online.

Connection to databases with ODBC connectivity is possible, CyberCash, ICVerify and First Virtual payment solutions are included. It is possible to create financial reports and additional tools for developing merchant applications

---

[17]http://www.icat.com/
[18]http://www.intershop.de/
[19]http://www.ifact.com/

are included. The merchant builder is a truly open solution, as the full source code is included.

Microsoft Commerce Server

Microsoft Site Server 3.0 Commerce Edition[20] is Microsoft's solution to the e-commerce problems. The solution is highly integrated into Microsoft BackOffice and its development tools. Simple sites can be designed by modifying some basic templates, while complex sites can be designed and customized through Visual InterDev.

Bundled with it is SQL Server, which gives you a complete database package. Built into the software are so-called pipelines, which are visual models that let you manipulate the order of the business processes. Two types of pipelines are available. One for the e-commerce online shopping solution and one for the ORM type business-to-business solution.

As all server features can be scripted and programmed through COM objects the pipelines can be extended to adapt to any scenario. This requires of course in-depth knowledge in the Windows platform and the product itself. Using the GUI pipeline editor, users can tweak or add code to various steps along the way, once the whole business pipeline has been implemented.

Cross-promotions are supported natively by the system. Any combination of rules and database fields can be use to create special sales, cross promotions and customer-based promotions. It also offers web site analysis tool that gives you feedback on how many customers are using the site and what their preferred products are.

ElMedia NetSell

NetSell, developed by ElMedia[21], is a product that is simple to use. The administration is done through a web browser, updates are made directly to the production data, which makes it suitable for smaller shops with only a few products. Larger shops won't want live updates, they will need a staging area, where they can test the changes first. A shopping basket and a customer database for registered customers is available.

The NetSell software is designed to work at an ISP site, which hosts the web server and the shopping software.

Open Market LiveCommerce

LiveCommerce by Open Market[22] is an Internet application that uses an embedded object-oriented database technology to generate a very flexible enterprise-scale catalogue system. LiveCommerce is designed for very large cata-

---

[20]http://www.microsoft.com/

[21]http://www.elmedia.de/

[22]http://www.openmarket.com/

logues with up to 100,000 items. It offers a fast and flexible navigation capability and offers customized searches according to the requirements of the customer by generating the desired catalogue page for the browser.

It is possible to use LiveCommerce as a stand alone Internet catalogue system, just as many others, but its strength lies in the integration with other system, such as transaction and inventory systems. The latest release incorporates a new store setup wizard, making it even easier for small to medium sized merchants to take advantage of the features. Dual currency support has been integrated to present prices in two currencies at the same time, such as Deutsche Mark (DM) and Euro, which is a legal requirement for the Euro participants since January 1999.

Yahoo Store

The Yahoo Store[23] is another product that cannot be bought, only rented. The software resides on the Yahoo-Server and merchants are able to administer their shop via the web browser. It uses an intuitive interface, has a built-in search engine and offers peerless statistical tools. The pricing options are very powerful and flexible.

The rental price per month depends on the number of items you want to sell via the web. Depending on your focus, it may make sense to outsource the hosting of the web server and the shopping software. In general, a company will outsource all parts that are not strategic for it. If shopping is just an add-on to your core business, then this can be a good solution.

7.2.4   Comparison of Online Shopping Solutions

Table 7.3 gives a short summary of the features and the types of solutions presented above. It is difficult to say which solution fits your requirements best; price, type and platform will be the first things you need to take into consideration and then look at the web sites of the independent software vendors for detailed information on the functionality of their solutions. The better the functionality matches your business requirements the better you will be positioned to make money through the online shop. The price normally gives an indication of the complexity of the product.

While all of these products are both interesting to companies that want to go online and ISPs that want to offer these services to their customers, a new type of selling shopping solutions has come up. Hewlett-Packard introduced in 1999 Commerce for the Millennium[24], a complete shopping solution designed for ISPs. Instead of selling a piece of software to the ISP, Hewlett-Packard sells a black-box to the ISP, which contains not only a shopping solution, but also the required back-end infrastructure, including a link to a bank for online payment

---

[23]http://store.yahoo.com/
[24]http://www.hp.com/

and a billing system. Hewlett-Packard has pre-integrated all the necessary components for this solution, making sure that all components are interconnected and allow the required flow of information between the store front and the business back-end. In addition to the business infrastructure, Hewlett-Packard also provides the Internet architecture consisting of hardware, such as servers and routers, that make it easy to add it the to existing equipment of an ISP.

What makes this solution unique is that ISPs do not have to pay up front for the hardware, software and installation, but rather pay on a transactional basis. Every time a business transaction takes place in one of the shops the ISP hosts, Hewlett-Packard is receiving a small fee. This makes it easy for ISPs to expand their business rapidly without having to put together single components and enables businesses to go online at a lower price as the cost is recuperated over time.

Comparison of Shopping Solutions

Product	Type	Platforms	Price
Beans Industry	Hosting	Java	low
Broadvision	Product	AIX, HP-UX, Solaris	high
HP Emporium	Hosting	HTML	low
IBM Net.Commerce	Product	Windows, AIX, HP-UX, Solaris	high
iCat ECS	Product	Windows, AIX, HP-UX, Solaris	medium
InterShop ePages	Hosting	HTML	low
InterShop Enterprise	Product	Perl	high
Internet Factory	Product	Unknown	low
Microsoft	Product	Windows	medium
ElMedia NetSell	Hosting	HTML	low
OpenMarket LiveCommerce	Product	Unknown	medium
Yahoo Store	Hosting	HTML	low

Table 7.3.

7.3 Implications of the New Economy

7.3.1 Generating Revenues

Using standard software solutions nowadays it is easy to set up and operate an online shop. But this is not enough to be successful. By paying attention to some basic rules, you can create an online shop that is very successful.

As prices become more and more irrelevant, it is necessary to create unique selling positions. This means that you must offer more than just what everyone else offers. As more and more shops offer the same products, it is necessary to distinguish oneself by offering value-added services.

Creating a new bookshop may seem stupid with such heavy weights like Amazon.com and Barnes & Noble already present on the web. But still it may make sense, if you do not try to compete with the size of these giants, but by finding a niche market where you have more expertize than a general bookseller. Creating a vertical portal site, where you also offer books will help generate sales in your book shop and at the same time generate hits on the rest of your site. A good domain name is also important; if people cannot remember how to access your service they won't come back.

7.3.2 Pricing on the Internet

While the price for production is going down, the actual final price for the end customer is not decreasing that much anymore. If we look at the prices, we can see that whenever a technology drops below a certain price, it is replaced by a newer technology. This is especially true for computer hardware. Although the speed of the computers is increasing rapidly, the prices are going down only moderately and older equipment it not available anymore.

As more and more services become digital, it is possible to customize them in such a way that they exactly fit the needs of the customer, without necessarily increasing the price. Instead of reducing the price, the price seems to tend to approach the maximum a buyer is willing to pay.

Many think that services and digital products in the information era should be free. The major reason is that many people cannot distinguish between the value of the product and the cost for replicating it. A film may cost 200 million dollars in production, but through the Internet replication, costs are nearly zero. Does this mean that one can give away the film for free?

The Internet is built on the premise of free information distribution, which was fine while it was an academic network. With the introduction of the world wide web, more and more commercial companies have become involved and they want to see money for their products. The problem is that once a product has been digitized it can be copied without problem. This can be one disadvantage of the open standards for commercial organizations.

On the Internet we will see three new ways that prices will be set (see also Table 7.4). The first pricing schema is based on the premise that the price is not based on the production costs anymore, but tends more and more to be determined by the buyer's willingness to pay. The market force behind this fact is the market power obtained by product differentiation. Even then, prices can be set at the consumer's value. Therefore, its price will not be zero unless the product is truly value-less.

New Paradigms on Pricing

The Internet offers new ways of creating revenues for a company, other than pricing the goods and services above the cost of production.

- **Advertising Pays the Product** – By adding advertising to the core product or service, it can be sold under production cost.

- **Buyer's Willingness to Pay** – The price is floating depending on demand and offers in the market. The Internet becomes a large auction.

- **Transaction Costs Based Billing** – The basic service or product is free and the customer needs to pay for every transaction a low fee.

Table 7.4.

In order to determine these new prices it is necessary to have more information on the customers' preferences. Sellers who can gather information on their customers will have an advantage as they can present the right products to the right customers at the right time and will be able to charge the highest prices. If we get back to the example of the film, this will mean that in the beginning the price for a copy of the film will be very high, as much more people will be interested in viewing it. As time goes by, the price will drop eventually to zero at a time nobody is interested in the film anymore.

This can be done because digital media has very low costs associated with digital replication. The viewer will not able to see a difference between the original file and the copied file and what is even more important, the viewer will not care. Artwork, on the other hand cannot be copied in such a way. The older the artwork gets the higher the prices become. A copy of a Picasso[25] can be downloaded at no cost, without having impact on the price of the original,

---

[25]e.g. http://www.compulink.co.uk/ phreak/picasso/

as the original picture is more than the frame, the canvas and the colors used to form the artwork.

The second pricing schema is based on the premise that it is possible to sell prices under cost of production and make money out of other revenue streams. The British magazine *The Economist*[26] asked an interesting question. Is it possible to sell dollar notes for 90 cents on the web? The short answer is yes, of course. While companies in the past calculated their prices on the cost of production, more and more companies are having additional revenue streams for making money. Actually all newspapers and magazines work this way. The are sold under price and earn money by putting in advertising. Television and radio content are sold at no cost and are financed entirely through advertising (at least the so-called Free-TV). The same applies to most web sites that offer content. But more and more web sites that offer goods and services use this paradigm to offer unbeatably low prices.

Free PC[27] is such a company. Free PC, as the name suggests, gives computers away for free. In order to qualify for a free computer, it is necessary to answer a list of questions and if the customer meets certain demographically attractive requirements, the customer will receive one of the computers for free. In order to qualify you need to be part of one of the target groups of the advertising, which you have agreed to view, whenever the computer is switched on. Half of the hard disk's space is reserved for advertising information, which is updated every time the customer goes online.

Other companies offer similar packages, which are good enough for the occasional computer user. Professional users will be hindered by this type of bombardment and will not be as productive as they could be.

The third way of pricing is basing on the transaction costs. Instead of paying a one-time price for a product, you are forced to pay for it every time you use it. The good old telephone service works this way in most European countries and more and more digital services require transaction payments instead of one-time fees. In Finland, Nokia[28] has started a web site where customers are able to compose new dial tones for free. They can use the composing software for free, but once they have decided on a new dial tone for their cellular phone, they need to call a special number and enter an ID. This will transfer the dial tone from the web site to the cellular phone and a transaction fee of approximately 40 cents is charged.

The same can be applied to online word processors, for example, which could be used for free, but every save of the document would cost a small transaction fee. The same could apply for loading, printing and spell-checking. By removing the initial cost, the product, service or piece of information becomes more pervasive. And if the transaction fees are low enough more customers are willing to spend some money on it. Instead of having 1,000 customers who are

---

[26]http://www.economist.co.uk/

[27]http://www.free-pc.com/

[28]http://www.nokia.com/

paying 100 Dollars or Euro for a product, you can have 1,000,000 customers who pay 10 cents per transaction. This generates a higher and more constant revenue stream for the company.

7.3.3 Implications on the Price

The Internet enables the free exchange of information, which also means that pricing information is flowing more freely. The cost of exploring alternative offerings and substitute products is nearly zero, the auction model described in the dynamic trade model becomes more real. In market segments where products and services are not differentiated sufficiently a price war will take place. Tickets, for example, are such products. Many airlines offer online auctions for empty seats on airplanes. Based on the last minute model, customers are able to bid for the seat. The core business of travel agencies, checking for flights and booking tickets and hotels, becomes more and more a self-service on the Internet. Other services, such as online banking make life difficult for many bank clerks. As the cost for the business transaction drops, the price for the customer drops as well.

Although many customers still prefer known brands, the low entry cost to the New Economy will drive down prices for established brands to the level of no-name products or services. Known brands perform a vetting function in the realm of overwhelming information availability. But the Internet offers a huge opportunity for newcomers to pose a threat to known brands. The cost for establishing a new brand are high, however. Amazon.com spends most of its money for the marketing campaign to market the brand. The costs for the operation of the business are almost negligible.

7.3.4 Implications on the Cost

By digitizing processes, such as moving distribution from physical products to digital products or using Internet based inventory tracking services, costs can be cut dramatically. The shortened duration of the time spent in the value chain provides both benefits and operational challenges. The technical challenges can be resolved easily through advanced hardware and software, but in order to stay in front of the competition it is necessary to resolve the operational challenges.

The companies need to handle all of their processes in parallel through real-time transactions. The Internet enables companies to drive down costs by introducing new processes, which either enhance existing processes or replace them. This requires resources to be re-deployed, particularly in the back office, as the front end is represented by a web application. Only very few online systems are self-funding at the time of writing, but costs can be saved in the back-end by changing the processes and adapting them to the needs of the New Economy.

7.4   Electronic Software Distribution

7.4.1   Benefits of ESD

Electronic Software Distribution (ESD) is a particular way of selling products via the Internet. The key feature is that it is not necessary to ship out products to the customers via traditional logistics companies. Shipping costs drop to nearly zero. The product and the manual are downloaded by the customer from the Internet.

The only shipping fee that occurs is the online time of the customers, if they are connected via a provider or telephone company that charges on a minute or hourly basis. I remember one incident in 1997, when I downloaded the Visual Café Java compiler package from Symantec[29] for the Macintosh, which had at that time already over 20 Megabytes. I had ordered it directly from the web site and downloaded it from the United States to my Mac in Europe, taking about six hours to download the complete package. My biggest fear was that the download would be interrupted and I would have to try again. Worse than trying again was the fact that I was allowed only one retry. I was lucky, the software was downloaded the first time. Electronic Software Distribution has evolved over time to overcome these problems. Faster modems and new concepts have made ESD a secure and cheap solution for the distribution of software. Not only software can be distributed through ESD, but also music, videos and books.

Customers, publishers and channel partners all can benefit from ESD. Customers, for example, experience a new shopping convenience as the delivery is immediate. No matter at what time of the day the customers access the web site, they will be able to download the product immediately. This also allows quicker access to updates and new releases for registered customers. ESD allows new pricing alternatives, such as try-and-buy and pay-per-use.

The benefits for the publisher include lower cost of goods sold compared to a physical distribution. The publisher does not need to replicate the product or the packaging, which makes also returns simple. There can be more efficient sales of niche and low-volume products and ESD also offers a more efficient channel for updates and selling upgrades. It allows also a faster time to market for new or replacement products. The paradigm of ESD improves the inventory management by avoiding stock-outs in the channel.

The advantage for channel partners is that they do not need to carry a physical inventory to manage and therefore do not have any inventory carrying costs. The sales environment is much more scalable without the traditional cost increases. Flexible and timely pricing and special offers with immediate feedback helps the channel partners develop new target markets and get returning customers to the web site by offering free upgrades, additional information and bug fixes. The channel partners also do not have to deal with

---

[29]http://www.symantec.com/

geographical boundaries any more. The products can be sold all over the world also allowing a faster time to market. The digital distribution chain makes it easier and more flexible to bundle and unbundle products.

7.4.2 Problems with ESD

Although ESD offers a lot of advantages, it also has some disadvantages, which can be overcome, if the traps are known and appropriate security mechanisms are implemented. Downloading software without special protection will allow the customer to copy the software to anyone and destroy the legal revenue stream of the software distributor. Forrester Research[30] calls it the "Digital Distribution Wars"[31], which we are seeing happening on the Internet.

The problem is not new. Software pirates have been copying software for years illegally, but the Internet offers new ways to spread the illegal software. In order to make ESD a success for a company it is necessary to protect the software in such a way that copying becomes impossible or infeasible. The faster the Internet connection gets, the more easily large software packages can be downloaded from the Internet. So far, university students and business people have the best connection to the Internet, but more and more households are getting high-speed access to the Internet, making it easier for anyone to get direct access to software over the Internet. Just as pirated software has helped the explosive growth of the personal computer, it now helps the explosive growth of the Internet, even though the content industry does not want to hear this. Already in 1985 the ftp tool enabled pirates to exchange software over the Internet and search engines today make the search for pirated software easy.

Another problem with ESD are new devices that are especially designed for pirated content. Diamond Multimedia[32] has set up the music industry when it released the Rio portable MP3 player in October 1998. Although there is some legal MP3 music available on the Internet, available at sites such as mp3.com[33] or orbos.de[34], most of the music available in the MP3 format on the Internet is illegal and that is the reason why the Rio portable is so successful. It also makes the copying of music much easier than it used to be.

Although most software or content is available digitally, only very few companies have so far put up their digital content for sale directly on the web. All the premium material has been held back. Media and software firms have extensive libraries of desirable content, but they will not distribute it digitally without a way to protect revenue. Some companies who are not able to cope with the quick change in technology. Instead of getting into the digital dis-

---

[30] http://www.forrester.com/

[31] The Forrester Report, Michael Putnam, Digital Distribution Wars, April 1999.

[32] http://www.diamondmm.com/

[33] http://www.mp3.com/

[34] http://www.orbos.de/

tribution they sue start-ups, which use the new paradigms and technologies to sell their content over the Internet. The recording industry, for example, tried to stop Diamond Multimedia from releasing the Rio portable, instead of working together with them to stop piracy.

7.4.3 Making ESD Profitable

The content industry is pursuing new digital formats, which make it possible to copy-protect the content. Threatened content owners are developing new secure publishing formats. To make the digital distribution business successful, technology firms and content owners must agree on protection principles and build a new digital infrastructure. To achieve robustness and flexibility, this framework surrounds content with compression formats, copy prevention methods, devices, media players, and licensing systems.

Agfa[35], Hewlett-Packard, Kodak[36] and others have responded to digital imaging piracy by creating the Digital Imaging Group[37] in September 1997. Their FlashPix format, together with copy prevention technology from cSafe, and fingerprinting from ImageLock forms a secure infrastructure for image commerce on the Web. More information on FlashPix and other image formats can be found in Chapter 12.

At the same time the music industry has responded to the threat of MP3 with the Secure Digital Music Initiative (SDMI) in February 1999. While the music industry backs the SDMI effort with the goal of settling protection and developing devices for the customers, they are also battling against the efforts by IBM[38] and Liquid Audio[39], which are proposing their own secure formats.

It is just a matter of time until people will start to download videos from the Internet. In May 1999 the first pirated copies of the new Star Wars films appeared on the Internet. The file was 1.3 gigabytes large, making it infeasible for most people to download in reasonable time and too costly. But it can be expected that within a few years bandwidth will be good enough for anyone to download the file within a few minutes or watch the movie in real-time over the Internet.

The software for real-time movie watching is already available. Realplayer from RealNetworks[40] and QuickTime by Apple[41], already offer today the possibility to view films and TV programs in low quality. The increased bandwidth will also increase the quality of service.

The Internet and other digital media have eroded the distinction between music, video, game and images. All these types of media merge into a new type

---

[35] http://www.agfa.com/
[36] http://www.kodak.com/
[37] http://www.digitalimaging.org/
[38] http://www.ibm.com/
[39] http://www.liquidaudio.com/
[40] http://www.real.com/
[41] http://www.apple.com/

of media, which is basically digital content. The newly formed content industry will have to create a multimedia rights clearing-house, to prevent unauthorized copying of the content. The existing clearing-houses, such as ASCAP and BMI will most probably merge into this new multimedia rights clearing-house, as these single industries merge. Imagine a racing simulation where the player is able to choose any type of music for the background music. It will become possible to download films, games, music and images from different web sites, with the licenses stored in a single location in the back-end.

Commerce Direct International[42] (CDI) is a clearing house, which runs its service on centralized servers and works directly with software publishers rather than resellers. McAfee Associates Inc.[43] and Corel Corp.[44] are using CDI's encryption, wrapper and transport technology to sell their security and photo library products through their own web sites.

Cable companies and broad band Internet access providers will merge into the single space of content providers, being able to charge for downloads and put it onto the ISP or cable invoice. This will mean that content providers will use new technologies and formats, as the current content formats are far too easy to copy. One problem with these new technologies is the encryption that is used therein. This will put the United States in a bad position as the export of encryption devices is very restricted. Other countries that are producing traditionally encryption software and content devices will benefit, such as Israel and Japan.

7.4.4 New Licensing Models

Electronic Software Distribution allows for new licensing models, which are slowly being adopted by the software publishing industry. This change has been inspired by advances in license management systems, which allow to bill for the actual usage of a certain digital product instead of having a fixed price for the software.

These license management systems have additional functionality, allowing developers the ability to monitor and track the usage of their products. With these technologies embedded into their products, developers can negotiate almost any license model shaped by various criteria, ranging from length of term and number of invocations to number of concurrent users. Software leasing may become viable for many companies.

These new license management systems do not only allow software companies to monitor the use of their applications and content providers to monitor the use of their audio or video data, but also local network administrators working for a certain company to create a software inventory of all connected computers that reside on a company Intranet. Employees will have the pos-

---

[42]http://www.cdi.net/

[43]http://www.mcafee.com/

[44]http://www.corel.com/

sibility to install software from anywhere, with a centralized license management. This also helps to reduce the amount of pirated software on company computers.

Software manufacturers and content providers are now able to provide new forms of licenses. Three types of licenses will become important in the future; concurrent licenses, licensed periods and licensed sessions. The concurrent licenses term allows a maximum number of users that are allowed to access a service or software at the same time. This type of license is often used for web software as it allows the control of the amount of users accessing a certain piece of software at a given time. Database management systems are also often sold on a concurrent use model, as their value increases with increased numbers of concurrent users.

The licensed periods model allows software manufacturers to operate a subscription business. The products are given out to the customers, which then can be used for a specific period of time, such as a month or year. Shareware or Tryware are typical pieces of software that are given out to customers for free for a certain period of time for testing purposes. Customers are able to test the software for thirty days and then are required to pay for the license or delete the software from their hard disk (see Chapter 14 for more information). Digital certificates are also often based on the licensed periods model. They expire after one or two years and require the owner of the certificate to go back to the certification authority to get a new one. The reason is twofold. It allows the certification authority to make money from the renewals and the certificate is rechecked every two years for security reasons, just as you have to renew your passport every few years.

The third type of licenses are the licensed sessions. This means that a certain piece of software or content can be used or viewed. This form of licenses gives customers a fixed number of sessions or a fixed amount of time. This is especially interesting for content providers. Most hotels around the world allow the viewing of pay television. Once you have paid for a film you are able to view the film for a certain period of time (normally one day) or a certain amount of times (normally twice). A similar license could be applied to content that is distributed over the Internet.

7.4.5   ESD Products

Products that allow electronic software distribution need to adhere to some rules to be accepted by the people who use them. Trying to invent bullet-proof protection is a waste of time. Every protection can be cracked, no matter how good it is, therefore the balance between ease-of-use and copy-protection should be maintained. The copy-protection should be transparent to the customers and should limit abuse to determined attackers. They are the real threat to your company and not the honest people who do make a copy for a friend from time to time.

The content industry needs to wrap content into a format that protects itself. This means that even if you are able to copy the content the source is always encoded into the content, so that pirates can be located easily. Watermarks are a good way to simply protect content. Companies like Channelware[45] have developed technologies that can decrypt files on the fly, while a game or application is being run. As soon as you exit the game or application the decrypted program is removed. In conjunction with digital watermarks and on-line registration, it protects the content even after the distribution.

To make ESD products more secure it is necessary to separate the license from the content. This means that one needs special software or devices to unlock the content. Just passing on the content will not enable anyone to use it. The license is personalized, meaning that it is very easy to trace back the origin of the license. To unlock protected content, the encryption key needs to be sent to customers via e-mail, for example. The advantage is that if a download could not be completed, it can be resumed based on the license records.

A good electronic software distribution product must be able to handle the complex tasks of delivering software and data to all systems dispersed on the Internet or on a company Intranet. It needs to be able to verify that the software was installed successfully and is ready to run. Problematic software should be de-installed and older versions restored if a problem occurs. A good ESD program also will help keep track of the versions of software and data that are currently installed. This will help to create an effective marketing initiative for Internet customers, as they can be informed about updates and bug fixes. On company Intranets, automatic updates can be executed and it can be verified that all users have the same version running on their system, making user support easier. A good ESD program should be able to distribute software to as few as one or two computers or as many as thousands of systems at various geographical locations.

It should be ensured that the ESD products do not require additional hardware for the customers. Dongles and other types of hardware protection have not been accepted by customers in the past and this won't change in the future. As the software changes so fast, new hardware would be required on a regular basis. A content-independent protection may be acceptable.

Companies like Reciprocal[46], Digital Delivery[47], InterTrust[48], GLOBEtrotter[49], Release Software[50] and Digital River[51] have already created ESD solutions for immediate use. It is expected that they will adopt new international standards, which are in the process of being defined.

---

[45]http://www.channelware.com/

[46]http://www.reciprocal.com/

[47]http://www.digitaldelivery.com/

[48]http://www.intertrust.com/

[49]http://www.globetrotter.com/

[50]http://www.releasesoft.com/

[51]http://www.digitalriver.com/

7.5   Configurator Tools

7.5.1   Reasons for Configurators

In order to create a product, collaboration is essential. Designers and engineers need to work together to create a product to its specifications. Through computer aided design (CAD) software this has been possible already for quite some time. Through the use of web-based configurator tools the collaboration can be easily extended to the customers so that they can create and buy unique products over the Internet.

Through a product configurator customers are able to assemble product components into a finished product. Through the configurator the customers are elevated to a level of technical abstraction, where they do not need to know which components fit together or how they do. These pieces of information are programmed into the configuration application. Through the Internet, customers from all over the world are able to assemble complex products themselves, directly at the site of the manufacturer, without needing the technical background required for every single piece, thus resolving the need for a technical expert as an intermediary.

The use of configurators reduces the number of technical people in presales and sales, as the customers are able to answer all questions regarding the configuration themselves. All major computer vendors, such as Dell[52] and Hewlett-Packard[53] offer online configurators for their computers. As computers consist nowadays of many components, it is important to know which sound card works with which main board and graphics accelerator. There are also many types of memory chips, processor upgrade cards and other hardware, which won't work together in every combination. Instead of letting customers order the hardware products one-by-one, they are now ordered through the configurator in a context. This context allows customers to select the appropriate hardware components. The number of returns is reduced through configurator tools and the customers are more willing to buy a product, as they are sure it will work with their existing configuration.

All major car manufacturers have been using configurators for quite a while on their web sites. See Figure 7.2 for the online configurator on BMW's homepage[54]. They were used by the sales people when talking to customers. Now that more and more cars are sold over the Internet, these tools are also accessible directly by the customer. Based on the component selections, a price is dynamically returned to the user, which makes the product configurator a good tool for web-based sales as well.

By using Internet-based configurator tools, companies are able to collaborate with a much broader audience and extend their business. In many cases

---

[52]http://www.dell.com/
[53]http://www.hp.com/
[54]http://www.bwm.com/

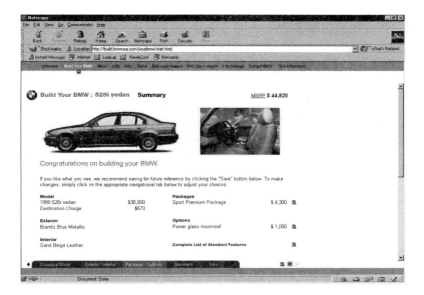

Figure 7.2. BMW Online Configurator

intermediaries were used to create configurations for the end customer. With the new generation of configurator tools, these intermediaries can focus their business on other services. Product-oriented companies need to look into Internet product configurators in order to survive.

Through the use of configurators customers are able to create customized solutions and receive pricing quotes in an instant. This helps also the manufacturer to reduce the time for producing the solution, as the orders can't be inaccurate or incomplete anymore. This also eliminates the order entry rework, which is necessary, if no configurator is used. This all results in increased customer satisfaction related to a higher-quality quote-to-delivery process. Configurators align solutions to the needs of the customers.

7.5.2   Configurator Products

Many configurator products are available and offer varying degrees of functionality on the Internet. The following list of products gives an overview of the best configurator solutions, which were available at the time of writing. The Internet enables customers to perform a number of "what-if" scenarios, without the need for understanding every component of the product in detail.

BT Squared Technologies

BT Squared Technologies[55] offers a packaged software application suite called "2order interactive selling system". The software is designed for client/server configurations, for stand-alone computers, such as laptops and offers Internet connectivity. Besides product and pricing configuration the suite offers solutions for interactive negotiation, quote and order management, proposal generation, a marketing encyclopedia and data synchronization. Through "2order interactive selling system" manufacturers are able to analyze the requirements of the customer more accurately. Once the requirements have been input by the customer, the system is able to configure, price, quote and sell the products and services. The software is available for the Windows platform, which makes it a good choice for sales people and their laptops, but less a stable solution for the general public on the Internet.

Cincom

Cincom[56] offer a whole suite of products. It is called iC solutions for configuration, which allows you to generate complete, accurate configurations. Cincom streamlines the configuration process by offering a complete suite of products for the sales force.

The iC Configurator Developer is the core product offering the possibility to manage information about customer requirements, products and services. It is possible to define attributes and features and add alternative configurations, in case the original configuration is not available. It is also possible to convert unique customer requirements into customer solutions.

Through iC Connect the sales people do not have to connect to a server, but have all information stored locally, making it a good solution for customer visits. The data is copied from the server, before going offline. Once the computer gets back online, all orders and updates for the configurator are exchanged.

Firepond

FirePond[57] offers a comprehensive set of tools for sales and marketing, called Signature Plus. One part of the solution is called Signature Plus Configuration and offers one of the best configuration engines available today. It allows sales people, partners and customers to create accurate product configurations. Through a mix of representation it is possible to create simple to complex product configuration models. This is achieved through optimized solvers, which address Boolean logic, conditional logic, fuzzy logic, spatial placement and many other deployment-proven modes of configuration. Signature Plus Configuration is the only solution to represent configurations in all of the modes at the

---

[55] http://www.btsquared.com/
[56] http://www.cincom.com/
[57] http://www.firepond.com/

same time. In addition to this it is even possible to use several solvers to mix inference engines to solve very demanding problems.

The configurator can be used, for example, first to determine which type of product fits the business needs of the customers and then the same configuration logic can be applied to further narrow the usage criteria, such as a specific model, options and engineering specifications. The final outcome is a highly customized product, which has been designed interactively by the customer, but is buildable by the manufacturer.

Through the graphical user interface customers are even able to participate in complex configuration processes. This reduces the need for training and speeds up the time for a deal to complete. The user interface is highly customizable depending on the output device and sales situation, such as a sales person talking to the customer or the end customer using the Internet to configure a system.

Friedman Corporation

The Friedman Corporation[58] offers an integrated, configurator for three key industries. Building and home products, capital equipment and consumer products are the industries supported by the multi-platform software, which is highly modularized. Specialized in ERP solutions for discrete to-order manufacturers it offers a good solution in high-volume and complex order-entry manufacturing environments.

Gedys

Gedys[59] offers a suite of products to implement product and service configurators. The suite consists of the products "net.select", "web.select" and "WebROM". Depending on the size of the company, you can choose either "net.select" or "web.select", which offer the possibility to start with a small core product and then add new modules as your needs grow. The third product "WebROM" enables the functionality of the Internet-based solution to be extended to sales people traveling with a laptop and to kiosk-based terminals without permanent connection to the Internet.

Planware

The Konfex configurator by the German software house Planware DV-System GmbH[60] offers a lightweight product, which is used by many small-to-medium enterprises in German speaking countries. The system is able to create an online configuration system for companies that offer highly customizable products. Konfex is sub-divided into four pieces of functionality. The actual config-

---

[58]http://www.friedmancorp.com/
[59]http://www.gedys.com/
[60]http://www.planware.de/

uration tool, a tool for checking the technical feasibility, price calculation and a template feature for web pages. One customer is Erwin Junker Maschinenfabrik[61], which uses it for the configuration of spare parts.

Trilogy

Trilogy[62] is the maker of the "Selling Chain Suite", which is a comprehensive, integrated sales and marketing solution. One of the most famous configurator tools, which is used at PC Order[63] on their web site, for example, the system is able to manage the flow of information between a company and its customers. It provides a company with appropriate customer information needed to price, market and sell its solutions, while giving the sales channel and end customer access to sales information needed to make an informed buying decision.

SC Config, Selling Chain's configurators delivers accurate solutions and quotes by incorporating the preferences of the customers and the choices made during the product selection. The user-friendly administration system allows non-technical staff to define product relationships.

7.6   Operational Resources Management

7.6.1   Reasons for ORM

Every company requires operational resources besides the goods that are required for production. These resources are the non-production goods and services that are required and managed on a daily basis to run the day-to-day business. The areas for operational resources include capital equipment (such as computer equipment) maintenance, repair and operating (MRO) supplies (such as office supplies) and travel and entertainment (T&E) (such as travel services).

In many companies the buying process for operational resources is managed by many different organizations and hundreds of different suppliers are providing services, goods and information. Although the operating resources do account for a large amount of company spending, the buying process is not well organized and managed. In many cases a paper-based process is used for ordering new pencils and phone lines.

Because of its decentralized approach in many companies, every department is able to handle the operational resources on an individual basis, which results in higher prices than through a central buying organization. Another cost factor is the maintenance of the relationships with the suppliers and the missing real-time features such as order status. Today many companies operate their buying process via telephone and telefax.

---

[61]http://www.junker.de/

[62]http://www.trilogy.com/

[63]http://www.pcorder.com/

Once a central buying organization has been put in place, the paper-based process needs to be digitized in order to automate, control and leverage it. As long as the process is not digitized, the company is not able to control the spending and the suppliers involved in the process.

Operational Resources Management (ORM) solutions put catalogues online and automate the purchases and the approvals. Beyond saving paper costs, the goal is to stop renegade spending and channel purchasing to selected vendors at pre-negotiated prices. ORM allows operational resources to be managed more strategically, by using the Internet and its connectivity to provide a communication infrastructure, where buyers and suppliers can work together on a direct basis without losing control over the spending. Actually the company gets more control over the spending through the electronic management system. Introducing ORM does not necessarily require additional hardware or software to be installed, as many systems run on standard web servers and browsers, which can be run on any computer platform. Through the use of electronic communication the cost per transaction can be lowered significantly and the process can be strongly automated.

Decision support tools enable the buyer to identify supplier discounts which have been introduced through a central buying process and are able to build strong relationships. ORM is not only reducing the cost per transaction, in most cases it also reduces the number of suppliers. In many cases different departments order their operational resources from different suppliers. Through central buying and ORM the number of suppliers can be reduced dramatically. The supplier consolidation will reduce costs even further.

ORM is one of the online services in the business-to-business area which will be implemented first as it presents a huge opportunity to cut down costs. Driving down the operational costs does automatically increase the profit for the company in return. In order to deliver the expected benefits, a complete solution must exist that provides a business-to-business connection between users, processes and systems.

By implementing an ORM solution companies are able to compare easily several suppliers of a certain product and track the orders on a buyer basis. An authorization of the buyer can be easily implemented and a workflow process can be implemented to replace the manual authorization steps. The ORM solution is able to provide an order status and an integration with the installed business systems.

The infrastructures on Intranet and Extranets enable companies to implement ORM solutions very efficiently. The purchasing catalogue of a company can be easily created by extracting the negotiated products and prices from the various catalogues of the suppliers. Thus; suppliers are able to offer one catalogue, which can be used for many purchasing departments of various companies. The purchasers are able to integrate all suppliers that offer their catalogues in the same standard without any trouble. A scalable connection between buyers and suppliers needs to be implemented in order to allow large and small partners to do business with each other. Purchasers and buyers need to agree on a price for every product or group of products. Price negotiation will take up most of the time.

ORM systems are moving business from proprietary EDI networks, which are mostly run over secure private networks, to the public Internet. These EDI networks are very costly to maintain and even more expensive to set up. Companies that already have them may want to stick with them to recoup their investments, but most companies are more than happy to give up these networks to eliminate the costs of maintenance. Those companies who haven't started yet, won't go into the risk of building up a private network, if the same business can be conducted securely over the Internet at a fraction of the cost.

7.6.2 Business Requirements

As mentioned above ORM can only be implemented successfully if the company already owns a central buying department. In addition to this a company-wide Intranet and direct links to the Internet are required to make the system work for everyone in the company. Therefore larger corporations are the most likely target market for ORM applications. Manufacturers are less likely to require an ORM system as a buyer as they have a lot of production goods which need to be bought on a daily basis and therefore already use a sort of ORM system. Manufacturers are ideal sellers in a digital ORM system. Large corporations offering services and information are more likely to be willing to invest in ORM systems as they do not buy operational goods on a daily basis.

In order to make the ORM even more successful, the supplier base needs to be consolidated. This process is being executed in many companies at the moment, as the cost for maintaining a large set of suppliers costs a lot of money. These companies are the ideal implementers for ORM solutions. Instead of sending out orders to many suppliers, the ORM system is taking the place of a virtual supplier, where all orders are sent. The ORM system then separates the orders and sends them out to the real suppliers. In batch mode, the ORM system is able to collect many small orders for a single product and then send out a larger order at the end of the day, receiving additional discounts.

A good ORM system should fulfill certain requirements in order to make sense in larger companies. Smaller companies may not need the complexity of large-scale ORM systems, but having all features will make the system more powerful and extensible. Table 7.5 contains a short summary of the required functionality.

The administration of the ORM system is very important and should be done through a web browser. The purchasing department should be able to administer the users and the system. The design of the ORM system should be possible through the administration, using HTML templates new pages should be easily set up within minutes. The ORM system should be customizable in such a way that it can look and feel like all other enterprise web applications.

Basic Features of ORM Systems

ORM systems should include at least the following functions to be a useful and extensible solution.

- **Administration** – Although this may seem trivial, a good ORM system needs an administration tool that can be used by non-technical persons.

- **Catalogue Support** – The ORM system should support multiple catalogues from different suppliers.

- **Enterprise Integration** – A good ORM system needs to integrate tightly into existing enterprise processes.

- **Localization** – Multinational companies need multi-lingual purchaser catalogues with local prices and products.

- **Reporting** – Tools for generating reports are a must.

- **Workflow** – Automated workflow should be possible directly through the ORM system.

Table 7.5.

More important is the administration of the users. Different roles should be assigned to people with different powers. Authorizers, requisitioners and buyers have different rights in the ORM system. Buyers for example, should only see the necessary products. Therefore it should be possible to assign product groups per user and a limit in spending for every single user should be possible. In most cases the users will be linked to group rights, as managing the rights of every single user will involve to much manual administration. Each buyer should also be assigned to a cost location, in order to retrieve the money for the order automatically from the correct department.

The ORM system needs to support multiple suppliers and their catalogues. The buyer front-end should integrate all the different suppliers and should allow a search over the consolidated catalogue and compare prices between different suppliers of the same or of similar products. The ORM system should automatically show the lowest price first. Ideally the system allows the import of different catalogue formats, making it easier for suppliers to become part of the system. In addition to an import feature, a connect feature is also useful.

Instead of uploading their catalogues, the ORM system connects to the original database, thus guaranteeing the most accurate and up-to-date data possible.

In order to automate all processes around purchasing it is necessary for it to be able to be integrated into existing enterprise solutions. Legacy systems should also be integrated, as they often contain the business logic for processes such as accounting.

Localization is very important, even if you have only a small regional company. If the catalogues and the ORM system are localized in your preferred language, you are able to choose from a far wider range of suppliers. If your company sits in the Czech republic and you have a supplier in Taiwan, then it would help if the catalogue would be in Czech in order to compare it better to a supplier from the Czech republic. Automatic price and currency conversions are also very important. In Europe support for multiple currencies is very important. Many companies operate on a European-wide basis. In the European Union the transition phase for the Euro requires every product to have prices in Euro and the local currency. Until 2002 this is a legal requirement.

A report generator is also a very important component of the system. In order to work effectively it is necessary to see how the system is used. Reporting is very important for the administrator to see if everything works flawlessly, but also for the management to see how effectively the work is done. The generator should typically have a set of standard reports and the ability to create new customized reports.

In order to integrate well with the existing enterprise applications, a workflow environment is very important. Typically ORM solutions do not contain a workflow component, but allow the connection to existing workflow applications. This makes it easier to integrate the ORM solution into the existing enterprise process environment.

7.6.3   Succeeding in the ORM Market

Although ORM systems have been available for some years, only very few are using it. The problem lies not in the technology. The software vendors have concentrated on the purchasing companies, as they will profit most from the ORM system. In order to convince the purchasing side, it is necessary to have many suppliers using the system and that is the problem. As long as the purchasers are not actively using the ORM systems in large quantity, it does not make a lot of sense for a purchaser to use the system.

Therefore the software vendors have started to change their business model and started to pay more attention to the suppliers. In March 1999 Ariba announced a partnership with Hewlett-Packard, whereby Ariba would host the catalogue of Hewlett-Packard on its web server and would keep it up-to-date. Although Hewlett-Packard still has to buy the software license, Ariba is taking over the costs for maintenance, which are much higher. By outsourcing the catalogue management, more organizations are able to participate.

Shortly after the implementation of Ariba.com, Commerce One started its own purchasing site[64]. Other than Ariba, Commerce One opened up its site to rival makers of ORM software. Commerce One is offering standard API, which allow other software solution to tie into the site. Instead of trying to push their own standard to the web, the ORM software manufacturers try to offer bridges between the solutions in order to create a larger market, thus offering a valuable service for more companies.

The ORM vendors are moving from a product price to a transaction price. Instead of licenses, transactions are becoming more important. Companies who want to use the service of one of the companies are required to pay per transaction, which will be around $1 US per purchase order.

Although it will still be possible to buy the software and install it, the transaction model will enable smaller companies to go digital in the ORM space, making them tough competition for the larger companies who can afford to install their own ORM system.

7.6.4   ORM Solutions

Many ORM solutions are available today and offer varying degrees of functionality on the Internet. The following list of products gives an overview of the best and most commonly used ORM solutions, which were available at the time of writing.

Ariba ORMS

Ariba ORMS[65] is a Java based solution, which runs on all platforms supporting Java. The system consists of several components, which talk to each other over the Network Application Architecture (NAA). Ariba ORMS contains a set of preconfigured business applications, which allow the automation of processes, such as capital equipment and MRO.

Over the NAA these business applications are able to talk to each other and link to legacy systems and databases using adapters. Ariba ORMS comes with a wide range of adapters, such as connections to Oracle[66], PeopleSoft[67] and SAP[68]. If the adapter is not available it is possible to write a new adapter that suits the needs of the company.

Through the use of Java, the user interface adapts nicely to the varying output devices, such as browser clients and enterprise servers and the business process needs of the enterprise. Finance departments, purchasing agents and suppliers can be nicely integrated into a single system, where everyone is able to communicate with the necessary partner.

---

[64]http://www.marketsite.net/

[65]http://www.ariba.com/

[66]http://www.oracle.com/

[67]http://www.peoplesoft.com/

[68]http://www.sap.com/

Ariba ORMS is able to subscribe to supplier catalogues on the Internet and aggregate the information into a single buyer catalogue. This is done automatically and requires no action on the buyer side, once a supplier catalogue has been subscribed. The internal workflow engine is able to manage most of the processes required for the purchasing department.

But there is a major disadvantage for companies outside of the United States. The software is not localizable in the current version, nor is a localized version available. This means that it is not possible to use other languages for the user interface, nor is it possible to have catalogues in several languages, using multiple currencies.

Commerce One Commerce Chain

The Commerce Chain solution by Commerce One[69] consists of two products, BuySite and MarketSite, which form together a complete ORM solution. BuySite provides a solution for internal processes, ranging from requisition to order. MarketSite starts to work from order to payment, which are the typical supplier tasks. Commerce Chain builds a bridge between these two solutions and offers a complete ORM solution.

The advantage of this is that this integration works perfectly. The problem is to get other supplier systems integrated. The connection is using proprietary protocols making it difficult for other supplier systems. BuySite offers all the tools to implement the most common processes required, while MarketSite offers the possibility to present the catalogues from various suppliers and allows the comparison of the offered goods and services.

The reporting feature is one of the best in the field. It is highly configurable and allows even buyers to create reports that suit their needs. Besides the configurable reporting part, many standard reports are included.

Although there are no standard interfaces to legacy or enterprise applications, Commerce One offers a service, where existing applications will be integrated into the Commerce Chain solution. Although this may seem a very good service, a standardized set of interfaces would be more useful, as customized interfaces will cost a lot of money.

The major problem with Commerce Chain is missing localization, just as in Ariba. Without this feature the software becomes unusable outside of the United States. International companies that want to implement ORM on a world-wide basis require this feature as well.

Infobank InTrade

InTrade, developed by the British company Infobank[70], is a newcomer in the ORM arena. Their software has been set on top of some standard Microsoft

---

[69]http://www.commerceone.com/
[70]http://www.infobank.co.uk/

products, such as the Internet Information Server, the Site Server, the SQL Server and the Commerce Server. This approach has the advantage that it is does not require large investments in hardware, but restricts the use to Windows NT. A porting is very unlikely as none of the underlying middleware components are available for other platforms.

InTrade is an open solution. Suppliers connect over the Internet to the purchasing server. If suppliers wish, they can use the InTrade supplier for offering the catalogue over the Internet. If they have another system already installed, InTrade Purchaser allows the import of data from other systems. In this case the purchasing system acts also as a supplier system. The advantage of the second alternative is that the supplier does not need to install software from Infobank, the disadvantage is that the supplier needs to create different catalogues for every purchaser and needs to upload them individually to the purchasing server.

With the supplier server installed, it can serve all purchasers at once. The data on the supplier server is replicated to the purchasing server through the standard replication methods, making the system faster for the purchaser, as all data is local available and only updates need to be replicated. The data between supplier and buyer can be exchanged through a proprietary protocol or via XML over the Internet.

The web-based administration tool allows the total control over the functionality of the system. InTrade is the only system that is fully localized, including language and currency. A German and a French version are already available; other languages are out soon.

Netscape CommerceXpert

The Netscape CommerceXpert suite of products consists of several modules for both suppliers and purchasers. The basic module ECXpert provides all the required functionality and infrastructure to set up a business-to-business operational resources management system. It provides interfaces to exchange information over existing EDI networks and the Internet and the integration into the ERP system.

On top of this module the purchaser needs to get BuyerXpert and the supplier SellerXpert, which provide the required functionality for the purchaser and the supplier respectively. BuyerXpert contains an order management system, a workflow engine and an online catalogue presentation system. SellerXpert on the other hand provides the same functionality as BuyerXpert, with the addition of the payment functionality.

CommerceXpert is compatible with OBI (Open Buying over the Internet) and allows the exchange of data via XML. The major advantage of Netscape's solution is that by adding new modules such as MerchantXpert and PublishingXpert the business-to-business system can be easily extended to become a business-to-consumer online shop at the same time.

CommerceXpert supports multiple currencies, date formats and languages, making it suitable for large companies which have subsidiaries around the world. It is also useful for non-native English speaking companies who can easily localize the application to suit their needs.

7.6.5   Comparison of the Procurement Solutions

From the following comparison chart (see Table 7.6) one can see where the ORM solutions have come from. All five solutions have their advantages and if you look at the row with the roots, you can see where each of the solutions was originally positioned and has its roots. That does not mean that you cannot mix the solutions or even choose a technology from one sector to deliver a solution in another. We have seen enough examples to prove this, but people tend to stay in the sector they feel comfortable with already.

Comparison of the Procurement Solutions

	Ariba	**Commerce One**	**Infobank**	**Netscape**
Administration	Java	HTML	HTML	HTML
Catalogue	Import	Import	Replication, Import	Connect
Integration	High	Good	Good	High
Localization	None	None	Full	Some
Platform	Java	Windows	Windows	Solaris, Windows
Reporting	Full	Full	Some	Full
Roots	Buyer, Purchaser	Value Added Network	Buyer, Purchaser	Buyer, Purchaser
Workflow	Built-in	Connect	Basic, Connect	Connect

Table 7.6.

7.7   Joining the Shopping and the ORM Solution

As we have seen in this chapter shopping and ORM solutions have a very similar functionality, but different target groups. While the typical shopping solution targets many end customers by offering the products of a single shop, the ORM solution tries to integrate as many shops as possible for a single buying organization. The shopping solution is a one-to-many relationship while ORM solutions target the many-to-one relationships.

This means that suppliers need to offer two catalogues, two databases and so on, in order to provide a service for both markets. In order to further reduce the overhead on the supplier side, shopping and ORM solutions will eventually migrate to offer many-to-many relations serving both the enterprise and the end customer market with a single database and a single, highly customizable catalogue.

This can be achieved quite easily using ORM solutions, actually with little modification by creating a new instance of the catalogue for a new company, which is the put onto the public web site allowing end customers to access it. For this catalogue the various roles for the ORM solution become less important and cost locations have to be replaced with credit card payment systems. The actual buying process is similar.

Typical shopping solutions will need stronger modification, as many components required for ORM solutions are missing, such as workflow. In order to migrate to a unified solution the software manufacturer needs to invest far more. But this investment will guarantee the survival of the software company, if it wants to remain a major player. Netscape is one of the first companies to offer a complete solution, CommerceXpert is able to deal with both scenarios.

In the near future we will see shopping portals that will enable end customers and companies to buy products through a unified interface, but with differentiated services.

Chapter 8

INTERACTIVE
COMMUNICATION
EXPERIENCES

8.1 The Basics

8.1.1 Communication Experience

The Internet started as a communication medium and any type of business, which we can see today requires at least a minimum of communication between the involved parties. Even though this communication may be automated and between computers only, without it the business cannot be executed.

The basic communication features of the Internet; Mail, News and Chat, are still the most used applications and will remain to be the number one in the future, as well. This is the reason why I have dedicated a chapter to interactive communications. There is no need to discuss how e-mail or news postings work, as everyone is able to grasp their functionality within seconds, as they are the digital replica of normal mail and bulletin boards. Online chat is nothing new compared to normal chit-chat, but the Internet offers new ways of communication and this chapter will focus on the new possibilities.

Although all technologies that are presented in this chapter can be used for private communication, the focus lies on how to add value to your business by using new and innovative communication technologies. These technologies do not offer radical new solutions, but try to integrate existing technologies to increase the effectiveness of the communication.

8.1.2 Talking to your Customers

Typical communication between a company and a customer is done either via normal mail, a phone call or through e-mail, if not on a personal basis. Although this is in theory very effective, it is possible to offer customers even better service by offering direct communication through online chats, for example. The advantage of online chats are that customers are able to help each other without contacting the company. Just as newsgroups offer this possibility, mail, e-mail and phone are direct communication methods which do require a lot of work in the customer care center.

As many customers are likely to have the same questions; by offering FAQ pages most simple questions can be answered. But more complicated questions cannot be answered through a static web page. In this case, it is often necessary to walk through the installation together with the customer.

By offering a dedicated chat group to the customers, it is possible to deal with more customer requests at the same time. Online chat offers written communication, which is done in real-time. In order to succeed it is necessary to obey some rules and to enable customers to use the new communication channels, such as online chat and newsgroups, it is necessary to implement them in a standard way. This reduces the overhead for learning how to use these new technologies and does not require any additional software installations on the computer of the customer. A web browser should be able to handle the requests of the customer.

If other software is required, it is necessary to give detailed description where to download and how to install the software. The easier it becomes for the customer to access this form of direct communication, the more success it will have. Implementing a bad solution (e.g. because it is too complicated, or takes too long to download) will increase the number of customers being unsatisfied by the service your company is providing.

Direct communication via chat or newsgroups does require the company to think about new communication standards. As the responses are very direct it is necessary to ensure that only qualified people are answering the questions and in the case they can't; a standardized process is implemented, which allows end customers to track their questions being passed from one department to the other. If the customers are not able to track the query, they will most likely submit the same query by another means, creating additional work for the customer care center and falsifying the statistics, which should be made on a regular basis to find out which problems the customers had in the past.

8.1.3 Interacting with Partners

Interaction with partners can be done over the same channels as the contact with the customers, but due to security reasons and traffic more complex methods of communication are involved. As information shared between partners needs to be treated confidentially, the communication channels need to be secured by encryption. In addition to this documents are being shared among the partners, making light-weight online text services, such as online chat or newsgroups, not the ideal solution.

As documents and applications are exchanged it is necessary to keep track of the version number and the person who made the last changes. This is also important from a legal point of view. Contracts, for example, could be created interactively through an advanced online forum, enabling both parties to revise the proposal and add comments from their legal departments.

Basic textual conversations between partners will most likely be nothing that is used on a day-to-day basis. This is mostly due to the mentality of the people. They are used to talking to partners over the phone, via e-mail or face-to-face. Especially among older employees, there is a resistance to the use of these new forms of communication. In some cases the employees prefer to send voice mails to others instead of e-mails, making it harder for the recipient to grasp the content. While communication costs are important for end customers, employees are less willing to save money by using advanced technical communication methods.

8.2 Moderating Online Meetings

The Internet and its technologies offer a great set of solutions for creating effective meetings. The solutions on the Internet include newsgroups where people can take part in a meeting on a certain topic in an asynchronous way. Instead of responding immediately to a question or request, the other members of the meeting are able to respond to it, whenever they have time for it. The same paradigm is used for mailing lists, which have the same functionality, but are based on the push methodology, while newsgroups used pull mechanisms. Push means that the content is brought to the computer of the participant actively, while pull requires the participant to look up the newsgroup, if new information is available.

While both technologies have proved to be very effective on the Internet, they do not truly represent a meeting, where decisions have to be made within a certain period of time. Online chats are getting closer to a virtual meeting, where all participants meet in a chat room to discuss a certain topic in real-time. The advantage over a real meeting is the fact that everything that is said is captured digitally, making it easy to follow-up or create a summary of the meeting. But online chats do not replicate the complexity of a real meeting. Missing are a dashboard to write down certain points, which may be of importance for the whole meeting and create drawings on the fly.

These missing features are included in newer versions of online chatting software. They allow participants to draw pictures online during the meeting, distribute documents during the conference and guide the other participants through a set of web pages, similar to a slide show.

These software products are good enough for day-to-day meetings where the participants know each other very well and do not require non-verbal expressions to understand the others. In business meetings with partners or customers, where you do not know each other, it is helpful to hear the voice or see the picture of the other participants. This makes it easier to get the real meaning behind the words. "I'm not sure." can be interpreted in different ways. It could be "maybe" or "no", depending on the culture of the person and the non-verbal expression accompanying the words.

Voice-over-IP and video-over-IP have become more common over the last few years and hopefully they will replace the business travels, where you are speaking for thirty minutes to someone on a certain topic. I, personally, have had quite a few of these travels, which took me a few hours to get to and a few hours to get back from, greatly reducing the efficiency of my working day. Using web cams, online voice, textual chats and web sites, it has become possible to reduce these costly and time consuming travels to a minimum.

8.2.1 Problems with Real-Time Applications

As connection speed is going up, more and more people are able to redirect normal phone calls to the Internet. The obvious reason for Internet telephony is to significantly reduce the cost of long distance voice communication. In addition to this, Internet telephony introduces entirely new and enhanced ways of communicating. Video conferencing, application sharing, and white-boarding are just a few of the applications that are already accompanying real-time voice communication over the Internet. More advanced systems hook up the telephone with the computer, which in turn is connected to the Internet. More simple solutions require some speakers and a microphone for the communication.

The Internet was not designed with real-time capabilities in mind. Its basic idea was to keep up service, even when some of the servers dropped out. Therefore stability was more important. In order to make phone calls over the Internet successful, a certain bandwidth needs to be guaranteed otherwise the call will become interrupted. E-mails do not require a guaranteed bandwidth, the connection can even break down. The e-mail server will just send out the e-mail whenever the connection is back up again. The same is true for web pages. If connections slow down, it will take longer for the web page to be loaded, but if you are in the middle of a conversation, this is not desirable.

The Internet is a packet-switched network, which has been used for applications where a variable Quality of Service (QoS) is tolerable, such as e-mail and file transfers. It does not matter if a file is a bit slower or if the transport of an e-mail takes five seconds longer. During the transmission it is possible to do something else. A phone call, for example, requires a dedicated line (or path). Packet switched networks do not dedicate a path between sender and receiver and therefore cannot guarantee QoS. Other than with telephone networks, the Internet allows many people to share a single line. In order to serve all people at the same time, the transmitted information is divided into packets, which contain a sequence number and a destination address. On the Internet there is no way to prioritize users or applications, as all packets are treated exactly in the same way, no matter what they contain.

It is also not important in which sequence the packets arrive at the destination; as they are labeled the destination host is able to re-compose the packets into the file or e-mail that was sent to it. You will get notified once the whole message has been transmitted. But a telephone call is more like a stream with constant transmission. It is easy to imagine that it becomes difficult to understand the other, if the words in a sentence arrive in the wrong order.

QoS becomes more important with real-time applications. Text-based chats work quite well on the Internet, as they require only very limited bandwidth. QoS products guarantee bandwidth over a network, enabling real-time applications.

The telephone network on the other hand is a circuit-switched network, which means that quality of service is guaranteed. When dialing a number a connection is built up that is exclusively used for the two participants connected. No matter how much traffic (in this case speech) is going over the line a dedicated circuit is ready to transport all voice data which is spoken during the telephone conversation. The same applies to television and radio transmission, where one channel is dedicated to one transmission. On the Internet many people share one circuit, which reduces the speed for every single person and it is impossible to predict how fast a connection will be at a certain time.

IP-based networks need additional hardware and software that is able to communicate the bandwidth with other network devices. ATM networks do offer QoS abilities in the protocol, making it easy to define minimum bandwidth requirements, but ATM networks are not one hundred percent compatible with IP networks.

So far very little software is able to talk to network devices and request a minimum bandwidth. Most applications just hope that there is enough bandwidth available.

8.2.2 Internet Telephony

The most popular application on the Internet that requires Quality of Service is Internet telephony. Although the quality is not as perfect as one is used to from normal phone services, it is good enough for many to use. The human brain is able to overcome transmission problems and the resulting reduced voice quality. Often it is even tolerable if single words are omitted, as the listener is able to get the word from the context. These are drawbacks of the current packet-switched Internet, which are more than compensated in exchange for the possibility of making long-distance calls at the price of a local call.

The quality of Internet telephony depends on two characteristics. First of all it depends on the quality of the connection. Typical Internet connections have some communication failures, which require the application to re-send certain packets until all arrive at the destination. This does not work with real-time applications. The packets need to arrive in the right order. Every packet that is delayed or lost will mean a decrease in quality, as the system will interpolate the missing packet. Interpolating means that the software makes a guess at what the missing packet may have contained, by analyzing the packets next to the missing one. The more packets that are missing the more distortion will be audible and the words fewer understood.

The other characteristic on the Internet that will determine the quality of the voice transmission is the connection speed of the parties involved in the conversation and the connection speed on the network segments in between. Depending on the speed a latency may occur. This latency can sometimes also be noticed when calling over a satellite, where the arrival of information has a slight delay. The slower the connection speed is the more delay in the conversation will be. Although latency can be annoying it will only slow down the conversation. It won't break it up in most cases.

Depending on how much each of these characteristics will really influence the conversation, it is possible to have good quality conversations that are very similar to telephone chats or very bad connections, which resemble more an alien transmission from outer space. In order to keep the latency factor low and the quality of the connection high, use Internet telephony when you know that less people are on the Internet, like at night; or for intercontinental calls look for times where either your continent or the other one is at sleep. As a rule of thumb, the overall connection speed on the Internet is best when corporate America is asleep.

With the introduction of IPv6 (see Chapter 3) and other schemes like the Resource Reservation Protocol (RSVP, see Table 8.1), you are allowed to reserve certain amounts of bandwidth for Internet applications requiring real-time communication. At the same time the available bandwidth is increasing all the time, making the need for quality of service less urgent.

One Internet telephony application is Netscape Conference, which is built into the Netscape Communicator Suite. If you have Netscape 4 or higher installed you can start using this application immediately, if you have a sound card, speakers and a microphone.

By entering the IP address of the other people taking part in the conference, a connection is set up and the people can start to conference. The disadvantage with the IP address is that many people who dial-up a provider get assigned a dynamic IP address, which changes with every dial-up. Finding out the IP address is not easy for a non-technical person, so before the Internet phone call starts, this issue needs to be resolved. Most software products propose a solution whereby the customer connects to a central repository and sends the current IP address to it. People who know that particular person will get to know that she or he is online and what the correct IP address is.

Unlike traditional voice conferences, Netscape Conference offers additional features. A "conference whiteboard" offers the possibility to draw and sketch some ideas. The digital blackboard offers the possibility of adding visual information to the voice conference. Another important feature is "collaborative browsing". This feature allows one participant to take the others through a

The Resource Reservation Protocol

The Resource Reservation Protocol (RSVP) seems to be the most prominent signaling protocol on the Internet. It reserves resources on the communication path as determined by the corresponding routing protocols. Since IP operates connectionless, different routes are possible, of course.

RSVP is not involved in data transfer as it currently operates over UDP and IP. It operates on so-called flows, which define "connections" for IP diagrams. It is the Flow Label that provides association of IP diagrams to RSVP reservations. The very important aspect is that RSVP supports multicast, i.e., it allows receivers out of a multicast group to issue their service requirements. It is based on a receiver-oriented approach, where the receiving node indicates to the network and the transmitting node the nature of the traffic flow that the node is willing and able to receive.

This enables supporting of heterogeneous QoS within a multicast group. The big advantage can be seen in the RSVP flexibility on the type of resource reservation that is signaled. There are two principal disadvantages – RSVP cannot provide hard service guarantees (because of the possibility of dynamic route changes during an established RSVP flow) and the fact that the flow state information that needs to be held inside the routers leads to a rather complex router design and implementation.

Table 8.1.

series of web sites while talking. The web pages may contain additional information about the topic of the phone conference. A file exchange is also possible. While talking it is possible to exchange files, and textual chat is also available, in case the sound transmission is so bad that one can't understand the other. Although this product is very basic, it offers many features that make phone conferences easier to manage. Within corporate networks, the software can be used if employees from different locations need to get in touch with each other.

A competing product is Microsoft NetMeeting, which can be downloaded from Microsoft's home page for free. It allows Internet telephony and application sharing. Application sharing is a similar feature as the collaborative browsing feature of Netscape, but extends the sharing feature to other applications of the Microsoft suite. It allows several Internet users to view and edit information simultaneously. This enables users to view the same Excel spreadsheet, talk about it and modify it during the conversation. Although this feature is good for the company Intranet it offers many ways for hackers on the Internet to steal information or interrupt the session.

Besides Internet telephony NetMeeting also offers textual chat, file transfer, a whiteboard, which can be used by all participants and the option for transmitting video.

The VocalTec Internet Phone[1] is another application strictly focusing on Internet telephony. It is one of the oldest applications for Internet telephony on the market. The current version is 5 and is from 1997. Besides the usual features, such as textual chat, file transfer, whiteboard and video transmission, VocalTec offers a direct integration with telephony gateways. The reason is that many companies use the VocalTec gateway software. A list of gateways can be found on the web site of VocalTec[2].

No matter which Internet telephony software you choose, the software will most probably be able to communicate with other software providing the same functionality. This has become possible by the H.323 standard, which was developed by the International Telecommunications Union (ITU)[3]. The H.323 standard provides a means for transporting voice, data and video over packet switched networks. This standard is supported by all of the above mentioned software packages. See Table 8.2 for more in-depth information on the H.323 standard.

Most of the products mentioned here do not require additional hardware besides the sound card, the speakers and the microphone, which are all part of the so-called "multi-media PC". For consumers it is difficult to get a computer without these components. But it is possible to enhance the experience by adding extra hardware.

One such product is the Internet PhoneJACK by Quicknet Technologies[4]. This hardware product offers a telephone socket, which allows normal telephones to connect to the computer and to the Internet. Any standard phone can be used to make phone calls over the Internet. Then you do not have to have a microphone and speakers anymore and the phone call over the Internet becomes more like a real phone call. In addition, a special digital signal processor (DSP) is able to reduce echo effects and provide real-time compression facilities. Compression reduces the size of the information that needs to be transmitted over the Internet therefore reducing the possible latency and may help to improve the quality.

---

[1]http://www.vocaltec.com/
[2]http://www.gold.vocaltec.com/iphone5/services/itsp_list.htm
[3]http://www.itu.int/
[4]http://www.quicknet.com/

The H.323 Standard

The H.323 standard provides a foundation for audio, video, and data communications across IP-based networks, including the Internet. The following list shows some of the highlights.

- **Bandwidth Management** – Special network managers are able to limit the bandwidth available to H.323 applications.

- **Codec Standards** – The compression and decompression of audio and video streams is highly standardized.

- **Flexibility** – Offers devices with different capabilities to take part in one conference.

- **Interoperability** – By adhering to the H.323 standard interoperability between applications is achieved.

- **Multicast Support** – Reduces bandwidth by sending out a single packet to many destinations at the same time without replication.

- **Multipoint Support** – Offers high quality support for conferences with more than two people.

- **Network Independence** – H.323 does not depend on a certain type of network, making it future-proof.

- **Platform and Application Independence** – H.323 is not bound to a certain type of hardware or operating system.

Table 8.2.

8.2.3 Internet Telephony Gateways

Through special gateways it is possible to extend the possibilities of Internet telephony to those who do not own a computer or do not have an Internet connection. Instead of routing a phone call through traditional phone lines a telephone company may decide to route it through the Internet. Therefore voice needs to be moved from the circuit-switched network to the Internet. This requires also a digitization of the data at one end and a digital to analog converter at the other end. In order to work efficiently and be cost effective the gateways need to be installed in every town that is connected to the Internet telephony system. This allows customers to make phone calls to every location at the cost of a local phone call.

The caller connects to the Internet telephony gateway by dialing a special prefix to the actual phone number. The telephony gateway takes the incoming call and identifies the country and area code where the recipient is located and looks for the nearest Internet telephony gateway. The second gateway makes a local connection to the recipient.

Jeff Pulver already introduced in 1995 his "Free World Dialup" project[5], which consisted of Internet telephony gateways to the public phone system in 42 countries around the world. The gateways were operated by almost 500 individuals that installed these gateways on their computers and people could use it for non-commercial phone calls. Unfortunately the Free World Dialup service has been abandoned.

These forward-thinking individuals were the first Internet Telephony Service Providers (ITSP). After a short test period, the traffic increased so much that an individual was not able to handle it on a free-of-charge basis. ISPs have started to become ITSPs.

There are a number of commercial Internet Telephony Service Providers, such as Internet Telephony Exchange Carriers (ITXC)[6] and TransNexus[7], that find Internet telephony gateway service providers around the world who will cooperate with one another. Another interesting example is in Germany the Deutsche Provider Network (DPN)[8], one of the largest backbone ISPs, which has started a co-operation with Interoute Telecom, a telecom company, to install an Internet telephony gateway for end customers.

In addition to the standard telephone to telephone conversations, it is also possible to talk from or to a computer-based user. In this case only one gateway is required, either at the caller or recipient site, depending on which of the partners is using a standard phone and who is using a computer.

More and more organizations are starting to allow web surfers with Internet telephony software to connect directly to agents in their call center by using an Internet telephony gateway. The Internet telephony gateway feeds calls from the Internet directly into their system. Some of the well-known providers of Internet telephony gateway products are VocalTec[9], MICOM[10], and Vienna Systems[11].

---

[5] http://www.pulver.com/fwd/

[6] http://www.itxc.com/

[7] http://www.transnexus.com/

[8] http://www.dpn.de/

[9] http://www.vocaltec.com/

[10] http://www.micom.com/

[11] http://www.viennasystems.com/

Another interesting product is Net2Phone[12], which is operated by the telephone company IDT[13]. It is the most popular telephony gateway, which requires a special piece of software installed on the computer. In order to use Net2Phone, it is necessary to get an account with IDT, which is debited whenever you call someone through their software. The account needs to be filled with money before one is able to phone someone. Before every call, the caller is notified about the account balance and how long the maximum phone call can take, based on this account balance.

Net2Phone is very good, if used for calls to or within the United States, but lacks quality when calling other countries. Everyone is able to test this piece of software for free, when calling 800 numbers in the US, which are free of charge. The complete list of the 800 numbers can be found on the Internet at inter800.com[14], one of many telephone directories.

Internet telephony can be used to build up call centers very easily. Many web sites operate under the premise of do-it-yourself. It is not uncommon that problems or questions arise during the web transaction and the customer needs to talk to someone directly to resolve the issues. Using Internet telephony it is easy to incorporate a "call-me" button into the web site that automatically sends out a request to the customer care center and initiates an Internet phone session. By pressing the button, the actual IP address together with the name of the customer is sent to the customer care center, which then is able to call the customer and go through the web pages to resolve open questions.

Today, small call centers need to buy their own hardware. With the introduction of Internet telephony it is possible to create Enterprise call centers (ECC), where multiple small call centers can share a single piece of hardware. This also makes it easy to move from traditional call centers to a multimedia call center where e-mail and faxes can be processed like any other call.

The advantage of such a solution is the tight integration and the interactivity that is possible with it. Banking solutions have already integrated web and phone into a single back-end. Edify[15], for example, offers the possibility of changing between phone and web in a single session. It is, for example, possible to type in the account number and use the phone to enter the password. In this case a real phone is used that has the gateway on the bank server.

8.2.4 Internet Fax Gateways

Internet Fax Gateways are just a natural extension to normal fax machines. They are slowly replacing fax machines in many locations. Although the importance of fax is slowly decreasing it still has one major advantage over the Internet. Documents that are signed and transmitted over a fax are regarded

---

[12]http://www.net2phone.com/

[13]http://www.idt.com/

[14]http://www.inter800.com/

[15]http://www.edify.com/

as legal documents. Another important point is that a fax machine costs much less than a computer and does not require any interaction in order to see an incoming document. It is printed and visible soon after it has arrived.

By introducing fax gateways it is possible to exchange documents with people who do not own a computer and where content is more important than clear print outs. The legal status is lost in the transition through the gateway, but the major advantage of having printouts wherever needed is still valid.

Fax gateways serve two purposes. Send faxes to people without a fax, but with an Internet connection and the other way round, send e-mails to people without Internet connection. Sending e-mails through a fax gateway, if both participants have e-mail is no good, but using two fax gateways to send faxes can reduce the cost for the transmission. Many fax gateways allow you to transmit faxes at the cost of a local phone call to any place in the world.

8.2.5 Video Conferences

Video conferencing software has the same problem over the Internet, the quality of service problem. Video transmission requires a lot more bandwidth than pure audio transmissions, but is based on the same standards, making it easy to integrate video over IP into existing networks. In order to make video conferencing possible it is necessary to install a camera and a microphone on the desk of every participant.

Today all computers are equipped with a sound card, making it easy to add the microphone, but the camera requires additional hardware and software to be installed. This and the additional cost have been show-stoppers in many cases. Although a web cam starts at 99 US Dollar or Euro many companies have not been willing to spend money on this equipment as they fear that it will congest their networks.

One of the best selling web cameras is the Connectix QuickCam[16], which is designed for video conferencing over the Internet and can capture 24-bit still images at up to 640-by-480 resolution.

The camera itself is a golfball-size black sphere with a lens that can be manually focused from one inch to infinity. There is no microphone or speaker built into the camera, so the video software automatically interacts with the audio card and any microphone and computer speakers. The camera is able to automatically adjust brightness, although there is a slider on the side for setting it manually. Clicking on the appropriate icon changes from still capture to motion.

The camera produces a maximum frame rate exceeding 15 fps at a CIF (Common Interchange Format) resolution of 352-by-288 pixels. This frame rate is just fast enough to avoid obvious jittery, jerky, and flickering animation. Videos are saved as AVI files, while still images are able to be saved in BMP, JPEG, or TIFF formats. The camera is bundled with Videophone 3.0,

---

[16]http://www.connectix.com/

Netmeeting 2.0, and VIVO Active Video Now, making it easy to do the first steps in video conferencing.

The most commonly used software for video conferencing is CU-SeeMe. It is a freeware product available for all major platforms, making it the de-facto standard for video conferencing. White Pine[17], the developer of the software has released an enhanced version of CU-SeeMe.

Enhanced CU-SeeMe supports video connections of 28.8 Kbps or faster and offers color video, a phone book, and a whiteboard. The software is easy to use. One simply logs on to the Internet, calls up Enhanced CU-SeeMe, and enters the IP address for the person or server you want to reach. The software supports three kinds of conferencing: point-to-point, in which you communicate with one other person via the Internet or a private network; group, in which you join an existing conference by connecting to that group's server; and one-way, in which you receive broadcast data from a server. You can open up to eight video windows at once, access numerous public CU-SeeMe videoconferences, and store your favorite IP addresses in the phone book.

The whiteboard module, enables users to type and insert colored lines into an online conference without a hitch. While the module supports many common graphics formats, you have to export your word processor and spreadsheet documents as plain ASCII before you can import them into the whiteboard.

Besides White Pine, other companies have started to use CU-SeeMe as the basis for their product. One of these products is called CU-SeeMe Pro, which has powerful applications such as collaboration on virtually any Windows-based application, full color video and audio support, exchange information on an electronic whiteboard, files transfer and much more.

The software is able to tap into the NetMeeting directory to find people and allows connections to people with NetMeeting, ProShare or other clients that adhere to the H.323 standard.

8.3   Internet Chat Solutions

8.3.1   Internet Relay Chat

The most popular open standard for real-time chats on the Internet is the Internet Relay Chat (IRC)[18]. AOL Instant Messenger[19] and ICQ[20] may be more popular with Internet newcomers, but these applications are based on proprietary standards and the protocols used are not supported by other companies or applications.

IRC has been available for many years, and was intended to be a replacement for the program "talk", which allowed two people to speak in real-time to

---

[17]http://www.whitepine.com/

[18]http://www.irc.org/

[19]http://www.aol.com/

[20]http://www.icq.com/

each other. IRC is a multi-user, multi-channel chat network that allows people to talk in real-time to each other, no matter where they are located.

In order to go onto the IRC network, you need to install an IRC client, such as ircII[21], ircle[22] or mIRC[23], or connect to one of the dozens web sites that allow access to the IRC network. IRC is based on the client-server model. Clients connect to a particular server and the server distributes the message sent in by a client back to all recipients that are on a particular channel. Most IRC networks consists of more than one server, so there is also a lot of server-to-server communication involved.

To get online, you need to choose an IRC server, a nickname and a channel where you want to meet other people. Everyone on the IRC network is able to open up a new channel, just by entering a name. If the channel name exists the user will enter the channel and meet the other people there, otherwise a new channel will be created. Some channels are focused on one topic, other channels offer a more generic platform for people with the same interests.

Channels with names like #Germany or #Italia have been designed for Germans and Italians or people who want to visit these countries (or hate these countries). As the topic is too general, these channels are crowded, often more than 300 people are on the channel and communication is almost impossible. Most channels range from two to thirty people, which makes it possible to participate in an on-going discussion.

Topics may vary from time to time and are influenced mainly by technical and political news. It often happens that technically focused groups start to discuss politics in the event of a crisis. IRC was very crowded during the Persian Gulf War, just as during the War in the Kosovo. As the IRC enables anyone who was an Internet connection to participate, it was possible to get first hand reports from people living in the area.

On other occasions, during large trade shows, Comdex[24] and CeBit[25], information is distributed rapidly throughout a community. People at the trade show are able to diffuse technological news to many people in one go by being present at the show and on the IRC network. Over the years, computer companies have held press conferences on IRC, where end customers could ask questions directly.

Other than the Web where most people are forced to understand English, the IRC offers enough space for people who do not understand English. There are discussion groups for every language, country and culture, and if one is missing, it is easy to open up a new discussion channel where that language and opinion are expressed freely. This is in fact much easier than developing a new web site.

---

[21]http://www.irchelp.org/
[22]http://www.ircle.com/
[23]http://www.mirc.co.uk/
[24]http://www.comdex.com/
[25]http://www.cebit.de/

The person who opens up a new channel has special powers, which allow her or him to throw out other people or ban them completely from that particular channel. These powers should be used to organize communication in the channel. If someone start to insult other people without reason on the channel, the so-called operator is able to throw the person out and if the person returns to the channel to continue with the insults, then it is possible to completely disallow access to that particular channel. These powers can be passed on to anyone else on the channel, in case the initiator is not available.

The operators set the standards on the channel. The way people should behave can be enforced by them and in many cases there exist web documents explaining how to behave properly on a certain channel. One such example is my home-channel #amigager, which was originally the home of the Amiga[26]–Fans in Germany, but now has evolved to a group of Internet experts who are either working for large companies, such as Hewlett-Packard, IBM, Peacock and the Deutsche Provider Network or are studying or teaching at a university. They use the forum on a daily basis for the exchange of information, opinions and programming tips.

The Netiquette for the channel is available online[27], of course, and if people do not behave accordingly, then they are warned once and asked to read the channel FAQ. Although the channel itself is fun and everybody would survive the death of the channel, it simplifies the work. Instead of looking up some programming constructs in a book or searching for information on a new standard on the web, the question is thrown into the channel and a highly qualified answer can be expected within a few seconds. Thus reducing the time spent programming and writing documentation. Just one piece of warning, if you consider coming into this particular channel. The channel has a reputation for ignoring beginner (or so-called newbie) requests. The channel lives off the exchange of information, it is highly unlikely that you can ask one thousand questions and get response every single question. In order to receive information, you need to show competence in some area and a perspective that you will also contribute in the future.

Many channels are up and running twenty-four hours a day. Virtual communities have been created, where people do not only meet so often on the same channel, but where they also start to see each other in real-life.

Although IRC has been around for a very long time, only very few companies have used it and no company at all is using it as part of its customer care center. There is a huge potential in it, as customers want a fast response, just as when calling in or sending an e-mail, and the transcript of the channel can always be used to update an existing FAQ.

Communication over standard IRC servers is not secure. The text you transmit to the IRC network is communicated in clear text to the server, which

---

[26]http://www.amiga.de/
[27]http://faq.amigager.de/

may pass it on to another server and then to the clients. It is very easy to eavesdrop on the IRC network, but this should not worry you. If you do not have anything to hide, then nobody will get at you.

Criminals, for example, have used IRC in the past for trading pornographic images of children which is forbidden in many countries. Identifying these people over the IRC network is very easy and gets them arrested within a very short time. Although some people may be rude, the IRC is a good place for communication.

8.3.2   Java Chat Rooms

As IRC requires the download of a special piece of software which needs to be installed and configured, it is not accessible to everyone, especially if the software is not available in your mother tongue. Therefore new chat software has been developed that is accessible to anyone who is able to use a web browser. Although there are some HTML based chat rooms available, the large majority of chat systems on the Internet are Java-based.

The Java applets, are downloaded at the same time as the HTML page. This may contain advertising or instructions on how to use the applet. Once it has been started, it connects back to the server, which then passes the text input from the user to other users who are also connected to the same server and have chosen to chat within a certain channel.

Gallery-Net[28], for example, is using a Java chat applet to allow its users to chat away while they are visiting the web site. This allows them to exchange ideas, e-mail addresses and news about art or anything they wish to talk about. The Java chat in this case is not moderated.

Two types of channels are used: Moderated and non-moderated. In moderated channels the participants cannot talk freely, but need to get permission to talk from an operator. In non-moderated channels people are able to express themselves freely without restrictions. The non-moderated channels are much more common and more accepted by the users. Moderated channels are normally used for interviews or press conferences, where you do not want everybody to chat at the same time. These two types exist not only with Java chats, but are a general feature for most chat technologies.

8.3.3   Virtual Worlds

As computers get faster it has become easier to create virtual worlds on the Internet where a three-dimensional person represents yourself while chatting, looking at images or buying goods on the Internet. Virtual worlds make the experience more personal on the web. Instead of being only an IP address connected to a server you are able to style yourself and appear on the screens of others as a human being (or as an alien, in some cases).

---

[28]http://www.gallery-net.com/

These virtual representations make it also easier for people who are not so knowledgeable the about Internet and its technologies. They can use the same paradigms they are applying to the real-world in a one-to-one manner to the Internet. A chat room becomes suddenly a living room where cakes and coffee are served, while an online shop has a real shop assistant that is able to answer questions, if necessary. While most shopping sites offer e-mail addresses and FAQs to resolve most questions, this does not reflect the real-world. Would you go into a shop and look for the FAQ or e-mail address to send off a question?

One of the more simple programs for virtual worlds is Microsoft Chat, which allows people to select a body, which everybody is seeing while they are chatting. The chat software is using the IRC protocol to connect to the standard servers, but it adds a graphical interface on top of the text based chat. Instead of seeing pure text, you have comic figures that can walk around in a chat room and exchange their opinions.

Besides this rather simple chat solution there are more sophisticated online shopping solutions that were implemented in a virtual world, in order to make the shopping experience as comfortable as possible. We will discuss them in Chapter 12. On of them is the "Virtual Reality Online Shopping"[29], which creates an integrated environment for E-Commerce using virtual reality and virtual communities.

Their virtual reality consists of several virtual reality shops, into which you can go and choose from a wide range of products. The mall does not only consist of the shops, but there is also a whole environment around the shopping mall, where you can get engaged in chats and watch artists. The project tries to emulate a real shopping experience and it is quite intriguing to enter this virtual world.

Instead of getting the users to find certain goods immediately, they are left to wander around, just as in a real shopping mall, where the experience is more important than the shopping, but customers are able to use short cuts through a search engine.

Another very interesting online shopping experience is Activeworlds.com[30], which is a virtual world featuring an online shopping mall called @Mart. More than 100 online businesses like Amazon.com and Beyond.com[31] have already opened shops in @Mart.

Shoppers walk around the @Mart virtual mall by pointing their mouse or using the arrow keys on their keyboard to proceed. Although the environment is 3D, the merchandise is displayed in 2D. A detailed description of the products is displayed when clicking on one of the graphics. The actual purchase and payment process is then done on the merchant's web site and not in the cyber mall, so that companies can add a fancy virtual shop, but do not need to replicate their existing infrastructure.

---

[29]http://www.vr-shop.iao.fhg.de/
[30]http://www.activeworlds.com/
[31]http://www.beyond.com/

Both shopping solutions allow customers to meet other customers in the shops and exchange opinions on the quality of the merchandise. Shop owners are also able to interact with customers and answer questions or discuss the price of the goods.

When the technologies get even better so that it is possible to recreate the real look of people in a three-dimensional world, it can be envisioned that business meetings can take place on the Internet. It will also become possible to conduct events, such as presentations directly on the Internet without anyone having to travel around the globe to attend. In many cases it is not necessary to be physically at a certain location in the business life, but participation is still desired. Through advanced Internet technologies this will become reality.

8.3.4   Internet Newsgroups

Internet Newsgroups support the efforts of virtual organizations or teams, which must work together, even though they may not actually be together, in either time or space. The newsgroups technology is a very old and proven technology and maximizes the human interaction while minimizing the interference of the technology.

Newsgroups allow asynchronous meetings and discussions on the Internet. Other than in the real-world where meetings and discussions are mostly synchronous. The advantage of newsgroups is that it is possible to answer questions whenever someone has time to do so, no matter where the person is located. This works only if the answer to the question does not inhibit your continuing with your work. It means that work in the New Economy is far more diversified and a single person is handling more than one task at a time. While computers in the early years where only able to execute one task at a time, they are now able to handle several tasks at the same time. This paradigm is taking over the working world as well.

Factory workers that execute a single task all day long are becoming slowly but surely the exception. The working force is moving to a more diversified workplace, meaning that several tasks are executed at the same time, even if this requires a change in the minds of many companies. Jobs can be executed much faster this way. If an employee has only one job to do, he or she will stop once there is a problem, such as waiting for the answer to a question. If the employees is working on several tasks she or he will put the task on hold and continue with the other tasks resulting is much less wasted productivity time.

This also requires that employees are more knowledgeable to be able to execute more than one task at a given time. Long-life learning is the only way to compensate for the changes in technology and business processes. Internet newsgroups are a good way to support the paradigms of the New Economy.

The virtualization of supply chains and teams make the development and execution of processes more efficient, but cannot be managed without the use of new technologies, such as Internet newsgroups. Virtualization means that a supply chain or team are put together on a case-by-case decision instead of putting together teams for all cases.

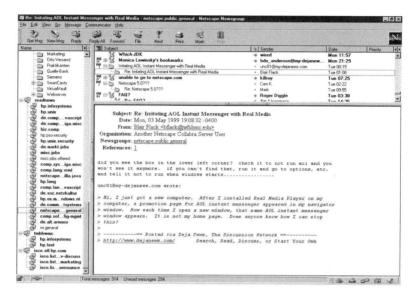

Figure 8.1. A response to a newsgroup posting

More and more companies are bringing traditional newsgroups to the web. DejaNews[32] and Supernews[33] are the most prominent examples of this trend.

8.3.5   Digital Communities

Very interesting are companies that provide a completely new service on the web. One of these companies is eCircle[34], which enables members to create the so-called eCircles on the web. eCircles are mailing lists or newsletters, which allow anyone on the web to become an editor of an online magazine on a specific subject without having to have the know-how on the technical details of how to publish and circulate it.

Every member in an eCircle automatically receives all messages sent to the mailing list via e-mail or are able to read the postings on the web, whatever a member prefers. Messages can be either forwarded automatically or approved first by the eCircle manager.

The creation and the maintenance of such an eCircle is free of charge, enabling any type of business or group of people to add value to their web sites.

---

[32]http://www.dejanews.com/
[33]http://www.supernews.com/
[34]http://www.ecircle.de/

This concept allows any type of group to stay in contact and issue a newsletter on a regular basis, which is sent out via e-mail and the members are able to respond. Through the web interface members are also able to look through an archive of previously posted newsletters and postings. The eCircle concept brings together the idea of mailing lists, newsgroups and newsletters to form a powerful platform for online chatting.

8.4 Internet-based Trainings

8.4.1 Reasons for Internet-based Trainings

As long-life learning becomes part of the working life, new technologies are needed to transport the information to the learner. In many cases it is not possible to conduct courses, as too few trainers know about a certain topic and are restricted by their location. Internet-based training, which evolved from computer-based training, offers a way to move knowledge fast to the people who need to know about a certain topic. It offers twenty-four hour availability and a strong personalization which adapts to the knowledge and the needs of every single learner.

Providing long-life learning facilities is more than just a necessity for a company. It needs to be part of the strategy of every company, as the results of the training have direct impact on the business results of your company. In order to make training more effective a new paradigm needs to be introduced and the training efforts need to be consolidated. It is very important for the training department to understand the company's business goals. A successful company needs to ensure that the majority of employees has knowledge of the company's overall strategy and their roles in achieving the goals.

Another problem for every company is that some business units are setting their own directions, creating a misalignment to the company goals. By having different goals and directions coming from different levels within the company, the employees will be confused and not know what the "right" direction is. This results in a waste of training investments.

Besides the bad business performance caused by the misalignment, training efforts will be less effective. Training will be held in parallel, multiplying the costs, as every course needs to be designed individually and resources are wasted. Although this is bad, it keeps the employees on track with the company goals. Much worse is the business unit that creates trainings that have nothing to do with the company goals and cannot be used for future projects and miss the mark in trying to help the company achieve its goals.

In order to overcome the problems with the rapidly changing business environment new training models are required. The new paradigm needs to be based on a company-wide training department, which co-ordinates and develops the training programs for the complete enterprise. This eliminates multiple efforts in developing training. As many companies have offices in several countries, the training need to be adapted to the needs of the country, as not all goals of the entire corporation may be of interest to for all countries, as some countries may not sell a certain product or service.

Not only does the products or services a company offers influence the training offered by the training department. Many training programs are designed around the products and services used within the company, such as software products like a word processor and a presentation designer. In order to simplify the exchange of information between departments and business units, computer software should be standardized. This also helps to reduce the amount of training required. If only one word processor is officially supported by the company, it is only necessary to offer one type of training for it. It also reduces the amount of training required, as employees are able to help each other.

Through the co-ordination of a centralized training department, not only new training programs can be introduced far quicker, but also the costs for training programs can be reduced significantly. Licenses, which need to bought, rented or leased from other companies, tend to get cheaper if ordered in larger volume.

In order to build up a centralized training department it is necessary to find out why so many departments and units are developing their own training programs. There are many reasons why departments choose to design them and these reasons need to be investigated, in order to create a successful corporate training department. One reason may be that the central training department is not responding to the needs of the business units. The ever-faster changing business rules need to be reflected also in the training department. New methodologies need to be created that allow the training department to create new courses much faster.

Courses, for example, need to be accessible before the are completed. If the training department finished the first unit, it needs to be made available digitally, so that the employees can start to learn, while the training department prepares the next unit.

Another problem of many traditional learning programs is that they are measured by the wrong units. Instead of measuring the number of days of training per employee, for example, new measurement methods need to be developed that reflect how the training helped to achieve the goals of the corporation, unit or employee.

8.4.2 The New Paradigm

The new training paradigm ties the training and learning activities to the goals of the company, group and individual and its success is measured by achieving the goals in all three cases. This also requires a change in the view of the managers. Training should not be considered as a cost that cannot be avoided. Long-life learning of all employees needs to become part of the business plan and seen as a key contributor to the success of the company.

The new learning can only be successful if the business goals are clearly defined and training is an integral part of it. This does not only require new thinking by the business managers, but also by the training organization. Instead of only supporting the goals, it should now help to define them. They should help to recognize the directions and communicate these goals to all employees in the company. This ensures that everyone knows about the goals and works together to achieve the company vision. Only if this can be ensured will the company be successful, as it does not waste resources and money on courses that lead into the wrong direction.

This does not only require the adjustment of business goals, but also the review of business processes and adjusting them accordingly. Once the goals and processes have been aligned and the training department has started with the new form of training, the training department should be measured on how accurately each individual employee, team, department and the whole company meet the expected goals. They should not be measured on the amount of training they have executed.

8.4.3 Just-enough Training

The cost for training can be reduced by developing training courses that teach exactly what the employees need to fulfill their work. This requires companies to create more dynamic training programs, which can be adapted to the needs of the single employee. An employee that needs to know how to print over the network does not need to know how to install a printer. Training therefore should not consist of massive blocks of knowledge, but of small modules, which can be assembled on the fly.

If the training programs can be assembled on the fly, it is also easier to provide just-in-time trainings. Whenever employees require specific training it will be available in an instant. The employees will be able to go to the Intranet training web site and choose the appropriate modules themselves online. All courses should be available online for self-learners, while it still makes sense to offer training with a trainer.

Learning should not be dictated by the training department. In many cases employees are able to learn from each other much faster than through the training department. The training department should offer courses for informal learning so that knowledge can be passed on among employees. In smaller companies this will happen on a daily basis between employees while they talk about problems, but larger companies or the Internet are too large to let everyone speak with everyone. Therefore mailing lists, newsgroups and chat groups can be very effective instant learning tools.

Chat groups offer the most immediate reaction to a query. A question posed in a newsgroup will get you answers within seconds or worst-case, minutes. Mailing-lists are a bit slower where response time is about one to five hours, while newsgroups are the slowest alternative (with typical response times up to 24 hours) they have the big advantage that the question and answer are available at any time after the question has arisen. Many newsgroups also carry FAQs to reduce the load of repeated questions.

The major problem with these technologies is that the employees do not get training certificates. Do-it-yourself training also does not give any visibility to your managers on how much employees learnt in the past year, but from my experience these self-paced training programs are far more effective, so maybe someone should come up with some statistical tools that allow you to count how many questions one has posed in newsgroups and mailing lists and how many answers the person provided (being effectively a trainer for that moment). This could make the use of newsgroups and mailing lists more accepted within companies who see these technologies just as a waste of time.

Although I discussed the long-life learning in a company in this subsection, the same rules are valid on the Internet. The Internet could be seen as a large company, with a lot of knowledge that is free, but not everyone knows what the others know. Long-life learning is not only a matter for business, but also for society. In order to ensure that people have access to new information technologies, they need to learn how to use them. Otherwise society will be split into two parts. One who have the knowledge, money and technology to further their knowledge and wealth and the other part, which has no access to these resources and is therefore at a disadvantage.

8.4.4 Training Management Software

To achieve the above-mentioned goals it is necessary to have the right software in place that is able to administer the whole process of training on a company- or Internet-wide basis. This means first of all that all training programs need to be developed by a single organization within a company in order to reduce duplicate training sessions, which cost money both to develop and to maintain. In many companies there is not only the training department developing programs, but also many other organizations for their internal use, as they think it would be easier to develop and deploy, as they have the appropriate knowledge and resources. This leads to many overlapping training courses. Organizational managers should try to encourage the development of training courses, but only if they are coordinated together with the training department. This will make everyone more happy, as the departments can ensure the high-quality content and the training department the high-quality of training management.

One software solution that is designed to manage and operate the training department is the software solution from Saba Software[35]. The training management software provided by Saba has been written entirely in Java making it easy to deploy on a type of system. It allows for the continuous assessment of how each learner learns best, as well as their competency, certification, and

---

[35]http://www.saba.com/

content needs. This feature is often used by managers to see how their employees have performed in the past and how this has changed since they last visited a training program. The software allows users to plan the best mix of online and traditional educational offerings, and online content purchase, conversion, or development based on global demand forecasts.

Education can be delivered using personalized mixes of traditional and online offerings available in any and all content delivery tools. It tracks the learning and financial results you deliver on a global basis. Customer satisfaction, education effectiveness, profitability, return on investment, and bottom line business results can be measured and improved instantly.

Saba provides innovative, comprehensive, global enterprise applications that help you gain a competitive advantage by accelerating the transition to online learning. The Saba Education Management System, for example, allows major enterprises around the world to create competency-driven, web-enabled learning environments that deliver personalized, cost- and time-effective online learning to employees, channel partners, and customers. It provides a truly web-based solution for all needs of learning.

It also supports all learning technologies. Because learning is driven by content availability, Saba can integrate with all open content delivery tools, including CBT, WBT, IBT, distance learning, EPSS, multimedia, CD, and synchronous and asynchronous delivery tools. At the same time Saba supports open industry standards such as AICC.

While Saba provides the whole infrastructure to set up a complete training management solution for a large corporation, many smaller companies would be happy to use existing infrastructures to save money and time for the implementation. Several companies have started to provide this infrastructure to allow small-to-medium sized companies to develop their own training programs or select from existing ones on the Internet.

One such company is the Internet University[36], which offers customizable courseware programs and a participant management platform that enables any type of organization or individual to extend their educational programs worldwide. Internet University has formed alliances with academic institutions that plan to launch or expand online distance learning programs. Clients and allies of Internet University receive a complete solution to their online distance education challenges.

The main features include a virtual campus, which features the online learning platform and a comprehensive student and online course management system. The management system enrolls students, handles secure online credit card transactions, tracks student progress, automatically grades and submits results to an online student record, provides feedback to students and reports to faculty and administration. Internet University's administration system allows you to add and delete class sections, edit and revise courses remotely.

---

[36]http://www.internetuniversity.com/

The second module consists of the course development tools, which can be used by faculty and instructional designers to create their own online courses. The third module is the Internet University Platform, takes care of the servers, communications lines, software, and staff to set-up and maintain the Internet server system for each individual organization that wants to offer courses for their employees or for all who are interested.

This and similar offerings enable companies and individuals to start a long-life learning initiative, which matches the needs of the individual, while it accommodates the needs of the company.

Part III

Internet Technologies

Chapter 9

COMPARING WEB
TECHNOLOGIES

9.1 Finding the Right Browser

9.1.1 The Browser Market

Although I promised not to use any statistics in this book, I will borrow a series of statistics to find out which browser is the preferred tool by users on the web. Actually I want to show that this knowledge is not relevant at all.

In the German online magazine Telepolis[1] Armin Medosch tried to find out which browser is the preferred browser: Netscape or Internet Explorer (IE). The background of this story was a news flash with the statement by Websidestory[2] that about two thirds of the Internet users use Internet Explorer and only about one third use Netscape. This headline brought up many Netscape users who could not believe that so many users were using IE. Medosch found out that these figures were based on a set of customers that used a certain program called HitBox, which is available to Microsoft platforms only and requires customers to apply for it. Therefore the data cannot be representative for the Internet as a whole. Table 9.1 shows some web sites and how much share the browsers Netscape and Internet Explorer have. This data has been compiled in January 1999 and should not be used for generalization. The results vary not only over the web but also over time.

As one can see, the results are varying and depend on the web site. One will get different results for different content on the web. There is no way to check if the data which is in the table is correct, but even if we assume that they are correct they are not really helpful. If you look, for example, at the main web site of the Heise publishers and compare it to the newsticker on the same server, you already get different results. It all depends on the customers of the site. Microsoft customers will more likely use Internet Explorer while Heise

---

[1] http://www.heise.de/tp/, Armin Medosch, 28 January 1999, "Zahlenspiele update: IE zieht doch nicht davon"

[2] http://www.websidestory.com/

Browser Usage

The following shows some web sites and the percentage of users which use Netscape (NS) or Internet Explorer (IE) to access them. The missing percent to 100 percent are users that use other browsers.

Web Site	NS	IE
http://www.heise.de/newsticker/	75%	22%
http://www.gallery-net.com/	71%	18%
http://www.nmr.de/	70%	24%
http://www.heise.de/	67%	30%
http://meta.rrzn.uni-hannover.de/	65%	33%
http://www.spiegel.de/	62%	35%
http://www.casinoplace.com/	61%	36%
http://www.rp-online.de/	57%	39%
http://www.mediatechbooks.de/	55%	20%
http://browserwatch.internet.com/	48%	38%
http://www.websidestory.com/	33%	64%
http://www.microsoft.com/	34%	62%

Table 9.1.

customers with its publications in the Unix market will attract more Netscape users. This example makes it quite clear, the Internet is not a mass media, it is the infrastructure for many mass markets and even more niche markets.

If you look at the numbers there is a gap of about ten percent on average on every web site. This percentage represents other browsers on the market. As a rule of thumb: No matter what business you do, do not expect users to have a certain type of browser. Textual information should be provided in such a form that it can be read by any browser. Web applications are something different. If you support the latest standards for your online banking solution, this is just fine, as this requires reprogramming for every version of the browser.

9.1.2 Sticking to the Web Standards

Many web sites do not comply to the web standards, defined by public bodies, such as the W3C or the IETF. Some people try to take advantage of proprietary standards or extensions to the web standards on their web pages to create a special layout, content or application. But many web pages are not adhering to the standards, because the programmer did not care or did not know about the exact standard. With a little work, it is possible to create web pages that conform to the web standards.

A standard is composed of elements and structures, in many cases some elements are used in the wrong context or structures have been extended without regard to the restrictions of the particular standard. Although the source code may be very similar, it won't be understood by all applications. Depending on the application it will either accept or ignore the extended standard or will fail. Unlike humans who are able to get one hundred percent of a meaning with only ninety percent of the information, a computer needs a hundred percent correct input to give out a fully functional output. Other than humans, computers are not good at guessing. By adhering to the standards it is possible to maximize the accessibility to the widest range of applications.

Many people think that checking the input against a certain application verifies that the source is correct. In ninety-nine percent of the cases, the input will fail in another application. A programmer should always test the source code against the standard and not against an application that tries to adhere to the standard (and most likely will have either bugs or an incomplete implementation).

A Java programmer, for example, could develop a special Java applet for every browser. But this is not desirable, as it requires a lot of extra work for the programmer. The programmer is forced to create work-arounds and wastes a lot of time maintaining several revisions of a single program version.

Web standards are designed to be both backward-compatible and forward-compatible at the same time. Older source code should always look good in new applications and new source code should also look good in older applications. Using extensions that are not part of the standard will break this compatibility and the interoperability between a set of applications which use the same input (e.g. HTML files).

9.1.3   Global Browser Player

This subsection gives you an overview on the most used browser software solutions and their main features. The four competitors are Netscape's Communicator, Microsoft's Internet Explorer, the text-based Lynx browser and the newcomer Opera from Norway.

Netscape Communicator

Netscape Communicator[3] is the best-known browser in the world. The browser is available for many platforms and other than Internet Explorer the non-Windows versions are available at the same time as the Windows version,

---

[3]http://www.netscape.com/

making Communicator the browser of choice if the user is working in a mixed operating system environment.

HTML 3.2, with all its proprietary extensions, such as Frames, are supported. Cascading Style Sheets are also no problem, but it does not quite conform yet to the W3C standards. JavaScript is understood by Netscape Communicator better than with any other browser. But this is no surprise, as JavaScript was invented and is being actively developed by Netscape.

The web casting feature of Netscape allows you to select a resource on the Internet, which contains a special type of content, such as information on Italian soccer and pushes the latest information to the desktop of the user. Other than a web page, where the user has to go actively and download the information (the so-called pull technology), the web casting feature allows servers to push actively information to the desktop of the user. The information will the be presented in a window or as the background of the desktop. This type of resource requires a constant connection to the Internet, in order to present up-to-date information.

Communicator is supporting Java 1.1 and Netscape is working on the Open Java Interface (OJI), which enables Communicator to accept third-party Java implementations. By releasing the source code on the Mozilla web site[4] and introducing a new feature called "Quality Feedback Agent" (QFA), the browser has become faster, more stable and more compact. The QFA is executed whenever the browser crashes and collects all the relevant information connected with the crash. This information is then sent back to Netscape and included into the bug database, making it easier to find out which bugs annoy many people and need to be removed first.

The built-in HTML editor allows the user to create web pages using a simple front end. The same editor can also be used to compose e-mails with HTML tags embedded. This allows users to create e-mails that are formatted and do not contain only simple text. A newsreader is also available and in the Enterprise Edition a Calendar makes Netscape Communicator a complete Internet work package.

If you are looking for a browser that is available on a vast majority of platforms, that supports newer releases of Java and JavaScript, then Netscape is the best choice.

Internet Explorer

Internet Explorer[5], which comes with every sold version of Windows and is freely downloadable for other platforms (MacOS, HP-UX, Solaris) is one of the most popular Internet platforms. Similar to Netscape's Communicator, its functionality goes far beyond the scope of a simple browser. Besides the browser part, web casting and a basic collaboration feature is built in.

---

[4] http://www.mozilla.org/
[5] http://www.microsoft.com/ie/

Just as with Netscape solutions, Internet explorer offers web casting, and the possibility of actively pushing information to the desktop of the user is also possible.

When running Internet Explorer on Windows, it can be highly integrated into the operating system. As this features is not cross-platform compliant, not many applications have appeared so far. Although the basic idea is good, the idea of supporting only Windows is not so good. It is possible to create local applications, written in HTML and JavaScript, that can easily interact with resources on the Internet.

In addition to support for JavaScript and Java, it also supports Active X components, media controllers, and VBScript, which are all Microsoft developments, available only on Microsoft platforms. Although these technologies provide some very good features, they are not designed for the web, which contains not only Microsoft power computers (although Microsoft would like to see it in the future).

A ratings services in the browser can be used to protect your family or business from inappropriate content. Web sites that are members of the PICS rating system[6] are automatically detected and displayed, when appropriate.

When installing IE, a cut-down edition of Outlook is installed, called Outlook Express. This is Microsoft's e-mail and news client, and it allows users to send and receive e-mails and newspostings. Besides Outlook Express, a cut-down version o FrontPage is installed, which allows the creation of simple web pages.

Although the latest release 5.0 has improved in many areas, there are still some inconsistencies and alterations to the web standards, which make it difficult to implement web pages which can be viewed in a consistent way in all browsers. HTML 4.0 is supported almost flawlessly, the same is true for cascading style sheets 1.0 support, but support for the DOM standard is not yet fully implemented. RDF and CSS 2.0 are not implemented at all.

All these features make Internet Explorer a complete solution, especially for users of Windows. The only disadvantage is that Java and JavaScript support is not up-to-date. The future of Java in Internet Explorer is not clear, Microsoft talked about removing it completely and the JavaScript implementation is always one version behind Netscape's browser releases. The JavaScript problem will disappear as soon as Microsoft take the ECMAScript standard on board, which is not a Netscape standard anymore.

Opera

Opera[7] is number three on the browser market. Although having only a very low market share, it is becoming very fast very popular, as it has some features that the two major browsers lack. While Netscape and IE are growing to

---

[6]http://www.w3.org/PICS/

[7]http://www.operasoftware.com/

become dinosaurs which require downloading packages of software exceeding fifteen megabytes, Opera is just over one megabyte. Opera is fast and functional, but lacks some features, such as Java and Active X support and it has only limited support for plug-ins.

As Opera is a new product it is much faster than Netscape and IE, as it has not been built on older versions whereby normally code gets added instead of completely replaced. Opera does not try to enforce new standards, but is built on the actual standards recommended by the Internet bodies, such as the World Wide Web Consortium[8]. Forms, frames, tables and fonts are displayed correctly and videos are displayed in-line without additional plug-ins. JavaScript and SSL are also supported, making this browser ideal for people who have little memory and slower systems.

Other than Netscape or IE, Opera opens windows within its own multi-pane interface. It does not include a full-blown e-mail client, but Opera allows simple e-mails to be sent out in order to reply to "mailto:" links. A simple newsreader is also included to read postings and post news into newsgroups.

Some of the most popular Netscape plug-ins are supported, such as Platinum's CosmoPlayer and Adobe's Acrobat reader, but it cannot be guaranteed that all plug-ins will work. As the software is produced in Norway, the software has been localized right from the beginning. French, Norwegian and German versions of Opera are already available and many other languages are to come.

The software is also being ported to other platforms than Windows, for example, to Linux[9], Amiga OS[10] and Mac OS[11].

As Opera is developed by a small software company they cannot afford to give the browser away for free. It is possible to download an evaluation copy for thirty days. If you are not in the need of the latest hype and don't require Java for online banking, for example, then Opera is a good choice.

Lynx

The smallest browser on the market is only about 500 kilobytes large. Lynx[12] is a text-based browser, therefore it does not support images, JavaScript, Java, Active X and sounds. Not even a mouse is supported. It is only capable of displaying textual information. Although this may seem strange to many people it actually displays what matters, the textual content. It is by far the fastest browser on the market.

Although it does not support the latest hype it is important for online business to know about the existence of the browser. It provides a very restricted view to your online offerings, which is similar to the view of embedded devices

---

[8]http://www.w3.org/
[9]http://www.linux.org/
[10]http://www.amiga.de/
[11]http://www.apple.com/macos/
[12]http://www.lynx.org/

and search engines. If you can view your web site through Lynx and do understand what it is all about, you can expect that people using mobile phones or other embedded device will be able to get the information provided on your web page.

Even if the customers are not able to execute a web based transaction, such as ordering stocks, they may want to see the actual stock price and then call their broker to place the order. Information therefore needs to be readable from any type of device. The same applies to search engines; if you are able to view your web page through Lynx, you can be sure that a search engine will be able to index your site properly so that it can be easily found by customers and visitors. Information that is hidden in Java applications, Plug-ins or images cannot be accessed by search engines, therefore it is necessary to add some text to explain the image or the application, so that search engines know what their purpose is.

Customers who are in need of information and have only limited resources, such as a very old computer (e.g. a Commodore 64 or MS-DOS computer) or a bad connection to the Internet because of a slow modem, or limited access to the Internet, such as a telnet account on a Unix server, will use this browser.

By checking your web site with Lynx you will also ensure that physically impaired people will be able to use the site. The information in textual form can be processed in a speech browser and can guide them through the web site. Images without additional information, for example, are like black spots on a web page and you will be able to detect them easily with Lynx.

Lynx cannot be used to do secure electronic business over the Internet, as it does not support SSL encrypted connections. Lynx can be downloaded for free, and every web designer should have a copy. Only if a web page is usable with Lynx you should then release it for the general public. Lynx can be used to verify if a web site is usable on network enabled devices, such as mobile phones and palmtops.

Many sites need JavaScript or SSL encryption, for example, to implement processing logic and security. But these technologies should really be used when there is a need for them and not because they are available. A Java ticker may be cute, but the same information can be presented in non-moving text. In any case, textual meta-information should be provided to explain the content of the web page and the reasons for using these advanced technologies.

9.1.4 Comparing Browser Technologies

Table 9.2 compares the four major browsers. As you can see there is no major difference in functionality; the problem is mostly in the implementation of the functionality. Every browser has a slightly different implementation, making it almost impossible to use the more advanced features of the browsers without running into trouble. Internet Explorer 5 and Netscape 5 promise to be more standards-based, but it is highly unlikely that both browsers will become truly interchangeable. Part of the marketing strategy of both companies is to provide something more valuable than the other and this is mainly achieved by adding new functionality. Therefore they have included functionality that is not part of any official standards and this will most likely also happen in the future.

Comparison of Browser Technology (1)

	Net-scape 4.5	IE 4.01	Opera 3.5	Lynx 2.7
Frames	Yes	Yes	Yes	Partly
Form	Yes	Yes	Yes	Yes
Tables	Yes	Yes	Yes	Partly
Fonts	Yes	Yes	Yes	No
CSS	Yes	Yes	No	No
JavaScript	Yes, 1.3	Yes, 1.2	Yes, 1.1	No
Java	Yes, 1.1	Yes, 1.0	No	No
Plug-ins	Yes	Yes	Yes	No
News	Yes	Yes	Yes	No
Mail	Yes	Yes	Yes	No
HTML Editor	Yes	Yes	No	No

Table 9.2.

With a delay of one or two releases the new functionality is becoming part of a standard. Therefore it can be expected, that all major browser soon be able to understand HTML 4.0 correctly, without any browser specific additions. The problem lies more in upcoming standards, such as XML, RDF and DOM. As these standards are still at their beginning, all companies will try to add some gimmicks, which break in other browsers. JavaScript will be a basic standard in Release 6 of the major browsers and expect release 7 of the major browsers to behave well on the XML, RDF, DOM and other standards described later in this chapter. By then new standards will have emerged, which will be fought over.

9.1.5 Other Browsers

Besides the four big players in the browser market, many other browser applications have been developed, which for one reason or the other have failed to become more popular. Some of the niche market browsers are presented here. Table 9.3 compares the runner ups.

Comparison of Browser Technology (2)

	Amaya	Arachne	iBrowse	iCab
Frames	No	Yes	Yes	Yes
Forms	Yes	Yes	Yes	Yes
Tables	Yes	Yes	Yes	Yes
Fonts	Yes	Yes	Yes	Yes
CSS	Yes	No	No	Yes
JavaScript	No	No	Yes	No
Java	No	No	No	No
Plug-ins	No	No	Yes	
News	No	No	No	Yes
Mail	No	Yes	No	Yes
HTML Editor	Yes	No	No	No

Table 9.3.

Amaya

Amaya[13] has been developed by the World Wide Web Consortium (W3C), which is maintaining and developing the HTML standard. It can be used to verify if your HTML pages are sticking to the standard. It supports the HTML 4.0 standard and Cascading Style Sheets (CSS), making it a good verification platform for web developers. Many web sites use features that are Netscape or IE specific and are not displayed correctly in Amaya. There is no support for JavaScript and cookies, which is used on many web sites nowadays, rendering these sites unreadable.

The major problem with Amaya is stability, rendering the browser unusable for daily browsing. It is a useful tool for developers, as it includes an integrated HTML editor and sticks to the HTML standards. Together with Lynx it should be installed on every web developer's computer. Amaya is freeware and available for several platforms besides Windows.

---

[13]http://www.w3.org/amaya/

Arachne

Arachne[14] has been developed by some Czech programmers for DOS-based computers. It uses less then a megabyte of RAM and fits on a floppy disk. Arachne supports HTML 4.0 and has a built-in mail client. Other than most DOS-based applications Arachne has a nice graphical user interface that allows the user to browse through web sites using a mouse, if available.

Arachne has been developed with people in mind who do not have any software for connecting to the Internet, so it does include software for dial-up accounts. This makes it a bit difficult to use with Windows-based computers as the drivers of Arachne interfere with the drivers of Windows, but with some configuration it is possible to use both.

Because it is using a DOS interface it is much faster than a Windows-based system. In addition to the browser and the e-mail client, there is a telnet and ftp application included. For people with very old DOS-based systems it is the only possibility to get onto the Internet with modest costs (for the software and the modem) involved.

As it has been developed in the Czech republic it is fully localized and supports many different languages. At the time of writing a Linux version is being developed, which then can be used to port it to other Unix flavors.

HotJava

HotJava[15] has been developed by Sun using the Java programming language. It's design is modular through JavaBeans-technology and is platform neutral. Sun wanted to develop a browser that runs on all network-enabled devices, ranging from appliances such as a mobile phone up to a large network server.

HotJava is the only browser that has 100 percent support for Java, as it is written in Java. But this is also its disadvantage, it is really slow. Both HTML pages and Java applets are slow compared to all other browsers and no JavaScript is supported. HTML is fully supported up to HTML 3.2, the browser accepts cookies and is able to encrypt communication through the SSL protocol.

It is possible to download either the source code or the binary version. The HotJava browser is available in two versions, as a full-featured web browser or as a JavaBeans component, which allows the display of HTML in any application that includes this JavaBeans component.

Although the browser supports all major standards it is not really an alternative to the major browsers, the latest version was far too slow for complex pages and Java applets.

---

[14]http://home.arachne.cz/
[15]http://www.sun.com/software/htmlcomponent/

iBrowse

iBrowse[16] is another browser that is at the time of writing only available for the Amiga[17] line of computers. Although many believe that the Amiga is dead, the supporters are even more vivid than the supporters of Macintosh computers. The Amiga hardware has stood still since 1991, but software is coming up, just as if the platform were still fully supported.

The Amiga platform has several web browsers, but iBrowse is the market leader. The browser does support JavaScript and supports HTML 3.2, just as Netscape and Internet Explorer do. But as Java is not fully supported in Amiga OS, no Java applets are supported. It allows the inclusion of plug-ins, but they need to be written especially for the Amiga platform, so only very few are available.

The browser does support most of the Netscape and Internet Explorer extensions and has a built-in mail client. It is one of the few browsers that supported the HTTP/1.1 extensions right from the beginning.

One nice feature is the netstat window, which shows all files that are currently downloaded. This allows you to see how fast each file gets downloaded and allows you to abort the download of files. This is useful for web pages with a lot of elements. If there are many images, it is possible to abort images that you are not interested in or that are too large.

The program is very compact compared to other browsers on the market and runs with only 2 megabytes of RAM, making the Internet accessible to people with older hardware.

iCab

The web browser iCab[18] created by some German developers may be able to compete with the big two browsers, Netscape and Internet Explorer. Although iCab is currently available for MacOS only, it immediately had a large impact on the relatively small market.

Highlights of iCab include a very user-friendly interface, a download manager for offline reading (which creates automatically a ZIP file for larger sites), and a special search tool that can be configured to use any search engine on the web. The browser requires only four megabytes of RAM and supports not only HTML 4.0 and Cascading Style Sheets (CSS) 2, but also all common extensions of the Netscape and Microsoft browsers. It has support for Java and a special feature to bookmark frames in the state of display. All other browsers are not able to bookmark pages with frames correctly.

If iCab becomes available for other platforms as well, it has the potential to become highly successful and a rival of Opera at least.

---

[16]http://cgi.www.hisoft.co.uk/amiga/ibrowse/

[17]http://www.amiga.de/

[18]http://www.icab.de/

9.1.6   Offline Browsers

In addition to the online browsers, many offline browsers have established themselves. Once you have decided which web site is interesting to you, you can simply download the complete site and read the content offline. All you need to do is to enter the starting URL and the program will download the web page and all elements on the web page, such as style sheets, images or sounds. Most programs offer the possibility to download recursively all links from that web page, eventually downloading the complete site.

Once you have downloaded the site, the normal web browser can be used to view the files on your hard disk. This works only with static HTML pages. If you come across a web site that builds dynamic web pages or uses CGI applications or Java applets that connect back to the server, then offline reading won't work properly.

The major advantage is that you can view the pages, whenever you need to and do not have to go online, but of course it may well be that you are downloading pages in which you are not interested.

Most programs that are available work similar to web spiders that index the content of web pages for search engines. Offline Explorer[19], developed by MetaProducts and WebZIP[20], developed by Spidersoft are programs that allow the retrieval of complete or partial web sites.

Cli-Mate[21], on the other hand, is highly specialized. It retrieves the weather forecast and installs it in the form of an image on the desktop of the computer. The information is updated automatically every time the user goes online. InfoNout[22] downloads the most recent movie listings automatically. This so-called push technology is discussed later in this chapter.

The third group of offline browsers are applications that scan through the the cache directory of the installed browser. Browsers use the cache to store the most recently viewed web pages in a special directory in order to save download time for the last few web pages. The files in the cache directory are not using the original file names, but use the date and time as a filename, therefore it is difficult to recognize which HTML page contains what. The cache browser reads the <title> tag and presents this information to the user instead of the cryptic filename.

9.1.7   The Impact on Business

The browser application has a huge impact on business on the Internet. It is the preferred piece of software to access online services, such as online shopping and online banking. The browser enables customers to self-service via the web. Although there are differences between the browser products, each of

---

[19] http://www.metaproducts.com/OE.html

[20] http://www.spidersoft.com/

[21] http://www.users.nac.net/splat/climate/

[22] http://www.boxoffice.com/download.html

them is capable of understanding and processing HTML, which is the building block for web pages.

The information on the web pages is displayed by the browser allowing customers to search for certain information within the web page, to print out the information for reference and can be used by digital companies to display and market products, information and services to customers around the world, no matter which language they speak or which type of computer they own. All they need is the web browser, which allows them to connect to the company's web site. Although there are other means to do business over the Internet, the browser has enabled almost anyone to do business, as the use is simple and very intuitive.

To expand your online business to a maximum number of customers you should use web technology, such as HTML to design and implement a web site. The browser window with information on your company is all the customers get to see, so you had better do it right the first time.

9.1.8 Browsing into the Future

With the start of the new Millennium (no matter if you think it starts in 2000 or 2001) the browser generation of today will be seen as prehistoric. The browser manufacturers included more proprietary features, which increased the size and the complexity of the software. As a result more and more bugs crept into the software making it more unreliable and more insecure.

But the biggest problem is that every browser manufacturer has bent the web standards a little bit into its own direction making the browsers advanced features incompatible. As a result most web pages use a design based on very old HTML standards, just to be sure that everyone is able to read the page. This chapter is full of new and emerging standards, which can enhance the web dramatically, but only if all browsers support them in a consistent way.

Another important point for the next Millennium is the upcoming era of pervasive computing. This means that more and more devices that had nothing to do with the Internet will become web enabled. The first microwaves with Internet connection are already on the market, allowing users to surf the web for recipes and order the required ingredients directly over the Internet at the local grocer. The microwave's job is it to heat up food and not to connect to the Internet in the first place, therefore the resources in the microwave will be very limited in order to maintain the price. Less memory, less colors, less speed will be most probable, or do you want twenty full-blown PCs all over the place? Most people could not afford it.

If we look at the latest releases from Netscape with its Communicator 4.61 (just under 20 megabytes) and Microsoft with its Internet Explorer 5.0 (just under 60 megabytes) and look at their sizes, we can see that these browsers were designed for the ever-increasing speed, memory and hard disk space of personal computers.

Features of Next Generation Browsers

The next generation of web browsers needs to adhere to the following features in order to meet the customers' expectations.

- **Internet Services** – Browsers need to integrate services on the Internet tightly, instead of offering them within the browser.

- **Open Source Code** – The source code needs to be available.

- **Real-Time Communication** – Live chats become more important.

- **Small Size** – In order to support devices other than standard computers, the size needs to be reduced.

- **Speed** – Network enabled devices are not as fast as full-blown computers, therefore the browser needs to be very fast.

- **Standards Compliance** – Web standards need to be implemented correctly.

Table 9.4.

Including these browsers in other devices than a computer is impossible. They have become so complex that it is not possible to simply remove some features from it to make it fit into a device with two megabytes of memory.

Some of the other browsers mentioned above are much smaller as they do not carry the burden of so much old code. But even Opera and the other browsers need to rethink the way they were written in order to fit onto other devices. Making browser technology available for other types of devices requires manufacturers to make the source code very modular, as some devices have more capabilities than others.

By strictly modularizing the browser technologies it is possible to create Web connectivity for almost any device, regardless of its features (e.g. limited memory, display). Netscape, for example, is working on two browser generations at the same time. The old one, which is based on Netscape 4 technology and on the old paradigm of creating software: New features are more important than speed and size, as computers get faster and equipped with more memory all the time. The new concept of connecting all devices to the Internet requires to omit features in order to make the application fast enough and fit into the possibly limited memory of the device. Therefore the new browser generation is modularized and completely rewritten using modern tools for optimizing size and speed. The first preview release of Netscape's new browser called Gecko has only as size of 1.6 Megabyte while maintaining all features of the old Netscape 4.61 release. By re-implementing all features, the new browser is also much faster and the Web standards are enforced by better control over the single modules.

In order to reduce the size of the browser, some of the browser services offered need to be moved to the Internet. Instead of offering natively a functionality, the functionality will be delivered from a web server. Your mobile phone won't have enough additional memory to add a full blown e-mail application. But this is not really necessary, as there are enough possibilities on the web to display, read and send e-mails. Web e-mail is able to offer the same functionality as a stand alone application, but does not require you to install a program on the client side.

All features except for the web browsing feature can be outsourced to the Web. Instead of opening up the news reader client, people can connect to Internet services offering all newsgroups. Instead of opening up a chat client, people can connect to a web server, which offers the same functionality. Every single service can be outsourced in this way.

The current generation of browser offers the choice between built-in functionality and the web functionality. As the connection speed to the Internet becomes faster, the web functionality becomes more accessible. Netscape offers a feature to look up stock quotes by entering "quote <symbol>", whereby <symbol> is the ticker symbol, such as AAPL for Apple and HWP for Hewlett-Packard. Just enter the above term and the browser will return a web page with all financial information about the selected company.

The address book is normally outsourced together with the mail functionality and companies have started to offer online calendar solutions. Online chats (sometimes called real-time messaging) is one of the favorite pastimes of the Internet community. It offers the possibility to talk to people from all over the world at the cost of a local phone call. In many cases online chats have replaced phone calls and therefore are becoming more and more important. The next generation of browsers will have a much stronger integration with chat, not only text-based chat as we know it today, but also voice conferences and video conferencing will become standard functionality for many devices.

The next generation of browsers will need to be strictly standards-compliant in order to succeed. As web browsers are given away for free, adding features that are not compliant won't be used, as web developers need to be sure that everyone is able to access a certain feature. By supporting the W3C standards new content and service sites can be implemented fast and cost-effectively. The most important move is the transition from HTML to XML as the base format for the Internet.

The W3C standards (such as XML, CSS2, DOM, RDF) enable the developers to create highly complex applications using the next generation of browsers. As current web browsers do not fully support these new standards, documents in these new formats need to be translated on the server to standard HTML and passed on to the browser. Over time these server translations can be removed. Currently the browser with the least standards support is the limit on standards adoption. By moving away from HTML to XML, features can be added without the need of updating the browser, making it easier for developers to create applications and services.

Experience has shown that closed development leads to non-standard implementations, limited hardware and software platform support, lesser quality and less interoperability. Open source on the other hand speeds up development, increases the quality and by offering the source code for free, everyone is able to port the application to another platform. But not only the software becomes available on more platforms, it also becomes available in more languages, as anyone is able to offer a translation for a specific language. More on open source and free software can be found in Chapter 14.

9.2 The Hypertext Markup Language

9.2.1 The Building Block

HTML, the HyperText Markup Language is the fundamental building block of the World Wide Web. Hypertext is a form of text that contains links to other text, therefore connecting texts in a non-linear way to each other. HTML is a non-proprietary format, developed by the World Wide Web consortium, based upon SGML (Standard Generalized Markup Language). The hypertext documents are plain text files that contain embedded codes for logical markup. These documents can be created by simple text editors or highly sophisticated authoring tools.

HTML is not a programming language, but a markup language. It only describes a logical structure of a document, rather than document presentation. It is, for example, not possible to alter the structure from within the document itself using only HTML.

HTML documents are stored on a web server, which distributes the files to the web browsers that connect to that particular server. The HTML files are then not only displayed to the viewer as they are, but are interpreted by the web browser that then creates the web page, according to the instructions that are part of the HTML code.

Originally HTML was supposed to be device independent. It was to be used on a variety of computer systems without change. The idea of HTML was to provide a means to structure a document. It was left up to the browser on any specific system to take care of rendering the document in whatever way the browser author thought most suitable. Tim Berners-Lee, the inventor of the world wide web was a researcher at CERN[23] and therefore more interested in structuring a document than creating a nice layout for it.

9.2.2   Web Page Layout

Over time the Hypertext Markup Language (HTML) and the World Wide Web had become very popular and commercial companies wanted to present information and goods on the Internet. The Web moved from being primarily a medium for exchanging scientific information to a marketing medium. Companies wanted their web documents to adhere to their corporate standards and needed to layout them accordingly. But the original HTML specification offered very little support for layout and presentation, so the demand grew for extensions. Various browser manufacturers introduced new HTML elements oriented towards presentation issues, which eventually became part of the HTML standard.

Over time HTML therefore has also become a language for creating a layout for a web page. HTML uses tags to describe certain text elements. In the beginning the tags were used exclusively to describe the structure of an element, such as a heading. The tag <h1> was used to describe a heading. In order to make the heading distinct of the body text, the web browser would display the heading using a font size of 36 points, while body text is 10 points. In later releases of HTML and massive pressure from the major browser producers the <font> tag was introduced, which allowed the HTML programmer to select a size of the font. Instead of <h1> this is a heading </h1>, it has become possible to use <font size=7> this is not a heading </font>. A short introduction to the use of HTML tags can be found in Table 9.5.

The problem with the <font> tag is that is does not tell anyone what the text element represents. The text could be a heading, body text, a signature, a code segment or any other type of text. Although a human is not able to see the difference in the browser, search engines, for example, will have trouble classifying this particular document as it is not able to distinguish on the importance of a text element. Automatic processing of documents is also very difficult as there is no or only little structural information stored in the document.

By using standardized tags the HTML code is independent of a particular web browser or operating system. Any web browser that understands HTML is able to read web documents, interpret them and create a layout for a web page. Using logical tags every browser is free to display a tag with a different style. While one browser displays emphasized text using bold text another one may choose to display it in italic.

The main reason for introducing layout tags was that web designers wanted to create web pages that looked consistent in all browsers. Their job was not

---

[23]http://www.cern.ch/

Introduction to HTML Tags

Most documents on the web are described by HTML tags. These instructions are embedded within a less-than (<) and a greater-than (>) sign to distinguish the instructions from the text that you want to display. HTML tags are used to describe text elements or define a layout. Therefore each text element is surrounded by two HTML tags, the start tag and the end tag. The end tag is the same as the start tag, but a slash has been added. An example could look like this:

```
<title>this is the title of the web page</title>
```

Although the current release of HTML is case-insensitive, this cannot be guaranteed for future releases. If you use HTML through XML, for example, case-sensitivity will be a basic requirement.

HTML tags cannot only define formatting options, but also attributes. The <font> tag allows for different attributes such as font size and color. A large red text could be created by <font size=5 color=red>. If attribute values use white spaces, then they need to be enclosed within quotes. The attribute information does not need to be repeated in the end tag. HTML is very powerful and simple at the same time. Anybody is able to create HTML documents within minutes.

Table 9.5.

to describe content, they wanted to create a special design. The latest release of the HTML standard, version 4.0, tries to reverse this development by deprecating most tags that deal with presentation and not structure. These tags are moved into style sheets. An example are the attributes of the <body> tag. More on style sheets can be found later in this chapter.

A deprecated element or attribute is one that has been outdated by newer constructs, and which may become obsolete in future versions of HTML. The browsers continue to support deprecated elements for reasons of backward compatibility.

9.2.3   HTML 4.0

In 1997 the World Wide Web Consortium[24] released HTML 4.0. It builds upon HTML 3.2 adding a host of new features. The new standard was developed by the HTML Working Group, which consists of many industry players, such as Adobe[25], Hewlett-Packard, IBM, Netscape, Reuters[26] and Sun, content specialists at HotWired[27] and PathFinder[28] and experts in the fields of accessibility and internationalization.

The major news in HTML 4.0 is that is has been designed with embedded devices in mind. Other than HTML 3.2, which was basically made for complex browser software only, the new recommendation allows access to web content from a broad range of devices, from smart television to cellular phones. The goal is to make HTML a fundamental building block for networked computers and mission critical information systems in the business world.

Just like it predecessors, HTML 4.0 is an SGML application, which enables hypertext documents to be represented using text-based markup, providing interoperability across a wide range of platforms. It includes features for basic document idioms such as headings, lists, paragraphs, tables and images, as well as hypertext links, and electronic forms.

These basic features can be rendered on graphical displays, such as the Netscape browser, text-only displays, such as the Lynx browser and speech-based browsers. These features were already present in HTML 3.2 and its Netscape and Internet Explorer version cousins.

Some totally new features have been introduced into HTML 4.0 to make it more appealing for content providers and users. The new HTML standard provides a way for authors to embed objects and scripts, and support style sheets in their documents. Although these features were already available in earlier versions, they have never been formally standardized, making it difficult to implement objects, scripts and styles across a set of different browsers. This enables content providers to dynamically update pages and change the appearance on the fly.

Electronic forms have been updated to allow content providers to display rich HTML in any button. Until now content providers could not control the design of the buttons in an electronic form. With the introduction of HTML 4 one can create read-only controls and group form controls together. Another very important feature is that it is now possible to provide keyboard shortcuts on controls making it easier for people who cannot use a mouse to control the complete form via voice control. Titles can now be added to any element, making the whole electronic form more appear like a standard desktop application.

---

[24] http://www.w3.org/
[25] http://www.adobe.com/
[26] http://www.reuters.com/
[27] http://www.hotwired.com/
[28] http://www.pathfinder.com/

Although I consider frames one of the less useful inventions of HTML, it has been substantially been improved in this new version. It now allows the creation of in-line frames in order to make compound documents by placing frames in HTML documents. This feature is very useful, but I still think that the basic frame architecture should be thrown out, except for this new type.

The basic table functionality has been enhanced to allow row and column grouping. The improved border control delivers additional design control to improve the performance and the power of the tables. Although these features may be very useful for creating tables, they may be again misused to create complex web page layouts. The layout should be controlled by the style sheets and not by tables.

Another very important feature update is the inclusion of new named entities, which now support important symbols and glyphs used in mathematics, markup and internationalization.

Flavors of HTML

In order to make HTML 4.0 a success, three flavors have been specified. By inserting a line at the beginning of the document stating which flavor you are using, the appropriate document type definition (DTD) will be used to validate the correctness of the document.

- **HTML 4.0 Frameset** – Should be only used if the documents use HTML frames to partition the browser window into two or more frames.

- **HTML 4.0 Transitional** – Should be used in order to support older browsers correctly, that do not understand style sheets, while allowing all the possibilities HTML 4.0 offers.

- **HTML 4.0 Strict** – Should be used when you want clean structural markup, free of any tags associated with layout. Requires Cascading Style Sheets to do the layout.

Table 9.6.

The new HTML standard has been developed with accessibility in mind. This means that embedded devices will be able to access the information, but also people with disabilities will get additional information describing images, labels for form fields and ways to associate table data with headers. This additional meta-information makes it easier to understand the content of an HTML page through a speech-based or Braille browser. Most web pages today contain information which can be easily extracted through the human eye, as they contain many images that are self-explaining, but are not accessible to these special browsers because of this missing meta-information.

The Web Accessibility Initiative (WAI) has developed authoring guidelines to support people with disabilities. For many web pages it will mean a major re-design, but hopefully when moving from HTML 3.2 to HTML 4.0 many web page designers will include this additional information. It will open up the web to millions of users who have been held back by pages designed only for people using graphical browsers. For online business this can mean a lot of additional traffic to their web sites.

Another important issue was the internationalization. In the past HTML already supported documents in other languages, but on a given web page, only one language was supported. HTML 4.0 now provides the markup needed for any language including multi-lingual documents. The advantage is that authors can now make their documents more accessible to users, whatever their language is. This is achieved by supporting the international ISO 10646 character set, and allowing authors to manage differences in language, text direction, and character encoding schemes. This makes it, for example, easier to create an English-Hebrew dictionary on the web. The English text will be written from left-to-right and next to it, the Hebrew text will be set right-to-left. The burden of internationalization is then passed on to the web page editors, which now need to support this new paradigm to make text entry easy. With current web page editors, it is necessary to write correct HTML 4.0 Hebrew web pages from back-to-front.

9.2.4 Relevance to Online Businesses

HTML's impact to the online business is very similar to the impact of the web browser. In fact, both technologies are linked together very tightly. HTML is the underlying technology for displaying content in a web browser. It allows customers to view product and service information easily and companies to develop such pages very easily. Although modern web browsers require a lot of memory, most web pages require only very little memory. The size of a typical web site is between twenty and fifty kilobytes, making the transport of information very efficient. Imagine if all the information on the web were only available via word processor file formats. This would multiply the download factor by ten to twenty without increasing the value for the customer or adding content. Actually most word processors now allow the direct output of HTML, making it easy for non-technical people to create web pages.

HTML is easy to learn and implement and therefore can be used by any company to present itself in a very interactive and multimedial way. HTML can reduce costs in a significant way. Instead of sending out tons of material via traditional mailing services, the customers are able to get the information on the web themselves and print it out, if required. This also reduces the amount of paper which is used for printing.

9.3   The Dynamic Web

9.3.1   Moving from Static to Dynamic Web Sites

Most companies have started out by using static pages to create web sites. The major advantage of this system is that no programming knowledge needs to be available and anyone with a web page editor is able to get some pages up and online. Once the information is online the only piece of software that needs to work is the web server, which has become a very solid piece of software over the last few years. Another very important issue is that static web pages do not require as many resources as dynamic web pages on a web server as the only action that the web server has to perform is to locate the web page on the hard disk and pass it on to the web browser.

But many companies will eventually want to do more and this requires them to tie web pages to their databases. Using the database model allows for dynamic web pages that let visitors add, insert, and delete data, while internal data is also available immediately on the Internet. Dynamic pages are a whole lot more flexible and useful than static pages, even though they may consume a little more resources on the web server.

Consider an online shop with ten thousand articles. Using static web pages, you would need to create a page for every single product resulting in tens of thousands of web pages, which are not manageable in any way. It becomes impossible to change the layout or add a link to every page. The same applies to online banking, ordering or any other service, which relies on data or information that changes over time. Using static web pages the whole web page needs to be rebuilt, even if only a single line has changed. The overhead for creating static web pages would consume more resources than dynamic web pages allocate.

Static web pages are still around, but used now only by individuals who have a few web pages online that they change every so often. A company offering an online service needs to have its web site always up-to-date and therefore all the information presented there needs to be up-to-date as well. Imagine a company selling printers via the web, but not having its latest model online for sale, because it took too long to add new static web pages to the site. Using a dynamic web site, the data on the new printer would be entered into the web server's database and the information on the printer would become instantly available to anyone visiting the site.

Through the use of dynamic web pages companies are able to create a standard layout, which is saved in a separate location apart from the data. At the time a customer accesses your web site the layout and the content are combined on the fly to form a highly individual web page, which answers the query of the customer.

Almost all business sites are using dynamic web pages. They make it easy to do changes in the layout as only very few layout templates need to be changed and this reduces the cost for the company and the time to market for a new web page design. This paradigm allows design agencies to create the web design without having to touch the content.

Dynamic web pages need not necessarily be pre-built on the server, using Cascading Style Sheets, the Document Object Model and JavaScript it is also possible to create client-side Dynamic HTML.

9.3.2 Cascading Style Sheets

As discussed in the section on HTML, HTML was developed to describe the logical structure of a document. In order to describe the layout of the document cascading style sheets (CSS) have been invented. They are supposed to help HTML to become again what it was once designed for.

CSS allows you to control the rendering of elements on a web page without compromising its structure. Fonts, colors, typefaces, and other aspects of style are defined in the CSS. Instead of using web terminology it uses desktop publishing terminology which addresses the needs of designers. The visual design can be addressed separately from the logical structure of the web page, just as layouters do. HTML does not have the possibilities modern desktop publishing (DTP) systems have.

Style sheets are templates, very similar to templates in DTP applications, containing a set of rules specifying the rendering of various HTML elements. These templates describe how a document is presented on the screen or when printed out.

What designers always missed most, was the typographic control. CSS allows web elements to be positioned to control the layout on web page and allows the fonts to be downloaded dynamically . Images and text can be layered and overlapped and can be dynamically moved around the screen with scripts. With CSS it is possible to control the layout of any given document in a web browser. Other than with HTML layout CSS, layout will look the same in all web browsers.

9.3.3 The Document Object Model

The document object model (DOM) is a model in which a document (such as a web page) contains objects (e.g. text elements, images, links) that can be manipulated. DOM has been recommended by W3C. Using DOM it is possible to remove, alter or add an element to a given document. It is also possible to change the content of an element or remove, alter or add an attribute. Through

DOM it is possible to get a list of all "H2" elements in a document or all elements with an attribute "SIZE=4".

Level 1 of the DOM specification allows the navigation around an HTML or XML document, and the manipulation of the content in that particular document. Level 2 allows the manipulation of cascading style sheets (CSS) styles which are used in an HTML or XML document, includes an event model and richer queries on the objects.

Depending on the hosting implementation the language for modifying objects in the DOM model, a web browser will most likely use JavaScript or ECMAScript (the standardization of JavaScript/JScript by the European Computer Manufacturer's Association [ECMA] defined by ECMA-262). This scripting language is embedded into the page itself and allows the manipulation of the objects on the page. An editor may also use a Java interface to manipulate the page in the editor. Java could also be used to create a DOM interface between a document and a database. But if not embedded into a web page, the interface could be in any language as the DOM is language neutral.

DOM is more than just a broker between scripting languages and a document, by providing a common syntax. Just as style sheets allow you to perform layout independent of content and structure, the DOM allows you to make interaction independent of content and structure. It uses the same paradigm from another point of view. This allows you to create code (and therefore interaction) independently of web pages, just as style sheets allow you to create layout independently of web pages.

In order to make the DOM language neutral it is necessary to define it in an interface definition language (IDL). Other than the component object model (COM) or the common object request broker (CORBA), which provide language-independent ways to specify interfaces and objects, the DOM is a set of interfaces and objects for managing HTML and XML documents.

9.3.4 Dynamic HTML

Although HTML is the best tool for publishing textual documents over the Internet, it is not designed to create interactive web sites and multi-media rich documents. Standard HTML is also limited to what concerns the layout. Therefore cascading style sheets have been invented, which allow pixel-level accuracy on the layout, which is comparable to traditional desktop publishing programs. This also makes the creation of online and offline documents from a single source easier.

Although it is possible to create dynamic web pages on the server, meaning that the content is brought together at the time of loading, most web pages are static once they are displayed in the browser, meaning that the content or layout cannot be changed without going back to the server. HTML, by definition, does not allow you to dynamically update content, change the appearance of content, and hide, show, and animate content.

To allow these features web pages need to become interactive. This cannot be done by HTML, so scripting languages such as JavaScript or VBScript have been invented to take over this role (see also the section on JavaScript later in this chapter). These languages allow to increase the interactivity of the web page, but only in a limited fashion.

If we now put all three building blocks together, HTML, Cascading Style Sheets and JavaScript/VBScript we are able to create highly functional, dynamic and interactive web pages that are similar to today's stand-alone multimedia applications. This is called DHTML or Dynamic HTML.

By exposing a document object model to the scripting languages web page designers get full control over the HTML document and its elements and are able to change the layout on the fly. The color of a heading can be changed, just as a block of text can be moved from the upper right corner into the lower left corner or hidden completely. The event model that accompanies the document object model extends the scripting languages' awareness of user actions, allowing keystrokes and a larger variety of mouse actions to be interpreted by scripting languages.

Through the use of DHTML it has become possible to create content dynamically on the client without having to reconnect to the server, which is often desired when working on a slow connection. Another very interesting feature is data binding, which is currently only supported by Internet Explorer, which allows the server and client to be connected in such a way that data in the database can be bound to elements in an HTML document. This allows you to view database content on a single web page. Most web sites reconnect to the server and get a new HTML page with database content. This functionality allows you to keep the HTML page and the layout and refill the content of single elements with new data entries.

DHTML allows the creation of complex client-side applications that do not necessarily need to interact with a server. Many games have been created in DHTML, such as Tetris, but also word processors, HTML editors and spreadsheets have already been created in DHTML. DHTML offers a way to provide applications on the web for a limited period of time. Similar to Java applets they allow user interaction, but are in general faster, as they are directly implemented in the browser and do not require a Java virtual machine to run.

9.4   Dynamic Server Concepts

Although DHTML is a good choice for smaller databases and web sites, the creation of dynamic web pages on the server will be more appropriate for larger companies with huge databases. In order to process input or data from the client and from other sources, such as databases, it is necessary to create interfaces for communication. The common gateway interface (CGI) is an established protocol for a web server application to receive data from a browser and prepare data before sending it back to the client. HTML pages may be embedded into the CGI applications. Server side includes (SSI) on the other hand can only prepare data before sending it to the client. SSI embeds commands into HTML pages.

9.4.1   The Common Gateway Interface

The common gateway interface (CGI) enables interaction between a web server and a browser using the hypertext transfer protocol (HTTP). HTML documents are static and served by the web server without changing anything to the client. A CGI program is executed and the results are delivered to the customers, such as a flight plan query or a news update.

CGI programs are able to handle information requests and return the appropriate document or generate a dynamic document. They can act as a gateway between databases and web browsers, which understand only HTML, but not SQL, for example. Customers are able to express queries using HTML Forms that allow the selection of items and the entry of free text, which then can be passed back to the server. The data a customer enters into the form is submitted to the web server, the CGI is able to pick up the information and pass them on to a program which can process the input and pass back the results to the web browser.

CGI programs are scripts or executables which are invoked by the web browser and then executed on the web server. CGI specifies how the data is handled between web page and executable, but does not limit this information to any specific language. C, C++, Python, Perl, Java are the most commonly used languages for CGI applications, but you can use any language. CGI applications are able to handle any type of application, depending on the imagination and ability of the programmer.

Although any programming language can be used to create server side HTML pre-processor applications, this section give a short overview on the most commonly used languages. Using Java, JavaScript, Perl and Python it is fairly easy to build applications that accept and provide data through the common gateway interface (CGI).

Java

Java[29] is a hardware-independent language that runs on all major platforms. Many people know Java in the form of applets in the web browser. As there are some problems with implementations in Java within web browsers, client-side Java is not always the best solution. Different browser manufacturers support different versions of Java, which are, of course, incompatible. Java on the server, on the other hand, has become one of the major drivers. Server-side Java has the advantage that it is browser-independent, if done properly

---

[29]http://java.sun.com/

and the server can be replaced without needing to rewrite or re-compile the software. Java is described in depth in Chapter 11.

JavaScript

Server-side JavaScript needs to be compiled and can then be used by the Netscape Enterprise Server, in a way similar to CGI programs. Server-side JavaScript is only accepted by the Netscape web servers, while the client-side scripting engine is supported and accepted by all major browsers.

Client and server-side JavaScript share the same basic functionality. Webmasters that know how to write JavaScript code for the browser will be able to write server-side JavaScript immediately. The advantage of server-side JavaScript is that the script is processed on the server and requires no special browser to view the page. The downside is that for every interaction a connection back to the server is required, just as with any other application that resides on the server.

Perl

Perl is the most popular programming language on the server side as it allows fast prototyping. Although many people think Perl[30] (Practical Extraction and Report Language) is a CGI language only, it is a regular programming language that can be used not only for the web. Perl is a scripting language that is interpreted by the Perl interpreter and which as been optimized for scanning text files, extracting information from files, processing the information and printing reports based on that information.

Larry Wall, the developer of Perl, has intended to create a language that is practical, therefore easy to use, efficient and complete, rather than beautiful. Unlike Java, Perl is hard to read. Perl combines some of the most useful features of other programming languages, such as C and Pascal and applications, such as "sh", "sed" and "awk".

Python

Python[31] is another good choice in the context of web server programming. It is an interpreted, interactive programming language that is based on the paradigm of object-orientation. It has many similarities with Tcl, Perl, Scheme and Java.

The syntax of Python is very clear, without reducing the power of the programming language. Classes, dynamic typing, dynamic data types exceptions and modules are the standard constructs of the language and it offers many interfaces to system calls, libraries and windowing systems, such as X11 Unix front-ends and Macintosh OS.

---

[30]http://www.perl.org/
[31]http://www.python.org/

Python can also interact with C or C++ applications, making it a suitable alternative for creating an extension language for applications that need a programmable interface. Python is very portable and is available on all major platforms, making it a good language if you run a multi-platform environment. The source code is freely available, making it possible to compile it even for currently not-supported platforms.

9.4.2 Server Side Includes

Server side includes (SSI) are commands that are included into HTML pages and are executed before the web page is sent to the client. The commands are a special kind of HTML tags, which are interpreted by the web server. The advantage for the web developer is that they do not need to learn any additional language, but need only add some more commands to the web page. The use is limited to the SSI extensions developed by the software company whose extensions you are planning to use.

SSIs offer a simple way of customizing a web page. It is, for example, very easy to define a variable that is replaced with the name of the customer identified by IP address, basic (login/password) or strong authentication (digital certificate) or via cookie. This feature enables you to welcome every single customer, without having different web pages on the server. It can also be used to omit or add specific information that may be uninteresting or valuable to the customer through simple "if-else" statements. SSI makes HTML highly dynamic, but the problem is that marketing won't be able to change the layout with a simple HTML editor, as the web pages contain a lot of programming information, which they would need to understand.

9.4.3 Net.Data

IBM Net.Data[32] is an application that allows Web developers to easily build dynamic internet applications using "Web Macros". They offer the simplicity of HTML with the power of dynamic SQL. Net.Data provides database connectivity to a variety of data sources including information stored in relational databases on a variety of platforms. The most prevalent databases can be data sources for your web application: DB2, Oracle, Sybase, DRDA-enabled data sources, ODBC data sources as well as flat file and web registry data.

Net.Data provides high performance web applications with robust application development function. Net.Data exploits web server interfaces (APIs), providing higher performance than common gateway interface (CGI) applications. Net.Data supports client-side processing as well as server-side processing with languages such as Java, REXX, Perl and C++. Net.Data provides conditional logic and a rich macro language.

---

[32]http://www.ibm.com/

With Net.Data, you get full support for Java, the standard for Web application development. You can use a Java applet to create a graphical chart, such as a pie chart, from the results of a Net.Data application. With Net.Data's support for JavaScript, you can validate data entered at the client's Web browser and call a Java application for additional logic. The solution offers a tight integration into databases and web programming languages to create an interactive environment on the web.

9.4.4   JavaServer Pages

JavaServer Pages (JSP) technology provides an easy and powerful way to build web pages with dynamically-generated content. It enables rapid development of web-based applications that are server- and platform-independent.

Web site owners can use the tools and interfaces they already know to create dynamic web pages. The application logic resides in server-based resources that the page accesses with HTML-like tags. By separating the page design from its content generation and supporting a reusable component-based design, JSP technology makes it faster and easier than ever to build dynamic and interactive web-based applications.

Through JSP the generation of HTML pages is simplified. HTML-like tags and scriptlets written in Java encapsulate the logic that generates the content for the page. Standard HTML or XML commands handle formatting and design. By separating the page design from the application logic that generates the data, JSP technology-enabled pages make it easier for organizations to reuse and share application logic through JavaBeans technology-based components or customized JSP specification-based tags.

The tight integration with the Java platform allows companies to leverage existing Java platform expertise and create highly scalable enterprise applications. This makes it also platform and server independent.

9.5   Web Application Servers

9.5.1   Reasons for Web Application Servers

Traditional web services are based on a two-tier architecture, meaning that two components are used to create the service, such as a web server or a database server. To make it easier for developers to isolate the business logic web applications servers are put in place, thus effectively creating a three-tier architecture, which has become the standard for network-based applications. In this schema the browser is not considered part of the architecture.

Web application servers do not only isolate the business logic from the program logic, but offer additional features, which are hard to implement in a two-tier architecture. Functions such as transaction management, clustering and load balancing are easily added to the three-tier architecture.

Another advantage of a three-tier architecture is that it becomes easier to access data and services that reside on legacy systems without direct connection to the Internet. The Web application server creates a unified messaging system, which allows each application that is connected to exchange information. Therefore the support code, which is used to connect the different applications, is encapsulated in a standard component, which is typically CORBA or COM. COM can only be deployed on PC platforms, while CORBA can be used on any platforms. The CORBA model is more open because of platforms and languages supported. Today most web application servers allow developers to write this support code in Java or C++. The development language is important because it may determine the application server platform and it affects the choice for the appropriate distributed computing model.

Through web application servers it is possible to consolidate functionality from all sorts of applications into a new user interface, the World Wide Web. Web application servers eliminate the need for the clients to connect directly all core subsystems in the back-end, as this requires extra knowledge for each application for every single employee. Through a web application server the back-end applications can be accessed through a browser.

By installing a web application server and integrating the business critical enterprise applications, it is possible to move away from mainframes, if desired without putting the service at risk. A transition has become much easier, as the underlying messaging infrastructure does not change. The first key architectural mechanism you will need to define in your new integrated system is data synchronization. All of your enterprise applications need to share the same data among themselves.

This leads to the databases, which are the backbone of any enterprise application. Most database vendors offer web application servers, which tightly integrate applications into their databases. Although this will guarantee the highest possible speed for applications that require that particular database, it may lock your company into using a certain database vendor, as these solutions use proprietary protocols to access data. This can become a problem, if you later decide to integrate applications that use another database system or choose to expand beyond database-centric applications.

9.5.2 Web Application Products

If we look at the market of web application products we can see that there is a lot of need and a wide selection of available software. At the time of writing more than one hundred professional products were released and available on the market. Other than with most software decisions where it is important to base your decision on the business idea, the decision on which web application server should be chosen depends mainly on the installed base of software and hardware. An up-to-date list of web application server products and background information can be found on the Application Server Zone web site[33]. The following is a selection of web application servers.

Avenida Web Server

Avenida Web Server[34] provides a powerful server-side Java technology (called servlet), which is not only easy-to-use, but has also a very small footprint. It is built on-top of Sun's Java servlet architecture and provides not only the same API, but also the plug-in capability into the web server. The standard edition comes with four servlets with the following functionality: file, proxy, redirect and virtual hosting.

The file servlet provides the functionality of a standard web server and is able to serve web content to the browser client. The second servlet, called proxy servlet allows the server to act as a proxy server to allow access from the Intranet to the Internet. It also has a tunneling feature built in, allowing the transport of HTTP requests transparently and securely to any given machine without revealing the source and the destination. The redirect servlet enables the server to redirect the HTTP request to another server with the same functionality. Through this functionality it is possible to introduce load balancing, which distributes the incoming requests over several servers. The virtual hosting functionality allows one web server to appear as a number of distinct hosts with their own domain names and IP addresses. This is a feature that ISPs are often using for their clients.

Although this product is a very good web server, especially for ISPs, it lacks the features required to build up an integrated virtual enterprise. Through the servlet architecture it is possible to build connections to the legacy applications in the background, but it requires quite a bit of additional work, as no standard adaptors are provided.

Bea WebLogic Enterprise

The WebLogic Enterprise product[35], developed by BEA Systems[36] provides an application server, which is very extensible and provides functionality for assembling, deploying and managing distributed Java applications. WebLogic is able to connect business components written in Java with heterogeneous databases, network information resources, such as online web services, and other business components, which do not necessarily need to be written in Java.

WebLogic is built on top of the BEA engine, which is a set of core technologies that BEA has acquired, integrated, and enhanced to create a high performing, easy-to-use, and comprehensive object management and transaction processing technology. Via the BEA engine, WebLogic is also able to leverage

---

[33]http://www.appserver-zone.com/

[34]http://www.avenida.co.uk/

[35]http://www.weblogic.com/

[36]http://www.beasys.com/

BEA's family of connectivity products that facilitate connection to other applications and data in the enterprise.

Through the Transaction Processing Framework companies are able to focus on their business logic instead of on infrastructure issues. It simplifies the programming of CORBA objects and automates many tasks that were previously the responsibility of the developer, such as management of transactions and object states.

To achieve high availability WebLogic has implemented a function to define replicated server processes that can take over the load when a server process fails. These server processes can be on the same or on a different machine.

WebLogic also tries to restart server processes that abnormally fail. The operator can specify the number of times it tries.

The application components can be managed through a graphical Java console that ensure security, scalability, performance and transaction integrity. BEA WebLogic Enterprise is one of the best web application servers on the market, as it provides a complete framework for the integration and many modules for standard applications to make the integration stable and simple.

Cold Fusion

Cold Fusion[37] by Allaire is one of the most popular products on the market. It allows the user to build and deliver scalable applications that integrate browser, server and database technologies. A special developer product, called Cold Fusion Studio enables developers to program through a visual interface and includes database and debugging tools in an integrated development environment (IDE). The pre-built building blocks in Cold Fusion Studio features an open integration with e-mail and directory services, database and enterprise systems.

The speed of Cold Fusion is achieved through its just-in-time compilation and the caching features, which allow developers to write portable Java code. Pages that are requested very often can be served from the cache to reduce the load on the server. Quality of service is a stronghold of the Cold Fusion system, as it natively supports multi-server clusters with built-in load balancing features and a fail over system, which passes on requests to another server when either a system is overloaded or fails. This make the system ideal for high volume and transaction intensive applications.

Through ODBC and native database drivers, Cold Fusion is able to connect to most database systems and through CORBA and COM it is very easily extensible. To round up the picture of an excellent development and deployment platform it has built-in security features that complement the security strategy of a company who wants to provide applications on the Internet that were available previously only in-house or via phone.

---

[37]http://www.allaire.com/

Enterprise Application Server

The Enterprise Application Server by Sybase[38] is a scalable enterprise integration platform. It consists of a component transaction server, the Jaguar CTS and a dynamic web server, the PowerDynamo.

The platform provides a single point of integration for heterogeneous back office systems and helps customers to extend their businesses on to the Web. PowerDynamo allows developers to create dynamic content for browsers and for automated transactions in a business-to-business scenario. The system provides a broad support for Internet standards, such as HTML, Java, C++, JavaBeans, ActiveX and CORBA. The business logic can be stored in multiple component standards to ensure the availability to any type of client.

eXcelon

The application server eXcelon by Object Design[39] offers high-performance and high-availability. It is a highly scalable data server that caches and serves all information to enterprise applications and Web servers using the new standard for data interchange XML.

The software provides adaptors for all major database systems, application servers and client software, and is easily extensible through the use of XML. eXcelon can be used as an application cache for existing data sources, meaning that it can relay database information to the web, for example. This reduces the number of interfaces to one, making it easy for customers to access multiple data sources and provides a security layer as the database servers are not exposed to the Internet.

The eXcelon server can also be used to create a complete data management system for new XML-based applications. In this case, eXcelon automatically stores, caches and delivers XML data across the middle tier of multi-tier applications. Through the use of XML eXcelon provides a very good architecture through the use of XML and is prepared for the future. What is missing is the pre-integration with standard business software to make it the preferred solution for large companies. Smaller companies that do not have much standard software installed will find it a very attractive offering.

Inprise Application Server

The application server by Inprise[40] has been designed to allow for rapid application development of platform-independent applications, built on open industry standards such as Java, C++, HTML and CORBA. By using these open standards, it is easy to build an integrated end-to-end solution for bringing your enterprise applications to the Internet. The development, integration, de-

---

[38]http://www.sybase.com/

[39]http://www.objectdesign.com/

[40]http://www.inprise.com/

ployment and management of the whole architecture can be done through the Inprise application server.

This new integrated enterprise platform allows support for multiple clients, the middle-tier business logic and back-end enterprise database management systems through a single interface. Access to legacy systems is added easily through a standard API.

The solution includes the Java Web Server by Sun, but supports all other standard web servers as well. To complete the picture of the application server, Inprise has added the Integrated Transaction Service (ITS) by VisiBroker that provides a flexible distributed and object-based transaction service that is fully compliant to the Java Transaction Service (JTS) standard. Also included is AppCenter, which is a distributed applications-level management tool.

Lotus Domino Application Server

The Lotus Domino Application Server[41] is an open and secure platform for developing and deploying web applications in a collaborative environment. The server allows dynamic business processes to be integrated with enterprise application systems.

It provides an integration with enterprise systems by leveraging current information assets with built-in connection services for live access to relational databases, transaction systems and ERP applications. The solution is optimized for collaboration by providing comprehensive application services like workflow and messaging. The simplified deployment and maintenance allows the use of integrated development tools. Standards support and server-to-server replication simplify the rollout, maintenance and rollback of enterprise applications. The billing services allow companies to track, report and analyze system usage for billing, charge-back and capacity planning purposes.

Netscape Application Server

The Netscape Application Server[42] is an Internet application server to develop, deploy, and manage enterprise-class business applications. The Application Server product line includes the Netscape Application Builder, for development of Java and C/C++ applications, and Netscape Extension Builder, for development of server extensions that enable connectivity to enterprise applications and legacy systems.

It provides the infrastructure for transactional, business-critical applications through pre-built system and application services. Netscape's solution includes optimized end-to-end performance features such as connection caching and pooling, results caching, which stores often-used database results on the web server, streaming, multithreading, and multiprocessing.

---

[41] http://www.lotus.com/
[42] http://www.netscape.com/

Scalability and high availability are services already built into the system. One very interesting feature is the Client-Independent Programming Model (CIPM), which reduces development time required to support multiple client types such as HTML clients, Java and C/C++ clients.

SilverStream

SilverStream[43] is an enterprise application server that allows corporations to build and deploy complex web applications (mainly HTML and Java) on which they can run their online businesses. It is designed and optimized for the Intranet, Extranet, and Internet. The solution delivers both client- and server-side Java and client-side HTML.

SilverStream provides the services required to deliver complex Web applications. It connects to multiple data sources including relational databases such as Oracle and Informix, host applications such as CICS, MQ Series, ERP systems such as SAP and PeopleSoft, and other data sources, such as Lotus Notes, document management systems.

SilverStream is a solution that provides support for large scale applications that can be deployed to tens of thousands, or even millions of users, with a scalable, reliable, secure and manageable platform. SilverStream enables companies to develop complex applications through an easy-to-use set of commands. The business logic is encapsulated in middle-tier objects that are handled in a distributed way. With SilverStream applications, developers can create and connect to these objects using COM, EJB and CORBA, making it a very comprehensive and complex solution.

WebObjects

Apple's WebObjects[44] is an application server environment suitable for large scale projects. It supports visual development of user interfaces and the direct connection to existing business applications and data resources. It comes with a palette of pre-built, reusable components, and provides a seamless integration with all kinds of enterprise information systems. WebObjects handles application server requirements, including load balancing, state management, HTML generation, and Java client interoperability. WebObjects is available on all major operating systems and works across applications, business systems, and existing business logic.

WebObjects provides a rich set of development tools, a solid performance and scalability, and a good set of enterprise data connectors. By design this solution requires more lines of code to achieve similar results as with other packages, but third-party add-ons can reduce the development time to match the times of its competitors.

---

[43]http://www.silverstream.com/
[44]http://www.apple.com/webobjects/

WebSphere Application Server

The WebSphere Application Server[45] by IBM combines a runtime environment for Java servlets with connectors to common database formats. It uses industry-standard object request brokers (ORBs) and enterprise middleware and runs on most web servers.

Three different editions of the WebSphere Application Server are available, which use the same basic set of technologies, but offer different functionalities, depending on the requirements of the customer. The Standard Edition, which is the basic package, combines the control and portability of server-side business applications with the performance and manageability of Java technologies to offer a comprehensive Java-based Web application platform. It enables powerful interactions with enterprise databases and transaction systems.

The Advanced Edition introduces server capabilities for applications built to Sun's Enterprise JavaBean specifications. Deploying and managing JavaBean components provides a stronger CORBA implementation that maps to portable Java technologies. The Enterprise Edition is IBM's flagship and offers a robust solution to growing e-business applications. It combines IBM's transactional application environment, TXSeries, with the full distributed object and business process integration capabilities of Component Broker.

Zope

Zope[46] is an open source application server and portal toolkit used for building high-performance, dynamic Web sites. It allows companies to develop dynamic Web applications easily. Zope is completely managed through the Web. Zope's framework provides a secure architecture, which includes access control, undo and private versions. Zope is based on Python, and offers support for CORBA, COM, XML, and leading databases. More information on Zope can be found in Chapter 14.

9.6   The Extensible Markup Language

9.6.1   Common Problems of the Web

In order to move on to do real electronic business on the web, it is necessary to understand why this is not possible with current technologies. Especially the HTML standard hinders the development of new applications on the Internet, as it was not designed to do anything else than presenting documents in a web browser. Electronic business has other requirements than displaying documents. Documents need to be displayed, processed, rearranged, stored, forwarded, exchanged, encrypted and signed, just to name a few actions. With HTML it is difficult to express the hierarchical relationship of data values

---

[45]http://www.ibm.com/

[46]http://www.zope.org/

(known from database records and object hierarchies). HTML reflects structure and presentation, but conveys nothing about the meaning of the marked up document.

The most commonly used version of HTML, 3.2, provides many ways of displaying content using Java applets, CGI scripts, JavaScript and plug-ins. But none of these technologies enables you to do anything useful to process the data without introducing an additional layer with middleware solutions. Many problems could be resolved by introducing new HTML tags into the standard, but there are several show-stoppers.

The biggest problem is that the HTML standard is only moving very slowly. For years HTML 3.2 has been the basis for the standard, although 4.0 was recommended already in December 1997. Unfortunately HTML 3.2 introduced many tags that have been introduced by the browser manufacturers and have become a de-facto standard (mixing structure and layout, as discussed previously). Remember all the sites containing "best viewed with browser X"? Although 3.2 is a standard, only very few sites adhere to it.

In order to enforce the use of HTML 4.0, it is necessary to create new browser versions that everybody needs to download and install. The document type definition (DTD) in all browsers is hard-coded, meaning that the introduction of a new standard won't change the behaviour of the browser (other than not understanding new structures and elements).

In order to resolve this problem, two things need to happen. The DTD needs to become more flexible to support the needs of electronic businesses and the browsers need to be flexible, in such a way that the DTD needs to become part of the document and not be part of the browser anymore. Every document will be able to include its own DTD, which formulates the elements in XML used in the document itself.

Today most applications are tied to the browsers, but many corporations have applications installed that are not able to display the information in HTML, but need to exchange the information over the Internet. Many customers also want Internet applications to have the look and feel of their applications, which can be achieved by launching external applications from within the browser. The best solution is to have web applications that understand the Internet protocols, such as HTTP and TCP/IP, but without requiring a web browser. This allows existing applications to be extended to talk to other resources, such as databases and applications, over the Internet. While the Internet protocols help to establish the communication, XML enables the exchange of data between applications that usually have totally different data formats.

In order to create intelligence on the web, search engines need to understand the content of web pages, but so far they are not able. If searching for a certain piece of information it is highly likely that you get one good result and at least one hundred false ones (some search engines are even worse by a factor of ten to a hundred). The problem is that search engines normally only index a set of words, document titles, URLs and meta tags, but do not know anything about the structure of the document. A search engine cannot decide if a document is a news article or a thesis, for example. There is no way to markup the significant portions of a document to focus on the important parts and ignore the noise (such as copyright statements, navigational bars, design elements). This would allow a much finer granularity of control over search engines. By adding additional attributes to web elements this can be achieved. Let's say you are researching information on a singer who also acts and writes (such as Cher or Madonna), then it would be good to have a classification of the function of the person on the web site. If tags like <singer>, <actor>, <author> could be used in HTML the number of direct hits would be much higher. With XML these tags can be easily defined and used.

Another common problem on the web is the collection of related pages and saving them to your hard disk or printing them out. The current method is to save or print them on a page by page basis, which can become really annoying, if there are more than ten pages. In many cases it is also difficult to identify the other parts of a particular collection, as the document that links all resources together is not known to the person who looks at a particular page (often a link is not provided, as the owner of the link is aware of the fact that the document is part of a larger collection). In order to express the interrelationship, special metadata should be attached to the documents, making it easier to find the other documents related to the topic of a particular search. Although adding metadata is possible in HTML, the information is restricted to the whole document and not only to parts of it, which may be of interest for a particular search. Using XML it is possible to create metadata for all text elements.

The current linking provided by the web is limiting, as it works only one-way. If you link to another document, the other document does not automatically link back to you. Links with multiple targets are also not possible and there is no way to automatically update the set of links you provide. Imagine you link to a document on another web server and the document moves from one location to another one; then you need to alter the link on your web site manually. But other linking mechanisms have been around for some time that provide these features such as the Hypermedia/Time-based Structuring Language (HyTime) and the Text Encoding Initiative (TEI).

9.6.2   Moving to XML

The extensible markup language (XML) is an ISO compliant subset of SGML (Standard Generalized Markup Language). XML is extensible because it is a meta-language, which enables someone to write a document type definition (DTD) like HTML 4.0 and define the rules of the language so the document can be interpreted by the document receiver. XML is like an alphabet for building new languages and gives companies a way to start with a common foundation and a common alphabet. Every industry is able to define the specific terms they use.

A document type definition (DTD) is essentially a context-free grammar like the Extended Backus Naur Form (EBNF) often used to describe computer languages. A DTD provide the rules that define the elements and the structure of the language. A regular markup language defines a way to describe information in a certain class of documents (e.g. HTML). XML on the other hand lets you define your own customized markup languages for any type of document classes.

An example could be an address markup language (AML), where one defines an element <address> which consists of <name>, <street>, <town>, <zip> and <country>. The element <name> consists of the elements <first> and <last>. Rules can indicate, if an element is optional, repeatable or has a default value. The advantage is that any application that is able to understand XML will understand a document using the address markup language, as the application is able to learn the rules by loading the DTD.

Table 9.7 displays a document in the AML notation, which I invented. Other than with HTML the layout is not defined, nor is the sequence of the text on the screen. The AML could be used to create a database of addresses. Searching for last names is very easy, as the information is correctly tagged. Presenting all sets of addresses beginning with the letter "A" in the last name, then presenting this piece of information in a browser, for example, is very easy. Other than that, the layout can be specified for different needs. In Germany the postal code is normally displayed in front of the city, while in the UK the postal code is at the end. In HTML you have to create to separate pages for the output of the data, while our AML is flexible and can detect in which country the address is and print it out in the required form. The layout is not defined in XML, but in a presentational language, such as the extensible style language (XSL) or the cascading style sheets (CSS). Using JavaScript and the document object model (DOM) it is easy to extract information.

The semantics and the structure of the data is preserved. The data is organized as in an object-oriented database. XML is about creating, sharing and processing information. The purpose of XML is to provide an easy-to-use subset of SGML that allows for custom tags to define, transmit and interpret data structures between organizations. These tags look like HTML tags, but describe the meaning of the information and so in a format that is precisely defined and predictable.

The introduction of XML will change the way we experience the web today and remove two constraints which are holding back web developments. Its dependence on a single, inflexible document type (i.e. HTML) and the complexity of the full SGML, whose syntax is very powerful but extremely complex. XML reduces the complexity of SGML and enables the development of user-defined document types on the web. Some say that XML provides 80 percent of the benefits of SGML with only 20 percent of the effort.

HTML has reached its limit of usefulness as it contains a pre-defined set of tags for describing documents. This has been extended by many manufac-

---

Address Markup Language (AML)

The following document is written in AML, which we have defined in XML.

```
<?xml version="1.0"?>
<address>
<name>
<first>Daniel</first>
<last>Amor</last>
</name>
<street>Kangaroo Lane 101</street>
<town>Yuppie Town</town>
<zip>12345</zip>
<country>Petrolistan</country>
</address>
</xml>
```

Table 9.7.

turers with new tags that mainly support the layout and not the structure. In order to represent a document in HTML it is necessary to conform to the existing tags. XML on the other hand allows organizations to create their own customized markup languages (and tags) for exchanging information in their domain (e.g. linguistics, knitting or dog-feeding).

Although it will continue to play an important role for the content it currently represents, many new applications require a more robust and flexible infrastructure. Electronic business on the Internet will only work if the information that is transported is not restricted to one make or model or manufacturer. Information can also not cede control of its data format to private hands. In order to save time and effort the information needs to be provided in such a form that it can be reused in many different ways.

The presentation of XML documents can be implemented by using the document style and semantics specification language (DSSSL), the cascading style sheets (CSS) specification or the extensible style language (XSL).

9.6.3 Business Requirements

In order to survive most companies need to improve the quality of the products, accelerate time-to-market and reduce costs at the same time. The Internet has increased the need for achieving these goals in short time.

This goal is not only true for the products, but also for the information associated with them. If information is the product then this subsection is also intended for the information product. To resolve the goal it is necessary to resolve the challenge of delivering information on paper, CD-ROM and on the Internet efficiently, accurately and fast.

This requires processes to be streamlined when creating the information. Therefore redundant work needs to be eliminated. This goal can be easily achieved by basing the information publishing process on the XML standard. This is especially important for companies who distribute information of great value, including medical, legal and business information.

As XML is format-independent it is possible to generate multiple outputs very easily. A document written in XML is able to generate documents for formats such as CD-ROM distribution, Internet delivery, help systems and printed documentation. If information is collected from multiple sources, the integration becomes much easier than if only one format is used.

Business Requirements

Information needs to adhere to the following requirements in order to reduce costs and enhance the productivity.

- **Conditional Information** – A means is required that is able to identify conditional information.

- **Durable Documents** – The information needs to be stored in a software and hardware independent way.

- **Integrated Reviews** – Reviews of information enhance the quality by adding meta-information.

- **Multiple Destinations** – A single document needs to be distributed in various forms, such as print, CD-ROM and Web pages.

- **Multiple Sources** – Different documents need to be integrated efficiently into a single document.

Table 9.8.

Another important issue is that computer data gets lost due to the fast change in formats. Much computer data has become unreadable because nobody is able to decrypt the information anymore. Many organizations need to store information for several years or decades and require; therefore; a format which remains readable in the future. With XML it is possible to create documents that are still useful, although the hardware and software that was used to create the data is not available anymore.

Information by itself is not always useful. By providing reviews of it, it is easier to classify the content and create intelligence. The reviews become part of the information and enhance the value of the information. Therefore means of storing and processing reviews are necessary.

In many documents information varies on external factors. These external factors change the content and a system is required to present the resulting information correctly. In a simple case, a product consists of several components and the document sums up the production cost. As the cost for the components may vary the document should always show the actual production cost. XML provides a means to identify information that is variable and to control the presentation of the information based on external conditions.

9.6.4 Reformulating HTML in XML

XML is on the verge of replacing HTML in the browser world. HTML won't vanish, but will become just one of the many possibilities of XML documents. This will make the Web even more dynamic and will simplify business over the Internet.

In May 1998 the World Wide Web Consortium held a workshop on the future of HTML and discussed ideas for the next generation of HTML[47]. The result was that the next generation of HTML will be reformulated in XML. Under the name of XHTML (extensible hypertext markup language) it will include a core tag set which will be used to mark-up headings, paragraphs, lists, hypertext links, images and other basic document idioms.

All other important tags defined in HTML will be grouped in a separate tags set, such as tag sets for forms, tables, graphics and multimedia. These tag sets will all adopt the XML syntax and will be able to be combined as need be. This means that the development of new tables functionalities can be conducted at a different speed as the development for graphics, without interference. Today all parts of the DTD need to be updated in order to support a new version of HTML. In the future it will be much easier, as one can partly update the feature set of HTML.

With the introduction of XHTML style sheets will become very important, as XHTML has no control over the layout anymore. Style sheets will take on the role of transforming mark-up for the purpose of displaying documents on different kinds of devices. With the imminent introduction of pervasive computing, people will not only want to access the web from their computer, but also from mobile phones, palmtops and other network enabled devices.

---

[47]http://www.w3.org/MarkUp/Activity.html

Advantages of XML over HTML

XML has many advantages over HTML. This table presents some of the reasons why your company should switch from HTML based documents to XML based documents.

- **Browser Presentation** – XML can provide more and better facilities for browser presentation and performance through the use of style sheets.

- **Information Accessibility** – Information is more accessible and reusable due to the flexibility of XML.

- **Richer Content** – Through the use of new markup elements it is possible to create richer content that is easier to use.

- **SGML Compatibility** – As XML files are compatible to the SGML standard, they can be also used outside the web in an SGML environment.

- **Tailored Document Types** – Document providers and authors are able to create their own document types using XML and are not restricted to the set of markup elements in HTML. It is possible to invent new markup elements.

Table 9.9.

In order to make web pages accessible to these types of information appliances, tools will help to provide the correct display on every device. Therefore conformance profiles have been introduced, which specify, among other things, exactly which HTML tags a given device has to support. The idea is that two different devices will present things in the same way if they belong to the same conformance profile and the document is within that profile.

Conformance profiles should greatly simplify matters when it comes to tuning mark-up to match the needs of the different information appliances. If the set of HTML features supported by a given class of devices can be precisely anticipated, then the mark-up can be transformed in a simple and reliable fashion. The transformation can take place either on the web site, at a proxy server or in the browser itself, depending on where the information about the device is specified.

9.6.5   Location of XML Documents

XML can be processed either in the browser (or any other client application) or on a web server (or any other type of server). Depending on the location of the XML document it will be differently processed and has other requirements.

Server-side Processing

Processing XML documents on a server will most probably be for one of two reasons, either for exchanging data between servers automatically without user interaction or for wrapping database data to create custom content (for a web browser that is not capable of displaying XML, for example).

If sharing data between organizations, it is necessary to agree on the tags and their meaning. Other than EDI, where the agreement needs to be sent to a third party for evaluation. XML is more direct by allowing two parties to agree on a DTD which is used for exchanging data. With XML it is very easy to send EDI messages over the Internet, so many people are working on XML/EDI bridges[48]. The Open Applications Group[49] is working on a set of XML DTDs for many kinds of businesses. Although these general DTDs may not suit your requirements, they help to set up fast business relationships on the Internet.

Sharing data, which is stored in databases is one of the applications that can be done automatically. By using XML it is possible to use the basic processing tools for any type of data and applications which are not dependent on the format and syntax used.

Syndication is one of the applications that can be easily implemented in XML. An information provider can easily integrate its service into many different sites with different layouts. The information provider can also provide only parts of the information to portal sites.

Creating dynamic content on a web server is also facilitated through the use of XML. The content can be stored in XML documents without the layout. Content contributors can write their content in specialized applications that suit their needs and create XML documents as output. These documents are then stored automatically in a database and can be accessed instantly over the Internet.

Client-side processing

The disadvantage of server-side XML processing could be that the data is processed and presented in a form that may not be viewable for a certain type of client. Think about a browser that is not able to display a certain type of tag or a client application that is not able to display the information provided by the server. In order to overcome these problems, it is possible to transmit the

---

[48]http://www.xmledi.com/
[49]http://www.openapplications.org/

"raw" XML document to the client and let the client decide what to do with it and how to display it.

All browser manufacturers are busily working on their next releases that will include support for displaying XML documents. This means that they are able to display XML documents without having a server to transform the document to HTML first. Through the use of the DOM, a standard for accessing and manipulating XML data web site authors are able to alter the content within a page through JavaScript.

Using XML it is also possible to transform XML to HTML in the browser. This allows a complete address book to be downloaded and a scripting search functionality to be used for displaying only the results you need. This will create a more individualized browsing experience, which has a slightly increased download time in the beginning, but then some applications can be executed without any interaction with the server.

9.6.6   XML Applications

Although XML is only slowly finding its way into Internet applications, many standards have already been created, which simplifies the processing of documents.

XSL

Similar to the Cascading Style Sheets (CSS) the Extensible Style Language (XSL) separates the content from representation. It specifies the formatting characteristics of XML documents on the Web while CSS specifies the formatting characteristics of HTML documents.

While CSS has its own proprietary syntax, XSL itself has been written in XML and can be extended through JavaScript. The formatting model is the same as in CSS and the highly complex Document Style Semantics and Specification Language (DSSSL).

Although it is possible to use CSS for formatting HTML tags, it is not necessary, as all HTML tags have a pre-defined representation in a web browser. XML tags are highly dynamic and none of them have a pre-defined representation in a web browser. A designer may create the tag <box>, which is perfectly valid in XML, if defined in a DTD, but no browser will know how to format this tag. XSL is able to add the missing style information to the XML tag.

Although CSS can also format XML documents, it can be only used for rather simple documents. But XML has been invented to create highly structured and data-rich documents. Other than CSS, XSL can also transform XML documents, moving an existing document in a form to another document in another form. XSL is able to render dynamically a page when elements need to be re-arranged, while CSS can only represent the data in the form it was originally placed in the file. XSL can be used, for example, to re-arrange web content for printing, to fit better on a printed page, without the need of downloading another version of the same document.

Although XSL is extensible through JavaScript, many developers feel that its features can be replaced by JavaScript and the document object model (DOM).

SMIL

Based on XML, the synchronized multi-media integration language (SMIL, pronounced "smile") has been created by the World Wide Web Consortium[50] and is a powerful way to synchronize any type of media (e.g. audio, video, text and graphics) and build time-based, streaming multi-media presentations without the need of learning a complex programming language.

Until now it was necessary to use either programming languages such as Java to implement complex TV-like content or multi-media applications such as MacroMedia's Director[51]. Using simple instructions that are similar to HTML and you can to build complex animations. The major advantage of this approach is that using this interpreted language, the time to download multi-media content decreases dramatically.

The major difference between SMIL and Director, for example, is that there is not one large file that needs to be downloaded, but the images, sounds and animations are downloaded one after the other in the order of appearance in the presentation. If components are used in several multi-media presentations the browser may have some already in the cache which reduces the download time even further. The customer is able to see the beginning of the multi-media much earlier and is able to decide if it's worth waiting for the rest of it.

Just as with HTML pages, replacing components is easy and does not require you to rebuild the complete page. With SMIL you can replace components and use the presentation in an instant without interrupting the service for your customers. The authoring process can be simplified by using SMIL.

SMIL is an application of XML and therefore supports hyperlinks in order to offer interactivity. SMIL has been recommended by the W3C in June 1998, but so far only Real Network's G2 Player supports the SMIL standard. As soon as the web browsers fully support XML they will also support SMIL.

SMIL has been developed to complement other web technologies, such as dynamic HTML (DHTML) and the document object model (DOM). Microsoft who initially supported the SMIL initiative, now contends the technology, as it has developed a media player at the same time, that is not compatible. Most other technology companies are jumping onto the SMIL bandwagon.

SMIL is not meant to be a replacement for existing multi-media technologies. It is a possibility to join the media formats and create an even richer experience.

---

[50] http://www.w3.org/AudioVideo/

[51] http://www.macromedia.com/

RDF

Another very interesting application, is the Resource Description Framework (RDF)[52], which has been developed by the World Wide Web Consortium, just as most standards discussed in this chapter. RDF adds metadata to Internet resources, whereby a resource can be any object on the Web, such as a web page, image or sound. The metadata can be used to find a resource by adding a detailed description and keywords to the metadata, to rate the content and to digitally sign an object on the Internet. Metadata is information on information and is an established standard for HTML pages using the tag "<meta>".

The problem with the metadata of HTML pages is that computers are not able to understand the information. If the description of two web pages is similar and point to the same type of information, such as "Germany is a country in Europe" and "Germany is a European country". Although a human understands that these two statements mean the same, a computer will not be able to detect this without extensive programming. RDF associates unambiguous methods of expressing these statements so that a machine can understand that they have the same meaning.

Although RDF is able to improve the search results on the web, it is not restricted to this application. It is able to describe individual elements and their relationships between them.

Therefore the W3C has developed a data model and a syntax for the RDF. The difference between RDF and similar frameworks is that RDF has been developed especially for the web. The syntax for RDF is based on a special data model, which defines the way properties are described. It represents the properties of a resource and the values of the properties.

Although RDF has been developed independently of XML, it can be easily represented in the extensible markup language. Therefore the names of the properties and the values are not pre-defined, but can be chosen by the responsible people of the Internet object. The creator of an RDF record can choose which particular properties or sets of properties will be used. In order to ensure the uniqueness of every RDF record, it uses the name-space mechanism, which is also used in XML and the Internet.

RDF is already used on the Internet. Netscape uses RDF to index site content in order to allow users to find information more quickly. The features "What's related" in Netscape Communicator 4.5 is using RDF to display related sites within the browser. Millions of users world-wide are using this feature and it is so far the most popular XML application.

9.6.7   Other Applications

XML applications are not only developed by the World Wide Web Consortium, but also by companies and other organizations. The W3 is offering a standard

---

[52]http://www.w3.org/RDF/

set of applications, but every company is free to develop new and innovative applications based on XML, which can be both private for internal use only or can be made public for external review and use. Engineers at NASA[53], for example, plan to use XML to develop an instrument control language for infrared devices on satellites and space telescopes. The XML syntax will be used to describe classes of infrared instruments, control procedures, communications protocols and user documentation. Computers will parse the tagged data and generate instrument control code, most likely in Java.

Siemens[54] is using a system that allows employees to submit their time cards and let managers approve them online. Each time card submission and approval is tied to basic human resource (HR) data such as name, serial number, and employee type. The time card validation depends on pay code rules and frequency tables. Managers have the ability to temporarily delegate approval responsibilities, and the entire system interfaces to the corporate-wide Directory Service database, as well as the Payroll system.

In order to achieve this goal, data between the different systems need to be interchanged and therefore a data format is required, which can be shared among the applications. XML serves as the data interchange format in a Time and Attendance System and enables the integrators to reuse interface code, extend and modify data structures to accommodate personalization and internationalization, and design the system without worrying about limitations imposed by data sources. Data fields can be added without disrupting the existing structure and applications. Global development and the different holiday schedules of each country can be easily implemented with XML. The developer can use the same pay-period DTD, but just drop in a new holiday attribute. XML makes the localization of an application easy, maximizing code and data model reuse. Many other companies, as well, have started to use XML to integrate their existing applications and exchange data between different platforms and database systems.

9.6.8 Business via XML

XML has become the standard for information exchange in an industry-neutral language. XML is used throughout the industry in a similar paradigm as EDI to exchange information in a very structured and pre-defined way. The difference between EDI and XML is that EDI had a limited set of structures that were accepted, and a new information structure needed months or even years to go through all instances to become a new industry standard. XML allows anyone to create new data structures on the fly. While this is great for the communication between two parties, it poses a problem for industry-wide exchange of information. If every company develops its own XML standards, it could lead to incompatibilities and additional overhead for converting the data. The prob-

---

[53]http://www.nasa.gov/
[54]http://www.siemens.com/

lem is less the different order of information, but more that some companies may omit or add information that another company cannot deal with.

To automate the value chain and the inter-company business processes, it is necessary to define XML data structures that contain all information for a certain industry with the option of omitting or adding information for the exchange of data. Many fear also that the independent software vendors will drive incompatible versions of XML that best fit their own product strategies.

XML has been integrated by PeopleSoft, Oracle, and Baan into their enterprise resource planning (ERP) systems. SAP is integrating XML into its Business Application Programming Interfaces (BAPI), which give developers access to the internal workings of the company's R/3 software. If the manufacturers of ERP software agree on a common XML format, developers will gain a standardized, vendor-neutral way to access human resources, financial, and manufacturing data stored in these systems. But if the software manufacturers are not able to find a common standard XML will not resolve the problem of proprietary APIs, which made life difficult in the past.

Today vertical XML vocabularies have already been implemented, which enable single industries to exchange information. So far these vocabularies have been introduced for the financial sector, the content management industry, air traffic control and the footwear business. Although this helps the single industry it can create a problem in such a way that the number of industry-specific dialects of XML may get out of control unless cross-industry standards are implemented within the business software products.

XML proponents fear that the major software makers will use their financial clout to hijack the consensus-building process, leading to proprietary and incompatible versions of XML schemas that favor a particular vendor's software and architecture. In order to make XML a success all companies need to get to a round table and agree on standards.

If you look at the computer industry then there should not be an XML schema for Hewlett-Packard and one for IBM, but one for the whole industry, which can be also used by other industries to order computers, for example. Otherwise the advantages of introducing XML cannot be exploited. Having several XML flavors accepted may be still valuable, but limited and won't achieve the actual goal of reducing costs and increasing automation.

While the independent software manufacturers need to adopt a generic XML standard, each industry needs to develop an XML schema at the same time. To stay with the example of the computer industry, it is necessary to define data structures for types of computers, reseller locations, configurator restriction and pricing models. These XML schemas are developed by standards bodies, such as the World Wide Web Consortium, Commerce.Net[55], Rosetta-Net[56] and the Organization for the Advancement of Structured Information

---

[55]http://www.commerce.net/

[56]http://www.rosetta.net/

Standards (Oasis)[57]. They are defining links within and between industries in a vendor-neutral way. Electronic business, supply chain and other areas have already been addressed.

9.6.9 Standard XML Schemas

The problem is that all the standards bodies are developing different standards for the same areas. For some time it looked like that the usual competitors would start a new standards battle over XML schemas just as we have seen battles over the right way to interpret HTML or the split in the industry over how Java should evolve.

Two portals have been set up, which represent the two industry camps that want XML to follow their ways. The first is XML.org[58], which has been developed by Oasis, which is backed by software makers, such as IBM, Sun, Novell and Oracle. The portal has been established since 1998.

On the other side of the fence Microsoft has launched its BizTalk[59] initiative in May 1999, which has been established as an XML design clearing house, developer resource and repository for XML schemas. To make BizTalk a success Microsoft is backed up by ERP software manufacturers, such as SAP, e-commerce software and service providers, such as Ariba[60] and partners in the industry such as Boeing[61].

The XML portals provide a form for XML schemas, which have been designed for specific industries, such as the financial sector, health care and insurance companies. Microsoft's BizTalk portal has raised suspicion among competitors, which fear that Microsoft wants to take over the XML software application industry by defining its own standards without the consensus of the rest of the industry. Parts of the industry fear that this initiative could splinter the XML market.

Fortunately Microsoft reconsidered its position regarding XML and joined Oasis in June 1999 to reduce the fears of the market. Companies have been stepping back from implementing XML as they feared a standards war on XML schemas. Microsoft's decision to back Oasis has eased these fears and made it possible to develop a common framework for XML applications on the Internet.

9.7 Plug-ins

9.7.1 Advantages of Plug-ins

Plug-ins are add-in programs for Web browsers, which are able to interact with the browser, web pages, resources on the Internet and local resources. Most

---

[57] http://www.oasis-open.org/

[58] http://www.xml.org/

[59] http://www.biztalk.org/

[60] http://www.ariba.com/

[61] http://www.boeing.com/

browsers nowadays support plug-ins. Plug-ins are normally used to add support for new file formats or add interactivity. The reason why plug-ins have become so popular is it is an easy way to extend the functionality of the web browser without the need of downloading a new browser. Especially in the early years, plug-ins have been very popular. Now that browsers have more and more features already built-in, the importance of the plug-ins is slowly vanishing, especially in the event of XML becoming the new basis for documents on the Internet. It will still take some years before browsers won't require any plug-ins anymore. The trend is to move away from plug-ins and offer Java or Active X solutions instead.

Plug-ins are native applications, meaning that the are bound to a certain processor and operating system. This poses a huge restriction on their use on the Internet, as a plug-in needs to be rewritten for every computer platform. Only very few companies do (Adobe, for example, has ported its Acrobat plug-in to fourteen platforms) and it requires the user to install something onto the computer, which may be beyond the capabilities of some users. Security is also a concern for plug-ins. As they have access to all your resources, a plug-in could easily format your hard disk or corrupt your data.

But there are some advantages that make plug-ins the best solution. Plug-ins are able to access any system resource without trouble, such as a printer, and allow high-quality printing of images and documents. Plug-ins are also much faster than a Java program could be.

9.7.2   Adobe Acrobat Reader

The Acrobat portable document format (PDF)[62] is the most widely used format on the Internet besides HTML. For textual documents that need layout and high-quality printing, many people use the PDF format, as the Acrobat plug-in is available for all major platforms.

It's integration with web browsers displays PDF documents seamlessly and the high-quality printing is supported on standard and postscript printers. Most web sites use PDF to distribute online brochure's and technical documentation via the Internet. Motorola[63], for example, uses the PDF format to give customers access to technical specifications of its computer chips. PDF offers some advantages over other text formats, such as Word's file format. It can be read on any platform and provides a high quality output across all platforms and printers.

The Adobe Acrobat Distiller product (which is not available for free) is able to convert HTML pages and Postscript documents directly into PDF documents. A special printer driver can convert all types of documents to PDF on the fly while printing, making it easy for anyone to create PDF documents.

---

[62]http://www.adobe.com/acrobat/

[63]http://www.motorola.com/

9.7.3 Apple Quicktime

QuickTime[64] was invented a few years back by Apple Computer and has become since then the most popular environment for multimedia CD-ROM and Internet productions. QuickTime was designed to simplify the task of working with and integrating the widest possible range of digital media types; not just sound and video. The QuickTime Movie format is actually so popular and good that it has become the basis for the MPEG-4 standard[65].

QuickTime is able to play many sounds and movie formats and the plug-in is able to communicate with JavaScript and Java applications, integrating the supported formats even better into the web pages. QuickTime is available for Windows and Macintosh platform only. More in-depth information can be found in Chapter 12.

Most films today are using the Internet as a marketing medium. In 1999 the first Star Wars prequel appeared and was heavily promoted on the Web. Many people went to the cinemas to see the trailer and left before the main film started. At the same time the trailer was put in QuickTime format onto the World Wide Web[66]. The QuickTime format guaranteed the makers of the film the maximum exposure on the web and the possibility of instant viewing through streaming technologies. While being downloaded to the desktop the customer was already able to view it. With other formats the customers would have had to wait for the complete transfer of the file before the first picture appeared.

9.7.4 Platinum Cosmoplayer

Platinum's Cosmoplayer[67] is able to display documents in the virtual reality markup language (VRML). VRML is an interactive format with its own scripting language. The interfaces to Java and JavaScript enable you to create not only 3D worlds, but to make them interactive as well. Using the fourth dimension of time, it is possible to move things around or change them. Using one of the above mentioned languages allows us to kick alive virtual people in a 3D world or to create virtual representations of people who wander through the VRML scene.

Cosmoplayer has been released as open source and binaries are available for Macintosh and Windows. It is expected that the source code will be ported to other platforms in the near future.

The CosmoPlayer is used by many companies to display their products in three dimensions on the screen, making the customers turn them around and look at the products from all sides. Besides this more traditional approach

---

[64]http://www.apple.com/quicktime/

[65]http://www.mpeg.org/

[66]http://www.starwars.com/

[67]http://www.cosmoworld.com/

to three-dimensional viewing, Platinum[68] is using VRML to display business data in three dimensions. Some people think that 3D business data views are not very useful, but in some cases they may offer some new insights on how to develop a business, which can be used to make the correct business decision.

9.7.5 Macromedia Shockwave

Shockwave[69] has become the standard plug-in for multimedia on the Internet. It is already installed with Netscape Communicator, therefore no additional download is required for Netscape users. The plug-in is able to play back interactive Web content, like entertainment software, business presentations, games and advertising.

The files for the shockwave plug-in are built exclusively with Macromedia Director, which is an authoring tool for creating rich multimedia applications. Shockwave is widely used and accepted on the Internet.

Casio[70], for example, uses Shockwave to inform its customers about their G-Shock watches[71] and enables customers to watch episodes of G-Gurl. Shockwave allows Casio to develop a very interactive and futuristic web site that matches the image of the watch.

9.8 JavaScript

9.8.1 Introduction to JavaScript

The JavaScript programming language is a very compact, object-based, platform-independent, event-driven, interpreted scripting language that can be used to develop Internet applications that can either reside on the server or on the client. Without any network communication, an HTML page with embedded JavaScript can interpret the entered text and alert the user with a message dialogue if the input is invalid (see Table 9.10 for a simple example). JavaScript can also be used to perform an action, such as playing an audio file, execution of an applet, or communication with a plug-in. JavaScripts are constrained to the client and cannot communicate with a server to exchange data with the server

JavaScript allows cross-platform scripting of events (e.g. key press or mouse click), objects (e.g. form elements or style sheets) and actions. JavaScript is also able to create interaction between HTML, plug-ins, and Java. Contrary to popular belief, JavaScript was never meant to be a scaled-down version of Java or a replacement for CGI scripts. JavaScript was developed by Netscape and not by Sun (who invented Java), but uses a similar name for marketing pur-

---

[68]http://www.platinum.com/
[69]http://www.macromedia.com/shockwave/
[70]http://www.casio.com/
[71]http://www.g-shock.com/

poses. JavaScript was originally called "Mocha", then renamed to "LiveScript" and finally became JavaScript, as it is referred to in most publications. The actual JavaScript interpreter in most browsers is based on the ECMAScript standard, which is the standardized version of JavaScript, supported by the European ECMA organization[72].

Integrating JavaScript into HTML

JavaScript can be easily integrated into HTML documents. A simple example is the following program, which checks if the first name of the user has been entered.

```
<html>
<head><title>The checkName JavaScript Example
Homepage</title></head>

<script language="JavaScript">
<!--
function checkName()
{
if (document.addressform.firstname.value=="")
{alert("Please enter a first name!");}
}
//-->
</script>

<body>
Hello.  Please enter your first name and press ok.
<form name=addressform>
<input type=text name=firstname>
<input type=button name=ok value=ok
onClick=checkName();>
</form>
</body></html>
```

Table 9.10.

Through JavaScript, even less-experienced developers are able to direct responses from a variety of events, objects, and actions. It provides anyone who

---

[72]http://www.ecma.ch/

can compose HTML with the ability to change images and play different sounds in response to specified events, such as a users' mouse click or screen exit and entry. It enables web developers to verify customers' input before it is sent to the server, reducing the load on the server and the required connections over the network. JavaScript runs also happily on very old and slow computers, as opposed to Java applets that may be far too slow to be of use in any on older computers.

9.8.2   Understanding the Value of JavaScript

JavaScript has many advantages over traditional programming languages. It integrates perfectly with the web browser. It is able to access all objects on a web page and manipulate them. This allows interaction to be created with the user without connecting back to the server.

JavaScript is a fairly universal extension to HTML that can enhance the user experience through event handling and client-side execution, while extending a web developer's control over the client's browser. JavaScript programs can be used for verifying input from the user, before sending it off to the client. This reduces the load on the network and increases the response times to the customer. Wrong input is detected immediately and the user has a chance to correct the input, without having to load a new page or reload the current page.

JavaScript can also be used for creating dynamic content. Depending on the type of browser, the JavaScript is able to display information in another format. Based on the user input the display on the page can be altered.

Depending on the type of network application and bandwidth, the combination of client-side applications and server-side applications needs to be evaluated. JavaScript is able to create and read cookies, making it possible to preserve the state. A cookie is a piece of information that is stored in the browser and can be retrieved by the server that placed the information there. This piece of information can be used to identify a user, for example. Using JavaScript, cookies and HTML pages it is possible to create complex applications without the need of a server application, making it possible to offer complex services without investing in expensive hardware.

Minivend[73], for example, is a shopping solution, which does not require any server software besides the web server. All information about the ordered products and information about the customer are stored in a cookie on the browser, and only when the customer decides to buy some goods, is the information transmitted to the Internet shop. This can be done sending an e-mail to the owner with the order.

Although the above mentioned example would not work with larger shops, it enables anyone to start-up business. This is not only true in the online retail business, but virtually any application can be implemented in such a manner.

---

[73]http://www.minivend.com/

In many cases JavaScript can replace client-side Java. It is a lightweight solution that users will be more willingly to tolerate.

9.8.3   VisualBasic Script

Besides JavaScript VisualBasic Script (VBScript) has established itself as a scripting language for web browsers. VBScript has been developed by Microsoft and is only supported by the Internet Explorer. It is a subset of the Microsoft Visual Basic language and is implemented as a fast, portable, lightweight interpreter for use in World Wide Web browsers and other applications that use Microsoft ActiveX Controls, Automation servers, and Java applets.

Like JavaScript, VBScript is a pure interpreter that processes source code embedded directly in the HTML. VBScript code, like JavaScript, does not produce standalone applets but is used to add intelligence and interactivity to HTML documents. The VBScript engine provides the core run-time functionality and includes a minimal set of basic objects. The majority of objects used are provided by Microsoft Internet Explorer. In general, anything that is specific to the Internet is provided by Internet Explorer, and anything that is generally useful is provided directly in VBScript. The Web author can insert additional objects through the <OBJECT> HTML tag.

The major advantage of VBScript is the tight integration into the Microsoft operating system, enabling it to create highly sophisticated web applications. Users that already have knowledge in Visual Basic will be able to create VB-Scripts without any additional learning. It is possible to debug VBScripts by using the standard Microsoft debugger, making it easy to trace down bugs in the script. The major disadvantage of VBScript is also its tight integration into the Microsoft operating system. It does not run on other operating systems or on other browsers, restricting it to people who use Internet Explorer and Windows. This is against the rules of the web, where everything should be accessible to everyone.

9.8.4   JavaScript versus JScript

As you now already know, JavaScript was developed by Netscape and has become since then the client-side scripting language of choice. As the early specifications were developed by Netscape only, Microsoft developed JScript, which is very similar to JavaScript and is supposed to be compatible with it. Nevertheless, there are quite a few differences that are of interest, as online businesses want their applications to be compatible with all browsers.

Some of the differences stem from bugs in the implementation while others stem from the actual implementation. In the early versions, where Netscape developed the standard by itself, the JavaScript implementation was always ahead of the JScript implementation. Netscape 2.0 had a comparable implementation to Internet Explorer 3.0, for example.

Microsoft's approach to client-side scripting offers the developer a choice between the C-style syntax of Netscape's JavaScript language and the VB-style that many Microsoft applications developers are already familiar with.

The differences between JavaScript and JScript are very subtle, but large enough make code break in one or the other case. While JavaScript is not case-sensitive for standard function names, JScript is. The function "onClick" can be written in JavaScript in any combination of capital letters (such as "OnClIcK"), but in JScript it needs to be written exactly as above stated. Another problem is the object hierarchy. This makes it more difficult to access objects on the web page, but with some work on top of your original script you can make it work in both browsers.

9.8.5 JavaScript Problems in Browsers

While JavaScript is now supported by all major browser manufacturers and even by the smaller ones, a problem remains, as the implementation is differing from browser to browser, just as you already know from HTML. This leads to web pages that are not displayed correctly in your web browsers and to applications that are not properly executed on the web, because you are using the wrong browser. It was already bad enough to have several HTML implementations, but with differing JavaScript implementations the web designers were even more restricted when creating new web sites. Either they would support only one version of HTML or JavaScript; then programming was easy, but they would get many complaints from their customers.

I know, for example, one online bank in Germany that uses JavaScript, but only the version that is in Netscape 4.04. If you try to use any other browser you will be stopped, as they do not support it. You can imagine how frustrated the customers will be, if they are limited to the exact browser version. They are not even able to update the browser in order to fix some bugs, as the server won't let them in anymore.

The other approach of supporting all versions can mean either that you restrict yourself to the minimum that is supported by all browsers, but makes your web site appear very dull, or you create multiple scripts for every browser. Although it means some additional work in programming and maintaining, the extra work is a must nowadays to keep the customers content and to implement the desired functionality.

9.8.6 Introduction to ECMAScript

In order to resolve the problem with the varying JavaScript implementations, ECMAScript was developed as the new standard for browser scripting. EC-MAScript[74], named after the ECMA organization, is based on several scripting technologies. JavaScript, developed by Netscape Communications and JScript,

---

[74]http://www.ecma.ch/ecma/ecma262.pdf

developed by Microsoft Corp. In late 1996 the development of the ECMAScript standard started and the first edition was published in June 1997. The ECMA standard was then submitted to the ISO organization, where it was approved in April 1998 as ISO/IEC 16262.

Manipulating computational objects and performing computations are the basic features of ECMAScript, which is a truly object-oriented programming language (as opposed to JavaScript). ECMAScript is not computationally self-sufficient, as there are no ways to input external data or output results to anything else than the host environment (in most cases a web browser).

ECMAScript has been designed to manipulate, customize and automate the facilities of an existing system. These systems have a user interface and EC-MAScript provides a mechanism for exposing the functionality to a programmatic control. The host environment provides a set of objects, which can be addressed by ECMAScript.

The initial idea of ECMAScript was to provide a mechanism to enrich web pages in the browsers and to perform programming tasks on the web server. But now more and more other hosts are beginning to use the ECMAScript engine, such as the KDE[75] project. The ECMAScript implementation will ensure that future versions of browsers will all understand the same scripting language without any variants.

In addition to the core language, the standardization process includes regular expressions, continues to support richer control statements and better string handling. Exception handling and internationalization and the above mentioned features are expected to find their way into the standard in the third edition, which is expected to be released in late 1999.

ECMAScript is able to provide scripting capabilities for different host environments, such as web browsers or web servers, but is not restricted to these host environments. Some of the ideas in ECMAScript are similar to other programming languages, in particular Java.

Web browsers allow ECMAScript access to objects, such as windows, menus, pop-ups, dialogue boxes and cookies. In addition the web browser provides a means to attach code to events, such as change of images and mouse-clicks.

The scripting code, which is used within a web browser scenario, is added to the HTML code. Most of the scripting is reactive and waits for the interaction of the user and therefore does not require a main program, which is run all the time in the background. The web server on the other hand, provides a host environment, which allows ECMAScript to process objects before sending them on to the web browser. The web server therefore provides a mechanism to lock and share data.

By using browser-side and server side scripting together it is possible to distribute computation between the client and server while providing a customized user interface for a Web-based application. Each Web browser and

---

[75]http://www.kde.org/

server that supports ECMAScript supplies its own host environment, completing the ECMAScript execution environment.

9.8.7 The Future of JavaScript

While many people still do not know what features the latest release (Version 1.3) of JavaScript/ECMAScript really has, the developers at Netscape and other companies are already planning the next major release of JavaScript (or ECMAScript), which will be version 2.0.

JavaScript was never designed to be a general-purpose programming language and this won't change in 2.0. Its strengths lies in the quick execution from source, making it a viable language for being distributed embedded in web pages. It can be used for fast prototyping by design. Its interfaces to Java and other environments and its dynamics are also strengths of JavaScript. The next major release will try to improve on these strengths, but add new features, such as JavaScript components and libraries, which can help in developing new applications and writing true object-oriented programs.

Also planned for JavaScript 2.0 are more security and robustness for the programs. Enhanced interfaces to existing languages and environments are planned and additional ones will be introduced. It is planned to improve JavaScript's reflection and dynamic capabilities and to enhance the performance and add support for threads, allowing a single program to run several tasks in parallel. In addition to this the language will be simplified where possible, reducing the possibility of errors.

These are the goals for the next release of JavaScript/ECMAScript, but the results may vary, as there is still a lot of discussion going on. All new features that will be implemented need to keep the language compact and flexible.

Chapter 10

SECURITY ON THE INTERNET

10.1 Creating a Security Strategy

10.1.1 Information Security

Communications via the Internet are by default open and uncontrolled. This conflicts with the needs of digital businesses, which require the privacy, the confidentiality and integrity of their transactions. The growing demand for electronic business also raises the awareness for security issues and concerns about achieving the goal of secure business via the Internet. The news is full of reports on Internet security that are hyper-critical and increase the fear that business on the Internet is dangerous. Network-based fraud is growing dramatically, and has made Internet security a business issue and not just a technical issue to be resolved in the IT departments of companies considering an Internet business strategy.

Today technology is able to make a system secure, but more than pure technology is required. Many problems have been reported in the past and it is sure that we will see even more incidents in the future. But if you look more in-depth into the reasons behind the attacks, you will often find human error, missing procedures and wrongly configured software to be the main problems. These errors can't be eliminated with more or better technology, but with an all-encompassing corporate security strategy.

The major problem on the Internet is the identity of the other users. In a real shop a customer is identified by her or his looks, on the Internet everyone looks the same. Although it is possible to pretend to be someone else in real life, on the Internet it is even simpler. On the Internet nobody can be sure about the identity of the other person without additional technologies. But even if a person can be identified, it is often not possible to do business, as this requires a signature, which can't be done without a legal framework. Information security is the major issue on the Internet, but it can't be implemented, if the basics aren't done right. Governments are starting to provide legal frameworks to punish attackers and allow creation of standardized digital signatures and certificates.

In order to enforce information security it is necessary to prevent unauthorized access to electronic data on the business critical systems of the company. The result of unauthorized access can be disclosure of the information, the alteration, substitution or destruction of content.

Organizations and people that use computers can describe their needs for information security and trust in terms of five major requirements: Confidentiality, integrity, availability, legitimate use and non-repudiation. Confidentiality is necessary to control who gets to read the information and to conceal the information to all others. Integrity needs to assure that information and programs are changed only in a specified and authorized manner and that the data presented is genuine and was not altered or deleted during transit. The availability needs to ensure that authorized users have continued access to information and resources. Legitimate use means that resources cannot be used by non-authorized persons or in a non-authorized way.

These five components may be weighted differently depending on the particular application. A risk assessment must be performed to determine the appropriate mix. A number of different technologies can be used to ensure information security.

Confidentiality and integrity can be implemented through cryptography, which offers a high degree of security. By encrypting the data no one is able to tell what the information is about. Through strong authentication it is possible to ensure that nobody sees, copies or deletes a certain piece of information. Using strong authentication and strong encryption the only way to break in is to have the necessary certificate for authentication and the key for the encryption. An authorization system is able to prevent access in a non-authorized way by authenticated people. Non-repudiation requires a trusted third-party which time stamps the outgoing and incoming communication and which is able to verify the validity of a digital signature. By putting a time stamp on every piece of information that moves between two parties, it becomes easy to find out if a certain e-mail had been sent out in time.

Security of the encryption key, assignment of liability, responsibility for the key, and audit of access to the key are all ongoing issues that must be addressed. There is no doubt that a cryptographic system, correctly managed and implemented, offers the highest security level for electronic information available today. But don't forget the education and security process re-engineering, as they will decide on the level of security of the whole company.

10.1.2   Information Policy

In order to ensure the security of the business-critical information, every company needs to develop an information policy, which ensures that processes are in place when something happens. The process for developing an information policy is like a circle, which returns always to the starting point to increase the safety. You cannot expect that everything works the first time. New technologies and ideas require you to continuously update your information policy. Just like your web page, which needs continuous updates, your security process requires continuous updates.

The first step of your information policy is to make a list of all resources that need to be protected. This does not only include computers, but also printers, routers, firewalls on the technical level, and also buildings that contain the hardware or where backups are stored. A process needs to be defined as to who gets physical access to the hardware and logical access to the software. Physical access is often neglected, but the best firewall software is useless, if the hacker can walk into the building and copy the required files onto a disk.

Once all resources have been listed, it is necessary to catalogue the threats for every single resource. This part will take the most time, but it is also the basis for a really secure system. Once the catalogue is complete, a risk analysis needs to be performed, which shows the percentage of each threat. As it is not possible to invest in preventing every threat, the company will need to evaluate, which threats can be ignored for the time being and which need to be catered to.

To prevent the most probable threats it is necessary to implement cost effective security systems. Cost are very important in the security industry. Security cannot be measured by return on investment. By implementing a secure system you add overhead and cost and there will never be a point where you will get money back from the system. The only thing that can be said is that it is highly likely that without the security system your company would lose a lot of money and business, but convincing upper-level management to invest in securing information can be difficult.

The processes need constant surveillance and updates in case of new threats or security holes. This will guarantee that your system is up-to-date and not penetrable by unauthorized people.

10.1.3 Threats and Challenges on the Internet

The Internet offers a wide range of possible attacks; although most of them are very unlikely it is necessary to evaluate how dangerous such an attack can be. The threats can be divided into four basic categories: loss of data integrity, loss of data privacy, loss of service and loss of control. See Table 10.1 for an overview on what these threats can mean to the company.

Computer hackers are people who try to achieve one or more of these goals at any given time. An online bank in Germany, for example, registers about one thousand attacks per day. It is not known how many of these attacks are really serious, but it shows that people try their luck.

Many people try to find holes in the software or the configuration to get into the system. Online banks are often the target of hackers, as the prospect of transferring money is a strong motivation for many people. In some cases hackers do not want to gain access to the system, but implement malicious

---

Threats on the Internet

Most threats on the Internet can be classified in one of the following four categories:

- **Loss of Data Integrity** – Information is created, modified or deleted by an intruder.

- **Loss of Data Privacy** – Information is made available to unauthorized persons.

- **Loss of Service** – A service breaks down due to the action of a hacker.

- **Loss of Control** – Services are used by authorized persons in an uncontrolled way.

Table 10.1.

---

procedures that cause a so-called "denial of service" (DoS) attack. The goal of the DoS attack is to deny access to the authorized users. This is achieved by attacking network components, such as routers or computer systems, by attacking applications or the operating system. This creates an inoperable condition, which may create a financial loss for the organization.

Modern security technologies have made attacks more difficult, but every day new vulnerabilities in application software and operating systems are published, which offer new possibilities for attacks. In order to keep a system secure, it is necessary to update the operating system and the application software on a regular basis.

There are many ways to attack a system. One way is to monitor the communication between two partners. The communication on the Internet is totally insecure by default. Information is transmitted in clear text. By monitoring the communication it is possible to get to know private information and passwords that may be transmitted. If you contact your mail server, for example, the login and password are sent to the server and anybody on the Internet is able to intercept the transmission.

Once hackers start to intercept the communication, they are also able to change the information before it arrives at the destination, it can be deleted or replaced. The recipient won't notice the changes made by a third party without special software.

Another possibility that can get a company into real trouble is to steal their software and hardware. Software, such as databases, may contain data such as private information and passwords, the hardware may enable the hacker to understand how the internal network is built up or contain hard-coded information, such as on a smart card and reveal in which context these smart cards are used (e.g. for opening the doors).

Instead of sniffing network communication it is also possible to intercept the electro-magnetic output of devices, such as monitors. Devices are available which are able to copy the content of a computer screen to another one, which is at a distance of a several hundred meters.

A denial of service attack can be executed by attacking known vulnerabilities of the operating system or application software or by exhausting the service by overloading the service with too many requests. The system is then so busy in dealing with these requests that responses to legitimate requests slow down and eventually fail.

Trojan horses are also a method for getting into a system. The Trojan horse is normally hidden in harmless looking software, which invokes the Trojan horse, when the software is launched. The Trojan horse will work in the background and collect information about the system and its users. These pieces of information are then sent out to the hacker, who then can use the information to enter the system or remote control it.

Masquerading (also known as spoofing) is also a very common type of attack. By pretending to be someone else a hacker is able to enter a computer system. IP spoofing is the way most attacks are conducted. Many systems are restricted to a certain set of IP addresses by pretending to be a certain IP address, it is possible to get automatic access to certain resources. Many systems ignore requests from non-authorized IP addresses. Through IP spoofing it is possible to appear as an authorized IP address. Although this will not automatically grant access to a certain system, it offers an entry point and may disclose information, which may be valuable to a hacker. By IP spoofing the system will start to respond and offer more points of attack for the hacker.

Another way to receive information and create intelligence about the target system is to look through the dustbin in front of the office for old media, such as floppy disks that may contain information which may be helpful to break into the system. This type of attack requires the attacker to be near the defendant, which makes it also easier to find the hacker after the attack.

Another way to get access to passwords and the internal architecture about the security system is to bribe the security personnel at the target site. If enough money is offered, some of the employees will be willing to disclose secret material. Although it is not possible to control every employee, the security system should never depend on a single employee. This is also important, if an employee is ill, had an accident or decides to leave the company.

Physical intrusion is a more traditional way of acquiring information or breaking down a service. The attacker enters the building, bypasses the access controls and gets the information. This also requires the attacker to be physically near the target to start the attack. This often helps to reveal the identity of the attacker, making this type of attack rather infeasible nowadays.

In connection with IP spoofing many attackers do not only present false information to the users, but also collect information, such as passwords. Imagine your favorite bookshop on the Internet gets IP spoofed. When you enter the URL of the bookshop, the domain name is resolved to the wrong IP address, therefore presenting the wrong home page. Damage can be done by insulting the customers with a special web page, but more professional hackers copy the content of the web page to the new location and will "only" collect information on the customers. When the user has chosen which books to take, existing accounts can be accessed by login and password. If this information falls into the hands of the wrong person, it is easy to imagine what damage can be done and it would take time until someone even the noticed.

Another method of letting hackers into the system is offering them information about the internal network. Many companies use domain names for computers which are enumerated, such as "system01.domain.org", "system02.domain.org", "system03.domain.org". This may make it easier for the internal staff to count how many systems are available, but it also makes it much easier for hackers to guess what machines are available and what their names are. Most companies use www.domain.org as their external web server domain name, but the www is often an alias for the real system name. I have already come across systems which were called "xxx07.domain.org" and were at the same time the external web server. By typing in "telnet xxx01.domain.org" it is rather easy to find out, if other systems are connected directly to the Internet and which operating system runs on them. Another weakness of some companies is to open the internal DNS structure to the outside world. If nobody is supposed to see the internal network, then nobody needs to know which machines perform what (such as mail servers).

10.1.4 Social Engineering

The most sophisticated and successful attacks are not on the technical side, but on the social side. Instead of using technology to break into technology, social engineering tries to get people to comply to the requests of the attacker. It does not mean that you control their minds and can remote control these people, as this would be too obvious and would most likely fail. Social engineering is about exploiting habits of people, so that they do not notice someone has stolen information from them.

Most attacks through social engineering involve that the hacker pretending to be someone else. This of course involves more than just calling the IT department of a certain company and asking for the passwords of the firewall computers. Even though you may not believe it, it can end with this phone call, but this requires a lot of preparation.

Social engineering concentrates on the weakest link in Internet security, human kind. In order to make a system secure in the Internet world, it needs to be taken off the Internet. But even this does not guarantee that your system is really secure. In April 1999 some hackers were able to steal information from a nuclear research institution in the US by using an insider who copied the relevant information onto a floppy disk.

Many business already rely on the Internet and in the future almost all companies will require an Internet business link in order to do business, therefore every company is a possible target for hackers. Social hacking makes it easy for hackers to get into any computer system, as it is independent of the attacking system platform, operating system and application software.

Social hacking works normally in a very indirect way. Anybody loosely connected to the people involved in securing the company network is already a potential security risk. By calling the receptionist it is possible to find out the names of people in certain organizations, which in turn are able to deliver additional information. After several phone calls, which cannot be traced back as well as e-mails (if they come out of the blue), the attacker has gathered enough information about the company and its procedures that it can call the responsible person at the security department and pretend to be someone else.

The information gathered are like little pieces of a puzzle, which will seem to be not useful to the person who provided the pieces of information. Only as a whole the information can be used to attack the company. In order to get the required information it is necessary to adapt the internal processes of the company. Organizational charts and the company phone book are also very helpful to appear as an employee. Internal documents that are thrown away should always be shredded to avoid anyone from stealing them from the dustbin. The use of floppies nowadays should be eliminated completely. It is just too easy to rip off information from a floppy that has been formatted. Hard drives and floppies that are no longer used should be completely destroyed. Social engineering does not require a lot of in-depth computer knowledge and enables anyone to become a hacker.

Another method of acquiring information is asking for it directly. Just call up the firewall administrators and ask for the password. In order to succeed you need to some insight on the company structure. The hacker may have read that the CEO of the target company is visiting another country in a time zone that is at least eight hours different and is going to hold a speech there. If the hackers get the timing right, they will call the headquarters half an hour before the speech starts and ask them for the password, because the laptop, which contained the presentation does not work anymore. Due to the time difference it will most likely be night and only few little staff will be available. The hacker will pretend to be the CEO and will request the information immediately in order to give the speech on time. In order to make the employee really believe that the caller is the CEO, the hacker will most likely reference the boss of the employee.

Think about it, would you give the password to the person calling or not? During the day, you would do maybe some background checks, but during the night, when you may be a little bit sleepy, then you will most probably just hand out the password. Social engineering works through information gathering and social pressure. Better hand out the information before getting fired, is one of the typical strategies.

Hackers will use strong arguments when doing the final step in the information attack, as weak arguments will most likely generate counter arguments. By presenting strong arguments most people will just obey. This will work especially well, if the person you are attacking is less competent than you are.

As you can see, no matter how good a system is protected, as long as people are involved in administration of the system, the system can be attacked indirectly. In order to make social engineering less likely, it is necessary to educate everyone in the company. Every single employee needs to understand the importance of security and what methods are available to eliminate the barriers by hackers.

In many cases it is easier to hack the people in front of the computer than the computer itself. At the same time it is also true that preventing people from hacking is also much easier than securing the computer. Constant education is therefore necessary.

10.1.5 Security through Obscurity

Many companies have been very restrictive with releasing information about their security systems. By avoiding talk about security many companies believe that nothing will happen. Other companies try to hide information on their web server, which is destined only for a few. Others have their extranets open to everyone and expect that if they release the URL only to a limited set of people that nobody will be able to find the information. Other companies think that their security technology is so complex that nobody will be ever to penetrate it.

These principles have been proven faulty and most security experts consider open discussion and education about security concepts and technologies. Open discussion on security standards is the key to successful technologies, just like open discussion on Internet technology has made the Internet a success.

Security through obscurity is still a very common strategy for many companies, which try to avoid coping with security holes. By ignoring security issues, the software vendors hope that nobody will document the holes and find ways to exploit them.

The best security products are discussed openly and even the source code for the product is available for everyone to review. Although this may seem strange at first, as hackers can find out how the algorithm works, it enables third parties to review the code and make it even more secure. This requires the security software vendor to develop algorithms, which provide strong encryption without making it possible to invert the algorithm. One very fine example is Pretty Good Privacy (PGP), where the processes and algorithms are well documented, without weakening the security.

10.1.6   Resolving the Security Issues

Now that you are scared and do not want to use the Internet anymore due to the security issues, I want to present solutions to the most common attacks. The first type of attack is the denial of service attack. Most DoS attacks are done by attacking indirectly the service you want to hit. In many cases another service running on the system is attacked, which is known to be vulnerable. A web server, for example, should block all non-HTTP traffic. By ignoring traffic on all other ports than port 80 for HTTP, the server is far less vulnerable to DoS attacks and does not spend processing power on illegitimate service requests from web clients.

Masquerading is also a very common threat to many digital business. By appearing as a legitimate user an imposter is able to access private information and execute commands, which are not publicly accessible. The problem here lies in most cases that the authentication is based on a single factor, such as a password or PIN. These pieces of information can be easily copied. In order to make authentication secure, a two-factor authentication is required, which involves not only the "something you know" factor, but also the "something you have" factor. By using smart cards together with a PIN, it becomes difficult for attackers to masquerade themselves as someone else, because two independent security barriers must be compromised before a successful attack can be made.

Although two-factor client authentication is far more secure, there are still possibilities to break into the system. The physical token, such as a smart card, contains a "secret", which is used to allow the customer into the system. This "secret" is unlocked by the PIN. In order to gain access, attackers need to know the secret or have the smart card and the PIN to authenticate themselves.

To prevent attackers gaining knowledge about the "secret", it is necessary to make the physical token tamper resistant. To avoid packet sniffing, the "secret" should never leave the token and it should never be able to read the "secret" to prevent brute force methods of decrypting it. To make a physical token unique, it is necessary to map the holder of the token to the identity of its owner. This prevents several people from sharing one identity. To prevent sniffing of the PIN number, the validation should be done on the card. This also requires that the keyboard used to enter the PIN is attached directly to the token, in order to ensure the privacy of the information.

A regular audit of the log files of the firewall, the web servers and the applications servers helps to prevent false authentication. A log file should log all failed attempts and should trigger a process, if the number of attempts is getting too high, for example, by adding mechanisms to control the life cycle of client authentication.

Another type of attack is DNS spoofing, which allows hackers to redirect customers to another server and capture sensitive client information. In order to ensure that the server a customer is contacting is the right one, it is necessary to add server-side authentication. This is done through a digital certificate on the server, which is unique for every domain name and IP address.

In order to prevent the alteration of information in transit, message integrity needs to be enforced. This is done by adding a message hash to the mail. The encryption of messages helps to prevent eavesdropping on confidential conversations. This makes it impossible for a private message between two parties to be intercepted and read by intermediaries.

One of the major problems on the Internet is the repudiation of messages, meaning falsely denying that a message has been sent or been received. This is often done in business transactions, such as online ordering and payment. People often order goods and then repudiate. In order to make business easier for the online businesses, it needs to be ensured that non-repudiation of the orders can be enforced. This is done through the use of digital certificates, which identify a customer in a very secure way.

10.1.7 Authorization

In order to move a business from a private network to the Internet, there are some security issues that need to be resolved. First of all it needs to be determined who has access to which business applications and company sensitive information. In many businesses there is no clear policy on who has access and why. This makes it difficult afterwards to determine who leaked certain information. This authorization list should also include information on what each person is allowed to do with each of these business applications.

In order to enforce this authorization list, a company needs to develop and implement a consistent set of policies for all users of a particular system (e.g. employees, customers, and partners) across multiple applications. A general authorization process needs to be implemented.

Authorization in general consists of a system architecture, which prevents the unauthorized access to services and data by strictly enforcing rules on what a user is allowed and is not allowed to do, based on their authenticated identity. The first step should be to move from a distributed administration of authorization to a centralized concept. Most applications have their own methods of implementing authorization. As more applications start to become available on the Internet, this distributed model creates additional security holes, as each application may have different bugs or holes that can be used to bypass the software. The costs for developing new software are also higher because you need to incorporate new authorization modules. Centralizing the administration and implementation lowers the costs for administration, implementation and maintenance. It allows a far more consistent view of security policies for security administrators.

A list should be maintained of each resource (such as a printer), file, database or application and the users/groups who have access to that particular object. With the new concept of using a centralized directory for administration each user or profile has a list of objects they are allowed to access. The database contains information on who has access to which application, and the policies/rules for what users are allowed to do within each application.

Most commonly, solutions use the Lightweight Directory Application Protocol (LDAP) service. Hewlett Packard's authorization server, which does not build on the LDAP service, was difficult to use, therefore it was superseded by the DomainGuard product, which uses LDAP. No matter which solution you choose, you need to be prepared to change parts of your existing applications in order to support centralized administration and maintenance.

10.2   Cryptographic Tools

10.2.1   Defining Cryptography

The prefix "crypto" comes from the Greek word "kryptó", meaning "hidden". Cryptology, from "kryptó" and "lógos" means therefore "hidden word" and is used to describe the fields of research in cryptography and cryptanalysis. The ancient Greeks already used this discipline to hide information. Cryptography is the art of keeping information private in such a form which is unreadable to another person without the right key. Cryptanalysis is the art of compromising algorithms developed in cryptography.

Cryptographic algorithms have been used throughout history mainly to keep communications private. During the Second World War the first computers were built to decrypt messages that the Germans used to send over the radio. Nazi Germany was using the Enigma machine, a wooden box with dials and wheels, to send and receive encrypted messages. The box was so small that it could be used from anywhere. U-boats, tanks, and offices were equipped with the Enigma. The code changed on a daily basis so decryption using traditional methods was not possible. If a German officer was captured the first thing he would have done was to destroy the Enigma as it was the most important device for the German military. British intelligence officers built a computer called Collosum, which was able to decrypt the information processed by the Enigma. Deciphering the Enigma codes helped to win the war.

After the World War II scientists turned away from cryptography and used computers for calculations. Only about thirty years ago, banks started to hook up networks of computers, as they connected all branches to a central mainframe. In order to secure electronic transfers the banks started to use encryption algorithms like the Data Encryption Standard (DES), developed by IBM in the seventies.

Encryption can be used for more than private communication. Encryption is able to transform data into a form that makes it almost impossible to read without the appropriate knowledge about the encryption schema. This knowledge is normally called a key. The key is used to allow controlled access to the information to selected people. The information can be passed on to anyone, but only the people with the right key are able to see the information.

Encryption is often believed to be a component of security, but actually it is a mechanism used to achieve security.

10.2.2 Reasons for Encryption

In Chapter 4 we have seen the legal issues with encryption technologies. Using encryption is important and will change the way businesses work. Strong encryption allows you to send confidential documents, like contracts or personal information by e-mail or save confidential information on your mobile computer, without having to fear that if someone steals it, the data will become public. Without strong encryption, all confidential information can be intercepted very easily and used against the owner of the information. One example could be the purchasing department of a company that communicates with its supplier base. or a company which exchanges all the proprietary component specifications, contracts, price sheets and new product information with its partners.

Businesses is exchanging more and more information over the Internet. In many cases this information is of financial nature and if these get into the wrong hands it can destroy businesses. In order to make electronic business feasible, the information needs to be kept private. Without cryptography the privacy cannot be guaranteed.

The most important application that needs to be encrypted is e-mail. Without cryptography e-mails are the electronic equivalent of traditional postcards. E-mails do not have a physical form and may exist electronically in more than one place at one time. If you have the right encryption/decryption software installed, it will hook up to your mail program and encrypt/decrypt messages automatically without user interaction. All you have to do is to say that you need a certain message encrypted. Encrypted e-mails are as if you have put the e-mail into an envelope which is put into a safe. Without the right key nobody is able to see the content, although anybody could take away the safe.

The more computers and networks became a commodity for the users, the more important it became to secure the information that was transmitted over the networks. As the computer world changed from mainframe systems to a server-client based world, cryptography started to look like an fundamental business tool. The Internet, which is the basis for most business transactions nowadays is an insecure network, as everybody is able to grab transmissions going from one place to the other. Security issues on the Internet are being resolved only slowly, as changing fundamental standards has become difficult.

Online banking and online payment are the most prominent Internet applications, which rely on encryption. Internet customers are very sensitive about privacy issues. Therefore all web browsers do support encryption of documents. There are some issues about browser encryption, as the standard key length is only 40 bit in the international version, which can be broken very easily. Additional encryption components are necessary in many cases.

Access control can also be implemented through cryptography. Television subscription channels work this way. As it is not possible to open or close channels to individual subscribers over a satellite, the information is encrypted and the key is distributed to the people who pay for it. This can be done either on a general basis or on a pay-per-view basis. Depending on the type of television channel a key is valid for the whole day or the key changes for every program. In the latter case, the key for a certain program is distributed to the customers, when they have paid for that particular program. The keys are stored in a receiver, which decodes the program. The receiver is connected to the television provider over a phone line, which is able to send the key or remove the key whenever necessary.

Business managers may think that they do not need to think about cryptography, as this is just another technical gadget for the technical people. Having or not having encryption in the communication can mean to have or to lose business. Using encrypted web sites and e-mail business managers are able to think of new business models that were not possible before.

10.2.3 Secret Key Cryptography

Secret key cryptography, also called symmetric cryptography, is the traditional form of cryptography. A single key is used for encryption and decryption. The two parties involved in the communication need to agree on the key before exchanging the information. The key should not be communicated over the same medium as the encrypted message. If you send encrypted messages over the Internet, you should agree on the key over the phone, for example.

The password (or key) is used to encrypt the outgoing messages, the so-called cipher-text is sent over the network and the recipient decrypts incoming messages using the same key. Some of the algorithms are based on strong mathematical foundations. These systems cannot be cracked by another algorithm. The only way to crack them is to try out all possible keys. In January 1999, an encrypted message with 56 bit was cracked in 24 hours by the Electronic Frontier Foundation[1]. The times for cracking encrypted messages is dropping dramatically.

Still there are some advantages over public key encryption. It is much faster and requires lower key length to get the same strength of encryption. The most common secret key techniques are stream ciphers and block ciphers.

Stream ciphers are known for their speed. The speed is achieved by operating on small units of the plain text. Normally stream ciphers operate on bit level. A so-called key stream, which consists of a sequence of bits, operates on

---

[1]http://www.eff.org/

the plain text using a bit-wise exclusive-OR operation. The encryption of a bit depends on the previous bits.

A block cipher on the other hand transform a block of plain text with a pre-defined length (such as 64 bits) into a block of cipher text with the same length. The transformation is done by providing a secret key, which is used for the encryption. Decryption works the same way, by applying the same secret key to the cipher text.

Secret-key cryptography is used, for example, in single user environments. If you want to encrypt your files on your hard disk, it would not make sense to use public key cryptography, as it would be far too slow and storing public and private keys in a single environment does not give any advantages over having only one key.

10.2.4   Public Key Cryptography

Public key cryptography or asymmetric key cryptography has one major advantage over symmetric algorithms. It does not rely on a secure way to exchange the password. Symmetric key algorithms need the two parties to agree on a common key, which can be intercepted while transmitting the key information from on to the other. This would make encryption over the Internet useless, if you sent the key before you sent the encrypted message. The key needs to be sent separately, but this prevents people or companies who do not know each other from doing business over the Internet.

In 1976, two professors at Stanford University, Whitfield Diffie and Martin Hellman proposed a system which they called "public key encryption". Public key encryption uses two keys for every encryption and works fine over insecure networks. Every user generates a pair of keys. Each of the keys is a large integer, sometimes with more than five hundred digits. The two keys are related two each other in a way that through special calculations it is possible to encrypt a message using one of the keys and decrypt it with the other, but you cannot decrypt the message with the same key.

In 1975, three researchers at the MIT developed an algorithm to implement public key cryptography. Ron Rivest, Adi Shamir and Leonard Adleman invented the RSA system[2], which was named after their inventors.

The RSA algorithm generates initially two distinct keys for every user. One of the keys is defined as the public key. The public key can be distributed freely to anyone using any means such as on floppy disk, via e-mail or on a printout. The public key cannot be used to decrypt any message, it can only be used to encrypt messages that can be sent to the owner of the public key. Only the person with the other key, called the private key, is able to decrypt messages that are encrypted with the public key.

Of course many mathematicians tried to find a way to break into the public key algorithm by doing some calculations (or even very many calculations), but

---

[2]http://www.rsa.org/

so far nobody has found an algorithm that solves the mathematical problem. Decryption programs use brute-force to break the key by trying out all combinations. Although it is not impossible, it is computationally infeasible, if the public key is long enough.

In most cases RSA is not used to encrypt messages, because of the timely computations it requires. For most messages it would become infeasible, as the time required to encrypt and decrypt would be too long. Instead, RSA is used to encrypt the symmetric key, which encrypted the message. The SSL standard, which is used to encrypt web pages (the URLs use https:// instead of http://), uses this feature. The key is generated on the web browser and then sent to the web server. Without public key cryptography you would have to send the key without protection over the Internet.

To make the transmission of the key secure, the web server sends its public key to the web browser. The web browser decides on a symmetric key and encrypts the message with the public key of the web server and sends it back. The web server is the only instance that is able to decrypt the public key with its private key. The RSA key is used as an envelope for the symmetric key. From then on the encryption is done by symmetric key, as this is much faster than public key encryption.

Through this system it is possible to choose symmetric keys at random. If one is able to break into an encrypted message, it would not give any information about the keys used in the other messages.

If you choose to encrypt e-mails, you can encrypt the symmetric key several times with different public keys. Each public key belongs to one of the recipients. So every recipient is able to decrypt the message. Every public key forms an envelope that contains the same key to decrypt the original message. This paradigm of secure messaging has been used in PGP, for example and used in a similar manner in SSL encryption on the web.

10.2.5 Comparison of Secret and Public Key Cryptography

The most important advantage of public key over secret key cryptography is that the private keys are never sent out. This makes this type of cryptography more secure and convenient. In a secret key system the keys need to be transmitted and pose a security risk. With secret keys it is also difficult to implement an authentication mechanism. A digital signature using a public key infrastructure is very easy, but in a secret key infrastructure secret information needs to be exchanged. In order to provide non-repudiation, a third party is needed to verify the authenticity.

But there are also some disadvantages to public key encryption. Most secret key technologies are much faster than public key encryption algorithms. They are faster by at least a magnitude, which means that public key encryption is no good for large files. In order to make a system secure and fast, both types of cryptography need to be combined.

In such a mixed environment the message will be encrypted with a secret key, as this would take ages with public key encryption and the secret key is attached to the message, but encrypted with a public key infrastructure. This way the speed and the security are enforced.

In SSL encryption, which is used for the secure exchange of information over the web, public key cryptography is used for exchanging the secret key. The web server sends its public key to the web browser. The browser creates a session key and encrypts the session key with the public key of the web server. The session key is then transmitted back to the web server, which decrypts the session key with its own secret key. This way it is possible to transmit session keys over an unsecured network. Once the session key has been transmitted it is used for encrypting the connection, as it is much faster. As long as computers are not at least a thousand times faster than today, secret key algorithms will remain important. The session key is secure as it is only valid for that particular session and cannot be reused.

10.2.6 Steganography

Messages that are encrypted using steganography look like harmless messages with attached images or sounds. People who would try to intercept the file would receive only a message that looks like there is nothing secret in it. Someone reading such an e-mail, looking at such an image or listening to such a sound would never detect any difference. In most cases the hidden messages are also encrypted to make it even harder to detect them.

Steganographic software tries to hide the information in the ordinary noise of digital systems of sounds and images. To remain undetectable, the hidden message has to have the same statistics as the natural noise of computer images or digitized sounds. The problem is that encrypted messages usually look much more random than the ordinary "noise" they are trying to mimic. Computer generated images are no good place to hide information, as they are too regular, but scanned images offer enough place to hide information.

There are some software packages available, that are freely distributable, that allow the encryption via steganography. But the quality is unfortunately not very high. If you analyze the data carefully enough, you will find the hidden message without too much trouble. The emulation of natural noise is often not good enough.

The commercial steganographic software packages offer much better hiding. Using this technique it is possible to transmit data without anyone noticing it at all. In countries where encryption is not allowed steganography is a way to avoid detection. Sending images over the Internet is nothing unusual and checking them for encrypted and hidden messages is very difficult, if not impossible.

10.3   Applications of Cryptology

10.3.1   Enforcing Privacy

Privacy is one of the major issues on the Internet. The Internet by default is unsecured allowing anyone who wishes to, to intercept messages going back and forth between two parties. In order to implement privacy it is possible to encrypt the messages, making them unreadable to third parties. They are still able to intercept the messages, therefore it is necessary to ensure that the keys are not transmitted in plain text over the Internet.

Privacy is not the only important issue on the Internet, but also on multi-user systems, such as servers, where several people share one hard disk for private information. The files are protected by passwords, so it is necessary to ensure the security of the passwords. This can be done by storing the hash value of the password instead of the password. Decoding the password is possible, but hash values are irreversible. When a user enters a password the hash value is calculated and compared to the hash value stored. This system makes it virtually impossible to steal data stored on that system without knowing the password.

10.3.2   Encrypting E-Mail

E-mail is the most used application in cyber-space. It is very simple to use and requires nothing special from your computer other than a connection to the Internet and a little mail program. The e-mail content is a plain text format which can be read by any computer system in the world. The easiness and friendliness of the application is also its problem. Every computer system in the world can intercept the message in transit and is able to read the contents without any additional software. A simple text reader will do.

If you send out an e-mail, the mail is not being sent directly to the destination, but instead the mailer looks at the destination and looks for some computers in between that are used to relay the message. This reduces significantly the cost of transmitting the information, as every computer needs to transmit the information only to the next one. The path between source and destination is built up as the mail gets sent off, an e-mail from Stuttgart, Germany to Oxford, UK may even have computers in between that are in New York, USA. Each of the computers in transit can easily check for certain senders and recipients and is able to save all the information in a file on the local hard disk.

Even if the attacker is not sitting on one of the computers in the path there are ways to filter message streams and get the required information. The attacker would require a hacker to install a piece of software on the relaying computer, which is called a "sniffer". The sniffer then scans all e-mails for certain keywords.

It takes normally only a few seconds to send an e-mail to any destination in the world. Nobody would notice, if someone picked up some information at a certain point; you would not even notice that someone has altered information, before sending it on, as there is no definite time limit for e-mail delivery.

Other than traditional mail (sometimes called snail-mail), e-mails do not have an envelope, which hides the information inside from viewing. E-mails are worse than postcards from a privacy point of view. Other than regular mails or postcards, e-mails on the Internet can be scanned for keywords easily and automatically. Scanning normal mail at an office will require a lot of time, which makes it impractical.

If you want to encrypt e-mail there are several ways of doing it. The most secure system for e-mail encryption on the market is currently PGP. If you use a version that has been proved to be secure and was compiled by a trustworthy person, you are on the safe side. The encryption algorithm based on public key infrastructure is unbreakable. The source code has been open on the market for years and has resisted all tries to break it. Only if the recipient of the mail reveals the private key are others able to decipher the message. PGP requires you to install a separate piece of software on your computer.

S/MIME (Secure Multipurpose Internet Mail Extensions) on the other hand is much easier to set up, as it is supported by both Netscape's Communicator and Microsoft's Internet Explorer natively. No extra software is required for using S/MIME. All you need is a digital certificate, which can be obtained from many sources, like TrustCenter[3] in Germany or GTE[4] in the US. S/MIME uses a similar method as PGP. It uses asymmetric encryption as an envelope to send a key to be used in the symmetric cipher that encrypts the message. S/MIME is far less secure than PGP as it uses a far lower bit-rate for the key outside of the United States and the source code was not public until recently, when Netscape opened the Mozilla web site and gave away the source code of its browser. Another problem: the strength of the encryption is weakened to near insignificance in browsers

Another way of encrypting your messages is the use of strong symmetric encryption algorithms that are not bound to the e-mailing software. Write your e-mail with a text editor, encrypt it with any strong encryption technology and then send off the encrypted file over the network. Blowfish, IDEA and triple-DES are common choices. But the software to decrypt the files need to be installed on all computers involved and a channel needs to be established in order to exchange the keys securely. The procedure of installing, maintaining and using this method is far too high to be of any value in a business environment. For private use it may be just ok.

If you need to transmit information secretly in such a way that you send it to an account which can be read by more than one person, you can use programs like WinZip[5]. Almost everyone has a copy and it is very easy to use. The encryption technology used is quite good, as well. The files are protected by password

---

[3]http://www.trustcenter.de/

[4]http://www.gte.com/

[5]http://www.winzip.com/

which can be cracked by brute-force, but you can change the password each time which requires the attacker to break in each time. The password can be easily transmitted via telephone.

10.3.3 Applying Encryption Technologies

If we look at encryption algorithms we will find many different types and many different levels of security. Some, like ROT13, which I described in Chapter 4, are broken very easily, others like PGP[6] cannot be broken by algorithm within a reasonable time frame (using a few thousand computers a few thousand years is not really reasonably). You would need to have the password and the key to decrypt the information sent in PGP format.

Encryption Strengths

Encryption technology can be divided into several encryption strengths, ranging from weak to unbreakable.

- **Weak** – Password protected text documents from word processors. These programs use very weak encryption, which can be broken in with simple tools.

- **Robust** – Using symmetric encryption technologies one can create robust encryption, but the weakness lies in the transmission of the key, which cannot be sent over insecure networks.

- **Strong** – Using public key infrastructure you can transmit the key over insecure networks.

- **Unbreakable** – One-Time Pads. This system uses a key that is as long as the message itself and can only be decrypted with the pad it has been encrypted on.

Table 10.2.

This section will give you an idea which encryption products suits which needs. Security and privacy are very important issues for your company and therefore a tiny bug in the encryption software can create much larger problems than a bug in a word processor.

---

[6]http://www.pgp.com/

A bug in the encryption software (or hardware) may destroy all your business, as your company secrets may become public. Most word processors offer the possibility to encrypt your documents, but these encryption algorithms are very weak and you never should rely on them, if you have confidential data on your laptop or intend to send it over an insecure network. They may be useful to keep colleagues from sniffing private data on a server, but won't stop professional hackers. AccessData[7] has even created a commercial software package that is specialized in breaking the code of such programs. They sell it for the purpose that one has forgotten the password, but it can be also used with the intention of breaking in.

Another very popular method of securing documents is to conceal them. Security through obscurity is a very weak system. Actually it is even worse than encrypting documents with a word processor. By placing documents in the wrong places, some people think that they can hide them from the rest, but other than with encrypted documents, all one has to do look for that file. Using simple file search one is able to retrieve most files. Using weak encryption one has at least the task of decrypting the information.

As most people use a system to hide files and data, (otherwise you would not find your information, anymore), it becomes easy to guess where other files may be hidden, once you have found a file.

Strongly encrypted files can be put on public web sites without having to fear that the information can be revealed, even though they may be stolen. Even the algorithms and the source code of the most popular encryption technologies is published, so that everybody is able to understand how the encryption works. The security comes from the algorithms and not from the system used to implement the algorithms. If one keeps the key secret no one else will be able to break the code.

10.3.4 Digital Signatures

Cryptography can be used more than just for encrypting and decrypting information. Authentication is one of the most important fields to build a trustworthy relationship. Only if I know to whom I am speaking can I trust her or him. Authentication is done in many cases by signing a document. In order to make electronic documents legally usable, it is necessary to have a mechanism that provides a means to authenticate the author of a document.

To make the system feasible for digital business, only a small part of the message is encrypted with the private key for signing. This part is called digital hash. The hash code is a function that reduces every possible message to a fixed number of bits. No matter how long the file is, the hash will always be the same length. The trick is that the hash code is different for every mail.

The hash function is a one-way function. It is not possible to create a certain hash code and find a message that would fit exactly that code. The hash code

---

[7]http://www.accessdata.com/

can be seen as a seal on the envelope. Sending along the hash code with an e-mail will guarantee that nobody has altered the e-mail while being in transit, but it does not allow you to prove who the sender was. Because the hash code uses a fixed length, the time for encrypting the hash code is always the same.

Digital signatures use public key encryption technologies, such as RSA, but not in the same way as standard encryption works. Instead of encrypting the message with the public key of the recipient, the hash of the message is encrypted with the private key and is then decrypted with the public key of the sender, which is known to the recipient. Of course, anybody would be able to decrypt the hash of the message, as the public key is public (as the name implies) and may be found on a public key directory server. But the fact that you are able to decrypt the hash of the message with the public key of a certain person already proves that it does come from that person. Only the person who owns the private key is able to create a message that can be decrypted using the public key.

There are two reasons for using the hash code for the digital signature. One is that it is takes too long to encrypt the whole message for signing purposes only. The second reason is that not everyone wants to encrypt a signed message. In many cases the message is meant to be public, but the author wants to certify the authenticity of the message.

In order to encrypt the message safely and sign it at the same time, one would encrypt the mail with the private key to prove that the message is from a certain person and on top one would encrypt the message with the public key of the recipient to make sure nobody is able to view the content.

A digital signature binds a document to the possessor of a particular key, but this is often not good enough, if the time, when it was signed is unknown. A contract signed digitally is not valid if there is no date or time stamp on it. An online purchase of an item at a reduced price, which is available only for a certain period of time, requires a time stamp to certify that the product was bought within the time frame.

A digital time stamp is therefore required to validate the time of the signature. This is done by adding the exact time and date to a document by a third party and encrypting this information with the private key of the third party. This digital time stamp binds a document to its creation at a particular time. This system cannot be used on a world-wide basis as there is no legislation, which guarantees a certain form of date stamp to be valid.

10.4 Privacy on the Internet

10.4.1 Footprints on the Net

Anonymity on the Internet is switched off by default on the Internet. Every person who is online leaves clear footprints behind. This fact is not known to many users. Every web site that is visited is able to create a personal profile of the user without special interaction with the customer. Marketing departments love the possibilities of the Internet to trace the preferences of the customers very accurately.

Most companies today have a privacy policy on their web page stating what they do with the information received from you, both voluntarily by filling in a form and involuntarily by clicking on a link. On-line businesses are eager to collect information to sell products and services that suit the interests of the customers. Some of the online businesses who do not have a privacy statement on their web site, collect information about the customers and visitors and offer the profiles to other organizations.

Internet browsing already reveals a lot about the customer. With every request for a new web page, the name of the browser (e.g. Netscape Communicator 4.61), the operating system (e.g. MacOS 8.6), the preferred language (e.g. French), the web site that has been last visited (e.g. http://www.yahoo.com/) and the IP address (e.g. 194.100.177.194) and domain name (e.g. foo.bar.org) of the computer are sent automatically to the server. JavaScript allows the server to get even more information about the computer of the client, such as screen resolution and number of colors.

These pieces of information are sent back automatically to the server and for most people there is no way to stop it. It is possible to switch off JavaScript, but still a lot of information is sent out. Although each single piece of information that is sent out does not harm your privacy, the sum of information may. Knowing the language and the domain name may reveal the region in which you live, while the browser and the operating system may reveal what type of customer you are. All this information can be used to guide you more precisely through the online offerings, but they can also be used to guide the customer to reveal more information.

Cookies are also very common when trying to accumulate information about a customer. The cookie is a file, which is saved on the customer's computer and contains site specific information, which can be retrieved by the site owner. The cookie may contain information about the password required for a certain web site, a user name, an e-mail address or purchasing information. The design of cookies prohibits the exposure of this information to other sites, but bad implementations in the past have shown that it was possible to extract information. Another problem is the general security issues of the operating system on the computer of the customer, which enables hackers to steal the "cookies.txt" file, without leaving a trace.

The very popular ICQ programs and its Unix predecessor "finger" allow you to retrieve personal information about the owner of a certain e-mail address. The programs also let you see when the person has read e-mail last and if they are currently online. While finger has no centralized database, ICQ stores all user information in a central repository. In order to use ICQ, the user needs to fill in a personal questionnaire, which is partly available to other visitors on the Internet.

Whenever customers use online services, they leave details about themselves, such as name, postal address, phone number, and e-mail address. This information is used in the event the customers returns to the web site. The problem is that the information needs to be stored in a secure place, so that nobody else is able to see the information. Misconceptions and misconfigurations of the web server have provided personal information to the public in the past and it can be expected that there will be incidents in the future as well.

The customer base is becoming more and more the capital of the online business. Getting access to the customer base of a competitor will enable you to target them directly with special offers or direct mailing (or even spam). The customer base also offers a good entry to understanding how the company works and which products are doing well.

Another means of gathering private information about a customer is to give away free software, free baseball caps, free t-shirts in return for personal information. A special type of new free software shows advertising on the screen, while being executed. The advertising is personalized to the profile of the user. One such program is Copernic 99[8], which allows the search of several Internet search engines at the same time. Before downloading the software, the customer is asked to fill in a questionnaire, which makes it easy to target advertising afterwards.

Another way to collect information about a person is to look through newsgroups. Persons who post messages into a certain newsgroup reveal their e-mail addresses and a lot about their personal preferences. People who read and post into a travel-newsgroup for Spain are most likely interested in traveling into that region. Spam mailers use this information to target their messages in a very direct and efficient way.

The Internet is by default an open system and provides means to reveal private information without being asked if nothing is done about it. Although personalization is a good thing to reduce the overhead for every task, the revelation of private information can also have a negative impact on your living.

Many privacy organization are fighting for setting up standards on the Internet, but as the Internet does not belong to anyone in particular it is not possible to enforce standards. New standards evolve slowly and need to bring advantages to the user in order to be accepted.

10.4.2   TRUSTe

The mission of TRUSTe[9], an independent, non-profit privacy organization, is to build customers' trust and confidence on the Internet. The goal is to accelerate growth of electronic business by certifying that a certain online business is trustworthy and that business with that particular site is safe. TRUSTe is a renowned organization, which gets a lot of support from established companies

---

[8]http://www.copernic.com/
[9]http://www.truste.org/

and individual experts and was founded by the Electronic Frontier Foundation (EFF)[10] and the CommerceNet Consortium[11].

TRUSTe issues a branded online seal, called "trustmark", which bridges the gap between users' concerns over privacy and Web sites' desire for a standard on self-regulated information disclosure. The "trustmark" is awarded to web sites that comply to the privacy principles established by TRUSTe and agree to allow third-party control over the enforcement of their privacy policy. A web site with the "trustmark" symbol means that the business has provided a special facility, where customers are able to check which information is gathered, how it is used and if this will be shared with others. By providing these information in a standard way, the customers are able to decide more easily if it is safe to give out additional information, such as postal address or credit card numbers.

The major advantage of TRUSTe over other similar initiatives on the Internet is the fact that the web site owners agree to let an independent third party check if the privacy policy is enforced. These checks are done both on a regular basis and if customers complain about the misuse of private information, additional checks are performed.

10.4.3 The Platform for Privacy Preferences

One of the initiatives of the World Wide Web Consortium is the Platform for Privacy Preference Project (P3P)[12]. The goal of the project to create a standard for privacy practices. Although TRUSTe provides a very good service, the privacy information provided on each TRUSTe site are not machine readable right now. The wording of every site can be different making it more complicated for the end user to understand what exactly will happen to the information provided. The P3P standard defines a way for web sites to inform the users of the site's practice on privacy, before the first page is presented. The information is presented in human and machine readable form, and should then be automatically compared to the privacy preferences of the browser.

Similar to the PICS (Platform for Internet Content Selection) standard[13], the web site owners have to describe the policy. A web service sends a machine-readable proposal in which the organization responsible for the service declares its identity and privacy practices. If a customer gets onto a web site that matches the preferences, the web site is presented without delay. Otherwise the customers will be notified of the privacy practices of the site and need to agree or disagree to these terms. The difference to PICS, which provides a static description of the content of a web page, P3P is able to respond to the wishes of the customer. If customers decide not to allow all information to be

---

[10]http://www.eff.org/

[11]http://www.commercenet.org/

[12]http://www.w3.org/P3P/

[13]http://www.w3.org/PICS/

passed on to the server, they have the possibility to choose which information is passed on and then will enter the site.

As a result of the "agreement" a set of personal information may be transferred automatically from the customer to the site. This will help both the customer and the Internet business to speed up a possible transaction by providing basic data about the customer that would otherwise have to be repeatedly entered. In addition to the list of information that is going to be transferred, a note shows how the data will be used.

Enforcing privacy standards on the Internet has become technically possible, but more important is to inform the electronic customers. Most of them are unaware of privacy issues on the Internet.

10.4.4   Enforcing Anonymity on the Internet

As every move on the Internet is traced by one or the other application or server it is rather easy to get identified. By using digital signatures it is even possible to authenticate each single individual. Enforcing anonymity is much more difficult. E-mails leave traces on the mail server and the transit server, making it possible to trace back the user of the e-mail; web servers log the IP address of the web client, making it also possible to identify the person.

To resolve this problem, anonymous remailers have been set up on the Internet. These are free computer services that privatize e-mail. A remailer allows one to send electronic mail to a newsgroup or to a person without letting the recipient know the name or e-mail address of the sender. Messages sent to such a service are processed in a way that all references to the original sender are removed. The header is completely stripped off and replaced with the e-mail address of the remailer.

Any new user sending e-mails through a remailer will get a new anonymous e-mail address, which makes it possible for others to respond to your e-mail, if desired. Replies to the remailer are then forwarded back to the originator without revealing the identity. In order to provide a successful remailing service, it needs to be easy to use and the system needs to be protected in a very secure way. Neither a hacker nor a governmental agency should be able to break into the system and get information on the users. Additional security can be built in by randomly adding time before sending on the message. This makes it harder to connect mails that have been sent out on your machine to mails that arrive somewhere else. Remailers that encourage the use of encryption software are even more secure, as the administrator is not able to see which messages are sent back and forth.

Anonymous remailers help to enforce privacy, but securing the remailer will not resolve the problem, as it is only part of the system. The mail is sent from your computer to the remailer over a set of computers, which can all be used to intercept the message, therefore it is really important to encrypt the message. Even if your mail is encrypted it can create suspicion. Analyzing the traffic going to and from the remailer can also be used to identify the origin of anonymous messages.

The certainty of anonymity can be increased by sending a message not only through one remailer, but through a chain of remailers. Not all attacks are of a technical nature. Legal action can be used to reveal the author of a mail. This has happened in the past and cannot be excluded in the future. If a response is not required, it is possible to forward e-mails without saving the original in a log file.

The Anonymizer[14] offers anonymous mails and web browsing, which can be tried out by anyone for free. Web browsing through the system is slower compared to direct surfing, but ensures that no information about your system arrives at the target. All system information your browser normally supplies is replaced by values provided by Anonymizer.com. This and similar services provide a valuable service for ensuring privacy on the Internet.

Another service specializing in e-mail is the Nymserver[15], which uses PGP and allows you to send e-mail pseudo-anonymously. In order to be secure that the services do what you expect them do do, visit your own web pages, where you can check the log files and send e-mails to your own address, to see if you can trace them back.

10.5   Fighting Virus and Hoax Virus Warnings

10.5.1   The False Authority Syndrome

Viruses are one of the most misunderstood concepts in the world of computers. Many people panic when they learn there is a virus on their system and start to delete files, format the hard drive, yell at colleagues or do other things that create more problems than the virus could create itself. The most important rule whenever you stumble over a virus is to stay calm and take the time to get more information on the topic or, even better, follow the company rules for anti-virus procedures, if any are available.

Be especially aware about people telling you about viruses. Rob Rosenberger has written an excellent article on this subject[16]. He calls the problem "False Authority Syndrome" (FAS) and the people "ultracrepidarian" (people who give opinions beyond their scope of knowledge). People suffering from FAS often assert conclusions from insufficient data and they habitually label their assumptions as fact. FAS is very common in the computer industry. Many people with a PC, for example, believe that they are able to do a good layout job for their documents just because they have the tools to do so (or at least they think Word is the ideal tool). But most of them have not received training as a designer. In most cases FAS does not do any harm (in our example, other

---

[14]http://www.anonymizer.com/

[15]http://www.nymserver.com/

[16]http://kumite.com/myths/fas/

people may just grumble about the design of the document), but with viruses, FAS does often create more harm than the actual virus does.

Developing a Strategy to Combat Viruses

In order to save your company from losing information or being brought into court because of receiving or spreading a virus, you should consider the following preventive measures for your company.

- **Anti-Virus Programs** – Install them on each desktop and at the firewall level. Provide updates on your Intranet.

- **Backup Strategy** – Develop a backup strategy for all important data. Be sure to do virus checks on your backups as well.

- **Education of the employees** – Organize introductory courses and have a direct link from your Intranet homepage to a frequently asked questions (FAQ) page.

Table 10.3.

In 1991 researchers discovered a new virus. This new virus would erase PC hard disks on March 6th, which is the birthday of Michelangelo, the Italian renaissance painter. Nothing spectacular happened until January 1992, when a computer manufacturer announced that it had shipped PCs with the virus by accident. The media got hold of the press release and built up a story. "Hundreds of thousands of computers" were already infected with the Michelangelo virus, they reported. Although many virus researchers dismissed the hysteria, the media would not stop the press coverage on Michelangelo. Self-made virus experts gave interviews in the news and explained how dangerous this particular virus was.

On March 6th 1992 no more than 20,000 computers world-wide were infected and only a few were really unprepared. Five years later, in March 1997, anti-virus experts could not confirm a single incident related to this particular virus.

Although this example is rather dated, it shows quite impressively how a virus, the media and the False Authority Syndrome can work hand in hand to create hysteria among computer users. The good thing about this event is, that from that time on all major computer manufacturers now include by default, an anti-virus program with their software. Laws have been established in various countries that forbid the distribution of viruses and heavy penalties may be the result of such an activity.

As discussed in Chapter 4, in the section about dark sites, developing a strategy in an emergency won't help you. It will be too late. Be sure to develop the strategy to combat the virus in advance. In case of an emergency everybody needs to know what to do. In case of fire everybody knows, but how many people know how to behave in case of an electronic emergency?

10.5.2   Understanding Viruses

In order to make the right decision in an electronic emergency it is necessary to understand what a virus is. In general, a virus is a computer program, just like any other program you have used. A computer program is composed of a set of commands that are either interpreted at run-time by certain language interpreters or are converted into machine-readable code that is executed at run-time. Computer programs are by themselves neither good or bad, Netscape Communicator or Adobe PhotoShop, for example, have been programmed to be highly useful applications. Viruses, on the other hand, have been programmed with the intention to be harmful. The difference may not be clear to everyone. The intention is not what counts, but the results. Some may think that a word processor is evil, because it has crashed already five times today.

There are three fairly common types of viruses:

- **Boot Sector Virus** – A virus that resides in your boot sector is the worst that can happen. Each time you start up the computer the virus is started as well. This could mean that the virus is infecting all files on your hard disk while booting. Once you start up the computer all files and removable media will become infected. In most cases you have to boot from another device, such as a CD-ROM to bypass the virus start-up, which in the worst cases recognizes anti-virus programs and deletes them before you can start them.

- **Executable Virus** – The virus works by infecting executable files (i.e. programs and libraries). In order to be able to do damage, the executable virus must be loaded into the system. Once it has been started, it attaches itself to all executable files that are started. By attaching the malicious code it is infecting the executable. Normally it adds the virus code to the end of the program. Once the infected file is executed, the virus is executed itself and loads itself into the system restarting the vicious circle. An executable virus remains in memory from the time it is executed until you turn off the computer, even if you exit the program it originally infected. If the virus infects Word, for example, every application that runs after Word will become infected as well, thus spreading the virus all over your system. Just don't start it until you have an anti-virus program run over the particular application. The Michelangelo virus is such a virus. In this case just do not start your computer on March 6th and you will be safe.

- **Macro Virus** – Macro languages are integrated languages within applications that allow automated actions of the application. Often macro languages are used to create automatic layouts or perform calculations based on the input of the user. They allow you to extend the functionality of the application. In most cases the macro-programs are harmless and useful, but due to missing security restrictions in many applications, it is also possible to create viruses. In most cases macro viruses are infecting Microsoft Word and Excel, the most wide-spread applications of their genre. They use Visual Basic to run their macros, which is easy to learn by anyone and very powerful. Unlike the executable virus however, the macro virus does not exist in memory once you close the host application. Loading Word or Excel documents into other applications is harmless. Other programs do not understand the macros. So removing macro viruses is fairly easy. If you load, for example, a Word document into Star Writer, just save it again and the virus is gone.

Virus attacks are a major issue on Windows and Macintosh computers and very common among users of standard applications with macro-languages. On Unix platforms there hasn't been a virus around for years. This is mainly due to the security restrictions of Unix systems and the open standards. Boot sector and executable viruses are less a problem on Intranets and company computers, but more a problem with software pirates. Employees normally tend to get their software from a single source within the company, which makes it easy to verify programs to be virus-free.

Viruses on HTML pages are also a myth. It is possible that certain web pages crash your browser, but this is normally because of badly written code within the browser and not because someone wanted to crash your computer.

Java applet viruses do not exist. Through the sand box principle of Java, it is not possible that Java applets are able to attack other resources. Java applets can't save to your hard disk, read from your hard disk or format your hard disk, unless you enable the applet to do so. But would you click on a button that says, "Please click me, then I will be able to erase your hard disk"?

Java applications on the other hand can be malicious, because they are just yet another executable on your computer. Please see Chapter 11 (Dealing with Java) on the difference between a Java applet and a Java application.

Active X components may be malicious because they are just ordinary executables who have all the rights of a normal program, thus being able to delete files or format your hard disk. Internet Explorer can be configured not to allow these features, but not everybody understands the security levels in the

Levels of Virus Damage

The level of destruction differs from virus to virus. Even the most destructive virus won't be able to do any harm, if you prepare yourself and your computer. With simple measures you are able to protect yourself against them. Viruses can be classified in the following way:

- **Level 1: Annoying** – Displays messages on your screen, but does not cause any real harm.

- **Level 2: Harmless** – Displays messages on your screen and prevents programs from operating, but will cause no permanent damage.

- **Level 3: Harmful** – Destroys the data for the program it has infected, but all other data will remain intact.

- **Level 4: Destructive** – Destroys all data, prevents the computer from operating, etc.

Table 10.4.

browser. A sand box model for Active X components would be nice to have, whereby the program is not able to see any resources on the computer.

As a rule of thumb: If you find a boot sector or executable virus on a company computer there is also a good reason to look for pirated software on that particular computer (and a good chance to find some). Other sources for viruses are fun-programs that are sent around. They are not useful, but some people think they are so funny that everyone needs to see them. Macro viruses on the other hand are a big problem on company computers, where people send their Word documents and Excel spreadsheets to their colleagues and partners. If one document gets infected it spreads fairly fast throughout the company if no protective measures have been taken. Large documents should always be zipped or, even better, should be put on a web page where the others can download the document. This prevents overloading the mail servers and recipients who work on low-bandwidth networks (e.g. working from home via modem) will especially be grateful.

The most malicious macro-virus, which was discovered in March 1999 is called "Melissa" and had a huge impact on the Internet. It is a cross-over between a spam mail and a virus, making the results even worse. Within hours the mail systems of large corporations had to be shut down because of the virus. Although the code is rather simple, the virus has been spreading with such a speed, that everybody is astonished. The message that is sent has a subject of "Important Message From " with the sender's name at the end, lending real credibility to the message. The text of the message is: "Here is that document you asked for ... don't show anyone else ;-)". Attached to the document is a Word document called list.doc, which contains a list of URLs for pornographic sites.

The document contains a Word macro, which is executed when you open the document. The macro, written in Visual Basic, connects to the e-mail client Outlook and pulls fifty e-mail addresses from every directory it can find and sends the document with your name as the sender on to these people. If you are lucky and do not use Microsoft Exchange as your e-mailing backbone, the virus will get fifty addresses and stop working. If you rely on Exchange it will go to the Enterprise directory and get fifty people from there as well. This will eventually lead to a collapse, as the virus is able to replicate itself throughout your company without trouble. Microsoft, the maker of the mailing software, was forced to turn off their internal mailing services for a while to get rid of the virus.

The virus infects the normal.dot template, which is used for every new document in Word normally. The template contains the standard settings of the user. Every document that is created after the virus has hit your machine will therefore become infected, spreading the virus very fast over the Internet. Just a few days later a cousin of Melissa appeared on the Internet. Instead of using Word, it was embedded into an Excel macro, which sends out sixty e-mails from the address book. Other than Melissa, which does this only once per computer, the "Papa" virus sends out the virus every time you open up Excel. But as anti-virus companies got to know Melissa first, Papa was not so difficult to detect and destroy. Papa also contained a bug, which prevented the world-wide distribution within a day.

This virus infected only users of Outlook and Word. If you were using Netscape and Word, or Outlook and Ami Pro, for example, the virus could not spread itself. Again, the intelligence of the virus was not in the code, but in the way the code was spread. Melissa was harmless compared to what could have happened. Using products from only one manufacturer does increase the vulnerability.

10.5.3 Deploying Anti-virus Solutions

As more and more businesses have an Intranet and a direct connection to the Internet, it becomes more and more important to protect not only single computers but also the network as a whole. Therefore it is not enough to install an anti-virus program on every computer. In addition to this standard measure which should not only be applied to network connected computers, but also to stand-alone computers. This protects the computers from being infiltrated by viruses via floppy, zip-disks and other removable media. Most anti-virus solutions are able to scan incoming e-mails as well, but this should not be necessary anymore. All mails should be checked at the firewall. That leads us to the second part of the anti-virus strategy. All inbound and outbound traffic of your company should be checked at the firewall. Incoming traffic needs to be checked in order to protect your data on the Intranet and all computers. It is just as important to check outbound traffic in the form of web pages and e-mail. No program or e-mail should leave your company without being checked for viruses. A virus in a mail or in a program on your web page can destroy the reputation of your company. Although firewall virus checking is very important applying, it to large installations is very difficult, because most of the anti-virus software runs on Windows NT only and not on high-performance Unix, so that scalability is an issue. Checking e-mail only is not such a big problem because e-mail is not a real-time application, but would you want to wait for ten minutes when downloading a file from a web server to have its virus checked?

Let's say you have an important document and need to send it out to a few hundred people. If the document contained a virus, you would spread this virus into dozens of corporations all over the world. Tracing back to the origin will take some time and effort, but it is possible and has been done successfully in the past. The distribution of viruses is illegal in most countries. So spreading the virus could have legal consequences, which could either hit the sender directly or the company she or he works for.

Regular backups are an important measure against computer viruses. This is true even if you are backing up the virus that eventually caused the damage. Even if the virus is in the backup, you can safely restore all of your data, obtain one of the anti-virus solutions and remove the virus before continuing with your work.

10.5.4 Required Software

As mentioned above it is important to install an anti-virus solution on every single computer within your company. There are many different solutions available on the market (see Table 10.5 for an overview). Most of them have the same basic functionality and vary in pricing, speed and support. Most important for any anti-virus software is the availability of the virus definition files. Virus definition files contain the information about the viruses and updates should be available on demand (via a web site, for example) and via push technology (e.g. an update every week), in order to keep the software up-to-date. The best solution is useless if the database is old.

No matter which of the solutions you choose, the following components should be always be included as a minimum:

- **Scanner** – This part of the solution scans all files on local hard disks, floppies, and network drives for viruses. It does not work automatically in the background; it needs to be started by the user.

- **Shield** – This part of the solution works in the background and looks out for viruses while downloading software from the Internet or inserting a floppy into the disk drive. This part of the process is automated.

- **Cleaner** – Once a virus has been found, it needs to be removed. This is what this part of the solution delivers. It scans the database for remedies. Often it is easy enough to delete the virus, but some viruses are destroying the actual data, making it impossible to restore the original state.

Anti-Virus Technology

At the writing of the book some of the most used solutions are the following (sorted alphabetically):

Company	URL
Datafellows Company	http://www.datafellows.com/
Dr. Solomons	http://www.drsolomons.com/
IBM Antivirus	http://www.av.ibm.com/
McAfee Associates, Inc.	http://www.mcafee.com/
Norton Antivirus	http://www.norton.com/
Thunderbyte	http://www.thunderbyte.com/
ViruSafe Virus Center	http://www.eliashim.com/

Table 10.5.

Once you have installed such a solution, viruses like the Michelangelo or Melissa virus won't have a chance on your computer and your local network anymore. Whenever you receive a new file, no matter how, the shield will start to check for a virus and an alarm goes off if something is found. Most anti-virus solutions erase the virus immediately, not requiring you to do anything about it. Just be sure to inform the sender of the file about the virus, so that the source of the virus is extinguished. In order to catch all incoming viruses, you need to update your virus definition file on a regular basis, such as every week. Otherwise the newest viruses will just slip through.

Even though firewall anti-virus solutions may not be a viable solution, some additional measures for your web and ftp servers should to be taken. If you cannot virus check all files on the fly, then let scripts run over your web server once a week to check for viruses to be sure that you are not spreading viruses all over the planet.

10.5.5 Ignoring Hoax Viruses and Chain Letters

Some viruses cannot be caught by software because of their implementation. They are not spread by computer code but by users (normally via e-mail). Therefore it is important to understand the threat.

In October 1998 the whole e-mail system at the U.S. Postal Service broke down. It appeared that a well-meaning employee forwarded the "Win a Holiday" virus alert to every email account in the usps.gov domain. Other employees hit the "reply to all" buttons, causing servers to overload. The administrators at USPS had to perform an emergency maintenance to get the e-mail back flowing again.

The "Win a Holiday" hoax

```
VIRUS WARNING !!!!!!
If you receive an email titled ''WIN A HOLIDAY" DO NOT
open it.
It will erase everything on your hard drive.  Forward
this letter out to as many people as you can.
This is a new, very malicious virus and not many
people know about it.  This information was announced
yesterday morning from Microsoft;
Please share it with everyone that might access the
internet.  Once again, pass this along to EVERYONE
in your address book so that this may be stopped.
Also, do not open or even look at any mail that says
''RETURNED OR UNABLE TO DELIVER"
The virus will attach itself to your computer
components and render them useless.  Immediately delete
any mail items that say this.  AOL has said that this
is a very dangerous virus and that there is NO remedy.
Send this to all your online friends ASAP.
```

Table 10.6.

The "Win a Holiday" virus alert is actually a simple e-mail. It tells the users not to open another e-mail titled "WIN A HOLIDAY". Someone within

USPS got so scared by this virus warning that she or he sent it to all employees who in return got even more scared thus creating an avalanche of e-mails that crashed the mail servers. This simple e-mail disrupted the whole communications network of USPS with a few lines of text. Viruses are not necessarily cleverly written programs, but may also be cleverly written e-mails (called virus hoaxes in most cases).

The virus hoax did not attack the mail servers directly, but targeted the employees, who (by default) are afraid of viruses. For many people the Internet is a mystery, therefore they believe whatever is written in e-mails, especially if renowned companies like AOL or Microsoft are mentioned. It is a myth that opening e-mails enables viruses to erase your hard disk (more myths can be found at Kumite's[17] web site). This applies only to the e-mail itself and not to its attachments which may be infected by viruses. And keep in mind, it is neither Microsoft's nor AOL's job to release virus alerts. If such an e-mail mentions a company which releases virus alerts, then go to that particular company web page and look in the news section to verify the e-mail.

If you receive virus warnings or chain letters in your e-mail, be careful about them. An Internet chain letter is a message, which is forwarded to hundreds of people. The recipient is requested to send it on. If each of them sends the letter on to only ten other people, the ninth re-sending results in a billion e-mail messages. Either delete it or send a copy of the mail to your local system administrators or security officer and they will be able to tell you if it is a real threat or just another virus hoax. Do not send it to your friends and relatives because you will be congesting the network and you lend the reputation of your company to the message (and your own as well), making it appear to be authentic even when that is not the case. Everybody in your company should understand what a virus hoax is. Have a direct link from your Intranet homepage to a FAQ section on viruses and virus hoaxes, where all employees can educate themselves on the latest developments.

Also be careful when receiving "updates" via e-mail. If you have not requested an update for a certain program, do not install the application that is attached to the e-mail, especially if the mail comes from a mass mailing or was posted in a newsgroup. In January 1999 a "bug fix" for the Internet Explorer was distributed via e-mail. It seemed to come from Microsoft Support, but instead of an update for the browser, it installed a Trojan horse on your computer. The file "IE0199.exe" displays an error message after starting the application, so that the user thinks that something went wrong during installation and doesn't bother about it afterwards, but the Trojan horse remains in memory and tries to connect on various ports to a Bulgarian server[18] and exchanges information with the server. The virus actually replaces a file in the Windows environment, so that it is started each time you reboot.

---

[17]http://www.kumite.com/myths/
[18]http://www1.infotel.bg/

The U.S. Postal Service example shows quite dramatically what harm false virus warnings can do to your company. Though these e-mails do not pose any real risk, they may lead to significant productivity loss and disruption in the environment, which may mean a financial loss for your company. Anti-virus programs are not able to stop virus hoax e-mails. Computer programs are not spreading the virus, but humans are doing it in good faith. Therefore it is very important to inform all employees and educate them. An excellent resource for more information on urban legends and net hoaxes is the urban legends web site of the Mining Company[19].

10.6   Conflicts in the Information Age

10.6.1   Information Attack

Although you may think that nobody is interested in information about your company, there may be someone out there who will be trying to do exactly this. Your security experts may have a tendency to concentrate on threats they are trained to deal with, but attackers do what they are good at doing, so your security experts may miss the protective measures that would actually have been necessary.

Most hackers are good at guessing passwords or good at stealing them. Many people buy software that uses pre-installed passwords. These passwords need to be changed, once the system is up and running, but unfortunately many people do not do this, enabling many people to enter a certain system without trouble. Even if you change your password, there is a good chance of guessing it. Many people use the company name, the name of a spouse, a birthday or any other information that can be remembered easily. Many people use "hello" or the login name as a password. Do a test, go to the computers of your colleagues or employees and try "hello" or the login name. I am sure you will find some computers that are easily unlocked.

There are many programs on the market, which allow you to test if a given login uses a password that can be guessed easily. These programs rely on multiple dictionaries with words from several languages. It encrypts a word from the dictionary and compares it to the encrypted password until it finds a match. One of these programs is simply called "Crack", which is freeware.

Complex software packages will most likely have bugs in them. Bugs normally terminate a program or refuse to execute a certain function, but some of them may lead to weakening the security of the system. A bug in a word processor most probably won't open up your computer to the Internet, but if a software server, such as the web server contains a bug, it may allow intruders to enter your computer by persuading the web server to let them in. Sometimes the reason for security holes is not buggy software but the configuration

---

[19]http://urbanlegends.miningco.com/

of software. Configuring a firewall in a wrong way may open up your Intranet and allow hackers to read your corporate data without trouble or maybe worse modify or delete the data.

In some cases the system is not insecure, but still data is revealed to people who should not have access to it. A person who has been authorized to enter a system uses resources to modify the status of their authorization and is able to access data and applications which should be not accessible to her or him. This is often done by using documented and undocumented weaknesses of operating systems and programs to bypass the security system. A viable way of doing this would be to let an intruder walk up to a certain computer and allow him or her to reboot the machine. After a reboot the intruder could install a virus or copy confidential data from the hard disk. With Windows-based systems it is especially easy to get into the system. If you, for example, protect Windows 95 with a password, pressing "Escape" will be enough to skip the password protection. On Windows NT you enter the system as guest and use the "getadmin" tool to receive super-user privileges. It could be even easier to steal backup tapes that were not encrypted.

Company phone books can be also stolen, or company literature simply asked for by phone. The attacker might pose as someone with something useful to sell, or pose as a customer trying to convince you that you should give them some information.

10.6.2   Information Warfare

Officially information warfare does not exist, but yet all governments are developing mechanisms to protect themselves in the event of an attack. Some may be developing tools to attack. Information warriors try to capture or destroy information, processes and systems of the enemy, while securing the information already known to the attackers.

Information warfare can be conducted on three different levels: personal, corporate and global. The methods are always the same. It is an attack on the privacy of certain persons, companies or countries. The attackers try to disclose information on them. The information is saved in many different databases, where the attackers try to get access. The bank has information on financial details, the doctors about the health and the corporations, information on new products. All this information can be used against you. They can be falsified and published. The difference between the three types of warfare is the dimension of damage

Battles are fought every day in information warfare, as individuals, companies and governments try to penetrate computer systems of enemies and competitors. The more technological advanced organizations or persons are the more vulnerable they become.

The weapons in the information war are most likely used by cyber terrorists, but it may happen in the future that armies will use the weapons in a

Weapons in Information Warfare

There are many weapons, which can be used in information wars, some of them are described here:

- **Chipping** – Replace standard chips with Trojan horses.

- **EMP Bombs** – Destroy the electronics of all computers through nuclear and non-nuclear detonation.

- **Human Engineering** – Pretend to be someone else to gain information over the phone, fax or e-mail.

- **Jamming** – Use this to block communication of the enemy by emitting electronic noise.

- **Logic Bombs** – A certain type of Trojan horse that is able to release a virus or a worm.

- **Nano Machines** – Little robots that attack the hardware of the enemy.

- **Spoofing** – Faked e-mails and TCP/IP packets that bypass the firewalls and other security measures.

- **Trap Doors** – Mechanisms to allow attackers to enter a system without being noticed by the security settings.

- **Trojan Horses** – Code fragments that hide inside of programs and perform undesired functions.

- **Viruses** – Code fragments that copy themselves into a program or modify it.

- **Worms** – An independent program that copies itself from one computer to another.

Table 10.7.

strike against the enemy. The information society is extremely vulnerable to disruption. Electronic communication and data exchange have become very important. Attacking the information backbones can create much more damage than a bomb could do.

10.6.3 Cyber-terrorism

The Internet reflects the real world using new technologies. So it reflects not only the pleasant side, but also the evil side of life. Terrorism is a threat in the real world and it is a real threat in the cyber world. Cyber-terrorism is a threat to everybody who is connected to the Internet, no matter if it is, for example, a single person, a club, a company or governmental agency. Terrorists use force to coerce others in order to promote their political or social objectives. There is no difference in motivation for "normal" and "cyber" terrorists. They use the computing resources to intimidate others.

Protection from Cyber-terrorism

In order to be protected from terrorist attacks over the Internet you should follow some simple rules:

- **Passwords** – No corporate computer system may have passwords that can be guessed or found in a dictionary. A regular password audit is necessary to check for compliance.

- **Network** – Change the network configuration as soon as vulnerabilities become apparent. Network audits on a regular basis are also necessary.

- **Patches** – Assign a security officer the task of subscribing to the important security mailing lists and informing everybody about new security leaks.

- **Audits** – Every system needs to be checked in regular intervals and log files need to be analyzed on a regular basis.

Table 10.8.

Cyber-terrorists are able to destroy the business of a large corporation, if the company did not take any measures to prevent any action that could be provoked by terrorists. Banks, which connect their internal databases to the Internet are just as vulnerable as companies who do business-to-business transactions over the Internet. As soon as you open a little hole into your firewall to let partners and customers participate in your processes and share your data, you create a potential security risk.

Terrorists have realized over the past few years that killing a president or CEO of a company just provokes anger among the employees and the public and does not do any damage to the attacked institution, as the function is not bound to the person anymore. Although it is a very tragic incident, if someone is being killed, it does not stop a company or government from working.

The Internet offers the terrorist many more possibilities of damaging an institution. Shutting down a power plant via computer networks (by infiltrating private networks or by using security holes on the Internet) can be done from remote locations, without having to fear being caught on site. Finding the terrorists is more difficult as masquerading techniques and stolen accounts can hide terrorists quite well. And companies are not very keen on publishing information about a threat, as they fear the bad publicity.

Cyber-terrorists have different strategies for attacking an institution. Depending on the type of institution they may have different strategies:

- **Virus Attack** – A software company could be attacked by planting a virus into a software package. The software is sold to customers and the virus destroys valuable information on their computers or opens a back door to their Intranets.

- **Alteration of Information** – A bank could be attacked by altering bank accounts. Money could be moved from one account to another thus ruining the image of some of the customers and of the bank.

- **Cutting off Communication** – An airline could be attacked by cutting off the communication between aeroplanes and the tower at the airport. In the worst case, the aeroplane is not able to land anymore and crashes.

- **Killing from a Distance** – A hospital could be attacked by changing patient information. The patient records could be altered in such a way that a kidney patient will get a liver transplant or the dose of a certain drug is altered to kill the patient.

- **Spreading Misinformation** – A company could be attacked easily by misinformation. The misinformation is spread over the Internet and hundreds of thousands of customers are misled by this information. Terrorist attacks can have different effects, ranging from a simple denial of service up to assassination.

In 1996 the US government created the "Commission of Critical Infrastructure Protection". The commission consists of all important companies in the field of power generation, communications technology and computer industry. The companies are united to develop solutions for an eventual cyber-terrorist attack against the United States. Another important goal is to create awareness for the problem in the private and public sector, as many companies and agencies are relatively ignorant about this topic.

There is no way to make your company 100 percent secure, except for shutting down all connections to the outside world, but this ruins your business. Nobody will be able to communicate with you and your company anymore. Mission-critical systems should be disconnected from public networks. Apart from isolation, the most common method of protection is encryption. Another solution is to use the firewall to monitor all communication between the corporate network and the public Internet.

Cyber-terrorists have nothing in common with hackers who try to break into systems. Most hackers try to break into systems for the sake of breaking in. Cyber-terrorists break into systems in order to harm the owner, by stealing, deleting or altering information, products and services.

Another type of online activism has begun to emerge called "hacktivism". These are online activists who break into web servers to demonstrate for something. In July 1998 protesters of the nuclear tests in India hacked more than three hundred sites and displayed an atomic mushroom on the home page instead of the normal content. One of the sites was the official Wimbledon tennis tournament web site[20]. The hacktivists want to create awareness for a political reason. They are not interested in destroying or stealing data. They claim that the use of the digital form of civil *ungehorsam* and online sit-ins is a right for everyone. Their cyber-demonstrations have nothing to do with cyber-terrorism, but as in real life the protest for a "good thing" is always relative.

On September 9th, 1998 the web site of the Pentagon was under attack by members of the "Electronic Disturbance Theater"[21] (EDT). The EDT wanted to protest against the treatment of the Zapatists in the Chiapas region in Mexico. By destroying the Pentagon web service they wanted to make a statement and urge the US government to reconsider its position on that topic. Unfortunately for these cyber activists the Pentagon was prepared for such an attack and responded to it by replying the requests that were sent, to the web server. The server of the EDT broke down before it could do any harm to the Pentagon server. This event shows quite clearly that the US government is prepared.

Another incident started in May 1999, when some hackers started an information war against the FBI[22], putting the web site out of service. Although the FBI was able to stop the attacks within a very short time, they could not get up the web site within days. While they were defending their web site the hackers broke into the web site of the US Senate[23] and changed the home page with their own. AntiOnline[24] documents these incidents, making it possible for everyone to see which web sites were and are under attack.

Governments throughout the world have recognized the threats and have started to protect the critical infrastructures, such as services in the telecom-

---

[20]http://www.wimbledon.org/
[21]http://www.thing.net/ rdom/ecd/ecd.html
[22]http://www.fbi.gov/
[23]http://www.senate.gov/
[24]http://www.antionline.com/

munication, finance, traffic, energy and water industries and emergency and governmental services. Although there haven't been any serious attacks on these vital services, there is no doubt that this will change in the future. The Internet enables anybody ranging from a country down to a single person to disrupt life for some people or even destroy a whole country.

10.6.4   The Eternity Service

In order to prevent terrorist attacks on Internet services, Ross Anderson from Cambridge University has developed a methodology[25] to manage data. By using many servers all over the world that are interconnected, it is possible to achieve very high reliability of storage of data and services. He called it the Eternity service, which provides new ways of creating, storing and handling copies of data of high importance with a very high degree of reliability. The Eternity service is designed to be resistant not only to threats such as natural disasters and vandalism, but also to political or court decisions, religious leader orders and activities of secret services.

The Internet was designed as a communication platform to be resistant to denial of service attacks; when parts of the Internet are destroyed it does not harm the Internet as a whole. Some services may be destroyed, but if backups exist, it is possible to reinstall them in another area. The Internet is supposed to survive a thermonuclear war.

The Eternity service proposes to construct a storage platform with similar properties using the Internet as the infrastructure. In order to replicate data across the Internet one has to use redundancy and scattering techniques.

Availability is a very important goal in the private sector. Actually far more important than confidentiality and integrity. There are many types of documents that need to be protected from destruction. Records of births and deaths, medical case notes and documents on property of real estate are just a few examples of documents that are vital for society in general and for a single person in particular. Without these documents a person can become a nobody.

Another problem in this rapidly changing world is the longevity of documents. Computer formats appear and disappear very fast, so data cannot be read anymore and programs cannot be executed anymore. Through the use of Eternity servers that are set up all over the Internet, important data can be saved in a very secure way. Although an attacker may be able to destroy parts of the Internet the stored information will be still available just as the regular Internet services won't be disrupted.

The Eternity service is not available right now, as the database servers have not been set up. All information from different customers are stored into the database and replicated all over the world. The data is encrypted in order to maintain anonymity of the customers and maintain the confidentiality of the documents. The information is buried in the vast amount of other information

---

[25]http://www.cl.cam.ac.uk/users/rja14/eternity/eternity.html

and even if the particular document can be found by hackers they are not able to pass on the information.

10.7   Client-based Security

10.7.1   Digital Certificates

A digital certificate is the most commonly used way for binding a cryptographic key with one or more attributes of a user. It allows the receiver of a message to verify the authenticity of the communication. Digital certificates have greatly helped to build up trust in electronic business on the Internet.

A digital certificate is a file, which is encrypted and password-protected that includes personal information about the owner of the certificate, such as the name of the holder, the postal address and the e-mail address. Other personal information can be encoded as well, such as the credit card number, depending on the business requirements. A public key is included and used to verify the digital signature of a message sender previously signed with the matching private key. Also included is the name of the certification authority which issued the digital certificate and the validity period of the certificate.

A list of certificate authorities that issue digital certificates can be found in Table 10.9. In order to issue a certificate the authority needs to verify the personal information of the holder. This can be done by different means, depending on the required security involved. The cheapest version of a digital certificate involves checking that the supplied e-mail address is valid. More secure solutions require the holder of the certificate to validate by presenting themselves in person or sending in a copy of their passport or driving license.

Digital certificates are used to secure the communication between browsers and servers (using SSL encryption), between customer and merchant (using credit card SET encryption) or between two e-mail partners (using S/MIME).

The client-server authentication using SSL is done through the following process. When accessing an online banking solution, for example, a series of messages is exchanged before the first secure page is displayed. The browser connects to the server and the server sends its digital certificate to the browser. This is done for two reasons, first of all, it is used to identify the server and second the public key, which is stored in the certificate is used to encrypt the session key. The identification of the server certificate is checked against the certification authority that issued it. If the identity is ok, then a session key is created, which is used for encrypting the following communication.

Once this has been decided on, a dialogue box pops up and informs the user of the digital certificate on the server and asks the user to select the appropriate digital certificate. The certificate is then passed on to the server, which checks the validity of the certificate and the certification authority.

Most Internet applications do not require the customer to have a digital certificate, as the process for distributing certificates in large numbers is still

Free Digital Certificates

Many sites offer a free digital certificate for private use. The following list contains some of the more popular certificate authorities (in alphabetical order):

Company	URL
Baltimore Technologies	http://www.baltimore.ie/
BelSign	http://www.belsign.be/
Thawte	http://www.thawte.com/
TrustCenter	http://www.trustcenter.de/
VeriSign	http://www.verisign.com/
Xcert	http://www.xcert.com/

Table 10.9.

complex and expensive to handle. It is expected that the process will be simplified and standardized to make digital certificates feasible for more applications on the Internet.

United Parcel Services[26] has started two services in Mid 1999, which allow businesses to send signed legal documents instantly over the Internet. The shipping company has launched a digital certificate-based confidential document exchange service and a service to exchange documents among disparate e-mail systems. Both services cost customers less than the price of shipping an overnight letter. Unfortunately the service came in too late for the contract of my book.

10.7.2 Smart Cards

Smart Cards have been heavily promoted in Europe and are slowly becoming popular throughout the rest of the world. In Europe applications in commerce, public transport and health care have been developed over the past few years and are highly successful.

Depending on the type of application, different levels of memory on the smart card are necessary. If you want to put data or applications on the smart card only once, it is sufficient to put a little chip on the card that contains read only memory (ROM). If your program needs to store temporary information on the card, for example, when exchanging data with a terminal, random access memory (RAM) should be added. Once the smart card has been removed from

---

[26]http://www.ups.com/

the terminal the information is lost, though. Most applications require electronically erasable programmable read only memory (EEPROM) which allows data and application to be stored permanently on the smart card. Other than with ROM only smart cards, the applications and data can be loaded, executed and removed onto the card at any time.

Types of Smart Cards

Smart cards have an embedded microchip instead of magnetic strip. The chip contains all the information a magnetic strip contains but offers the possibility of manipulating the data and executing applications on the card. Three types of smart cards have established themselves:

- **Contact Cards** – Smart cards that need to inserted into a reader in order to work, such as a smart card reader or automatic teller machines.

- **Contactless Cards** – Contactless smart cards don't need to be inserted into a reader. Just waving them near a reader is sufficient for the card to exchange data. This type of cards is used for opening doors.

- **Combi Cards** – Combi Cards contain both technologies and allow a wider range of applications.

Table 10.10.

Today actually all smart cards on the market use EEPROM chips. Some factors limit the size of EEPROM on the smart card. While 128 or 256 Megabytes are fairly common in computers today, smart cards only store up to 16 Kilobytes. This is more than a thousand times smaller, but still enough to hold complex applications. In the early eighties 16 Kb actually were more than most applications needed, but as graphic user interfaces have become popular and the complexity of the programs continues to rise, the amount of memory a program requires has increased dramatically, just to name a few factors. Smart cards have many restrictions that do not allow them to use so much memory and fast processors. Smart card chips have standardized dimensions and no power supply other than when introduced into a smart card reader. The price for EEPROM is still very high, as computers use mainly RAM. These are some of the factors that limit the size of memory.

The newer releases of smart cards are able to hold more than a single application. The applications do not even have to be from one organization only. The application of electronic cash provided by your bank can be on the same card as the access control to your office. In order to allow multi-functionality it is necessary to ensure security for every application. If an application runs on the card it should not be allowed to view data stored by other applications on the same card. Each application needs to have its own compartment on the smart card. The limitation to multi-functionality is the amount of memory on the smart card itself.

Information on smart cards can be accessed in four different ways, depending on the type of application you want to provide and the type of memory you are using. With read only smart cards information is loaded once onto the card. Once information has been stored on the card, it can then only be read. It is not possible to add, modify or erase information. An application could be, for example, to allow access to a building. The smart card would contain some information on the user, such as the name and employee number. The information could be stored in a ROM, as the information will not change for a given employee.

Some smart cards, such as the telephone cards, allow you to add information only. Every time someone makes a phone call using a phone card, the application checks how many units have not been used and allows a phone call to be made. Every unit that is used during the phone call is added to the list of used units. The cards do not allow the modification or deletion of information thus preventing fraud by putting the cards back into their initial state.

Some smart cards do allow information to be deleted or modified, just like on a hard disk; these are often used for storing data. Some data on the smart card is stored in such a way that it can never be accessed. The application is brought once onto the card and can then only be executed without access to the source code or data associated to it. Key generation and password processing are two applications that should never be revealed to the outside world in order to protect all other applications on the card. Table 10.11 contains a short overview over the different types of smart cards.

Security is the major issue with smart cards. If a hacker is able to copy or manipulate the content of one card to another one it may destroy the business of the smart card application issuer. This means security functions have to be at the core of all smart cards. However, different applications require different levels of security and absolute security cannot be guaranteed.

In order to make the smart cards secure against manipulation, the basis to ensuring effective protection against manipulation or copying of smart cards requires a secure hardware whereby physical countermeasures need to be taken. A secure operating system and system security is necessary, which means that the communication between all components involved in the security system is encrypted. The overall level of security is only as good as that of the weakest element in the chain.

Information Access

Information on smart cards can be accessed in four different ways, depending on the type of application you want to provide and the type of memory you are using:

- **Read Only** – Information can only be read from the smart card.

- **Add Only** – Information can only be added to the smart card.

- **Modify or Delete** – Information can only be modified or deleted.

- **Execution Only** – Programs can be executed only without seeing any information.

Table 10.11.

Common threats for smart cards are loss of authenticity (the uniqueness of the card cannot be guaranteed), integrity (the completeness of information cannot be guaranteed), confidentiality (the privacy of the information cannot be guaranteed) and availability (the service on the card cannot be guaranteed).

Smart cards are protected by the PIN code. The security issue is that the PIN code needs to be entered via a keyboard. Technically it would be possible to intercept the communication between the keyboard and the smart card reader. Therefore newer smart card readers such as the GemPlus GCR 410, are connected between computer and keyboard therefore ensuring that the PIN code is not transmitted to the computer.

Today smart cards are already widely used. Typical smart card applications include the following:

- **Health** – Smart cards containing personal health information. This information allow the transfer of patient information between doctors.

- **Finance** – Cash cards, such as the Mondex card in the UK and the Geld-Karte in Germany (see Chapter 13).

- **Mobile Communications** – The GSM (Global System for Mobile Communications) network uses smart cards for identification of the user. It allows users to switch phones and keep their numbers.

- **Stationary Telecommunications** – Typically pre-paid phone cards are based on the smart card system. It reduces the cost for maintenance and handling and prevents fraud, theft and credit loss.

- **Transportation** – Payment for underground tickets is a very common application, and the payment for parking tickets.

Smart card applications become more popular as they enable customers to pay for goods and services. The number of smart card readers attached to computers is still very low making the smart card not yet a viable solution on the Internet. As more and more keyboard makers include smart card readers into their keyboards and the latest releases of operating systems include drivers for smart cards in the standard installation, it is only a matter of time until smart cards will become the preferred method of authentication and payment on the Internet.

10.7.3 Biometric Identification

The most common way to identify a person is a password-based solution, such as with digital certificates or smart cards. But passwords are not perfect. In order to make them secure, they need to be difficult to guess. But this makes them also difficult to remember. This is acceptable as long as one has only very few devices to operate. But as more and more become available electronically, more and more passwords and PINs need to be remembered. Your mobile phone, your bank account, your e-mail, your computer, your online shopping sites all require passwords or PINs in order to recognize you. Biometrics offers a solution to the password problem by replacing the authentication method, so that no passwords have to be remembered.

Biometric identification is a means for automatically identifying persons, based on their unique physical characteristics or behavioral traits. It is an upcoming alternative to digital certificates and smart cards, with the advantage that it is strictly based on the physics of the human and does not rely on any files, which could be copied or on passwords, which can be cracked. Instead of using a technology that is based on something you know or something you possess, biometrics is based on who people are or what they do.

Everyone has unique and stable features, such as fingerprints and eyes and standard ways of doing things, such as speaking and writing. These features are much harder to forge and are almost always available. Only in a very few cases are the features not available, such as when you break your arm and are not able to write for a certain period of time.

Biometric technologies include fingerprint, iris and retina scanning. The analysis of handwriting is also a common method for biometric identification. Voice and hand print recognition are also upcoming technologies, which have started to become promising.

Although the technologies have been available for a few years, very few companies are using biometric technologies so far. The technology is still immature and too expensive. The rate of false identification is often too high to be tolerated and users resist some forms of biometric identification. The scan of the retina is a procedure most people will be unwilling to support, for example.

As accuracy is lower than with digital technologies, trade-offs needs to be compensated. This is often done by using more than one technology to identify the user. A fingerprint scan in combination with voice recognition will be more reliable than one of the technologies alone. Biometric applications are very CPU intensive and therefore require high-end computers to support a large base of users.

Issues with Biometric Identification

The identification via physical attributes has many advantages over passwords and digital certificates, but there are also some drawbacks:

- **Acceptance** – Biometric identification is still not widely accepted.

- **Accuracy** – By design no biometric approach is 100 percent accurate.

- **Costs** – The cost for implementing and maintaining biometric systems is higher than a password based system.

- **Privacy** – Personal information is required for biometrics to work. This information needs to be kept in a secure place, otherwise it is possible to replicate it or otherwise misuse it.

Table 10.12.

Biometric authentication requires the users to register fingerprints, voice prints and faces first. These features are then digitized and key features are extracted and converted to templates. This templates are then compared with the person in front of the identification device. Matches will never be exact, as the conversion from analogue to digital always includes loss of information. In order to reduce the number of false rejections or acceptances, it is necessary to adjust the sensitivity threshold very carefully. Other than digital technologies, which either have a completely correct answer or completely false answers, biometric technologies deliver answers like "most probably", "very likely", "probable" and "unlikely". Depending on the hardware and software used the threshold needs to be set in such a way that wrong answers are eliminated.

It is rather unlikely that every computer will be equipped with a biometric device in the near future. But manufacturers of embedded systems, such as mobile phones may more easily embed such a functionality into their devices. In order to operate a mobile phone a fingerprint could be used instead of the PIN, making the system more secure without the need for a larger infrastructure. The mobile phone would allow the caller to scan in its fingerprint and store it in the device. Every time callers switch on the phone, they would need to identify themselves via fingerprint.

Another very promising technology is voice recognition as it can be used at a distance, just like a password. It is possible to use voice recognition to deal with your bank and initiate money transfers, for example. The major disadvantage of voice recognition is the ability to record the human voice and replay it by another person whenever necessary. Therefore additional security measures need to be implemented.

Signatures have been used widely in the past, but they were also very easy to forge. In order to enhance the security for signatures, biometric sensors do not only register what you have written, but also how you have written it. Such a device measures the speed and direction of your hand movements as you form your signature. In order to make it even more secure, some devices also measure the force with which you press the pen against the paper and the angle at which you hold the pen.

Besides the traditional biometric applications, more and more companies have started to develop more unusual systems. Security systems that detect the body odor of the individual are planned. BTG[27] has developed a technology that identifies individuals by the blood vessel patterns in the back of the hand. These are just two examples of what can be measured from the body. There are even more patterns which are unique and characteristic for every single person.

With the introduction of new, more powerful hardware and more intelligent software, biometrics will become the solution for personal identification.

10.8   Server-based Security

10.8.1   The Need for a Firewall

As more and more companies become Internet-enabled, by setting up public web servers and internal networks, the necessity for security also rises. Network security can be implemented through different means, but most commonly through a firewall.

---

[27] http://www.btg.co.uk/

Firewalls are systems that protect trusted networks from untrusted networks and vice versa. A firewall implements an access-control policy, which allows users from either network to access certain resources on the other network. Every owner of a network needs to determine if there are any resources that need protection. Companies will most likely need a firewall to protect their internal documents from the outside world.

Firewalls are designed to prevent access to certain systems even though they are connected to the Internet. This access-control is helping to protect the software and the data on that particular device. Firewalls help to protect systems against vandalism and theft, which are the main threats to every system.

A system connected directly to the Internet offers in most cases one or more services. In order to protect this service a firewall can deny all other access to the computer. A web server, for example, should serve web pages to customers. In order to maintain the server additional services are running, which are necessary for the administrator to add files or applications. These services should only be open to the administrator. Other users should not even have the possibility to determine if these services are run. A firewall can help to determine in advance where the user is coming from and offer the services the client is allowed to see. Normal customers will then see the web page, while the administration services (such as ftp, telnet) are restricted to a certain range of IP addresses.

In order to secure these services several strategies can be used. The most conservative would be to place the Internet services on an isolated web server, which has no connection to the internal network. This offers the best security, but also the least value to the customers, as the information will never be up-to-date. The second strategy is to use application proxies that require no additional investment in software and hardware, but require a blind trust in the used proxy software and the proxy administrators. The third alternative is to use a multi-layered firewall, which does not require additional investment in consulting, but a lot of configuration.

Firewalls play a central role in any security strategy. They allow internal clients to access resources on the Internet without exposing the internal client to external threats. For the outside world, the whole company is accessing the Internet as one person through the use of proxies. This strategy does not reveal anything about the internal networking structure of the company.

More sophisticated firewall solutions are using a multi-layered approach, whereby an external firewall is followed by a demilitarized zone (DMZ) and a second firewall, which protects the internal network. In the DMZ a company would typically put all servers that are needed for customer interaction, such as web-server, ftp-server and mail-gateway. Every service that you offer to your customer will require an additional hole through your firewall. Every hole increases the possibility of a security breach. Therefore a multi-layered approach offers a good solution for adding functionality, without decreasing the security level.

10.8.2   Server Protection

Companies that connect servers to the Internet need to be concerned about hackers abusing the offered resources for illegal purposes. This can range from adding pirated software to the web server and publishing the URL to people who are looking for that software to using the resources, such as processor speed to do large calculations or printers to print out thousands of pages and get them distributed. Often break-ins are used appearing as someone else and attacking other more protected systems.

The result of the launched attacks are often false claims by law enforcement agencies and other Internet sites claiming that the owner has tried the break in. Even if the claims are proved to be wrong, it can damage the business of a web site. In order to help law enforcement to find the hacker it is necessary to make backups of the log files on a regular basis and ensure that all applications and services are producing log files correctly.

An alarming signal for a break in is when a log file has been deleted or the history of the unix shell is empty. Hackers will try to attack the system by breaking the passwords of legitimate users. This makes it easier for the attacker to move around the system without other users being suspicious on the system at the same time.

Most Attacks are successful because of configuration errors of the external systems or errors in the operating system, the network devices or the applications that run on the external servers and are run in super-user mode. Bugs in these programs can open up the system to an attack by passing on the powers of the programs to the attacker.

Another common way of breaking into a system is missing protection of important files. In the past many hackers have been able to break into a system, because they could get hold of the password file, which they could easily download via ftp or http. The passwords are encrypted, but breaking the encryption can be done easily on the system of the hacker, so nobody will notice a hacker trying to guess a password. The hacker will decrypt the password file and then enter the system as a legitimate user.

Although web servers are common points of attack, newer releases of the software offer good protection and only configuration accidents allow attackers to bypass the software. The situation is far worse for application servers connected to the Internet. Often the software was not designed to incorporate security, which makes them vulnerable and the major point of attack.

By invading the external servers, it is possible to gain information about the internal servers, which contain far more critical information about the company. It is therefore necessary to implement strong host security for the external web servers. Strong host security needs to be implemented in disregard of a firewall. Only if the server itself is secured will a firewall be able to block all the unwanted traffic. A firewall is not able to enhance the security of a server platform.

This has major implications, if the Intranet is connected directly to the Internet at the same point where the web server is placed. If hackers are able to break into the web server, there is a good chance that they will also be able to get into the Intranet. Strong host security can prevent this type of attack.

A secure system needs to be able to detect break-in attempts. New paradigms or newly found bugs in the software will always be a threat to security, therefore several precautions should be taken. Hackers often change configurations to work in an environment that they are more comfortable with, lower security parameters or add users to the system. By periodically performing a system integrity check it is possible to verify changes in the configuration. The integrity check should be able to confirm that the key files, such as the password file or the security settings, of the system haven't been tampered with. An unauthorized change in the configuration may indicate a security breach.

In addition to the regular system integrity checks, it is necessary to start an audit system, which monitors constantly if the security has been compromised. This allows administrator to intervene and limit the damage. See Table 10.13 for an functional overview of an audit system.

Automatic audit reports need to be evaluated and analyzed. This is a time consuming task, therefore it is necessary to create an alarm mechanism, which automatically detects certain patterns in the audit, which may be part of an attack. In order to work effectively the alarms need to be configured in such a way that only the relevant attacks are displayed on the screen of the administrator. The threshold needs to be fine-tuned in order not to miss some attacks, but on the other hand also not to receive thousands of unnecessary reports. Typical alarm patterns include users logging in from unknown IP addresses. If a user logs in from somewhere in Korea and Switzerland within twenty-four hours, the system should give alarm. It is very possible that the user has moved from Korea to Switzerland, but this can be verified rather easily. Port scans from a certain IP should also ring off the bell, as someone is trying to find out which services are available and repetitive failed logins are also a reason to be concerned about a loss of security.

The alarm system should be flexible and allow either automated actions or manual interaction of the administrator. An automated action could be to deny access to a certain IP address, if a port-scan is identified. This can be used by a hacker to create a denial of service attack, by spoofing IP addresses. A manual interaction is therefore necessary immediately afterwards to verify the automated action was appropriate. The alarm should be able to send off e-mails, trigger mobile phones or alert applications.

10.8.3   Attacks from the Inside

Although securing the internal system from the outside world is very important, about 80 percent of all break-ins are done from within the company, by trusted users. Employees are able to get administrator or root passwords on a

The Audit System

An audit system needs to fulfill the following requirements to complement a security strategy.

- **Adaptable** – The audit logs should be provided in a standard format, which allows tools to create audit reports for the management.

- **Automated** – In case of a resource problem, the auditing mechanism should be able to resolve it either by freeing up other resources or shutting down the system to prevent further damage.

- **Configurable** – Adding, editing and removing subsets of system activities should be able at any time.

- **Dynamic** – It should be possible to check out the session log files to free up hard disk space.

- **Flexible** – The consumption of system resources should be controlled in a flexible way.

- **Manageable** – Tools for managing the files of various sessions need to be included.

- **System-wide** – The audit system needs to be able to monitor a wide basis of system activities, on the operating system and application level.

Table 10.13.

system rather easily by asking the responsible person for it. In many cases the access to the super-user account is granted because someone needs to install a new application or create a backup of some data. Although most employees will only limit the use of the root password to what they are asked for, some of them will use super-user power to explore the system and do direct damage. A more indirect way would be to introduce security issues, either voluntarily (by lowering the security parameters) or involuntarily (by installing buggy software), which can be exploited afterwards without having to know the root password anymore (which was changed by the administrator, for example).

To reduce the risk of internal attacks a system-level authorization control needs to be implemented. By breaking up the super-user powers into single powers, which can be attributed to single users, the total control over the system by unauthorized people can be prevented. Each user on the system has a set of powers associated with the tasks they are required to fulfill. A user adding software to the system, for example, does not need the power to add or remove users to or from the system and a user who wants to backup data, does not need access to the kernel configuration. Although this makes user administration more tedious, it makes it much easier to find out who modified what.

Authorizations should be added or removed whenever the administrator thinks it is necessary and automatic reduction of authorization is also very helpful. A user that makes a backup every Friday should not have the authorization to do this on any other day, without the consensus of the administrators. The authorizations should be assigned at login time, after the user has been authenticated.

In addition to the system-level authorization an application-level authorization system can provide additional security for every single application. This system prevents authenticated users from using a system in a way they were not authorized to do so. Guest users in an application not be able to perform administrative tasks, for example or should access services and data they are not authorized to use; they could otherwise obtain services and data that they haven't paid for.

In order to make the application-wide authorization secure it is necessary to log all attempts by a client to access unauthorized services and data. Automatic alerts inform the administrators which then can intervene and protect the system from further damage.

10.8.4 Protecting Digital Businesses

In order to ensure the availability and security of your digital business, you should distrust all networks it is connected to. This encompasses the internal networks, Extranet and the Internet in particular. A firewall can provide means to allow controlled access to certain resources. Firewalls are normally placed on the boundary between Internet and Intranet, but this is often not enough. It does often make sense to place firewalls on the Intranet to protect resources that should not be available to every employee. Personnel information needs to be protected to ensure the privacy of the information, for example.

Firewalls are also used to control the access within the company. Imagine a company distributed all over the world, forming a global Intranet. Each company site will be protected via firewall from the other to ensure that a break-in in one site does not effect the other subsidiaries.

But firewalls are not general-purpose access-control systems and are not able to detect insider's abuse of authorized access. By installing a firewall it is not possible to detect or prevent insider attacks, which are responsible for about 80 percent of all attacks. Therefore the firewall needs to be integrated into an overall security strategy that not only prevents attacks from the outside, but also the attacks from the inside.

Another problem is tunneling used by malicious programs. Tunneling uses application protocols to pass malicious applications or data. Firewalls also cannot protect networks from malicious programs, such as viruses and Trojan horses. A firewall is not designed to scan the huge amount of data that is going in and out. Some firewall solutions offer APIs to integrate a virus scanner, but the problem is that virus scanners are far too slow for real-time applications and for high volumes of traffic.

Firewalls also cannot protect against attacks that do not go through it. Although many companies are afraid that Internet connectivity may leak internal data to the outside world, this can be done easily through social engineering and theft of media. Therefore it cannot be said often enough that a firewall will not resolve all security issues a company will have in the information age. For a firewall to work, it must be a part of a consistent overall organizational security architecture. Firewall policies must be realistic, and reflect the level of security in the entire network.

It doesn't make sense to set up a firewall, if there are no security policies for floppy disks, fax machines or phone calls. It does not make sense to build a large house, lock the front door and leave all the windows open.

10.8.5 Trusted Operating Systems

A firewall serves a very specific function that that is based on the premise that the Internet is used for browsing, content serving, and mediating access to internal servers such as mail, news and ftp servers. It is placed in the data path between the external and internal clients and servers and the configuration of the firewall tells who is allowed to talk to whom. Firewalls work on the TCP/IP protocol level allowing ports (i.e. services) to be opened or closed. If the data is not encrypted, it can even do some content filtering, which enables checking if outgoing mails contain company internal documents or if incoming mails are infected by a virus.

But this is already not standard functionality of the firewall anymore. The goal of a firewall is to determine how to direct traffic and who is allowed to see what. The firewall manufacturers "harden" the operating system by applying the latest security relevant patches and removing all services from the firewall machine that are not really necessary. A so-called "trusted computing base" is formed by the firewall software and the operating system, which works in a highly specialized and security-oriented way.

Firewalls are only secure as long as no other applications are executed on the firewall machine. By adding non-trusted applications to the firewall machine it is possible to circumvent the firewall rules. Firewalls are highly specialized gateways, which cannot perform any other tasks such as application services.

In order to work efficiently, today's electronic business needs to run middle tier application which operate on the boundary between Intranet and Internet or Extranet. This requires a new philosophy for security. This new philosophy won't eliminate the need for firewalls, but will add the need for trusted operating systems (TOS), for handling the electronic business applications.

Real-time applications require this middle tier to access internal databases directly. In mission-critical applications the access to the original database is a must. In these cases a solution with a traditional firewall will either not be secure enough or not fast enough. Fast access to critical resources allows companies to take advantage of current business opportunities.

In order to make the business available to as many people as possible, it is necessary to create a web front-end. This poses new security issues, especially with the browsers. With web enabled applications, companies expose the heart of their business to the whole world. Attacks on the companies' mission critical applications and information is significantly more damaging then a shut down of a single desktop.

As businesses are moving to phase four of their electronic business evolution, not only the speed and profit is increasing but also the risks are getting higher. Companies are moving from only providing information about their business to providing queries and updates to information, which provides a much higher value to the customers. In phase four real business transactions are conducted over the Internet, which offer the highest value to the end customer, but also put the company at risk, if security cannot be guaranteed.

To ensure the security for the business transactions, the mission-critical systems should not be placed on a standard computer, but on a system with a TOS. These systems have been certified to support the tough B1 and B2 level US defense industry standards and E3 European standards.

The advantage of a TOS is that they use data partitioning and are based on the least privilege paradigm. Data partitioning means that operating systems provide means to place data on the machine in several partitions. Programs, files, communication resources, and network interfaces can be put into separate partitions. Other than partitions on file system level, these logical partitions allow only programs within a certain partition to see the data of exactly this partition. A special mechanism allows the exchange of information between partitions. As there is only one little tiny hole between the partitions it is easy to define rules for the exchange of information. In a traditional operating system, applications can protect their own files. If the application makes a mistake, the data in the file can be disclosed or damaged. It is up to the application to set file permissions properly. By segregating information into partitions the probability of errors can be reduced.

A typical trusted operating system consists of two partitions, one connected to the Internet (outside) and one connected to the Intranet (inside). The only two applications on the outside partition running is a web server and a daemon that allows connections to the inside partition. No data is placed on the outside. Requests from the Internet are accepted by the web server and passed on to the daemon, which then decides if the request is valid or not. The business logic is placed on the inside partition and every application has its own set of privileges, which are stored in a database. By default an installed application is not allowed to do anything on the trusted system. Every application needs to be examined and it needs to be determined which privileges the application requires to run without compromising the security. This information needs to be stored in the database and attributed to the application. If the entry in the database and the attributes of the application do not match the application is not launched, creating an additional layer of security.

Trusted operating systems also offer the ability to remove the root account from the kernel. Instead of checking against the root, the checks are made to a set of privileges, each of which grants a specific power. Instead of associating power with users the powers are associated with programs. This allows the power to be given the program only for the time it is running.

Hackers will need to hack into program accounts instead of user accounts. The problem for them is then that the rights they will get when hacking a program account is that these powers are only available for that particular application. A take over of the system is then very unlikely. Privileges are not inherited, making it difficult to exploit security flaws applications may have. An error within an application will not bring down the whole system, like on traditional operating systems.

A trusted operating system can be used to allow real-time collaboration for research and development via the web. By offering the necessary information in real-time to the researchers and developers they can add information much faster. The product designs teams need to protect their future designs from unwanted access, in order to stay ahead of their competition.

The same applies to financial institutions who need to provide real-time services to their customers. They need at the same time to ensure that no unauthorized users gain access to account information. Financial services companies are showing individuals and businesses that the efficiencies gained from the Internet are extremely compelling.

Health care companies are able to cut costs through the use of real-time information services on the Internet by transferring their policy management services to the Internet and insurance companies, for example, are able to allow independent salespeople to shop for the best policies through special real-time access to the internal information.

These new strategic services create a critical gateway between users and the application resources on the Intranet that support the online services. With traditional operating systems and application programming practices, the Web server becomes an extremely vulnerable point for security attacks that are difficult to stop.

10.8.6   Trusted Solutions

Two trusted operating systems are mainly used for securing electronic business on the Internet. Hewlett-Packard's Virtual Vault and Sun's Trusted Solaris, which are described in this subsection.

Hewlett Packard – Virtual Vault

The Virtual Vault[28] trusted Web-server platform consists of a military-grade operating system, which is based on HP-UX. The operating system complies to the US Department of Defense Trusted Computer System Standards and is binary compatible to HP-UX making it possible to run standard applications in a high security environment. The additional security is built into the operating system and network layers to protect sensitive information. In order to make the system Internet-ready, it is shipped with the Netscape Enterprise Server, which has been slightly modified to comply to the same standards.

A common problem with most operating systems is the super-user account, which allows total control over the computer to those with access. Virtual Vault has a special mechanism to address this problem. It breaks down the powers of the "root" into more than fifty distinct privileges. By applying the least privilege paradigm each application is granted only the minimum privileges required to run properly. This makes it impossible for "Trojan horses" to attack a system, if they are able to get into it.

The web run-time environment is strictly partitioned, meaning that a security layer has been put in place to protect internal information from the outside. It had been originally developed to protect highly classified intelligence information in the army, but it is now used by all installations of Virtual Vault to meet the security needs of the companies on the Internet. See Table 10.14 for an overview of the standard partitions.

A program that needs access to data or a program in another compartment needs special privileges to do so. The communication between "inside" and "outside" are secured by a so-called trusted gateway, which protects the applications that reside in the "inside" compartment from malicious attacks or bugs in middleware that might otherwise do damage to internal applications.

The static HTML files, for example, are stored in the "system" partition, which helps to protect their integrity. As no programs are allowed to run in "system", it helps them from being exploited by hackers looking for security flaws or misconfigurations. Programs can also be executed in another partition (often also called compartment), with no direct access to the "system" partition.

The trusted gateway provides the assurance that CGI, programs, which are installed on the Virtual Vault system, do not contain malicious code. In many cases hackers replace the actual CGI program to gain access to personal customer information and knowledge about the Intranet. By using the trusted

---

[28]http://www.hp.com/security/products/virtualvault/

Data Partitioning with Virtual Vault

Four partitions are used with Virtual Vault in a standard configuration. The access between these partitions is very limited.

- **Inside** – Is used to store and execute databases, CGI programs, Java servlets and middleware services.

- **Outside** – Contains the web server and some middleware clients.

- **System** – Is the place to save the external static web pages.

- **System High** – Contains audit trails, for example.

Table 10.14.

gateway checksums for all existing CGI applications are created and the powers are stored in a database. Every change within the CGI will result in the application not being executed anymore.

Unfortunately not all applications are Internet-ready and consist of a single, monolithic component. This architecture makes it difficult to protect the underlying server. To make the system secure it is necessary to transform the monolithic application into a more distributed component architecture. As this requires a rewrite of major parts of the software, it is necessary to offer means to go online for the time being. While the programmers work on the distributed solution, Virtual Vault offers the trusted gateway proxy, which allows access to monolithic applications without putting the server at risk. The trusted gateway proxy provides a proxy component that fields all Internet requests and forwards valid data securely to the middleware server that resides on the Intranet.

Another core functionality of Virtual Vault has been implemented through the integration of Hewlett-Packard's free product Web Quality of Service (WebQoS)[29]. WebQoS adds so-called peak usage management, which prevents an overload of the server and minimizes the impact of unexpected surges in demand while maximizing the volume of completed transactions. This protects performance levels of already active customers, which are about to complete transactions. As long as the resources are tied up with these customers, new

---

[29]http://www.hp.com/go/domain/

transactions are not permitted onto the site. The newly arriving customers will be redirected to another server in a defined cluster, making sure that the available resources are used up to a maximum.

As more and more businesses start to use Java on their business servers, it is necessary to take special precautions for the Java Virtual Machine (JVM). In order make the business application secure the JVM needs to run on the "inside" compartment. Making it inaccessible to the web server and to the attackers from the web server.

Through the web administration interface it is possible to administer the system remotely from another Intranet server. The interface is using standard web pages, making it easy to understand with little training. Audit trails and alarms help administrators to ensure system security by providing valuable checks and balances. The audit reports reside in another secured partition, which is inaccessible by unauthorized applications. Virtual Vault also offers a tight integration into Hewlett-Packard's OpenView[30] software.

Sun – Trusted Solaris

Trusted Solaris[31] is a special release of Sun's operating system Solaris, which complies to the US Department of Defense Trusted Computer System Standards. It includes CDE, as the graphical desktop environment and Solstice AdminSuite, which controls access to information and what users are permitted to do on the system.

Just like Virtual Vault, Trusted Solaris offers additional safeguards against internal and external threats, beyond the protection features of standard Unix systems. While Virtual Vault is designed more to be the application firewall sitting between Internet and Intranet, Trusted Solaris offers the possibility of connecting multiple servers and workstations to create a distributed system, whereby security can be implemented at multiple levels. Although this approach allows for more flexibility it also offers more ways of attacking the system.

Trusted Solaris is binary compatible with the standard Solaris operating system allowing most applications to run without any modification on the secure system. Multi-level versions of some essential applications, including trusted databases, have also been developed to run on Trusted Solaris.

Trusted Solaris divides administrative tasks among a number of administrators, reducing the risk of a take over through a hacker. Administrators entering the system need to log on in the normal way and then assume a role. This enables all administrative activities to be traced back to a specific authenticated user. Three different types of administrators are available on the system; a security administrator, a system administrator and an operator. A fourth root role is provided for software installation purposes.

---

[30]http://www.hp.com/go/openview/
[31]http://www.sun.com/products-n-solutions/government/trustedsolaris.html

The Solstice user and database manager enforce a "two-role control" for the configuration of user accounts, devices, hosts and networks. This is achieved together with a new device allocation and profile manager. The profile manager allows the administrator create execution profiles, which bundle sets of applications and actions with optional security attributes. Without an execution profile, a user cannot do anything on the system. Execution profiles are also used for configuring the powers of the administrators. It is possible to redistribute administrative responsibilities among administrators.

Trusted Solaris provides different types of labels that are assigned to files, windows, hosts, devices, networks and other system objects, which users are able to access. These labels indicate the level of trust of anyone accessing the system by assigning a clearance, which defines the maximum and minimum sensitivity labels.

Mandatory Access Control (MAC) is used to compare the sensitivity label of the user with the object being accessed. If they do not match, the user is not allowed to access the object. This is similar to the data partitioning model of Virtual Vault. Discretionary Access Control (DAC), on the other hand, uses file permissions and optional access control lists to restrict access to information based on a user's identity or group membership. DAC is used along with MAC to control access to system files.

It is possible to set security attributes for each host and network, which enables the communication. By default no communication is allowed. The communication can be fine-tuned for communication between Trusted Solaris and other trusted systems.

Similar to Virtual Vault, Trusted Solaris use the least privilege paradigm, which removes the risk that occurs in standard operating systems because programs running as root are exempt from all policy controls. The root privileges are divided into almost ninety distinct privileges (compared to the fifty in Virtual Vault). Trusted Solaris provides a tool that helps to identify, which privileges are required to run any given application properly.

10.8.7 Certification Authority

In order to have digital certificates it is necessary to have them issued by a trusted third party called certification authority (CA). The role of the CA is to issue a means of personal identification that is recognized on a country or world-wide level. A CA can issue different types of digital certificates, which are required by individuals (e.g. in a web browser) and organizations (e.g. on a web server) who want to identify themselves on the Internet. The certificates are available to any requesting party and can be obtained with different levels of assurance, such as Class 1, 2 or 3. Depending on the level of assurance it can be verified if the certificate really belongs to the person who has done a particular business transaction on the Internet. Class 1 certificates require only a valid e-mail address to obtain the certificate, while Class 3 requires a higher level of personal identification, such as presenting the passport at the certification authority.

In addition to the general digital certificate companies may decide to issue special digital certificates, which can be used only for a special purpose, such as online banking or health care information. These special certificates are not available to everyone, but only to individuals who are eligible, determined by the organization's membership or subscriber rules. These so-called private label digital certificates contain information specified by the organization to extend brands and end-user customer relationships into cyberspace.

In order to become a certification authority it is necessary to do significant investments in technology, infrastructure and practices. As digital signatures and cryptography are both required for managing a CA it is necessary to handle a high volume of computing-intensive traffic. In order to support the servers, special devices must be bought that only handle the encryption. To manage high-volume deployments, it is necessary to combine the required cryptography and security protocols to support trusted applications with Web-based front-ends, scalable transaction engines and secure databases. As the database is the capital of the company, special physical security measures need to be taken. The building needs special protection, and the server room needs guards and ID checks just as the Internet connection needs a trusted operating system sitting in between to monitor the activities.

In order to serve customers on a world-wide basis the CA needs to have redundant communication links, automated backup and recovery facilities that ensure the availability of the system at any given time. Trained customer service and help desk personnel are also required to ensure that customers are able to resolve their problems.

Most important are the practices, which are providing the core business values of the CA. The practice statement consists of a set of documents that establish the legal infrastructure and metrics for operating as a trusted third party on the Internet. It is a defined model of trust and a legally binding framework. The practice statement describes in detail the certification infrastructure, together with the foundation for the operations of the certification authority. Also described is how the application for a certificate works and what validation requirements are used for the application. The complete procedure of issuing is described in the statement and when certificates are accepted and how they are used. Sections on the suspension, revocation and expiration of the certificates are also required, just as the obligations of issuing authorities and the certification authority. All this information is necessary to ensure the proper working of the CA, for the sake of the customers and in front of the law.

Chapter 11

DEALING WITH JAVA

11.1 Introducing Java

11.1.1 Definition of Java

Sun defines Java with the following two short sentences. "Java is a simple, object-oriented, distributed, interpreted, robust, secure, architecture-neutral, portable, high-performance, multi-threaded, dynamic, buzzword-compliant, general-purpose programming language. Java supports programming for the Internet in the form of platform-independent Java applets."

Although this is quite a concise definition of Java to understand the features of Java for a technical person, non-technical people and especially business people will not have a clue why Java is such a success in the Internet world and what the above sentence implicates for their online businesses. This chapter tries to explain the technical virtues of Java and how they can help to enhance the electronic service of the online business.

The sentence which is used most to describe Java's advantage is "Write once, run anywhere". It describes the unique feature of Java. It is totally hardware and software independent ("architecture-neutral" is the word Sun used in its definition). There are no restrictions on which platform you develop your Java software. If you develop your application, for example, on an Apple PowerMac it will run on the Windows and Unix families as well (the Sun buzzword here is "portable"). It does not matter if you run MacOS[1], BeOS[2] or MKLinux[3] on the PowerMac.

You do not have to change anything within the program, nor do you have to re-compile the source-code. Once the program has been written and compiled, it will run on all platforms that support Java. As of today, all mainstream clients (Windows and Mac-OS based, Intel and PowerPC-based) and servers (all Unix flavors) support Java. Besides the original implementation by Sun and porting done by IBM, Hewlett-Packard and others, there are several open

---

[1] http://www.apple.com/macos/
[2] http://www.beos.com/
[3] http://www.mklinux.apple.com/

source communities who write run-time environments and compilers for Java (e.g. ElectricalFire[4], Kaffe[5], Japhar[6] and Jikes[7]).

The promise of portability and architecture neutrality is delivered by the Java Virtual Machine (JVM), which provides a software environment and a translator for the Java applications to the system platform they are run on. System platforms could be, for example, Windows NT 4.0 on an Intel Pentium processor or HP-UX 11.01 on the HP PA-RISC processor. As input, the Java compiler builds the application by generating an executable representation called byte-code. Byte-code is unique in that it is a set of execution instructions for the JVM rather than for the actual system hosting the execution. The JVM defines the execution engine for application logic written in Java. To execute, the Virtual Machine interprets byte-code to emulate the execution of applications on the host system. It is the actions performed by the JVM, which represent application execution. This is unlike the traditional model where the host system performs the actions representing application execution. This model allows the program to be resource independent. Although it may be slower than a comparable C program, it fits perfectly into the Internet world, where you, most probably, do not know what hardware and software platforms your customers have.

11.1.2 Validating the Business Case

One of the chief virtues of a Java environment is its ability to support real-time updates of information exchange across applications, across different platforms, and even outside the enterprise to business partners. Another virtue is the ease of the application development. Querying databases on several platforms and different locations becomes easy with Java, which has a standard way of doing such transactions. As society morphs into an information society, databases and information-driven applications become more important. Therefore using the appropriate tools and programming language becomes important. Java will succeed first in the applications that benefit from enhanced information exchange.

Applications nowadays need to be "Internet-enabled". Therefore using programming languages that have integrated support for Internet features, such as opening ports on the lower level and transferring web pages on a higher level, is helpful as it reduces time to implement. In Java it is really easy, for example, to build a chat server. The chat server source code will have in its smallest form about 20 lines and the client maybe 200 lines. Building applications that connect to databases or other services over the Internet are done fairly easily and consistently over all platforms.

---

[4]http://www.mozilla.org/projects/ef/

[5]http://www.kaffe.org/

[6]http://www.japhar.org/

[7]http://www.research.ibm.com/jikes/

Java Business Value Proposition

Java offers unique features for the development of new services
and products. The most important features are the following:

- **Ease of application development** – As a programming
  language, Java contributes to developer productivity by
  dramatically shortening software development time. Developers see that software that would take weeks to write
  with other tools can now be written in days with Java.

- **Application mobility** – Another advantage to developer
  productivity. This feature permits Java-based applications to run on any hardware platform that supports a
  Java Virtual Machine.

- **Real time information updates** – In a Java environment, information can be updated in real time across applications, across platforms, on the inside and the outside
  of a business enterprise. Many classes of applications are
  enhanced by this standardized flow of information – this
  is a major business benefit of Java.

- **Growth** – New ways of communication and collaboration
  have been created by the Internet. Java is able to support
  these services and enhance them through its language
  features. Your applications can grow at the same speed
  as your company.

Table 11.1.

Application development with Java becomes fairly easy as soon as you have
to support more than one platform. Write it on a certain hardware platform
and if you stick to the Java specifications it will run without changes on other
platforms as well.

Java technology enables the exchange of information in real-time throughout enterprises and beyond company boundaries, and so enables new classes of
software technology for e-business, especially for electronic commerce, supply
chain management, management – repair – operations (MRO) and customer
interaction.

If we look at enterprise-wide applications, Java applets are not really of interest. They may be useful for certain applications where users have to interact with certain Java servers, but in order to save bandwidth, simple web forms will do it in most cases. Java really makes a difference on the server. Java technology for server-side applications permits more innovation and efficiency than ever possible in the past.

Java should be used in enterprise business solutions, server-side and infrastructure applications and end-to-end application deployment. Server-side and infrastructure applications are those which require information to be updated in real-time throughout the enterprise. Supply chain management and enterprise resource planning are examples of such applications.

Java applications have occasionally failed to provide real application mobility, since early versions of the Java environment were specified rather loosely: A Java platform could be completely compliant, yet inconsistencies between implementations prevented true compatibility. Each version of Java code gets closer to delivering on the promise of true application mobility.

Let us consider an online shopping example. When ordering a product via the Internet, the web application at the merchant accepts your credit card number and sends it on to the bank to another application for a credit check. Another application at the supplier will check availability for the product you have ordered, and if it is not in stock, will place an order with an outside vendor for additional supply. That particular application must reply with availability and all the information must be consolidated fairly quickly so that you, the consumer, may be informed that your order has been accepted and will be fulfilled by some specified date.

We now have a minimum of five applications involved. In the worst case, each of the applications runs on a different platform with incompatible APIs. If all the parties involved had used Java instead, the exchange of information would have been very easy.

By itself, Java has attracted considerable media attention and industry hype. Realistically, businesses will incorporate Java technology as it enhances their own corporate goals, and not because they have read about it in a computer magazine.

11.1.3 Embedded Devices

So far, we have discussed Java from an enterprise computing perspective. As it evolves, however, Java technology has implications for many classes of electronic devices: peripherals, instruments, measurement and consumer electronics, which are also called embedded devices.

All large electronic producers recognize the growing importance of Java technology in the emerging market of embedded devices. Java is able to play a major role in embedded devices in two ways. Using JavaOS, an operating system written in Java, it is possible to write complex applications on these devices with little memory resources and processing power. The other way of using Java is using the Java API to control these devices from another machine, such as a PC. On the embedded device a real-time operating system (RTOS) receives the messages from the Java application and is able to respond in the appropriate way. If you look around your house, for example, you will find many devices that already use chips, like for example, the washing machine and the TV set. All of these devices have their own hardware inside and their own operating system. They are not able to talk to each other nor can they be controlled from remote by a single device. Having a TV and a VCR from two different brands already forces us to use two different types of remote control, because they cannot speak to each other. Using Java and standard APIs, it would become possible to control all devices in a household from a single remote control or over the Internet. But this may not be the best thing to do. Without the necessary security infrastructure, hackers would be able to switch on your TV during the night and turn off the heating in winter.

When introducing Java into embedded devices these devices are also network enabled, meaning that they are able to communicate with other devices or services. Pervasive computing is about to become real. Based on this new paradigm several companies have started to develop new technologies and strategies. Lucent Technologies[8], for example, developed the Inferno technology to allow the connection of devices and Hewlett-Packard[9] developed a complete new vision for the future of the Internet. Their E-Services initiative works at a level higher, not on the device level, but on the service level. See Chapter 15 for more detailed information on pervasive computing.

11.1.4   Java versus JavaScript

In December 1995 Netscape announced LiveScript, which then became JavaScript. It was developed independently of Sun's Java programming language. The first browser to support JavaScript was Netscape 2.0. The target is the group of less experienced developers, who want to add interactivity to their web sites. Unlike Java, JavaScript is a scripting language, which allows the programming of events, objects, and actions. Java and JavaScript interoperate well but are technically, functionally and behaviorally very different. JavaScript and Java are able to exchange variables and functions via a special API, called LiveWire, which was also developed by Netscape.

Java and JavaScript are distinct languages, with different purposes and features. JavaScript was designed to provide an easy way for Web authors to create interactive Web pages. Unlike Java, which is meant for experienced programmers, JavaScript is a simpler "scripting" language (such as AppleScript) aimed at those with less programming experience. Like Java, JavaScript is a cross-platform language that can work with any compatible browser.

---

[8]http://www.lucent.com/
[9]http://www.hp.com/

Comparison of Java and JavaScript

Although Java and JavaScript have very similar names, they are quite different. This table shows the largest differences between Java Applets and JavaScripts.

JavaScript	Java Applet
Interpreter – Interpreted by client – not compiled.	**Byte-Code** – Compiled on server to byte-code format before interpreter execution on client.
Object-based – No classes or inheritance; built-in, extensible objects.	**Object-oriented** – Classes and inheritance; built-in, extensible objects.
Integration – It is integrated with and embedded into HTML.	**Attachment** – Applets distinct from HTML (accessed via HTML Pages).
Loose Typing – Do not declare variables' data types.	**Strong Typing** – Must declare variables' data types.
Dynamic binding – objects references are checked at run time.	**Static binding** – references to objects must exist at compile-time.
Secure – cannot write to or read from HD.	**Secure** – cannot read from or write to HD, without explicit permission of the user.

Table 11.2.

Table 11.2 consists only of a little overview on the differences between JavaScript and Java Applets. A more in-depth analysis on JavaScript can be found in Chapter 9 as it is tightly integrated into the web browsers and the HTML code. Microsoft implemented its own version of JavaScript called JScript, which is partly compatible with JavaScript. As a rule of thumb, Internet Explorer's is one version behind Netscape Navigator, i.e. IE's 4.0 JScript is compatible with Netscape's 3.0 JavaScript.

JavaScript is an interpreted language, meaning that is not necessary to compile the code, making it easy to use for anyone without in-depth programming knowledge. Only a browser and a text editor are required to write JavaScript applications. The language is not truly object-oriented, as it is not possible to create new classes or inheritances, but has a built-in set of objects, that can be extended and accessed. Other than Java, JavaScript does not require the user to declare variables' data types and objects are checked at run time (as opposed to the compiler checks of Java). JavaScript does not allow access to system resources, such as printers or hard disks, but many bugs in the implementations have showed that there have been holes which make it possible to read from a hard disk. Therefore keep an eye on the browser manufacturer site and download updates or patches that resolve these security issues.

11.1.5 Example Business Cases

In order to make Java technology successful on the Internet a sound business case needs to be behind it. If the new possibilities of the technology do not help you make more profit, reduce costs or help you in any other way, most businesses will refuse to use them. This section describes four business cases, which will be checked against the described technologies in the following sections. This will allow us to see if that particular Java technology will add value to the electronic business.

The Online Bank

A financial institute or bank operates in the conventional way, by offering its services over its branches and the telephone. It wants to add online banking to its portfolio and create special web pages for accessing information on the balance of people's accounts and enable transactions through HTML forms. The interaction between web browser and server is done through CGI programs, which talk to the back-end system, most probably a legacy system, that does not even understand TCP/IP. How can this process be simplified?

The Fashion Manufacturer

A fashion manufacturer designs and produces a collection every half year. In order to promote the collection, the manufacturer organizes a show where it presents its products. The retailers are invited to participate and choose the appropriate products that fit the style of their shop. As the show is organized in one place, and retailers from one country or continent gather there, many smaller retailers do not go there, as it is too expensive. Instead of going there, they go into larger shops and look at what they have chosen and order on that basis their goods. In order to reach the smaller retailers as well, the fashion manufacturer chooses to create an online service where retailers can view the products, choose them and combine them. The first step would be to install a shopping system from which the retailers can choose goods. But to make the system really valuable, it needs to be interactive. How can this be achieved?

The Cargo Service

A cargo service offers the transport of goods at short notice. In order to automate the process, the company offers a web page with an HTML form, where customers can enter the necessary data and can check flight availability and arrival times of the packet at the destination. Offering this service is not a great enhancement over ordering the pick up of the packet. In order to make the service really valuable, tracking and tracing needs to be implemented and payment should be made possible directly over the Internet. How can this be achieved?

The Car Designer

A team of car designers needs to access the designs of a new automobile over the network. The information is stored in multiple databases throughout the company. In order to simplify the work of the designers, the information should be accessible through one interface and it should be able to combine resources to gather intelligence that is created by the wealth of information. How can such an interface be built and the information be joined?

11.2   Java Foundation Classes

11.2.1   Technical Overview

When Java was introduced the abstract window toolkit (AWT) was the graphical user interface (GUI) that was supplied with it. It provided a very simple library for building Java applications and applets. Java developers encountered many limitations when attempting to create a modern looking application. Still the AWT provided 100 percent portability from a single set of source code and assumed a native look and feel on the deployment platforms.

The idea of the AWT was to provide a portable GUI library, which works on all platforms. Instead of emulating the native look and feel of a single toolkit, the AWT uses a layered toolkit model, where each Java component creates a native component. Each Java component class wraps the native implementation, which is a rather complex issue as every native toolkit uses a completely different event model, for example. This resulted in a somewhat limited use of a user interface.

In version 1.1 of the Java Development Kit (JDK) AWT became part of a comprehensive set of GUI classes called the Java Foundation Classes (JFC). It provides a range of new features, such as a better event model, printing capabilities, a lightweight user interface framework and is JavaBeans compliant.

Using Swing it has become possible to create applications with a professional looking GUI, not only for the web browsers, but also for standard applications. The AWT provided little integration into a desktop environment and limited functionality for creating larger applications.

Features of the Java Foundation Classes

- **JavaBeans Compliant** – A consistent API is used to handle events.

- **Lightweight UI Framework** – Enables components to be peerless and completely written in Java.

- **Delegation Event Model** – Support of visual development environments and development of distributed and multicast applications.

- **Printing** – Support for printers has been integrated.

- **Data Transfer/Clipboard** – Elements in AWT did not support the clipboard functionalities, such as cut, copy and paste.

- **Desktop Colors Integration** – Java application will integrate seamlessly into the desktop.

- **Graphics and Image Enhancements** – Extended support for rich graphical user interfaces.

- **Mouseless Operation** – Every operation that can be done with the mouse, can also be executed via keyboard.

- **Popup Menu** – Opens context-driven menus.

- **ScrollPane Container** – Implementation of a highly configurable and resizable user interface.

Table 11.3.

The features of the JFC introduced in JDK 1.1 include the following (a summary can be found in Table 11.3). The JFC is JavaBeans compliant, which means that an architecture and platform neutral API for creating and using dynamic Java components is used. The advantage of the JavaBeans approach is that Java programs are able to interoperate with legacy applications and can be easily distributed over the Internet.

The lightweight user interface framework, which is used in the JFC allows components to be completely transparent. The components can be written completely in Java and do not carry overhead from the native windowing system. The JFC components have a consistent look and feel across all platforms. This means that applications with a GUI load and run faster. AWT was much more restricted, as it did not allow developers to extend the components or change their look and feel. Converting existing AWT components to JFC is easy, making it easy to upgrade the existing applications to the new paradigm.

The delegation event model used in the JFC is very different to the simple event model in the AWT. Using AWT it was necessary to create complex if-then-else constructions to handle events, with the introduction of JFC events identified by their class instead of their ID. The event listener communicates with the objects interested in a particular event, reducing the load on a system.

With JFC printing has become possible. Now it is possible to send text or graphics to a printer using Java code. With AWT it was necessary to include native code, but then printing was restricted to a particular platform. JFC introduces printer support that can be easily integrated into applications.

One problem with AWT was, that it was not possible to cut and paste text from or to the Java program. The JFC introduces full clipboard support, which enables dynamic data type to be created, registered and transferred. It is now possible, for example, to cut an image out of a Java application and paste it into Photoshop. Other than the old AWT, the JFC is able to adhere to the system color scheme, which makes it easier for users to adapt colors to their preferred settings. The Java Foundation Classes enhance the graphical capabilities, by introducing functions to clip an image or flip it horizontally or vertically.

The JFC introduced the mouseless operation, which enables users to use a Java program without a mouse. The advantage of this is that data entry and operational applications can be created and speeds up the use of certain features. People who access computers through voice-control can access these applications more easily if there is a voice layer on top, which translates voice to letters. In addition to the mouseless operation, pop-up menus have been introduced which open up menus that contain all the functions relative to the object the mouse pointer is on. These so-called context menus reduce the failure rate and increase the speed for using a program.

ScrollPane containers have been introduced to support automatic scrolling for a single component. It allows the content of a pane to be updated much faster than was possible in AWT. The introduction of the ScrollPane container greatly simplifies the task of displaying information in a fixed area.

11.2.2 Checking the Business Cases

If we look at our four business cases, then we can see that all from them profit of the JFC. The Java Foundation Classes are able to create highly dynamic and modern graphical user interfaces for all types of applications. The online banking solution will profit from a nice Java interface that allows the customers to choose all functions of the banking application. The application is able to change its looks and appear as a standard application for corporate customers who have strict design rules for computer programs.

The fashion manufacturer can create an easy to use interface using Java and the JFC. Imagine a desktop for retailers where they can order goods and create arrangements, which can be used for the decoration of the shop. Instead of going to fashion shows, the retailers are able to select skirts and blouses online, by using virtual models. The Java Foundation Classes offer a wide range of functions, which make it possible to create a virtual showroom without spending months on development. The Java applet is able to connect to the order system and automate much of the manual work which many retailers have to do on a regular basis.

The cargo service will not profit a lot from a Java graphical interface. The customers of the cargo service won't have additional functionality through the Java Foundation Classes. Instead of providing an extra graphical interface through a web browser, cargo customers would prefer to have an integration into their existing ordering system.

Car designers can profit a lot through an advanced graphical interface. The interface allows the designers to navigate through a design and describe the parts of the design in more detail. Using VRML scenes, the designers are able to check their designs in detail and can give direct feedback on certain elements. Introducing an Internet based design and review process enhances the collaboration between people who work in different locations.

11.2.3 Online Experience

Although the Java Foundation Classes are part of Java 1.1 web browsers do not support the features natively. In order to use the features, it is necessary to install the them separately onto the computer or install the latest Java plug-in from Sun, which supports all features of Java 1.1. As it is not a standard component of web browsers only very few Internet solutions support the Java Foundation Class. It is to expected that new releases of web browsers will support Java 2 and all of its components, so it will only be a matter of time until JFC will be natively supported.

The Zürcher Kantonal Bank[10], one of the largest Banks in Switzerland uses the Java Foundation Class to create an interactive banking experience. Using a Java applet for online banking outside of the US is especially important. Although there is a special agreement that financial institutions outside of the United States are able to receive 128-bit keys for encryption, it is easier to use the standard 40-bit encryption and add a security level on top of the SSL encryption. This can be done easily through Java, but the standard AWT interface is more than ugly. With the introduction of the Java Foundation Class, Internet Java applets are becoming modern applications.

---

[10]http://www.zkb.ch/

11.2.4 Required Software

Up to release 1.1 of the Java Development Kit the Java Foundation Classes needed to be added manually to the system. With the introduction of Java Version 2 the JFC has become part of the distribution and is the new standard GUI package used for all new applications. The AWT package is still available and will be used to maintain backward compatibility with older systems.

11.3   JINI

11.3.1 Technical Overview

Jini[11] is the latest initiative by Sun Microsystems, which allows all types of devices to be connected into so-called impromptu networks. Jini allows access to new network services and delivers them in a simple way. Built on the Java standard, Jini technology creates a network consisting of all types of digital devices without extensive planning, installation or human intervention. Each device broadcasts the services it offers to all other devices in the community which they can use.

An impromptu community is created when two or more devices create a network to share their services. They do not need to have prior knowledge of each other in order to participate. The communication is established dynamically and does not require the devices to exchange drivers to offer their services to the other devices in the community.

Other than traditional networks, an impromptu community will not only consist of servers and clients, but all devices that create, modify or receive information. The consumer appliance market, with products such as mobile phones, television sets and personal digital assistants can be easily included into a Jini network. Pervasive computing becomes reality.

Every electronic device today is able to handle information and contain a certain type of microprocessor. The devices are ready to communicate with the other devices, but today's networks are not prepared for the required pervasiveness. Jini is written in Java and can therefore be run on all devices that include a Java run-time environment (JRE). It will also run on existing networks, no special network protocols are required.

Devices using the Jini technology use a process called "discovery" that searches for other devices using the Jini technology. When connecting a new device to the network, it will try to to locate the look-up server and register its services. Once the connection between the devices has been established, Java objects are sent to a look-up service, which represent the services as well as their characteristics and attributes. When a device in the impromptu community wants to use a service offered in a community, it can download the required data from the look-up server, such as applications, drivers or interfaces.

---

[11]http://www.sun.com/jini/

Jini enabled devices need to update their registration periodically. If they fail to do so, the look-up service removes the services from the list. Removing a device does not interrupt the services offered by the other members of the impromptu network.

If a device has no Java installed it still can become a participant in a Jini network. This is done by moving the objects to another device, which acts on behalf of the other system. The system talks to the look-up server and sends out the Java objects. The system acts as a proxy between the Jini network and the non-Jini enabled device.

If there are enough resources (memory and hard disk) on the device left, it is also possible to install the Jini software to broadcast the services offered by the device to the Jini network.

Any Java application can use Jini software by creating a connection to the look-up server. The server will send back a list of services, which can be retrieved by the application. If the application is interested in a certain service the look-up server will send a Java object which handles all requests to the service. This object handles any device-specific details and the machine running the application does not need to have a driver for the device.

In the most simple case Jini can be used to attach a device to a computer, such as a printer, monitor, or hard disk, which all are Jini enabled and are to work immediately without any driver installation. The paradigm of "Write once, run anywhere" enters a new dimension. With Jini it is very easy to create distributed systems that share responsibility and resources.

Through Jini it is possible to associate devices, such as printers, to people and places. Imagine you need to print out a text in another office. Just press print and it will be printed on the printer that is next to you, no matter what type of printer it is.

11.3.2 Checking the Business Cases

The business case behind Jini is to improve productivity, save costs and simplify the use of a network. The interaction with the network and the connected nodes (i.e. devices) become easier. It allows the simplified delivery of new products and services over a network.

Jini enables bank customers to deal with their bank from any Jini enabled device, if the online bank has a Jini connection network. Customers in a car, which has a Jini connection are able to make financial transactions without the need of a normal computer with a web browser. Depending on the functionality of the network device in the car, the bank is able to offer certain operations. If the device offers a graphical display, the bank could send images, which show the development of your portfolio. If the device contains a voice recognition feature, online banking can be mixed with telephone banking to achieve the most convenient way for the driver to communicate with the bank.

The fashion manufacturer could web enable all of its clothes. Although this may seem far-fetched, first test have already been made. A small chip is woven into the label, which identifies the type of clothing and how it needs to be treated. When you put the clothes into a washing machine it would automatically check if all clothes can be washed together. If not, the washing machine would report exactly which piece does not fit.

The cargo company will be able to use Jini to facilitate the tracking of goods. Today every station needs a computer to communicate if a packet has passed it. Stations include the pick-up at the customer, the airport check-in, the boarding onto the plane, and the same station at the destination. The logistics partner who is picking up the packet at the customer site will not have a computer to connect to the Internet. With Jini a mobile phone could be used to communicate the pick-up to the tracking system. The airport check-in will probably have access to the Internet and could communicate directly to the tracking system. During boarding a person with a bar-code scanner is not able to communicate directly back to the tracking system, but adding a Jini interface to the scanner would create a hand-held networking appliance that would immediately report back which packets have been boarded. Through Jini the devices in use could be also used in the future. This would make the transition easy, as the single stations would not be required to learn a new technology. Jini would work transparently and quietly in the background.

Through Jini the car designers will benefit from Jini when they build the first prototypes. These prototypes could contain several Jini-enabled devices which allow the designers to track the availability and functionality of their design components. An impromptu network can also be set up with other devices outside of the car. Devices that measure traffic congestion could interact with the car, by telling the GPS system in the car which route is the fastest, for example. Or as mentioned in the preface, the car could interact with petrol stations and start to ask for petrol prices. This process could create highly dynamic petrol prices, as petrol stations with low demand would try to become more attractive by lowering the price for some minutes. Without the connectivity there is no reason for petrol stations to lower prices for minutes, as only the cars that pass by would notice. More and more cars contain GPS satellite navigation systems and mobile phones. In Dublin, Ireland it is possible to get taxis with Internet connectivity and in Helsinki, Finland it is possible to pay for automatic car washing with the mobile phone. Device-independent interconnectivity becomes more important and Jini is one possible way of implementing it.

11.3.3 Online Experience

Jini was introduced officially with Java 2. Although pre-release versions have been around for some time and tests have been conducted, there is no live system available yet. The major problem is less the software, but to have appropriate hardware devices that understand Jini.

For simple tests it is possible to install Jini on standard computers. But Jini's full strength lies in the interconnectivity of different types of devices.

11.3.4 Required Software

The required software can be downloaded from Sun[12] at no cost. The source code is also available and can be modified to the needs of the business case. Although there are some restrictions in the license, the software can be used freely.

The base software required for building a Jini federation consists of the latest Java Virtual Machine, extended remote method invocation (RMI), which has been enhanced to work with Jini. In addition, a lookup service is required, which consists of a database for services available in the federation. A discovery service is required to allow resources to register their services with the lookup service and distributed security is required, which is a security framework built on top of Java's built-in security.

11.4 JavaBeans

11.4.1 Technical Overview

The JavaBeans component model enables developers to write reusable components in Java. It is a portable, platform-independent component model written in Java. JavaBeans can be manipulated visually and can be combined to create traditional applications. The advantage of creating components rather than monolithic applications enables developers to create complex applications much faster and reuse some of the components for other projects as well.

JavaBeans also acts as a bridge between proprietary component models and provides a seamless and powerful means for developers to build components that run in ActiveX container applications, for example. JavaBeans can be used to develop or assemble network-aware solutions for heterogeneous hardware and operating system environments.

Two different types of JavaBeans components will be in use. Either a Java-Beans component is used as a building block in order to compose a larger application or a JavaBeans component is used as a regular application, which can be embedded into web pages, for example. These two aspects overlap programming. A calculator may live within a composite application as well as within a more normal compound document. There is no sharp cutoff between the so-called "composite applications" and "compound documents".

A reusable software component is a piece of software that provides a well defined functionality. The functionality is presented in such a way that other pieces of software are able to access this functionality. The functionality of a JavaBean can be something very simple, such as a certain type of button

---

[12]http://java.sun.com/

or something very complex, such as an application. Imagine a company that wants to put a copyright statement into every program. Normally the company would need to write the code and embed it into the application. Although the code is not difficult to implement, it still can be responsible for bugs as it needs to be recompiled with the application. Moving the copyright statement into a JavaBean means that the code needs to written only once and only compiled once. Then the functionality then can be used by any application through the standardized JavaBeans API.

Features of Java Beans

Although the functionality of every JavaBean is different, there are some features that distinguish JavaBeans from other types of applications.

- **Customization** – Visual application builder tools are able to customize the appearance and the behavior of a JavaBean.

- **Events** – Allow JavaBeans to connect and communicate with each other.

- **Introspection** – Visual application builder tools are able to analyze how a JavaBean works.

- **Persistence** – After customization in a visual application builder, the Beans can be retrieved with customized features, for future use.

- **Properties** – Developers are able to customize and program with JavaBeans.

Table 11.4.

JavaBeans is a complete component architecture supporting properties to program with Beans. A public interface defines the way a bean interacts with other beans. The interface consists of properties, methods and events. Properties are named attributes of JavaBeans that can be read or set by other Java-Beans. Public methods can be triggered by other JavaBeans and events are used to communicate with one another. JavaBeans can be automatically analyzed (called introspection) and their appearance is easily configurable (called customization) through a visual application builder tool. JavaBeans can be used to create both Java applications and applets. Applets can be designed to work as reusable JavaBeans. But applets are not automatically beans.

The JavaBeans API tries to ensure portability. A JaveBean developed on a certain platform should behave in the same way on every other platform. In order to reduce the risk of having unsupported features, the API tries to remain simple and compact.

11.4.2   Checking the Business Cases

JavaBeans reduces the time to develop applications, which makes the development easier and less costly. If we now look at our business cases, we can see some advantages. JavaBeans does not influence the business case, but it does influence the way the business process development is organized. The reusability is a very important factor. Instead of offering the same software package to all users, the JavaBeans model allows for highly configurable and dynamic application solutions.

The online bank is able to write JavaBeans, which can provide a basic functionality, both for customers and employees. Depending on the type of users, additional Beans can be loaded. Using JavaBeans it is also possible to start online banking simply, by offering the account balance at the beginning. Adding functionality is then very easy. Through the JavaBeans model it is rather easy to add new JavaBeans when they become available, making the initial offering available very soon in the development phase. As every JavaBean is separate it is possible to update the functionality of every JavaBean individually. In monolithic applications in many cases interdependencies are much higher, requiring at least a recompilation of the whole source code.

The fashion manufacturer can gain the same advantages as the online bank through the use of Java. By using JavaBeans the development can be done partly in-house and some of the development can be outsourced. For the online presentation, web pages and JavaBeans can be intermixed, allowing the optimal presentation for the fashion. Standard HTML pages will be used for the textual description. The order form can be done using a HTML form, while the three-dimensional representation of the models can be written in VRML (see Chapter 12 for more information on VRML) and the interactivity can be written in Java. Using JavaBeans, features can be used in different applications, for different target groups.

The cargo company is able to write many components, which can be used not only for customer interaction, but also for internal processes. By re-coding their internal business processes by using JavaBeans, it becomes easy to extract the necessary JavaBeans, which are required for the customer interaction.

As cars already contain many electronic devices, and given the need for programming these devices it may make sense to code the functionality into JavaBeans. This can reduce the time and cost for the availability of new devices and functionalities. New devices can be introduced into the next generation of cars much more easily if the functionality is coded into another JavaBean than the connection to the physical device.

11.4.3   Online Experience

As JavaBeans has become part of the Java standard with version 1.1, it is still not supported by all browsers and therefore only limited use has been made of it on the Internet. So far most use of JavaBeans has been made in application development offline.

One example for Intranet use is Charles Schwab[13], a Web-based securities trading company, which uses JavaBeans to provide a common interface to its core systems for use by its business units.

The application built in JavaBeans allows users to enter an account number and the system returns financial information from the core system. Two types of Beans have been used to create the application. Data access Beans allow access over the interface to the back-end system and the viewer Beans display the data graphically on the desktop of the employee.

In order to achieve mission-critical application performance, the JavaBeans standard was enhanced by BeansExtender developed by IBM[14], which offers several enhancements over the JavaBeans standard: the ManagedBean class, the instance-based aggregation model, "Bean Dipping," and the Assembly Surface builder tool. These features together with the Java Active X bridge make a perfect solution for Charles Schwab, as existing Active X applications could be integrated into the JavaBeans model without modification.

Another application developed by IBM in its AlphaBeans programs is BeanMachine, which is an easy-to-use multimedia tool for enriching Web pages with special effects. BeanMachine consists of several JavaBeans components that can be used together to create applets with a few mouse clicks. The Beans included offer sound effects, animations, text effects and access to the database of your choice in JDBC.

11.4.4   Required Software

JavaBeans do not require extra software to be included. Java 1.1 does support JavaBeans natively and all major development tools for Java, such as Visual Café by Symantec[15] or VisualAge for Java by IBM[16] make it easy to implement and use JavaBeans. Their visual interface allows the beans to be clicked together and work together.

Many portals have been created that allow the download of freeware, shareware and open source JavaBeans. These sites offer a wide range of JavaBeans,

---

[13]http://www.schwab.com/
[14]http://www.alphaworks.ibm.com/
[15]http://www.symantec.com/
[16]http://www.ibm.com/

which make it easy for developers to create complex applications without need-ing to rewrite every single function. One such directory is Components.com[17].

11.5 InfoBus

11.5.1 Technical Overview

InfoBus is a very compact Java API, which allows the co-operation of applets or JavaBeans. The applets or JavaBeans can be either on a web page or in any other Java application and are able to exchange data through InfoBus. Java-Beans can become "data providers" and "data consumers", which are defined in the InfoBus architecture. A JavaBean that acts as a provider connects to a database and offers the data onto the InfoBus. JavaBeans that act as data consumers are able to retrieve the data from the bus and process it. The advan-tage is that the processing JavaBean does not need to understand data formats and can concentrate on the implementation of the data processing. This seg-regation of provider from consumer is extremely powerful in that it enables applications to be independent of their data. JavaBeans are also able to act as consumer and provider at the same time.

The InfoBus specification extends JavaBeans by providing a set of enhanced interfaces to share and exchange dynamic data. The current release requires the JavaBeans to "live" within the same Java Virtual Machine. Although the design does not include provisions for connecting to other JVMs on different devices, it does provide facilities for writing a bridge between the JVMs. It can be said, that all JavaBeans loaded from a single class loader are able to connect to each other.

The InfoBus interfaces allow application designers to create "data flows" between co-operating components. Other than the traditional event/response mode, the InfoBus interfaces use only very few events and an invariant set of method calls for all applets. The semantics of the data flow are based on interpreting the contents of the data that flows across the InfoBus interfaces as opposed to responding to names of parameters from events or names of call-back parameters.

The standard communication between JavaBeans is based on the so-called introspection model, which we discussed above in the subsection on JavaBeans. The InfoBus interface offers a tightly typed contract between co-operating beans. The interface allows data flows to be created between co-operating beans through direct procedure calls.

11.5.2 Checking the Business Cases

Device and format independent data solves most of the problems, which pro-grammers encounter in today's computer environments. Every application and

---

[17]http://www.components.com/

The InfoBus Process for Data Exchange

The data exchange on the InfoBus consists of the following elements:

- **Membership** – By implementing the InfoBusMember interface any Java class can join the InfoBus.

- **Rendezvous** – This protocol allows data producers and consumers to send out requests and accept requests.

- **Data access** – InfoBus has a set of standard interfaces for the direct data transfer between a producer and a consumer.

- **Change notification** – Once data has been transmitted, the consumer can be notified in the case of modifications of the data.

Table 11.5.

device is using another format to encode data. InfoBus does not impose applications to use other formats of data, but converts data into a neutral format. This neutral format can then be used by any application that is connected to the InfoBus.

The online bank can greatly enhance the data flow between the legacy system in the back-end and the front end systems. Instead of converting the data to a format the front end application understands, the data is offered to the InfoBus. The InfoBus is then able to deliver the information to any kind of device or application that is connected to the InfoBus. This enables the bank to switch front end applications whenever a new version becomes available. The integration with the back end system does not need to be considered in such a way as it needs to be today. Security can be an issue if the InfoBus is not only used for communication between legacy and customer, but also for internal data exchange. Although very powerful, security measures would need to be implemented, so that end customers are not able to see internal data.

The fashion manufacturer is able to present the same data in many different ways through InfoBus. By offering the data to the InfoBus, different applications are able to pick up the information and present it either graphically or textually to the customer. The information can the be presented in a visual way to the retailers, so that they can use the data for deciding which clothes fit into their shops. The same data needs to be presented in a textual way for the invoice and for automatic order processing.

The cargo company will be able to create a highly sophisticated tracking and tracing solution by combining the strengths of Jini and InfoBus. Jini will provide the networking infrastructure for all devices involved and the InfoBus protocol allows the exchange of information. This solution enables totally different types of devices to communicate with each other and pass information on.

The car manufacturer is able to create virtual team using different hardware devices for the development and in addition to this, the InfoBus protocol could be incorporated into the design, allowing technical checks to be made easier. Every device in the car is able to provide its information to a console, which checks the availability and the quality of service of each.

11.5.3   Online Experience

The concept of InfoBus is very new and so far no applications have been sighted on the Internet. Due to its nature, this type of information sharing will most likely happen first on company Intranets. The next section that will benefit from InfoBus are information services, such as online banking, where web applications serve as front-ends to legacy systems and databases.

Internet applications with interactive and dynamic features will be most likely using InfoBus, as the information used in the application can be updated easily in an instant. Normal HTML pages are very restricted. The current applet-servlet connections will be replaced with the InfoBus architecture in the near future. Instead of applets and servlets JavaBeans will be used.

One offline application is Lotus eSuite[18], which uses the InfoBus for seamless application integration allowing programmers to write custom extensions using eSuite and other off-the-shelf Java applications.

11.5.4   Required Software

The InfoBus specification is also available for free from Sun[19]. No special development tools are required for writing applications adhering to the InfoBus standard.

Distributed InfoBus (DI), developed by IBM[20] extends the InfoBus standard in such a way that it is able to operate across devices and JVMs. This removes the restriction mentioned above, that only JavaBeans within a single JVM can communicate with each other. DI works like a bridge for JVMs and supports several network protocols, namely HTTP and IIOP.

---

[18]http://www.lotus.com/

[19]http://java.sun.com/infobus/

[20]http://www.alphaworks.ibm.com/

11.6   Resolving Possible Java Issues

11.6.1   Speeding up Java

There are several ways of speeding up Java programs. Byte-code can be translated to native machine code. The JVM then directly executes, rather than abstractly emulates, the code according to the actual processor architecture of the system hosting execution. This performance improvement can be either done by "Just-In-Time" (JIT) compilation, i.e. when running the program it will be compiled, or by using a native compiler like TurboJ[21] which translates the Java program to native code and saves it in this format to the hard disk. The disadvantage of the second approach is that once you have compiled the Java program using TurboJ it is not hardware independent anymore. You would have to recompile it for another platform, which is still a lot easier than rewriting the whole application for the other platform. If performance is an issue, this may be the best way of doing it. The native compiler will appeal to large customers with known configurations who are willing to give up mobility for even better performance.

The latest invention from Sun is their HotSpot[22] technology. Most people will prefer this so-called optimized dynamic compiler to native compilers for the good performance that maintains application mobility.

There are some problems with JIT compilation. Due to the fact that the JIT compiler runs just before the application is executed, it does not have much time to do the compilation, otherwise the users would become impatient before they would have a chance to see to program itself. In order to save time it is not possible to perform extensive and advanced optimizations, which would really speed up the code, but slow down the start-up. HotSpot uses adaptive optimization to resolve the problems of JIT compilation by taking into account an interesting characteristic of most programs. Almost 100 percent of all programs spend most of their time executing a small part of their code. The relation between executed time and code part is about 80 to 20. About 80 percent of the time is spent on 20 percent of the code. Maybe you have already noticed earlier on that this relation has appeared several times throughout the book, in totally different situations. This particular relation is known as the Pareto principle or the 80/20 principle. More information on this topic can be found in Richard Koch's book "The 80/20 Principle"[23].

Instead of compiling the whole program when it starts, HotSpot runs the program immediately and tries to detect the critical areas of the program, which are called "hot spots". The global native-code optimizer then focuses on these hot spots. By avoiding compilation of infrequently executed code (on average about 80 percent of the program), the HotSpot compiler can spend more

---

[21] http://www.camb.opengroup.org/openitsol/turboj/
[22] http://java.sun.com/products/hotspot/
[23] Richard Koch, "The 80/20 Principle", Nicolas Brealey Publishing Ltd., London.

time on the performance-critical parts of the program, without increasing the start-up compile time. While the program is running, HotSpot monitors the activity of the program and adapts itself to the needs of the user. If, for example, someone is using a spread-sheet, the person may first do some calculations, so HotSpot will try to speed up this part of the program, and then do some graphics, so the optimization moves on to this part on the fly, to the needs of the user.

Applications can also have some parts compiled dynamically, and other parts compiled through the native compiler. Hewlett-Packard, Sun and Symantec[24] are developing tools to help users determine best compilation strategies for their applications. No matter how the code is compiled, it can share the same runtime environment and interact with Java applets that can come from anywhere in the organization.

As a rule of thumb, the performance will depend a lot on the application mix, but the Hewlett-Packard Java labs estimate that the optimized dynamic compiler offers five times the performance of the standard Java environments. The native compiler offers a boost of approximately six to seven times.

To get the best performance from a Java-based configuration, it's not enough to tune just the Java applications. In order to improve performance it is necessary to tune the entire configuration, including the Java runtime environment (JRE) and the underlying operating system. Although hardware tuning may make sense in some cases, Sun's hardware Java chips, for example, failed, just as many other specialized chips such as for Pascal and other languages failed before. The performance boost was too small to encourage users and developers to switch from multi-purpose chips to highly specialized CPUs (central processing units). Some businesses, for example, have seen dramatic performance improvements by tuning the way Java applications make calls to other applications or databases.

Hewlett-Packard's Java Environment Tuning Center (JETC)[25] draws expertize from several HP lab organizations to evaluate and tune customers' applications and computing environments. One company to visit the JETC was Ariba[26]. By improving the way the Ariba applications made procedure calls across class libraries and fine-tuning calls to the Oracle database, performance was improved by about 250 percent. HP engineers from the Java organization worked with HP-UX kernel engineers and the Developer Alliance Lab to characterize the Ariba application performance and improve the overall implementation.

Other companies, like IBM and Sun have similar organizations within their companies that help customers to speed up their Java development and improve the execution of their Java applications.

---

[24]http://www.symantec.com/
[25]http://www.hp.com/go/java/
[26]http://www.ariba.com/

Java Optimization Problems

If a JIT had time to perform a full optimization, it would be less effective than for other languages, like C for the following reasons:

- **Type Testing** – Dynamic type-tests need to be performed frequently, because the virtual machine must ensure that programs do not violate language semantics, or access unstructured memory.

- **Object Allocation** – Object allocation rates are much higher for the Java language than for C++, because it allocates all objects on the heap.

- **Method Invocations** – In Java, most method invocations are "virtual". This means not only that method invocation performance is more dominant, but that static compiler optimizations (especially global optimizations like in-lining) are much harder to perform for method invocations.

- **Dynamic Loading** – Java programs can change on-the-fly due to the powerful ability to perform dynamic loading of Java classes.

Table 11.6.

11.6.2 The 100 Percent Pure Java Initiative

100 percent Pure Java means that an application is written completely in Java and does not rely on external class libraries or native code. It is possible to integrate third party technologies, such as special classes, but they need to be distributed with the applet or application, so that it can run on any computer supporting Java. With smaller third party contributions this works fine, but there are some problems with large third party frameworks. First of all because of the size and then, of course, because of licensing issues. Another issue is that the technology used in the classes may be unknown and use proprietary technologies.

Java applications and applets should not rely on proprietary technologies, as these limit the program to a certain platform, which is opposed to the goal of Java. Using the standard toolkits for the user interface, for example, allows customers to see your application on any given platform, without any restrictions. Although there were many deficits in Java 1.0, from 1.1 on, these deficits have been addressed and compensated. There is, for example, no need to use any proprietary extensions to build a modern looking user interface anymore.

The 100 percent Pure Java initiative frees the developer from incompatibility concerns and lets them take advantage of the full benefits of the Java platform. As large third party contributions are difficult to integrate into a 100 percent Pure Java application, many developers asked to expand the JDK to support the needs for the most commonly used components. This has the advantage of an improved overall performance as they are more highly integrated.

11.6.3 Java Applet Security

Security is the major concern for going online. Many myths have contributed to this factor and new incidents seem to prove that the Internet as a whole is very insecure. Some companies block all types of applications as they may contain a virus which can destroy information on a company computer.

Although viruses are a major concern they are often associated with Java applets, which is simply wrong. In theory it is not possible to write software that is malicious as Java applets run in a so-called sandbox, which does not have any connection to the resources on the client's computer. In practice there have been some problems with the implementations of the browsers, which did not prevent all attacks.

In order to understand better why applets are secure, it is necessary to know what the difference between applets and applications are. By design, applets are embedded into web pages and do not run outside of the web page context. Applets are downloaded like HTML documents, but unlike HTML documents, are executed on the client computer.

Applets loaded over the net are prevented from reading and writing files on the client file system. Although this would already be enough to secure the computer of the client, additional security has been built in to prevent misusing the client's computer as a gateway by allowing Internet connections only back to the originating host.

Applets are also not allowed to start or access any application that has been already installed on the client, nor are they able to load libraries or define native method calls, preventing direct access to the operating system and its resources.

As you can imagine these security restrictions also restrict the usability of the Java applets. By default it is not possible to print documents or save documents. Java is able to print and save, but the web browsers prevent these functionalities when an applet is loaded. This is because you cannot trust applets, as you do not know where they come from.

If your applet requires additional features, such as printing or saving, then you can ask the clients to allow these features. Adding access to local resources requires the applet to be signed. By signing the applet the identity of the programmer is revealed. Once the applet has been loaded over the network, a browser requester pops up and asks the user if she or he wants to trust the applet of a certain person or company. Every single additional resource needs to be accepted individually. Saving, printing, loading would require three confirmations. The signature together with the confirmations make Java applets very secure.

This is only true, if the applet is loaded over the network. Applets that reside on the local hard disk are automatically trusted.

11.6.4   Java versus Active X

Active X and Java offer the possibility of adding functionality to static web pages, without additional server connections. By downloading an Active X control or a Java applet, web pages become more dynamic and interactive.

This basic advantage also brings some problems with it. Active X and Java pose an additional security risk to the data on your computer. By downloading a program it may contain back doors, which try to access or destroy data on your computer. In order to make Java and Active X useful and accepted by the users, both approaches implement measures to ensure the security and privacy of your data.

Active X is supported natively in Internet Explorer and can be used through a plug-in in Netscape as well. Through the security settings it is possible to accept Active X controls without warning, with warning or refuse them altogether. If you decide to accept Active X controls then you need to rely on your judgement, as there is no way to tell what the Active X control will be trying to do. Active X controls are like any other application, with all rights on the computer to read, delete and modify data.

Active X controls may contain a digital signature by the author. This digital signature tells you who has written the control and asks you to accept the control or to refuse it. In theory digital signatures are a good idea, but once you have accepted an Active X control, it is able to take over the computer. And don't expect to remember all signatures you have trusted in the past.

Java on the other hand restricts the access to local resources with untrusted applets. By default all programs are run in the Java "sandbox" as we have seen in the last subsection. As long as nobody finds a hole in the Java sandbox, you can be sure that your data and the resources on your computer, such as printers and hard disks are protected.

Therefore the major difference between accepting an Active X control and a Java applet is the level of damage that can be done by accepting unknown programs. Most Java applets and Active X controls are harmless, but only one malicious piece of code can destroy all your data. The more people download

Active X controls and Java applets which are hamless, the more they will trust the next one as well.

By accepting a Java applet, you do not permit access to local resources, but with Active X control you do permit this by accepting the download. If the Java security sandbox breaks down, then the Java applet will also gain access to all resources. The major difference is that in the Java case you did not permit access, while in the Active X case you did. In the case of an Active X control that tries to save a file to your hard disk and destroys by accident some data, you will have difficulties in suing the company for destroying your data, as you granted access to it. In the case of Java it is quite clear that you did not permit access to the data.

In order to be on the safe side, one should refuse all programs from the Internet, and decrease its value at the same time, as many applications rely on Active X controls or Java applets.

Signed Java applets offer a slight advantage over Active X as it is possible to partially trust programs. By offering access to the printer, the program is not able to see data on your hard disk. Active X requires you to fully trust it or refuse it. Java in general also offers better protection against accidental damage caused by a bug in the program.

Due to the nature of Active X programs it is possible to implement programming languages and let programs run in that environment. This is not only restricted to Active X components, but is also valid for browser plug-ins. By accepting these programs you are trusting only the plug-in or Active X control, but have no control over the programs, which are run within it. Shockwave is such a plug-in, which executes applications created by Macromedia Director. If the plug-in or Active X control has a security problem, it can be exploited easily by the program that is running within the component.

Fortunately only very few attacks are known through Java, Active X or Plug-ins. But nobody can guarantee that this will be like this forever. The possibilities are there and it is just a matter of time until someone sits down and writes some malicious code.

In order to reduce the risk, you should not generally trust a component by a single user or company. Every time you download a new component, think about its necessity. Is it really necessary to run it, or does it pose a security problem? In order to reduce the risk even further, trust only components that have a single functionality, such as displaying a new graphic format. If you trust a complex application the risk is higher that something may go wrong, intentionally or non-intentionally.

Download always the latest release of your favorite web browser and look out for patches that close identified security holes. This will reduce the risk that the browser is responsible for the accident. The computer that you use for browsing the web should also not contain critical information that may be important for you or interesting for others. Keep these files on a server with password access and you should be fine. In the case that a program destroys the content of your hard disk, you should be up and running again fairly soon, if there is only standard software running on it.

11.6.5 Moving from C++ to Java

As Java is becoming more important every day, many companies want to port their existing code, written in other languages to Java, in order to benefit from the object-orientation and the cross-platform abilities of Java. It has significant advantages over C++ in terms of portability, power, and simplicity.

C++ was developed by Bjarne Stroustrop of AT&T Bell Labs during the 1980s. It was derived from the object oriented language Simula and the procedural language C. C++ was developed to allow programmers to build object oriented software without sacrificing C's efficiency. C++ is now widely used, its speed of adoption due to the fact that the transition from C to C++ was considered to be relatively simple. Another probable reason for success is that it is a hybrid language; you can use it in a procedural manner and/or an object oriented manner.

But this is also the reason why C++ provides all the opportunities to shoot yourself in the foot just as C did. Its Achilles heel is the freedom it gives the programmer in dealing with pointers. Pointer arithmetic, casting and explicit memory management using "new" and "delete" are the major causes of bugs in C++ programs, just like in C. This is not possible in Java, making it more fool-proof than C++.

Many programs have been written in C++, so that object-orientation is no problem, and it is not necessary to change the programming paradigm. These advantages are leading many people to consider replacing C++ with Java, not only for web applets, but increasingly for client and server applications as well.

This subsection will highlight some of the most important things a programmer has to think about when moving from C++ to Java. IBM[27] has an excellent online tutorial for people who require more information on this topic.

The major differences between C++ and Java are syntactic, so that the Java compiler will be able to discover the differences, in case you have forgotten to change them. The Java compiler is much more rigorous than that of C++, so much of the code that needs to be changed will be found by the compiler. But in some instances the same code in C++ and Java has dangerously different consequences.

There are several differences that need to be taken into account when moving code from C++ to Java. The Java language does not support three data types that are part of the C and C++ languages: struct, union, and pointer. These data types can be emulated in most cases. There are also some differences in how certain operators in the Java language work as compared to both C and C++. And the command line arguments passed to a Java application are different in number and in type than those passed to a C or C++ program. An-

---

[27]http://www.ibm.com/java/education/portingc/

other important difference is string handling. In C and C++, strings are simply a null-terminated array of characters. The Java language uses the String class provided in the java.lang package. In C++ you can have multiple-inherited classes where Java only has single-inheritance. Other features not present in Java, but are in C++, include global variables, stand-alone functions, friend functions (everything in a package is a friend of everything else in the package) and non-virtual functions.

A number of features have been added to Java to make it safer including true arrays with bounds checking, concurrency, interfaces and packages. There is no need to explicitly allocate or free memory in Java, as this is handled by the garbage collector.

As Java follows C++ conventions in many cases, large parts of the original C++ can remain unchanged. This includes variable names, the flow of control, names of primitive types, operators and comments, for example. Just as in C++, Java allows you to write classes, override methods, overload methods, write constructors and instantiate objects.

Moving from other languages may prove to be more difficult or in some cases to be easier. Languages belonging to the group of Wirth are very easy to convert to Java, as they follow a similar syntax. Moving programs written in Pascal, Modula or Oberon can be easily re-compiled in Java, while Ada and Lisp require some more in-depth review of the original source code, before they can be moved to Java.

11.7 Avoiding the Java Wars

11.7.1 Hewlett-Packard

Through 1998 we have seen two major fights over Java. Hewlett-Packard developed its own version of the Java API for embedded devices in conjunction with Intel and other partners and Microsoft got sued for its implementation of Java in Internet Explorer 4. Many people were concerned that the Java standard would vanish after these wars, but actually the opposite happened. Probably the opposite happened, because of the media attention on both fights; Java became even more popular.

Hewlett-Packard realized after evaluating the draft specification of Sun's embedded Java implementation that practical considerations for manufacturing Java into these devices have not been taken into account. As Sun is not producing embedded devices they were not aware of the possibilities and problems of the embedded devices market. Because of the unfortunate licensing scheme of Sun, HP would need to become a licensee of the Sun code and would have to renounce control over the intellectual property. Hewlett-Packard was not willing to participate in such a controlling process.

Hewlett-Packard wrote its own embedded virtual machine called Chai (Russian for Tea), and referenced published specifications to ensure compatibility with functional specs and upward compatibility with any enterprise Java implementation. The Hewlett-Packard virtual machine is a complete implementation, but the Java APIs are assigned to different devices based on the devices' function and memory. Microwave ovens and medical instruments, for example, require different functions and have a different amount of memory available. One of the things an embedded system requires is flexibility. The original Sun embedded virtual machine required all devices to incorporate all APIs, which would add cost and memory overhead in the manufacturing process.

Java's automatic garbage collection is a big problem with Java for embedded systems. Garbage collection is used to automatically release memory from objects that are no longer needed. This makes it easy to write programs, but occupies the system for an unpredictable period of time, making it unsuitable for real-time applications. Hewlett-Packard's modified version of the JVM uses a variant of the original garbage collection, called "incremental garbage collection", which allows for more determinacy than Sun's original implementation.

The paradigm of write-once-run-anywhere is much less important in embedded systems where functionality is carefully defined in the design. Users normally do not program these devices, all software comes from the manufacturer. The real attraction of Java lies in its high-level object-oriented nature and the uniform development and target environment. Another problem lies in Sun's Java licensing model, as embedded devices are shipped in much higher volume, the price per device is too high to make it cost-effective.

Many people thought that Hewlett-Packard wanted to go its own way, but the truth is that they wanted to show Sun how it should be done. Widespread approval of this approach and support from a range of leading Real-time Operating System vendors, such as Intel and Wind River have influenced Sun to alter its original design.

But unfortunately Sun halted half way through, which resulted in the creation of the J Consortium[28] formed by several companies such as Hewlett-Packard, NewMonics[29] and Plum Hall[30], which tries to push new features into the Java language for embedded devices independently of Sun. These companies have formalized an effort to define a standard for "real-time" extensions.

The J Consortium is an incorporated version of the Real-Time Java Working Group. Incorporation gives the effort a better ability to set a real-time Java standard. The J Consortium wants to deal with the real-time extensions to Java, but won't touch the rest of the Java technology.

Sun is not happy with this development of course, as it createss two versions of the real-time extensions. The J Consortium members are unhappy about Sun, because the process of creating the real-time standard is controlled by Sun only. The J Consortium claims that Sun does not have enough knowledge in the area of real-time applications and devices.

---

[28]http://www.jconsortium.org/

[29]http://www.newmonics.com/

[30]http://www.plumhall.com/

In any case, this fight over Java shows quite clearly the status of Java in the industry. Every company tries to pull Java in its own direction to appear as the market leader in developing applications and devices. Although the fight over the real-time extensions won't change anything in the Java language standard, it shows where most companies see the future of computing. Pervasive computing will incorporate embedded devices and therefore gaining control over the programming language, which will run on these devices will give the company the decisive advantage for the business of tomorrow. It seems that Java has won the race, now the race is on which Java is going to be used. More information on Java in embedded devices can be found in Chapter 15, which deals with the new paradigm of pervasive computing. There embedded devices and Java play an important role.

11.7.2 Microsoft

The fight between Sun and Microsoft on the other hand did have another reason. For Microsoft the Java standard meant a threat to its market share, as the operating system suddenly became irrelevant. The operating system was the core business of Microsoft. Windows in all its flavors had more than 95 percent of the market share. But if people started to implement software in Java it suddenly didn't matter which operating system you were using.

Nonetheless Microsoft became a licensee of the Java language in order to incorporate it into its web browser Internet Explorer and it Software Development Kit (SDK) for Java.

In 1998 Sun sued Microsoft and asked them to remove the Java from their products, as they did not seem to adhere to the Sun Java standard. Neither of the two programs passed the Java compatibility test, which meant that Java applications written with the Microsoft tools might not run on other platforms (such as the Mac OS) or in other browsers (such as Netscape Communicator).

Sun's complaint against Microsoft included trademark infringement, unfair competition, breach of contract, false advertising and others. Sun's claim was that Microsoft was trying to break Java's success by tampering its "write once, run anywhere" promise. Microsoft was suspected of adding Windows-specific code to the Java language that would inevitably break the cross-platform operability. See Table 11.7 for a list of differences in the implementations.

Although Sun may be right with its claims, the claims are just a sort of marketing gag. Not many developers are using Microsoft tools to develop Java applications anyway, as there are much better tools on the market and those who do not stay with the Java specification are not interested in achieving true cross-platform compatibility. Buying a reference book with the Java specification does not cost much and the specification can even be downloaded from the web. Microsoft on the other hand should not try to sell its software as 100 percent Java, it should write on its products "loosely based on Java" or something similar.

Differences in Microsoft's Java

The Microsoft Software Development Kit for Java contained several alterations to the original specification provided by Sun. In January 1999 a patch was released by Microsoft that resolved the described changes.

- **New Classes** – Sixteen new classes were introduced into java.awt that you should avoid.

- **New Methods** – There are at least fourteen methods that you should not use unless you only want to run your applications on a Windows platform using IE.

- **New Instances** – There are two instance variables for you to avoid also.

- **No Portability** – Forget portability, if you choose to use the classes in com.ms.

- **Method Missing** – A toString() method of ByteArray-OutputStream is missing.

- **Object Locking** – This may be performed at a different level from the one you expect, so it may favour one platform over another.

Table 11.7.

In January 1999 Microsoft had to put the Service Pack 2 for their developer products onto their web sites, which includes patches to make its software compliant with the Sun specification. Microsoft had lost this round in the fight in court for Java.

Developing new solutions with Java give you the edge over your competitors as it is the right tool for developing Internet services and products. With Java release 2 Sun has opened the license of Java to allow others to modify the source code. If you do use Java, be sure to get in contact with Sun and try to influence them to release Java as open source which will make it the true and only standard for Internet applications for the next years.

11.8 The Future of Java Computing

11.8.1 New Java Technologies

Many other Java technologies are emerging, among them additions like Java 3D, offering an API for developing applications with three-dimensional graphical objects. The Java 3D API gives developers a set of high-level constructs for creating and manipulating 3D geometry. Tools for constructing the structures used in rendering that geometry are also made available in the same package. Integration with other web standards is also very important. The integration between Java and XML is a very important step into the future.

Sun is developing a Java standard extension for XML. The basic functionality includes the reading, manipulating and generating of XML text, which are the core features required to form the building blocks for developing fully functional, XML-based applications. This extension is planned to become a standard extension for Java, enabling every Java application to understand XML, if desired. By extending the JavaBeans architecture to understand XML it becomes even easier to integrate it into existing applications.

XML is changing the way electronic business is implemented on the Internet. Together with Java it is enabling a new generation of Internet applications. XML and Java form together a complete, platform-independent, Web-based computing environment, which is able to produce portable "smart" data. Code written in Java can be embedded into an XML document. This allows data to be created with its own data manipulation application. While XML enables the information exchange, Java is able to automate the exchange. XML contributes to platform-independent data, in the form of portable documents and data, while Java contributes to platform-independent processing through portable object oriented software solutions. IBM has created a dedicated vertical XML portal[31], which contains a lot of Java applications and example source code for business applications.

11.8.2 Outlook into the Future

As Java 2 has only been released for a while it is difficult to predict which direction it will take. So far Java's fate was decided by Sun. With the introduction of Java version 2 the license has been made a little more friendly, allowing third parties to develop additions to the standard. One of the major contributors to new development in Java was IBM and its AlphaWorks[32] web site.

More and more free implementations of Java appear, making it possible to implement and use Java without having to rely on Sun, making it a truly open programming language for anyone in every situation. But Java will only become a standard for the future, if it becomes an official ISO standard.

---

[31] http://www.ibm.com/developer/xml/
[32] http://www.alphaworks.ibm.com/

Java won't make other programming languages superfluous, but it can be expected that new libraries for other languages will appear that will make cross-platform availability of the application easier. One such framework is FoundationWare, developed by Hewlett-Packard, which unifies and simplifies Windows NT and HP-UX development and deployment, by bundling industry-leading middleware technologies with HP-UX. A set of common middleware services, such as CORBA ORBs and the LDAP Integration Kit, are made available for HP-UX or Windows through a set of APIs. This creates a single development environment for HP-UX and Windows NT applications.

The accompanying FoundationTools allow developers to use a single-source code stream for both Windows NT and HP-UX versions of an application. This common development environment and the single source code stream enable faster, easier, less costly development of robust, scalable applications that run immediately on Windows NT and HP-UX. The application can be developed in Visual C++ and then compiled at the same time for NT and HP-UX.

A similar product is Tributary by Bristol Technology[33] that enables software developers to use Microsoft Visual C++ as their integrated development environment for Sun Solaris and IBM OS/390. Tributary extends the Visual C++ IDE, leveraging existing knowledge, to write, compile, link, and debug enterprise applications. The software allows developers to combine the power and reliability of Solaris and OS/390 with the ease of use of Visual C++ application development. The ability to integrate with third party tools allows developers to write native Solaris and OS/390 applications from Visual C++, and to easily port Windows 32-bit applications and applications using the Microsoft Foundation Classes (MFC) to UNIX.

Similar products are under development by other companies to simplify the development and deployment of non-Java applications across several operating systems and types of devices. In addition to these new cross-platform compilers, there have been introduced new cross-language converters, which allow you to convert source code from one programming language to another. Many cross-language converters have been written to allow programmers to convert their code from Basic, Pascal or C++ to Java, for example, to make the transition easier and to combine new and old code more easily.

Java has put pressure on other programming languages to become cross-platform compatible and support the Internet. Java is still leading, but other languages are getting nearer. We will see what Java 3 will look like, but it can be expected that it will remain in lead.

---

[33]http://www.bristol.com/

Chapter 12

IMAGING ON THE INTERNET

12.1 Image Business

12.1.1 Reasons for Better Quality Images

The reason I have dedicated a separate chapter to images is easily explained. Although many people browse the Internet for information, they mostly get from it textual information. The quality of pictures is poor compared to magazines, for example. This is the main reason most Internet users do not buy goods online that rely on high-quality pictures to show their design. Selling books, tickets and CDs over the Internet is easy, as nobody is really interested in the fabric of the cover or the information that is printed on the ticket. Content is more important than design in these cases.

If we now look at businesses that rely on design and not so much on content, we can identify the following: Goods that are bought on an emotional basis need good graphics on the Internet to sell. These emotive goods are bought not only because of their price or their features, but also because you like what you see.

If we look at the business opportunities on the Internet for high-quality imaging, we can identify the two following areas where they have the biggest impact:

- **E-Catalogues** - High-resolution images in your e-commerce storefront, especially for emotive goods.

- **E-Business Communications** - Newsletters, publishing and banner advertising will also profit from the higher resolution of images.

Web sites using high-resolution imaging will enhance communication, collaboration and commerce.

Customers on the Internet want a better and more interactive experience while browsing their preferred online shop. The online-merchants on the other hand want to increase their volume of online sales (Customer: "I can see the product"). They want to reduce product return costs (Customer: "It's what I

451

thought it was") and they want to increase the number of repeat orders per year (Customer: "I like it, I'll do this again"). This also allows the online-merchants to sell higher-value goods online that would not have sold otherwise (e.g. cars, appartments, jewellery, clothing).

12.1.2 Business Requirements

In order to realize the full potential of an image-rich web site for business-to-business and business-to-consumer requirements, the Internet Imaging technology needs to meet the following requirements:

- **High resolution** – Viewing and printing of high resolution images should be feasible by as many users as possible, without having the need for more resources on the client, server and network side.

- **Download speed** – Download times for high-resolution images must be kept to a minimum. Download times should be optimized for the output device, e.g. low resolution at 72 dots per inch (dpi) for the monitor and 600 dpi for a laser printer.

- **Universal format** – A multi-functional, information-rich format, that allows a bandwidth efficient display on the web and printout. It should need neither special plug-ins nor additional software.

- **Universal access** – The users should be able to receive the pictures that they desire from any source without being restricted by their own location.

- **Free choice of browser and image processing software** – The users should be able to use any browser or image processing software to download, print or alter images.

- **Scalability** – The Internet imaging solutions and technologies must enable companies and webmasters to manage the fast-growing number of images quickly and efficiently.

- **Integration with existing solutions** – Every new imaging technology must enable the users to include downloaded images in existing applications.

- **Open standard and open source** – Open standard means that the format is developed in a public forum, and Open Source means that the source code of the viewer is free to use and be modified by anyone.

12.1.3   Example Business Cases

Having the technology to display high-resolution graphics is one thing that can be achieved by creating new standards on the Internet. But more important is the business case. If the new standard or technology does not help us to sell more of our products online or reduce the costs of production, then there is no reason to use it. There are many cases on the Internet where people used hyped up technology and failed because the business case was not good enough. So we will now develop four business cases and see if the technology is adding value to each electronic business.

The Photographer

An artist wants to sell her artwork online. She is a photographer and a painter. Customers are able to connect to her site and look at the images. Using static images, they can get a rough idea of what is in the picture. They will send off an e-mail to the artist asking for a catalogue in order to get a higher resolution of the desired picture. As you can see, this involves many additional steps in between before the deal can be closed. Why are the customers not able to get higher resolution images for the desired picture? Why can't they just print out a high-resolution image from within the web page?   .

The Fashion Designer

A fashion designer needs some new cloth for his designer clothes. He connects to the web site of several cloth factories and wants to find out about their new material. He can easily compare the prices and the relative availability. But how about the fabric of the cloth? He needs to send e-mails out and ask if they can provide samples. Why can't the designer print out a high-resolution image of the cloth to show the fabric? In this case, of course, he still needs to order samples because he needs to feel the difference, but he can at least reduce the number of requests.

The Car Manufacturer

A car manufacturer wants to sell cars online. The customers connect to the Internet site of the manufacturer. They are able to find out all the technical details about the car, they can see some pictures and even buy it online. But if they want to do a test drive they will need to find out where the nearest car dealer is (a little database on the web site will do that). The next thing would be to check when it would best suit everyone to come along for a test drive (an e-mail to the dealer could be sent). But how about walking around the car while online? How about sitting in it and drive around a little without going to the car dealer at all?

The Retailer

A retailer has different means of transporting content to its customers: either sending out a traditional printed catalogue, a brochure, a multimedia CD-ROM or distributing information on the products via the Internet. Most retailers will have a unit working on the catalogue, a unit working on the CD-ROM and one working on the web site. The reasons in the past were manifold, but the most important one was that the technology for producing these different types of media was too different. Wouldn't it be a good idea to unify the images and texts for all three media and get all the information from a single resource?

12.2 Image Concepts

12.2.1 Static Image Formats

If we now look at the commonly used formats on the Internet, we can see that only static image formats are directly supported by the web browsers. Here, static means that the image itself cannot change its colors, perspective or resolution. All browsers understand the static file formats GIF, JPEG and PNG (there are still some souls out there who put BMP graphics on their web pages and do not notice that the majority of people see only a broken link). This section will give you a short overview of these formats and explain their advantages and disadvantages before moving on to the dynamic formats that will enhance your web presence tremendously.

If we look at the market share that GIF, JPEG and PNG have, we will see that PNG (pronounced "ping") is not very common yet. But when creating web sites with static images, you should nowadays consider PNG to be the best solution.

Static images should be used nowadays to create a flashy layout on your site. As soon as you try to sell something, you should consider moving on to dynamic formats.

So why bother with PNG, when GIF and JPEG have been around for so long? Both of them have problems. The GIF was developed by CompuServe and has a bad reputation for being the format of choice for pornographic images that were exchanged on the CompuServe network. GIF uses the patented LZW compression algorithm from Unisys, so that actually every GIF-supporting program would require paying licensing fees. As far as I know this was never enforced, but this could change anytime, so it is better not to rely on this format. GIF images support only up to 256 colors. This was fine until true color graphic cards became the standard in all computers.

JPEG on the other hand is a so-called "lossy" image format. Depending on the strength of compression, the image loses information. The compression algorithm tries to remove data that cannot be distinguished by the human eye, so that makes it a good format for viewing. But as soon as you try to change a JPEG image, you will notice that this hidden information is missing. When applied to photos you won't notice the loss, but with clip arts, text, etc. you can see the difference immediately. The advantage of JPEG is that the files are compressed at a ratio of 1:10 or more, so that your 500 KB images become less than 50 KB to download.

When CompuServe announced at the end of 1994 that the GIF format uses a patented algorithm, the Internet society started developing a new format (after the obligatory inflammatory weeks on Usenet) that would be free of charge and better than GIF and JPEG together. The PNG project is a perfect example of Internet co-operation and efficiency (similar projects are Linux[1], Mozilla[2] and Apache[3], see also Chapter 14 for more information on open source projects). Using mainly E-mail and Newsgroups, developers from all over the world have designed and implemented this new standard. The goals for the new image format where the following:

- **Portability** – Make it portable across platforms, operating systems and implementations.

- **Network-friendly** – Make it network-friendly by reducing the size of the image.

- **New Graphic Format** – Create a new graphics format to replace GIF and partly JPEG.

PNG does not support animation. For animations there is another format called MNG ("Multiple-Image Network Graphics"). It is based on PNG and will do everything that GIF animations do and more (e.g. sprites, multimedia features).

Starting with Version 4 of Netscape Navigator/Communicator and Internet Explorer, PNG is directly supported by these browsers. Older browsers can be PNG-enabled by downloading a plug-in [4]. Depending on the customers, the webmaster needs to find out how many of them still rely on older versions of browsers. If you are, for example, creating web pages for your Intranet and know that everybody is using Netscape 4.5 or higher, then it is quite easy to switch from GIF to PNG. Always check the log files of your web server and your user profile before moving on to a new format. See also Chapter 9 for more browser-related information.

Do not stand still. The Internet is constantly changing. And change is good. Remember to keep changing as well, otherwise you will fail. Users with PNG-enabled browsers will notice the difference in image quality and faster download times.

---

[1] http://www.linux.org/
[2] http://www.mozilla.org/
[3] http://www.apache.org/
[4] http://browserwatch.internet.com/plug-in.html

What Is New in PNG?

The PNG image format is the new standard for static image files on the Internet. Officially PNG stands for "Portable Network Graphics". The unofficial acronym for PNG is "PNG's Not GIF" (just like "GNU's Not Unix", a recursive acronym). The most important features of PNG are:

- Greyscale images up to 16-bits (GIF and JPEG: 8-bit)

- True-color images up to 48-bits (GIF: 8-bit, JPEG: 24-bit)

- Up to 65536 levels of transparency/translucency (GIF has one, JPEG none).

- Automatic "brightness" compensation across platforms (not supported by GIF, JPEG)

- Two-dimensional interlacing, which provides an initial impression of the image after just 1/64 of the data has arrived (GIF, JPEG: after 1/3 of the data has arrived).

- Free of patents and better compression (1/3 of GIF, comparable to JPEG).

Table 12.1.

To get back to the business case, static images are the best choice for images that do not contain content, but are for web page design purposes only, for low-quality images or non-interactive pictures. Many companies nowadays use static image formats for delivering high-quality and interactive imaging, but this requires a large overhead and limits use.

A simple example would be to offer a small thumb nail of an image on a web page and then by clicking on the image, you could get a higher resolution image of the same picture. Many people think that this may be a good solution, but it becomes highly complicated as soon as one has thousands of images on the web site and wants to offer them all in five different resolutions. Using a static format one will need some good conversion tools, a database and some other tools (CGI-scripts, content management systems, etc.) to manage the site. The use of interactive image formats will simplify the administrative procedure, as we will see later on.

Animations can be done quite easily with static image formats, but the size of the images will increase dramatically. Please ask yourself first if you really need to rotate the e-mail button before uploading it onto your web site. The animation may attract more customers to click it but on the other hand, if the download takes too long it will get fewer people onto your web site. Creating animations using dynamic image formats may require a little more work, but the files will be much smaller (e.g. a small ASCII text containing the co-ordinates of the movement of an object, instead of saving each frame of movement). Again, depending on your customer profile one should decide on the complexity of the web page design (see also Chapter 5). Before developing a visual strategy one should always decide on the purpose and the message of the site.

From a business point of view, static image formats will be important to your web designers but won't help increase sales over the Internet. The future of static image formats is PNG (and for animations MNG), so use them to show that you are using state-of-the-art technology. Static image formats become useless as soon as one tries to create an interactive experience for the customers. It's not worth the effort. Looking at the assumptions made in the section "business requirements", one can see that not all of the requirements are met by the static image formats.

12.2.2   Dynamic Image Formats

If we now look at dynamic image formats, we can see that there is a whole range of different products on the market right now. Dynamic image formats are able to change their resolution, change the perspective, the lights, colors, etc. In the context of Internet imaging, dynamic does not mean Java applications, Director movies or Active X controls that can also deliver dynamic and interactive image formats. They need additional programming. Dynamic image formats do not require programming. They do require design, though.

Dynamic images contain meta-information about the picture itself, allowing one to modify its appearance without having to create a new picture. Think, for example, of an apple that can be viewed from all sides without having to reload the web page. Looking at an apple in GIF format one cannot change the perspective of the apple; one cannot view the apple from the other side, because the GIF format hasn't stored any information on what the other side may look like. Adding meta-information to the data is crucial for processing it and for creating added value to the customer (as already discussed in Chapter 6).

Most of the dynamic image formats use browser plug-ins or need special viewer programs. This limits the use of the formats if the plug-ins are not available for all target platforms (one of the few plug-ins that is available for all platforms is the Adobe Acrobat Reader plug-in[5], making PDF files the standard for distributing documents over the Internet). Using Java applets will resolve

---

[5]http://www.adobe.com/

the platform dependency, but this may require you to write a Java web application (called Applet). This may be overkill. If you rely on browser plug-ins like
Apple's QuickTime[6], Platinum's CosmoPlayer[7] or Real Networks' RealPlayer[8],
you have a good chance of being on the right track. All of them are already installed when downloading Netscape Communicator, for example. The following
three sections are about technologies that enhance your online business case
or enable a new business case to be taken online.

FlashPix, QuickTime VR and VRML are three breakthrough technologies,
which have been chosen on the basis of this section on business requirements
for Internet imaging. There are many other formats out there, but none of
them fit as well into the business requirements.

12.3   The FlashPix Format

12.3.1   Technical Overview

FlashPix is unlike any other imaging technology available today. The key to
FlashPix is a multi-resolution, tiled file format that allows images to be stored
at different resolutions for different purposes, such as editing or printing. Each
resolution is divided into 64×64 blocks, or tiles. Within a tile, pixels can be
either uncompressed, JPEG compressed or single-color compressed.

FlashPix objects are stored in structured storage container files and the
image data is stored in defined color spaces called sRGB, which are close to
most commonly used RGB color spaces, but which are calibrated to known color
values. By defining the color space options and providing standard ICC color
management profiles, FlashPix delivers consistent color on standard systems
as well as with color managed systems.

Editing is easily handled thanks to a set of image manipulation features
known as the image view. The image view works like two co-ordinate systems;
the source and the result co-ordinate system. Viewing parameters include area
selection, a filtering parameter, a spatial orientation matrix, a color twist matrix, and a contrast parameter.

The FlashPix format is also rich in non-image data definitions. This meta-
data includes information such as content description, camera information and
scan description. Finally, FlashPix has the ability to add numerous extensions.
With FlashPix, applications can add new storage, streams and/or property sets
that can be maintained across editing sessions of the file. Audio, for instance,
can already be embedded into FlashPix images.

The communication between web browser and web server is handled by
the Internet Imaging Protocol (IIP). This new protocol, developed by the same
team as the FlashPix format, is designed to communicate tiled image data

---

[6]http://www.apple.com/quicktime/
[7]http://www.cosmoworld.com/
[8]http://www.real.com/

FlashPix Features

Some of the highlights of the FlashPix format are the following:

- Resolution-independent co-ordinate system

- Multiple image representations

- Defines a standardized color space that keeps colors consistent when viewed across various displays and printers

- Contains compression header information shared between all files at all resolutions in all sub-images, reducing file size dramatically

- Structured storage makes FlashPix easily accessible

- Allows creation of new extensions such as an audio extension which allows you to attach audio data to an image in a single complete package

- Scaleable and portable

- Specifies operations to be applied to image data acquired from a source

- Resulting image data can be cached independently of the source format

Table 12.2.

and related information efficiently over network connections. To maximize performance over the Net, IIP reduces messaging overhead by bundling multiple requests into a single message that an IIP server can parse (for incoming messages), and format (for outgoing messages). This allows efficient access to multi-resolution images. IIP is designed to work especially well with images in FlashPix file format but does work with non-FPX files just as easily and transparently.

12.3.2 Checking the Business Cases

Looking at the business case examples from the first section one can see that FlashPix is able to meet the expectations of the customers extremely well in the first two cases and the last one. The artist is able to deliver high-quality images to the customer using the FlashPix technology. Using a conversion tool or a paint program (e.g. Adobe's PhotoShop), she is able to transform her artwork into high-resolution web-enabled images. The customers are able to surf the artist's web page using low bandwidth network access (e.g. via modem), looking at all the images online, but always with the possibility of high-resolution prints. The major issue with high quality images is copyright protection. Digital watermarks have not proven to be effective so far. So additional protective measures need to be taken. One of them should be that the name of the artist and the license scheme should come with each picture (What is the end-user allowed to do with it? How many copies are they allowed to print?).

But this really depends on the type of artwork. If one is painting large format pictures, there should be no need to add security, there are too few large format color printers around.

Poster designers and painters, creating small format pictures, on the other hand, have a problem giving out high-resolution images. It may ruin their business. In this case one should consider selling the high-quality images over the Internet. Right now it is not possible to limit the number of prints a user makes. But future releases of the FlashPix technology will eventually allow this type of licensing scheme. Two scenarios are possible:

1. **Pre-Paid** – The customers download a picture, pay for a certain number of printouts and are able to make the printouts whenever they want. As soon as they have reached the maximum number of printouts the software will refuse to print the image until the artists receives a new order from the user.

2. **Post-Paid** – Encoded into the picture are the payment details (e.g. credit card, debit card, etc.). As soon as one tries to print out a picture, the information is sent to the artist via Internet and a little fee is collected for each printout. In conjunction with large-format printers this could create a new dimension in selling art. A poster shop would consist of some terminals and a large format printer. The customers would choose their preferred poster online. Then they would give this information to one of the shop assistants who would print out the poster for the customer in the desired size. The customers could also access the poster shop from home and get the poster shipped. The customer is more satisfied because he has a greater choice of images and the shop manager is happy because he does not need to buy a large quantity of posters in advance, but can produce the posters on demand.

The fashion designer in our second example is able to choose the color and fabric online without printing at all. Being online, he can zoom into the pictures for more details, so that there is no need for a print anymore. He can get a look at the details of the fabric and then decide which of them need to be examined in real life, saving him a lot of unnecessary work. Adding a "feel-device" may resolve the problem of not being able to touch and feel the cloth, but being realistic, such a thing won't be available within the next few years (but then again, maybe there is someone out there just creating such a device). The fashion designer himself can use FlashPix himself for his online catalogue. Using FlashPix he can allow users to take a closer look at the fashion presented online.

The third business case does not profit so much by the FlashPix technology. The only thing you can do with FlashPix here is to offer a selection of views of the car and let the user zoom into the details. It will be hard to create a 3D type of experience with the current versions of the FlashPix format. Future releases of FlashPix are expected to have a type of panoramic view built in that enables users to create 3D environments.

Our retailer in the fourth business case could use FlashPix to generate a type of meta-catalogue for images. Just as with text, which will be basically the same for catalogue, CD-ROM and web site, the creators can now join the image resolutions into a single database. From there they can extract the required resolution (e.g. 1200 dpi for the catalogue, 144 dpi for the CD-ROM and 72 dpi for the web site). The image will automatically be available in the required resolution. Even without using the client software of FlashPix the designers of the catalogue can make a large impact on costs by using a unified source for images.

12.3.3 Online Experience

If we now look at the web, we can see many companies already using the Flash-Pix technology to deliver high-quality images to their customers. Fat Face[9], a UK based retailer of fashion for the Generation X has re-launched its web site in November 1998 using FlashPix technology which has been integrated into their existing InterShop shopping solution. More than 2,300 products are now available in high resolution on the Internet. Customers now have the possibility to choose, for example, a pair of trousers and are able to zoom in and see embroideries, stitching and other details.

Another fine example is the web site of PowerDisc[10]. PowerPics, which is their online service, is a digital stock photography site for business use in presentations, brochures, and newsletters. On the web site you can find images through keyword or category search engines. Images then can be added to the shopping basket and are ready to be purchased. One can choose a resolution and a license agreement. The cost depends on both the resolution (Customer: "What size do I need?") and the license agreement (Customer: "What do I need the pictures for?"). PowerDisc used to distribute images on CD-ROMs before moving its operation to the Internet.

---

[9]http://www.fatface.co.uk/
[10]http://www.powerpics.com/

Figure 12.1. Zoom on a picture by Nicolaj Romanov

Gallery-Net[11] is using the technology to show paintings in high quality. Figure 12.1 shows the difference in detail of FlashPix (left) and a JPEG (right) file, when zoomed in.

Pornographic web sites were the first to adopt and use the SSL encryption for credit card payments. After it proved to be a secure and viable way for Internet payment, other online businesses have taken over the SSL encryption for doing secure business over the Internet. The use of HTML forms and SSL substantially reduced the cost for many companies. Suddenly they could automate the whole payment process. FlashPix is in a similar position. It lowers costs for businesses using it, so soon it will be more widely adopted. The Digital Imaging Group has promised a simple freeware implementation of FlashPix thus enabling everyone to use it.

12.3.4 Required Software

In order to view FlashPix images over the Internet, some software needs to be installed on the web server. Among the server products there are "Netgraphica/IIP Server" by TrueSpectra Inc[12], Hewlett-Packard's "OpenPix ImageIgniter"[13] and Live Picture's "Image Server"[14]. FlashPix images used to be

---

[11]http://www.gallery-net.com/
[12]http://www.truespectra.com/
[13]http://image.hp.com/
[14]http://www.livepicture.com/

displayed with a plug-in in older versions of the software servers. Newer re-leases of the server software allow the use of cgi-bin applications, Java applets, ActiveX components or even flat images. The most common way is to use a Java applet because it works on all platforms and requires no additional soft-ware to be installed. In some cases, though, it may not be the fastest way to view the images.

A very innovative feature has been introduced into Version 3.0 of the Open-Pix ImageIgniter Software. It automatically detects the type of browser and serves the images in the format that suits your browser best. The Netscape browsers use a Java applet, Internet Explorer an Active X component and all other browsers use a CGI-based solution. Although this is not the ultimate solution, it is the optimal solution for the current situation on the market, with different browsers adopting different standards (it would be optimal, if all browsers would understand the same standards in the same way). The other companies producing server software are catching up and are trying to top the feature list. For a complete list of FlashPix enabled products, you can always go to the web site of the Digital Imaging Group[15]. There you will find an up-to-date list of products, ranging from digital cameras and scanners to image software that support the FlashPix format and a freeware implementation of the FlashPix server software. Although it is far from being as powerful as the commercial products, it is good enough for a trial.

12.4 QuickTime VR

12.4.1 Technical Overview

QuickTime was invented a few years back by Apple Computer and has since then become the most popular environment for multimedia CD-ROM and In-ternet productions. QuickTime was designed to simplify the task of working with and integrating the widest possible range of digital media types; not just sound and video. The QuickTime Movie format is actually so popular and good that it has become the basis for the MPEG-4 standard[16].

QuickTime VR is the virtual reality component that allows viewing 360-degree panoramic images. Having panoramic images means that one can ei-ther look around from a point of view or that one can walk around a certain object, depending on what one wants to display. In the first case, a webmas-ter could use it to show a room in which the users are standing in the middle. Depending on the quality of the image, one can zoom into details like curtains, pictures on the wall, etc. The same method of zooming in and out can be applied to objects that can be viewed from all sides, e.g. a sports car.

Many games and educational software are using QuickTime VR. But the use is not limited to these areas, as we will see in the next section.

---

[15]http://www.digitalimaging.org/
[16]http://www.mpeg.org/

QuickTime Elements

QuickTime consists of three distinct elements:

1. The QuickTime Movie file format defining

   - means of storing digital media compositions
   - container format storing not only media assets but also the description of the media composition

2. The QuickTime Media Abstraction Layer defining

   - access to software tools and applications to the media support service
   - hardware acceleration for critical portions
   - means for extending and enhancing the media services

3. And a rich set of built-in media services:

   - Comprehensive set of built-in capabilities to reduce development time.
   - Interoperability between QuickTime applications.

Table 12.3.

12.4.2 Checking the Business Cases

If we now look again back to our sample business cases, we can see that we have a hit for the first three cases.

In the first case the artist would be enabled to present more than just images. She could put objects, sculptures or installations online that can be viewed from every angle. The user can zoom in and out for more or less detail. Another thing the artist could do is to take pictures of the gallery and let the users wander around the gallery. Using QuickTime VR the user is able to walk around and approach pictures. The advantage over the FlashPix format here is that once you have downloaded the QuickTime file the speed is amazing, you zoom in and out in real-time, you can walk around the object in real-time as well. But this is also the disadvantage: You have to download the complete file first, and they tend to be large for good quality examples (ranging from a few hundred kilobytes up to several megabytes). The download of a 400 KB file using a 28.800 modem would take about 2 minutes, for example. This is something you can go for; most people will have the patience to wait that long for a cooler view of the world. But don't forget to mention on the web page what the user should expect. Another disadvantage is that QuickTime VR does not adapt itself to the required resolution. QuickTime VR is a format that is made for on-screen viewing. It has no special features for printing, in contrast with FlashPix.

Looking at the second business case, we discover some similarities. The fashion designer will not be really interested in "walking around the cloth", but the feature of zooming in is essential for him. The cloth manufacturer does not gain anything by using QuickTime VR over FlashPix, so he would stick to FlashPix. But the fashion designer can gain a lot through QuickTime VR. This technology enables him to present his fashion in a very attractive way on the Net. Just like having models wearing his clothing for a printed catalogue, he can use them for creating 3D models on the Internet. The creation of QuickTime VR is a little more complex than just doing a photograph, but it will allow users to walk around the models and see what the clothing is like from all sides. QuickTime VR images actually consist of 12 or 24 photographs of the same object from 12 or 24 different angles.

The third business model does profit from using QuickTime VR as well. It would even profit more when using QuickTime VR in conjunction with the FlashPix technology. The car would be photographed from 24 different angles to create the 3D experience. The user can zoom in and out, can walk around the car. Clicking on certain points of the car, the wheel, for example, would cause the server to send a FlashPix image to replace the QuickTime VR image to give greater control on details. This could work for all objects that do not need a 3D experience to reduce download times. If you need to turn the wheel, then the web site would offer the option to download another QuickTime VR image or to use a VRML object (see section about VRML).

In our fourth virtual business case we cannot really gain anything by using QuickTime VR. We can create wonderful 3D experiences for the CD-ROM and the web site, as described in the paragraph above. But we won't be able to create a unified image database with QuickTime VR, which was the business requirement for this business case.

12.4.3 Online Experience

One of the most prominent users of the QuickTime VR format was NASA[17] in July 1997, when Pathfinder[18] landed on Mars. A little rover called Sojourner drove around on the surface of Mars and took pictures. The pictures were taken in a form that enabled you to create panoramic photographs without any

---

[17] http://www.nasa.gov/
[18] http://mpfwww.jpl.nasa.gov/

additional overhead. Having panoramic photography meant that conversion
to QuickTime VR was just a matter of hitting some buttons. The QuickTime
VR model allowed users to look around Mars, as if they were there themselves.
They could zoom into details, look around the landscape and enjoy the strange
red panorama of the planet. During the Pathfinder mission, NASA had to set
up numerous mirror web sites in order to maintain normal service on their
main web site, due to the huge demand for information. Most people didn't
know that they were watching QuickTime VR because the necessary plug-in
was already installed in their browsers. But still, this single event meant a
huge boost in awareness for this technology (by the way, FlashPix and VRML
technology got better known as a result of the same event, but it didn't have
such a large impact on them). Although NASA hasn't made any money from
their multimedia images, they have resulted in US congress being more willing
to spend money on space flights, due to the good coverage of the event.

Hewlett-Packard in Europe is showing its benchmark center on the company Intranet using the QuickTime VR format. Visitors are able to wander
around the benchmark center and see what equipment is available there (See
Figure 12.2).

Figure 12.2. Hewlett-Packard's European Benchmark Center

Another good example is Seiko Corporation[19] in Japan. They use Quick-
Time VR to present their watches online[20]. At the moment of writing Seiko

---

[19]http://www.seiko-corp.co.jp/
[20]http://www.seiko-corp.co.jp/Kinetic/outer.html

is using its web site for marketing purposes only, so using our definition from the introduction we can classify their web site in category 2. You are not able to buy watches online, so far. Although the technology of presenting them is very good already, the only way to buy a watch is to select a country and send off an e-mail to the country headquarters for more information on the nearest dealer. Checking if the stock is available at a particular is not possible, as it is on Hewlett-Packard's web site.

Another beautiful web experience is the Reebok[21] web site for men's training shoes[22]. Here we have the same issue as with Seiko's online experience. It is a good marketing instrument, but there is no way for Reebok to measure if it is increasing its market share. It gives the company the feel of being innovative, but on top of that one should always try to reduce costs and/or increase profit when introducing a new technology. Depending on how important "coolness" is for a company one could do it like Reebok or Seiko and use technology just to show off. In most cases this won't work, though, or will not be enough for the company and their customers. QuickTime is more a "feel-good" software than FlashPix is, due to its speed, but FlashPix has the advantage of the well-defined business case. QuickTime has been used traditionally by creative people, whereas FlashPix is more the type of technology a business manager would choose.

12.4.4 Required Software

Software for developing QuickTime VR images can be obtained from Apple and third party vendors. In contrast to FlashPix QuickTime is not an open standard. Development and implementation are done entirely by Apple. The client software comes in the form of a stand-alone player and a browser plug-in, both free in the standard version. You can upgrade the standard to the professional edition with higher speed by paying some money to Apple, but so far I haven't found a site that would work with the pro version only, so it remains to be seen if it's worth the upgrade.

On the web server side no additional software needs to be installed. QuickTime files are just stored in the path of the web server documents in order to be retrieved by the browsers. In order to create the QuickTime files you need specialized authoring software. A complete list of tools can be found at Apple's QuickTime developer's homepage[23]. In order to create QuickTime VR movies without interaction, you can download a freeware tool from Apple's web site[24], but it is only available for Mac OS. If you need to develop it on Windows, then you have to go for the commercial applications[25].

---

[21]http://www.reebok.com/

[22]http://www.reebok.com/training/

[23]http://www.apple.com/quicktime/developers/tools.html

[24]http://www.apple.com/quicktime/qtvr/

[25]http://www.apple.com/quicktime/authors/

12.5 VRML

12.5.1 Technical Overview

The Virtual Reality Modeling Language (VRML) is the file format standard for 3D multimedia and shared virtual worlds on the Internet. It is an open specification for creating, viewing and manipulating 3-D objects and spaces. Just as the Hyper Text Mark-up Language (HTML) led to an explosion on the Internet by implementing a graphical interface and being the basis for the exchange of information, VRML adds the next level of interaction, structured graphics, and two extra dimensions to the online experience. The third dimension, depth and the "fourth" dimension, time, are added to the flatlands of the Internet.

What Is VRML?

VRML, which is pronounced either "vee-are-em-ell" or "ver-mul", is an abbreviation for Virtual Reality Modeling Language. You may see some references to "Virtual Reality Mark-up Language", which is what VRML was called at the beginning, taking its cue from HTML, the Hypertext Mark-up Language. The main features are:

- **Open Standard** – VRML was recognized as an international standard (ISO/IEC-14772-1:1997) in December 1997 by the International Organization for Standardization (ISO) and the International Electrotechnical Commission (IEC).

- **3D Multimedia** – Long before its standardization VRML became the de-facto standard for sharing and publishing data between CAD, animation, and 3D modeling programs.

- **Shared Virtual Worlds** – Being able to talk and work in a 3D shared virtual space was one of the earliest motivations of the VRML pioneers.

- **On the Internet** – Unlike previous 3D applications, using the Internet to share 3D objects and scenes was built into VRML from the very beginning.

Table 12.4.

VRML is the most interactive format of the three discussed in this chapter. Having its own scripting language and interfaces to Java and JavaScript enables you to create not only 3D worlds, but to make them interactive as well. Using the fourth dimension of time, we can move things around or change them. Using one of the above mentioned languages allows us to kick alive virtual people in a 3D world or to create virtual representations of people who wander through the VRML scene. One could imagine having online meetings using VRML offices in the near future, whereby the quality of the human representation would improve with every meeting. The approach to VRML is totally different to the approach we have taken with FlashPix or QuickTime VR. You cannot just scan in an image and convert it to the VRML format. The format has evolved from the Inventor format designed by Silicon Graphics. The VRML language describes the objects you want to see on screen. The language contains constructs for displaying cubes, cylinders, spheres and many other simple and not so simple geometric figures. The structure is similar to the HTML language. Using these relatively simple elements you are able to build up quite complex scenes. Architects, who build houses, for example use this method. While the initial work is more complex than just drawing a two-dimensional picture, you can extract more information from the images afterwards. Since you have the additional two dimensions, you can create complex 3D worlds where you are able to walk around and things may change over time. The only issue with VRML is that it requires a lot of processing time and that renders it unusable for low-end personal computers. More complex scenes require Pentium-II or PowerPC G3 chips that run faster than 400 MHz, supported by a fast graphics card. But as you know, it is just a matter of time until these processor speeds become low-end and therefore available to low-budget consumers. Getting to know the VRML format now is strategic for the future of your company if you are interested in close relationships with your customers.

12.5.2 Checking the Business Cases

VRML worlds offer advantages over "normal online shops". The dynamic virtual reality environment allows merchants to implement stronger marketing and branding initiatives and the retention period of a typical shopper is much longer in a 3D world, as there is much more to explore. It is much easier to create interaction between customer and merchant, and customers are able to see other customers and chat with them.

If we now look back to our business cases, we can see quite easily now where VRML fits and where it does not fit that well.

Getting back to our first case with our artist, you will see that we cannot enhance the quality of her paintings and photos at all. But we can build a virtual gallery around the pictures. Using textures we can actually used scanned images for the VRML world. This allows users to walk up to a wall and see a picture. The quality is normally not as high as with non-moving pictures, but we can add some functionality that allows the user to view a high-resolution image by clicking onto the textured image. As you can see here immediately, we cannot enhance the quality of the product presentation itself, but using VRML we can design a comfortable environment for online shopping. Using Avatars we would be able to see other visitors in the gallery and could even start to chat with them, just as in real life. You can exchange opinions and experiences online. Buying in a group, you may receive a group reduction and the site administrator could create personal agents to help customers.

If you now compare a 3D virtual reality shop with a standard HTML shop, most people would prefer the one where one can actually talk to other people who are interested in the same things. Many shops already offer online chats, but using Avatars takes the shopping experience to a new level.

If we now remember the second business case where we had a fashion designer looking around for his preferred cloth, then we could imagine cloth manufacturers using programs to design the fabric and then converting the design of the fabric to VRML. This would allow the fashion designer to zoom in as far as he wanted. He could also use the VRML file to add the fabric to his clothes while designing them on the computer. In this case the fashion designer could create virtual models wearing his latest fashion. They could walk around in a virtual shop and present the dresses, trousers, etc. Although this sounds highly unlikely today, it may be something real tomorrow. The reality of tomorrow is what we dream of today.

Our car manufacturer would gain a lot through VRML. He can use his original CAD design files and transform them into VRML files for online viewing. Internet users would be able to create their cars online, by configuring them to their wishes. Changing the color or the type of tires would become very easy, for example. This would allow even far more interaction. After having configured the car you desire, you could choose a lovely place to go for a drive, like Tuscany in Italy. A virtual representation of the country roads could be reproduced onto your screen and you could drive around in your new car. Although this would never replace the real test drive, it would draw lots of people to your web site. Although this scenario is still a little way off; today's computers are still too slow for such a simulation, we will eventually see this come alive.

If we look at the fourth case, we can see a good use for VRML in the area of replacement pieces, for example. These are small parts are designed on computers. They are normally stored in a CAD format. If we convert all these drawings into VRML files, we could use them for all three types of media. Depending on the resolution we can output whatever may be required. Using VRML we would be able to build a unified database of drawings. The advantage over other CAD formats would be the instant availability on the Internet.

Another example would be an architect who is selling architectural designs of houses. He has all the data in CAD format and converting it to VRML would enable his web presence within minutes. With VRML we have the issue of copyright infringements; as we get the complete source code in readable form, any VRML file could be easily copied. Therefore an architect or producer of replacement parts will use some type of conversion to reduce the high quality of the original drawings that will still be good enough for customers to view, but won't be good enough for competitors to copy.

12.5.3 Online Experience

Siemens KWU[26] in Germany is using VRML to speed up the development of new power plants. The new nuclear power plant EPR (European Pressurized Water Reactor) is built using the Internet for communication and the VRML standard for visualization. Siemens is exchanging information on new parts within a power plant with customers and production partners. The web clients are able to navigate through a virtual power plant and select elements to get more information on that particular element. Once an element has been chosen, it is possible to download CAD documents that need refinement. Siemens KWU only does a raw design of the plant and lets selected partners develop the fine-grained version of the design. The VRML scenes are used to navigate through the documents that are on the server (see Figure 12.3).

Figure 12.3. Siemens KWU EPR

Once a partner has submitted the design of a particular piece of the building to Siemens, everyone involved in the construction phase is able to check that all components have been brought together in the right way, or if, for example,

---

[26]http://www.siemens.de/kwu/e/

some pipes do not fit together. After having constructed the power plant on the Internet the same system can be used to show potential customers what the power plant will look like. There is no shopping solution used here and the 3D server does not handle payment. Having only a handful of customers and only a few power plants to select from online, shopping is not feasible as there is no fixed price for such a project and buying a nuclear power plant by credit card seems a little odd.

The quality of the VRML worlds is very high and demands a lot of CPU power from the web clients. In this case, where we have only a very few customers, setting up a high end computer at each customer site is a problem that can be solved without spending too much money. The first EPR is expected to go online in 2008 near Marseille in France.

This is also the reason why there aren't many examples of successful e-business applications on the Internet. The demand for resources is extremely high. Many companies use VRML for fun (sometimes called marketing). Skoda[27], the Czech car manufacturer, uses it for a virtual showroom online, but walking around in the showroom the animation is either too slow or the quality is not high enough. Neither the customer nor the manufacturer really gains anything from this.

Lenin's Homepage in Russia[28] uses VRML, too. The web site offers general information on Lenin and allows the visitor to view the famous Mausoleum in Moscow, Russia. One can virtually tour the mausoleum and learn more about the organizer of the October Revolution in 1917. It is possible to do a guided tour through the mausoleum or walk through it on your own.

In December 1997 a pan-European project consortium lead by Mellon Technologies[29], a Greek company specializing in electronic payment systems, and the Greek software house Exodus[30], started an 18-month research project on "Virtual Reality Online Shopping"[31]. The latest technologies were used to create an integrated environment for e-commerce using virtual reality and virtual communities. A virtual reality mall has been built up with several virtual reality shops inside. You can go in them and choose from a wide range of products. In addition to the shops, there has been built up a whole environment around the shopping mall, where you can get engaged in conferences and talks and where street artists juggle with balls. The project tries to emulate a real shopping experience and it is quite intriguing to enter this virtual world. The use of VRML right now is not perfect and complicates the Internet shopping experience. Instead of getting the users to find certain goods immediately, they are left to wander around, just as in a real shopping mall, where the experience is more important than the shopping. As it is using many high resolution ob-

---

[27] http://www.skoda-auto.cz/

[28] http://www.lenin.ru/

[29] http://www.mellon.gr/

[30] http://www.exodus.gr/

[31] http://www.vr-shop.iao.fhg.de/

jects it can become really slow if many objects are on the screen at the same time. Being a research project you cannot really buy anything, but many e-businesses will profit from the results of this project.

Activeworlds.com[32] is a 3-D virtual reality environment featuring an online shopping mall called @Mart. Many 3-D online stores have already been built using Activeworld's drag- and-drop store building technology. More than 100 online businesses like Amazon.com and Beyond.com[33] have already opened shops in @Mart.

Shoppers walk around the @Mart virtual mall by pointing their mouse or using the arrow keys on their keyboard to proceed. Although the environment is 3D, the merchandise is displayed in 2D. A detailed description of the products is displayed when clicking on one of the graphics. The actual purchase and payment process is then done on the merchant's web site and not in the cyber mall, so that companies can add a fancy virtual shop, but do not need to replicate their existing infrastructure.

12.5.4   Required Software

All CAD software is able to design VRML objects and scenes. There are specialized VRML software products, but if you look at them, most are just stripped-down versions of CAD software. Interactivity can not be designed with CAD software. We need to do that using the programming interface, either Java or JavaScript. There is no software that needs to be installed on the web server, but the Internet customer needs to download one of the VRML plug-ins. In November 1998 Sony[34] released the Java source code of its VRML player, enabling other programmers to enhance the existing code. This open source initiative will enable more and more people to enjoy virtual reality on the Web.

12.6   Comparing Imaging Technologies

Now that we have looked at the three most promising technologies, I just want to review the business requirements from the second section. Table 12.5 shows which technology meets which requirement.

All three technologies have their advantages and if you look at the row with the integration of existing software, you can see where each of the technologies was originally positioned and has its roots. That does not mean that you cannot mix the technologies or even choose a technology from one sector to deliver a solution in another. We have seen enough examples to prove this, but people tend to stay in the sector they feel comfortable with already.

Open Standards and Open Source have become more important. Having an open standard means that you do not have to rely on one company for the image

---

[32]http://www.activeworlds.com/
[33]http://www.beyond.com/
[34]http://www.sony.com/

Comparison of Imaging Technology

	FlashPix	**QuickTime VR**	**VRML**
High Resolution	Yes	Yes	Yes, requires a fast computer.
Download Speed	Fast	Slow	Fast
Universal Format	Adapting itself to the browser	Requires Plug-in	Requires Plug-in
Universal Access	Yes	Yes	Yes
Free Choice of Browser	Yes	Yes, requires Plug-in	Yes, requires Plug-in
Scalability	Yes	Yes	Yes
Software Integration	Image processing	Multimedia	CAD
Open Standard	Yes	No	Yes
Open Source	No	No	Yes

Table 12.5.

format. There is a consortium behind the format that is driving the development. Open Source means that the source code can be adapted to the needs of the webmasters and their clients, and that one does not have to pay license fees. See Chapter 14 for more information on the Open Source Community.

12.7   The Future of Imaging

12.7.1   Fractal Compression

The future of imaging is manifold. One addition to the portfolio of important graphics formats is the use of fractal compression technologies. Many structures in Nature are similar to themselves, e.g. mountains, coastal lines or leaves of plants. These self-repeating patterns can be used to save complex structures in rather simple equations. You can zoom into the structure without losing information. Fractal compression tries to save the whole picture in a transformation matrix. As a result the image becomes resolution independent. No matter what resolution you require it will be delivered to you. While JPEG images are tied to pixels, fractal compression images are tied to mathematical relations. Using these algorithms it is no problem to print out a picture either as a thumb nail or as a poster always having the highest resolution possible, using a very little image file.

The disadvantage of fractal compression is the time it needs to compress and decompress, because the transformation matrix is highly complex. The more detail the image has the more complex the matrix will become. Eventually faster hardware will become available and we can therefore expect a breakthrough in fractal compression technology. But hopefully better algorithms will also become available, as well. Faster algorithms should always be preferred over faster hardware.

12.7.2 DjVu

AT&T[35] has invented a new format, the so-called DjVu pictures (pronounced "déjà vu") that tries to overcome the deficits of JPEG with scanned documents. The major problem with JPEG is that sharp contrasts cannot be reproduced perfectly. For example, black and white images and images with text, should be saved in GIF or PNG format instead, due to this restriction.

The AT&T labs have developed a format that separates the background information from the foreground image. The background and the foreground use different compression algorithms to achieve the best possible result. The compressed file is about five to eight times smaller than a comparable JPEG, but with a much better resolution than JPEG could achieve for scanned documents. A sample of a scanned document would take up 31.2 MB in TIFF Format, 604 KB in JPEG format and only 134 KB for the same document in the DjVu format. The compression rates are extremely good, but limited to present scanned images on the web. It will never replace an all-purpose format like JPEG.

More information on AT&T's DjVu format can be found at their research site[36]. At the time of writing a plug-in is required to view DjVu images, but this will be replaced by Java applets and native browser support in the future.

12.7.3 JPEG 2000

Of the existing standards, the JPEG standard is being pushed at the moment. Code named JPEG 2000, work on an update for the existing JPEG format is in

---

[35]http://www.att.com/

[36]http://djvu.research.att.com/

progress. Some of the planned features are the following. Grey-level images, black & white pictures and computer generated images will have less distortion through the use of new algorithms in the lossy format, by adding a new lossless compression algorithm to the basic set of compression algorithms. This will also result in better performance.

The JPEG standard today offered only resolutions up to 65536×65536 pixels. Although this is more than enough for most applications, there still may be some people who require an even higher resolution. Instead of supporting multiple decompression architectures as in the current version, JPEG 2000 will contain a unified decompression architecture.

What Is New in JPEG 2000?

Based on the JPEG standard, JPEG 2000 has a set of new features, which will move it closer to other formats, such as PNG.

- **Distortion** – Less distortion for highly detailed grey-level images.

- **Lossless Compression** – Includes lossless and lossy compression in a single code stream.

- **Large Images** – Support for images that are larger than 65536×65536.

- **Decompression architecture** – Creation of a single common decompression architecture.

- **Noisy Environments** – Enhanced support for transmission in noisy environments.

- **Better Performance** – Better performance on computer generated images.

Table 12.6.

Many other formats are in the pipeline and we will see which will become a standard. Keep in mind that a standard can only become highly successful if it is supported by all the major browser software packages.

12.7.4   X3D

In February 1999, the Web3D Consortium[37] (formerly known as the VRML Consortium) announced that it has initiated the process to define X3D, a next-generation componentized 3D standard that includes integration with XML. Standing for "Extensible 3D," X3D is defined as an interoperable set of lightweight, componentized 3D standards that flexibly address the needs of a wide range of markets.

X3D incorporates a number of component specifications allowing extremely lightweight applications to be deployed on a variety of platforms, from workstations to set-top devices. Initial components include a lightweight 3D runtime engine with state-of-the-art rendering capabilities, a platform-independent 3D file format and integration with the XML standard. Additionally, by integrating real-time 3D graphics with text, plus 2D graphics and streaming sound and video, X3D will enable a wide range of web- and broadcast-based applications including entertainment, online shopping and enterprise data visualization.

X3D is building upon the VRML 97 ISO standard with clearly defined backward compatibility with existing VRML content. X3D will be interoperable with other standards and technologies such as MPEG-4 and HTML. A first prototype has been released in mid 1999 and it is expected that X3D will replace VRML over the next few years. Companies are already shifting development focus from VRML to X3D.

---

[37]http://www.web3d.org/

Chapter 13

PAYING VIA THE NET

13.1 The Payment Business

13.1.1 Business Requirements

In the information age electronic payments are becoming more and more important. New financial procedures and monetary structures have been introduced to reflect the technological possibilities and economic necessities of our time. Through globalization and the Internet end customers and companies have changed the way they pay.

Traditionally payment means that a value is transferred using a variety of techniques, either via cash or documents. Cash has been provided in the form of bank notes and coins, which are mainly issued by national governments and documents for payment have been provided in the form of bills of exchange, cheques drawn on a bank, money orders written by an accepted authority such as a national post office, letters of credit and payment card vouchers.

These different payment mechanisms have differing characteristics. The extent to which the parties are identified ranges from total anonymity with cash to total identity with credit cards. The traceability of the transaction ranges and the taxability of the transaction varies among the different payment methods. The reason that so many mechanisms exist is that there are many different circumstances in which value is exchanged, and each of the mechanisms has niche-markets in which it is perceived by at least some parties to have advantages.

As with traditional payment methods, the biggest problem is to ensure that nobody is able to copy your digital money or steal your credit card information. The financial transactions between banks have been already digitized for some time. The SWIFT-Network (Society for World-Wide Interbank Financial Telecommunication) is a private network, but more and more connections are being established with public networks such as the Internet.

Electronic payment systems need to fulfill certain requirements in order to emulate the properties of the existing payment schemes. Internet payment systems need be flexible. They should support different payment models for different situations (such as credit card, cash, check). The timing of the payment should be agreed on by the parties involved.

Converting digital money from one system to the other should be allowed. A payment infrastructure should allow multiple forms of payment and digital currencies and, in addition to this, agreements with providers of other digital and real funds need to be signed, in order to create mechanisms that allow the conversion of funds into their system.

In order to make the payment infrastructure successful, it should allow anybody to use it and needs to be accepted widely. Users should be able to limit their losses, by creating thresholds, that require additional approval, before the payment occurs. The monitoring of the payments should be easy as well. It should be easy to use, and most payments should be done automatically. Everybody should be able to pay with it or to cash in the money without the need for an intermediate, such as a bank. The payment solution should be an open standard, which can be used by any business.

Therefore not only buyers and sellers should be independent of the standard, but also the transaction servers. Anybody who wants to process the payment should be able to do so. In order to be attractive, both for customers and merchants, the customer and merchant base needs to be large enough. The developers of the payment system need to get as many merchants as possible on board in order to attract the customers.

All financial transactions could be performed via the Internet, but for security reasons existing financial networks should be used for clearing. Every transaction involves a buyer and a seller of products, information or services. In order to perform a financial transaction a financial institution is required that enables the money transfer. In most cases two financial institutions are involved. The issuer is the financial institution used by the buyer and the acquirer is used by the seller.

Electronic payments start with the communication between buyer and issuer, whereby the buyer asks the issuer to release money by withdrawing it from a bank account or issuing a credit card, for example. The money is then sent to the acquirer for clearing. If the acquirer validates the money, a message will be sent on to the seller. The reseller can then start the order processing and the money is put into the seller's account.

Security is the most important issue with digital payment systems. Since payments involve actual money, digital payment systems are a prime target for criminals all over the world. In the real world, copying coins or bank notes is hard, but not impossible, if you have the right equipment. But replication of real cash takes time and money, and the false bank notes are in most cases easy to detect, as they all have the same serial number. On the Internet, replication costs are near zero and changing the serial number is made easy. Therefore one must ensure that the payment system is secure, otherwise it will not be accepted by the customers. The Internet is an open network, which allows anybody to eavesdrop on the traffic, so modification of messages needs to be

Digital Payment Requirements

In order to make a digital payment system successful, it needs to adhere to the following requirements:

- **Acceptability** – In order to be successful, the payment infrastructure needs to be widely accepted.

- **Anonymity** – If desired by the customers, their identity should be protected.

- **Convertibility** – The digital money should be able to be converted into other types of funds.

- **Efficiency** – The cost per transaction should be near zero.

- **Flexibility** – Several methods of payment should be supported.

- **Integration** – To support existing applications, interfaces should be created to integrate with the application.

- **Reliability** – The payment system needs to be highly available and should avoid single points of failure.

- **Scalability** – Allowing new customers and merchants into the system should not break down the infrastructure.

- **Security** – It should allow financial transactions over open networks, such as the Internet.

- **Usability** – Payment should be as easy as in the real world.

Table 13.1.

prevented by the use of digital signatures. Another important factor is that the money must arrive at the desired destination. If you pay in a shop you give the shop assistant the money, but if you make payments via the Internet, transactions can be diverted to other bank accounts without anybody noticing it initially. Therefore digital signatures and encryption technologies are required to make every financial transaction secure.

In order to make micro-payments feasible the payment system should not create additional costs and not decrease performance. If you pay, for example, by credit card today in the real world, the merchant has to pay about four percent to the financial institutions involved thus making credit card payments infeasible for small payments (so-called micro-payments), such as paying for visiting a web page.

Once you have received the digital money you should always be able to pass it on to a bank or partner or keep it in a safe place. It should be accepted just as your credit card or cash. Therefore a high acceptance is necessary. The acceptance should actually be so good that the digital money will also be accepted by people who do not use the Internet.

Transactions via the Internet need to be private. Some or all parties may wish confidentiality, therefore third parties should never have the possibility of intercepting the transaction and even it they are able to do this, they should not be able to read the transaction, so it should be encrypted. The buyer, seller, and order should only be known to the participants involved; actually only to the participants who need to know certain data.

The integrity and the authentication of financial transactions needs to be maintained. The buyer message sent out to the seller needs to be signed in order to guarantee that nobody else is able to withdraw money from the buyers account or credit card without his or her consent. Every message should also be unique in order to guarantee that a financial transaction can only be executed once. Once the transaction has been completed the seller sends an acknowledgement to the buyer.

The availability and reliability of the financial system needs to be ensured. Hackers and online vandals will try to create Denial of Service (DoS) attacks, whereby payment services are premium targets. An interruption of the infrastructure could mean a loss to all participants. All parties should be able to perform their part in the financial transaction whenever they want or need to do so. In order to make a transaction reliable it must be atomic. A transaction should never be incomplete. Either the payment is accepted or rejected, but there must never be an unknown state. Otherwise this would mean that money could get lost via the Internet. The payment protocol needs to handle cases where the network or one of the participating computers breaks down. In most cases the complete transaction becomes void and needs to be repeated, but some payment systems are able to continue at the point the transaction stopped at the moment of the crash.

For cash like payment systems anonymity and untraceability need to be implemented, as these are the main advantages of real cash. This can only be maintained if no third party is required for the transaction. Anonymity allows one to hide the buyer's identity, while untraceability means that different payments of a single buyer cannot be linked, either to the buyer or to the other payment. It should be impossible to monitor an individual's spending patterns or determine the source of income of that particular person. By encrypting all messages between the participants of a financial transaction, it is possible to make the transactions untraceable to others, which may be good enough for most transactions. On the other hand it is also possible to implement anonymity and untraceability of the seller. Where anonymity is important, the cost of tracking a transaction should outweigh the value of the information gained.

As the Internet grows, the demands placed on payment systems will grow as well. The payment framework should be able to handle a growing number of customers and merchants without losing performance. In order to keep the system alive, a distributed system should be preferred, whereby payment servers are placed in different locations on the Internet, in case one of the connections or servers break down.

The payment infrastructure should be able to support existing Internet applications through a programmable interface, so that no or only very little modification of the application is required.

Online Payment Categories

As in the real world, on the Internet several payment systems will co-exist. Depending on the value of the order, three types of payments have been established on the Internet:

- **Micro-Payments** – transaction with a value of less than approximately 5 Euro or Dollar. Suitable payment solutions are based on the electronic cash principle, as the transaction costs for these systems are nearly zero.

- **Consumer Payments** – transaction with a value between about 5 and 500 Euro or Dollar. Typical consumer payments are executed by credit card transactions.

- **Business Payments** – transaction with a value of more than 500 Euro or Dollar. Direct debit or invoices seem to be the most appropriate solutions.

Table 13.2.

Each of the payment systems mentioned in Table 13.2 has different security and cost requirements. Micro-Payment systems are very similar to ordinary cash, while consumer payments are most likely done by credit or debit card. Business payments are executed in most cases by direct debit or invoice. The following sections give an overview of the possible payment methods. A common framework for Internet payment needs to be developed, in order to support the above-mentioned requirements and payment systems. So far, many isolated solutions have been developed and the following sections will go move into detail, before discussing some payment frameworks that allow more than only one payment system.

13.1.2   Psychology of Micro-Payments

Over the last few years many developers have tried to push micro-payment solutions to the Internet, but only very few have succeeded. The problem was never the technical implementation, but the Internet itself. Every company on the Internet gives away small pieces of information for free. So it is hard to justify the need to pay for small bits of information, even if the price is only a fraction of a cent. The other issue is a psychological problem. If you have the choice of paying a one-time fee of 20 Dollars or Euro or paying 50 cents for every transaction, about 80 percent of the people will either pay the one-time fee or use the service only very seldom as it requires a new payment each time. It makes financial calculations more difficult as you do not know in advance how much money the service will cost and spending money means always thinking about it for a while. Most people will prefer to think once about it and use the system as often as they need it. Otherwise they will first think about the costs and how they can be justified and then decide maybe not to use it. Therefore the subscription model is used in most cases on the Internet.

I actually tried it out myself. I got 10 "CyberEuros" from one of the banks and wandered around the Internet to see what I could get there. There were many offerings of viewing certain web pages, which cost around 10 cents, but I was reluctant to spend the money because I was not sure if it was worth it. I got the 10 "CyberEuros" for free in order to test the system, but was still reluctant to spend them, as I wasn't sure if I could not find similar information for free. Paying 5 Dollars for an ongoing service would have been fine, as there may be lots of rubbish, but sometimes you will find the information that helps your business. Pay per view may work for certain online offerings, but it will have a difficult stand in the digital world.

13.1.3   Minimizing the Risk

Customers have already decided that the Internet is secure for paying. The number of transactions is rising every year significantly, but how secure is it to accept orders via the Internet? The explosive growth adds also an explosive risk to online retailers.

Although we will see that there are many different payment technologies available on the Internet that are declared to be secure, one should take precautions to protect yourself when accepting orders via the Web. Fraud is nothing new, but the Internet offers many possibilities to automate the payment process. Even with customers who are willing to pay with their own money transmission errors can lead to incurring losses.

Credit card transactions via SSL especially do not guarantee that the credit card payment can be fulfilled successfully. Even if the money has been transferred to your account the card holders are able to enforce a charge back to their accounts. Because Internet credit card transactions are classified as Card-Not-Present transactions, merchants are 100 percent liable for losses, even when the bank has authorized the transaction. While electronic soft goods don't carry a high cost of goods, theft represents a loss of revenue and the potential for further fraud through illegal distribution.

The major problem is getting the information right in the first go. Therefore your payment web page should include the following information, the customers need to include, before they can send off the order. The credit card number and the expiration date are the most important items. Using a little JavaScript[1] I have written it is possible to check if the checksum of the number is correct. Although this won't reduce the possibility of fraud, it does reduce the number of false entries.

An e-mail address and the full postal address and the name should also be present and the order confirmation should be sent to that e-mail address. If the address turns out to be wrong the order should be cancelled. The postal address can be verified by various online services. These first checks should be supplemented by a credit card check at the bank.

Internet customers often claim a shipment because of the following reasons. They may deny the transaction, therefore it is necessary to record all details of the transaction. Through the use of digital certificates it is possible to enforce non-repudiation. Others may claim that the credit card has been used fraudulently, either because the card has been stolen or the card has been used without their authority. Another common problem is that customers claim that the goods never arrived, were defective or of poor quality.

Fraud has been simplified through the anonymity of the Internet. Therefore the growth of the electronic business also attracts criminals. Through simple measures the risk of fraud can be reduced significantly.

Customers not known to the online business should only be able to pay upto a certain predefined limit, which is much lower than for the customers which are already known to the company. By offering a confirmation web page before accepting the order, customers can verify their order details and accept the terms and conditions, which should be present on that page as well. If you have some doubts on the credibility of a customer just reject the order by sending out an e-mail that it is not possible to serve the customer.

By accepting only orders where the customer and card holder name match, you can further reduce the risk of fraud and confirm the order before fulfill-

---

[1]http://www.net-factory.com/javascripts/

ment. If you really want to be sure, call the customer, otherwise send out an e-mail. Document the completed transaction in order to have evidence in the event of problems.

Once a customer has ordered, the goods should only be shipped to that particular address and nothing should be handed over to a third party. In order to keep control over your shipping you need to find a trustworthy logistics partner, which enables you and your customers to track shipment once the goods have left your warehouse.

When shipping digital goods ensure that a unique key is sent through a separate message identifying the customer. This enables you to ensure that only people who have paid will get access. In case of a charge back you can disable the key. This is especially important if you offer a subscription fee.

If you are afraid that these risks are too large for your small start-up (or large corporation) then you can outsource the payment service completely. This lets you concentrate on your business and ensures that you get your money in any case and that the outsourcer is responsible for getting back the money in case of a problem.

13.1.4 Fraud Detection

Dealing with fraud impacts business productivity as online businesses need to invest into resources that manually scrutinize orders, track down bad transactions and negotiate in case of trouble with the bank. Companies that implement too strict fraud techniques, on the other hand, will lose customers and revenues as they pose additional burden on the customer's side to ensure security and liability. Customers will most likely go on to another online shop, where paying is made easier.

In order to level out fraud, several companies have started to offer fraud detection programs. One of them is ClearCommerce[2], which helps online merchants to reduce the number of charge backs and fraudulent transactions. Negative databases, with records of e-mail addresses, card numbers and phone numbers of those who have initiated charge backs makes it easier to detect fraud. In addition to this, modules are in use that check the number of times an individual card is used in a single week. By limiting the purchases to a single card per week fraud can be reduced significantly.

Instead of monitoring the transactions manually the FraudShield product by ClearCommerce allows companies to set up rules that validate the transactions automatically and lock out all transactions that are suspicious. The software checks online, if the card holder and card number match with the corresponding bank and if the customer has enough credit to buy the good. It offers real-time, automated fraud-checking that performs numerous Internet-specific checks that substantially reduce your risk from fraud while lowering your costs. Merchant-configurable fraud rules enable you to establish fraud

---

[2]http://www.clearcommerce.com/

screens tailored specifically to your business. ClearCommerce's fraud protection software enhances, rather than duplicates, checks performed by the card processor.

Fraud checks include guards against processing invalid credit card numbers, checking for duplicate orders, the recognition of suspicious spending patterns, and guards against automatic card generator programs.

The fraud checklists let you establish criteria for lock-outs based on combinations of individual fraud checks for increased sophistication. These Boolean statements allow you to combine a number of variables in the rule. For example, if the transactions occurs at midnight to 2:00 a.m. and includes item #579243 (leather coat) and is initiated by a Hotmail user and ships to Eastern Europe, then decline it.

By using address verification services it becomes easy to verify if a given name lives at a certain address. This works quite well for individuals ordering services or goods from a web site. In Germany, for example, the Deutsche Bundespost[3] offers an address verification service for online businesses that are interested in selling goods in Germany. In the United States, for example, Visa[4] offers an address verification check in conjunction with the credit card. The card number and the address can be sent off to Visa and they will check if the shipping or billing address match the address of the card owner. This requires the hacker not only to have a credit card number but also additional information on the owner of the card.

Cabela's, Inc.[5], a catalogue and retail merchant for hunting and fishing equipment, uses real-time credit authorization and fraud detection to expand their customers' purchasing options to include the Internet. The payment back end software was integrated with a storefront, the legacy systems in the company and the bank to make it a cheap and efficient solution. This allowed Cabela's to integrate the payment services data from Cabela's bank and pass it through the process to the settlement point, saving time in addition to being customized to the requirements of the Cabela's fulfillment system.

13.1.5   Example Business Cases

New standards on the Internet can be achieved by using advanced payment technologies. In order to make a payment technology successful, it needs to support a solid business case. If the new standard or technology does not help us to sell more of our products online or reduce the costs of production, then there is no reason to use it. There are many cases on the Internet where people used hyped technology and failed because the business case was not good enough. So we will now develop four business cases and see if the technology is adding value to that particular electronic business.

---

[3] http://www.post.de/
[4] http://www.visa.com/
[5] http://www.cabelas.com/

The Internet Bookshop

The standard example for online business. A company wants to sell books via the Internet. A digital shop has been set up where customers are able to browse through a large set of books and can choose from there the desired books. How should customers pay for the books?

The Translation Service

A freelance translator offers her services on the Internet. The customers are able to send in their texts via e-mail, ftp or fax and will receive price quotations and the finished translation by the same communication means. How should customers pay for the services?

The News Agency

A news agency delivers its content to the web and is able to provide highly customized news to individual customers and portals. The news flashes can be either pushed to the customer through push channels or e-mails or pulled by putting the content onto a web page. How should customers pay for this information?

The Software Company

A software company sells its products via the web, offers updates, online help and an online call center for the customers. What would be the most appropriate payment method for the software and the call center?

13.1.6   Internet Payment Methods

Just as in the real world, three different types of payment systems have been established on the Internet: pre-paid, instant-paid and post-paid systems. As the term pre-paid already suggests you have to pay first and then can buy a product or service. Pre-paid systems basically work by saving digital money to the hard disk or to a smart card. They could be seen as the digital equivalent of cash. The file containing the digital money is called virtual wallet. The electronic money can be used at any time to pay for goods and services online. The advantage of electronic cash is that it is anonymous. Nobody is able to trace back who paid for the service or goods. As soon as goods have to be delivered physically this advantage is gone. The disadvantage is the storage on the hard disk or the smart card. If you lose the file the money is gone, just as if you lose your wallet. Anybody who "finds" the contents of the wallet, can use it to pay with it. Instant-paid systems are based on the concept of paying in the moment of the transaction.

Instant-paid systems are the most complicated to implement as they require direct access to the internal databases of the banks in order to make the payment in an instant. Security needs also to be implemented more strictly than in the other cases, as instant-paid systems are the most powerful systems. A limit for the instant-paid payment solution may make sense to reduce the possibility of fraud.

In pre-paid or post-paid transactions access to a bank is done either before or after the actual order process is executed. The money is debited from the bank account in the same moment as the transaction takes place. Post-paid systems on the other hand allow you to buy a product and pay afterwards. Credit cards are one of the most common post-paid systems, both in the real world as in the cyber world.

Credit-cards are appropriate in particular circumstances. They are, however, very expensive. This is primarily because of the low level of security (which relies on embossing, magnetic-strips, signatures and stop-lists), and the resultant high and increasing cost of fraud. In addition, transaction processing costs are significant.

Debit cards are relatively highly secure, because they require the customer to confirm that they know something that only the card-owner should know: the PIN. But whereas the costs from error and fraud are very low, the communication costs associated with fully on-line transactions are high.

13.1.7 Political Impact of Digital Currencies

Many concerns regarding the impact on the money supply and governmental control have been raised since the introduction of digital currency. In the short run, governments will retain control over the currencies by adjusting the control of the money supply. The reason is that companies mostly deal with invoices and end customers in most cases use credit cards. These types of payments do not require a new currency, but use currencies that are under governmental control. Customers who pay in Dollars, Euros or Yen won't influence the value of the currencies directly.

But new digital currency systems that are not directly linked to a physical currency may affect the monetary system in two ways. On the one hand, these currencies may influence the supply of money by changing the way money is multiplied. Price levels and interest rates could also be affected by digital currencies, if they reach a critical mass.

Governments make money by issuing money, as the cost of printing a bank note is lower than the value of it. This so-called "seigniorage" and interest-free lending to the government by the public are the revenues, which a government receives every year. Through the introduction of digital currencies, some portion of the government's revenue is taken away. Introducing a digital currency by a private company is like printing private money. As a result the central banks relinquish their legal monopoly to issue money or money substitutes.

Most states are not intending to issue electronic money. In most cases private companies are offering the electronic cash, with one exception being Finland, where an electronic wallet is being issued by a company wholly owned by the central bank.

If private companies are allowed to print money, the revenues related to seigniorage will be shared between the governments and these companies. The acceptance of a currency depends on the public confidence. If there is enough confidence in these companies, these companies will start to develop a competition. Other than a government, which does not let consumers participate in the profits, private companies may distribute the profits to their customers, which will lead to totally new perspectives in the currency industry and lead to new forms of convenience, service and quality. Online banks, for example, could compete with the governments by paying interest on digital currency deposits.

At the time of writing, no legal framework had been established that allows private companies to create commercial types of digital currencies. Many tests have been done, but governments fear that digital currencies will be used for criminal activities, such as money laundering. For the Internet to succeed digital currencies are not necessary, but the Internet has deregulated many markets and won't stop at the currency market.

13.2 Post-paid Payment Systems

13.2.1 Credit Card Solutions

Credit card payments are nowadays the most common and preferred payment method on the Internet. The use of credit cards is simple, and they are accepted on a world-wide basis. Customers browse through a web site, decide what services or products they need and enter their credit card information into a HTML-form. The contents are sent to the web site, where the information is either collected and sent once a day to the bank, or the web site owner has established a direct link to the bank, whereby it is possible to check on-the-fly, if the user has enough credit to pay for the goods.

The credit card payment system has some advantages over other forms of payment. They are issued and accepted world-wide and offer consumers the ability to collect all charges and pay the total at a later time (for example, at the end of the month). The credit card system provides good consumer protection, as customers have the right to give back goods within a certain time frame and dispute charges, as they are not charged directly to the account of the customer. Credit cards are not bound to national currencies. No matter where you buy your products, the currency conversion is done automatically for the customer. The mechanism of using credit cards via the Internet is very similar to the system of mail and telephone order transactions, therefore almost everybody is able to understand how it works within a few seconds.

In the credit card payment system there are four players: the customer, the merchant, the issuer and the acquirer. In order to use a credit card the customer and the merchant need to establish relationships with the issuer with respect to the acquirer. The issuer gives the consumer a credit card. The merchant applies to an acquirer for the ability to accept one or more card brands. Customers who now go to the merchant and want to buy goods or services, present their credit card to the merchant. The merchant verifies the validity of credit card by sending the credit card information to the acquirer. Over the financial network the request is then passed on to the customer's bank. The bank then verifies the information and returns the authorization to the merchant through the acquirer. This may sound highly complicated, but it is the way it works today, if you go into a shop and buy something.

Although there are still some companies who want you to give them your credit card number without encrypting the transmission, most companies use encryption to protect the private information about the credit card, the order and the customer. Without the encryption it would be to easy for hackers to intercept the messages and use or alter them for their own purposes.

Using special programs, called sniffers, criminals are able to copy the decrypted information and use it to pay for other things. As long as you do not need a shipping address the credit card information can be misused easily, for example, to pay for online services. Although stealing credit card information is nothing new, the Internet enables attackers to do the stealing more systematically.

In order to make credit card payments secure two standards have been established over the past few years: SSL encryption developed by Netscape and Secure Electronic Transactions (SET)[6] developed by Visa and MasterCard. The differences between SSL and SET are evident. SSL only encrypts traffic between the web browser and web server (the user's computer and the merchant's computer). SET on the other hand offers a complete payment solution, which involves not only the customer and the merchant, but also the bank, which is needed for credit card payment.

SET

SET was designed exclusively to secure Internet financial transactions, SSL is a generic encryption system which can be used to transmit any data. SET combines existing security technologies with public key encryption using digital certificates for both credit card holders and merchants. The public key infrastructure (PKI) is defined within the scope of SET. The PKI is used to verify that a participant in the transaction is really the person or institution he or she pretends to be. This is important as the Internet provides no standard mechanism to verify a person or institution. With this mechanism, it is possible to introduce the concept of non-repudiation to Internet-based transactions. Customers who pay via SET cannot dispute afterwards that they did not do the transaction, as all orders are digitally signed. The digital signature cannot be forged. In addition to this feature, the PKI is used to send encrypted information via

---

[6]http://www.setco.com/

the Internet. Using strong encryption it is possible to transmit the credit card transaction over public networks, such as the Internet.

What Is SET?

SET was developed by MasterCard and Visa in 1996 and has established itself as one of the leading standards in credit card payments via the Internet. The SET specifications include the following:

- **Highly Secure** – The transmission of credit card information can be transmitted over public networks using strong encryption technologies.

- **Low Visibility** – Only the information a partner needs to see is displayed. The merchant does not need to see the credit card information and the bank does not need to see which orders have been placed.

- **Recognized Standards** – Transaction flows, the message formats, integrity, authentication, confidentiality and the encryption algorithms are all defined in the SET standard.

- **Non-Repudiation** - The SET standard defines a public key infrastructure, which is used for verification of the participants and to encrypt/decrypt the messages sent between the partners. A digital signature is used to identify the participants.

Table 13.3.

SET has been developed to provide a confidential way of payment and order information. All information in a SET transaction is encrypted. The integrity of the transmitted data is ensured through the digital hash code, which is appended to every message and enables the receiver to verify that the message has not been altered in transit. Through the use of digital certificates it is possible to show that a card holder is the legitimate user of the credit card. The authentication is also required for the merchant in order to be properly identified by the acquiring bank. The SET protocol is not dependent on transport security measures and does not prevent their use, such as using additionally

SSL on top of the SET encryption. As SET programs are developed by several software vendors, interoperability is very important.

SET provides some privacy features which make it harder to gain information on the customer. Only the information a participant really needs to see will be revealed. A merchant, for example, does not really need to know the credit card details. This information can be routed directly through to the bank and the bank can confirm the validity of the information back to the merchant and authorize the money transfer. SET defines more than just encryption. Transaction flows, message formats and encryption algorithms are provided as standard in order to guarantee the integrity and confidentiality of the messages, and the authentication of the users.

Additional security will be introduced in SET 2.0, when smart cards will be supported. Credit cards will then have an additional chip on the plastic card, which will contain the digital certificate and the public and private key of the user that is required to perform a SET transaction. Currently only debit cards have the chip. The chip card solutions provide additional security and convenience for the card holders. This will also enable more people to use it. Today it is still difficult to get a certificate and install it.

Using a chip card, customers will be able to use any SET enabled network device anywhere, such as computers and TV set top boxes at home, computers in the office and kiosks in the public. An additional benefit for the card industry is the similarity between SET transactions and conventional POS and ATM ones, when a chip card is used. It will simplify processing and operating procedures.

Several pilots for the C-SET (Chip-secured Secure Electronic Transactions) are under way at the moment of writing in the European Union. The European Commission has adopted C-SET as a recommended specification. The smart card provides authentication and encryption. The design also includes an enhanced banking gateway that handles most of the payment processing, thus reducing the cost and complexity for the merchant.

In order to resolve legal issues with the encryption, the cryptographic functions are implemented on the bank side, in order to prevent regulations that prohibit widespread deployment of cryptographic software.

There are many other possible ways to pay via credit card. The disadvantage of these solutions is mainly that they are not open and are bound to a certain service provider. The following list will give a short overview on three solutions.

WireCard

The WireCard[7] solution consists of several modules making it suitable for business to consumer and business to business transactions. The secure online payment module, which is of interest here, allows the secure transmit of credit card

---

[7]http://www.wirecard.de/

information from the customer to the merchant, by using a Java applet, that encrypts the information with 2048 bits. The applet uses the RSA and Blow-Fish algorithms for encryption making it very secure. With today's technologies it would take approximately 10^{22} (10,000,000,000,000,000,000,000) years to decode the credit card information.

As the company resides in Germany the software can be exported to any other country without restrictions. The solution is also not bound to a certain browser or operating system, making it a very good solution for online credit card payment.

Once the credit card information has been entered, the applet encrypts the data and sends it off to the server, which takes the information and passes it on to a bank for validation. Once the credit card has been validated successfully, the merchant will receive a notice to proceed in the transaction. The back end validation is done by the clearing module, which allows credit cards to be checked in real time (which is more secure) or in a batch (which is cheaper).

CyberCash

The CyberCash[8] solution encrypts credit card details, just as SSL and SET do, but the procedure is a little bit different. The credit card information is sent from the customer to the merchant encrypted in such a way that the merchant can't decrypt it. The merchant passes the information on to the Cyber-Cash server together with the sum of the customer order. From the CyberCash server the payment is initiated through the financial networks.

First Virtual

First Virtual was founded in 1994 and is the only online payment system that is secure without encryption technology. Security in the First Virtual[9] system is guaranteed by requesting a confirmation e-mail from the customer. If the customer does not respond in a given time-frame with a certain code, the order will not be executed. In order to prevent sniffing of credit card information, special IDs are exchanged instead of the credit card information. The credit card needs to be stored once on the First Virtual server and a VirtualPIN is assigned to the credit card number, which is used for transactions. The user needs to call First Virtual and tell them the credit card number; the information is never sent via the Internet. The First Virtual server initiates the payment transaction with the financial networks.

During the most successful phases in 1996 more than 2000 merchants and 200,000 customers where using the system to pay for goods on a global scale. In late 1998 First Virtual's credit card payment system was put on hold, as there was not enough demand as many invested into the SET standard, which was

---

[8]http://www.cybercash.com/
[9]http://www.fv.com/

struggling to become the standard credit card payment system at that time and the general purpose SSL encryption technology.

13.2.2 Invoice

While credit card transactions are very common in the business-to-consumer area, invoices are more common in the business-to-business sector. In many cases the business-to-business transaction volume is too high for credit card transactions. Consider the example where your company needs to buy one hundred computers, printers and monitors. The sum would be too high for the limit of most credit cards. Buying each computer on its own would be possible via credit card, but this would certainly be more expensive than buying all at once, for both the buyer and the seller.

Another important reason to consider payment via invoice is that many companies traditionally have paid via invoice and changing the type of payment would require a reorganization of the process, which would cost too much. A third reason could be that the credit card companies want up to four percent of the transaction in fees, for many smaller companies these four percent can mean the difference between profit and loss. In countries where credit cards are not as common, payment via invoices is also a viable way to substitute online payment solutions.

Lufthansa Cargo[10] digitized its SameDay[11] Service in January 1999. Same-Day allows you to send documents and small packages throughout Europe in a maximum of six hours, hence the name SameDay. As this service is too expensive for private use, the target customers are businesses that need to send spare parts and documents throughout Europe, that need to be delivered very fast. As most of their target customers have an infrastructure for paying via invoice, in the first phase of the project only payment via invoice is accepted. The next step for Lufthansa was to introduce a way to connect the financial systems of the customers and their own in order to send invoices electronically via electronic data interchange (EDI). Only then did they start to build up an infrastructure for people who want to pay via credit card, for freelancers and small companies who do not use EDI nor have an SAP R/3 installed.

In order to make invoices a good solution for the Internet, it is necessary to make it a secure solution. Therefore some sort of user identification is necessary. In the Lufthansa example, a SameDay employee calls the customers to tell them when the courier will be picking up the package. With an expanding business, calling up all customers is not a good way. Actually it is only necessary to check the identity when a customer uses the service for the first time. The next time the customer returns to the web site, it is only necessary to enter a login and password to identify themselves. As the SameDay service involves non-electronic procedures such as picking up the goods at a certain address,

---

[10]http://www.lhcargo.com/
[11]http://www.sameday.de/

the possibility of abuse is limited. With a totally digitized product or service, such as an online newspaper, this can be a much bigger problem.

For these services printed bills would mean extra costs that are larger than the purchasing price itself. Online billing therefore offers the possibility to cut costs and automate manual processes. Two of the first banks to implement electronic billing are Bank One Corp.[12] and the Bank of America[13], which have started to offer integrated electronic billing to their online banking customers. Another very important advantage of online billing versus printed billing is the fact that billing errors can be reduced substantially.

Online billing creates a new service sector on the Internet, the online billing service. Instead of going to many different places for paying invoices, billing services can aggregate all bills and the customer is able to pay all bills in a single location. This billing portal sites are very interesting for many companies as every customer is going to return to the site at least several times a month, making it easy to start cross-selling activities based on the user profile, which could include the billing information. Therefore not only are banks trying to get into the online billing market, but also traditional Internet portals such as Yahoo and Excite.

Although end-customer billing will be the first step on the Internet, the real advantage lies in offering invoices to business customers on the web. Business-to-business transaction costs will be lowered because of this new technology.

13.2.3 Internet Cheques

Internet cheques have no great importance on the Internet, so far, but still it is important to understand the way they can be used. It may be of value for your particular business. Electronic cheques work similarly to conventional cheques. The customers receive digital documents from their banks and need to enter the amount of the payment, the currency and the name of the payee for every payment transaction. In order to cash in the electronic cheque it needs to be digitally signed by the payer.

The use of cheques in the US and Europe differs quite a lot. Most existing electronic cheque solutions are based on the US American system, whereby the cheque needs to be signed by the payer and the payee. The payee brings the check to the bank, cashes in the money and then the cheque is sent back through the bank to the payer.

NetCheque

In 1995 the NetCheque system was developed by the Information Sciences Institute of the University of Southern California[14], which implements all of the above requirements.

---

[12]http://www.bankone.com/

[13]http://www.bankofamerica.com/

[14]http://www.usc.edu/

The buyer and the seller need to have an account at NetCheque. In order to make it really secure, a Kereberos-identification and a password are used. In order to pay via cheque it is necessary to install some special client software, which works like a cheque book. A customer is able to send an encrypted cheque with this software to the merchant.

The merchant is able to get the money from a bank or can use the cheque for a transaction with a supplier. A special accounting network verifies the cheques and gives an OK to the merchant who then delivers the goods.

Although the system is also suitable for micro-payments, it never really took off. The main problem is the public key infrastructure that is needed to exchange certificates and sign the cheques. In 1995 this was not available, and at the same time credit card based transactions took off. Another weakness of NetCheque was also its small initial customer and merchant base.

PayNow

The PayNow service developed by CyberCash supports micro-payments in the form of electronic checks. The CyberCash Internet wallet contains the PayNow checks which can be used in online shops that support the CyberCash standard. The electronic check will work in a similar manner to stored-value chip card transactions where the consumer pre-loads a CyberCash wallet with value though the real money remains in the bank.

echeck

The FSTC Electronic Check (echeck)[15] is currently being piloted at the US Department of the Treasury. The echeck leverages the check payment system from the real to the virtual world with fewer manual steps involved. It fits within current business practices, eliminating the need for expensive process re-engineering. The echeck system is highly secure and can be used by all bank customers who have checking accounts. Checking accounts do exist in the US, but are unknown, for example in Europe.

Echecks contain the same information as paper checks and are based on the same legal framework. The electronic cheques can be exchanged directly between parties and can replace all remote transactions where paper checks are used today. Echecks work the same way traditional cheques work. The customer writes the echeck and gives the echeck to the payee electronically. The payee deposits the electronic cheque, receives credit, and the payee's bank "clears" the echeck to the paying bank. The paying bank validates the echeck and charges the customer's account for the cheque sum.

Echecks offer the ability to conduct bank transactions in a safe way via the Internet. The validity of the echecks can be verified automatically by the bank, which reduces fraud losses for all parties involved. Using the Finan-

---

[15]http://www.echeck.org/

cial Services Markup Language (FSML) and the use of digital signatures and certificates make the system highly secure.

13.2.4 Cash on Delivery

Another post-paid model that works offline is cash on delivery (COD). Customers are able to order goods and services online and pay when the goods or services arrive at their doorstep. Arktis[16], one of Germany's largest resellers of Macintosh software, uses this system for its online business. Customers are able to browse through the online (or printed) catalogue, order via telephone, fax, mail or e-mail and get the goods delivered to their doorstep. The employee of the postal service who delivers the goods gets the money from the customer. This system has the advantage that Arktis gets the money from the postal service and does not need to verify in every case that a customer is willing to pay for the goods. If the customer is unwilling to pay at the doorstep the package is sent back to the sender and the postal service asks for a refund.

This system makes it easier to sell goods and services to people whom you do not know and who are not willing to pay via credit card for one reason or the other. And you do not have to wait until the customer pays the invoice. COD is normally more expensive, as it involves the postal service. The costs for COD are normally paid for by the customer.

13.2.5 Checking the Business Cases

Based on the economics of an Internet bookshop, which is our first business case example, we can see quite easily that all post-paid solutions are viable options for the online bookshop. Credit cards are most likely supported as the bookshop will use them if it has shops in the physical world. If this is the case knowledge in this area is already there and the relationship to the bank has been established. Invoices are also very common in the bookshop business, as the goods are not so expensive that one order not paid in time will ruin the complete business. If the online bookshop is spending money on new technologies it will most likely allow electronic cheques or gift vouchers that can be exchanged for books. The advantage of this system is that a customer can purchase a cheque or a voucher and give it to a friend as a present. Due to the large number of customers a niche payment system such as electronic cheques may still be useful to implement. The cash on delivery system also works for bookshops very well, as the necessary infrastructure is already in place. The connection to the logistics partner have been established and can be used to receive the money from them.

The translation service won't use all of the post-paid solutions as they are not suitable for freelancers. A freelancer won't accept credit card transactions, as they have far fewer financial transactions than a bookshop, for example.

---

[16]http://www.arktis.de/

Paying four percent credit card fees may be viable for a shop that has thousands of transactions a day, but translators will most likely have only a limited number of financial transactions a month. So setting up the credit card infrastructure and then paying the credit card fees is too expensive. A translator will most probably use invoices to initiate payments as this only requires a bank account and no interaction on the translation service side. All transaction costs are on the customer side. Freelancers won't use electronic cheques as this is not suitable for this type of business, because the number of customers is limited and it is not likely that many of the customers will have the technical infrastructure to support the system. Cash on delivery is also highly unlikely as the translation service is more business-to-business than business-to-consumer. And in the B-2-B world it is not likely that companies have thousands of Dollars or Euros lying around just in case a business partner sends a completed translation by COD.

The news agency services can be paid by almost all post-paid systems. Two types of payment can be envisioned here. Either micro-payment for every single news item or a subscription fee that needs to be paid every week, month or year. Credit cards are not designed for micro-payments, but can be used to pay the subscription fee. The same applies to invoices. Sending out invoices for every single electronic transaction would cost more than the transaction is worth. Electronic cheques can be used to do both, micro-payments and pay subscription fees. This may be he most economic solution for the news agency and the customer, as the service and the payment are fully digital and do not require the switch to an analogue medium. Cash on delivery is not possible in this case, as the goods are only delivered digitally. It would be possible to extend the cash on delivery model to the Internet by paying with electronic cash of course. We will see that with the pre-paid model later in this chapter.

The software company would most likely support all post-paid payment systems. As with the news agency service, the online call center could be paid either by micro-payments or through a subscription fee. As I have already pointed out, credit card transactions are not suitable for micro-payments, so if you have a credit card infrastructure it would be easier to support the subscription model. The software itself would most probably be paid by credit card. The software could also be paid by invoice and the support through the online call center, if based on the subscription model. Just as with the news agency service, electronic cheques will be an adequate solution for both, selling software and offering online support. Cash on delivery would only make sense for the software, but not at all for the online support service.

13.2.6 Online Experience

Credit card payment is, without doubt, the most successful payment system on the Internet. It is actually more difficult to find a site that does not accept credit card payment, but I will mention a few examples of how different sites use credit card payment systems. About 99 percent of all web sites that accept credit cards use a simple SSL encryption to ensure the privacy of the credit card information.

On the web site of the Florists Transworld Delivery[17] it is possible to select a bunch of flowers and pay for them directly online with credit cards. All the customer has to do is to enter the credit card details, which are then transmitted electronically to the payment server using SSL encrypted communication. Once the order has been authorized by the credit card company the order will be sent to the local flower shop. Once the local flower shop has accepted the order, the credit card is debited and the order is executed by delivering the flowers to the recipient.

Discos Castello[18], a compact disc online shop in Spain, uses the SET standard for accepting credit cards in its shop. The SET standard uses a much stronger encryption through the use of digital certificates and a public key infrastructure. In order to allow customers to pay with their credit cards, they need to ask their bank for a SET certificate which identifies them against the system. In Spain, the credit card processor 4B[19] and more than forty banks are participating in the SET program and give out the certificates to their customers. Once a customer has applied for the certificate and has loaded the certificate into the electronic wallet which needs to be installed on the computer of the customer, the wallet is able to talk to the point of sale (POS) software which is installed on the web server of Discos Castello. The wallet software encrypts the order information with the public key of the merchant and the credit card information is encrypted with the public key of the bank. Using this mechanism the merchant is able to see the order only, but not the credit card information. The merchant passes the credit card information on to the bank which authorizes the order and sends an "ok" back to the merchant which then processes the order. Other than in the first example, the communication between merchant and bank is highly standardized and strongly supported by the credit card processors.

Another possibility is to use an online bank to ensure the accuracy of the credit card transaction. The *Internet Business Magazine*[20] in the UK is using this system for reader subscription. The readers who would like to subscribe to the magazine go to the web site and are redirected to NetBanx[21], where the credit card details are collected. The bank receives an up-front fee for every transaction which would be much higher than if Internet Business did it themselves, but they do not need to think about digital certificates or install special software on their system for the payment process, as there is only one product that can be paid for.

---

[17]http://www.ftd.com/

[18]http://www.discoscastello.es/

[19]http://www.4b.es/

[20]http://www.ibmag.co.uk/

[21]http://www.netbanx.com/

The official Japanese Titanic homepage[22] offers Titanic cups, t-shirts and all the other Titanic goods, which can be bought through CyberCash. The German web site Referate Online[23] offers scientific reports for pupils who are too lazy to write their own for school. Through CyberCash payment the pupils are able to download reports for any school subject.

The German online poster shop 3W Art[24] enables its customers to browse through their online catalogue and select posters and other art-related articles for ordering. Once the customers have decided on the goods to order, they are asked for their addresses and the products are sent out. Together with the goods an invoice is sent out which asks the customer to pay via money transfer. Although this may seem risky as there is no guarantee that the customer will pay in the end, as the goods are not costly and need to be sent out to a real address it is a risk that many companies, especially in Europe are taking. Many of them are connected to address databases provided by postal services, such as the Deutsche Bundespost[25]. Using these databases it is possible to verify if a given person lives at a certain address.

Billserv.com[26], an online billing services has create a billing portal called Bills.com[27], where consumers are able to pay their bills.

Another example for online business paid via invoice is Travel Overland[28]. The online flight booking service which allows customers to choose their flights online and book them directly into the systems of the airlines. The customers will receive a confirmation via e-mail and the invoice is sent via normal mail. If the flight has been booked more than four weeks in advance then the customers need to pay 75 Euro per person in advance. The rest of the money needs to be paid two weeks in advance. The tickets will then be sent out to the customers about ten days before their departure.

Two of the above mentioned payment solutions, NetCheques and PayNow, have been out of business for quite a while. There are no real life examples on the web anymore, but knowing that these solutions have failed and why they have failed is very important in order to prevent your business from failing. It does not help to have the right business idea and an excellent web site, if people are not able to pay because the business is using a payment solution nobody knows how to use or has access to.

Arlt[29], a reseller of computer hardware uses the cash on delivery method, but restricts it to Germany. Using this payment option you have to pay an additional 10 DM (5 Euro or Dollar) extra.

---

[22] http://www.titanic.co.jp/
[23] http://www.referate.de/
[24] http://www.poster.de/
[25] http://www.post.de/
[26] http://www.billserv.com/
[27] http://www.bills.com/
[28] http://www.travel-overland.de/
[29] http://www.arlt.de/

13.2.7   Required Software

In order to allow credit card payment using SSL encryption all that is needed
is a digital certificate on the web server that encrypts the traffic between customer and merchant. The certificate can be created by a certificate server that
can be installed on any system at the merchant site or can be bought, for example, from VeriSign[30], as these certificates are accepted in all browsers. For
certificates that are created by non-trusted partners, such as a merchant, the
customers need to acknowledge the certificate before using it the first time. The
problem with SSL is that no standard mechanisms on the server exist that allow for communication with the bank. This issue needs to be resolved on an
individual basis.

As mentioned above many banks offer the outsourcing of payment methods.
You have your shopping site and they will take care of the payment. This
is the best solution especially for smaller shops. Besides NetBanx there are
many other payment service providers such as MasterMerchant[31], which offers
special payment services for Sport Books, Adult web sites and online casinos.

The SET standard requires the installation of special software on the client
computer, the merchant server and the bank gateway. This software regulates
the communication which is required for the credit card transaction between
the parties involved. Hewlett-Packard and IBM offer complete solutions for the
SET standard. Hewlett-Packard's solution is based on the Verifone[32] software,
which they bought in 1997 and is called vSuite[33]. It contains four products,
vWallet for the customer, vPOS for the merchant, vGATE and Omnihost for
the bank. IBM proposes its IBM Payment Suite[34] which consists of the IBM
Consumer Wallet, IBM Payment Server, IBM Payment Gateway and the IBM
Payment Registry. There are many other smaller vendors of SET software. A
complete list can be found at the SetCo site[35].

Verifone has developed a new product called PayWorks, which can act as the
foundation and central hub of any Integrated Payment Solution application
configuration, the IPS Switch application component that switches payment
messages from one IPS component or option to another. The software handles
a broad variety of information including credit transactions (via SET, SSL, for
example), debit transactions, payments and other payment-related messages.
The IPS Switch is just one of many application components that are a part of
IPS. IPS contains a wide variety of application components to handle credit
and debit, draft capture and settlement, private label credit, issuer interfaces
and even Internet security. Through the modular design, it is possible to select
the capabilities that match your business needs and build a powerful electronic

---

[30] http://www.verisign.com/
[31] http://www.mastermerchant.com/
[32] http://www.verifone.com/
[33] http://www.verifone.com/solutions/internet/
[34] http://www.software.ibm.com/commerce/payment/
[35] http://www.setco.org/matrix.html

payment system, customized to your business requirements. When a business requires a new form of payment, it can plan for it and add it easily. The whole solution is based on Java and XML, making it ready for the future.

Traditional invoices require companies to get the information through their ERP system to a printer and then send the print outs out to the customers. One provider of online billing software is BlueGill Technologies[36], which has developed applications for four vertical industries. Edify[37] has built online billing into its banking platform software. E-Bill, developed by CheckFree[38], allows banks to convert legacy billing data and present it on the Web.

All other payment solutions are proprietary. Please contact the vendor for more information on the particular implementations. Credit card is the way to go for post-paid transactions right now, as the technology is proven and there are many different vendors.

13.3   Instant-paid Payment Systems

13.3.1   Debit Cards

Debit cards are also used a lot, in fact, they are used a lot more in Europe than in the US, where credit cards are more common. The difference between credit cards and debit cards is that in order to pay with a debit card you need to know your personal identification number (PIN) and need a hardware device that is able to read the information that is stored in the magnetic strip on the back, unlike with the credit card, where all the information is also printed on the front of the card.

So far the business with debit cards is non existent on the Internet. As no computer is equipped with a hardware terminal that is able to read the magnetic strip. As the prices for such devices drop they will become a commodity that will be sold together with every computer, replacing the floppy drive. The trend is moving from magnetic strips to electronic chips on smart cards. Smart cards nowadays are used mainly for electronic cash, but in the future they will replace the debit and credit cards as well.

13.3.2   Direct Debit

Direct debit is another post-paid solution which is used in online transactions. The German ISP PureTec[39] uses this system for the payment of their services, which consists of domain name registration and web site offerings. Instead of asking the user for their credit card number, PureTec asks the customers for their bank account number and the bank code. The money can then be debited

---

[36]http://www.bluegill.com/
[37]http://www.edify.com/
[38]http://www.checkfree.com/
[39]http://www.puretec.de/

directly from the bank account. The only problem with this system is the signature. In order to get the money from a bank, you need a valid signature of the customer on the same sheet as the order. As long as no legislation for digital signature has been established, it is necessary to print out the completed order, sign it and fax it to PureTec (see Figure 13.1).

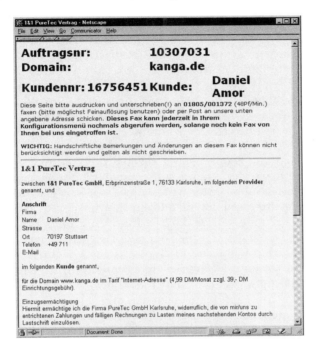

Figure 13.1. PureTec's Direct Debit Model

Direct debit is not yet a fully instant-paid solution, but with digital certification laws in the making, it is just a matter of months, until the first web sites and banks will accept digital signatures from their customers to debit their accounts.

13.3.3 Checking the Business Cases

The bookshop would profit from the instant-paid model as the money would be coming in at the time of order which would reduce the possibilities of fraud. There is one slight disadvantage over post-paid models in the case of a return. As the post-paid payment systems are not debited immediately from the bank account of the customers it is possible to send back the books before any financial transaction has taken place. In the instant-paid model the money needs to be credited back to the bank account. The major obstacle for debit cards are the implementation issues. There are no standards that are accepted on a country-wide, continent-wide or world-wide level as the type of debit cards differs so much. With direct debit we have a similar problem, transferring money from your own account to the account of someone else is possible world-wide, but someone else debiting your account is not possible throughout the world because of the missing standards. On a local national basis this is possible, so if you limit your target group to a certain country then the direct debit model will work.

For the translation service the same restrictions apply as with the post-paid models. The implementation on the Internet would be far too expensive for the number of transactions, and the other limiting factors described in the bookshop example above do not help with the business model.

The news agency may work with the instant-paid model. It would be possible to envision a free newsletter where people can sign up and pass on their bank details with the authorization to debit the account in the case of an information transaction. People would receive the free newsletter with short summaries of the news stories and will receive a login and password in order to identify themselves when entering the news web server. There they can read through the whole story and download it in their preferred format. Every time they do this, some money will be debited from their bank account. The transactional costs need to be low in order to make this an efficient way of payment. The far better solution would be to charge them a monthly fee allowing the customers to read through all stories that come up in that particular month. This, of course, does not give you the control over what a customer is able to see. Depending on the exact business model and the customer base it needs to be decided which model is more useful.

For the software company the same rules apply as with the bookshop. It will be able to handle all transaction by instant-paid systems in a very efficient way. If the online support is paid by subscription fee it can be bundled into the product and sold in one transaction to the customer. Micro-payments are possible, but it remains to be seen how much a single transaction would cost. As long as digital signatures are not accepted by banks the manual process involved will hinder an efficient use of the payment model.

13.3.4 Online Experience

No online shops use debit cards so far for online business, but it will not take long until the first shops will support this payment model as it is very useful for small to medium payments.

Travel Overland[40], which normally uses the invoice payment model, requires customers to use the direct debit model for special offerings and last minute flights. The customer books the flight the normal way, but will be redirected to a special web page for payment where they need to enter their bank

---

[40]http://www.travel-overland.de/

details. The page then has to be printed out by the customer, signed and faxed to Travel Overland. They debit the card and send out the tickets, if there is enough time, and the customer is willing to pay packaging and postage. Otherwise they will be left at the departure airport for pick up.

13.3.5 Required Software

For direct debit no special software is required, as digital signatures are not yet accepted by the banks in most countries. In Germany, the HBCI standard is about to be established, which allows not only direct debit, but also other banking applications. A special web form suffices to gather all relevant information from the customers, which they then need to print out and fax to the merchant. The whole process is manual, but the data entered in the form can help save time, as the bank details are saved in digital form. The faxed form is used to authorize the money transfer. Once digital signatures are accepted, special software on the merchant server will pass on the transaction to the bank where the money transfer will be initiated in an instant.

13.4 Pre-paid Payment Systems

13.4.1 Electronic Cash

Electronic cash solutions use software to save the equivalent of cash onto a hard or a floppy disk. Coins and bank notes are replaced by digitally signed files. The advantage of this system is that the cost of passing on the money is nearly zero (the only real cost you have is the internet connection). In order to receive the money, you need to go to a virtual automatic teller machine on the Internet or to a real world ATM, where you can get electronic cash by direct debit from the bank account or by credit card payment. The difficulty with electronic cash is to implement it in a very secure way. As the money is stored in files, it should be made clear that by copying the files the value of the cash is not increased nor should it be possible to alter the amount of the digital money on your hard disk. Electronic coins and notes should have digital marks that make it impossible to use them more than once. The use of encryption technologies, digital signatures and electronic signatures helps to reduce the possibility of fraud.

In order to emulate coins and bank notes, digital money should not reveal the identity of the person who has paid with it. Payment should not require a bank in between. Electronic money should be exchanged directly between the two partners involved. Splitting up the value is also very important. Instead of one digital bank note, you should be able to split it up into several bank notes and coins, which can be passed on to different people. Some implementations of electronic cash are the following solutions.

DigiCash

The electronic cash by DigiCash[41] is called eCash. Other than the previoulsy mentioned system, DigiCash tried to establish a network of service and product providers that accepted eCash. Bookshops, casinos and online newspapers accepted the money in exchange for goods, games and information.

The DigiCash solution is one very successful electronic cash solution. The Deutsche Bank[42] in Germany decided to become a partner and now is able to issue eCash to its customers. Some other banks around the world have become issuers as well, such as the St. George Bank[43] in Australia.

In order to use eCash the customer has to open an account at a participating bank, such as Deutsche Bank or Mark Twain Bank. The customer then needs to transfer a certain amount of money to that particular account and will receive the money in the form of electronic cash, which can be stored on the hard disk of the customer. The money is stored in the form of tokens. The electronic cash that customers get from their bank is also transferred to a special bank account from which the merchants are then paid for the financial transaction. The eCash system is a one-way token system that allows the money to be used only once. Only one transaction can be executed between customer and merchant. The merchant cannot use it to pay for something else. It needs to be brought back to the bank to be cashed in. Peer to peer transactions between customers are possible but require a bank in between to convert the tokens. Every token contains the sum it represents, a random number which is used as the serial number and a digital signature of the issuing bank. The bank is able to validate the electronic cash without knowing who used it, allowing the anonymous use of the electronic money. This is achieved by using a system called "blind signature". Table 13.4 explains in detail how this works.

The consumer is then able to go to a web site that supports DigiCash and is able to pay with the files on the hard disk. A merchant that wants to accept DigiCash money needs also to set up an account at a DigiCash supporting bank, in order to cash in the accepted money. The transaction costs are zero for the DigiCash model. In 1998 more than 150 web sites accepted DigiCash money until DigiCash went bankrupt in late 1998. Credit card transactions have destroyed the business for DigiCash, although they are seeking new investors to rebuild the service with a better business model.

A support site for German eCash shops[44] has been established, where you can find a list of shops that accept eCash from Digicash. The eCash system has established itself in many different areas of online selling, such as providing information, entertainment, digital goods, such as software products and with traditional online retailers.

---

[41]http://www.digicash.com/
[42]http://www.deutsche-bank.de/
[43]http://www.stgeorge.com.au/
[44]http://www.ecash-shops.de/

What Is a Blind Signature?

The blind signature is a patent-pending algorithm that was invented by David Chaum, the founder of DigiCash. To put it simply, a customer that acquires electronic cash creates raw tokens. A serial number is added to the token and sent to the customers' bank. The serial number is made invisible to the bank by multiplying it with another random number (the so-called blinding factor). The bank adds a digital signature to the token and sends it back to the customer. The customer is able to divide the serial number by the blinding factor and get the original serial number back. Using this mechanism, the bank is not able to trace back the tokens to the customers, as the bank does not see the original serial number.

Table 13.4.

NetCash

NetCash was also developed by the University of Southern California in 1995 and is not in use anymore. Although it was a very good implementation it was too early to be successful. It required a complex infrastructure that was too difficult to implement and use by many Internet users in the early days.

NetCash provides anonymous payments on the Internet. It is an electronic currency that supports real-time electronic payments. In order to get money from a currency server, the customer needs to have an account on a NetCheque server. The NetCheque system which was discussed above, provides a secure framework for online payment systems, which can be extended to include electronic cash. Offering the combination of NetCash and NetCheque, customers have the possibility of choosing their level of anonymity.

The anonymity is not as great as in the DigiCash system, as the NetCash coins can only be purchased through NetCheques. The currency server used to distribute the NetCash coins is able to trace the customers who purchase the coins. This is not likely to happen, as the customers can freely choose which currency server they use.

Once coins have been purchased by a customer, they can be passed on to other customers or merchants without revealing the identity of the buyer although a currency server is involved to ensure that the coins are valid. Only persons who want to cash the NetCash coins into real currency need to identify themselves at a currency server. In the NetCash scheme it is possible to transfer coins without the need of a currency server, but then there is no assurance that a coin is valid.

CyberCoins

Besides the CyberCash credit card solution, which was mentioned above, there is also a system for micro-payments called CyberCoins. CyberCoins enable merchants to sell, and consumers to buy, digital products via the Internet. CyberCoins can have a value ranging from $.25 up to $10, denominations too small for use in credit card purchases.

For every customer and merchant, special "cash-containers" are provided on a special Internet server, which act as CyberCoin accounts. Using the Cyber-Cash wallet, it is possible to move money to the CyberCoin account. In order to pay with the wallet a special command from the web browser is sent to the wallet which requires the customer to accept the payment. Once the customer has accepted the money it is transferred electronically from the customer's account to the merchant's. The communication is secured through encryption. The customer's order is sent to the merchant which adds the merchant data to the order and sends the completed order to the CyberCash gateway, which then moves the money between the accounts.

IBM Micro Payment

The system developed by the payment division of IBM Israel in Haifa[45] is a micro-payment system that allows the alteration of simple HTML links into payment links. Therefore it is necessary to put the Internet Service Providers in between customers and merchants. The system uses the existing payment infrastructure of the ISPs. The clicks on a certain link are registered in the log files of the merchant and can be attributed to a certain customer. The required payment is then passed on to the ISP which debits the money from the bank account of the customer. So far only some pilots are available on the Internet.

MilliCent

MilliCent[46] has been developed by DEC (Digital Equipment Corporation). It is based on the system of vouchers, which allow payment below the cent limit. These vouchers are called "scrip". In order to enable the electronic business, brokers are required for the payment. The brokers are typically Internet Service Providers and financial institutions. The brokers sell broker-scrips to the customers and manage the scrip of the merchants, which are different for every merchant. In order to pay, a customer needs to exchange a broker-scrip for a merchant-specific scrip. The scrips are managed then in the MilliCent

---

[45]http://www.hrl.il.ibm.com/mpay/

[46]http://www.millicent.digital.com/

wallet. Using a merchant-scrip the customer is able to pay for goods, information and services at a certain merchant without the interaction of a third party. This makes MilliCent a cheap solution for micro-payment businesses. Although several pilots are on the way, it is not clear, if the system will have a future, especially as the system does not guarantee anonymity.

13.4.2 Smart Cards

Smart Cards are very popular in Europe and their acceptance is increasing in the United States. Phone cards, Health Care cards and debit cards have embedded chips which contain money, health information and account information. Every debit card issued in Europe (called an EC Card) contains information on the owner and the account. In addition to these pieces of information, systems have been developed to store cash onto the chip.

The money on the card is saved in an encrypted form and is protected by a password to ensure the security of the smart card solution. In order to pay via smart card it is necessary to introduce the card into a hardware terminal. The device requires a special key from the issuing bank to start a money transfer in either direction.

Smart cards give shops the advantage that they need not carry around a lot of money after closure each day, but can transmit the money electronically to their bank account at the moment of payment. Actually the virtual money that has been used to pay for the goods can be transmitted in an instant to the bank of the merchant. The major advantage of smart cards is that it is possible to use them in both worlds, real and cyber. Using the smart card it is possible to go to a bank, load the card and pay on the Internet. The other way round is just as possible. Offer a service on the Internet, charge your customers who then transfer their money to your card and you can cash the money in at your bank or pass the money on to pay for another service. Electronic cash as described in the last subsection can only be used on the Internet. Smart cards can act as a bridge. Online auctions where everyone can offer something will profit a lot from smart cards, as people can exchange money directly, without the need for an intermediate.

Their great advantages are relative security, and simple, off-line operation. Together, these translate into low transaction costs. In Europe two standards have been established, the Mondex card in the United Kingdom and the "Geld-Karte" in Germany.

Mondex

The Mondex company, a subsidiary of MasterCard international, has become established in the United Kingdom and is becoming increasingly popular in the US. The money can be transferred by smart card readers that are attached to telephones, ATMs and through special electronic wallets. The reader is able to dial into a bank and enable the transfer between user and bank. One you have loaded money to your smart card, you are able to transfer the money to your business partners using the electronic wallet. Using the wallet, ATMs and Mondex telephones, it is also possible to check the balance on the card. Money can be exchanged between anybody in possession of a Mondex card. The Mondex system supports up to five different currencies on the card at the same time, which can be exchanged at a bank for any other currency. So far there is no mechanism on the card itself to convert a given currency into another one, as the smart card is not aware of current exchange rates.

It is not required to have a bank as an intermediate in every case. The system guarantees anonymity just as real cash does. This is also its disadvantage, it is not possible to track down criminal transactions. Only very few sites accept the Mondex card today, but it will just be a matter of time until more sites do, as it offers a great possibility to implement micro payments with no transaction costs are charged (the users have to pay a monthly fee of about UK Pounds 1.50).

The Mondex system is based on some strong security features that make it virtually impossible to forge the money. Mondex uses the Value Transfer Protocol (VTP), which uses strong cryptography to protect the movement of the money. Mondex values can only be moved between Mondex cards, which makes it a closed system.

The Mondex system allows customers to lock the value on a given card, in case of a loss. Banks are then able to operate a reward system to incentivize the return to their rightful owners. The persons who find the card can't do much with it, as it requires entry of a PIN to operate it.

GeldKarte

In 1997 the banks in Germany started issuing new debit cards with an embedded chip. This chip contains the functionality of electronic cash, which is called the GeldKarte (MoneyCard). As debit cards are replaced every two years, by the beginning of 1999 every debit card in Germany had become a smart card. The difference to Mondex is the way the cards are loaded with money. A special teller machine is necessary to get the money.

In order to pay with the smart card, existing devices need to be enhanced. Hardware devices for personal use are not planned. This would allow a person to log all transactions between smart cards. If more money is coming from the card than originally had been loaded onto the card, it would be inactivated. This also allow you to re-substitute money, in the case of a loss. Privacy is an issue with the log files, but the banks assure that they do not misuse the logging information. Sellers are not seeing personal information from the buyer; all they see is the number of the smart card, which then can be used by the bank to identify the user.

There are no sites that accept the MoneyCard at the time of writing due to its infrastructure, but its acceptance in shops and ticket machines is very high. The MoneyCard is a very attractive alternative for electronic businesses. Other than credit card companies which charge approximately 4 percent of the transaction, the MoneyCard enabled banks only charge 0.3 percent (or a minimum of 0.01 Euro). Because of the low transaction costs, the MoneyCard is ideal for micro-payments, which can be used to pay for web pages, documents and pictures, for example. In addition to this, the merchant receives the money during the ordering process and not after. The process is only completed if enough money is on the smart card.

The disadvantages of the MoneyCard for customers are that they have to pre-load the money onto the smart card (as with all pre-paid solutions) and risk losing interest on the money earned, if it had been left it in as bank account. The major drawback of the system is that it is a national solution. So far only Germany is using it. To make it really successful, other European countries need to adopt it or it will be replaced by international systems, such as the Mondex card. Even more important is that smart card readers become a commodity integrated into the keyboard, for example, and do impose additional costs on the customers.

Technical specifications for the use on the Internet have been issued in 1998, but only pilots have been set up, so far. There are no digital companies that accept the MoneyCard live. The major obstacle is the wide use of smart card readers.

VisaCash

VisaCash, the electronic wallet, has been tested in several countries so far. Two different cards are available, the one-way card, which works similar to a telephone card and a card that can be reloaded, which works similar to the Mondex card and the GeldKarte.

The VisaCash card works on the Internet so far only a prototype has been demonstrated at the CardTech/SecurTech Conference in Orlando, Florida. But during the Olympic Games in Atlanta it was used as the preferred payment method. Since then not much has happened with the VisaCard.

13.4.3   Checking the Business Cases

Pre-paid solutions are the preferred solutions of the banks and the online shops as they require the user to pick up the money in advance (which is good for the bank, as it does not have to pay interest on the money anymore) and can hand it over to the online shop at the instant of buying the product (which prevents digital fraud). The system works like in the real shops, where people come in and buy products for cash. It is easy to understand, especially for people who do not have a lot of knowledge in the area of payment.

Our bookshop would most probably accept electronic cash, as long as the books do not get too expensive. Due to the fact that the money is on the hard disk of the customers they won't pick up hundreds of Dollars or Euro and store them until they find what they were looking for. Ideally the bookshop would accept mixed payments in that one part is paid using a credit card and the other part is paid with the electronic money. Smart cards would not be accepted right away as the necessary readers are not available with every computer and there is no established standard that is accepted on a continent-wide or world-wide basis. Technically there is no issue, but it will take some time before smart cards payment are established. Once there is a standard the bookshop will most likely pick up this payment method.

For the translator again this would not be a viable solution, as the costs for building up the infrastructure would be too high. The amount of money paid for the services would also normally be higher than the pre-paid solutions are suitable for. The translator does not provide services that can be paid with micro-payment solutions nor are most of the translations in a price range below 200 Dollar or Euro.

For the news agency pre-paid solutions would fit perfectly if the business model is based on fees for every single transaction. The pay per view model works perfectly together with the micro-payment solutions that are offered by the pre-paid models. Even with a subscription model it will make sense, as long as the subscription fee is reasonably low.

The software company would accept pre-paid payment solutions for smaller software packages and of course for the online call center. Typically micro-payments and pre-paid solutions are supported by end customers but not by businesses as they need an invoice first to pay for a certain article.

13.4.4 Online Experience

The DPunkt Bookshop[47] in Germany allows the download of their books. The content can be downloaded chapter by chapter. Every chapter is available in PDF (Adobe Acrobat) format, which can be viewed with any browser. In addition to this DPunkt has a database of images and textures which can be bought online.

NetCash and CyberCoins had been widely used until 1998, when new standard came up which made the developers give up and the shops shut down the NetCash and CyberCoins option. In 1997 the First Union Bank[48] in the US had started a pilot with CyberCoins and had even built a Mall on the banks own web site, where people could shop for CyberCoins. Research I conducted on the Internet lead to many dead links for these payment schemes. But still they need to be mentioned in this chapter, as they have had a large impact on the Internet is today and help you understand which payment schemes are available and useful.

So far no online businesses accept smart card based systems such as Mondex or the GeldKarte. There are several trials underway. One example is the

---

[47]http://ecash.dpunkt.de/
[48]http://www.firstunion.com/

University of Exeter in the UK, which has developed a set of tools to deal with Mondex cards on the Internet[49].

13.4.5   Required Software

None of the above mentioned solutions are based on open standards. Therefore it is necessary to contact the companies that have developed the standards for particular software. Please refer to the above mentioned URLs for further information.   None of the payment solutions mentioned in this chapter can really be recommended, as they are lacking the open standard.

13.5   Comparing Payment Technologies

Now that we have looked at the three types of online payment, I just want to review the business requirements from the second section.   Table 13.5 shows which technology meets which requirement.

Comparison of Payment Technology

	Post-paid	Instant-paid	Pre-paid
Acceptability	High	Low	Low
Anonymity	Low	High	Middle
Convertibility	High	High	High
Efficiency	Low	High	High
Flexibility	Low	Low	Low
Integration	High	Low	Middle
Reliability	High	High	High
Scalability	High	High	High
Security	Middle	High	Middle
Usability	High	Middle	Middle

Table 13.5.

It becomes quite clear that post-paid systems are scoring the highest marks, as they have been established on the Internet for a while. Pre-paid and instant-paid systems are not as common on the Internet. There the standards have not

---

[49]http://www.ex.ac.uk/ecu/mondex/JTAP/

been settled yet and many things are still in movement. Although this may seem bad, it is good, as it opens up the possibility of integrating new technologies and paradigms. SSL-based credit card payments are so established that other standards like SET have difficult uphill battles to fight.

13.6 The Future of Payment

13.6.1 SEMPER

In the future highly integrated frameworks will help to conduct secure business via the Internet. Payment solutions will be only one segment in the infrastructure as payment does not address the broader "trading" process in an open extensible way. Trading is more than making payments and includes, for example, offers, receipts, proof of delivery and customer care – which consumers demand in the real world and must therefore be present in the virtual world. This section will focus on two projects, two for the business-to-consumer area (SEMPER and the Open Trading Protocol) and two, which focus more on the business-to-business transactions (Global Trust Enterprise and OBI) and identify the payment solutions used therein.

SEMPER (Secure Electronic Marketplace for Europe)[50] is a research project founded by the European Union to allow payment with electronic money via the Internet. The SEMPER project tries to identify the required infrastructure for such an environment. Its predecessor project CAFÉ (Conditional Access for Europe) already identified the technical requirements for electronic passports, digital driving licenses and cyber money in real world applications. Terminals and Teller Machines are able to identify the user and allow the storage of electronic money.

As we have already seen in this chapter, many different, incompatible Internet payment systems compete with one another. Most online shops accept only a limited subset and some accept only one payment system. Ideally every online shop should be able to support any available method of payment, but without increased costs on the merchant side. Without a unified framework for payment, the solution architect for an online business needs to implement every payment method, one after the other, which makes it costly. A general payment service framework therefore is necessary that separates the business model from the payment model. The framework needs to make different payment models transparent to the business application.

The SEMPER framework consists of a security kernel and different services that surround it. The services are divided into modules. At the time of writing modules for encryption, certification and payment existed. These modules can be called from business applications through the security kernel by using a special application programming interface (API).

---

[50]http://www.semper.org/

The connection between the payment and the business process needs to be defined through a hierarchy of APIs that represent payment models, such as credit card payment systems or electronic cash solutions. The following features need to implemented in order to complement the APIs. Payment models need to be selected automatically, so that applications do not need to bother about this. They should only need to think about the value and the recipient of the payment. And tools will need to be created that allow the incorporation of payment models into this generic payment service.

For the SEMPER system a java-based generic payment service has been created. It can be fairly easily extended, by adding new classes to the generic payment service class. So far SET and DigiCash have been implemented, so that users of the generic payment service are able to exchange financial transactions with people who use either SET or DigiCash. It is just a matter of time until other modules will become available and make the whole system valuable. Through the modularity of Java and the open framework the implementation is not a big issue. It is more difficult to convince owners of propriety standards to support an open standard infrastructure, as this means they have to reveal the source code.

13.6.2 The Open Trading Protocol

The Open Trading Protocol (OTP)[51] complements today's electronic payment protocols by addressing the process of doing business. The OTP provides a means to negotiate trade and buy and sell by invoking the underlying payment protocols, which can be one of the above mentioned.

The aim of the OTP is to lower the cost of trading. This is done by using the Internet as a distribution channel that is consistent, inexpensive and secure. The required framework is described as part of the OTP. OTP enables new models of trade that are available only on the Internet. The framework allows payment models with two (direct payment) or three parties (indirect payment). The protocol is open, flexible, extensible, robust, and vendor neutral making it ideal for the Internet. Open means that the specifications are not secret and the flexibility allows the creation of differentiated service offerings to be created. The extensibility means that new or enhanced trading and payment models can be integrated without disrupting the service of the other components. The robustness of the protocol means that the whole infrastructure is able to cope with errors or downtime of the participating servers and clients. As the protocol is open, any interested independent software vendor (ISV) is able to create software that adheres to the standard. This offers businesses the ability to choose from a range of products with similar feature sets and make it therefore independent of the ISV.

Costs for customer care can be lowered significantly by using the OTP, as it has a very flexible, but standard way of providing information on a certain pay-

---

[51]http://www.otp.org/

ment. The information can then be extracted to resolve issues of payment. The OTP supports the delivery of goods both digitally and physically. The whole trading chain is linked by the information, so that the delivery information can be brought together with the payment information.

13.6.3   Open Buying on the Internet

OBI[52] is a freely available framework for business-to-business transactions. The standard contains a detailed architecture, concise technical specifications and guidelines, and information on compliance and implementational issues. Any organization or individual can acquire a copy of the OBI standard and use it to build a product, service, or solution.

The OBI architecture is based on the idea that process owners should be responsible for the information associated with their business processes. Suppliers should, for example, be responsible for the content of the online catalogue and the prices while purchasing organizations should be held responsible for profile information and account codes.

The architecture normally has three organizations involved; the supplier, the purchaser and the payment authority. Part of the purchaser organization is the requisitioner who actually places the orders via the Internet. In order to identify the requisitioner a digital certificate is used. The purchasing organization handles the server, such as the OBI server for receiving order requests and returning orders and the people there handle, for example, the profile information of the requisitioners. The purchasing department also maintains the relationship with the suppliers and deals on the prices.

The payment authority provides the processes needed for the authorization of the payment between the purchaser and the supplier. A payment authority is in most cases a financial institution, such as a bank. If the payment is done via bulk invoice, the responsibilities could also be part of the supplier.

The supplier maintains a dynamic electronic catalog that presents accurate product and price information for every purchaser. The information needs to be kept private, as one purchaser should not be able to see the prices and product range of the other purchasers. The product and price information are displayed as agreed on in the contract with a buying organization.

Communication between the trading partners is done over standard HTTP protocol and the use of SSL encryption using standard web browsers to keep costs on the purchaser side down. The information is transported via the Internet. The more companies adopt to the OBI standard, the cheaper a purchasing order will become. So far some OBI pilots are being conducted, but no real implementations have been spotted on the Internet. It remains to be seen if the OBI standard will become successful in the MRO/ORM business.

---

[52]http://www.openbuy.org/

Properties of OBI

OBI is designed for business-to-business purchasing, which is different from consumer purchasing and is built on the following principles:

- **Common Vision** – The OBI standard is based on the expectations for B-2-B solutions of the participants and the common issues that arise. The standard tries to be as general as possible.

- **Cost Effectiveness** – Maintenance costs need to be reasonable and the OBI solutions need to integrate easily with the existing IT infrastructure.

- **Flexibility** – The standard needs to be flexible enough to accommodate variations of different implementations and upcoming business needs.

- **Robust Infrastructure** – The infrastructure needs to be able to allow transactions securely and reliably.

- **Value-Added Services** – Service providers have the possibility to differentiate themselves through value added services on top of the standard with its protocol and message formats.

- **Vendor Neutrality** – To encourage a diversity of product offerings from a variety of software vendors the standard is open and includes interoperability tests.

Table 13.6.

13.6.4   Global Trust Enterprise

Global Trust Enterprise has been developed by CertCo[53] in the US together with many partner banks throughout the world, such as the HypoVereinsbank[54] in Germany. The reason for building up the service are manifold, but the basic idea was to create a powerful enabler for business-to-business trans-

---

[53] http://www.certco.com/
[54] http://www.hypovereinsbank.de/

actions. The idea is founded on the principle of broad participation by financial institutions and more and more banks are taking part in the initiative. Other than business-to-consumer transactions on the Internet that rely on one-to-one authentication models, the global trust enterprise seeks to extend this model into a multilateral (many to many) environment, as businesses tend to have more than one employee.

The major obstacle to implement world-wide business-to-business networks is the issue of identity trust. Through the new system companies doing electronic business will be able to identify the trading partner. CertCo is issuing identity warranties that enables buyers and sellers to manage the risk. This confidence in the business partners enables enterprises to conduct high-integrity, authenticated and trusted business-to-business transactions with already known and unknown trading partners via the Internet. As mentioned earlier, payment in the business-to-business area is mostly done via invoice, so sending out the invoice is not the problem. The problem is to be sure about the identity of the business partner.

International trade, corporate purchasing and content delivery represent some of the typical business-to-business transactions covered by the global trust enterprise. Let us look at an example: Consider a Danish ice cream company that wants to expand its market reach, minimize the cost and conduct business with several importers in the Americas and Asia. Digital certificates issued by participating banks allow the exporters and the importers to trust each other as they negotiate the prices and sign the contracts. The certificates can also be used to audit the transactions. Once the participating companies have obtained the certificate from their banks, they are able to conduct business with any other company that has registered at any of the participating institutions via the Internet.

The reason why CertCo chose to work with financial institutions to provide the authentication of business partners, is explained easily. The banks are experienced in identifying corporate customers and their employees for the online initiation of electronic transactions, as they have done this for years on the private financial networks. Signature guarantees, check and credit card verification are tasks that banks already perform and are able to extend easily to the Internet. Trading partners on the Internet will therefore trust the identity of the others, because they trust the financial institution they are working with.

Using the global trust enterprise framework, corporate customers will be able to use services provided by the participating banks. A typical buy-sell transaction would require the seller to ask the financial institution to verify the digital signature of the buyer. The bank of the seller and of the buyer would get in contact automatically through the network and exchange the required information. In this case, the buyer's bank would take the signature and verify it and send back an attestation that the signature is valid. Likewise as the buyer may ask to verify the digital certificate of the seller.

In order to enable communication between the participants, a standardized system and process for identity certification has been established. The global trust enterprise will act as a root certification authority for the financial institutions and will be able to perform an audit to monitor the adherence to a set of predefined system rules and business practices.

Advantage of the Global Trust Enterprise

The global trust enterprise compared to previous efforts differ in several ways.

- **Interoperability** – Businesses are not dependent on a particular software vendor or financial institution, as the identity trust is based on common business practices and open technical specifications.

- **Support** – The framework is sponsored by financial institutions throughout the world, making it an efficient way of doing business via the Internet.

- **Digital Identity** – Businesses will require only one digital certificate for all their virtual business activities.

Table 13.7.

The elements of identity trust that will be addressed are the following. Based on common legal and business practices a foundation for trust is created by establishing a uniform set of identification and operating practices. The global trust enterprise will provide the technology to identify trading partners in real-time via the Internet. The digital signatures and hash codes are used to verify that the information transmitted has not been changed during the transmission. Through these technologies non-repudiation can be guaranteed and they will provide strong legal evidence of the existence of the message, including additional information such as the signature, time and date and the certificate of the sender.

The global trust enterprise does not require participants to obtain special proprietary standards. It is built on open standards, in order to facilitate interoperability between the participants. Digital signatures, certificate and business practices are shared throughout the framework to expand the business-to-business transactions.

Part IV

The Present Future

Chapter 14

THE OPEN SOURCE COMMUNITY

14.1 Information Wants to Be Free

14.1.1 Free Software

Other than in the real world, people on the Internet have been willing to share information, programs and media files for free. This already happened long before the current open source movement. The so-called free software movement containing public domain software, freeware, cardware, mailware, giftware, shareware are the concepts in the programming era that dominated the web before the large companies decided to give away their software for free.

Placing a program into the public domain meant for programmers that others could grab their programs, use them, and even modify them without even mentioning the original author. Only very few programs have been released as public domain software. But the educational value of having such programs is very high. The source code can be used by others to understand how to program something and use it for their own projects.

A little stricter is freeware, which allows users to use a program for free, but the author retains the copyright and does not allow the commercial use of the program. In many cases the source code is not available, and where the source code is available, the code is not allowed to be used in other programs without the permission of the original author. Giftware, cardware and mailware are special types of freeware, where the the author requests a gift, a postcard or a letter from the users. These requests are never enforced, but the author is happy about every reaction from the user.

The intention of these forms of free programs is to provide a service to the online community, to become known in the community. Most projects were based on programs that solved a personal computing problem and were then extended to solve problems of the general public. The programmers work for the non-market economy. They are not interested in money, but in the beauty and utility of their programs.

Shareware is a little different. The author releases the software for free, but requests the users pay a fee if they like the program. Many programs do not enforce this payment. Others use special keys that allow potential customers to use a certain program for thirty days or restrict the functionality (saving is not allowed, for example). Today these programs are called evaluation copies. The shareware concept allowed many people to earn some money without the need of building up a company. Homegrown programs could be easily distributed over the Internet without the need for much marketing. The chat client mIRC[1], for example, is distributed as shareware. Anybody can download the software, try it out and then decide to keep it or to remove it. Much pirated software is used only once before it is removed from the customers' computers. The shareware concept enables customers to test a product legally, as opposed to the previous model, where the customer had to buy a product in order to test it, as distributing a demo or evaluation version via floppy or CD always involved replication costs.

Another good example of shareware is the Group-Graphic Editor by Kessler-Design[2], which allows owners of Nokia mobile phones to create graphics, upload them to their phones and share them with their friends, customers and partners. The software has been written by a student in his spare time. The Internet is the only channel for marketing and distribution. Customers are able to download a thirty-day version of the tool and need to pay a fee to receive a key that will allow them to continue the use of the tool. Without the Internet such a business could not be operated.

"Free software" has two meanings in English; without cost and freedom. Free software means actually both, it is free to use, but even more important the user is free to change the source code, redistribute it and extend it by improving the source code. Richard Stallman of the Free Software Foundation (FSF)[3] has a concise definition of free software on his web page: "Think free speech, not free beer".

Free software means that with it the users have the freedom to look at the source code, are allowed to copy the programs and are able to change or enhance the applications in order to adjust it to their needs. This does not mean that software needs to be available free of charge. Free software in the sense of the FSF may also be sold.

The reason why software should be free in this sense is that a computer program can be compared to a recipe. Both describe steps, which lead to a certain result. Just as exchanging recipes is something very common, the exchange of software should also be free. Or would you want to prohibit the exchange of recipes? Although this is a very good definition of free software in my humble opinion, a new term has been introduced: open source software, which is similar but not the same.

---

[1]http://www.mirc.co.uk/
[2]http://www.kessler-design.com/wireless/
[3]http://www.fsf.org/

14.1.2   The Impact of the Internet

Software that can be used for free and contains the complete source code is gaining market share and will eventually dominate the market. Therefore it is necessary to understand what free software means and what it implicates. To start with two examples; the Apache[4] web server and the Linux[5] operating system are the fastest growing software packages for their respective market segments. Apache accounts for more installations than all other server packages combined, and its market share is growing. The Linux operating system is the fastest growing competitor for the still Windows dominated world. The software can be downloaded for free and it is even possible to participate in the development of new releases.

The Internet has become so successful, because all of its standards are free; Free of charge and freely extensible. Anyone can download the specifications and use them to implement new applications or even enhance them by submitting a new request for comment (RFC)[6]. Another problem has arisen with the Internet. It has become fairly easy to copy programs. Once a person has circumvented a copy-protection and puts it onto a web site, millions of people have the possibility to download a certain file. Making money from programs has become more difficult. In order to make money out of software it is necessary to give it away for free. This may sound illogical, but it was the only way Netscape could survive the threat of Microsoft.

In order to retain its market share, Netscape had to release its browser software for free, just as Microsoft did a few months earlier. But it topped the free offer of Microsoft by offering the source code for free as well, making Netscape the good guy in the browser war. In an instant thousands of people were downloading and reviewing the source code. They found bugs in the source code the developer's at Netscape had not found during their revision. Thousands of eyes see more than two. Even if a company is able to pay for thousands of testers, free source code is better, as it enables the testers to rewrite the code and present the bug fix to the Internet community, which then flows into the next update of the program.

The major difference between software development in a company and on the Internet is that the Internet community is more chaotic, therefore the development cannot be managed in the traditional way. Product design on the Internet is not driven by a predefined time line or a traditional top-down or bottom-up design. It is driven by the ideas of the programmers involved and can be bottom-up and top-down at the same time. These ideas make it more difficult to have a product ready at a certain time, but enable innovation and let ideas into the product that may seem unconventional and too costly for a company.

---

[4] http://www.apache.org/

[5] http://www.linux.org/

[6] http://www.ietf.org/rfc/

14.1.3   The Cathedral and the Bazaar

In 1997 Eric Raymond held a keynote speech at the Perl (another open source product) conference. Entitled "The Cathedral and the Bazaar"[7] it compares traditional software development methods with the new open source paradigm. The cathedral stand for a closed group software development method, whereby the design and the implementation are done within the group without or only with limited interaction with outsiders.

The members of the bazaar work in a loose-knit collective in a public way that allows people to move in and out during the process. Old-style programming is based on a set of programmers, each having a certain task, that may not necessarily be interchanged with the work of the others. All traditional software companies work in the cathedral way; even older open source movements such as the Free Software Foundation[8] are considered to work in the Cathedral way, as not everybody is permitted to work on the source code.

The management style of the new open source movement was quite different. Instead of managing a tight group of experts, the managers of the open source communities try to get as many people on board as possible, generating a much larger effect, as new ideas are flowing more freely. This results in the fact that bugs are found much easier, as everyone can inspect the source code and improve it. The motivation for people to take part in an open source project is to crave recognition.

Many people fear that open source software will lead to a balkanization of the program, which means that many different versions of the original software appear on the market confusing the users. The owners may start a battle over which version is better and this will drive users to get completely different products. So far this has not happened, due to the concept of centralized integration of new source code. The chaos and confusion have not appeared, but malicious programmers will always try to create confusion. With good control over the integration process, this won't happen.

14.1.4   Building a Successful Open Source Project

If we look at the successful open source projects on the web, it is easy to see what makes them so successful. First of all they need a modular design. In order to allow many developers to work at different parts of the project, it is necessary to create modules that work independently. This makes the project really strong, as it allows everybody to work at their own speed, without breaking up the whole project. The communities are also able to exchange programmers much more easily, as the modules tend to be small and easy to understand. The modules should be so small that a programmer can finish it within reasonable time before moving on to the next module or project.

---

[7]http://www.tuxedo.org/ esr/writings/cathedral-bazaar/
[8]http://www.fsf.org/

A leader is necessary to co-ordinate the efforts of the different groups working on the project. A flat hierarchy is necessary otherwise chaos will prevail. The leaders are also needed to inspire the developers, as they are providing their skills and time for free and won't do this if they are forced to. A leader needs technical and people skills on the same level. Perl has Larry Wall to supervise the developments, while Linus Torvalds is the leader in the Linux project. Apache works slightly different, where a committee of thirteen people forms the leadership. No matter how the leadership looks, only if there is a clear message as to who is in the lead will a project succeed.

In order to make the project a success, the software product should solve a general problem. An operating system, a web server or an online library are projects that many are interested in. A program for measuring network devices will not attract many developers, but in the context of a larger project could well work out.

14.1.5 Open Source Definition

The portal site of the open source movement[9] defines open source in the following way. In order to qualify a program as open source it needs to be freely re-distributable, include the source code, allow modifications, and protect the integrity of the original version. Further, the license should not discriminate against any person, groups or fields of endeavor. Re-distribution should be possible without additional interaction and the license should not be specific to the product, and not place restrictions on bundling it with other software packages. Reliability and quality are guaranteed through independent peer review and the rapid evolution of source code.

This means that the license may not restrict any party from selling or giving away the software as a component in a software package. No fee needs to be paid for such a sale. The source code needs to be distributed with the executable. If the source code is not included into the distribution pack, a way of freely downloading the source needs to be documented. The source code should not be obfuscated and intermediate forms such as the output of a preprocessor or interpretable byte-code are not considered as source code.

The author must allow modification of the original source code and the distribution under the same terms and conditions of the original software. The author may restrict the distribution of the modified source code without changing the name or version of the original source code, in order to prevent the liability for that piece of software that has been modified by a third party.

The author must not discriminate against any person or groups, by preferring or neglecting someone. The software may also not be restricted for a certain form of business. It must be allowed to use a program for private and commercial use without any restrictions. To make a license valid, it should not depend on a particular software and not place restrictions on other products.

---

[9]http://www.opensource.org/

14.2   Free Software Projects

14.2.1   The Gutenberg Online Library

One of the oldest movements on the Internet is the Project Gutenberg[10]. It started in already 1971 when Michael Hart typed the "Declaration of Independence" into a mainframe computer. The philosophy behind Project Gutenberg was to create electronic texts (such as information, books and illustrations) that everyone in the world is able to read and they should be available in the simplest, easiest form. Their goal is it to have 10,000 books available before the year 2001, which enables the users to read, use, quote and search these documents over the Internet. People should be able to look up quotations they heard in conversations, films, songs, other books, easily with any text editor that supports a search functionality.

Therefore the electronic texts in the Gutenberg online library are made available in the standard ASCII format. These files can be read by any computer without problem, as they do not contain any layout information. Italic, underline and bold words have been replaced by capital letters. Having the electronic texts in this format guarantees that no matter how old or new the computer is, if the computer is able to display text, then it will be able to display Gutenberg's electronic texts.

Just as with the file format, the Gutenberg Project tries to reach 99 percent of the general public by offering texts that most people want and use. Texts that are interesting for only a small group are not considered for inclusion into the electronic library. The same applies to the editions that Gutenberg puts on the web site. The content is king, punctuation is not so important and the people at Gutenberg won't start any discussions if a colon is more appropriate than a semi-colon in a particular case.

The copyright of an edition has expired and therefore has been placed in the public domain. The copyright expires normally at a certain time after the death of the author, depending on the country of origin. In the United States, for example, the copyright expires 50 years after the death of the author. The staff at Gutenberg then enters the book into a computer and releases it to the Internet community.

The Gutenberg online library is divided into three sections (see also Table 14.1). The light literature section contains books such as "Alice in Wonderland" and "Peter Pan". It is designed to get readers interested in computer based texts. It should provide a reference book site for people who want to read a book the movie of which they have seen at the cinema or on television. These are books that everybody knows by name, but may not have read, as it was not available because of one reason or the other.

The second section is the so-called heavy literature section, that contains books such as the Bible and the collected works of William Shakespeare and

---

[10]http://www.gutenberg.org/

The Project Gutenberg

In order to qualify for the Project Gutenberg a book, text or piece of information needs to fit into one of the following three categories:

- **light literature** – Stories for anyone who is interested in reading. Books include "Peter Pan" and "Aesop's Fables".

- **heavy literature** – Literate highlights, such as "Moby Dick" and "Paradise Lost".

- **references** – Books that do not contain literature, but references such as dictionaries and encyclopedia.

Table 14.1.

Victor Hugo. This section is provided for the power user who needs to look up quotations and text parts in these books. The books can also be used to create a new printed edition by adding the layout to the text.

The third section is the references section which contains many useful resources, such as Roget's Thesaurus, dictionaries and almanacs, which provide support for anybody who is involved in creating new texts.

14.2.2 The Linux Operating System

The now famous Linux[11] operating system was started by Linus Torvalds, a student at the University of Helsinki, Finland. Work started in 1991, when Linus started to enhance the Unix derivate Minix. In 1994 the first release of the Linux Kernel was released. Linux started to become more and more popular, first in the scientific community, as it offered the power of Unix on low-cost Intel-based hardware. Small ISPs use Linux systems, as the investment in hardware is much lower and the software is available for free. Linux has evolved into a completely new operating system that is similar but not identical to UNIX.

The term Linux refers actually to the kernel, the core of the operating system, but nowadays it is used for the complete package, just as many people think that Office 98 is an operating system and actually mean Windows 98. The complete packages on top of the Linux kernel are called distributions.

---

[11]http://www.linux.org/

Although the source code is freely available to everyone through the GNU General Public License, the distributions are put together by companies who may charge for the collection of software. The GNU public license allows the reselling of the configured software packages, with the limitation that the source code needs to be published with the sold package. This limitation also means that all software that is created on top of the Linux kernel needs to be available in source code form as well, if the kernel is required in any form.

Today several commercial companies are offering distributions, such as Red Hat[12], Caldera[13] and Suse[14]. These companies started with compiling and configuring the software available for Linux, but nowadays they are actively writing software to add value to their distributions.

Linux is available on all major platforms, such as Intel-based Pentiums, that are normally used to run Windows; PowerPC-based computers, that normally run Mac OS and most Unix hardware platforms run Linux as well.

One major problem of Linux at the beginning was the missing commercial applications. Today the situation has changed, all major vendors of software support Linux, "Corel Draw", "WordPerfect", "Star Office" and "Netscape Communicator" are just a few of the applications that run on Linux. WABI[15], a Windows emulator allows 16-bit Windows applications to run under Linux.

The Linux community has its own mascot, the penguin, which was selected by Linus to represent the image he associates with the operating system. Due to the popularity of Linux the merchandising business is up and running, and it is possible to buy t-shirts, mugs, mouse pads and other stuff with the Linux penguin on it.

14.2.3 The Open Directory

The Open Directory project[16] evolved from the NewHoo directory, which was developed and maintained by some free spirited minds that wanted to create an alternative to the commercial search engines of the Internet. In November 1998 Netscape bough NewHoo and included it into its open source web site Mozilla. The goal is to provide a comprehensive directory of the web, by relying on a vast amount of volunteer editors.

Commercial directories that rely on humans to do the categorization are unable to handle the thousands of submissions they receive each day. An entry into Yahoo takes months. Therefore the quality and comprehensiveness of the commercial directories has suffered a lot lately. While web crawlers often retrieve thousands of documents, only very few of them are really relevant to the search query.

---

[12]http://www.redhat.com/

[13]http://www.caldera.com/

[14]http://www.suse.de/

[15]http://www.wabi.com/

[16]http://www.dmoz.org/

In order to regain the quality and the comprehensiveness of a directory the Open Directory project tries to provide a means for the Internet to organize itself. At the pace of the Internet, the number of users is also growing, which can be recruited to do a little work at the Open Directory. It provides the opportunity for everyone to contribute. Every person has certain areas of interest, where she or he collects information and links. Open Directory editors can use this knowledge to add a URL to a certain zone and organize it. They are responsible for an up-to-date zone which does not contain bad links.

Everyone who is able to use a browser can become an editor and instantly add, change or reject entries.

14.2.4 The TEX Typesetting System

TEX is a typesetting system written by Donald E. Knuth, which is intended for the "creation of beautiful books – and especially for books that contain a lot of mathematics". And although this book does contain only very little mathematics, it has been set in TEX, as the system creates a pleasant and consistent layout that can be used directly by the printers. It also reduced the amount of stress put onto the author (aka myself), as the text is plain ASCII and can be written in any text editor, reducing the risk of system crashes by overblown and buggy word processors.

Knuth developed a system of "literate programming" to write TEX, and he provides the literate source of TEX free of charge, together with tools for processing the source into something that can be compiled and something that can be printed. By offering the source for free, TEX can be ported to virtually any operating system and platform. Not only is the system itself highly portable, but also the documents that are created.

The TEX typesetting system consists of a macro processor, which offers powerful programming capabilities, making the system also rather complex to use. To support TEX Knuth has written two additional packages, called Metafont and Metapost. TEX is able to define the layout of the glyphs on a page, but Metafont is able to define the relations between the shapes of the glyphs, details the sizes of the glyphs and details the rasters used to represent the glyphs.

Over the years Knuth and many others have designed many sets of fonts using Metafont, but fortunately TEX is not restricted to these, but is also able to use any Truetype or Postscript font, once they have been be converted to the TEX format.

Metapost, on the other hand, is used to implement a picture-drawing language that outputs Postscript, which can be incorporated into the documents.

As TEX is rather complex, more advanced macros have been written. The most famous macro package is LATEX, which provides a document processing system. Similar to HTML, LATEX allows markup to describe the structure of a document. The author does not need to think about presentation, this is handled automatically by the system. The layout can be controlled using a doc-

ument class or add-on packages. L#T#X tries to balance between the required
functionality of the author and ease of use. I used L#T#X for the book, as using
plain T#X would keep me busy all day with typesetting issues and people on
the IRC channel #TeX would have hated me even more (for my rather stupid
questions).

T#X is free, because Knuth wanted it to be so. This decision was made long
before anyone talked about Linux or open source and Knuth also did not mind,
if anyone earned money by selling T#X-based services and products. Unlike
with many other projects, the development of T#X has come to a halt. The
decision was made soon after T#X 3.0 was released. Knuth is continuing to bug
fix the current version, and every bug-fix release adds a digit to the version
number, slowly approaching the number π. The release of T#X which I used
to write the book was 3.14159, which has a copyright notice of 1982! This is
something very special. Most software that you are using is not older than a
year!

The source code license agreement is also very special. When Knuth dies,
he wants T#X to be frozen at version π. Thereafter, no further changes may be
made to the source code. Metafont is bound to a similar license agreement, but
the version numbers tends version e and is currently at 2.718.

These restrictions haven't stopped the development of new projects in this
area. People have already started to develop a successor to T#X, one of them
is the Omega Project. The Omega Project is an extension of T#X supporting
Unicode, which allows authors to use any alphabet in the world (e.g. Cyrillic
or Kanji). Omega uses a powerful concept of input and output filters that work
with existing transliteration schemes. At the same time L#T#X 3[17] is becoming
the new standard for document processing.

14.3 Open Source Projects

14.3.1 The Jabber Instant Messaging System

Jabber[18] is an instant messaging system, providing online status and instant
message delivery to participating users via the Internet. It is similar in functionality to ICQ[19], IRC[20] and AIM[21], which is already used by many millions of
users on the Internet.

The developers of Jabber offer an alternative to these two commercial systems by providing an open source initiative and have overcome first generation
problems and the commercial attitude of those systems. The key features of
Jabber include an architecture of distributed servers, which allows customers

---

[17]http://www.latex-project.org/latex3.html

[18]http://www.jabber.org/

[19]http://www.icq.com/

[20]http://www.irchelp.org/

[21]http://www.aol.com/aim/

to connect to their nearest server, reducing the traffic to the outside world and speeding up the connection. Jabber will provider an ISP-level service, similar to most other Internet services. The protocol is based on the XML standard for the data exchange and while simple in functionality it allows pervasive clients to be created, which can be easily embedded or extended. The major advantage of this system is that it tries to maintain back-end compatibility with other instant messaging systems, such as ICQ, IRC and AIM, thus creating a unified instant messaging solution for the Internet.

At the time of writing the Jabber team was discussing how to integrate the Jabber instant messaging engine into Mozilla to make the browser even more useful.

14.3.2 The Jikes Compiler

Jikes[22] is a Java compiler developed by the T.J. Watson Research Center at IBM. It has been rewritten from scratch in C++ and translates Java source files into byte-code.

The original Java compiler by Sun was written in Java and is therefore slow. The Jikes compiler speeds up the compilation, but has no effect on the execution of the program afterwards. It has been created as a replacement for the original compiler and can also be used to verify that your source code conforms to the specification. If your program can be compiled by Sun's and IBM's compiler, chances are very high that it conforms to the Java standard.

The reason why IBM released Jikes as Open Source was mainly that more and more people were asking for a Linux version (until then only a Windows binary was available). In July 1998 IBM released the Linux version of Jikes and received an overwhelming response. Not only was the Linux version very successful, the Windows version also became more popular.

IBM was receiving many bug reports and people started to ask for the source code, especially people who have Linux installed. Therefore IBM Research has released the source code to make Jikes more reliable and accessible. Since then many people have taken the source code and have ported it to other platforms and the compiler has become faster and more bug-free.

IBM also used Jikes to learn more about open standards and the open source movement. Although it is highly unlikely that IBM will release all software as open source, the very successful example of Jikes may eventually lead to other open source projects coming from IBM. IBM is, for example, already co-operating with the Apache open source movement, and it has integrated the Apache web server into its product line.

Mailing lists and newsgroups are used to offer support for users and developers. The source code has been published in CVS form, which helps IBM to track changes to the source code and enables volunteers to contribute to the source code.

---

[22]http://www.research.ibm.com/jikes/

14.3.3 The KDE Graphical Desktop Environment

The graphical desktop environment KDE[23] is an add-on for operating systems that use X11[24] as the graphical user interface. X11 is used by all Unix implementations. The commercial Unix systems have a graphical desktop called CDE (common desktop environment, which makes using and administering the Unix system a lot easier.

As CDE is commercial it is not available for free Unixes, such as FreeBSD[25], NetBSD[26] or Linux[27]. KDE has been created as a free substitute for CDE. Today KDE offers more functionality than CDE.

The KDE project is being developed by several hundred enthusiasts from all over the world. The complete KDE code is made available under the LGPL/GPL licenses. This license allows anyone to modify and distribute KDE code freely, under the premise that it remains free of charge.

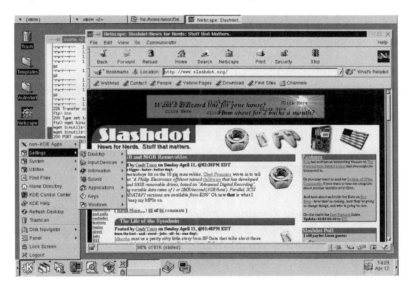

Figure 14.1. KDE Desktop running on HP-UX

Although X11 is very powerful, there is a need for KDE, as more and more users want a common feeling for all platforms. X11 does not have a common drag and drop protocol, meaning that different applications provide different means and processes for drag and drop. The desktop configuration cannot be done through an easy-to-use dialogue-based interface. Another problem is that

---

[23]http://www.kde.org/
[24]http://www.x.org/
[25]http://www.freebsd.org/
[26]http://www.netbsd.org/
[27]http://www.linux.org/

there is no unified application help system, which is common on Mac or Windows, for example.

KDE overcomes these problems and offers some great new features. The desktop can be easily adjusted to the wishes of the customer through so-called themes. Besides many newly invented themes, it is possible to install a Windows 95 or MacOS theme, giving Unix applications the look and feel of a Windows-PC or Apple Macintosh computer. Although this may seem like a toy for Unix users, it will help newcomers to get accustomed to the new operating system. A consistent feel and look also makes it easier to learn new applications. Menus, toolbars, keybindings and color-schemes, for example are standardized. KDE is fully localized and available already in more than twenty-five languages. Any application that runs on X11 will also run on KDE, but in order to exploit the possibilities of KDE, more and more applications appear that run exclusively on KDE, such as an Office Suite.

In Figure 14.1 you can see KDE running on a computer running HP-UX 10.20 and nicely replacing the CDE desktop.

14.3.4 The Mozilla Browser

In January 1998 Netscape made two announcements that changed the browser market situation. From that time on the Netscape browser was free of charge and at the same time, the source code of Netscape Communicator was released to the general public. These two announcements were the desperate attempt to survive in the browser war against Microsoft. The decrease in market share has been stopped and new, more stable browser versions have been released since then.

When Netscape announced the release of the browser source code, the Swiss newspaper "Neue Zürcher Zeitung" (NZZ)[28] called this a new type of software communism. Free software has nothing to do with communism, but deals with the freedom of the individuals to do whatever they like with a piece of software. Although the wording may be a bit strange, it showed the general change in attitude regarding software. Newspaper like the NZZ who were not interested in free software suddenly became very interested in this new development. Not only in Mozilla, but also in other open source or free software projects.

In order to co-ordinate the work on the source code, Netscape sponsored a web site[29] and named the open source effort "the Mozilla Browser", which opened in March 1998. The mission of the web site was to allow the product to grow and mature and continue to be useful and innovative. The various changes made by disparate developers across the web need to be collated, organized, and brought together as a cohesive whole.

Unlike with other open source efforts, where the originating company retreats from the development, Netscape created a special Mozilla division that

---

[28]http://www.nzz.ch/online/01_nzz_aktuell/internet/internet1998/nzz980306kommunismus.htm
[29]http://www.mozilla.org/

chartered to act as a clearing-house for the newly-available Netscape source. The Mozilla people from Netscape are the code integrators. The Mozilla organization started to provide a central point of contact and community for those interested in using or improving the source code. The people behind the Mozilla organization collect changes, help to synchronize the work of the submitting authors and release the source code on the web site.

Mailing lists and discussion forums have been set up in order to speed up development and allow the exchange of ideas between the developers. The Mozilla organization tries to help people reach consensus and guide them into the right direction, by coordinating the efforts of the different developer communities. The web site contains roadmaps to the code, co-ordinate bug lists and keeps track of the work in progress.

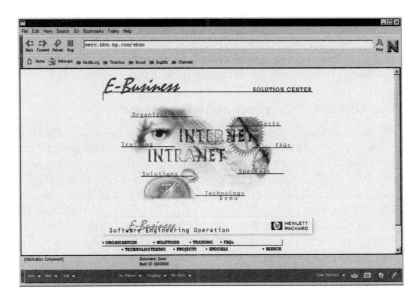

Figure 14.2. Mozilla Build 27 March 1999

The open source project lead by Netscape is trying to base its principles on the bazaar style proposed by Eric Raymond, which was discussed earlier on in this chapter. The development is done in a distributed manner, while the integration is done at a central point, the Mozilla web site.

Netscape calls its system a meritocracy, the more code participants contribute the more responsibility they will gain. Becoming a member of the team is simple, just write some code. The code is then reviewed by the Mozilla core team, which decides then if the code can be included into the source tree or not.

Figure 14.2 shows a pre-release version of the Mozilla browser. The displayed version was compiled on 27 March 1999 and is far from complete.

14.3.5 The Open Firmware ROM Code

The Open Firmware (OF) initiative provides a non-proprietary open standard boot firmware, which is independent of the processor or bus type. The specification defines a device interface, which allows peripheral cards to identify themselves and uses a boot driver that works on any CPU supported by the OF initiative. In order to facilitate programming a user interface is provided that allows powerful scripting and debugging. An API has been developed that allows the operating systems and their loaders to make use of services provided by OF to assist in the configuration and initialization process.

Although the firmware is only a very small piece of software within the computer, without it the computer would not do anything, therefore it is very important and several companies have started implementing the OF specifications. One of them is FirmWorks[30] in Mountain View, California. The FirmWorks solution provides a processor independent configuration and booting support for plug-in devices. The ANS Forth interpreter is used for programming, debugging and configuration. A range of drivers is already included in the package and a framework for creating new drivers is included.

14.3.6 The OpenPGP Cryptography Framework

OpenPGP[31] software uses a combination of strong public-key (PKI) and symmetric cryptography to provide security services for electronic communications and data storage. These services include confidentiality, key management, authentication, and digital signatures. The standard is defined in a RFC (request for comment), which is "the Internet way" of openly publishing new standards. All basic standards, such as mailing, news and http are available as RFCs.

The idea for OpenPGP was born after Phil Zimmermann released his program PGP that allowed the encryption and signature of files. The OpenPGP project tries to implement these ideas in a public standard, so that anyone is able to create programs based on the OpenPGP standard to exchange encrypted information with other applications. The OpenPGP standard does not only describe the encryption/decryption, but the complete infrastructure necessary to operate. OpenPGP is based on PGP 5.x.

14.3.7 The OpenSSL Toolkit

OpenSSL[32] has been started as a response to the commercial implementations of the SSL protocol. The OpenSSL is a robust, full-featured toolkit for secure sockets layer (SSL version 2 and 3) and transport layer security (TSL version 1). The source code is available and is based on the open source paradigm. It provides a full-strength cryptography for the whole world, as it has been

---

[30]http://www.firmworks.com/

[31]http://www.ietf.org/rfc/rfc2440.txt

[32]http://www.openssl.org/

developed outside of the United States, therefore not needing a export license from the United States.

Volunteers from all around the world are working on the OpenSSL project and use the Internet to communicate, plan and develop the toolkit and the documentation related to the project. The OpenSSL project is based on SSLeay, which is a library for including support for the SSL protocol into any program.

The project is managed by a small core team of developers that co-ordinate the effort of the OpenSSL community.

14.3.8   The Zope Web Application Platform

Zope[33] is an object-based, open source web application platform, which allows powerful, high performing and dynamic web applications to be built easily. It uses an integrated object database, which provides a facility for servicing content managers and web application developers.

The Zope architecture competes with commercial products, such as Cold Fusion[34], Netscape's Application Server and SilverStream[35]. But other than these products that are aimed at systems programmers and relational databases, Zope uses a scripting model and the built-in object-oriented database.

The Zope platform consists of several components, namely the Z Publisher, which provides a means for publishing objects and integrates with common web servers using a number of protocols, such as Zope's Persistent CGI. In addition to the Z Publisher, the Z Framework exists, which contains the foundation for the environment and built-in objects such as folders, documents, and images.

Dynamic page generation is handled through the Z Template system. The integrated Z Object Database is able to handle large volumes of files and is tightly integrated with the object model of Zope. The Z SQL Methods and Z Database Adapters provide the integration of the object-oriented data in relational SQL servers.

Unlike many other software products presented in this section Zope was not created by some people in their free time, but was developed by a Digital Creations[36]. The product was a commercial product with a price tag before the company decided to move from a product company to a consulting company. Digital Creations used to offer two versions of their software; Bobo, a free, open source toolkit for web-object applications and Principia, which is its commercial cousin. Both products were maintained in different groups, splitting the engineering efforts. In an effort to consolidate the two software projects, the company found out that the real value of the product could be better exploited by creating a new product by joining the best features of both products and releasing the new software for free.

---

[33]http://www.zope.org/

[34]http://www.coldfusion.com/

[35]http://www.silverstream.com/

[36]http://www.digitalcreations.com/

At the beginning there was resistance within the company as the value of the intellectual property of the software was considered an important asset to the company. But it was not hard to convince them that open source can actually increase the value of the company, as it brings along some advantages. By marking the well-known software as open source, the user base has been multiplied within little time, which in return leads to a more-known brand. This leads to more activities in the consulting area and an increased valuation of the company.

By moving the product to open source, it became available for more platforms and could be easily extended by other people, adding more capabilities much faster and with less errors. By fostering a product community an army of messengers was created, which extended the marketing of the product and the consulting and made it more pervasive.

The investment in releasing the source code of the application made it easier for the company to grow, as it could spend less on engineering and marketing and put more efforts into building up a consulting force. Another important issue for customers of such a rather small company was the longevity of the software lifecycle. By placing it in the open source community the software could live forever and by supporting an open source community the company is able to add new technologies much faster.

By moving to open source, Zope has established itself as an alternative to Cold Fusion, which dominated the market until then. There would have been no other way to get so much market share in so short time and with so little investment.

14.4   Moving Your Company from Products to Services

14.4.1   Supporting the Software

As we have seen in the last example of the last section, Zope, open source software does not automatically mean that a company is not able to make money from it. Although the companies behind the open source software are not always very well known, they provide the missing parts that make the software project a product. In the early years of the software business the software was the core product to sell, but nowadays the prices are dropping and more and more companies are releasing the source code, as it becomes too complex to maintain within their own company.

The major advantage for software developers in the open source arena is that they can freely create their software without having to cope with support for customers and can concentrate on the program. But the major issue for companies not to use free software is no matter how good a product is, if there is no 24 hour support available, companies are very reluctant to use it. Internetborn software has a lot of support, but this support differs from the traditional software support, where you can call someone.

Newsgroups and online chats offer great support to the communities of free software. Ask a question and within a few hours you will most likely have the answer to your problem, in many cases even the answer to a problem that has not occurred yet. Web pages with in-depth information, FAQs and other resources offer everything a customer may need. But the support cannot be guaranteed. Nobody and everybody is responsible for your receiving an answer to your question and this is not very well-received by companies using certain products. Cygnus Software[37] offers support, documentation and customization for software that is released under the GNU public license and Red Hat Software[38] offers technical support for the Linux operating system. Both companies charge for the support and the services around the software.

14.4.2 Improving the Software

The results of Cygnus' efforts, for example, by adapting the GNU C Compiler to other CPU architectures is brought back into the original source code stream in order to provide a sound basis for the core product, but still Cygnus is the only one making money of the adaptation by delivering not only the adaptation, but also the knowledge that is required for support. The open source community has nothing against profit, as long as it comes from add-on value that these companies provide and distribute for free.

Apache is creating business for several companies. The commercial version of Apache called Stronghold, developed by C2Net[39] is one off-spring. The company combines the free web server Apache with the free SSL software SSleay, to create a secure web server and the necessary infrastructure around it. A web-based administration part, scripting, an integrated search engine and digital certificates have been added by C2Net. The company also developed the support for SSL v3, integrated it into Stronghold and then gave the source back to the developers of SSleay, which had developed only the code to support SSL v2.

Organic Online[40], is another company lead by one of the chief developers of the Apache team and provides web site services to large customers using Apache as the core product.

Caldera[41] is a company in the Linux business that integrates software and creates a simplified administration interface for Linux. Instead of selling Linux to customers, Caldera provides solutions for different market segments. It is possible to buy a server where the software (such as a web server, DNS server and mail server) has been pre-integrated for web hosting, or a general purpose workstation with Netscape Communicator and WordPerfect pre-installed.

---

[37] http://www.cygnus.com/
[38] http://www.redhat.com/
[39] http://www.c2.net/
[40] http://www.organic.com/
[41] http://www.caldera.com/

14.4.3   Integrating the Software

Netscape is using the Open Directory on its portal. Instead of investing in resources to build up the directory, it uses the free time of the people on the Internet. This lowers the investments for the company while providing a useful service for free. Anybody is able to get the data behind the open directory and include it into their own site. Anybody who wants to provide a portal is able to use the data and extend the service section with this one.

The latest to profit from open source software are the hardware companies. In late 1998 and early 1999 almost all large computer manufacturers in the Wintel (Windows/Intel) world have announced support of Linux as an alternative operating system. The most prominent examples are Corel Computer[42] (a division of the software developer Corel) which introduced a complete line of computers which exclusively run with Linux and Hewlett-Packard, which introduced a twenty-four hour support hotline for Linux. These and other companies responded to the market by offering the open operating system on their existing hardware. Another reason for introducing Linux was that the operating system does not cost a license and development for hardware drives was done by third-party companies without financial support from the hardware vendors.

14.4.4   Problems with Open Source

But there are also problems with the open source paradigm. Caldera, for example, has only access to the integration, but no influence on the implementation of the underlying software. If a bug appears in the operating system and breaks down the service on one or more of the installed computer bases, Caldera can only submit a bug report to the Linux community and hope that the bug will be resolved. The same applies to the introduction of new hardware devices. Caldera is not in the position to write drivers for new hardware devices and therefore needs to wait until the Linux community responds to the request. There is no way to be pro-active without investing in developers who know the source code and are able to react in the case of an emergency. But this is still cheaper than maintaining the whole source code.

On the Internet the costs of replicating software is zero and protecting programs has become almost impossible, therefore more and more companies release their software as open source. If the Internet community accepts the open source it guarantees the software product a long life, while companies are able to provide the services around the core product. As the services are very individual to the customer, the companies are able to charge more per customer and software pirates have no means of copying the services.

While Netscape retains control partly over the software by actively contributing to the development and providing the forum, other open source pro-

---

[42]http://www.corel.com/

jects, such as Linux are developed totally independent of any company and provide their own funding for the infrastructure.

A company that wants to release the source code of a program to the public needs to be aware that just releasing the source code won't help at all. Someone may pick it up, rip off some of the code and use it for something else. But this is not the expected result for the company that released the code. Keeping control over the source code is essential in developing a high quality software product that can help not only their own company.

14.4.5 Releasing New Open Source

The reasons for releasing the code can be manifold. In Netscape's case it was necessary to improve the quality of the program and to stabilize the market share of the browser software. Other companies may be forced to release the source code because the people who knew the source code left the company or it is not longer strategic to improve the code. Other open source software is developed by employees in their free time and then placed on the Internet for the happiness of all and used to build new services within the company.

In order to make the open source project work it is necessary to set up a web site, newsgroups and mailing lists. Software for code management and bug tracking is also necessary. All the required software can be found for free on the Internet, so the investment is not very high. In addition to the installation of software and hardwarem processes need to be set up on how developers are able to retrieve the code and submit the changes.

If the infrastructure is not in place, the project will fail. In addition to the infrastructure it is necessary to electrify the community and support them in the first phase to get the open source project up and running. If the program has a base of developers who use it, for example, to develop services on top of the program, then they can be invited to embrace the source code and continue development. If the program is designed for end-users without developers in between, someone needs to be nominated who will lead the effort; either someone who is working on a similar product or someone within the own company. In Netscape's case it has been someone from within the company.

14.5 Introduction to Open Hardware

14.5.1 Differences to Software

Open Hardware is the logical extension of Open Source Software. Unlike software, hardware is much more difficult to reproduce. Hardware companies spend billions of dollars for the construction of new chip production plants. For that reason I thought there wouldn't be many people investing time in creating open hardware. But my investigations on the Internet proved me wrong. Actually there are many projects in progress.

Like software, hardware requires most of the time to design a new product and only a small percentage to distribute it afterwards. In order to develop a successful open hardware project all the requirements of the open source are valid, but depending on the type of hardware it is necessary to find a partner who will be able to reproduce the hardware design. Typically universities and research institutes provide the facilities for the test phase and commodity manufacturers a forum for mass reproduction.

The first step will most likely be to create virtual hardware that runs on existing hardware and can be used to verify the design and start to implement applications for that particular hardware, as it is always difficult to convince someone to use a certain hardware product if no applications are available. On the other hand, the application designers won't start programming, if nobody buys the hardware.

Like software, hardware is always designed using software that speaks a hardware description language, such as VHDL[43] or Verilog[44]. These products not only allow the design, but also the circuit testing before they are prototyped or produced.

The problems begin after testing. In order to verify the correctness of the chip design, it is necessary to create a physical representation of the design to create benchmarks and allow bug tests. Therefore a partner is required. Fortunately most universities already have the capability to produce basic circuit boards and many are able to create circuit boards of a higher complexity. Students involved in an open hardware project are able to use these facilities to create the necessary hardware.

Examples of open hardware projects could be the following. Creation of special chips that support hardware acceleration of certain applications could be created. An open-design kit could be created, which has several interfaces that connect an FPGA board with your computer. Specially designed compression/decompression and encryption/decryption chips could be implemented. General-purpose processors could also be the target of open hardware developers. Signal processors to support audio applications, such as speech recognition and music synthesis are also targeted by the hardware developers.

14.5.2 Open Hardware Projects

14.5.3 The Common Hardware Reference Platform

The common hardware reference platform (CHRP) architecture specification provides hardware-to-software interface definitions. Although the chips are based on the PowerPC processor architecture which is copyrighted, the interface definitions are free. Though the PowerPC microprocessor is the most widely used RISC processor, substantial legacy software exists and a mecha-

---

[43]http://www.vhdl.com/

[44]http://www.verilog.com/

nism for running the major part of this legacy software is a requirement. The system address map has been defined with a specific objective of assisting efficient x86 emulation. Additionally the PowerPC microprocessors support Bi-Endian operation which is a key attribute important to running the supported operating systems and applications.

An important feature of the architecture is the ability to implement freely below the designed interfaces through device drivers, the use of open firmware, a run-time abstraction service (RTAS) and a hardware abstraction layer (HAL).

The idea of the architecture is to combine leading-edge technologies to create a superior computing platform, by supporting a wide range of computing needs. The goal is that as many operating system are able to run on this system as possible. The architecture was developed with support for legacy hardware without restricting itself to it. It helps protect the customer's investment while moving on to a more advanced computing platform. Systems based on this architecture are expected to offer price/performance advantages and to address the expected growth in computing performance and functionality.

Apple was the first to implement the CHRP architecture in its PowerMac product line. By opening up its systems, standard peripherals could be used more easily, but before the first system was due to appear, Apple changed its mind, decided against it and remained with its proprietary architecture. In August 1999 IBM released an open-source CHRP board to support the PowerPC-Linux community. Although IBM does not sell the boards, it enabled third-party vendors to build dedicated Linux computers based on the PowerPC chip, which is built by IBM.

14.5.4   The Freedom CPU

The first chip developed in the Freedom CPU line is called F1-CPU. Freedom, which is the name of the architecture, can be used in the GNU/GPL sense, where you are free to take the design and masks and manufacture your own chips. The developers of the F1-CPU opposed the idea of calling it O-CPU (where "O" stands for open), as requested by some people, because they do not like the definition of open source and prefer to be part of the original free software (and hardware) movement.

The basic idea of the F1-CPU is to create a RISC processor with increased performance. In order to solve performance issues it is necessary to remove bottlenecks, such as the context switch latency, caused by saving and restoring register sets. The F1-architecture provides near-zero context switch latencies by providing a memory-to-memory architecture as opposed to the register-to-register architecture implemented by many RISC processors.

The design of the F1-CPU will have an external floating point unit (FPU) due to space restrictions on the die. The sequel chip F2, which will be implemented in a higher density will most likely have four FPUs on the die working in parallel.

In order to support multiple processors working together, the Freedom CPU team opted to implement a NUMA-style multiprocessing architecture, which allows both shared memory and message-passing. Symmetric multi-processing (SMP) as used by Intel is not supported, as it creates a new bottleneck.

The goal of the F1-CPU is to provide an alternative to the upcoming Merced processor. Although the F1-CPU will run at lower clock rates than Merced, it will be faster because of optimizations on the chip and in software (especially compilers). It is expected that integer performance will be comparable to or better than the Merced. FPU performance will basically depend on the number of FPUs plugged on the CPU bus. With two FPUs the F1 will probably provide better performance than a Merced. With four FPUs it should be much faster than the Merced.

Linux will be the first operating system to run on the F1-CPU with other operating systems following later on. A port of Linux is being developed at the same time as the F1-CPU development.

14.5.5   Open Design Circuits

The ideas for the open design circuits (ODC)[45] architecture have not been implemented so far, but present a typical approach to open hardware. ODC are chip designs that are openly shared among developers and users, similar to the open source software. The ODC approach captures the advantages of open-source software, and applies them to hardware. The approach by ODC avoids the large initial investments usually needed for hardware development, and it allows for the rapid design sharing, testing, and user feedback which are key to open-source software success.

ODC offers an approach that differs quite a bit from other open-design hardware initiatives. They resemble more closely open source software. Open-design circuits are very close to reality, even though no development community exists for them at the time of this writing.

When considering chips, the fabrication costs are particularly high for the relatively small quantities needed for development versions. Also problematic are the long fabrication delays, and the effort required to get test boards working on many sites. And, last but not least, manufacturers are very secretive about their fabrication processes and cell libraries, while documentation is necessary to create open-source design tools.

The reason why the initiators chose the name open design circuits over open design hardware is that the term is too general. The ODC approach is specific to designing digital circuits for chips. Writing device drivers for existing hardware or creating new motherboard designs are not part of the initiative.

In order to avoid the above mentioned problems, there are two fairly obvious alternatives to manufacturing. A simulator is often used to test a design. By distributing the simulator and the design and masks as open-source software it

---

[45]http://circu.its.tudelft.nl/

is possible to simulate the results and detect logical errors. The problem arises when it comes to performance testing. A simulator does not offer the possibilities to test the time a certain program needs to execute, as the simulator is bound to the the the underlying hard- and software.

Field programmable gate arrays (FPGAs) provide an interesting alternative, as they contain large numbers of programmable logic blocks (logic gates and registers), and a programmable interconnect. These chips are like usual gate array chips and can be programmed without the need for a wafer processing plant. SRAM FPGA are the interesting for ODC development, as the configuration is stored in RAM on the chip. This enables the developers to re-program the chip simply and fast. As developers using FPGAs have hardware to test, it is possible to measure hardware performance without the need for a large up-front investment by producing silicon wafers. Still FPGAs are relatively expensive for someone who just wants to play around a little bit with a design. By developing open chips over the Internet, prices for FPGA will decrease and the development will take off.

In order to push the open chip development, it is necessary to create interesting ideas for open design activities, to connect a group of people with the appropriate FPGA hardware and create a better price/performance ratio for the hardware to attract more people to come on-board. While many people have at least basic knowledge in the software area, only very few people know anything about hardware design and manufacturing.

Several technical issues need to be addressed in order to spread the ODC initiatives. As the ODC initiatives use FPGA devices, it is necessary to rely on some important properties. The devices need to have an open specification in order to connect them to the design tools that may be written by the initiative. The device should be robust and not break with design mistakes. Portability is also an issue, in order to make designs portable, the hardware should not use proprietary extensions that would cause the design to break on a future hardware device.

The development process for ODC is divided into several phases, which are also very common in open source software. A small group of people connect over the Internet to build up a virtual community that sets the goals for the open design tools, data formats and the hardware. They set up a web site that promotes their activity and create newsgroups and mailing lists for technical and administrative discussions. Before starting the design this group will decide which tools will be selected and integrates them into a basic package that every interested developer can download from the web page. If the required tools are not available, then the team will evaluate the effort for developing a new tool or changing the design. Once the tools and the design have been decided on, the appropriate FPGA devices are selected for initial development.

By spreading the information and with better open design tools becoming available, more and more people will be joining the initiative and starting to work on comprehensive design libraries and large designs. As soon as interesting designs become available, more people will begin buying FPGA boards and start testing and improving the designs.

Universities and smaller companies will then come on-board and will use the tools and designs in courses, in in-house applications and even product development. These low-cost solutions won't replace the mainstream hardware, but will find many niches where they can play an important role. A new type of consultant emerges; the open design circuit consultant. On the hardware side, FPGA manufacturers and ODC initiatives will try to improve the performance of the hardware.

Once the solutions have matured and become comparable to commercial offerings, the open design community will have established a movement with a large number of designers and larger corporations will integrate the open technology into their own products.

Although the presented ideas are still wishful thinking, it could work out. Just as Linux is becoming more important than some commercial operating systems, the same could happen to an open design chip.

14.5.6   The Open Hardware Certification Program

The Open Hardware Certification Program[46] is a program for hardware manufacturers who would like to certify their hardware devices as open. This means that a manufacturer promises to make available a set of documents for programming device-driver interfaces of the particular hardware device.

Although this does not guarantee that for every single piece of hardware a driver will be available, it will ensure that people who are interested in writing a driver will have the resources to do so. Hardware manufactures are able to go through a simple self-certification procedure and use the open hardware logo on their packaging.

Although the certification program does not ensure the development of new hardware or access to the design documents of the chip, it allows anyone to access the functionality of the hardware. This makes it accessible for open source programs, such as Linux, which has a constant lack of drivers, as many companies only develop drivers for Windows.

14.5.7   The Open Hardware Specification Project

The Open Hardware Specification Project (OHSpec) is an attempt to respond to the hegemony of the Wintel (Microsoft Windows/Intel). It's goal is to create a truly free and open hardware design to compensate for the decreasing impact of alternative architectures on the market, such as the Sun and SGI chip architecture for low-end workstations.

OHSpec does not try to attempt to license or register hardware components whose interfaces are available publicly, such as the open hardware certification

---

[46]http://www.openhardware.org/

program[47], but to create a new computing platform as an alternative to the existing platforms. It will be released under a variation of the GNU General Public License, adapted to hardware projects.

The OHSpec project tries to create a new hardware design from scratch, which requires a lot of dedication and hard work. The goal is to overcome the limits and design flaws of the current computers. The design tries to integrate with existing hardware without restricting itself to these paradigms. If a choice needs to be made between support for existing hardware compatibility and introducing a better hardware paradigm, the OHSpec will choose the latter.

In order to let as many people as possible participate in the project, the most important design principle is simplicity, in order to constantly extend and improve the OHSpec platform. The OHSpec team is still at the very beginning and is trying to define how far they want to break away from current hardware designs and which standards will be used to implement the system.

Other than software development, hardware manufacturing is not a no-cost venture. Therefore some sort of funding needs to be established in order to maintain a supply of necessary components. OHSpec wants its funds controlled by a non-profit organization, like the Free Software Foundation. Money could come from printed documentation, production of reference platforms or support from research and industry.

Development is organized via the web site and mailing lists that let developers exchange ideas and information.

14.6 Outlook into the Future

The future of free software looks good. More and more companies offer the source code of their programs for free or new programs are directly developed for free. The move to free software and hardware is a move away from the industrial age to the information age, where money is made in services such as customizing and consulting and not so much in product sales.

Prices for software replication have dropped to zero with the introduction of the Internet and prices are dropping for hardware replication all the time. In the ideal world, hardware and software will be both free in the future and people would offer their services. As the ideal world is unlikely to happen we will still have to pay for most hardware and software in the future, but with fierce competition from free products activists.

Currently the free product movements are not very coordinated. In the near future the open source and free software movements will enlarge, but won't move together. Although the basic idea is very similar, the implementation of a free product is divers.

Free hardware will be boosted by new inventions that make replication easy and a low-cost operation. The lower the cost for a certain piece of hardware and

---

[47]http://www.openhardware.org/

the more standardized the hardware is, the more services can be run on top of it and the larger the market for such services and solutions are.

Vertical open source portals, such as Mozilla.org or Linux.com, and horizontal open source portals, such as SourceXChange[48] become more important in the future. SourceXChange, for example, is designed to let companies tap into the pool of open-source programmers while letting those developers get paid for their efforts.

The Web site will let programmers bid for projects that companies don't want to do on their own. Companies will offer a variety of compensation, including cash or free equipment, and the resulting software will be released to the open-source community. Projects will have formal schedules and milestones, and will take away some of the last excuses people have not to use the open-source development model.

SourceXChange will be hosted by O'Reilly and Associates[49] and be backed by Hewlett-Packard and other companies. O'Reilly will get a part of the proceeds that change hands, similar to online auction web site eBay[50], which receives a fraction of every transaction. The developers and the organizations sponsoring the research will be able to rate each other. In the near future we will see other similar initiatives coming up onto the Internet.

---

[48]http://www.sourcexchange.com/
[49]http://www.ora.com/
[50]http://www.ebay.com/

Chapter 15

PERVASIVE COMPUTING

15.1 Internet Services

15.1.1 Enabling Technologies

Pervasive computing is today becoming slowly reality. The concepts have been available for several years now and the companies who are driving the web are recognizing the value of an extended Internet; a universal network. Some companies are already fearing the end of personal computer-based computing. To calm down the hardware manufacturers; this won't happen, but the growth rates will drop. Not everyone wants to have a personal computer with Windows or MacOS sitting on their desktops. In many cases, people would like to have access to the Internet through their mobile phones or their TV sets. The Nokia Communicator[1] offers not only Web access, but also E-mail and file transfer. Many companies have started to provide access to the Internet through so-called set-top-boxes, allowing web content to be viewed on the TV and write and send e-mails without having to know what a device driver or a DLL is. These Internet appliances have been around for quite a while, but basically they just take the functionality of a PC into another device.

Pervasive computing goes a step further. It replicates not only the standard functionality of the web into embedded devices, but offers services provided by the device to other entities on the Internet. The idea is to reap the benefits of ever-broader networks without having to deal with obtuse, unwieldy technology. The first generation of embedded devices were passive, meaning that they relayed existing services to other devices, such as the TV. The second generation of embedded devices is more intelligent and is able to look out for services on the Internet, collect them and bundle them into a "meta"-service.

Today companies are forced to build their entire offering virtually from scratch. Online businesses provide all services required for the complete solution; they are not able to outsource parts of it. Amazon.com[2], for example, provides the service of selling books to its customers. All services required for

---

[1]http://www.nokia.com/
[2]http://www.amazon.com/

selling books have been implemented by Amazon.com and are maintained by them, making their web site proprietary, massive, and costly.

Inventory management, distribution, billing and web store management are all services required by most online retailers in order to implement the service of selling goods on the Internet. Although it is not part of their core business, these services need to be implemented, maintained and operated by the online retailer. Next generation online retailers will be able to outsource these services to inventory management, billing, distribution and web store management solution providers, which are able to provide these services at a lower price and a better quality.

In order to make the outsourcing of services feasible on the Internet, every service needs to be able to communicate with the other. The concept of service is, on this level, rather abstract. The service of billing can then be further divided into several more simple services. One of them will be physical printing of the bill. The bill is printed on the local printer of the retailer and then sent out to the customer. The bill could be printed out at a local billing office, which reduces the costs of shipment. If the printers of the customer have a direct web connection, the bill could be printed out at the customer site, which eliminates shipping costs for the billing company. Additional costs could be reduced even further if the bill is entered directly into the ERP system of the company and paid automatically.

In order to make this new paradigm work fast and efficiently all levels of service need to be integrated. While the Internet enabled the communication between different services, HTML/XML enabled the data exchange between different services, a new layer needed to be added on top of these layers to enable services to accept other service to connect and create new meta-services or simply broadcast the availability to the network.

As today's networking capabilities are too cumbersome or limited for the next generation of applications which are about to appear, several companies have created technologies that connect everything from light switches to supercomputers in one ubiquitous network. The race is on to create the standard for the next generation of the Internet and as it often happens with high-technology efforts in their infancy, companies will compete to establish their own vision of the universal network.

Sun and its Jini technology are probably the best-known promoters of the universal network or pervasive computing vision. But many other well-known companies have started to create similar technologies and incorporated the idea of the universal network into their corporate vision. Besides Sun, Hewlett-Packard, IBM, Lucent Technologies and Microsoft have technologies and paradigms available for their customers to take them onto the next level of computing, on to pervasive computing.

This chapter gives an overview on the available technologies and the visions of the companies behind the technology. The race has just started and it is impossible to say who will win in the end. It may be worth to note that most technologies presented in this chapter are inspired by the Star Trek television and film series and therefore relate their names to it trying to bring part of the 23rd century Star Trek vision to the beginning of the 21st century.

The technologies are part of the corporate vision or company strategy, so that it cannot be expected that it will spread rapidly throughout the world. The tactical goal of these new technologies is in most cases to make the companies developing the software and architecture to appear as innovative and drive sales of more traditional products such as operating systems, servers and printers.

15.1.2   Business Opportunities

The new paradigm of Internet services allows businesses and consumers to use the Internet as a cost-effective access to a wide range of high-quality, dependable services. Areas of services will include traditional Internet services such as financial management, procurement, marketing, travel and data storage, but will also create new digital services, such as partner collaboration services and health care monitoring.

The advantages for businesses using these services means that the time-to-market is increased, the costs are decreased and it becomes easier to adapt to market change. These advantages also mean a growing opportunity for businesses to become Internet service providers themselves. Software suppliers, for example, have already started to make their products available on a usage basis over the Internet, rather than through the traditional software licensing model.

15.1.3   Internet Services Standards

To make Internet services just as successful as the World Wide Web it is necessary to create standards that are just as wide-spread and accepted as HTML. The standards include protocols and APIs for accessing and deploying services on the Internet that need to be added to these content-oriented Internet standards.

The standards need to support the core functions of electronic services, such as the description and virtualization of the Internet services. On the web catalogues, icons, files, and entire Web pages represent actual products, databases, or organizations. The creation of virtual representations of Web objects is proliferating rapidly, yet there is no standard means of doing so. Many of the methods are homegrown or less than functional. A component that virtualizes Web objects lies at the center of many current and new commerce, content, and collaborative services.

In order to add value to the Internet service it is necessary that it supports tracking and monitoring. This functionality is crucial to the commercial viability of Internet-based services. This needs to be built into the core components to allow a quick deployment of intelligent Web services. Results can be observed easily and the quality of service can be guaranteed by adjusting it to the usage of the service and changes in business and technology.

The third important point that needs to be provided by the core functionality of an electronic service standard is to ensure the security and privacy of the service. A core Internet services platform function needs to support building blocks for rapid security and for privacy-enabling the service.

These core functions provide the Internet service engine that are required to operate a service on the Internet. They support and integrate with the services and embed core capabilities within the services themselves. It is, for example, possible to create services directories, which allow users to track activities, virtualize objects and identify service components, access types and participants. By monitoring and adjusting quality of service it is possible to guarantee service level agreements (SLA). Another important feature that becomes available instantly is billing. It supports secure transactions and authentication of the participants. By giving service customers and service providers tools for the interaction, they are able to negotiate service level agreements and transactions. This also allows access to be virtualized and the delivery of the service.

Virtualization means that a service, such as a file, that you want to be visible to certain people gets a virtual name on the computer of every person who is allowed to view it. The source name and target name are therefore different, making it possible to move the original location of the file without having to change the name at the destination or even notify them about the change.

15.1.4   Moving Applications to the Web

The first step in pervasive computing has already taken place. More and more services and applications are available on the Web, which were not part of it originally. Online e-mail and calendar services are very popular and will become the standard in the near future. By putting these services onto the web, any device that contains a web browser can be used to access these services. People using a cell phone, a handheld, a notebook and a desktop computer are able to access their e-mail, for example, from any place.

The problem is that not all files are on the web right now. A text written in Star Office, for example, is saved in most cases on a local hard disk and is not available from other computers or embedded devices. By moving applications such as word processors to the web, the files can be easily saved on an Internet web server. This allows customers to access their data from any Internet-enabled device.

As moving a word processor to the web is no trivial task, companies are looking for other ways on how to access documents through a web interface, which are distributed all over the place. FusionOne[3], for example, has built an Internet-based technology that recognizes and updates information across a

---

[3]http://www.fusionone.com/

personal network of unrelated devices of different sizes and platforms. A traveler using an Internet-connected kiosk, for instance, could call up FusionOne's site and access documents, which reside in that personal network.

FusionOne has developed a software called Internet Sync, which allows customers to indicate which files they want to access on their personal network and allows the seamless synchronization of the digital information. Internet Sync allows customers to access the most recent updates to almost any file on their own personal hard drive back at the office, including word processing documents, spreadsheets, MP3 music files, browser cookies, as well as calendar and contact information. This allows content to be moved to any device the customer is using at the moment. It does not allow you to move applications.

While sharing files over the network is fine, it does not help to have a certain image file, if the device you are using at the moment is not able to display or change the image. Pushing applications to the screen of any device will require changing the paradigm of programming to allow for automatic detection of the capabilities of embedded devices. A framework for programming applications for different devices needs to be established as a standard to allow the creation of such an application without additional overhead for the programmer.

15.1.5 Open Internet Services

By using open standards businesses can offer their Internet-based services to as many people as possible. At the same time, the single service can be combined to work together with other services to create an even more valuable service. Services providers will also benefit as the costs of standards-based products are lower.

In the past there haven't been clear standards on how to provide the core functionality for Internet services. Putting an additional layer on top of traditional standards, such as HTML will not help the effectiveness of the proposed services and will make them dependent on these other standards. The new standards should propose a way to provide the basic features without requiring intensive technology engineering to shield the user from the pain of learning proprietary solutions.

Although the Internet and Web are clearly based on layered protocols, the profusion of non-standard technology and engineering to adapt proprietary solutions to generic usability are all-too-familiar themes to the computer industry. The Web's accelerated growth and continued success continues to be an opportunity to change industry patterns. In fact, the rapid pace of adoption often rules out time to architect the complex solutions of the past. New services have to be deployed instantaneously. They must be done with the assurance that core functions will be in place to support them.

By deploying a standard-based Internet service solution, customers will experience a more valuable and more personalized service, while businesses will be able to provide more efficient and mission-critical services to their customers without having an overhead on complex technologies. Service providers can create new services much faster, as the core functionality is already provided. These new standards will drive more traffic to the electronic services, as more people are able to use and find it, and will allow faster, lower-cost deployment of value-added services with partners or on their own.

This is the ultimate goal of pervasive computing, making service the prime directive on the Internet, while extending it to reach out for devices that were not connected yet. Several companies have started to build technologies and visions to reach this goal and the rest of this chapter will try to explain which company has already done what and how they have implemented it.

15.2   Device-to-device Communication

15.2.1   Introduction

The lowest layer in the pervasive computing technology architecture, which allows embedded devices to be connected to a network. This layer defines how the communication is established, the information is transported and how the connection is terminated. It does not specify how the information needs to be structured or what a service is. Jini, ChaiServer, Inferno and Universal Plug and Play are technologies that have been developed respectively by Sun, Hewlett-Packard, Lucent Technologies and Microsoft.

15.2.2   ChaiServer

As we have seen in Chapter 11, Hewlett-Packard contended the implementation of Sun's Java for embedded devices. The reason was that embedded devices have different requirements and that Sun's Java implementation does not take this into account. Embedded devices can be simple that require only minimal or no administration, such as a palmtop, or more complex, which require administrative and management features, such as printers.

Chai, the name of Hewlett-Packard's implementation of the Java Virtual Machine, means "tea" in many languages such as Russian, Czech, Turkish or Hindi and "life" in Hebrew. Tea is one of the most popular drinks throughout the world. Hewlett-Packard decided to call its virtual machine and embedded technologies family of products "Chai" to convey the notion of a world where virtually every device, process, or service (analogous to the pervasiveness of tea) is improved (that is, given life) just by virtue of being empowered by Chai. Another reason for calling the product Chai is the connection to Java, which is a type of coffee. With Chai, these devices, process, or services are able to combine measurement, computing and communications capabilities to attain a new level of local sophistication and intelligent interoperability.

Unlike Sun's embedded Java Virtual Machine, ChaiVM takes the differences in embedded devices into account and enables manufacturers of embedded devices to get the maximum out of the hardware. The ChaiServer[4] adds new functionality to the ChaiVM by extending it to allow web-based connections to other devices on the network. The connectivity is implemented in using existing Internet protocols and technology standards and extends the capabilities of the embedded devices. HP ChaiServer has a scalable architecture that allows appliance designers to install only those portions that are required by the appliance. It provides a scalable, compact, robust web server with a very small ROM footprint, ranging from about 200KB-400KB, making ChaiServer perfect for embedded applications with footprint constraints.

The ChaiServer creates information appliances that are able to manage appliances and devices remotely through the World Wide Web. The appliance would be able to download and run new diagnostic routines in devices remotely and receive notification of events in the devices and take action on them. The embedded devices are able to upgrade software dynamically in the devices with new releases.

By adding the ChaiServer to the embedded devices it is possible to add additional capabilities to a device with only little additional costs, as most of the existing infrastructure and software can be retained. Every device is able to have its own web pages that may contain information on the functionality of the device or could be used to securely manage and administer the device through a set of dynamic web pages.

ChaiServer also provides an execution environment that allows users to update the appliance with platform-independent, dynamically loadable, plug-in objects called Chailets. A Chailet is an HP ChaiServer object written in Java that performs functions ranging from creating a home page to complex operations (such as diagnostics, measurements, or computations) based on input from remote devices. Chailets implement one or more methods that may perform some computations and then sends information to, and retrieves it from, a host. A Chailet communicates with other network entities using protocols like HTTP, SMTP (electronic mail), or through the ChaiServer Notifier Chailet. Chailets can be loaded at runtime using the Loader, and they can interact with the host device(s) via the I/O interface. Chailets have their own Uniform Resource Locator (URL) with which they can be directly accessed via the Internet using any web browser. Chailets may also include native code using standard Java Native Interfaces (JNIs). Chailets require the ChaiServer to run, which in turn runs on any Java-enabled platform ranging from a small embedded device to a large Unix server.

Some of the main features of ChaiServer are the support for HTTP 1.1 (ChaiWeb is an HTTP daemon that enables a web browser to access the functionality of Chailets), the installation, update and loading of remote Chailets and event notification and propagation. Chailets can be used to generate dynamic web pages.

---

[4]http://www.chai.hp.com/

15.2.3 Inferno

Inferno[5], developed by Lucent Technologies[6], is one of the oldest technologies available. The first version of Inferno appeared already in March 1997. The technology consists of a small footprint operating system that can connect to networks or run programs within a virtual machine. It has been designed with smart phones, Internet appliances or set top boxes in mind and supports programs written in two languages: the Limbo language developed by Lucent technologies, which translates Java applications on the fly, and Personal Java, the stripped down version of Java, developed by Sun for embedded devices.

Inferno can run directly on hardware platforms or hosted on standard operating systems such as Windows NT and Linux. It is a distributed architecture-independent network operating system, which models all available resources as files. The virtual machine is used to hide the differences in hardware and the name spaces are personalizable. Security is one of the strongholds of the Inferno architecture. Built-in are security mechanisms that enable encrypted communication between the devices and the Limbo language making Inferno a good solution for enabling particular applications in the universal network. Inferno has been developed with the telecom world in mind and is not a general solution for the converging universe of computers and information appliances. For the telecom world it offers one of the best solutions by providing a common API, which enables the exchange of information and services.

The idea of treating all resources in a universal network as files may make it easier to access them by the user in the end, but does require quite a lot of overhead and makes it difficult to exploit all the features of the single resource. Inferno is a good native operating system for embedded devices and network appliances. In order to make Inferno a full blown implementation of a pervasive computing framework it is necessary to add, for example, dynamic extensibility, scalable lookup and brokerage services, identity through attribute descriptions and an inter-machine trust and interaction model.

Another problem with Inferno is that almost nobody knows about it. Although it is well-designed and works very well in the above mentioned niche markets, Lucent has spent no time on marketing the solution. Inferno fits well into today's sight of things and lacks the vision for the future of the Internet. It enables embedded devices to participate in a network without allowing other services or applications to exploit the resources of these embedded devices.

Lucent has three target sectors for its Inferno technology: the network element manufacturers (such as Cisco[7]), the consumer electronics manufacturers (such as Philips[8]) and network service providers, which allows them to introduce a wide array of new devices and new customer-focused service offerings.

---

[5] http://www.lucent-inferno.com/

[6] http://www.lucent.com/

[7] http://www.cisco.com/

[8] http://www.philips.com/

Inferno-based services offer the possibility of increased customer satisfaction and strengthened customer loyalty. The Inferno system is backed by a complete infrastructure, which is able to support highly interactive applications. Lucent has developed scenarios for sending and receiving e-mails on mobile phones or receiving pay-per-view films over a set top box which can be connected to any type of network.

Some of the products that have been announced in the past are the following. Lucent has introduced a new firewall concept, which is based on Inferno technology allowing network devices to talk to the firewall software on a server making it easier to detect intruders and prevent attacks. Philips introduced the first Inferno-enabled mobile phone, the IS-2630, which is able to connect to the Internet. Intel and UMEC[9] have also announced reference designs for a web phone, a telephone with a web browser and e-mail program built in.

The advantage of Inferno is its maturity. At the time of writing Lucent had released version 2.3 of the Inferno software package, making it a stable solution. It runs on most personal computer operating systems making it easy to develop applications for and every developer receives a CD-ROM with a reference manual and many examples, making it easy to build new services. The downside of Inferno is that the software and the CD are not free of charge. Within the three target markets Lucent has a long list of well-known partners, which will help to guarantee the success of the product. Another factor, which will help to bring Inferno to a broader audience is the well-organized "University Partners" program, which ensures that many students will have access to the technology and are able to develop applications for it. A seed financing programs for Inferno projects tries to get independent software vendors on-board.

Inferno is a device-centric software solution, making it difficult to implement complex services, which require the co-ordination of several types of devices and their services.

15.2.4 Universal Plug and Play

Universal Plug and Play (UPnP) by Microsoft is another technology that allows the creation of networks for the exchange of services and information. It is an extension of the plug and play hardware recognition system, which was introduced with Windows 95 (and is also known as plug and pray), allowing people to tie devices together without needing a computer. Devices are able to announce themselves and their capabilities when plugged into a network.

Universal Plug and Play is designed to work with "smart objects" such as light switches or volume controls and intelligent appliances such as Web-enabled telephones, or computers; devices that are currently not connected to a network. Unlike the other approaches described in this chapter UPnP is an evolution of an existing technology, taking on the burden of the underlying technology. This makes UPnP more complex and less innovative and elegant.

---

[9]http://www.umec.com/

Microsoft calls this approach more secure as it leverages a big heritage of existing technologies and brings Internet technologies into a new class of devices. The conservative approach is typical for Microsoft.

UPnP only works together with devices that are based on one of the Microsoft operating systems, making the system not truly universal as the name tries to suggest, but tries to further the market reach of the Microsoft products into the embedded devices market. Microsoft has found support from Compaq, Intel, ATI, 3Com, AMD, Kodak, and others.

UPnP, which is conceptually related to Jini, works nicely as a complementary technology to Jini, because UPnP could handle much of the grunt work required to secure blocks of IP addresses, for example. This would allow Jini to concentrate on the interaction between the intelligent appliances themselves and the network.

15.2.5 Jini

We already talked about Jini[10] in Chapter 11 in the context of Java and its usefulness to the Java community. Jini is part of the pervasive computing initiative by Sun Microsystems, which allows all types of devices to be connected into so-called impromptu networks. Jini allows the access to new network services and is able to create a network consisting of all types of digital devices without extensive planning, installation or human intervention. Each device broadcasts the services it offers to all other devices in the community, which then can be used by all members of the network.

An impromptu community is created when two or more devices create a network to share their services. They do not need to have prior knowledge of each other in order to participate. The communication is established dynamically and does not require the devices to exchange drivers to offer their services to the other devices in the community. Jini is designed to bypass computers altogether. The only thing that is required is Java someplace on the network.

Other than traditional networks, an impromptu community will most probably consist of information appliances, such as mobile phones, television sets and personal digital assistants. Every electronic device is able to handle information and contains a certain type of microprocessor. Jini adds the functionality to connect to a network and exchange information and services. It enables the discovery of any device or program on the network and make that device or program seamlessly available to authorized users.

Jini makes it possible to associate devices, such as printers and scanners, to people and places. Imagine you need to print out a text in another office, just press print and it will be printed on the printer that is next to you, no matter what type of printer it is and to whom it belongs. Jini allows instant access to any network program or service by providing an object-oriented approach to distributed computing.

---

[10]http://www.sun.com/jini/

The most significant feature in Jini are the Federations (another reference to Star Trek), which consists of a bunch of loosely connected devices that are regulated in a decentralized manner. It is assumed that every device connected is friendly. This concept makes it easy to integrate new devices into the impromptu network, but also creates security issues. The first release of Jini did not include distributed security features.

The benefit of Jini is that it is not necessary to invest into new equipment in order to enable the vision of pervasive computing. Jini runs on all types of devices that can be fitted with a Java Virtual Machine and allows dynamic change of the network. Jini heavily depends on the existence of an underlying operating system in order to work, requiring embedded devices to install and load an operating system, requiring a certain amount of memory. As Jini works as as add-on it is rather easy to program applications and services on standard personal computers with Java and Jini installed. If users connect Jini-enabled devices to their personal computers no drivers need to be installed in addition to the Jini software on the computer.

One possible application of Jini could be to tap multiple processors across a network to work in parallel and resolve highly complex computations. This type of clustering enables computers on the network to use the available capacities to a maximum. Imagine twenty computers connected to each other, a user starting a computing-intensive application on one system will broadcast the request for processing power to the other computers. Every computer that has processing time available will be able to donate it to the application. This, of course, requires a rewrite of traditional single-processor applications.

Scalability is one of the major issues with the current implementation of Jini. It can run in work groups of up to 200 objects only. This makes Jini a workgroup solution in which participants share the same security model. Jini does not scale well to a wide area network (WAN) nor does it provide functions to cross firewalls, which protect company networks from the rest of the Internet. The reason for the lack of scalability is that all changes are expected to be consistent. An additional drawback to scalability is that all members of an impromptu network need to share a single clock at which they operate. If one device gets out of sync it needs to be resynced in order to share its services and data. This does takes time and resources.

Less a problem is its dependency on Java. It is difficult to enable devices to talk the Jini way of network communication that are not Java enabled. As Java is available for almost any type of hardware it should not be such a large problem. It may be more of a problem to introduce Jini into a company with zero knowledge of Java. The meta-data system of Jini requires suppliers and consumers of services to agree on a common description of the services and devices to find each other. Java supports only a global name space, making it impossible to create local names for devices and services that are located in other locations. Therefore the whole name needs to be used to address such a service or device.

Jini can work as an extension to CORBA (Common Object Request Broker Architecture), just as most solutions presented in this chapter. Actually most of the solutions presented here were built at a time when CORBA was not as powerful as it is today. Jini can be viewed as a Java directory and lookup service, which are nowadays also available in CORBA. But this can also be said of most solutions provided in this chapter. The difference is that for the first time all types of devices are able to exchange information and services in a standardized manner.

Jini is a good device architecture through its installable interface and many companies have started to license the technology to create new devices and services. Cisco[11], for example, has created a Jini-powered cable modem and Quantum[12] demonstrated a free-standing Jini hard disk.

15.3   Information Exchange

15.3.1   Introduction

The middle layer is responsible for the exchange of data between devices. While the bottom layer connects the devices and the top layer connects the service providers with the service customers, the middle layer is responsible for the flow of information between service provider and service customer. By defining standards, Hewlett-Packard with JetSend, IBM with T Spaces, Lucent Technologies with InfernoSpaces and Microsoft with Millenium offer solutions for solving the problem of inconsistent types of data. The problem with data is that it is saved on every device in another format, making it difficult to transport the information to another device that does not understand exactly that format. The middle layer is providing a means for devices to negotiate the appropriate format in advance. It would be, for example, possible to choose the JPEG format for the communication between a scanner and a printer. The other function of the middle layer is the creation of a device independent format that can be understood by all participating devices. XML, for example, could be used for the communication between a word processor and the hard disk. The following technologies promise to solve this problem.

15.3.2   JetSend

Hewlett-Packard[13] introduced the JetSend[14] technology in 1997 to reduce the complexity in handling different document formats. The technology complements most of the presented solutions here, such as E-Speak, Jini and Universal Plug and Play.

---

[11] http://www.cisco.com/

[12] http://www.quantum.com/

[13] http://www.hp.com/

[14] http://www.hp.com/go/jetsend/

The idea behind JetSend is to allow devices to negotiate the best way to share documents. A JetSend-enabled scanner could send images to a JetSend-enabled printer directly, for example, without the interaction of a personal computer in between. Another example could be a cable television operator who sends out video on demand to its customers and does not need to worry about the format of the film. The JetSend enabled devices at the operator and the customer are able to determine the right format automatically. The two devices involved need to be on the same network and will negotiate through the JetSend protocol, which format is known to both of the devices that can be used to interchange the information without losing information.

As Hewlett-Packard offers a wide range of printers, scanners and digital cameras, it is obvious that these devices were the first that learnt the JetSend protocol. But now also computers support the protocol. This will allow them to take over JetSend communications for non JetSend-enabled devices.

Hewlett-Packard tries to position JetSend as the Esperanto of the computing world, promising universal viewability of content. The JetSend technology already has been licensed by several companies, including Panasonic, Minolta, Siemens, Xerox, and Canon, which are all producing printers, scanners and cameras.

15.3.3 T Spaces

T Spaces[15], developed by IBM[16] is working on a Java-based technology that lets computers and embedded devices share data, such as e-mail or database queries. T Spaces is just one of IBM's many projects that applies to the future and tries to complement Sun's Jini to achieve the common goal of pervasive computing.

As IBM puts it: T Spaces allows you to connect all things to all things, whereby a thing is a chip-based device. It is a network communication buffer with database capabilities and enables communication between applications and devices in a network of heterogeneous computers and operating systems. The technology makes it easy for resources such as printers, scanners, fax machines, or software services to be shared across networks with lots of different kinds of computers. T Spaces is designed for the local area network (LAN) and will help to reduce the hardware costs in homes and small offices first. T Spaces has not been designed with thousands of devices attached to a single network. There is also no way to cross firewalls without compromising the security.

The vision of IBM is targeting the home market. Unlike Hewlett-Packard, which tries to create a global pervasive computing vision, IBM is targeting the home market with its T Spaces product, thus creating a local vision of pervasive computing. Pervasive computing in every household requires a dedicated server, which controls the flow of information and services between the devices

---

[15]http://www.almaden.ibm.com/cs/TSpaces/

[16]http://www.ibm.com/

and IBM hopes to be the company, which will sell these hubs into the house of the next century. IBM is looking at a way to provide a virtual terminal and a broker between resources, but so far only on a local level.

T Spaces has many advantages over other technologies. Data is de-coupled from programs, meaning that data can outlive its producer (because once it's produced, it lives in tuple space) and can be produced before the receiver exists. The communication is anonymous and the sender does not need to know anything about the receiver, and vice-versa. Sender and receiver only need to know about tuple space, which mediates all communication. The communication is also asynchronous, whereby the sender and receiver have to be on the network at the same time for the communication to happen. The producer produces when it's ready and the consumer consumes when it's ready.

T Spaces has been implemented in Java and consists of a very small core, which can be loaded into most embedded devices with very little memory on board. The persistent data repository and the database indexing and querying capabilities are the strongholds of the T Spaces implementation. New operators can be defined dynamically and used immediately making the whole system very dynamic and interactive. Event notification is also integrated into T Spaces, making it possible to react immediately to changes on the network.

T Spaces has been available for some years now and has matured over time, but still some flaws are visible. So far it does not perform well on Windows NT and the built-in HTTP server will fail if the there is no network connection, e.g., on a laptop that has been disconnected from the network.

15.3.4   InfernoSpaces

The InfernoSpaces technology provides a framework for building distributed computing applications. It extends many of the Inferno NameSpace capabilities to non-Inferno platforms and allows application deployment across a heterogeneous environment, independent of the hardware platform, the network protocols, the programming languages and the operating systems. InfernoSpaces contain of a set of software libraries that allow, for example, legacy applications to take advantage of a distributed computing environment. An application created with InfernoSpaces will be able to interoperate with other Inferno or InfernoSpaces applications.

InfernoSpaces is a flexible, scalable and distributed computing technology that allows any device to be connected seamlessly and easily with any other device. The creation and the sharing of network services and devices becomes much easier. It can be used to create any type of distributed application in a network and can be used with any programming language and operating system. This last promise is not yet true, as InfernoSpaces only supports C, Java, Limbo, Windows, Solaris and InfernoOS at the time of writing. Other than the Inferno package, InfernoSpaces is free of charge, making it accessible to anyone with an Internet connection.

The advantage of InfernoSpaces is its simplicity making it possible to learn it in days. It is based on a file model, which is known to all developers. It flexibility allows the developers to separate application design from the underlying network configuration and the software scales very well from the smallest embedded device to large network elements and servers. Through its design model it is possible to write networking application without writing specific networking code. The simple-to-use and elegant framework allows even beginners to develop networked applications.

Some of the applications that can be written with InfernoSpaces are IP telephony and distributed call processing. Internet Games and instant messaging solutions can be also developed without too much hassle. Directory services and online billing solutions are also typical applications for the InfernoSpaces architecture.

InfernoSpaces is a highly sophisticated technology, which will work well in conjunction with other pervasive computing products presented in this chapter.

15.3.5 Millennium

To complement Microsoft's pervasive computing strategy, the company works on a next-generation distributed operating system called Millennium that lets computers share tasks across a network, automatically adjusting to new components being added or removed. The goals of this technology include seamless distribution, worldwide scalability, transparent fault tolerance, security, resource management and resource discovery.

Several prototypes have been implemented so far: Borg, Coign and Continuum. Borg (another reference to Star Trek) is a stripped down version of the Java virtual machine (using the Microsoft flavor of Java, see Chapter 11) that can create a cluster of computers that look like a single one when running Java programs. The discovery of new devices in the network is based on a notification-oriented system.

The second prototype, Coign is an automatic distributed partitioning system (ADPS). It can automatically convert local COM applications into distributed client-server applications without access to source code. Using a scenario-based profiling system, Coign discovers the internal structure of an application and cuts the application into client and server components; choosing a distribution that minimizes communication between client and server. Coign does not only support Microsoft's flavor of Java, but also Visual Basic and C++ based on the distributed COM architecture written by Microsoft. A program is started and Coign decides how to distribute a program and automatically accomplishes that task in a way that maximizes the network performance. This is combined with a discovery protocol that measures bandwidth availability, latency and the speed of the available CPUs.

Continuum (and again a reference to Star Trek) has the same functionality but is not restricted to a particular application, but will work with any application. The designers of Continuum have had the ambitious goal of distributing the Windows API to create a single computing environment (i.e. one single system image) across multiple machines. The goal of Continuum is to provide a distributed single system image environment to a large class of applications regardless of their source language.

The advantage of this system is that it allows application designers to continue with their existing applications and the underlying Millennium component will take care of it and make it distributed. The distribution is handled automatically after the application has been written. This approach is far easier than with Jini or CORBA, for example, which requires the application to adapt to the new paradigm during the development.

The downside of the system is that it is still only released as developers pre-releases and the prototypes run only on Windows. Millennium is built on top of Microsoft's Component Object Model (COM) and future releases will rely on COM+, which will be strictly limited to the Windows platforms, making it a homogeneous environment with a central server.

15.3.6 InfoBus

InfoBus was presented in Chapter 11, just like Jini, as part of the overview on Java. So this section won't go into technical details anymore, but will try to explain where InfoBus fits into the pervasive computing strategy of Sun.

InfoBus allows the co-operation of applets or JavaBeans. They can exchange data through the InfoBus architecture. JavaBeans can become "data providers" and "data consumers", which are defined in the InfoBus architecture. A Java-Bean that acts as a provider connects to a database and offers the data onto the InfoBus. JavaBeans that act as data consumers are able to retrieve the data from the bus and process it. The advantage of InfoBus is that participating objects do not need to understand data formats and can concentrate on the implementation of the data processing. This segregation of provider from consumer is extremely powerful in that it enables applications to be independent of their data.

The InfoBus specification provides a set of interfaces that allows you to share and exchange dynamic data. It is possible to create so-called "data flows" between co-operating components. The semantics of the data flow are based on the interpretation of the data content, which flows across the InfoBus interfaces as opposed to responding to names of parameters from events or names of call-back parameters.

InfoBus complements Jini, which allows device-to-device communication, by implementing a way to exchange data over a standard interface. Through Jini and InfoBus it is possible to extend the functionality of the web to other devices, without introducing a new paradigm, such as the e-service strategy of Hewlett-Packard.

15.4   Service Broadcasting

15.4.1   Introduction

The top layer of the pervasive computing architecture is the service layer, which allows the exchange of services over a network. Services that reside on a device can broadcast their existence and offer them to other devices, business objects or human beings. While Jini offers some basic functionality for local service exchange it lacks the scalability and the security to make it a product for the Internet. The only product that is able to scale well on the Internet is the E-Speak product by Hewlett-Packard.

15.4.2   E-Speak

Jini's vision is not unique to Sun. Many in the industry today and over the last several years have had a vision of interconnecting devices. Hewlett-Packard also has a similar vision of connected devices working together to provide services to end users, and announced it in March of 1998 with ChaiServer.

HP's E-Speak technology, code-named Fremont, takes this vision even further by adding new, dynamic capabilities such as scalability, security and heterogeneity. Jini is an architecture for device interaction in a small, trusted workgroup (LAN) or home environment, whereas Fremont is an architecture for service interaction in a large, unsafe, distributed environment, such as the Internet. It offers services that include computing resources, information and even access to applications on a pay-per-usage basis, in a similar way information has been available for some time now on the web.

The difference with the old web and the new infrastructure is that the availability and the quality truly become the most important aspects of the service. It is not necessary to know how it is managed, who provides the service or where it is installed and configured. The Fremont technology will take care of the basic issues with services on the Internet.

Fremont is a network middleware layer that lies on top of the operating systems, making services independent of the operating system. One could call this type of solution "install once, serve anywhere" in addition to Java's "write once, run anywhere".

Fremont is designed to make any computing resource, such as disks, files, Java objects, legacy applications and device drivers available as services over the network. It also allow these electronic services to advertise their capabilities and discover new capabilities as they are added or become available anywhere on the network. Fremont provides unique mechanisms and protocols for negotiation, brokering, bidding and billing between these electronic services. The Management, the monitoring and the fine-grained, dynamic access controls and security make it easy to create service solutions that are not only powerful, but also secure. The Fremont architecture makes it easy to combine electronic services, thus creating a new service in a modular way.

E-Speak Overview

Hewlett-Packard's E-Speak Technology offers very interesting features.

- **Independence of Language** – Unlike other pervasive computing implementations it does not depend on a single programming language, such as C++ or Java.

- **Meta-Data System** – Attribute-based lookup is supported, making it easy to exchange information and services.

- **Name Virtualization** – The virtualization of resources makes it easy to move the original resource without reconfiguration of the clients.

- **Revocation of Privileges** – Fremont is able to configure itself to revoke access to materials lists and other secure information.

- **Scalability** – Unlike Jini, for example, Fremont is able to handle resources on the Internet, not just on an Intranet or closed network.

Table 15.1.

These "meta-services" do not need to reside on a single device. It is possible to combine services from different devices to create a new service. Imagine a weather report service that uses different devices such as a thermometer and a barometer. If each of these devices were Fremont enabled it would be easy to present the actual weather data on a web page with only very little programming knowledge (mainly HTML).

Fremont links services, not just repositories of data, making a real leap into the future of computing. It has been designed to be a universal language and protocol for electronic services. Hewlett-Packard sees Fremont as a technology platform for open services. An open service is a state where end-user services can be dynamically composed of best-in-class and competitive service components and resources using standardized, non-proprietary interfaces.

To put the features of Fremont into a nutshell: It is a federated software infrastructure that runs on top of an operating system, similar to the web, and is a living system, similar to an operating system, but unlike most middleware such as CORBA, which consists basically only of a set of tools. It simplifies and secures the creation, management, and access of services over the Internet.

Most pervasive computing technologies enable device to device connectivity, but this is not sufficient to enable electronic services. ChaiServer allows devices to talk to each other, but it does not specify how to do this. In order to create electronic services, it is necessary to advertise, broker, compose and maintain the service. The broker, for example, is able to handle sets of services, sets of data types, and sets of access devices.

Fremont allows the creations of instant Extranets, providing business partner collaboration. On a case by case decision it becomes possible to allow partners access to single services on your Intranet, if necessary, without compromising the security. The ability to connect services spontaneously allows people to collaborate in a far more direct and efficient way than we know today. The creation of an Extranet takes months to decide and implement, as you are giving access to your Intranet. With Fremont, particular services can be relayed in a secure way to the Internet, making the service available only to the partners who are allowed to see and use it. This reduces the risk of someone being able to break into your corporate network.

Partners that use the Internet to share services need to start up a client application. It represents an interface to the originator. This interface allows the originator to choose a file from a directory on his machine and make it available to a partner who is running the client application. A "gateway" process, running on the originator's machine, presents the client application with its interface to the FireScreen service. The FireScreen gateway is responsible for "pushing" shared information to the external FireScreen "connector" and for retrieving requests found at the connector site.

A "connector" process, running on a separate host, somewhere on the Internet, will allow gateway processes to "post" information. Gateway processes will post one of three types of information to the connector: "availability" messages which represent sharing authorizations, "consume" messages which represent file transfer requests, and during a transfer the actual file contents. A second gateway process, running on the consumer's machine, acting in much the same role as the gateway process on the originator's machine will provide consumer's with information about file availability. This gateway will also post "consume" or fetch requests as directed by the consumer's client application. A second client application, running on the consumer's machine, will allow the user to see the files made available with his identity and retrieve those files. This application will actually be identical to the application run by the originator. The consumer and originator simply use different features as they exchange roles.

This concept allows businesses to create next generation portals, which are also called electronic service brokers (ESB). The ESB allows online services to charge other systems for its resources and creates a new business channel for the delivery of electronic services in the following ways.

It creates additional revenue opportunities for telephone companies by allowing them to provide services beyond basic connections to consumers and it creates new business opportunities for companies desiring to deliver electronic services to their customers. Consumers can gain access to a wider range of functionality without having to purchase or install applications on their own and it lowers the cost barrier for access to sophisticated capabilities. This allows customers to access services without having to pay for the underlying infrastructure. Instead of buying applications that need to be installed locally, for example, you rent them over the Internet for the time you need them.

Fremont aka E-Speak sits on top of other consumer-device focused technologies, such as Jini, ChaiServer or Universal Plug and Play. While Sun is promoting Java everywhere and Microsoft Windows everywhere, Hewlett-Packard does not care about the operating system nor about the implementation language for accessing the electronic services. It can use any of the mentioned technologies to implement these services.

Several E-speak pilots are under development, such as at Uniscape[17], Captura[18] and Helsinki Telephone[19]. At Uniscape, for example, E-speak is used to find translators and allow them to bid for services. Customers can select translators based on speed, quality and price.

15.5   The Vision

15.5.1   Introduction

Although pervasive computing is being implemented by several companies, as we already have seen in this chapter, it can only be successful if the company is having a vision. The vision will align all organizations within the company to ensure that the vision becomes reality. So far only Hewlett-Packard has presented a complete vision of the future of computing.

15.5.2   E-Services

Hewlett-Packard has created a unique vision based on the above mentioned products, which is their so-called e-services strategy. Hewlett-Packard is forecasting an explosive growth of specialized, modular electronic services that pervade the fabric of life and Hewlett-Packard is aligning all of its organizations, resources and expertise to make their customers take full advantage of the e-services vision.

It's no longer only web sites or portals that matter, but electronic services that are integrated into all kinds of devices and utilities and are made available via brokers. An e-service is a service or resource that can be accessed on the

---

[17]http://www.uniscape.com/
[18]http://www.captura.com/
[19]http://www.hpy.fi/

Net by people, businesses, and devices, such as computers and mobile phones. Several e-services can be combined automatically to perform virtually any kind of task or transaction.

In order to understand better the new opportunities it is necessary to look at today's business on the Internet. Most Internet business is based on web servers and browsers that communicate and exchange information and follow pre-defined processes. The Web enabled start-ups rock whole industries by reaching out for customers that were not accessible to small companies before. Amazon.com is the perfect example of a start-up that nobody took seriously in the beginning and suddenly was the biggest fish in the pond. Traditional book companies, such as little bookshops, large chains of bookshops, publishing houses and large resellers suddenly had to start-up their own online ventures to counter-attack the attacks of the Internet start-ups. Slowly companies have started to think about their businesses differently. They adapt the rules of the start-ups and redefine their customer service. Customer-centric business has become more important and customers have been enabled through the web to serve themselves.

Extranets have helped to unify communities of partners and have saved the participating companies a lot of money. New services start to appear on the Internet every day. But the problem with today's websites is the fact that each company has built their services in a proprietary, massive and costly way. The companies were forced to create their entire offerings from the ground up.

The open service paradigm developed by Hewlett-Packard makes electronic services more modular, which allows them to be assembled on the fly as they are based on the open-services interface. They can be combined more easily to offer new types of services. The paradigm of "Do-it-yourself" evolves into "do-it-for-me" through the open-services interfaces the services can talk to each other without human interaction. The interface allows for integration of any type of device into an e-service.

It is expected that the shift in paradigm will be followed in the business world and in the IT area. Web sites will become less important. The automated services will work more likely in the background. Most people would rather only think about all the things they want to get done and not how they get done. With e-services this will become reality.

By implementing e-services it has become possible to offer traditional services, such as banking to more people, via a wider variety of devices and implement new services. Business-to-business web sites will profit from the new paradigm, as it will become easier to implement billing systems, automated supply-chain management, procurement solutions and a modular ERP system. All kinds of of business-to-business transactions can now be handled by combinations of intelligent e-service systems.

The IT department will also be able to benefit greatly from the introduction of e-services. Certain services, which are not required daily and are not part of the core business can be outsourced, such as processing power, data storage and data mining. E-Services will help to ensure the availability and security of these services. E-services will give companies much more flexibility in the way they manage their IT infrastructures, making more efficient use of resources both in-house and outside. The IT department will transform to a service provider, which will use outsourcing strategically to lower costs and gain flexibility. It will enable e-services of all types and plan profitable e-services solutions, such as the extended supply chains and ensure the quality of service and the consistency of the user experience. Everything on the Net (both inside the enterprise and the outside world) is treated as an online service.

The most important battle is the long-term one. In an e-services world there is going to be more choice, and thus more competition. Customer loyalty will be based on the reliability of your systems, how easy they are to use, and how useful they are.

Another interesting field for the paradigm of e-services is the pay-per-use service. All types of consumers are able to pay for services on demand, such as software, video or audio services. Pay-per-use e-services will be tightly woven into daily life. People will plug into them via e-service utilities, such as corporate networks, phone companies, and ISPs, using a variety of devices. And they can take advantage of a much wider range of services, because they'll pay only for what they use.

E-services are highly modular, making it attractive to a large group of customers, who do not want to buy enormous, monolithic systems. Customers are able to subscribe to the specific services they want to use. This reduces the initial cost for accessing a service and companies will be able to generate more stable profit streams as the money is coming on a more regular basis and from more customers. The basis for the profit is broadened and by streamlining whole chains of transactions companies are able to save a lot of costs. Another advantage of the e-services is that they can be developed, tested and put on the market much more quickly because of their modular architecture.

E-services make it possible to focus on the real work and neglect the underlying technology and processes. End users will be able to take advantage of much more sophisticated services because they don't have to buy the whole thing. They can just subscribe to the services they need, paying for some of them on a pay-per-use basis. The aim of Hewlett-Packard is to turn any service or computing resource into a building block for e-services.

15.6 Comparison of Pervasive Computing Technologies

Table 15.2 gives a short summary of the functionality of the different pervasive computing technologies. It is difficult to tell which technology will prevail. It can be expected that the technology that gets most companies behind its vision will make it. Probably two or three technologies will fight for the next few years to become the standard for pervasive computing.

As we have seen pervasive computing technologies can be divided into three different layers. The bottom layer is responsible for the device-to-device communication, the middle layer is responsible for the exchange of data between devices and the top layer is the service level, which allows the exchange of services between devices. These three layers need to be present to make pervasive computing successful. The above mentioned technologies often represent more than one layer in the layer model. By using the layer model it is also possible to integrate technologies from different vendors. It is, for example, possible to use Jini in conjunction with E-Speak or T Spaces with ChaiServer.

Mobile phones, video cameras, CD players, car stereos and other electronic mobile devices, which already use today a lot of technology, will be most likely the first devices to be connected to the Internet. Refrigerators, microwave ovens and other household devices will become connected only later on to the rest of the world. The security issues have not been resolved yet, to let every device participate in the Internet. But companies like Hewlett-Packard and Lucent Technologies have thought about security, resulting in a more secure infrastructure for any type of device.

15.7 The Future of Pervasive Computing

The future is still wide open; as standards are just about to develop it is hard to predict what the future of pervasive computing will bring. One thing is clear today, it will change the way we have used computers in many ways.

Software, for example, won't necessarily be installed anymore on a computer. It will be able to use a certain piece of software on many different devices, meaning that software becomes a service, which is paid on demand. A request will be sent out and the appropriate service will send back the answer. This paradigm is true for any type of information or service. Information and services will become available, whenever there is need for them. Imagine the car from the preface. It does not need to have a petrol station search engine built in. It is enough to know that one is available and how to get to it when the petrol is low.

This may change the way we work: it will require a lot of changes in the working world, as everything is moving to the just-in-time paradigm. Products, for example, won't be built and then sold at a time when the customer is ready to buy. The products will be built when the customer is paying and services will be offered at the time the customer needs them.

Pervasive computing may also change the way we see advertising. Why should I present advertising for things I do not need right now? Just like spontaneous networks can be created, spontaneous advertising will be available to match the needs of the customer.

Pervasive computing also makes it easier for freelancers (or e-lancers) to make money on a world-wide basis. Through pervasive computing it is possible

Pervasive Computing Technologies

- **ChaiServer** – Java Virtual Machine extended to allow web-based connection to other devices on the network.

- **JetSend** – Technology that lets networked devices negotiate common file formats for data exchange.

- **E-Speak** – Architecture for service interaction in a large, unsafe, distributed environment, such as the Internet.

- **E-Services** – Modular architecture for online services that can be accessed on a network.

- **Inferno** – Small-footprint network operating system to let any type of device plug into the network.

- **InfernoSpaces** – Framework for building distributed computing applications, independent of the platform.

- **T Spaces** – Java-based system that allows any type of device to share messages, database queries, print jobs, or other network services.

- **Millenium** – Lets collections of computers automatically divide up computing tasks across networks.

- **Universal Plug and Play** – Extends hardware recognition and connection of any type of devices.

- **Jini** – Devices are able to share services for "spontaneous networking" with other Jini devices.

- **InfoBus** – Cooperation of applications across devices. They can exchange data through the InfoBus.

Table 15.2.

to deliver a small building block in a highly specialized area to other services to make them more sophisticated, without interfering with their business. This will also mean that we are moving from software developers to service developers. The quality of the service idea becomes more important than a particular implementation.

Therefore two types of new entrepreneurs will be around for the next few years: service developers and service providers. The service providers of today will eventually merge to the service providers of tomorrow, but it gives start-up companies the chance to take away market share from traditional service providers, as they may be slow to move to the next generation of services.

As technology is changing very fast in these early days of pervasive computing, keep an eye on the book's web site[20] for updates on this topic.

---

[20]http://www.ebusinessrevolution.com/

Chapter 16

BEYOND PERVASIVE COMPUTING

16.1 Technical Outlook on the Future

16.1.1 Opening Internet Access

If we look at a future where pervasive computing has been fully implemented what will happen next? Although this may be ten to fifteen years away, it is still important to think about the future and how one can help to design it. The following chapter presents some of my ideas how the future may evolve; I may be completely wrong, but I try to provide a vision that really may happen. I may also be wrong on the time frame, meaning that the vision may be here already here in five years time or as far away as fifty years. In any case, I hope that this chapter will help you to develop new ideas on how to create the future. A forum for the exchange of these new ideas can be found on the web site[1] accompanying this book.

Pervasive computing will change the way we work and live. But it will be a transition rather than a revolution, from a technological point of view. Just like the telephone did not replace direct human communication and the television did not replace the cinema, pervasive computing will not replace current computing technologies. Desktop computers will still be part of everyday life, but they won't be hot technology anymore, just a commodity for some of us. The big business will move on to new paradigms, technologies and devices.

Pervasive computing will add a new facet to our lives, giving us the opportunity to do more things in a shorter time and more easily. Many things will become instant. Many services will be able to anticipate the need of the customer and will act appropriately.

The cost for accessing the Internet will drop to nearly zero for most parts of Europe and Northern America and other countries will be able to catch up with the Internet as new devices become available, such as the PDSL (power digital

---

[1]http://www.ebusinessrevolution.com/

subscriber line) technology from Northern Telecom[2], which allows Internet access over power lines, instead of telephone lines. This reduces the investments in infrastructure for the poorer countries.

BellSouth[3] is about to release its passive optical network (PON), which is already available in Atlanta, Georgia to selected customers and will offer a bandwidth of 100 MBits/s to its customers. The new standard does not require active network components to be installed at the customer's site. Lucent Technology[4] and Oki Electric[5] provide the network termination module. This module translates not only the network traffic from ATM to Fast Ethernet, but also extracts automatically radio and television content, so that radios and television sets can be used in their usual ways, without any additional hardware components. The test installation allows the transmission of 100 MBits/s and 120 digital, 70 analogue television programs and 31 digital audio channels at the same time. The new access is available at 60 Euro or Dollars a month. This is a huge step in advancement.

Wireless communication will also become more important making the single individual even less dependable on a certain location, on certain devices or certain software. Most important the bandwidth will become adjustable in such a manner that anyone will get the speed he or she needs at a certain moment. Delays and disconnects will become errors of the past. Quality of service becomes a standard on the Internet allowing customers to buy certain service level agreements from their content access providers.

The biggest change in technology will be less advanced and faster processors or new operating systems, but the free choice of technology. It suddenly will not matter anymore how fast your computer at home is or which operating system you are using. Through Internet services you can acquire processing power for a short period of time, whenever necessary, which will then be much cheaper than buying a new computer and the operating system will not matter anymore, as the services offered over the Internet are not depending on a certain piece of hardware or software anymore. The services will adapt to the environment of the customer and offer always the best performance.

16.1.2 Consumer Device Integration

With the unlimited availability of bandwidth, we will also see a total convergence of media over the next few years. Instead of having a radio, a television set, a compact disc player and a computer, which most people have today, only one device will be around, which is able to replace all consumer devices. Physical media, such as compact discs and video cassettes, will become obsolete. What may remain will be the cover, with the lyrics and photos of the artists,

---

[2]http://www.nortel.com/
[3]http://www.bellsouth.com/
[4]http://www.lucent.com/
[5]http://www.oki.com/

which you can buy in a shop or have shipped to your home. In addition to the usual booklet information the former CD booklet will contain an access code to download the music from the Internet to your local audio device. The audio or video will be saved onto a local or remote hard disk in a format similar to MP3, but with better compression and security features built-in, in order to prevent the illegal copying of music. It won't prevent the copying of the music, but if one copies the music from one device to another one, the price will be deducted from the credit card of the owner of the target device. Traditional compact disc and video sellers will have a few years remaining before they need to change their business, in order to support the new paradigm.

Television and radio will become just another set of packets on the Internet. They won't disappear, but the diffusion over the air will disappear. Instead of an aerial, you will need a broadband Internet connection in order to watch digital television. The same will happen to radio, which is already today one of the most popular services on the Internet. I, for myself, love to listen to Radio Deejay[6] from Milan, Capital Radio[7] from London and CoolFM[8] from Belfast at work. By moving television and radio to the Internet, aerial frequencies become available that were blocked by the television and radio transmissions. This will allow new sorts of devices to communicate in a wireless manner with each other.

Obviously with broadband Internet access, the next device will be the telephone that will move from being a separate device to an integral part of the, what I call, new media center. Already today ISDN offers the possibility of not only hearing the voice, but also seeing the picture of the other participant. With broadband access and this new media center, you will be free to choose between only audio or audio/video calls.

The next generation of cellular phones is expected to have a bandwidth of 2 megabytes/second allowing it to serve more information over the mobile phone than ever before. Right now the GSM standard is restricted to approximately 9 kilobytes/s making it even unusable for larger e-mails and web sites. As we've seen in Chapter 3 there are ways around this limit. The MegaCar is the first mobile media and business center, which allows high-speed Internet connection on the road. It achieved the high-speed connection by multiplexing 16 GSM channels. Imagine multiplexing 16 channels of the new standard of 2 megabytes/s, making it possible to transfer 32 megabytes/s to and from a moving car. Phone calls, television, radio, computer application, electronic services, audio and video will become available anywhere as long as your media center supports the output. The next generation of mobile phones will all have color displays making it easy to display video and live transmissions, while audio can be played back even with the current generation of mobile phones. Imagine your phone acting as a projector to increase the size of the image.

---

[6] http://www.deejay.it/

[7] http://www.capitalradio.co.uk/

[8] http://www.coolfm.co.uk/

With the migration of the traditional consumer electronic devices to the new media center consumers gets rid of another problem which was rather annoying in the past. The format problem: remember the beta versus VHS video cassette wars, the MPEG versus AVI movie format wars or the compact disc versus the mini disc war. There is a long list of format wars, which were basically a lot of wasted time in the past, as they did not allow the further development of technologies. With the integration of consumer electronics you will get the electronic content you requested and do not have to know which format is has been and how it has been transported to your screen or your speakers. If a new format is required, the appropriate software will be delivered with it on the fly.

Other devices in your household won't likely merge, as a dishwasher is not capable of washing your clothes nor is a refrigerator able to act as a stove. Pervasive computing will still have an impact on these devices. Today these devices are already fitted with computer chips, so connecting them to a local network will be the next logical step. Control from a central point may be useful, but then again there is still a lot of manual work involved, like putting the clothes into the washing machine or getting the dishes out of the dishwasher. It will also most probably not be of interest to you how much energy was spent on washing the clothes. But this information may be of interest to your energy broker, which tries to get the lowest price for energy for you. The future will bring along a rich set of brokers, as we will see in the next section.

By handing out all the relevant information regarding your usage of energy, the energy broker is able to determine which power supplier will be the most cost efficient for your use and may offer some advice on how to lower the cost even more. The energy broker could tell you that it would reduce costs to switch on the washing machine on Monday evening, as there seems to be a surplus of energy, which can be bought at a low price for that particular action. The broker will therefore update your local database with this information, which in turn will trigger your washing machine at the right time. This still requires you to load it with dirty clothes, but if you do it then or now may not make a big difference. In any case the energy broker will check with your Internet-based calendar to see if this conflicts with an evening at the cinema.

Another example could be the refrigerator, which is connected to your food broker, who selects the shops where you can buy your preferred food at the best price and quality. While you may be buying your food on Saturdays, this may change in the future, as the price won't be fixed for food anymore, but depend on the demand of the market. Therefore the food broker will try to match your food preferences with the offerings on the market and try to buy the food which costs less. This will mean that you will have to be a bit more flexible in order to get the lowest prices for your food or eventually pay a bit more for exactly what you requested.

16.1.3   Privacy and Security in the Future

As every device is collecting data on your spending and usage, one-to-one marketing can become even more effective. The more information about yourself that becomes available to merchants the easier they can make the appropriate offers to you. This has the disadvantage that you may eventually lose control over your privacy, if you give out all this type of information to every merchant that passes by on the Internet.

The big brother from George Orwell's Book "1984" could easily become reality now, but not like he envisioned it. Most probably it will not be the government stealing your privacy, it will be the advertising and marketing agencies, who are interested in your profile in order to make you buy even more things you do not need. This tendency can be seen already on many web sites today.

In order to prevent such a situation, a new form of trust needs to be built up. The brokers I have been talking about in the last section won't be humans, but most likely very intelligent agents sitting in the media center and controlling the flow into the house and out. They will be the only ones to see your detailed profile. The energy broker, for example, won't send out your profile to every power supplier in the world to get the best prices, but in order to retain the privacy, will ask the power suppliers to provide the broker with a detailed price list with up-to-date information, so that the broker can compare the needs of the customer with the price lists of the suppliers and choose from every supplier the appropriate pieces to have the solution that fits the needs of the client.

Most probably there will be a constant connection between power suppliers and energy brokers, so that the energy brokers are able to get the lowest prices for the washing machine, which is switched on once a week and get instant power, whenever the customer switches on an additional digital device. The communication between energy broker and power supplier needs to be encrypted in order to make sure that nobody is able to intercept the complete transaction. As the energy broker will most likely buy energy from several power suppliers at the same time, they won't be able to get the full picture of the customer, but by intercepting the communication with all power suppliers someone would be able to benefit from this information. Encryption technologies will hopefully be allowed on a world-wide basis at a high-level making break-ins impossible.

Security also becomes very important. As the energy broker orders energy whenever it is required, it needs to be ensured that nobody can break the energy broker or its connection to the power suppliers. The whole installation needs to be therefore highly redundant and highly available, meaning that the envisioned five nines of Hewlett-Packard (99.999 percent, which is equal to five minutes down-time a year), will need to increased to at least six or seven nines. Only if this high level of availability can be guaranteed can it be used on a day-to-day basis. Hackers would otherwise find ways to black out whole towns with a few commands.

In order to keep your privacy and ensure that nobody else is able to switch devices in your household on or off, a next generation type of firewall will be required that allows the secure access to your devices, while you are on holiday, for example, but prohibits any other access to them. New forms of authentication will therefore be required, which make it impossible for penetrators to appear as someone else.

Digital and biometrical authentication and authorization methods will be combined to form a new biodigital form of access to your home, car and anything else that needs to have a form of restricted access from the public.

16.1.4 Next Generation Internet

The future of the Internet will be tightly integrated with the technological advances and the change of business models in the future. Several programs are in progress to create new Internet technologies, such as the Internet 2[9] initiative in the United States, which brings us to the infrastructure that is required to build up highly interconnected homes, which allow us to bundle all types of media into a single media center.

The World Wide Web which dominates today's online business will evolve into a more interactive and multi-medial type of place. Many services that are available on the Internet have already become part of the World Wide Web. Group calendar services, online chats, newsgroups are all merging to the web platform making it easy to integrate all other types of services. The teletext system, which is part of your television will be replaced by the web that allows you to view the television program in a more interactive manner. You will be able to choose a show, read information on it and then set a reminder so that the television will remind you five minutes before the show starts. During the show, you will be able to click on everything that you can see during the show and get more information on it. Imagine a scene in a kitchen, where you are able to get more information on the stove and order it directly over the Internet. If you think the last James Bond film was overloaded with advertising then think again. The next generation of Internet will allow you much more direct or indirect advertising over the different channels it will provide.

A similar paradigm will be available for the radio. Listen to the radio and click on a button, if you like a certain song. This will lead you to the web site of the singer, where you can get additional information and buy the song. Radio and television will become streaming content on the Internet.

The web as we know it today will disappear or at least become less relevant. The simple linking of pages will be substituted by a more powerful way of linking content to each other. Multiple targets will become common, meaning that clicking on one link will provide you with more than one resource at a time. This will for example eliminate link lists. Instead of providing a list of links on a certain subject you provide one link and the possibility to specify the

---

[9]http://www.internet2.edu/

content and it will automatically select the right content for you. Although this is already possible through search technologies, it will be available to anyone through a simple command in HTML.

Searching on the Web will also become easier as search technologies evolve and become more mature. Instead of typing in cryptic keywords natural sentences and search engines with built-in voice recognition will ask you to clarify the sentence. They will become standard on the Internet.

16.2 Looking into the Future of Business

16.2.1 Content Brokers

In the future we will see new intermediaries appearing in between consumers and providers. The new providers will either provider content, products or services. Unlike traditional intermediaries the new brokers will have access to all providers at the same time and will most probably have fixed contracts with one or a few providers, as we have seen in the past. They will be free to choose whatever may be the best for their customers and will earn their money by receiving a fraction of each transaction. The money will probably be paid half by the provider who is content to have a new customer and half by the customer who is content to have the best provider regarding price, quality or speed, depending on the needs of the customer.

The content providers will deliver the content to the new media center, which will replace all the consumer electronics which used to be in most households. The content is delivered on top of broadband Internet access, meaning that Internet networking and content standards will be used. New technologies will be necessary to ensure the quality of service, as customers are used to from traditional television and radio services, for example.

The traditional model of selling goods at a fixed price will also change from pay-once towards the pay-per-use model. The advanced technologies in billing will allow companies to charge customers on a pay-per-use basis with very low costs incurring for both the customers and the suppliers. Digitized products and services will benefit most of the new model, as they can be easily uploaded and removed from the premises of the customer. Digital certificates and one-time passwords will allow access to content once, for example, and then the content will be automatically deleted or locked until the customer enters a new valid one-time password.

New rights management and metering systems will allow copyright holders to implement these new pricing models. The metering systems will allow for charging on a micro-transaction basis if the copyright holder wishes and if the user agrees. These micro-transactions would entail any or all of several operations, including the searching within the content, the modification, the duplication, the printing, the export from the controlled environment, the browsing and the transmission to others. Instead of using pricing models based on subscriptions or units, content providers, authors, and publishers could choose to charge a very small amount for small transactions. Instead of downloading a complete book, you would pay-as-you-read, for every chapter that is delivered to your doorstep, in whatever form, either as a file or as a printout or as an audio cassette. The same may apply to magazines. You pay only for the articles that you are really interested in.

The transaction-based revenue stream will eventually exceed the revenue stream of the traditional print products. To succeed content providers will have to cannibalize their existing print, subscription, and connect-time businesses. If they don't, start-ups will most likely take over the lead in content providing. A problem is how to move from traditional pricing to the transaction-based pricing without destroying the traditional business. In order to move, you need to take a longer period of declining revenues into account. Many traditional companies will be reluctant to move forwards, but as the major benefit they will get a stable transaction-based set of businesses. Start-up companies will have an easy life, if they do not have the burden of the legacy they have to keep up with.

16.2.2   Product Brokers

As already mentioned above the future of business will be bright, but only for companies that adapt to the new paradigm of service and selling. While the Internet revolutionized computing and adapted business, pervasive computing is just the logical extension of Internet computing, but provides a revolution in the business area.

Remember the example from the preface, where a car automatically selects the cheapest petrol station nearby for refueling. This is a basic product broker, which is also location bound due to the fact that the car cannot get the petrol from anywhere, but requires it within the next 10 miles. The request for petrol and the demand will eventually set the price the driver has to pay.

From this example you can see that the most important change will be that fixed prices will disappear over the next ten to fifteen years. If we look at the prices of the flight tickets of Lufthansa[10] or British Airways[11] you already will see today that they do not have any fixed prices anymore. A flight from Stuttgart to London can cost anything between 100 and 800 Euro or Dollar. The initial prices, which were set by the company will start to move either up and down immediately after they have been released, depending on the demand for that particular flight. If it is a flight that nobody wants to take, you will see ticket offers near the 100 Euro limit, while almost full flights will cost up to 800 Euro. In May 1999 I looked for a flight to London and found that there was no price difference between economy class and business class. The reason was that the economy class was booked out, so no matter which class you chose, you

---

[10]http://www.lufthansa.com/
[11]http://www.britishairways.co.uk/

paid business class and would fly business class. British Airways could have easily said that economy was booked out, but many companies pose restrictions on the use of the business class. By offering an economy class ticket, the travel department would be buying it, as it is normally cheaper than business class and the traveler would arrive in London at the desired time, without having to discuss the use of the business class with his or her managers.

As prices start to flow, it becomes harder to handle for the end customers. Therefore a new set of intelligent agents will be introduced that will help to decide, which offering is the best in a particular situation. We are already seeing the first generation of intelligent shopping agents appear on the web, with Acses[12], being one of the most prominent examples for buying books. These intelligent shopping agents will be refined over the next few years to give you even lower prices. Imagine that you need to buy a certain book, but do not necessarily need the book tomorrow. In this case the shopping broker will be given a week to find the cheapest offering. During that week the prices may go up and down at a single shopping site because of the varying demand, but on the other hand the shopping broker will accumulate orders from different customers. After three days the shopping broker may have found ten people who are interested in the same book and place a bid for ten books at every single online bookshop. The shops would then reply with their price back to the shopping broker, which then would further negotiate prices and get the best price for your request.

16.2.3 Service Brokers

Besides shopping brokers a new class of service brokers will appear, which will be able to handle mass-customized services, such as a television program and highly-individual services, such as a translation. Besides the television channels with a preset selection of programs, highly customizable films and shows will be presented in the future, where you can choose to view a film or show at any give time. This is already possible in some cases, but this sector will grow very fast in the future. As the showing of a film or show does not require any additional service other than broadcasting it can be easily mass-customized. Again, prices will be varying a lot. Top titles will be rather expensive, while older films may have lower prices assigned to them, depending on the preference of the customers.

In addition to this, films that nobody wants to see, will be free of charge. This may seem unorthodox, but as nobody is viewing them, you are not losing money on offering these films free of charge. Offering films for free will get the attention of the customers and eventually demand will start to rise for these films and so will the price increase over time. If nobody is interested in the films, keeping them in the archives won't cost a lot of money, as memory prices will drop with every month, just as they already do nowadays.

---

[12]http://www.acses.com/

Service broker's for translators will use a similar schema to determine a price. It will be based on the quality, reputation and availability of the translator. Imagine a company that needs a twenty pages of technical text translated within a week and two translators bidding for the contract through the translation broker. There is a young translator, inexperienced and seeking work, who is offering his service at 1 Euro or Dollar per line translated as a base price. The more experience translator offers her service at 2 Euros or Dollars per line translated. The number of pages and the time frame until it needs to be completed determine the real price of the bid. This is still a partly manual process. First of all both translators need to check if they have time for twenty pages, which would take about two days. Due to the fact that the text is of technical nature, then the price of the first translator rises to 1,75 Euro and of the second to 2,10 Euro. The difference in increase is linked to the experience in that particular field. The experienced translator has already done several translations on that particular technology, while the other one has never done such a translation. If we now look at the availability, the young translator has a lot of other translations to do in that particular week, so it would be difficult to do this translation as well, therefore his price rises to 2,40 Euro per line, as he is reluctant to take on this work as well. The more experienced translator revises her calendar also and finds it also difficult to include it into the time schedule, but is willing to take on the extra work in the evening, so the price rises only slightly to 2,30 Euro.

The translator broker will pass on these two prices to the company who requested the translation service and they will be able to determine which offering is the better one. The choice will not be made only on the basis of the price, but also on the existing relationships with the translators. It could well be that they will choose the young and more expensive translator for that particular case, because they know him well and he knows the company, while the other one may be a very good translator, but hasn't had any experience with the company.

As you can see, service brokerage will not be able to make automated decisions on who should provide the service, but it offers a good way to determine the market price at the moment a service is required and reduces the overhead for finding the right service for that particular moment. Prices will vary depending on demand and offerings on the market. At another given time it may be possible that two hundred translators will bid for single translation.

As you can imagine this will increase the competition on the already very competitive market. It can be expected that manufacturer, retailers and content producers will all need to change the way they do business. Instead of offering complex products, they will only offer small building blocks that are compatible with the offerings of the competition. Car manufacturers, for example, will most likely disappear in their current form. Over the last few decades they have evolved from manufacturers to parts assemblers. The parts come from third parties, which are tightly integrated into the supply chain of the car manufacturer. The car manufacturer today decides on the design and the technical specifications of a car and assembles the car from pre-built parts. In the future it can be imagined that car manufacturers will evolve to car assemblers that accept parts from any third-party vendor.

Customers will then be able to use a highly sophisticated online configurator to build a strongly personalized car. Imagine a future, where you will be going to BMW's[13] web page, selecting the chassis of a Ferrari[14] and the motor of a Rolls Royce[15]. As in this future all parts will be compatible, just as services are becoming compatible in Hewlett-Packard's E-Services vision, this is something car manufacturers have to get accustomed to. This does not only apply to the automotive industry, but also to any other industry that builds complex products out of pre-built components. The computer industry will not be different; already today we see the dominance of the computer platform decreasing through the Internet, HTML and Java. Computers will become commodities, offering the basic computing service, which can be enhanced in real-time over the new Internet. The boxes that you will buy in the future will contain a computing broker that will get the appropriate resources over the network for you. Additional memory, hard disk space or processing power will be made available to you whenever you have a need for it. This reduces the cost of the computing broker to a minimum making it possible for anyone to get such a box, which delivers the basic functionality required to connect to the Internet.

The move from agriculture over to industrial age to the service era will be completed within the next ten to fifteen years. This does not mean that we will be able to live without agriculture and industries, but they will become commodities that are expected to be in place with technological advances occurring also in the future, requiring even less people in these areas. The place to make big money will be the service area.

The biggest problem I have right now is that I cannot imagine a post-service era. What will come after service? Maybe it is like asking for the fourth dimension of space, which may be mathematically easy to prove, but almost impossible to imagine. Maybe there is nothing after service, but I think the world should dedicate some resources on defining a new type of business culture and model that will lead us through the twenty-first century.

16.2.4 Broker Software

While auctions have always played an important role in all economies around the world, the Internet has brought us to a new level, where the paradigm of auctions start to dominate the economies. The reason is that the Internet reduced the high costs for receiving information on an auction and participating does not cost anything anymore. The Internet makes it possible to reduce the

---

[13]http://www.bmw.de/

[14]http://www.ferrari.it/

[15]http://www.rollsroyce.co.uk/

transaction costs to such an extent that almost anything can be sold through the auction/broker model over the Internet. Typical auctions are used for the following market segments. Last-minute tickets, electronic components, used goods and consumer products.

The Internet is the ideal platform as it removes the limits of traditional auctions, such as a short time for the offer and the low number of bidders. In order to offer an auction service on the Internet, a broker information system needs to be installed at the auction site. One solution is the Auction Server, developed by AIT Gmbh[16], which provides a complete infrastructure for developing online auction and brokering services. Anything from a small auction to a complete auction server can be implemented by the Auction Server software.

The software offers more than just a simple bidding process. Automatic bidding agents are able to act on behalf on customers who have no time to attend the auction themselves. The bidding agents can be programmed to bid up to a maximum price automatically. The first site that uses the Auction Software from AIT GmbH is QuickM@rket[17], which acts as an "auction mall", where small and large customers are able to create auction services.

The German site of eBay[18] uses the auction software from Living Systems[19], which is built on a multi-threaded service architecture. The Auction Broker uses advanced features such as JIT compilation and caching that ensure high performance on the most demanding sites. The deployment platform supports multi-server clusters with native load balancing and fail over to serve high volume, transaction intensive applications reliably.

The Auction Broker Software allows companies to create and design their own customized auction and/or virtual store. It's a fully functional user friendly auction tool with an e-commerce solution. It's designed to be simple to navigate yet fast and powerful. It offers maximum flexibility, for any size of business. The back-end administrator (Auction Control Center) has powerful features to customize the software to the needs of the company. The Auction Broker Software is available for rent or purchase, making it possible to run the business yourself or to outsource it to Living Systems.

16.2.5 Total Automation of Business

The use of next generation brokers will eventually lead to a complete automation of business, making human resources superfluous for electronic services. Dealing for the best price will become an automatic feature of your company, requiring less resources on the sales side and on the procurement side. Although production may still need human resources, the administrative part of the company will reduce itself to the minimum required.

---

[16]http://www.aitgmbh.de/
[17]http://www.quickmarket.de/
[18]http://www.ebay.de/
[19]http://www.living-systems.de/

The introduction of global Internet laws will make it easy for intelligent agents to discuss contracts with other intelligent agents without any human interaction. Human intelligence will only be required to feed the intelligent agents and to use the service in the end. As more and more services run fully automated in the background, the need for human business is reduced, leaving the field open to new ideas.

As more and more people are superfluous in large companies, they eventually become electronic freelancers who do work for many people at the same time and offer a set of highly specialized services. Through the Internet one person and some high-speed hardware will be able to handle many thousands of requests at the same time, instead of doing one job after the other. This will reduce the amount of human resources in the freelancers space as well. Only very few people will have a job in agriculture, production and the service area. Most people will have time to do whatever they like. This means that they are able to explore new things, become artists or sit in front of the media center and get bored to death.

The total automation of business may make large companies collapse as they are too expensive to maintain and will bring the electronic freelancers into a perfect position to produce goods or services, both online and offline. Smaller manufacturers may find it easier to produce highly specialized goods at a good price, as opposed to large companies which produce many types of goods at the same time.

The Internet will allow the creation of virtual value chains instantly for the production of certain goods, which can be highly personalized. The need for rock-solid value chains will be reduced and the power in business will be re-shuffled.

16.3 The Societal Impact

16.3.1 The Transition Phase

Advances in technology will always influence society, but neither only in a positive or only a negative way. It needs to become the role of the politicians to think about ways to give everyone a role in this new society, which allows them to be happy. As national politics will lose control completely over the global network economy in the future, the national politicians have enough time to think about new social structures and programs to help people in the transition phase.

After the transition phase the people will hopefully have found a new sense in life and will have a new income stream to support themselves and their families. The major obstacle for such a future are the politicians who do not know much about technology and are slow to respond to the changing needs of the ever-faster rotating world. But a new generation of politicians will eventually appear that has grown up with the Internet and will know what to do.

Internet technologies offer a huge opportunity for the whole world to concentrate on the important things in life and forget about the stupid work that is done better by computers. The downside of this example is that if the world wants to depend on so much technology it will have a problem if the power supply fails at any given time. Therefore the free time that has become available should be used to show people how things worked in a world without electricity, computers and networks.

Farmers should learn how to produce fruit without the help of machines, just as everyone should learn how to write with a pen and learn how to cook or make fire without high-end technology. Already today this knowledge is getting lost, where school children have seen cows only on television and think the milk is made in the supermarket. While technology may make life easier, the roots should not be forgotten and taught in school.

While technology advances people should think on how to simplify the use of technology. Today operating a VCR is often a very complicated mission, just as changing the time on the car stereo. Technology should enable everyone to use it, not only the highly educated specialists.

16.3.2 Responsibility for the Society

The Internet has already become the major form of communication for educational institutions and businesses all over the world. The governments are catching up fast. While the access for them is no issue, it needs to be ensured that everybody will get access to the Internet. This does not only mean that everybody should be provided with the hardware and software, but also with the necessary knowledge to make use of the content and services on the Internet. This type of knowledge is called information literacy.

Today print literacy is still a major problem around the world. In many countries around the world many people still cannot read or write and before they can go on to learn how to use the Internet society needs to solve this problem first. Otherwise the Internet becomes an elite information infrastructure, which will be accessible only to those who have the resources, skills and knowledge. This would increase the gap between the rich and the poor even further.

In order to ensure the global access to the Internet the education standards around the world need to be raised. In addition to print literacy information literacy will need to be part of the curriculum for all school children. At the same time new paradigms of accessing information need to be implemented that allow the less-fortunate to access the basic services via graphical symbols, for example. A lot of web-based services need to be accessed as well over a standard phone to allow people without Internet access or reading skills to access electronic services.

The Internet may create psychological dependencies on networked communication, thus reducing the demand for relationships in real life. The Internet allows people to appear every time they connect to be another person. People may associate more freely online because they are not bound to geographical or temporal limits.

16.3.3   Next Generation Work Life

Through the automation of standard business processes the amount of work as we know it today will be reduced significantly. This poses a huge problem for many people who built their life around work. The importance of work for making enough money to live a decent life becomes less important. In an automated business world, products and services will be available at the fraction of the current costs, making them available to anyone.

It remains to be seen if the reduced amount of work will be distributed evenly among the working force or if it becomes a status symbol for the new information elite. The current trend is moving towards a working elite and this won't be stopped if politics do not do anything about it. This will require a shift from a work-life balance to a new form of making sense of the life. Without a goal in life suicidal tendencies will increase, just as will crime, which is not provoked by hunger, but by boredom. This is something we see already today.

It may well be that people will still work, not to earn a living, but to be occupied. In a positive future this will mean that work shifts to scientific research, art, music and sports, but it also may have a negative impact, where a government forces people to work.

16.3.4   Politics in the 21st Century

Governments and politics have always been bound to geographical limits. The limits defined the areas of influence a government had. Laws are enforced within these limits and taxes need to be paid by the people living within these limits. The taxes are used to pay for the infrastructure and the security, for example, of the inhabitants of a country that is defined by its borders.

The globalization of the economy has also created a situation where companies reside in a certain country, but pay taxes in another country. BMW[20], for example, which is a German company, does not pay any taxes in Germany anymore. There is also no way to enforce them, as they would move the whole production to another country, making employees lose their jobs. The New Economy has a large impact on the politics, much more than ever before. The Internet increases this dilemma for national governments. While governments will still be needed to keep up public safety, for example, their influence on the economy will vanish.

The European Union is one example of a transnational government, which sets rules on a transnational level. While taxes are still differing among the members of the Union, the laws are merging. At the same time as we see the creation of a transnational government, the influence of national governments

---

[20]http://www.bmw.com/

is largely reduced. But the influence of regions has increased over the same period of time. The European Union has become less a Union of national states,
but more a Union of regions, whereby the local identity becomes more important than the national identity. The economies of these regions are competing
against each other, as each region can be seen as a single economy competing
against other economies under the same law and taxation system.

Politics will have to focus on regional and transnational issues in order to
survive. The existing national states will not have a very bright future, if they
do not adapt to the changing environment.

Appendix A

GLOSSARY OF E-BUSINESS TERMS

This appendix contains a list of all the buzz-words used throughout the book. You can use this glossary while reading the book or as a future reference.

Acceptable Use Policy A former set of formal rules that govern how a network, application or piece of information may be used. See also *netiquette*, *Terms of Service*.

Active X Software technology developed by Microsoft for including applications into HTML pages. Lack of security let many people prefer Java over Active X.

Address An address on the Internet is described as a uniform resource locator, which can be used for any type of addressing, such as e-mails (mailto:info@gallery-net.com), web pages (http://www.news.com/) and ftp sites (ftp://ftp.netscape.com/pub/communicator). Instead of using domain names, it is also possible to use IP addresses. See also *ftp*, *e-mail*, *IP*, *uniform resource locator*, *web page*.

Address Resolution Protocol Used primarily with IP – Network Layer to resolve addresses.

ADSL See *asymmetric digital subscriber line*.

Advanced Research Projects Agency Network A computer network that has been developed in the late 60s by the US Department of Defense to allow communication in a post-nuclear war age. Predecessor of the Internet. See also *internet*.

Ad-Server A program or server that is responsible for handling the banner advertisements for several web sites. These servers offer statistics about visits and movements of customers. They offer also functionality, such as banner rotation, so that a single customer will not see a certain banner twice, when visiting the same web page.

590

Ad Transfer An ad transfer is the successful arrival of a customer at the site of the banner advertisement. See also *banner advertisement*.

AFK Net-language for "away from keyboard".

Agent Application that acts for a customer by completing transactions, seeking information or prices or communicating with other agents and customers.

AI See *artificial intelligence*.

Anonymous FTP See *ftp*.

Anti-aliasing Process used to remove jagged edges in computerized graphics.

American Standard Code For Information Interchange A standard for the representation of upper and lower-case Latin letters, numbers and punctuation on computers. There are 128 standard ASCII codes which are represented by a 7 digit binary code. The other 128 codes are used differently on most computers. In order to display non-Latin codes, Unicode is used in most cases. See also *binary code*, *unicode*.

API See *application program interface*.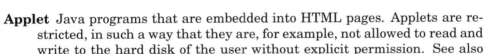

Applet Java programs that are embedded into HTML pages. Applets are restricted, in such a way that they are, for example, not allowed to read and write to the hard disk of the user without explicit permission. See also *HTML*, *java*, *servlet*.

Application A program, which is self-contained and that executes a set of well-defined tasks under user control.

Application Program Interface Interface, which allows the communication between programs, networks and databases.

Archie Piece of software for finding files on anonymous FTP sites. It searches only for file names and has been replaced by more powerful web-based search engines. See also *anonymous FTP*.

ARP See *address resolution protocol*.

ARPANet See *advanced research projects agency network*.

Artificial Intelligence A branch of computer science that studies how to endow computers with capabilities of human intelligence.

ASCII See *american standard code for information interchange*.

Asymmetric Digital Subscriber Line ADSL is becoming the alternative to an ISDN line. It allows much higher bandwidths over a standard digital telephone line. It needs to be configured similar to a leased line in such a way that it can connect only to ISPs that are near you. A typical ADSL setup allows download speeds up to 1.5 megabits per second (about 200 kilobits per seconds), but upload is restricted to 128 kilobits per second (similar to two ISDN lines). ADSL works asynchronously, therefore the different up- and download speeds. See also *bit, bps, ISDN, leased line, xDSL*.

Asynchronous Transfer Method A fast, intelligent hardware switch which can support voice, data, image, and video. Cell-switching (as opposed to packet) technology which replaces variable-length packets now in use with uniform (53 byte) cells. It promises any-to-any connectivity and networks that scale easily from a few nodes to global deployment. Combines packet switching's efficient use of bandwidth with circuit switching's minimal delays.

ATM See *asynchronous transfer method*.

Attached File A file, for example an application, image or sound, that is embedded into an email message. See also *e-mail*.

Audio Video Interleaved Windows format for saving video with sound.

Authentication The process of verifying a person.

Authorization The process of allowing access to a system to a person.

AUP See *acceptable use policy*.

Avatar Three-dimensional representation or digital actor of a customer in a web shop or in a chat room.

AVI See *audio video interleaved*.

Backbone The top level of a hierarchical network. Major pathway within a network offering the highest possible speed and connecting all major nodes. The main pipes along which data is transferred. See also *network, nodes*.

Bandwidth The maximum size of information that can be sent through a connection at a given time. Usually measured in bits per second (bps). See also *bps, bit, T-1*.

BASIC See *beginners all-purpose symbolic instructional code*

Baud It is commonly used in the same way as bits per second. See also *bit, bps, modem*.

BBS See *bulletin board system*.

BCC See *blind carbon copy*.

Beginners All-purpose Symbolic Instructional Code A computer language that is easy-to-learn and highly flexible, which was invented at Dartmouth University.

beta A pre-release of an application that is made available for the purposes of testing.

binary Mathematical base 2, or numbers composed of a series of zeros and ones. Since zero's and one's can be easily represented by two voltage levels on an electronic device, the binary number system is widely used in digital computing.

Binary Digit A single digit number in base 2 (therefore 0 or 1). The smallest unit for computerized data. See also *byte, kilobyte, megabyte*.

Binary Hexadecimal Algorithm to convert binary files into ASCII-text. Used mainly on Macintosh computers. See also *binary, ASCII, MIME, uuencode*.

Binhex See *binary hexadecimal*.

Bit See *binary digit*.

Bits per second Measurement unit for transferring data. A 33.6 modem can move 33.600 bits per second. See also *bandwidth, bit*.

Blind Carbon Copy Copies people onto e-mails that cannot be identified by the person to whom the e-mail message was originally addressed to. See also *carbon copy, e-mail*.

BOFH Net-language for "bastard operator from hell".

Bookmark A file that contains references to web pages that you have already visited, which then can be organized and used to return to a particular page later on.

Boolean Search A search allowing the inclusion or exclusion of documents containing certain words through the use of operators such as "AND", "NOT" and "OR".

Boot To start up or reset a computer. When a computer is booted the operating system is loaded. There are two different types of booting a computer. A cold boot means that the computer needs to powered up from an off state and a warm boot means that all data in the memory is erased and the operating system is loaded from start. See also *memory, operating system*.

Bot Net-language for "roBot".

Bozo Filter A feature to screens out incoming e-mails and news postings from those whose correspondence in not valued. See also *e-mail, news, spam*.

Bps See *bits per second*.

Browser Client application that is able to display various kinds of Internet resources. See also *Client, homepage, internet explorer, mosaic, netscape, URL, WWW*.

BTW Net-language for "by the way".

Bug A programming error that causes a malfunction of the computer software or hardware. See also *hardware, software*.

Bulletin Board System A computer based system that allows people to discuss topics, up and download files and send and receive e-mails. Bulletin boards can either run independently on a single computer where people dial in, or can connect to other bulletin boards to form a network, such as the FidoNet. See also *dial in, e-mails, network*.

BWOTD Net-language for "bad word of the day".

Byte Eight bits for a byte which is used to represent a single ASCII character, for example. See also *bit*.

Carbon Copy When people use the CC function of their web browser they use it to copy additional recipients to an e-mail. See also *blind carbon copy, e-mail*.

CBT See *computer based training*.

CC See *carbon copy*.

Central Processing Unit The main chip inside every computer that is used to run the operating system and the application software.

CERN European Laboratory for Particle Physics, Geneva, Switzerland and birthplace of the World-Wide Web.

Certificate Authority Issuer of digital certificates, used for encrypting communication and signing documents. See also *digital certificates, digital signatures*.

CGI See *common gateway interface*.

Chat Direct communication over the Internet with multiple persons. Other than e-mail, responses are made in real-time. See also *IRC*.

Checksum A special calculation applied to a piece of information. If the information is transmitted and the calculation achieves the same result, then the transmission was successful.

Class In object-oriented programming, a category of objects, or the applet file itself. For example, there might be a class called shape that contains objects which are circles, rectangles, and triangles.

Client Application that resides on the customers computer and contacts a server to communicate. Examples: IRC clients, Web Clients. See also *IRC, web*.

Clipboard A piece of memory that stores information only temporarily. See also *memory*.

CODEC Program or device that COmpresses/DECompresses digital video.

Common Gateway Interface A standard that describes how a web browser passes on information to a web server. CGI programs are able to read the information, process it and pass the results back to the web browser.

Compiler A program that translates a programming language into machine code. See also *programming language, machine code*.

Compression Technology to reduce the size of files and save bandwidth. See also *bandwidth, lossy compression, non-lossy compression*.

Computer Based Training Way of learning to use a computer and a software package, offering information on a certain subject and a test for the pupil.

Concept Search Instead of searching for documents that contain a given keyword, a concept search will search for documents related conceptually to a given keyword.

Connection Established path for exchanging information.

Control Prog/Monitor Operating System created by Gary Kildall in the 70's.

Cookie Piece of information that is stored in the browser and can be retrieved by the server that placed the information there. This piece of information can be used to identify a user, for example.

CP/M See *control prog / monitor*.

CPU See *central processing unit*.

Cracker A person who tries to break the copy protection of software.

Credit Card Processors Offer services for electronic businesses, such as processing credit card transactions and verifying credibility of customers.

Crosspostings A message that is sent simultaneously to several newsgroups. See also *message, newsgroups*.

Cyberculture A collection of cultures and cultural products that exist on and are made possible by the Internet, along with the stories told about these cultures and cultural products.

Cyberspace First used in Neuromancer by William Gibson. It is used to describe the Internet. See also *internet*.

Daemon A background process waiting for a client to start-up the service, such as the pop 3 daemon, which runs continually, but is activated only when people retrieve e-mails using an e-mail client.

Data Encryption Key A string used to mathematically encode a message so that it can only be decrypted by someone with either the same key (symmetric encryption) or with a related key (asymmetric encryption).

Data Encryption Standard Encryption scheme, developed by IBM in the 1970s.

Database Collection of data formatted in a special way, to make it easier to retrieve a particular piece of information.

Dedicated Line A phone line that connects two computers permanently to keep up service.

Demilitarized Zone Zone in multi-layered firewalls, which contains public Internet services.

DES See *data encryption standard*.

DHCP See *dynamic host configuration protocol*.

DHTML See *dynamic hypertext markup language*.

Dial-Up A temporary connection between two computers established over a phone line.

Digerati The digital elite, invented by *Wired* magazine. Derived from the word literati.

Digital Certificate File containing information about its owner that can be used to identify the owner. See also *certificate authority, SSL*.

Digital Signal Processor A separate processor, built into some sound cards, that relieves audio processing from the computer's CPU.

Digital Versatile Disk A new standard for recording video on CD-ROM's using MPEG2, thus boasting better-than-broadcast TV quality. Costing about the same as a CD, DVD-ROM's hold 8 to 40 times more data. DVD will replace videocassettes, laserdiscs, CD-ROM's and audio CD's.

Disk Operating System Outdated operating system with a command line interface. See also *operating system*.

Dithering If a color is not available, it can be made from the available colors by placing a pattern of colors next to each other to visually mix. For instance the illusion of "orange" can be made by placing red and yellow pixels next to each other.

DMZ See *demilitarized zone*.

DNS See *domain name system*.

Domain Name The name of a computer connected to the Internet. The Domain name is used to form a URL. See also *URL*.

Domain Name System Database that links IP addresses and domain names. See also *domain name*, *IP*.

DOS See *disk operating system*.

Download To receive files from another computer on the Internet by actively requesting it.

DSP See *dynamic signal processor*.

DVD See *digital versatile disk*.

Dynamic Host Configuration Protocol Internet standard, based on RFC 1541, for the automatic allocation of IP addresses.

Dynamic Hypertext Markup Langauge An extension to HTML, which allows a better user interaction and introduces dynamic web page creation.

E-Cash See *electronic cash*.

EDI See *electronic data interchange*.

E-Mail See *electronic mail*.

Electronic Cash Electronic money that can be exchanged on the Internet for goods, information and services. It is mostly used for micro-payment solutions. See also *micro-payment*.

Electronic Data Interchange A standard for the inter-organizational computer-to-computer exchange of structured information.

Electronic Mail Exchange of digital documents via the Internet.

Emoticon Sideway faces express emotions without words on the Internet using special characters on the keyboard. The best-known emoticon is the smiley :-). If you can't see the face, turn you head and look again. Other emoticons include the smiling pirate .-) and the sad person :-(.

Encryption Procedure to render a message illegible to anyone who is not authorized to read it.

Ethernet Standard for connecting computers on an Intranet. See also *bandwidth*, *intranet*.

Extranet Extranets are extended Intranets to share information with business partners over the Internet in a very secure way. See also *intranets*.

FAQ See *frequently asked questions*.

FDDI See *fiber distributed data interface*.

Fiber Distributed Data Interface Standard for computer connections on optical fiber cables at a rate of 100 Mbit. See also *bandwidth*, *ethernet*, *T1*, *T3*.

File Transfer Protocol Internet protocol to move files from one Internet site to another one. Public FTP servers allow the up- and download of files, creating public file archives.

Finger Tool to locate people on other Unix servers. It helps to see if a certain person is online.

Firewall A tool to seperate an Intranet from the Internet by disallowing connections on certain ports, making the Intranet very secure. See also *network*, *intranet*.

Firewire Serial interface technology, which allows the connection of devices at speeds up to 50 Mbytes/s. Used for devices such as video cameras so that they can feed real time video to a computer.

Flame A crude or witless comment on a newsgroup posting or e-mail. See also *flame war*.

Flame War Instead of discussing positions in an online discussion, personal attacks (or flames) against the debators are exchanged. See also *flame*.

Flat File A database in ASCII format that separates records by a special character. See also *ASCII*, *database*.

Font Typographic style such as Times Roman or Helvetica.

Forward Sending on an e-mail to a third person. See also *e-mail*.

Frame HTML tag that allows the browser window to be segmented into several sections. See also *browser*, *HTML*.

Freenet Internet access provided on a non-profit basis.

Freeware Software that is available to anybody without the need for paying a fee, while the author retains the copyright.

Frequently Asked Questions A web page that lists and answers the most common question on a particular subject.

FTP See *file transfer protocol*.

Full-Text Index Database containing every word of every document, including stop words. See *stop words*.

Fuzzy Search Finds matches even if the keyword is misspelled or only partially spelled.

FWIW Net-language for "for what it's worth".

FYI Net-language for "for your information".

Gamma Correction As not all screens or printers are the same, colors have to be adjusted from the computers idea of "normal" before they are displayed.

Gateway Architecture for bridging between two networks that work with different protocols.

GIF See *graphic interchange format*.

Gigabyte 1024 Megabytes, but some use 1000 Megabytes, as it is easier to calculate with. See also *Byte*, *Megabyte*.

Glitch Small malfunction in the hardware or software which does not cause an interruption.

Graphic Interchange Format Image format, very common on the Internet. See also *JPEG*, *PNG*.

Gopher Internet protocol for presenting menus of downloadable documents or files. It is still around, but has no real importance anymore. See also *HTTP*, *Hypertext*, *WWW*.

Graphical User Interface Graphical environment to simplify the use of the operating system and applications.

Grep Unix command to scan files for patterns, also used as a synonym for fast manual searching.

GUI See *graphical user interface*.

Guru Synonym for expert.

 Hacker Persons who spend their time breaking into systems and networks in order to steal, change or delete data that does not belong to them.

Handle See *nickname*.

Hello World! The program that every computer student learns first, outputs "Hello World!".

Hit The download of an element on a web page. If a web page consists of the HTML text, two images and a sound file, then there have been four hits on the web server. It is a way to measure the load of the server. See also *HTML, web server*.

Homepage The main page on a web server.

Host See *server*.

HTML See *hypertext markup language*.

HTTP See *hypertext transport protocol*.

Hypertext Web documents that contain links to other documents.

HyperText Markup Language The language for developing documents for the World Wide Web. See also *client, server, WWW*.

HyperText Transport Protocol The protocol for transporting files from a web server to a web browser. See also *client, server, WWW*.

IBT See *internet based training*.

Icon Mnemonic convention to replace functional names by images.

IDE See *integrated drive electronics*.

Identity Hacking See *social hacking*.

IMAP See *internet mail access protocol*.

IMHO Net-language for "in my humble opinion".

Index A searchable database of documents created automatically or manually by a search engine.

Integrated Drive Electronics A 16-bit parallel interface transferring only data. Cheaper than ESDI medium-range capacity (40-200Mb). Can't perform a physical (low-level) format because it is not a device-level interface.

Integrated Services Digital Network Digital version of the good old analogue telephone line.

International Organization for Standardization A federation of national standards bodies such as BSI and ANSI.

Internet The computer network for business and leisure based on the TCP/IP protocol. All other computer networks have become irrelevant. Evolved from ARPAnet. See also *ARPANet, network, TCP/IP*.

Internet Based Training Evolution of the computer based training, which offers real-time learning over the Internet with a teacher. See also *computer based training*.

Internet Mail Access Protocol RFC 1730[-33] IMAP4 allows a client to access and manipulate electronic mail messages on a server. This should be viewed as a superset of the POP3. The IMAP4 server listens on TCP port 143. IMAP is definitely an emerging technology and functionally completely outperforms the older POP environment.

Internet Protocol See *TCP/IP*.

Internet Protocol Number Unique address for every computer connected to the Internet. Currently it is composed of a series of four numbers, separated by dots. Example: 127.0.0.1. Domain names refer to IP numbers. See also *domain name, internet, TCP/IP*.

Internet Relay Chat Multi-user chat facility on the Internet. Many servers around the world are interconnected to allow hundreds of thousands of users to chat at the same time. Special IRC clients are necessary to connect.

Internet Service Provider Company providing access to the Internet.

Internet Society Non-governmental international organization for global co-operation and co-ordination of the Internet and its technologies and applications.

Intranet Private network that is based on the same technologies as the Internet, but restricted to a certain user group. See also *internet, network*.

IP See *internet protocol*.

IRC See *internet relay chat*.

ISDN See *integrated services digital network*.

ISO See *international organization for standardization*.

ISOC See *internet society*.

ISP See *internet service provider*.

JAR See *Java Archive*.

Java Programming language developed by Sun with cross-platform neutrality, object-orientation and networking in mind. See also *applet*, *JDK*.

Java Archive A file format used to bundle all components required by a Java applet. JAR files simplify the downloading of applets since all the components (.class files, images, sounds, etc.) can be packaged into a single file.

Java Development Kit Basic development package from Sun distributed for free in order to write, test and debug Java programs. See also *applet*, *java*.

JavaScript Scripting language developed by Netscape that allows interaction within HTML pages. See also *HTML*, *scripting*.

JDK See *Java development kit*.

Jini Infrastructure and programming model which allow devices to connect with each other to create an instant community. Jini technology enables devices to work with each other, so users can create their own personal networks or communities no matter where they are located.

JIT See *just in time*.

Joint Photographic Experts Group Multi-company commission that develops new image formats.

JPEG Image format for the Internet using lossy compression algorithms. See also *joint photographic experts group*.

Just In Time The concept of reducing inventories by working closely with suppliers to co-ordinate delivery of materials just before their use in the manufacturing or supply process.

Kill File File that contains rules for filtering unwanted messages.

Kilobyte 1024 Bytes, sometimes 1000 Bytes. See also *bit*, *byte*.

Knowbie Expert in computer networking. See also *newbie*.

LAN See also *local area network*.

LDAP See also *lightweight directory access protocol*.

Leased-Line A permanently established phone line that is used to offer twenty-four hour access to the Internet.

Lightweight Directory Access Protocol A technology that provides access to X.500 for PCs.

Local Area Network Computer network limited to a certain location. See also *ethernet, WAN*.

Login Account name to gain access to a system. See also *password*.

LOL Net-language for "laughing out loud".

Mailing List A system to redistribute mails from one person to many other people who are interested in that mail. Mailing lists are used to create online discussion, similar to newsgroups, with the difference the mails are sent automatically while newsgroups require the user to actively retrieve the information. See also *e-mail, newsgroup*.

MAPI See *messaging application programmable interface*.

Megabyte 1024 Kilobytes, sometimes 1000 Kilobytes. See also *kilobyte, byte, bit*.

Message Handling System X.400 series of recommendations of abstract services and protocols used to provide electronic mail services in an OSI networking environment. X.500 is a series of recommendations that provide a distributed, user-friendly subscriber directory to help users address X.400 messages. These services are called simply the Directory.

Message Transfer Agents Part of the X.400 OSI stack. Responsible for the actual transport of the message between user agents. MTA's typically reside on separate machines.

Messaging Application Programmable Interface Microsoft standard for accessing mail on a server, similar to IMAP. See also *IMAP*.

MHS See *message handling system*.

Micropayments Payments that have a value between a fraction of a cent and roughly ten Dollars or Euro.

MIME See *multipurpose internet mail extensions*.

Mirror Sites Sites that contain exact copies of the original site. They are used to spread the load over several sites and to speed up the download for the customers by placing the server nearer to them.

Modem See *modulator demodulator*.

Modulator Demodulator Device between computer and phone line that converts computer signals to a form that can be used to transport the data over telephone networks.

MTA See *message transfer agents*.

MUD See *multi-user dungeon*.

Multipurpose Internet Mail Extensions Format for attaching binary files to e-mails. Enables multi-part/multimedia messages to be sent over the Internet. This standard was developed by the Internet Engineering Task Force (IETF). See als *binhex*, *uuencode*.

Multi-User Dungeon Environment for multi-user role games. Every user plays a different role in the game and is able to communicate and interact with others. Example: telnet 130.149.19.20 7680.

Netiquette Code of behaviour on the Internet.

Netizen Responsible citizen on the Internet.

Network The connection of two or more computers in order to share resources is a network.

Newsgroup Discussion group on USENET. See also *USENET*.

Network News Transport Protocol Standard protocol for exchanging postings and newsgroups over the Internet.

NNTP See *network news transport protocol*

Node A device connected to a network.

Object Oriented Programming Art of programming independent pieces of code, which are then able to interact with each other.

Offline Not connected to the Internet.

Online Connected to the Internet.

OOP See *object oriented programming*.

Operating System Software that is loaded right after the boot time. It provides the basic functionality to run applications, based on a single set of instructions.

OS See *operating system*.

Packet The smallest unit for transmitting data over the Internet. Data is broken up into packets, sent over the network and then reassembled at the other end.

Password Secret code to identify a user when logging onto a system.

Perl Powerful scripting language, often used to write CGI scripts.

PGP See *pretty good privacy*.

Phrase Search A search for documents on the Internet containing an exact sentence or phrase specified by a user.

Plug-ins Software that adds functionality to commercial applications, such as the Netscape browser or Adobe's Photoshop.

Point of Presence Local access to the services of an ISP. See also *ISP*.

POP See *point of presence*.

POP3 See *post office protocol*.

Port Interface for accessing services on a server.

Portal Point of entry web site to the Internet.

Post Office Protocol Protocol for receiving mails via a client.

Postmaster Administrator of the mail server. In case of problems, you can contact the postmaster. The postmaster of someone@foobar.org is postmaster@foobar.org, for example.

Pretty Good Privacy Encryption algorithm developed by Phil Zimmerman.

Protocol Rules how computers and applications interact.

Proxy Server A proxy server retrieves documents on demand from a server and passes them on to a client. The advantage with a proxy server is that it normally caches documents. It is considerably faster to retrieve documents from the proxy rather than directly from a web server, especially if someone else has already retrieved that particular document.

PSTN See *public switched telephone network*.

Public Switched Telephone Network The normal telephone network.

Push Technology Also referred to as "Web-casting" or "channel-casting", this technology broadcasts personalized information to subscribers.

Query Request for information from a database.

Query-By-Example Find search results similar to a search result the user finds particularly useful.

Queue Sequence of objects.

RAM See *random access memory*.

Random Access Memory Memory, that is used for executing applications and storing documents while working on them.

Readme A text file containing information on how to use the file you want to access.

RealAudio Software tool that supports transmissions of real-time, live or pre-recorded audio.

Remote Login Logging into a computer system from remote.

Request For Comments The process for creating an Internet standard. New standards are proposed and published in form of a request for comments document. When a new standard has been established, it retains the acronym and a number is added.

RFC See *request for comments*.

Root The administrator account that has super-user rights on a system. See also *sysop*.

ROTFL Net-language for "rolling on the floor laughing".

Router A device to handle the connection between two or more networks. See also *network*.

RTFM Net-language for "'read the f*cking manual". Answer to a question that users could have answered themselves by reading the manual.

Search Engine Web service that allows you to query a database for keywords and returns matching web pages.

Secure Sockets Layer Protocol invented by Netscape to encrypt communication between web browser and server. It provides privacy, authentication and integrity.

Server A device that provides one or more services to several clients over a network. See also *client*, *network*.

Servlet A Java application that runs on a server. The term usually refers to a Java applet that runs within a Web server environment. This is analogous to a Java applet that runs within a Web browser environment.

Shopping Cart It keeps track of all the items that a customer wants to buy, allowing the shopper to pay for the whole order at once.

Simple Mail Transport Protocol The protocol to send electronic mail over the Internet. See also *e-mail*.

Simple Network Management Protocol Protocol to manage and monitor devices connected to a network.

Smart Card Plastic card of credit card size with an embedded microchip. The chip can contain digital money and personal information about the owner.

SMDS See *switched multimegabit data service*.

Smiley See *emoticon*. :-)   .-)   :-(

SMTP See *simple mail transport protocol*.

SNMP See *simple network management protocol*.

Spam Inappropriate use of e-mail and postings by sending information and advertising to people who did not request them.

Spider See *web crawler*.

SQL See *structured query language*.

Stop Words Conjunctions, prepositions, articles and other words, which appear often in documents yet alone may contain little meaning.

Structured Query Language The preferred programming language for communication with databases.

SSL See *secure sockets layer*.

Switched Multimegabit Data Service A proposed new standard for very high-speed data transfer.

Sysop See *system operator*.

System Operator Person who is responsible for the operations of a computer system or network resource.

T-1 A leased line with a bandwidth of 1,544,000 bits-per-second (about 1,5 Megabit/s). See also *bandwidth, bit, byte, ethernet, T-3*.

T-3 A leased line with a bandwidth of 44,736,000 bits-per-second (about 44 Megabits/s). See also *bandwidth, bit, byte, ethernet, T-1.*

Tagged Information File Format A compressed graphic file format developed by Aldus as an international standard format. Unfortunately there are different versions of TIFF around, notably the MAC and PC versions have differing ways of compressing the data.

TCP/IP See *transmission control protocol / internet protocol.*

Telnet Program to perform a remote login to another computer.

Terabyte 1024 or 1000 Gigabytes. See also *byte, kilobyte.*

Thin Client A cut-down network terminal with no local processing power.

TIFF See *tagged information file format.*

Transmission Control Protocol/Internet Protocol A set of protocols that are the foundation of the Internet, which enable the communication between computers.

Triple-dub Net-language for "WWW".

Trojan Horse A program that seems to be harmless and starts harmful functions after it has been installed.

Unicode Text encoding scheme including international characters and alphabets.

Uniform Resource Locator Addressing scheme on the Internet to locate Internet resources.

Universal Serial Bus Serial interface that allows connection of up to 127 devices at speeds of either 1.5 or 12Mbits/s. It supplies power for those devices and allows the devices to be added and removed without rebooting.

Unix Operating System, developed in the early seventies.

Unix to Unix Copy Software to exchange e-mail and news on a store-and-forward basis.

Unix to Unix Decoding Method of converting text files to binary files. See also *binhex, MIME.*

Unix to Unix Encoding Method of converting binary files to text files. See also *binhex, MIME.*

URL See *uniform resource locator.*

USB See *universal serial bus*.

USENET A decentralized world-wide system for newsgroups. See also *newsgroups*.

UUCP See *unix to unix copy*.

UUDECODE See *unix to unix decoding*.

UUENCODE See *unix to unix encoding*.

Viewtime This is the time a banner advertisement is visible on a web page. See also *Banner Advertisement*.

Virtual Memory System A multiuser, multitasking, virtual memory operating system for the VAX series from Digital Equipment.

Virtual Reality Markup Language A scripting language that is used to define three-dimensional worlds.

Virus Malicious piece of code that can be hidden in programs and destroy data on a computer.

Visit A visit is a complete session of accesses to a certain web server conducted by one person. A visit is concluded when the customer hasn't viewed any page for a certain period of time (60 seconds in most cases).

VMS see *virtual memory system*.

VRML See *virtual reality markup language*.

WAIS See *wide area information servers*.

WAN See *wide area network*.

Web See *world wide web*.

Web Crawler Service that scans web documents and adds them to a database. After having indexed one page it follows all links and indexes them as well. See also *search engine*.

Webmaster The person in charge of a web server. Most web servers will allow mails to be sent to the webmaster. The web master of http://www.foobar.org/ can be reached at webmaster@foobar.org, for example. See also *postmaster*.

What You See Is What You Get The promise that what you see on screen will also be what you get when you print out the document. Only very few software packages are able to fulfill this promise.

Wide Area Information Servers Software package that allows the indexing of large quantities of information. Uses a separate protocol from HTTP and is not used very much anymore. See also *HTTP*, *search engine*.

Wide Area Network A network that is distributed over several locations. See also *LAN*.

Wintel The majority of computers today run the Wintel combination; the Windows operating systems and Intel processors.

World Wide Web The part of the Internet, which is accessible through a web browser. The Web is not the Internet, but a subset.

Worm A program that is designed to replicate itself over a network. Although not all worms are designed to destroy anything, most of them will try to attack your resources.

WRT Net-langauge for "with respect to".

WWW See *world wide web*.

WYSIWYG See *what you see is what you get*.

Yahoo The original and most famous web directory.

YMMV Net-language for "your mileage may vary". A warning that not everything described in a manual will work exactly the way it promised to.

Appendix B

EXAMPLE INTERNET BUSINESS ARCHITECTURE

B.1 The Business Idea

The following is based on ideas I developed for my father's business, who after working as a freelance editor several years for a large publishing company in Germany wanted to go back and restart his editing, translation and recording service, which he had almost dropped in favor of large contracts for the publishing company. The proposed solution here has not been implemented at the time of writing, it has been developed during the writing of this book and will be implemented after the book has been finished. You will find the link to this web site on the book's homepage[1].

In order to restart the business and reach out for new customers, it was necessary to build up a web site that represents his service and shows customers what he and his potential partners are able to do. Although my father had been using e-mail for several years, he did not have a web site with information about his company ETS.

If you remember the six phases from the preface, you will notice that we were at Phase 0 right now. Some basic Internet knowledge was available, such as using e-mail and a web browser, but no knowledge at all about how to build an online business and what is necessary to create one. As you can see here, it is not only important to find the strengths, but also the weaknesses to build up a successful business online.

In order to see how the online business could be created, it was necessary to look at the services offered and see how they match on the Internet. Editing, translating and recording are all tasks that cannot be done in real-time over the Internet, as these tasks are far too individual for each customer for a software to handle it. The Internet can only be used to market and promote these services. It cannot be used to automate these services. But the Internet allows us to create value-added services on top of these basic services.

---

[1]http://www.ebusinessrevolution.com/

In order to make the web site a success ETS had to build up a business portal for each of these services. By offering the value-added service for each of the services, it becomes easy to guide a large number of people to these sites and generate new profit streams such as banner advertising.

We will develop one of the three business portals in this chapter as an example. If we look at the recording service ETS wanted to offer over the Internet, we need to understand first exactly what the job consists of. Until now companies who had a German promotional image or training film called up ETS and asked if my father was available to voiceover the translated text in English. In many cases ETS would also do the translation work before the actual recording. The recording work is done in various studios in the region. While it is quite easy to make the deal on the Internet, the actual recording will still have to take place in a studio, making it not very useful to offer the recording service to companies outside of the region (Southern Germany and bordering areas), if they have their own sound studios.

This brings us to the point to think about the target customers. Who are the potential customers and where are they located. As we've seen in the last paragraph it is not possible for my father to travel the whole world for recordings that may take only a few hours. As the Internet offers your content to be viewed by anyone, it is either necessary to exclude most of the world for this type of service or enhance the service in such a way that he will talk to some sound studios in the region who will accept material from customers who are not located in the region. Many customers will already have their preferred recording studio, so that this may be a problem. This means that the selected sound studios need to promote themselves as well so that customers are more willing to give out their film to that particular studio.

Imagine companies from Australia, Russia and South Africa selecting the services of ETS. They will most probably have their preferred sound studios locally, but traveling would take up too much time to be cost effective. So they would be forced to choose a sound studio proposed by ETS. By making agreements with several sound studios in the region, ETS would be able to attract customers from all over the world, who are in need of a native English speaker for promotional films.

In order to offer additional value on the web site, the business portal needs to be built up. In this case it is a vertical portal regarding all facets of recording. There needs to be a directory of recording web sites and resources, possible links to books on recording (although I haven't seen any), links to recording studios and speakers. The portal can have all recording studios and speakers in there to offer the customers a choice. In order to keep the business with ETS, the speakers and recording studios would need to pay a transactional fee for every customer that comes from the business portal. This guarantees that the speakers are not taking away business and ensures a high quality of speakers as they are hand-picked. The directory could also be made up out of two parts. A general part that includes all available resources and a more specialized part where ETS proposes selected studios and speakers. As ETS is specialized in English-speaking recordings, supporting speakers for other languages will increase the value of the web site without reducing the amount of work ETS receives in the end. The final goal may be to delegate all the work and use the web site as a transactional site for other speakers, including native English speakers.

B.2 Marketing on the Web

In order to market the capabilities of ETS, the service needs to be explained in detail on the web site. The web site is first and foremost the business card of ETS. In addition to a written description, which is similar to the document ETS used to send out to customers, the Internet offers additional possibilities. Many companies request a tape in order to hear the voice before deciding to make use of the service. Instead of sending out the document with the service description and the tape it is possible to set up a few web pages that have the same result.

In addition to the service description, it is possible to set up sample web pages, that contain the audio in conjunction with the speaker's text. Five different texts for five different situations would be enough to give most customers a good feeling of how the voice would be for their film.

In order to market the web site efficiently it needs a domain name that reflects the content of it. Actually two domain names would be suitable, one that carries the name of the company. In this case "ets" and the content of the business portal, something connected to the recording. Before deciding on the exact second level domain name, one should think about the top-level domain. If the offering a regional one, then a country domain would be more suitable or if it is a general service for the whole world, then a ".com" would be probably more suitable. As we've seen above, the service can be offered to the whole world, therefore a ".com" top-level domain would be suitable. In addition to this we would try to target the German market in particular, so the complete web site would be English and German and the German web site would get a ".de" domain to make it a more regional offering for Germany.

To find out which domain names are available, we look at the web site of Internet Solutions[2] in the United States and Ripe.net[3] in Europe to find out which ".com" and ".de" domain names are available.

The most obvious domain names "ets.com", "ets.de" and "ets.net" were already taken so that we had to look out for similar names that made it easy for customers to find the site and remember the domain name. The same applied to "recording.com", "speakers.com" and "aufnahme.de" and "sprecher.de". Finding a solution for the second domain name was easier as attaching something

---

[2]http://www.internetsolutions.com/
[3]http://www.ripe.net/

like -net was easy, making it "recording-net.com". But the first one was more difficult to resolve. How should the domain name for the company name be chosen if the most appropriate names were already taken. PureTec[4] offers a service that proposes up to thirty domain names, if the domain name is already taken that you wanted to use. In the end my father decided to take a totally different domain name that did encompass all fields of work: text-projects.de[5]. The ".de" at the end indicates where the company is located and the English domain name provides an idea about the type of work he is doing. As you can see choosing a domain name can be difficult if you do not have a well-known brand name or well-known products.

Once the domain name has been decided on, it is necessary to create the site (this will be explained later on) and to publish the address in as many locations as possible. First of all, the URLs need to put into the footers of the e-mails sent out to existing customers, so that they can have a look at the site. The next step would be to submit the URLs to as many search engines as possible. This will ensure that people who are looking for that particular service through a search engine will be able to find the site of ETS.

On the web there are many sites dedicated to recording so that a banner and link exchange with these site will increase the traffic directed to this web site. In order to keep visitors and customers returning to the web, the site needs to be updated on a regular basis. A news section should keep the customers informed about the changes on the site and news from the recording industry should keep them coming back at regular intervals.

A frequently asked questions (FAQ) page will help customers to resolve the most common questions regarding the service, reducing the load of questions coming in through e-mail. At the same time it is important to set up a feedback page, allowing customers and visitors to express their opinions and wishes, making it easier for the company to extend the service into the right direction and meet customer demand individually and dynamically.

Known customer should have the chance to login and receive personalized information. It would be, for example, possible to handle all the communication on the web site instead of e-mails, making it easier for both parties to track the comments of the other. The personalized web site can offer special information or updates on work that is in progress.

In addition to the actual service and documents around the service, a mailing list and newsgroup can be set up to allow the exchange of ideas between customers, sound studios and speakers. In this case four newsgroups would work quite well, one more general and three dedicated lists for customers, sound studios and speakers. The content would most probably be about the business and new technologies changing the business, but as other examples have shown in the past, it won't be restricted to this.

---

[4]http://www.puretec.de/

[5]http://www.text-projects.de/

B.3   Implementation of the Service

In order to implement the service on the Internet it is necessary to buy the domain names, which costs per domain name about 35 Euros or Dollars per year. In addition to the domain name one has to decide if the web site should be hosted on its own system or put onto a web server hosted by an ISP. In this case, as ETS has only a small company, with no resources dedicated to Internet technology, it would not make sense to set up a computer locally and lease a phone line to connect to the Internet. Maintenance would be a problem. Therefore outsourcing the web server option to an ISP is the simplest and cheapest solution in this case. A typical ISP web server hosting solution would cost about 20 to 30 Euros or Dollars per month, for about 30 Megabytes of web space and unlimited traffic per month. This basic web server package normally includes a POP3 e-mail address and unlimited e-mail aliases for that particular address. One such ISP would be cihost.com[6] in the United States; many other providers throughout the world offer similar services at similar costs.

The one POP3 e-mail address will allow ETS to retrieve the e-mail from the server and read it in an e-mail program, while the e-mail aliases will help customers to speak to the right person within the company. ETS would be able to set up multiple e-mail addresses very easily. Typical e-mail addresses for a company include "webmaster@domain.com", which deals with questions regarding the technical implementation, "info@domain.com", for general requests about the web site and the service, "orders@domain.com" for ordering enquiries and status updates and "stuart@domain.com" for personal mail.

The different domain names would all link to a single web server, but to other directories. The ".de" domain would show the site in German, while the ".com" site would present the content in English. Through a simple HTML link the customer will have the possibility to switch languages at any time.

In this case the aliases all link to one e-mail address, making it easy for ETS to respond to any type of query from a single mail program without the need of setting up multiple configurations. For the customers it looks like there are many different people working for the company, which may be true in the future, but as a start-up it is easier to appear as a competent company.

In order to make communication easy between customers and company the customers should use a web-based form for sending back e-mail to the company. This makes it easier for the customer to decide to whom the e-mail is sent by selecting the appropriate e-mail address and function and by guiding the customers to information that gets a qualified response in a very short time. In the recording business information about the recording will help to qualify the type of recording and its price. As the service is very individual it is not possible to put up a price list onto the web site. By offering a web form that includes fields for the length of the film, the type of film and other details that are of interest in determining the price, an upload button for adding the text could

---

[6]http://www.cihost.com/

also be easily implemented, sending out the text automatically for review to ETS. By disallowing new customers to send e-mails directly to ETS, it is easier to classify e-mails and respond to them.

The business portal, which should contain a directory of recording and speaker related sites can be built up quite easily by extracting the relevant parts from the Open Directory[7] project, which allows other sites to take the complete database or parts of it and include it into their own web site. We would need to search for the relevant parts for our vertical business portal and need to define a way to automatically extract these parts on a regular basis to keep the data up-to-date. A Perl[8] script can be used, for example, to extract the necessary parts on a monthly basis and put it into the web page design of the web site. The license of the Open Directory asks for a link back to the original and the add site link, which also leads automatically back into the database. These two links are created easily and voluntarily as the Open Directory is an invaluable service for any portal.

In addition to the Open Directory database sound studios and other speakers need to be integrated into the site. This leads us to the next step the design of the web pages. As ETS had no knowledge of web page design this work needs to be outsourced to a web design company who creates the initial set of web pages according to the company design. As the costs for the web design company is high, they won't be used for the ongoing business. A short introduction to the web and HTML should be sufficient to let ETS maintain and operate the site themselves.

Therefore a tool needs to be selected that enables ETS to change the web site at any given time, moving pages around, changing content, adding new pages or deleting pages without having to know how HTML works and how the update process works to move the changed site to the Internet. For this matter we have chosen NetObjects Fusion[9], which makes it easy to change the web site, once the basic templates have been created. The program uses an interface that is similar to desktop publishing systems and word processors, making it easy for a non-technical person to understand how it works and how to change, delete or add pages. The software offers a staging area, where the changed web pages can be viewed before they are uploaded to the production server, making sure that only web pages are uploaded that are really ok. The editing process is very easy to understand. The software costs less than 200 Euros or Dollars.

Payment won't occur over the Internet in this business-to-business scenario. Invoices will be sent out after the recording has been completed, so there is no need to implement an online payment system for this web site. In order to create additional revenue streams, the web site should carry banner advertising. The banner advertising can be organized on a one-to-one basis, meaning that

---

[7] http://www.dmoz.org/

[8] http://www.perl.org/

[9] http://www.netobjects.com/

ETS would have to negotiate or it is possible to go to one of the many online banner advertising offices. In order to keep work low in this area we will chose an online banner advertising office.

The personalization of the web site can be managed through a set of Perl scripts that need to be written in order to allow access to private parts of the web server which are dedicated to single customers. These private directories may contain documents, such as contracts, texts, sound files, and video files, which need to be exchanged before and after the recording session. The private sessions should be controlled by login and password, which is a standard functionality of all web servers. If the material contained in these directories is sensible, such as contracts, the web server should exchange the data only encrypted, therefore SSL encryption needs to be switched on, which is also a standard functionality of all web servers. In order to enable SSL encryption, a digital certificate needs to be purchased, which is available for 100 to 200 Euro or Dollar on the Web. A local search engine for the web site is integrated into most web servers and if not, Perl scripts are available that offer this service.

Problems with cultural differences are not be expected, as the web site is business-to-business only and contains only business information. This reduces the risk of offending a certain culture.

This site starts between phase three and phase four from the preface, which I called "Trying E-Commerce" and "Doing E-Business", where the company is trying to sell a service online. The system is not connected to the real databases on the Intranet, as there is no Intranet and would not make any sense in this case. The costs are very low, if you look at the prices mentioned through the chapter. Startup costs are about 1,000 to 2,000 Euros or Dollars, depending on the costs of the web design agency. The ongoing costs are very low in this model. Once the site is up and running online the web space and the domain name need to be paid, as the maintenance work on the web site is done by ETS themselves. As the site is very specialized and much of the site automated, the need for change is not very high.

The personalized web site offers security through standard login and password authentication and the communication is secured through SSL encryption. As implementation and operating costs are low, it is easy to focus on the actual work, which results from the customer deals, made over the web or traditional channels.

B.4   Outlook into the Future

If we look at the future and pervasive computing there are good chances to integrate the recording service into the new paradigm. The new paradigm connects all sorts of devices and integrates them into the Internet. In our case we could envision a future where the customer provides the film, the sound studio the recording equipment and the speaker sits at home using a microphone.

The film is broadcast to the sound studio and the speaker at the same time, allowing the speaker to add the text and the sound studio to record the text.

This requires the speaker to have a dedicated room for recordings, equipped with a microphone, a computer and a television set. Each device is connected to the Internet. The computer is used as a teleprompter, which shows the text in real-time, while the microphone sends the voice to the sound studio, which records and alters the voice to fit into the film. The television set shows the film from the customer in real-time. This enables each of the participants to deliver its best service without having to care much about how these devices connect and how content is delivered. Once the film and the voice are synchronized and the customer is happy, the film can be sent off to a video copying firm who can instantly produce video cassettes and at the same time the company can make the film available on its Intranet, enabling the employees to see the film before it is used or make it even public on the company's web site.

Everything is available the instant it is required. Instant private business networks will become more important in the future, where most of the business will be conducted over the Internet.

Appendix C

USEFUL WEB ADDRESSES

The following sites are not representative and are a selection of my favourite sites if you want my private bookmark file. I collect keywords in my memory, as the facilities for administering bookmarks in the browsers are not very good, in my humble opinion. The URLs are changing very fast so that it does not make any sense to remember them. In order to find information I rely on meta search engines, so that I only have to remember the keywords in order to find a certain site again. Have fun with the following sites.

C.1 Business

This section provides some links to highly valuable business sites on the Internet.

http://www.etrade.com/ One of the best known online investment and financial services, which comes with a portal site for financial matters.

http://www.stock-world.com/ Another investing portal with many information.

http://www.turtletrader.com/ TurtleTrader teaches the Turtle trading techniques. These trading techniques are used by some of today's most successful traders and can help all traders earn above-average profits in most futures and stock markets going both long and short.

C.2 Comics

The following are some of my favourite comic sites on the web. They deal with lost souls either in the working or Internet world.

http://www.dilbert.com/ The Dilbert Comic Zone is a must read for everyone working for a cubicle company.

http://www.kimble.org/ The mighty Kimble in his fight against the evil powers of the world.

http://www.pcweenies.com/ The comic strip with typical nerds in it.

http://www.userfriendly.org/ The daily Unix friendly comic strip.

http://www.webcomics.com/ Portal site for online comics.

C.3 Computers

These web sites are always useful to find out more information about the hardware you are using.

http://www.amiga.de/ Although they lost the battle, some lost souls still hope for a new Amiga.

http://www.apple.com/ The ultimate user-friendly computer. If you want an easy to use computer, take a Mac.

http://www.compaq.com/ One of the largest PC makers in the world.

http://www.digital.com/ Bought by Compaq.

http://www.hp.com/ The inventor of the open systems has moved to become the company of open services.

http://www.ibm.com/ The Big Blue.

http://www.sun.com/ The inventor of Java has always some interesting new ideas, concepts and pieces of software.

http://www.sgi.com/ Former Silicon Graphics has evolved from a graphic processor company to a general computer company with lots of interesting hardware.

C.4 Fun

Fun web sites that provide no value other than a good laugh.

http://www.thenia.com/ The Nerd Intelligence Agency provides all computer users with very important information.

C.5 Hacking Related Sites

Not only hackers will find these resources interesting. Anyone interested in Internet security will find information here that will make their systems more secure. Only if you know the threats you can do something about it.

http://www.antionline.com/ AntiOnline's mission is to educate the public about computer security and hacking related issues.

http://www.hackers.com/ A very complete resource for hackers.

http://www.l0pht.com/ Commercial site for security tools, plus hacking info, exploits and news.

http://catless.ncl.ac.uk/Risks/ Forum On Risks To The Public In Computers And Related Systems.

http://www.technotronic.com/ Technotronic Security Information provides the network administrator with up to date security related information.

C.6   Internet Organizations

The following organizations have influence on the Internet and its standards. To find out what the Internet in the future will look like, have a look at the following sites.

http://www.iesg.org/ The Internet Engineering Steering Group is responsible for technical management of IETF activities and the Internet standards process.

http://www.ietf.org/ The Internet Engineering Task Force is the driven force for new Internet standards. It is an open international community of companies, who design and operate networks, do research in new technologies and sell products based on these technologies. Although it is open to anyone, the task force is driven by companies, which try to agree on new standards, which enable new services on the Internet, while running more smoothly. Internet Standards proposed by the IETF are the so-called Request For Comments (RFC).

http://www.isoc.org/ The Internet Society is an organization of Internet experts that comment on policies and practices. It oversees a number of other boards and task forces dealing with network policy issues.

http://www.w3.org/ The World Wide Web Consortium, the inventor of the World Wide Web.

C.7   Mailing Lists

http://www.allEC.com/ The allECommerce mailing list provides news and updates in the ecommerce sector.

http://www.geek-girl.com/bugtraq/ BugTraq is the mailing list for security relevant bugs and flaws in applications and operating systems. A must for anyone connected to the Internet and who is concerned about security.

http://www.alistapart.com/ A very lively mailing list on all topics around the web.

http://www.nua.ie/ New Thinking – Free weekly email contributing to a philosophy for The Digital Age.

C.8   News

These online news sites are all concerned about Internet, related technology, the New Economy and the webified society. Each of these sites also offers a free newsletter.

http://www.news.com/ Leading source of computer and Internet related information.

http://www.techweb.com/ News central with lots of interesting information on computers and the Internet.

http://www.slashdot.org/ The news service for extreme Geeks.

http://www.wired.com/ News source for Internet, computer and political issues.

C.9   Search Engines

While more and more search engines appear on the Internet every day, I prefer meta search engines that search across several search engines.

http://www.metacrawler.com/ My favourite meta search engine that provides in most cases the best results.

http://www.savvysearch.com/ If I cannot find something with metacrawler then I look here for the missing pages. If I cannot find a web page in metacrawler and savvysearch it probably does not exist.

http://www.metager.de/ My third instance for meta-searching.

C.10   Software Development

For those who are in need of a piece of source code or hints on programming.

http://www.developer.com/ The meta-resource for developers covering all important programming languages.

http://www.cgi-resources.com/ If you are looking for CGI scripts to pep up your web site then this is the right resource.

http://developer.netscape.com/ Provides all the information that a person on the Internet needs regarding JavaScript, HTML and Netscape products.

http://developer.java.sun.com/ The ultimative web site on Java technology.

SUBJECT INDEX

Hewlett-Packard Computer Education and Training

Hewlett-Packard's world-class education and training offers hands on education solutions including:

- Linux
- HP-UX System and Network Administration
- Y2K HP-UX Transition
- Advanced HP-UX System Administration
- IT Service Management using advanced Internet technologies
- Microsoft Windows NT
- Internet/Intranet
- MPE/iX
- Database Administration
- Software Development

HP's new IT Professional Certification program provides rigorous technical qualification for specific IT job roles including HP-UX System Administration, Network Management, Unix/NT Servers and Applications Management, and IT Service Management.

In addition, HP's IT Resource Center is the perfect knowledge source for IT professionals. Through a vibrant and rich Web environment, IT professionals working in the areas of UNIX, Microsoft, networking, or MPE/iX gain access to continually updated knowledge pools.

http://education.hp.com

In the U.S. phone 1-800-HPCLASS (472-5277)